Cloud Computing: Systems and Technologies

Cloud Computing: Systems and Technologies

Edited by Amanda Wegener

Clanrye International
www.clanryeinternational.com

Clanrye International,
750 Third Avenue, 9th Floor,
New York, NY 10017, USA

ISBN: 978-1-63240-794-8

Cataloging-in-Publication Data

Cloud computing : systems and technologies / edited by Amanda Wegener.
p. cm.
Includes bibliographical references and index.
ISBN 978-1-63240-794-8
1. Cloud computing. 2. System analysis--Computer programs. 3. Information technology.
I. Wegener, Amanda.
QA76.585 .C56 2019
004.678 2--dc23

For information on all Clanrye International publications
visit our website at www.clanryeinternational.com

CLANRYE
INTERNATIONAL

Contents

Preface

Cloud computing is an information technology tool that allows storage of data on internet entities called 'clouds' that are constantly available for faster sharing of data. Cloud computing employs tools of virtualization softwares that convert storage devices into virtual structures thereby allowing universal access of stored information across multiple levels. Such elaborate frameworks are significant for minimizing IT infrastructure costs, user involvement, possibility of human errors, and expediting data processes. This book covers all significant aspects related to cloud computing in detail. It is designed to keep readers up-to-date with the advances in this field. Those who want to gain a deeper understanding of this field will be immensely benefited by this book.

All of the data presented henceforth, was collaborated in the wake of recent advancements in the field. The aim of this book is to present the diversified developments from across the globe in a comprehensible manner. The opinions expressed in each chapter belong solely to the contributing authors. Their interpretations of the topics are the integral part of this book, which I have carefully compiled for a better understanding of the readers.

At the end, I would like to thank all those who dedicated their time and efforts for the successful completion of this book. I also wish to convey my gratitude towards my friends and family who supported me at every step.

Editor

1

An efficient and traceable KP-ABS scheme with untrusted attribute authority in cloud computing

Hanshu Hong and Zhixin Sun*

Abstract

ABE has been widely applied for secure data protection in cloud computing. In ABE, user's private keys are generated by attribute authority, thus, attribute authority has the ultimate privileges in the system and can impersonate any users to forge valid signatures. Once the attribute authority become dishonest or be invaded in cloud systems, the system's security will be at risk. To better solve the problem mentioned above, in this paper, we propose a key-policy attribute based signature scheme with untrusted authority and traceability (KP-ABS-UT). In our scheme, the signer's private key is composed by two components: one part is distributed by attribute authority and the other part is chosen privately by the signer's self. Thus attribute authority cannot forge any signatures which should be signed by legal users. Besides, our scheme introduces an entity "tracer", which can trace the identity of signer when necessary. By security analysis and efficiency comparison, we prove our KP-ABS-UT scheme meets the requirements of unforgeability as well as lower computation cost.

Keywords: Access structure, Untrusted authority, Traceability

Introduction

With the various information resources increasing rapidly in the cloud, users are faced with urgent problems like how to make data sharing among resources efficiently and securely. On this occasion, Sahai proposed a new cryptographic primitive named "ABE" (attribute based encryption) [1]. In ABE mechanism [1–4], a user's identity is described by several attributes rather than a single string. A data receiver is capable of getting access to the data when the attributes he possesses match with the structure made by the data owner. KP-ABE [2, 3] is a typical class of ABE.As is shown in Fig. 1, a user's private key corresponds to an access tree structure. Each leaf node stands for the attribute a user owns; the non-leaf node describes the access policy of these attributes. The ciphertext corresponds to an attribute set such as {Attr1, Attr4}. Due to its capability of providing flexible access control for data sharing between users, KP-ABE is gradually becoming an effective tool for secure data sharing in complex networks.

After the proposal of ABE, ABS (attribute based signature) has been developed as a primitive to solve the data authentication problem in attribute based cryptosystem. ABS was originally proposed by Maji et al. in [5]. In ABS mechanism [6–9], a user is capable of signing a message using the private key component of the attribute set he owns. A receiver validates the signature by utilizing system public parameters. The signature can be verified to an attribute set or access structure which the signer possesses. Since the advent of the notion, many ABS schemes have been proposed. However, most of the existing ABS schemes have one thing in common, that is the attribute authority has the ultimate privileges in the whole system. In order to keep the whole system running safely, attribute authority must be honest and highly protected. In the open network systems, attribute authority are vulnerable to external as well as internal threat. Once being invaded, it can impersonate any users to forge legal signatures, which will threaten the whole security of the system. What's more, anonymity is an important feature of common attribute based signature

* Correspondence: sunzx@njupt.edu.cn
Key Lab of Broadband Wireless Communication and Sensor Network Technology, Ministry Education, Nanjing University of Posts and Telecommunications, Nanjing, China

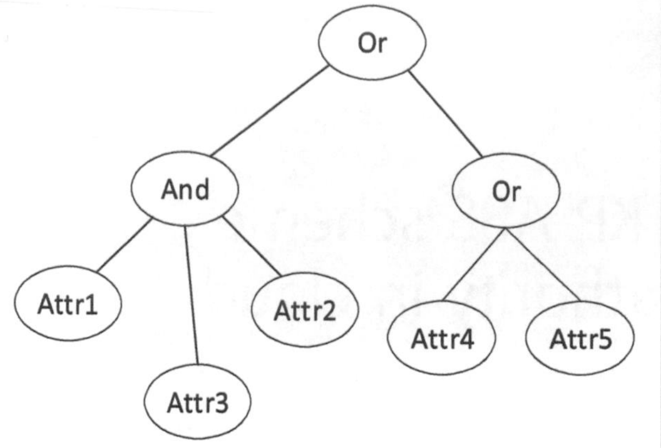

Fig. 1 Access structure for KP-ABE

mechanism. However, some malicious users may take advantage of this feature to release illegal information without taking responsibility.

To better solve the problems discussed above, in this paper, we construct a KP-ABS-UT (key-policy attribute based signature with untrusted authority and traceability) scheme, which has the following merits: (1) the signature is unforgeable, even attribute authority cannot impersonate any users to forge legal signatures; (2) the overall computation cost of the whole process of signing and verifying is reduced sharply; (3) the signer's identity can be traced by the system administer if necessary.

The rest sections are arranged as follows:

In section 2, we give the literature review and fundamental mathematical preliminaries and notions. The security model and detailed algorithms of our KP-ABS-UT scheme are constructed in section 3 and section 4. Section 5 gives the security proof and performance comparison of our scheme. At last, the conclusion of this paper and prospects on future directions are made in section 6.

Related works and preliminaries

Related works

The notion of ABS was first proposed by Maji in [5]. Since then, many ABS schemes have been proposed by researchers worldwide. Existing literatures of ABS can be classified to three types in terms of the data access structure :(1)ABS using threshold structure [10–12]; (2) ABS using LSSS access structure [13–15];(3) ABS using access tree [16], which has been illustrated in Fig. 1. Besides access structure, different ABS schemes have different advantages and performances. A. Escala et al. in [13] proposed a user-revocable attribute based signature. If a user drops some of the attributes, his signing privilege can be exactly withdrawn. Their scheme also achieves adaptively security in the standard model. S. Shahandashti et al. in [10] construct a threshold ABS and applied it to credential systems. Their scheme enables a signature holder to prove possession of signatures by revealing only the relevant attributes of the signer, hence providing signer attribute privacy for the signature holder. S. Kumar et.al in [11] proposed an ABS which is equipped with multiple threshold access structure. Their scheme is efficient as well as stretchable. Tatsuaki et al. in [16] proposed a decentralized multi-authority ABS. In their scheme, due to the introducing of multiple authorities, thus no central CA is needed. However, this also brings about other problems such as parameter synchronization, time synchronization, etc. Besides, the efficiency of their scheme can be further improved. S.L Ding et al. proposed a traceable ABS in [14], which allows PKG and the issuing authority join together to trace the identity of a malicious signer. However, since the trace algorithm needs frequent participation of PKG, it may be exposed to more internal and external security risks. Li et al. in [15] proposed a novel ABS with hidden attribute property. In their scheme, anonymous user revocation is achieved. Liu et al. in [17] proposed an attribute based multisignature scheme, which allows a number of users to participate to authenticate a message with only one signature. Their scheme is shown to be secure and is more appropriate to be applied for wireless communications. Chen et al. in [9] proposed a new paradigm named "Outsourced ABS". The computation load in their scheme is reduced sharply by delegating most of the computation work to a semi-trusted server, thus this will relieve the terminal devices from heavy computation burden. The high efficiency and security level makes their scheme an excellent method for providing data authentication in cloud computing. Xu et al. in [18] propose an ABS scheme with dynamic user revocation. Their scheme has superior performance with regard to scalability, which is able to be applied to massive data storage environments.

The above schemes have laid solid foundations for filling the gap between theoretical proposal and practical application of ABS. However, in the above schemes, the attribute authority has the ultimate privilege in the system. Even worse, it can forge as any legal users and generates a valid signature. Once the attribute authority become dishonest, the system will be exposed to potential risks. Although ABS with multiple attribute authorities has been proposed in [16], if these attribute authorities collude with each other to obtain a user's private key, a legal signature can still be successfully forged. Thus, it is of significance to cut down the privilege of the attribute authority in ABS systems.

Bilinear pairings

Denote G_1 and G_2 to be cyclic groups of prime order q. Let g be a generator of G_1. A bilinear pairing $\hat{e}: G_1 \times G_1 \rightarrow G_2$ has three features [19]:

Bilinearity: For $a, b \in Z_q$, $\hat{e}(g^a, g^b) = \hat{e}(g, g)^{ab}$.
Non-degeneracy: There exists $P, Q \in G_1$ which satisfy $\hat{e}(g, g) \neq 1$.
Computability: The value of $\hat{e}(u, v)$ can be calculated for any $u, v \in G_1$.

Hardness assumption

Decision Bilinear Diffie-Hellman problem:

Picks random numbers $a, b, c, z \in Z_q^*$, assuming that the value of (g, g^a, g^b, g^c, z) are given, no probabilistic polynomial-time algorithm can distinguish the tuples $(A = g^a, B = g^b, C = g^c, \hat{e}(g, g)^{abc})$ and $(A = g^a, B = g^b, C = g^c, \hat{e}(g, g)^z)$ with a non-negligible probability.

Lagrange Interpolation function

For a polynomial $p(x)$ in Z_q of order $d - 1$ and a set S in Z_q with the size $|S| = d$ is computed by $p(x) = \sum_{i \in S} p(i) \prod_{j \in S, j \neq i} \frac{x-j}{i-j}$.

Our model and assumptions

Formal model of our scheme

In order to clearly describe our KP-ABS-UT, we define some notations listed in Table 1.

The model of our system is shown in Fig. 2. Our model consists of 4 entities: "AA" (Attribute authority), "tracer", "signer" and "receiver". AA provides system's public parameters, generates part of user's private key and distributes them to users. After receiving the original key generated by AA, signer re-generates his own private key by adding a secret component. Then signer signs the plaintext using the private key generated by himself and uploads the signature to cloud center. Cloud center provides secure data storage and responses the access request made by data receiver. Receiver verifies if the signature is a valid one. Tracer is responsible for revealing the signer's identity when necessary.

Table 1 Notations and their corresponding meanings

Notations	Meanings
G_1, G_2	Groups
$\hat{e}$	Bilinear paring operation
H_1	Hash function
PK	System public parameters
MK	System master key
AA	Attribute authority
U	Global attribute set
A_i	Attribute i
D_i	Private key of attribute i
M	Plaintext
T_i	Access structure
x	Node in the access tree
$\Delta_{i,S(x)}$	Lagrange interpolation function
q_x	Polynomial defined by AA
p_x	Polynomial defined by signer
v	Signature to be verified
id_l	Identity of user l

Formulized definitions of algorithms in KP-ABS-UT:

Setup$\{1^\lambda\} \rightarrow \{PK, MK\}$:This algorithm is operated by AA. Take in a security parameter, it generates PK and MK. PK is shared by users while MK is kept private by AA.

Private key generation$\{PK, MK, T_k, s\} \rightarrow \{D_{i,T_k,id_l}\}$: The private key generation algorithm is an interaction between AA and a user with an access structure T_k. On input PK, MK, T_k, AA firstly returns D_{i,T_k} to be the initial attribute private key for T_k. Then each signer embeds a secret component into D_{i,T_k} to re-generate his own private key D_{i,T_k,id_l}.Signer sends certain information referring to the secret component to tracer. Tracer assigns a unique identity number to the signer and stores the relationship of each signer with his identity.

Sign$\{D_{i,T_k,id_l}, PK, M, \sigma_{id_l}\} \rightarrow \{v\}$: This algorithm is run by a signer which the systems public parameter PK, a plaintext M, signer's private key D_{i,T_k,id_l} and a mathematical constant σ_{id_l} which can reveal signer's identity as input. Then the algorithm outputs a signature v for the plaintext M.

Verify$\{PK, v, M\} \rightarrow \{\theta\}$: This algorithm is run by the receiver. On input PK and the plaintext M with the signature, it outputs a value θ. If $\theta = 1$ then the signature is a valid one, if $\theta = 0$ then the signature is invalid.

Trace$\{MK, v\} \rightarrow \{id_l\}$: This algorithm is run by the tracer. On input the signature v,the tracer can pinpoint the exact identity of a signer.

The essential unforgeability of our KP-ABS-UT

Definition 1

Our KP-ABS-UT has the existential unforgeability if no *Adversary* has non-negligible advantage in the following game played by a *Challenger* and an *Adversary*.

Setup : *Challenger* runs *Setup* procedure to obtain the system parameters and sends *PK* to *Adversary*.

Sign queries: *Adversary* chooses an access control structure T_i,a plaintext M. *Challenger* calculates the attribute private key D_{i,T_k,id_l} and runs the *Sign* procedure to calculate the signature $v = Sign(PK, M, D_{i,T_k,id_l})$.After then, *Challenger* sends the signature v to *Adversary*.

Challenge : *Adversary* chooses a plaintext M^*,a challenging access structure T_c , and calculates the signature v^*.

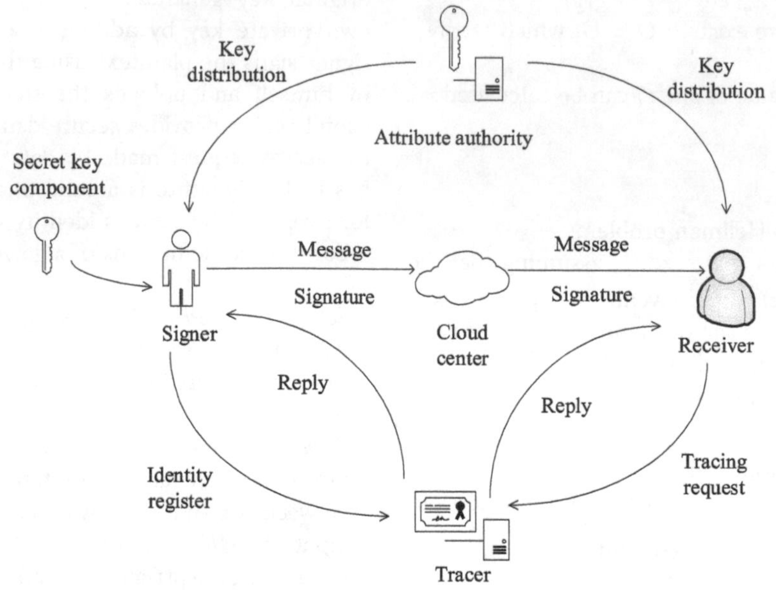

Fig. 2 The system model of KP-ABS-UT in cloud computing

Challenger verifies the signature by running the procedure *Verify*(PK, v^*) and outputs a value θ.

Adversary wins if the output of *Verify* algorithm is valid.

Denote $Adv(A) = |Pr[\theta = 1]|$ to be advantage of *Adversary*.

Our construction to KP-ABS-UT scheme

Concrete algorithms:

Setup: Let G_1 and G_2 be two cyclic groups of prime order p, while g is the generator of G_1. Let $\hat{e} : G_1 \times G_1 \rightarrow G_2$ be a bilinear paring. Define $H_1 : \{0, 1\}^* \rightarrow Z_p$.AA picks $t_i \in Z_p^*$ for each A_i in the system. Besides, AA picks another secret number $y \in Z_p^*$ and calculates $\hat{e}(g, g)^y$.Set MK to be $\{t_i, y\}$ while PK to be $\{G_1, G_2, p, g, H_1, \hat{e}(g, g)^y, g^{t_i}\}$.

Private key generation: AA randomly chooses a polynomial q_x for each node x in the access tree and sets the degree d_x of q_x to be one less than the threshold value k_x of that node ($d_x = k_x - 1$). For any other node (except root node) in the access tree, let $q_x(0) = q_{parent(x)}^{index(x)}$. For the root node AA sets $q_{root}(0) = y$. To avoid the signature forgery which can be made by AA, the signer also chooses a polynomial p_x likewise and picks a secret number s. For the root node AA sets $q_{root}(0) = y$ while the signer sets $p_{root}(0) = s$. Once the polynomials have been decided, the private key is of each leaf node x in the access tree can be denoted by $D_{i,T_k,id_l} = \left\{g^{\frac{q_x(0) \cdot p_x(0)}{t_i}}, i \in T_k\right\}$. Signer sends the value of g^s to tracer.

For each signer, tracer chooses a global unique identifier $id_l \in Z_p^*$ to describe his identity (Without loss of generality, the signer's identity is denoted by id_l). Tracer calculates $\sigma_{id_l} = (g^s)^{id_l}$ and sends σ_{id_l} back to the signer. Meanwhile, it stores a list recording the relationship between singer's unique identifier and σ_{id_l}.

Sign: For a plaintext M, the signer picks a random number $r \in Z_p^*$ and calculates:

$$C_0 = \hat{e}(g, g)^{yrs}, C_1 = \hat{e}(g, g)^{ys}$$
$$C_2 = \left\{D_{i,T_k,id_l}{}^{H_1(M||\sigma_{id_l})^s + r}\right\} = \left\{\left(g^{\frac{q_x(0) \cdot p_x(0)}{t_i}}\right)^{H_1(M||\sigma_{id_l})^s + r}\right\} \tag{1}$$

The signature can be denoted by $v = \{C_1, C_2, C_3, M, \sigma_{id_l}, g^s, H_1(M||\sigma_{id_l})^s\}$. The signer sends v to the receiver.

Verify: After receiving the signature $v = \{C_1, C_2, C_3, M, \sigma_{id}, g^s, H_1(M||\sigma_{id})^s\}$ from the signer, receiver firstly calculates: $\hat{e}(H_1(M||\sigma_{id})^s, g) = \hat{e}(H_1(M||\sigma_{id}), g^s)$.

If the equation is set up, then calculates *VerityNode* $(x, PK, v) = \hat{e}(g^{t_i}, C_2)$.

If x is a leaf node, then the calculation process is as follows:

$$VerityNode(x, PK, v) = \begin{cases} \hat{e}(g^{t_i}, C_2) = \hat{e}\left(g^{t_i}, \left(g^{\frac{q_x(0) \cdot p_x(0)}{t_i}}\right)^{H_1(M\|\sigma_{id_l})^s + r}\right) \\ = \hat{e}\left(g^{t_i}, g^{\frac{q_x(0) \cdot p_x(0)}{t_i}}\right)^{H_1(M\|\sigma_{id_l})^s + r} \\ = \hat{e}\left(g^{p_x(0)}, g^{q_x(0)}\right)^{H_1(M\|\sigma_{id_l})^s} \cdot \hat{e}\left(g^{r \cdot p_x(0)}, g^{q_x(0)}\right) \\ \perp, otherwise \end{cases} \tag{2}$$

All the value calculated from *VerityNode(x, PK, v)* will be stored as F_z. For any $F_z \neq 0$, the algorithm calculates F_{root} (the value of root node) using Lagrange interpolation method.

If x is a non-leaf node, z is the child node of x,then the value of *VerityNode(x, PK, v)* is calculated as follows:

Let $i = index(z)$, $S'_x = \{index(z) : z \in S_x\}$

$$\begin{aligned} F_x &= \prod_{z \in S_x} F_z^{\Delta_{i,Sx'}(0)} \\ &= \prod_{z \in S_x} \hat{e}\left(\left(g^{p_z(0)}\right)^{\Delta_{i,Sx'}(0)}, g^{q_z(0)^{\Delta_{i,Sx'}(0)}}\right)^{H_1(M\|\sigma_{id_l})^s + r} \\ &= \prod_{z \in S_x} \hat{e}\left(\left(g^{p_{parent}(z)^{(index(z))}}\right)^{\Delta_{i,Sx'}(0)}, \left(g^{q_{parent}(z)^{(index(z))}}{}^{\Delta_{i,Sx'}(0)}\right)\right) H_1(M\|\sigma_{id_l})^s + r \\ &= \prod_{z \in S_x} \hat{e}\left(\left(g^{p_x(i)}\right)^{\Delta_{i,Sx'}(0)}, \left(g^{q_x(i)\, \Delta_{i,sx'}(0)}\right)\right)^{H_1(M\|\sigma_{id_l})^s + r} \\ &= \hat{e}\left(g^{p_x(0)}, g^{q_x(0)}\right)^{H_1(M\|\sigma_{id_l})^s} \cdot \hat{e}\left(g^{r \cdot p_x(0)}, g^{q_x(0)}\right) \end{aligned} \tag{3}$$

Then, the algorithm calculates F_{root} (the value of root node) by recursive function.

Finally, the algorithm verifies if:

$$F_{root} = C_1{}^{H_1(M\|\sigma_{id_l})^s} \cdot C_0 \tag{4}$$

If the equation is set up, then the signature is a legal one and the signer's attributes satisfies the claimed structure.

Trace: The tracer searches the list recording the relationship between $id_l - \sigma_{id_l}$, then the identity of the signer can be pinpointed.

Security proof and performance evaluation

Correctness proof

To calculate the value of F_{root}, it is essential to obtain the value of leaf nodes which satisfy the access structure.

Since the value of $VerityNode(x, PK, v) = \hat{e}\left(g^{p_x(0)}, g^{q_x(0)}\right)^{H_1(M\|\sigma_{id_l})^s + r}$, whether x is a leaf node or non-leaf node, consequently, the value of root node F_{root} can be calculated by:

$$\begin{aligned} F_{root} &= \hat{e}\left(g^{p_{root}(0)}, g^{q_{root}(0)}\right)^{H_1(M\|\sigma_{id_l})^s + r} \\ p_{root}(0) &= s, q_{root}(0) = y \end{aligned} \tag{5}$$

Consequently, if the signature is valid then the equation is set up:

$$\begin{aligned} F_{root} &= \hat{e}(g^s, g^y)^{H_1(M\|\sigma_{id_l})^s + r} \\ &= \left(\hat{e}(g,g)^{ys}\right)^{H_1(M\|\sigma_{id_l})^s + r} \\ &= C_0 \cdot C_1{}^{H_1(M\|\sigma_{id_l})^s} \end{aligned} \tag{6}$$

Unforgeability

Theorem 1

If our scheme can be broken by an *Adversary* then it can be constructed that a simulator with a non- negligible advantage solves the DBDH problem successfully.

Proof

In the challenge game, if an *Adversary* can break our scheme with advantage ε, then a simulator be constructed to solve the DBDH problem with an advantage of $\frac{\varepsilon}{2}$.

The construction process of the simulator is as follows:

Phase 1 *Setup*:

Challenger sets the parameters as follows:

Defines a global attribute set $U = \{1, 2, \ldots n\}$.

Denotes id_l to be the unique identifier of *Adversary*.

Defines G_1 and G_2 be two cyclic groups of prime order p. The generator of G_1 is denoted by g.

Defines a bilinear paring $\hat{e}: G_1 \times G_1 \to G_2$.

Picks $\mu \in \{0, 1\}$, $a, b, c, z \in Z_p$.

$$\begin{cases} (A,B,C,Z) = \left(g^a, g^b, g^c, \hat{e}(g,g)^{abc}\right) & if\ \mu = 0 \\ (A,B,C,Z) = \left(g^a, g^b, g^c, \hat{e}(g,g)^z\right) & if\ \mu = 1 \end{cases} \tag{Let}$$

The aim of simulator is to output a value μ^* as a guess of μ.

The simulator runs *Adversary* as sub-program and plays the role of *Challenger*.

Adversary defines attribute set γ.

Simulator randomly chooses $r_i, \beta_i \in Z_p$ and sets PK to be $Y = \hat{e}(g^a, g^b) = \hat{e}(g,g)^{ab}$, $T_i = \begin{cases} g^{r_i}, & if\ i \in \gamma \\ g^{b\beta_i}, & if\ i \notin \gamma \end{cases}$

Phase 2 *Queries*:

Private key generation queries:When *Adversary* asks a *Private key generation* query for access structure T_k, simulator responds as follows:

Chooses two polynomial q_x, p_x for each node x in the access structure T_k and sets the degree d_x of q_x, p_x to be one less than the threshold value k_x of that node ($d_x = k_x - 1$). Besides, simulator sets $q_{root}(0) = y, p_{root}(0) = s$. For any other node (except root node) in the access tree, let $q_x(0) = q_{parent(x)}^{index(x)}$. Then simulator calculates the private key and sends D_{i,T_k,id_l} back to *Adversary*.The format of D_{i,T_k,id_l} is as follows:

$$D_{i,T_k,id_l} = \begin{cases} g^{\frac{q_x(0)p_x(0)}{t_i}} = g^{\frac{q_x(0)p_x(0)}{r_i}}, \text{if } att(x) \in \gamma \\ g^{\frac{q_x(0)p_x(0)}{t_i}} = g^{\frac{q_x(0)p_x(0)}{b\beta_i}}, \text{if } att(x) \notin \gamma \end{cases}$$

Sign queries: When *Adversary* asks a *Sign* query for access structure T_k and a plaintext M, simulator responds as follows:

Firstly, simulator calculates the private key $D_{i,T_k,\sigma_{id_l}}$.

Obtaining the private key of access structure T_k by running

Randomly chooses $r \in Z_p^*$, let $\sigma_{id_l} = (g^s)^{id_l}$, then calculates:

$$C_0 = \hat{e}(g,g)^{abrs}, C_1 = \hat{e}(g,g)^{abs}, C_2 = \left\{ D_{i,T_k,id_l}{}^{H_1(M||\sigma_{id_l})^s + r} \right\} \tag{7}$$

Then signer outputs $v = \left\{ C_1, C_2, C_3, M, \sigma_{\sigma_{id_l}}, g^s, H_1\left(M||\sigma_{\sigma_{id_l}}\right)^s \right\}$ and sends it to *Adversary*.

It can be seen that the simulator is consistent with our scheme.

Phase 3:*Challenge*:

Adversary outputs a new signature v_l with a challenging access structure T_l and plaintext M.

Adversary cannot make *Sign* queries about T_l and v_l is not gained by a previous *Sign* query.

Adversary forges the signature as the following process:

Chooses a polynomial p_{lx}.Sets $p_{lroot}(0) = s_l$. Picks $r_l \in Z_p$, returns g^{s_l} to simulator.

Simulator chooses sends $\sigma_{\sigma_{id_l}} = (g^{s_l})^{id}$ back to *Adversary*.

Adversary forges the private key $D_{i,T_l,\sigma_{id_l}}{}^*$ of the access structure T_l.

$$D_{i,T_l,\sigma_{id_l}}{}^* = \begin{cases} g^{\frac{q_x{}^*(0)p_{lx}(0)}{t_i}} = g^{\frac{q_x{}^*(0)p_{lx}(0)}{r_i}}, \text{if } att(x) \in \gamma \\ g^{\frac{q_x{}^*(0)p_{lx}(0)}{t_i}} = g^{\frac{q_x{}^*(0)p_{lx}(0)}{b\beta_i}}, \text{if } att(x) \notin \gamma \end{cases} \tag{8}$$

Adversary calculates $v_l = \left\{ C_0, C_1, C_2, M, g^{s_l}, \sigma_{\sigma_{id_l}}, H_1\left(M||\sigma_{\sigma_{id_l}}\right)^{s_l} \right\}$:

$$C_0 = \hat{e}(g,g)^{abs_l}, C_1 = \hat{e}(g,g)^{ab.r_l s_l}$$
$$C_2 = D_{i,T_l,\sigma_{id_l}}{}^{r_l + H_1(M||\sigma_{id_l})^{s_l}} = \begin{cases} \left(g^{\frac{q_x{}^*(0)p_{lx}(0)}{r_i}} \right)^{r_l + H_1(M||\sigma_{id_l})^{s_l}}, \text{if } att(x) \in \gamma \\ \left(g^{\frac{q_x{}^*(0)p_{lx}(0)}{b\beta_i}} \right)^{r_l + H_1(M||\sigma_{id_l})^{s_l}}, \text{if } att(x) \notin \gamma \end{cases} \tag{9}$$

Verify :

Simulator firstly calculates $VerityNode(x,PK,v_l) = \hat{e}(g^{r_i}, C_2)$.

$$VerityNode(x,PK,v_l) = \begin{cases} \hat{e}\left(g^{r_i}, \left(g^{\frac{q_x{}^*(0)p_{lx}(0)}{r_i}} \right)^{r_l + H_1(M||\sigma_{id_l})^{s_l}} \right), \\ \text{if } att(x) \in \gamma \\ \hat{e}\left(g^{b\beta_i}, \left(g^{\frac{q_x{}^*(0)p_{lx}(0)}{b\beta_i}} \right)^{r_l + H_1(M||\sigma_{id_l})^{s_l}} \right), \\ \text{if } att(x) \notin \gamma \end{cases}$$
$$= \hat{e}\left(g^{p_{lx}(0)}, g^{q_x{}^*(0)} \right)^{r_l + H_1(M||\sigma_{id_l})^{s_l}} \tag{10}$$

By recalling the recursive function, the value of root node F_{root} can be calculated by:

$$F_{root} = \hat{e}\left(g^{p_{lroot}(0)}, g^{q_{root}{}^*(0)} \right)^{r_l + H_1(M||\sigma_{id_l})^{s_l}} = \hat{e}\left(g^{s_l}, g^{q_{root}{}^*(0)} \right)^{r_l + H_1(M||\sigma_{id_l})^{s_l}} = \left(\hat{e}(g,g)^{s_l q_{root}{}^*(0)} \right)^{r_l + H_1(M||\sigma_{id_l})^{s_l}} \tag{11}$$

According to the setting in *Setup* phase, let $s_l = c$, $r_l + H_1(M||\sigma_{id_l})^{s_l} = f$, then

$$F_{root} = \left(\hat{e}(g,g)^{s_l \cdot q_{root}{}^*(0)} \right)^{r_l + H_1(M||\sigma_{id_l})^{s_l}} = \begin{cases} \left(\hat{e}(g,g)^{abc} \right)^f, \text{if } \mu = 0 \\ \left(\hat{e}(g,g)^z \right)^f, \text{if } \mu = 1 \end{cases} \tag{12}$$

Then we will discuss the advantage of simulator in breaking the DBDH assumption.

When $\mu = 0$, *Adversary* forges the signature successfully. According to our assumption, the probability of this incident is $\frac{1}{2}+\varepsilon$. When *Adversary* successfully forges the signature, simulator guesses $u^*=0$ and simulator has a $\frac{1}{2}+\varepsilon$ probability of making the correct guess of u^*. The probability of simulator making the correct judgment can be denoted by:

$$Pr(u^* = u|\mu = 0) = \frac{1}{2}+\varepsilon \tag{13}$$

When $\mu=1$, *Adversary* fails to forge the signature. The result of output is rejected symbol $\perp$. Under this condition simulator guesses μ^* randomly. The probability of simulator making the correct judgment can be denoted by:

$$Pr(u^* = u|\mu = 1) = \frac{1}{2} \tag{14}$$

As is mentioned above, the advantage of simulator is:

$$\begin{aligned}&\frac{1}{2}Pr(u^* = u|\mu = 0)+\frac{1}{2}Pr(u^* = u|\mu = 1)-\frac{1}{2}\\&=\frac{1}{2}\left(\frac{1}{2}+\varepsilon\right)+\frac{1}{2}\times\frac{1}{2}-\frac{1}{2}\\&=\frac{\varepsilon}{2}\end{aligned} \tag{15}$$

Unforgeability with untrusted authorities and traceability

In attribute based signature mechanism, users' attribute private keys are generated and distributed by AA. Under this circumstance, AA is capable of forging any signatures without being detected. To keep the whole system running safely, AA must be honest and highly protected from being invaded. However, in the complex network systems, there are variety risks which may result in the fault of AA. Consequently, for the sake of safety, AA's rights in the system should be reduced to some extent. In our KP-ABS-UT, the private key used for signature is generated by joint efforts of both AA and user, so it is computational infeasible for AA to forge any signatures which should be signed by legal users. Besides, since different users randomly choose different secret numbers to embed into their initial private keys distributed from AA, it is computational infeasible for a user to personate any other users to forge a legal signature in the system.

Anonymity is another important feature of common attribute based signature mechanism. However, some malicious users may take advantage of this feature to send out illegal information without taking responsibility. To prevent such incidents happening, in our KP-ABS-UT scheme, the signer's identity can be revealed with the introducing of "tracer". When data receivers receive illegal information from a malicious signer, they can send the signature ν to tracer. Since tracer has stored $\sigma_{id_l}=(g^s)^{id_l}$ with user's identity, the signer's identity can be located by searching the id_l–σ_{id_l} list. Then tracer calculates $\sigma_{id_l}{}^{-id_l}=\left((g^s)^{id_l}\right)^{-id_l}=g^s$. Since s is the secret number used in the *Sign* algorithm and g^s has been sent to tracer, a signer cannot deny the message he signed before.

Efficiency and comparison analysis

In our KP-ABS-UT scheme, assume "n" to be the amount of attributes which a signer owns. The *Sign* algorithm needs (n + 3) times of exponential operation and 1 hash operation. The computation of *Sign* algorithm is low since it does not need any paring operation. The *Verify* algorithm needs (n + 1) times of paring operation and 1 hash operation. Since the computation cost of paring operation is much more than any other operation, in this paper, we mainly compare the number of paring operation with other ABS schemes [9, 14, 18] with respect to efficiency. The efficiency and performance comparison results are listed below in Table 2.

From the result we can see that the computation cost is lower in our KP-ABS-UT since the number of bilinear paring operation is reduced. Thus our plan has a higher efficiency. Besides, our KP-ABS-UT uses access tree as control structure, each signer's private key corresponds a certain structure. It is computational infeasible for different users to collude their private keys with each other to forge a legal signature. With the introducing of user's secret key component and the entity "tracer", the signature cannot be forged by AA and can be traced to identity if a malicious user releases information illegally. The overall comparison shows our KP-ABS-UT is of better performance and is more appropriate for secure data verification in open network systems such as cloud computing, etc.

Conclusion

In this paper, we propose a KP-ABS with untrusted authorities and traceability, which is also of high efficiency. In our scheme, the signer's private key is composed by two components: one part is distributed by attribute authority and the other part is chosen privately by the signer's self. The signature cannot be forged by any other users including attribute authority. What's more, the identity of signer can be traced. Our scheme is proved to be secure and of better performance with respect to efficiency.

Table 2 Efficiency and performance comparison

Scheme	Access method	Traceability	With untrusted AA	Computation cost
[14]	LSSS	Yes	No	(n + 3) paring
[9]	Threshold	No	No	4 paring
[18]	Threshold	No	No	(n + 4) paring
Our scheme	Access tree	Yes	Yes	(n + 1) paring

Our future work should focus on the attribute revocation and key refreshing in our KP-ABS scheme. Once key exposure happens, although the system can trace the traitor, however, user's private keys still need to be refreshed for the safe of privacy. Consequently, research on the attribute based refreshing mechanisms should be taken into our future research direction. Besides, outsourcing ABS [9] with untrusted attribute authorities also merits attention.

Competing interests

The authors declare that they have no competing financial interests.

Authors' contribution

Dr Hanshu Hong: Participated in the design of scheme and drafted the manuscript. Dr Zhixin Sun: Participated in the performance analysis of the proposed KP-ABS-UT. All authors read and approved the final manuscript.

Acknowledgement

This research is supported by the National Natural Science Foundation of China (60973140, 61170276, 61373135).

References

1. Sahai, A, Waters, "Fuzzy identity-based encryption". Proc. Int. Conf. EUROCRYPT 2005, pp. 457-473, Aarhus, Denmark: Springer; 2005. http://link.springer.com/chapter/10.1007%2F11426639_27
2. V. Goyal, O. Pandey, A. Sahai and B. Waters, "Attribute Based Encryption for Fine-Grained Access Control of Encrypted Data", In ACM conference on Computer and Communications Security, pp. 89-98. 2006.
3. Attrapadung N, Libert B, De Panafieu E. Expressive key-policy attribute-based encryption with constant-size ciphertexts, Public Key Cryptography—PKC 2011, vol. 6571 of LNCS. Taormina, Italy: Springer, pp. 90-108, 2011.
4. Bethencourt J, Sahai A, Waters B (2007) Ciphertext-Policy Attribute Based Encryption. Proceedings of the 2007 IEEE Symposium on Security and Privacy, Washington DC, pp 321–334
5. H. K. Maji, M. Prabhakaran, and M. Rosulek, "Attribute-based signatures: Achieving attribute-privacy and collusion-resistance," IACR Cryptology ePrint Archive, pp. 328 – 351, 2008.
6. B. Z. J. S. Dan Cao, Xiaofeng Wang and Q. Hu, "Mediated attribute based signature scheme supporting key revocation," in Proceedings of the 8th International Conference on Information Science and Digital Content Technology. Jeju Island, Korea: IEEE; 2012; 277–282.
7. S.Q. Guo and Y.P. Zeng, "Attribute-based signature scheme", In International Conference on Information Security and Assurance, pp.509-511, 2008.
8. H. K. Maji, M. Prabhakaran, and M. Rosulek, "Attribute-based signatures", in CT-RSA, 2011, pp. 376–392, 2011.
9. Chen X, Li J, Huang X (2014) Secure Outsourced Attribute-Based Signatures". IEEE Transactions on Parallel and Distributed Systems 25(12):3285–3294
10. S. Shahandashti and R. Safavi-Naini, "Threshold attribute-based signatures and their application to anonymous credential systems," Progress in Cryptology–AFRICACRYPT 2009, pp. 198–216, 2009.
11. Kumar S, Agrawal S, Balaraman S, Rangan C (2011) Attribute Based Signatures for Bounded Multi-level Threshold Circuits. Public Key Infrastructures, Services and Applications (EuroPKI 2010), Berlin Heidelberg, pp 141–154
12. J. Herranz, F. Laguillaumie, B. Libert, "Short attribute based signatures for threshold predicates", Topics in Cryptology–CT-RSA 2012, pp. 51–67, 2012.
13. A. Escala, J. Herranz, and P. Morillo, "Revocable attribute-based signatures with adaptive security in the standard model," in AFRICACRYPT, pp. 224–241, 2011.
14. S.L Ding, Y. Zhao, "Efficient Traceable Attribute-Based Signature", in IEEE 13th International Conference on Trust, Security and Privacy in Computing and Communications, pp 582-589, 2014.
15. Li J, Kim K (2010) Hidden attribute-based signatures without anonymity revocation. Inform Sci 180(9):1681–1689
16. Okamoto, T., Takashima, K, "Decentralized attribute-based signatures", Public Key Cryptography-PKC. Nara, Japan: 2013; 125–142.
17. X. Liu, J. Ma, Q. Li, J. Xiong, and F. Huang, "Attribute based multi-signature scheme in the standard model," in Proceedings of the 9th International Conference on Computational Intelligence and Security (CIS'13). Sichuan Province, China: IEEE; 2013; 738–742.
18. Zhiqian Xu, Keith M. Martin, "Anonymous User Revocation for Using Attribute-Based Signature in Cloud Computing". 6th International Conference on Cloud Computing Technology and Science. Singapore: IEEE; 2014; 358-365.
19. Boneh D, Franklin M (2001) Identity-Based encryption from the weil pairing. In: Advances in Cryptology-CRYPTO 2001. Springer-Verlag, LNCS 2139, Berlin, Heidelberg, pp 213–229

2

Dynamic spatial index for efficient query processing on the cloud

Ibrahim Kamel[2], Ayesha M. Talha[1*] and Zaher Al Aghbari[3]

Abstract

Data owners with large volumes of data can outsource spatial databases by taking advantage of the cost-effective cloud computing model with attractive on-demand features such as scalability and high computing power. Data confidentiality in outsourced databases is a key requirement and therefore, untrusted third-party service providers in the cloud should not be able to view or manipulate the data. This paper proposes DISC (Dynamic Index for Spatial data on the Cloud), a secure retrieval scheme to answer range queries over encrypted databases at the Cloud Service Provider. The dynamic spatial index is also able to support dynamic updates on the outsourced data at the cloud server. To be able to support secure query processing and updates on the Cloud, spatial transformation is applied to the data and the spatial index is encrypted using Order-Preserving Encryption. With transformation and cryptography techniques, DISC achieves a balance between efficient query execution and data confidentiality in a cloud environment. Additionally, a more secure scheme, DISC*, is proposed to balance the trade-off between query results returned and security provided. The security analysis section studies the various attacks handled by DISC. The experimental study demonstrates that the proposed scheme achieves a lower communication cost in comparison to existing cloud retrieval schemes.

Keywords: Data outsourcing, Spatial queries, Encryption, Dynamic updates

Introduction

With increase in spatial data, data owners require the services of untrusted remote servers that can store huge amount of data and allow fast access to outsourced data. Cloud computing allows a third-party service provider to manage the data and provide services directly to the end-user. Cloud computing provides attractive features such as scalability, cost-effectiveness and high-computing power. Popular examples of cloud-based services include Google Maps and Amazon EC2. In recent years, mobile devices and navigational systems have become common and this has created the need for location-based services (LBSs). Mobile users issue queries from devices with limited storage and computational resources. Spatial range queries performed at the cloud server must be completed in real-time and only relevant results should be returned to the user.

The cloud model consists of three entities, namely the Data Owner (DO), Cloud Service Provider (CSP) and the Trusted User (TU). The DO outsources the spatial data and index for fast retrieval to the CSP, while the TU issues encrypted queries to the CSP. The query is processed directly on the encrypted data at the CSP without additional communication overhead between the TU and CSP. The relevant results are returned in a secure format to the TU, where decryption reveals the actual data points.

The fact that the data is controlled by an untrusted third-party [1–4], raises security concerns about data confidentiality. Data confidentiality requires that data is not disclosed to untrusted servers, as they could release sensitive information to competitors. Therefore, when outsourcing spatial databases in the cloud, the data should not be visible to the service provider or adversaries. The CSP provides services to multiple DOs and hence cannot be trusted. Another prime concern is efficient query execution, which can be resolved by using a spatial indexing structure for fast data access.

To achieve total confidentiality, the naïve solution is to encrypt the whole dataset and send only the encrypted

*Correspondence: atalha@sharjah.ac.ae
[1] Research Institute of Sciences & Engineering, University of Sharjah, Sharjah, United Arab Emirates
Full list of author information is available at the end of the article

data to the cloud service provider. During the query phase, the TU retrieves the entire encrypted data from the server, decrypts it and searches for the required data points. This makes ideal security achievable, but it is clearly not practical in real-time applications as the resulting data communication cost would be high, especially if only a small portion of the data is queried. Furthermore, the high processing power of the cloud environment would not be utilized in this case.

This paper focuses on the development of an efficient retrieval technique that can be executed on encrypted data at the cloud service provider. Several specialized retrieval techniques have been proposed to answer queries on encrypted data. Researchers have adopted two different approaches to resolve this issue. The first approach is to use spatial transformation techniques to obfuscate the original data prior to sending it to the CSP [5–8]. The other approach is to use cryptographic techniques [9–12] to protect the confidentiality of the outsourced data. To provide a double layer of security, we apply both transformation and encryption techniques on the outsourced data.

In cryptographic approaches, some existing works use the Advanced Encryption Standard (AES) [13], which can be used only to answer exact-match queries. While others use the Order-Preserving Encryption (OPE) technique [10]. OPE is a class of cryptographic techniques that preserves the relative order of the encrypted objects, executing range queries on the encrypted data directly at the server without having to decrypt it. Although the security of OPE falls short of the targeted industry standards, there is a lot of interest by researchers in OPE as it allows comparisons directly on the encrypted data. Since this paper supports queries on encrypted data at the CSP, we employ the OPE technique for the index and the secure AES for the spatial data points.

Security and query processing efficiency are important when designing schemes applicable in a cloud environment. In this paper, the **DISC** (**D**ynamic **I**ndex for **S**patial data on the **C**loud) scheme is proposed for answering spatial range queries on encrypted databases at the CSP. In DISC, a combination of transformation and encryption is used to provide a fair balance between data confidentiality and query execution. Another key advantage of the proposed approach is that there is no need for the DO to install an additional trusted front-end i.e. a tamper-resistant device [14–16], between the user and cloud service provider during query processing.

Briefly, the DISC retrieval scheme works as follows. The DO transforms the spatial data points and indexes them. The index is encrypted using the OPE technique for fast data access at the CSP, while the spatial data points are encrypted using the more secure AES. Next, the indexed data is outsourced and encrypted queries are processed entirely on the encrypted data at the CSP. Encrypted query results are returned to the TU, where they are decrypted using the key provided by the DO and then false positives are filtered to obtain the actual query results. With DISC, it is also possible to perform updates dynamically on the encrypted index at the CSP, where the DO issues an encrypted update request to be partially carried out at the CSP.

Contributions:

- A retrieval scheme is proposed to answer queries over encrypted data at the CSP, ensuring confidentiality of data outsourced by the DO.
- DISC provides efficient communication between the TU and CSP (one round of communication).
- The proposed scheme supports dynamic updates such as insert, delete and modify on the encrypted data at the CSP.
- An enhanced and secure scheme, DISC*, is proposed as well to further obscure the data at the CSP.
- Furthermore, a comprehensive security analysis against known attacks used in the literature is provided.
- Simulation experiments were conducted on real data to evaluate the performance of DISC and the proposed scheme is compared to an existing cryptographic transformation scheme in terms of communication cost.

The remainder of the paper is organized as follows. The next section surveys some existing work in this area. "Problem statement" section briefly discusses the cloud system model. Then, "DISC: a retrieval scheme" section describes DISC used in our approach. "Indexing spatial data" section discusses the indexing scheme in detail, and "Answering spatial range queries at CSP" section presents the spatial query phase, i.e., processing encrypted queries at the service provider. "Dynamic updates at CSP" section focuses on dynamic updates on DISC at the CSP. "Secure scheme: DISC*" section proposes a secure and enhanced DISC* scheme, which discusses the trade-offs between efficiency and security. Next, "Security analysis" section provides a security analysis on the transformation and encryption technique incorporated in DISC. Lastly, experiments are conducted on two real spatial datasets, and the results with comparative and evaluative measures are offered in "Experimental evaluation" section, followed by conclusions in "Conclusions" section.

Related work

The issue of secure outsourcing of data has been addressed in several recent papers. Hacigümüs et al. [17] were the first to formally propose database services outsourcing to a third-party service provider. The typical model comprises of the data owner, service provider and authorized users. The data owner outsources data and query services to the untrusted service provider. In Location-based services, trusted users issue queries to the service provider. Despite the fact that the cloud environment provides on-demand services along with scalable storage and extensive computational power, it poses data security and privacy challenges. The primary goal is to secure data by encrypting it and allowing queries on encrypted spatial data at the cloud service provider. Batten et al. [18] propose a cloud storage model, which comprises of cloud customers, cloud service provider and cloud service operator. The customer rents storage from the service provider, which owns the cloud resources and maximizes storage resource utilization between numerous customers, and the management of data storage is taken care of by the service operator.

One of the existing work by Yiu et al. [5] proposed several transformation as well as a cryptographic scheme for outsourcing spatial databases. In data transformation schemes, the data points are relocated in the space based on an equation. In these schemes, the attacker can gain knowledge about nearby points with limited background information. The encryption based scheme inherits the security of AES, where the DO stores the encrypted R^*-tree index in the cloud. To process a query, the data owner retrieve encrypted nodes of the R^*-tree level by level, decrypts them and select intersected nodes. They are able to hide the spatial data from the CSP, but cannot provide range query processing at the server. Thus, answering queries requires multiple rounds of data communication between the server and user.

Similarly, Kim et al. [19, 20] designed a transformation scheme based on the Hilbert curve. The space is transformed by clustering the data points and reducing the dimensionality to $1 - D$. The data is encrypted using the conventional AES and stored at the server. To process a range query, the entire encrypted file has to be sent to the user to search for relevant records. The user then requests for required data, hence requiring multiple rounds of communication.

Both [5] and [19] result in a high communication cost between the service provider and user owing to multiple rounds of data exchange. To overcome this, Talha et al. [21] present a dual transformation approach that allows query processing on encrypted data at the server. The original spatial data points coordinates are hidden using the Hilbert space-filling curve and grouped in packets. The encrypted data is stored at the server. The user sends encrypted spatial range queries and the results are decrypted by the user. This lowers the communication cost as it is limited to a single round.

However, the above-mentioned transformation-based and cryptographic approaches are designed for static data and therefore cannot handle dynamic updates. In the event of any insertions, deletions or modifications to the data, the dataset would have to be indexed and encrypted again before outsourcing it to the CSP. Whereas, the DISC scheme proposed in this work can handle dynamic updates from the DO.

To support range queries over large datasets efficiently, Damiani et al. [14] build a tree-index and store the nodes of a B+ tree as encrypted blocks. To process a range selection, the user repeatedly retrieves a node, starting with the root, and decrypts it to identify the child node to traverse to. Upon reaching the target leaf node, he then follows the sibling pointers in the leaf level.

On the other hand, Hore et al. [16] partition the data into a set of buckets. The data owner builds indices for buckets which are not hierarchically structured, so the index search must be linear in the number of buckets. Increasing the bucket size improves privacy but reduces efficiency, since the indices must be locally stored, and index searching is linear.

Data privacy and query integrity is assured by Ku et al. [22] for outsourced databases. The points are encrypted with a symmetric key and indexed based on the Hilbert curve. A probabilistic approach is applied to a portion of data encrypted with a different key to ensure reliability of query results.

Recently, Wang et al. [9] proposed a framework that provides both security and efficiency. They use an $\hat{R}$-tree index that is encrypted using Asymmetric Scalar-product Preserving Encryption (ASPE) scheme. However, it does not provide a privacy guarantee, nor does it provide confidential query processing because it leaks information on the ordering of the MBR of the leaf nodes and requires result post-processing as it introduces false positives.

Wong et al. [23] propose a scheme for secure kNN (k-Nearest Neighbors) queries on encrypted data. Distance comparisons between an encrypted query and data points are achieved using ASPE, with query points and data points being encrypted differently. Given two data points and a query point, the cloud can determine which data point is closer to the query point. Lu et al. [24] proposed an outsourced range query scheme using predicate encryption. This scheme provides provable security and can achieve logarithmic-time search since it orders the encrypted data points. However, it is not very practical as it only supports 1-D data.

In contrast to the approaches mentioned above, Hu et al. [3] propose that the DO outsources decryption keys to the server, and provides users with encrypted data. In a query process, a user first sends encrypted data and query to the cloud, then the cloud uses the decryption key to decrypt data and query, and return the result. The novelty of this paper is that they use homomorphic encryption to ensure that the cloud cannot learn anything during the query process. However, fully homomorphic encryption [25] is highly impractical in practice.

To overcome the limitations of the existing schemes, our approach is modeled to achieve a balance between data confidentiality and efficient query processing i.e single round of communication. To allow range queries over encrypted numeric data, Agrawal et al. [10] propose the Order-Preserving Encryption (OPE), where a plaintext is converted to ciphertext through order-preserving mapping functions This scheme is secure against ciphertext-only attacks and fails when the data distribution or the plaintext are known, as it is then straightforward to associate an encrypted record with its plaintext counterpart.

Yiu et al. [26] utilize OPE in a metric-preserving transformation, where each data point is assigned to its closest pivot. The index reveals information about the space by not hiding the number of points per pivot. The query is evaluated with regards to the original space but the query point is mapped to a pivot point. Furthermore, adaptive chosen-plaintext attacks can reveal the secret key and help identify dense areas in the space.

Problem statement

System model

In this paper, DISC is proposed, which is a Dynamic encrypted Index for Spatial data on the Cloud. The DISC cloud system model is shown in Fig. 1, and it comprises of three distinct entities. Namely the Data Owner (**DO**), Cloud Service Provider (**CSP**) and the Trusted Users (**TU**). Briefly, the process works as follows, DO outsources spatial data to CSP which is queried by TUs. The database is transformed, indexed and encrypted before it is stored on the cloud. The keys are sent to the users by the DO. The CSP processes encrypted range queries and modifies the dynamic index with encrypted updates sent by the DO. TUs issue encrypted range queries to the CSP and obtain encrypted query results in a single round. Lastly, the TU decrypts the results returned.

Notations

The DISC retrieval technique can be generalized to several domains. Given a spatial dataset, D, at the DO with s two-dimensional spatial data points, $D = (d_1, d_2, \ldots, d_s)$, represents physical locations in the space. The domain of each dataset is normalized to the unit square $[0, 1]^2$ in 2−D Euclidean space, $\mathbb{E}^2$. Table 1 lists the notations that will be used throughout the paper.

Preliminaries

Hilbert Transformation: Space-filling curves are used to map multidimensional data to one-dimensional data where they pass through every partition in a given space without any intersection with itself. The mapping has to be *distance-preserving* such that points closer in space are mapped onto nearby points on the curve. One of the widely used curves is the Hilbert curve due to its superior clustering properties [27]. Spatial points are traversed exactly once and indexed based on the order in which they are visited by the curve. We begin by representing the area of an N x N grid as a single cell. We iterate, and in the ith iteration, $i = 0, \ldots, n-1$ (for $N = 2^n$), we partition the area of the N x N grid into $2^i.2^i$ blocks. Next, the points are assigned Hilbert cell values based on the curve. The grid is spanned according to the curve using the Hilbert Space Key (HSK) [22]. The HSK = $\{x_0, y_0, \theta, g\}$, where (x_0, y_0) is the curve's starting point, θ is the curve's orientation and g is the curve granularity. Based on the HSK, it is possible for two or more points to have the same cell value in the curve.

Order-preserving encryption: It is a type of homomorphic encryption scheme. Fully Homomorphic

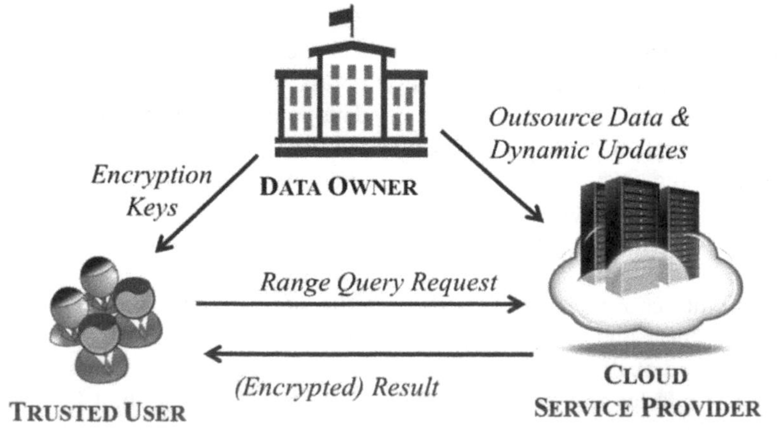

Fig. 1 Proposed system model for spatial data outsourcing

Table 1 List of Notations used

Notation	Description
DO	Data owner
CSP	Cloud service provider
TU	Trusted user
D	2D spatial data point set
F_{HSK}	Hilbert transformation function
H	Hilbert cell value
K_{OPE}	Order-preserving encryption key
K_{AES}	Advanced encryption standard key
LHV	Largest Hilbert value
$nodeCapacity(n_L)$	Node Capacity of a leaf node
QR	Query Hilbert value set
R	Query result set

Encryption [25] would be ideal as it allows query execution on encrypted data and is completely secure, however, its high computation cost makes it prohibitive in practice. Therefore, we employ the order-preserving encryption (OPE) scheme proposed by Boldyreva et al. [28], which allows range queries to be evaluated on the numeric data. The order of plaintext data is preserved in the ciphertext domain through a random mapping without revealing the data itself. For an encryption key K_{OPE}, if $x < y$, then $E_{K_{OPE}}(x) < E_{K_{OPE}}(y)$. OPE allows efficient access to the encrypted data by maintaining a set of indexes for simple comparisons, such as relational and logical operations between values in a spatial range query request. For OPE applied to integer values, the output set is bigger than the input set meaning that no two values will have the same encrypted value.

Hilbert R-tree: It is a hybrid structure based on the R-tree and B^+-tree that utilizes the Hilbert space-filling curve. The nodes in the tree are sorted on the Hilbert value of their rectangle centroid. A defining characteristic of the Hilbert R-tree is that there exists an order of the nodes at each tree level, respecting the Hilbert order of the Minimum Bounding Rectangles (MBRs). Searching procedure is similar to that of R-tree. Each internal node entry consists of the MBR that encloses all the objects in the corresponding subtree, the largest Hilbert value (LHV) of the subtree, and a pointer to the next level. Each leaf node of the Hilbert R-tree stores the Hilbert coordinate of the MBR of each data point stored and has a well-defined set of sibling nodes. Thus, the Hilbert R-tree can keep spatial data ordering according to Hilbert value when it is updated dynamically. Dynamic Hilbert R-trees achieve high degree of space utilization and good response time, while other R-tree variants have no control over space utilization. The Hilbert R-Tree allows around 28% saving in response time compared with existing structures. Moreover, the R-tree index is non-deterministic as the tree structure differs based on the sequence of insertions, whereas the Hilbert R-tree does not suffer from this.

System model data flows

With DISC, it is possible to process user queries in a secure and efficient manner. The data index is built and encrypted at the DO and stored at the CSP, while the TU issues encrypted spatial queries. There are four different data flows in the model:

1. **DO to CSP:** Outsources the encrypted spatial index to the CSP as well as the encrypted dynamic updates. The Hilbert curve is used to transform the location of spatial data points. Following the formal definition of the Hilbert space-filling curve in [27], H_{2D} with granularity, $g \geq 1$ is used for a two-dimensional space. This implies that any point in the 2−D set, D, is mapped to a 1−dimensional integer set $[0, \ldots, 2^{2g} - 1]$ using the Hilbert transformation function $F_{HSK} = f(d)$ based on the HSK (cf. "Preliminaries" section). Next, the DO forms the Hilbert R-tree. The encryption function $E_{K_{OPE}}$ is applied to the internal nodes in the index and $E_{K_{AES}}$ is used for the spatial points. Encrypted updates, $U = E_{K_{OPE}}(u)$, are sent individually to the CSP as required.
2. **DO to TU:** The transformation key, HSK, and encryption keys, K_{OPE} and K_{AES}, are sent by the DO. Communication channel between the DO and TUs is assumed to be secured under existing security protocols such as SSL.
3. **TU to CSP:** TU converts the range query request to a set of 1−D Hilbert indices, $QR = (q_1, \ldots, q_m)$, using F_{HSK}. This integer set is encrypted using $E_{K_{OPE}}$ and sent to the CSP to be executed over the encrypted index.
4. **CSP to TU:** The encrypted query is processed entirely at the CSP and the resulting data point set, $R = (E_{K_{AES}}(d_1), \ldots, E_{K_{AES}}(d_r))$, encrypted using AES, is returned to the TU where it is decrypted using $E_{K_{AES}}$ and filtered to remove false positives.

DISC: a retrieval scheme

The data owner stores data on remote servers that provide querying services to trusted users. Data confidentiality in an outsourcing retrieval scheme is key as data is managed by an untrusted party i.e. CSP. A common mechanism to ensure secure data outsourcing is encryption, so that the CSP can learn as little information about the plain data as possible. In this work, DISC is proposed to process encrypted queries directly on encrypted data, in order to keep the data and query results confidential from adversaries. It is required to have a balance between data confidentiality and query execution. A spatial indexing structure is built to provide fast data access and in turn, efficient query processing.

Indexing spatial data

Spatial index is a data structure used to improve the efficiency of spatial data operations on data objects. Common spatial index methods include the R-tree and its variants. **DISC**, a **D**ynamic encrypted **I**ndex for **S**patial data on the **C**loud, uses the dynamic Hilbert R-tree [29] with regards to the Hilbert transformation used to discretize the data points. The index structure is then encrypted using the Order-Preserving Encryption scheme (OPE [28], while the actual data is encrypted separately with a secure symmetric encryption method, AES.

The indexing scheme used by the DO is illustrated in Figs. 2 and 3. The index construction process at the DO is initiated with static 2−D spatial data points in the space. Next, each spatial point in the space is assigned a Hilbert cell value in the grid. In the example in Fig. 2, the space is partitioned into 64 cells by applying a Hilbert curve of granularity 3 with starting point $(0, 0)$.

Next, the Hilbert R-tree index is constructed bottom-up based on the ascending Hilbert cell values. The DO then encrypts the Hilbert R-tree internal nodes and Hilbert values in leaf nodes using OPE, while the data points in the leaf nodes are encrypted using AES before being outsourced to the CSP, since it is not a trusted entity. This protects the sensitive data from being leaked by the CSP (i.e. to third-party vendors). The CSP does not have the ability to decrypt the encrypted data without the secret keys. The DO sends the transformation and encryption keys only to TUs.

The encrypted index and data points at the CSP are shown in Fig. 3. The leaf and non-leaf nodes are encrypted using OPE [enclosed in a red dashed box] to support range queries and dynamic updates, while the data points in the leaf nodes [enclosed in the blue solid box] are encrypted individually using the secure and traditional encryption scheme, AES [13]. The parent-children relationships (i.e. pointers) in the index are not encrypted in order to allow efficient query search. Additionally, the DO sends the OPE key and the AES key to the TUs so that they can send encrypted queries to the CSP and decrypt the returned query results.

Algorithm 1 lists the pseudo-code for the dynamic index construction process. In the first loop (Lines 1–4), each spatial data point d_i in D is normalized to $[0, 1]^2$ and then its Hilbert cell value is computed using the Hilbert transformation function, F_{HSK}, based on the Hilbert Space Key. In Line 5, the resulting Hilbert cell values for all data points are stored in C and sorted before building the Hilbert R-tree Index (Line 6). Lines 7–12: all the nodes in the tree are encrypted. If it is an internal node, MBR and LHVs are encrypted using the OPE scheme to allow for comparisons on the encrypted data. While, data points in the leaf nodes are encrypted using AES. Lastly

Algorithm 1 Encrypted Index Construction (by **DO**)

Input:
Spatial Data Points, $D = (d_1, \ldots, d_s)$
Encryption Keys, K_{OPE} and K_{AES}

1: **for all** d in D **do**
2: Normalize d_i
3: Compute Hilbert value, c of d_i using F_{HSK} and add to C
4: **end for**
5: `I = BuildHilbertR-Tree()`
6: **for all** n in I **do**
7: Encrypt MBR and LHV using K_{OPE}
8: **if** n_i is a leaf node **then**
9: Encrypt data points in n_i using K_{AES}
10: **end if**
11: **end for**
12: Send Encrypted Index, I_E, to **CSP**

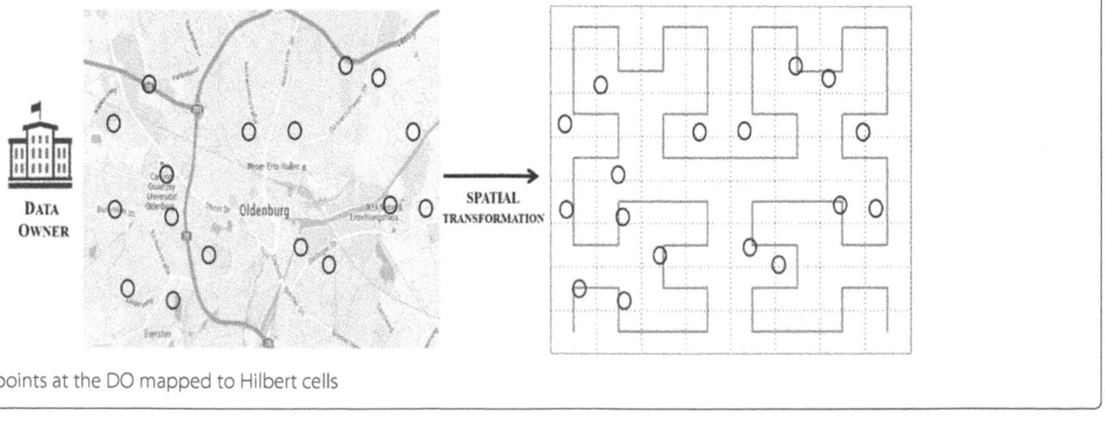

Fig. 2 Spatial data points at the DO mapped to Hilbert cells

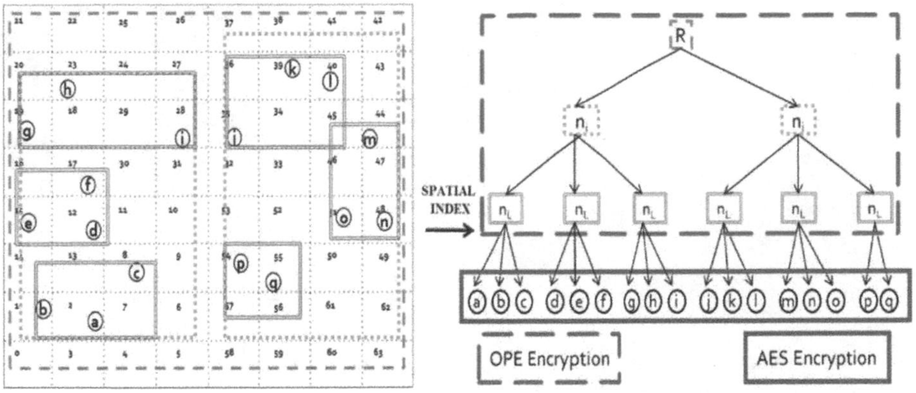

Fig. 3 Index construction process based on transformation

(Line 13), the index is outsourced to the Cloud Service Provider.

Answering spatial range queries at CSP

The key requirement for query processing at the cloud server is fast response time. The encryption scheme in DISC encrypts nodes without modifying the index structure, hence faster than linear search is possible. The DISC retrieval scheme deals with 2−D spatial range queries due to their popularity. In spatial range query algorithms, the index search propagates downwards starting from the root node, considering whether node entries overlap with cells in the query region.

When a query request is initiated by the TU, the rectangular region of the range query, (QW ([(cx_0, cy_0), (cx_1, cy_1)])), is converted to a set of 1-D Hilbert cell values [30] by the TU, which includes cells that may partially or completely overlap with the query region. Since some of these cells only partially overlap with the query region, the set of cells might retrieve irrelevant data points (i.e. false positives) in the query response. Having false positives in the results is a reasonable trade-off for security, given that the ordering information and data points are securely encrypted in DISC. The Hilbert cells in the query set are then encrypted by the TU using the OPE key. The CSP is responsible for processing the encrypted query request over the spatial index.

Figure 4 shows the spatial range query procedure. Queries are formulated in terms of their OPE encrypted Hilbert values and AES encrypted data points corresponding to encrypted Hilbert values are returned. The CSP searches the index created by DISC, performing comparison tests level-by-level, and proceeding to a node's children if and only if the node's LHV is greater than the query value. The CSP thereby obtains all leaves contained in the query region, and then returns data points in leaf nodes to the TU with Hilbert values corresponding to the queried values. We assume that the granularity for the Hilbert curve transformation is high enough, such that each data point is associated with a unique Hilbert value. The CSP cannot query the data points themselves as comparisons cannot be made on data encrypted using AES.

The Hilbert R-tree index improves the search performance as it uses Hilbert cell values to impose a total order on the entries. Algorithm 2 shows the complete spatial range query procedure. Lines 1 − 6 and Line 18 list the process at the TU, while Lines 7 − 17 highlight the query processing procedure at the CSP. First, the rectangular query region, QW ([(cx_0, cy_0), (cx_1, cy_1)]), is converted

Algorithm 2 Spatial Query Processing on Encrypted Data (CSP)

Input:
Query Window QW, [(cx_0, cy_0), (cx_1, cy_1)]
Encryption Keys, K_{OPE} and K_{AES}
1: Q = Hilbert cells contained in QW ▷ At **TU**
2: **for all** $q \in Q$ **do**
3: $QR = QR \cup K_{OPE}(q)$
4: **end for**
5: Send encrypted QR to CSP
6: **for all** n nodes in Index **do** ▷ At **CSP**
7: **if** (n_i is a leaf node **then**
8: Check for intersection between QR and all Hilbert Values in n_i
9: Add corresponding data points to R
10: **else if** LHV(n_i) is greater than QR_i **then**
11: Search recursively in the subtree under n_i
12: **end if**
13: **end for**
14: Return encrypted spatial data points, R, to TU
15: **TU** decrypts R using K_{AES} to obtain actual data objects

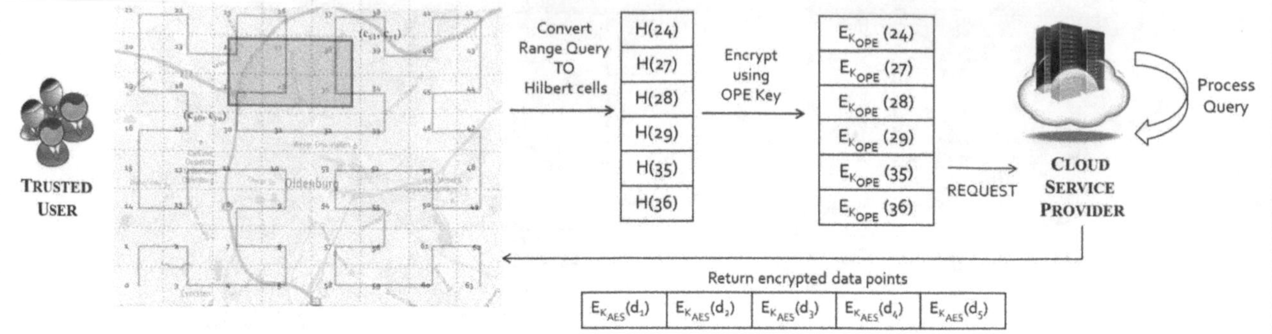

Fig. 4 Query processing at the cloud service provider on encrypted data sent by trusted users

into a set of ascending Hilbert cell values (Line 2) and stored as *QR* at the user end. Next, in Lines 3 – 5, the TU encrypts *QR* using the encryption function K_{OPE}. The encrypted *QR* is sent to the CSP as *QR* along with the encrypted query window *QW*. In Lines 9 – 16, starting from the root, the search descends the tree structure and examines all nodes, *n*, that have Hilbert values less than the queried values, *QR*. If n_i is at the leaf level, each Hilbert value in the leaf node is checked against query Hilbert values in *QR*. The encrypted data points of matched values are returned as the query response, *R*, to the user (Line 17). In Line 18, the TU then decrypts the retrieved data points using the K_{AES} key and generates the actual query response.

Dynamic updates at CSP

Besides processing spatial range queries efficiently at the cloud service provider, DISC allows dynamic updates on encrypted data. DISC takes advantage of the total ordering based on Hilbert transformed values in order to support updates. The proposed scheme is capable of updating an OPE encrypted index at the CSP without revealing the underlying index structure. Dynamic data includes three update operations on the encrypted index: insert, delete and modify. In order to update a spatial data point in DISC, the data owner first needs to issue an update request. Based on the request, the CSP has to locate (i.e. query) which leaf nodes of the index are directly affected. Lastly, all updates applicable to the parent nodes are propagated upwards till the root.

Insert: The new spatial data point to be inserted is sent in an encrypted format by the DO to the CSP. The data point is encryped using AES and the corresponding Hilbert value (H) of the MBR centroid is computed and encrypted using OPE, so that comparison operations can be made. For insertion, the Hilbert R-tree index performs binary search on the total ordering of Hilbert values and these are used as the key value to find the insertion location in the encrypted index, based on simple value comparisons. Starting from the root node, at each level the node with the minimum LHV greater than H of all its sibling nodes is chosen. When a leaf node, n_L, is reached, insertion can be done. If the node capacity of n_L has not exceeded the node capacity, $nodeCapacity_{max}$, the AES encrypted data point is inserted in n_L along with the H value. If the leaf node, n_L, is full, overflow has to be handled by by splitting the leaf node into two and moving half of the ordered entries to a new node. Lastly, the index has to be adjusted such that the LHV values of the parent nodes reflect the newly inserted value. The algorithm at the functional level is listed in Algorithm 3.

Algorithm 3 Insert Encrypted Data in DISC

Input:

Encrypted Data Point, K_{AES}(d) ▷ Sent by **DO**
Encrypted Hilbert Value, K_{OPE}(H)

```
n_L = FindLeafNode(K_OPE(H))          ▷ At the CSP
if n_L < nodeCapacity_max then
    Insert(K_OPE(H), K_AES(d)) in n_L
else
    HandleOverflow(n_L)
end if
Invoke AdjustTree()
```

Delete: To delete a data point, the Hilbert value of the data point to be deleted is sent in an encrypted format by the DO to the CSP. The Hilbert value (H) is encrypted using OPE, so that comparison operations can be conducted on the index. In the Hilbert R-tree deletion process, the entry with the Hilbert key value (i.e. leaf node, n_L, with H) is removed without visiting multiple paths in the index. A delete update on the leaf node may cause n_L to go under the minimum node capacity, $nodeCapacity_{min}$. In the event of an underflow, sibling nodes can be merged together. A functional-level algorithm is listed in Algorithm 4.

Algorithm 4 Delete Encrypted Data from DISC

Input:

Encrypted Hilbert Value, K_{OPE}(H) ▷ Sent by **DO**

```
n_L = FindLeafNode(K_OPE(H))          ▷ At the CSP
Delete(K_OPE(H)) in n_L
if nodeCapacity(n_L) < nodeCapacity_min then
    HandleUnderflow(n_L)
end if
Invoke AdjustTree()
```

Modify: In order to modify a data point over encrypted DISC, the CSP conducts an insert and a delete operation on the index at the server. Thus, the DO has to send the data point to be deleted and the new data point to be inserted. For the modify operation, the CSP needs to first locate where the point to be deleted lies in the index, then delete it. It is not feasible to insert the data point in the same location as the deleted point as their positions in the indexed tree may differ. Lastly, updates are propagated upwards till the root node of the tree.

Secure scheme: DISC*

The data owner creates encrypted range queries, and sends them to the CSP, where they are processed over the encrypted index. The CSP performs the search starting from the root and proceeding to a node's children if the query value is less than the largest Hilbert value. In DISC, the lowest level of the index comprises of leaf nodes which stores the data points in a particular Hilbert cell. Thus, the CSP returns the encrypted data points matching the query Hilbert values (in OPE) to the TU. The CSP is unable to query the spatial points themselves as they are securely encrypted using AES. DISC is a retrieval scheme which is capable of returning the exact set of encrypted points. Given that the LHVs in the leaf nodes are encrypted using OPE, the ordering information of points within the Hilbert transformation can leak over time. Given a series of spatial queries over a period of time, the attacker can rebuild the order of data points in the transformed space based on the intersection of query results. The DISC index can be fine-tuned to accomodate the trade-off between security and false positives in the query result. Therefore, we propose DISC*, a more secure retrieval scheme that protects the ordering of spatial points in the leaf nodes of the index. As displayed in the index in Fig. 5, the leaf node level along with the data points is encrypted in AES [enclosed in blue solid box]. This may induce a number of false positives in the query results returned and thus filtering will have to be performed at the user-end. This is a reasonable trade-off, given the additional layer of security at the CSP.

Secure spatial range queries at CSP

The query processing is still done entirely at the CSP and follows the same procedure as listed in Algorithm 2 (cf. "Answering spatial range queries at CSP" section). The query processing time is reduced in DISC*, as there is no need to compare Hilbert values in the leaf (Line 8). The search space is restricted to the non-leaf nodes in the index and this helps locate the leaf node whose Hilbert value is closest to the query value. In Line 9, instead of returning relevant data points, the whole leaf node is returned. This will induce some additional points that are not part of the query result, and can be filtered by the TU after decryption in a post-processing step.

Secure dynamic updates

In DISC, it is possible to update the index at the CSP given the update operation and encrypted data from the DO. But in DISC*, given that the entire leaf node is encrypted using AES and not just the data points, it is not possible to update directly at the CSP. Thus, secure updates require a single round of communication between the DO and CSP. The complete procedure is illustrated in Fig. 6. First, The update request is initiated by the DO. The DO sends the OPE encrypted Hilbert value corresponding to the update operation. Second, the CSP searches the

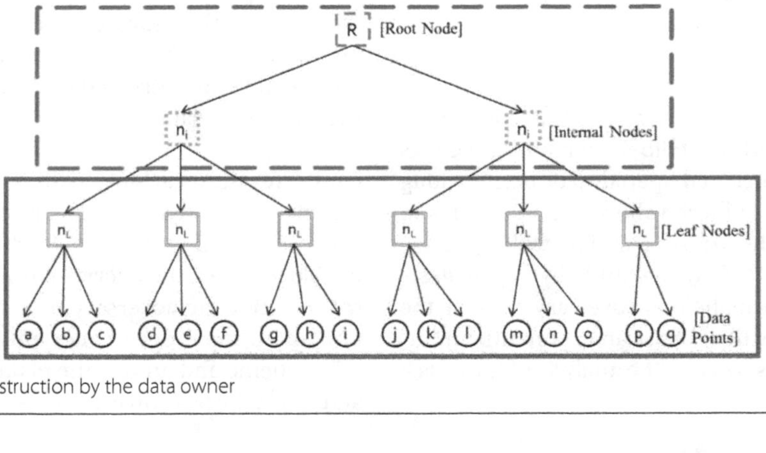

Fig. 5 Spatial data index construction by the data owner

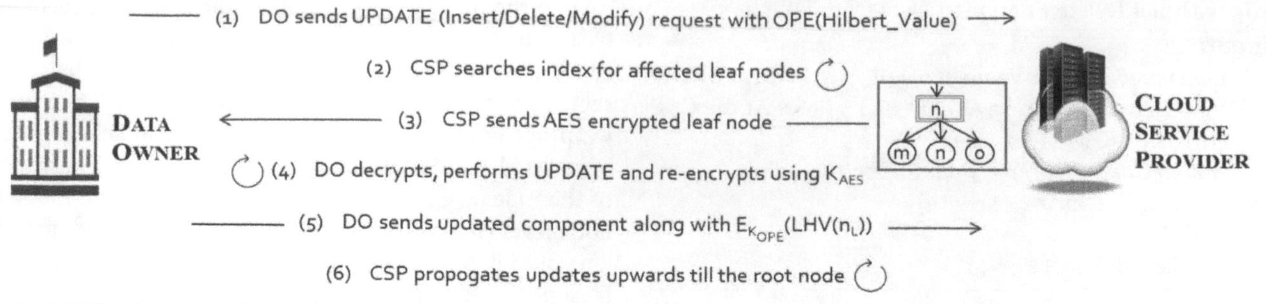

Fig. 6 DISC* scheme procedure for dynamic updates between data owner and cloud service provider

encrypted index and locates the leaf node corresponding to the Hilbert value. Third, the leaf node is sent from the CSP to the DO. Fourth, in order to perform the update, the DO has to decrypt the AES encrypted node and perform the respective update. Next, The DO encrypts the node using AES and sends it to the CSP along with the LHV of the node encrypted using OPE. Lastly, the CSP replaces the updated node in the index and propogates updates upwards till the root based on the updated Hilbert value. Even though partial update is performed at the DO, it is clear that hiding ordering information in DISC* enhances data confidentiality.

Security analysis

The key requirements of a secure data outsourcing scheme demand that: 1) data confidentiality at the server and 2) queries are efficiently processed by the CSP and results are returned to the user without any alteration. As mentioned previously, the TUs are trusted by the DO and hence have been provided with both the HSK, as well as the encryption keys. We focus on the *curious intruder* model [31] to analyze the attacks posed to DISC, which requires Hilbert transformation of the data points before encryption. Moreover, the Hilbert cell values of data points are encrypted using OPE, while the actual data points are encrypted using AES. AES provides the standard security guarantee and hence, is not susceptible to common attacks triggered by obtaining background knowledge of a subset of the data.

Hilbert transformation

It is intuitive that if an attacker is aware of the space transformation technique used (i.e. Hilbert curve in DISC), as well as a subset of the original spatial data points along with their transformed Hilbert values, the attacker can determine the key of the transformation technique i.e. Hilbert Space Key (HSK). But, the study by [7] suggests that it is infeasible for a malicious adversary to infer the exact HSK being used as there exist an exponential number of possible HSKs, as shown in the analysis of the attack below.

Brute-force attack: In the event of a brute-force attack, the attacker will have $2^b * 2^b * 2^b$ elements for x_0, y_0 and θ in the entire search space. The number of possibilities for the curve granularity g as G. To accurately find the curve's starting point, it should lie on the intersection of two edges. Using b bits for each x_0 and y_0, the attacker can generate 2^b values on each axis and this will require an exhaustive search over the grid. Likewise, for the curve orientation, the entire continuous 360° space should be discretized to generate 2^b values. Since $G \ll 2^b$, the complexity of the brute-force attack to find the transformation key is $O(2^{3b})$, where b is the number of bits used to represent each parameter in the HSK. Choosing a large enough value for b, will make the Hilbert mapping irreversible. Given that b is chosen to be 32 bits, the complexity of finding the HSK parameters would be $O(2^{3*32})$ for different possibilities of the curve granularity.

Order-preserving encryption

In OPE, the ciphertext is in the form of numeric data. Since OPE schemes can support comparison operations on the ciphertext, it is infeasible to achieve ideal security for OPE. Boldyreva et al. [28] were the first to provide a complete security analysis on OPE. The higher the security provided by the encryption scheme, the lower its efficiency and support of operations. Therefore, to achieve a low communication cost and a single round of data exchange between the CSP and TU, we settle on a weaker OPE scheme that leaks as little information of plaintext as possible. Also, with traditional encryption methods, it is not possible for untrusted CSP to process user queries on the encrypted data.

Ciphertext-only attack: This is the most common attack for encryption techniques. The *one-wayness* property of encryption was proven to hold, where the adversary is unable to invert the encryption without the knowledge of the key. But the adversary may be able to gain information about the order of encrypted values revealed by the OPE scheme and predict the plaintext values (i.e. if (p_1, c_1) and (p_2, c_2) are known for $p_1 < p_2$ and no other known plaintext-ciphertext pairs occur between these two). If the adversary knows a certain number of plaintext-ciphertext pairs, the scheme splits the plaintext and ciphertext spaces into subspaces. On each subspace, the analysis under each *one-wayness* definition reduces to that of the random order-preserving function domain and range of the subspace. The ciphertext space must be at least twice the size of the plaintext space. Thus, in the OPE scheme adapted by the DISC/DISC* approach, the OPE parameters are chosen in such a way that subspaces are unlikely to violate this condition.

Discussion: The AES encrypted spatial points are stored along with their OPE Hilbert values in the index at the CSP. The security of the scheme can be exposed if the attacker can gather limited background knowledge about the data distribution without the encryption keys. However, Hilbert R-trees do not expose the complete ordering of spatial data points. In some cases, even if it is possible to gather some information regarding the ordering of the leaf nodes from queries over a period of time, the attacker cannot infer the actual location of the spatial point (cf. Lemma 1).

Lemma 1 *Considering the worst case, assuming that an attacker can decrypt the ordering of a subset of Hilbert cells in the grid, the attacker can estimate the Hilbert value of the actual spatial data point as one of the $O(2^{32})$ different possibilities of the Hilbert curve granularity, g.*

Proof Given the total number of spatial points in D, and the granularity of the Hilbert curve, g, the average number of points assigned to each Hilbert cell is computed as follows:

$$cell_{avgPoints} = \frac{size(D)}{2^{2*g}} \quad (1)$$

Therefore, selecting a small value for the Hilbert curve granularity, g (i.e. $g << size(D)$), results in multiple spatial points being assigned to the same Hilbert cell. This increases the security provided by DISC and DISC*, but increases the number of false positives returned in the query result. □

Experimental evaluation

To evaluate the performance of the proposed approaches, DISC and secure DISC*, several experiments were conducted. We compare and analyze the difference in communication cost based on the query size and node capacity of the index. DISC and DISC* are empirically compared with the Cryptographic Transformation (CRT) method proposed by Yiu et al. [5]. Experiments were performed on an Intel Core i7-3770 CPU @ 3.40 GHz with 16 GB of RAM running the 64-bit Ubuntu operating system and implemented in C++.

Experiment on all datasets are conducted with varying query sizes ranging from 5 to 20%, where each spatial range query is a randomly distributed region in the normalized domain space. Each MBR in the non-leaf and leaf nodes is represented by 4 coordinates. Each LHV in the nodes is the Hilbert value and is represented by 4 bytes (an integer), and each spatial data point consists of x and y coordinates in double precision (16 bytes). The results shown in the experiments below are averaged over 100 runs for 4 varying query sizes.

Spatial datasets

Our experiments are performed on four real-world spatial datasets obtained from [32]: (1) City of Oldenburg (**OL**) Road Network comprising of 6104 points, (2) City of San Joaquin County Road Network (**TG**) having 18,263 points, (3) North East USA (**NE**) consisting of 123,593 points, which represent the real postal addresses and (4) Road Network of North America (**NA**) with 175,813 points is approximately 2800 KB. The domain of each dataset is normalized to the unit square $[0, 1]^2$ and two of these datasets are shown in Fig. 7.

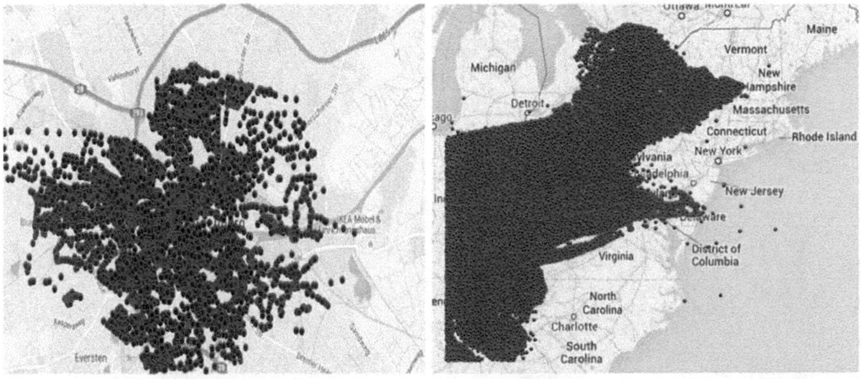

(1) Oldenburg (**OL**) (2) North East USA (**NE**)

Fig. 7 Two real-world spatial datasets: road networks. (*1*) Oldenburg (OL), (*2*) North East USA (NE)

Table 2 Index construction time (s) for various node capacities

	Index construction time (s)			
Node capacity	OL	TG	NE	NA
10	0.26	1.51	4.31	8.14
20	0.29	2.36	5.50	9.72
30	0.35	3.91	7.36	11.19

Index construction time

In DISC, the Data Owner builds an index over the spatial dataset which is based on the Hilbert R-tree. The dataset is transformed using the Hilbert curve. An empty Hilbert value means that there is no data point associated with it and these empty values are discarded during the initialization process. The index construction time is averaged over 100 runs. The DISC construction time is proportional to the number of spatial points in the dataset and Table 2 shows time taken to build the index for all 4 datasets. DISC is constructed initially at the DO and outsourced to the CSP where it is used to answer queries and handle dynamic updates from DO.

Effect of node capacity

The value of node capacity is the maximum number of data points per node, which dictates how the index is constructed. An optimal value of the capacity reduces the amount of pages searched at the server as well as the amount of data sent from the CSP to the TU. Figure 8 shows the effect of the node size on the query processing time on the DISC index at the cloud server for a small and big dataset, with node capacity ranging from 10 to 30. It can be seen that the query time and node capacity have an inversely proportional relationship, the query search time decreases when the node capacity is increased. This is due to the fact that Hilbert R-tree index will have a greater height (i.e. more levels) when a smaller node capacity is used. Other datasets and query sizes follow a similar trend, as does DISC*.

Query processing time on the cloud

The search performance of the DISC index is faster-than-linear with regard to the number of spatial data points. Figure 9 shows the time taken to process range queries on an encrypted index at the Cloud Service Provider. The experiments have been conducted on all datasets and results of OL and NE are displayed due to space limitations. The other two datasets display a similar trend. The range query size in this experiement is 20% and the average query time is measured in *ms* over 100 runs for varying node capacities of the index in DISC. The x-axis shows the node capacity, while the y-axis shows the average query processing overhead in milliseconds. When the node capacity is small, the average query time is more, but as the node capacity increases, the query time drops and this is appropriate for a CSP as they have adequate computing power. With a smaller node capacity, more levels in the tree have to be navigated through. Comparing DISC with the more secure DISC* reveals that DISC* has a faster processing time as the leaf nodes are encrypted in AES and its values cannot be compared against Hilbert values. The most time-consuming task in DISC is to sequentially check overlapped leaf node for queried Hilbert values. As the size of the query increases, the time taken to process the query also increases.

False positive rate

Both DISC and DISC* induce a number of false positives in the query result. Given that false positives increase security, a significant false positive rate is not a major concern in a secure outsourcing scheme such as DISC. Hence it is expected that the more secure scheme DISC* has a higher false positive rate than DISC. As we have noted previously, data owners can tune the spatial index for different tradeoffs between security, query efficiency and false positives. Figure 10 shows the average false positive rate for 100 queries over the larger data set NE, while other datasets follow a similar trend. We compare both schemes and show the impact of different query sizes

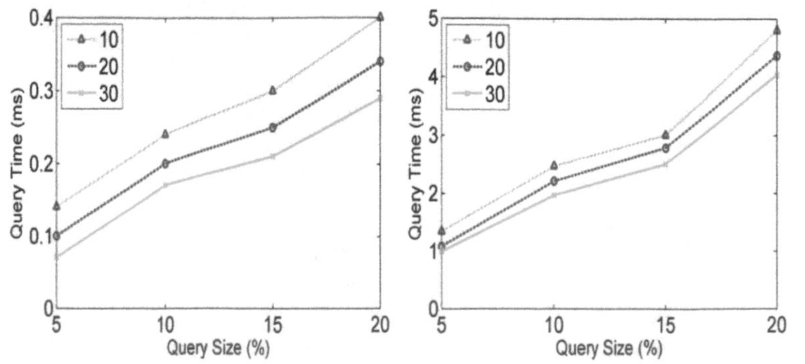

Fig. 8 Query processing time (ms) based on various node capacities (Datasets: OL & NE)

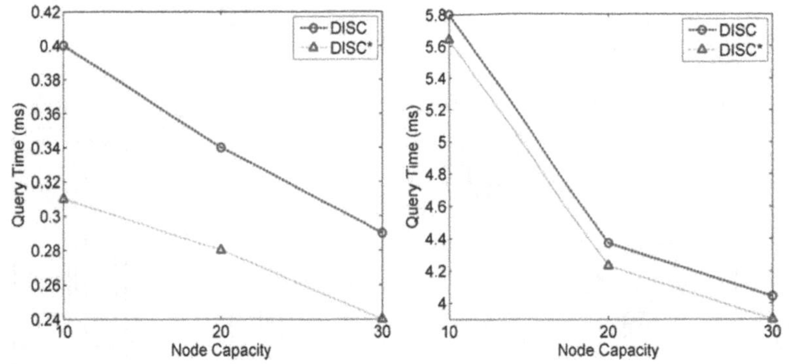

Fig. 9 Query processing time (ms) at the CSP (Datasets: OL & NE)

and various node capacities on the false positive rate. For larger query sizes, the false positive rate increases as more data points are returned. For larger node capacities, the false positive rate is usually less than 50% and the increase in the average false positive rate becomes steady.

End-to-end time for a query between the DO and CSP

Figure 11 illustrates the average end-to-end user time of the approach evaluating spatial range queries (10%) on the **OL** and **NE** datasets for both schemes. The TU makes use of an Android mobile phone (HTC) in this experimental evaluation. The transfer bandwidth of the network considered here is 1 Gbps [33]. The round-trip network delay time is the time taken for one round-trip between the TU and the CSP, which is 125 *ms* [34]. It is not shown in the graph as our approach requires only one round between the CSP and TU and is hence fixed for all query sizes. Other network delays and faulty packet transmission issues due to network errors is not taken into account. The *end-to-end user time* comprises of four components:

- Query Encryption Time (**TU**): Is the amount of time taken to encrypt the query Hilbert cell set using Order-Preserving Encryption.
- Query Request Time (**TU**): Is the amount of time taken to transform the range query window to the Hilbert cell set and send it to the CSP over the network.
- Query Response Time (**CSP**): Is the amount of time taken to process the spatial query over DISC and generate the result set to send back to the user over the network.
- Result Decryption Time (**TU**): Is the amount of time taken filter the false positives and decrypt the query result set using the AES key. The decryption time taken for 1 KB of data is 0.015 ms using the AES scheme at the user-end [35].

Figure 12 shows the network transer time in milliseconds over a 1 Gbps connection. The query request from the TU to the CSP as well as the query response from the CSP to the TU over the network is shown for different query sizes for the NE dataset. The end-to-end time relies on the size of the query as well as the indexed dataset. It is visible that the bulk of the time is taken to return the query result from the CSP to the TU. The CSP has scalable computational power and this does not affect the performance of the location-based services provided. The main idea is to have minimal processing done at the

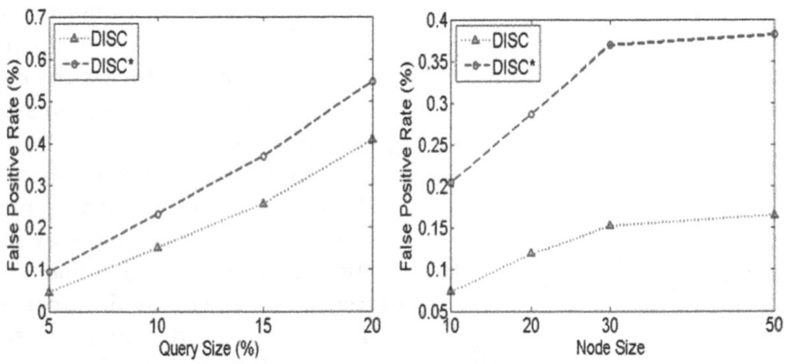

Fig. 10 Average false positive rate (%) for query sizes and node capacity

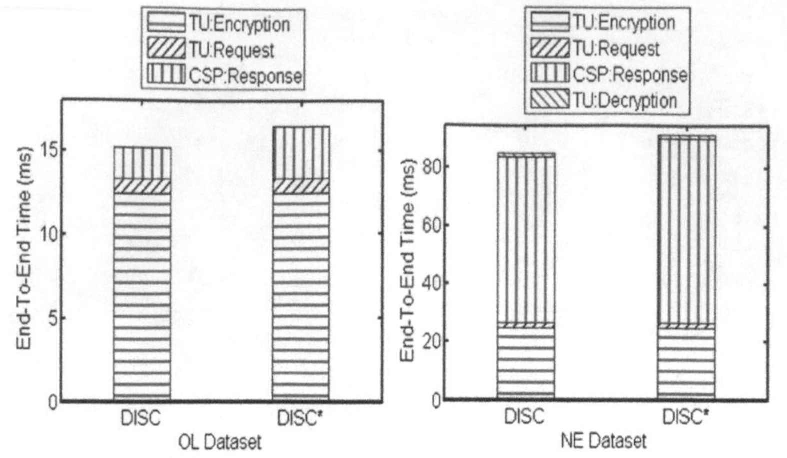

Fig. 11 User to cloud service provider: end-to-end spatial query time (ms)

user-end as they have limited resources. Forming the query takes a minute amount of time and the efficient encryption scheme (AES) allows fast decryption of query results. Since the OL dataset is small in size, the decryption time is almost negligible and hence not shown in the graph. The secure DISC* scheme has a higher time at the CSP as a larger result set is returned.

Query communication cost between user and CSP

In the experiment shown in Fig. 13, 100 random spatial range queries of varying sizes were generated and the amount of data (i.e. average communication cost in bytes) exchanged between the CSP and TU is measured. The communication cost includes: 1) Query Request: TU transforms the query region into a set of Hilbert cell values and transmits the encrypted set of values to the server, 2) Query Response: the CSP searches DISC for corresponding leaf nodes and returns the encrypted data points as the result. The query sizes ranging from 5 to 20% are used in the experiments.

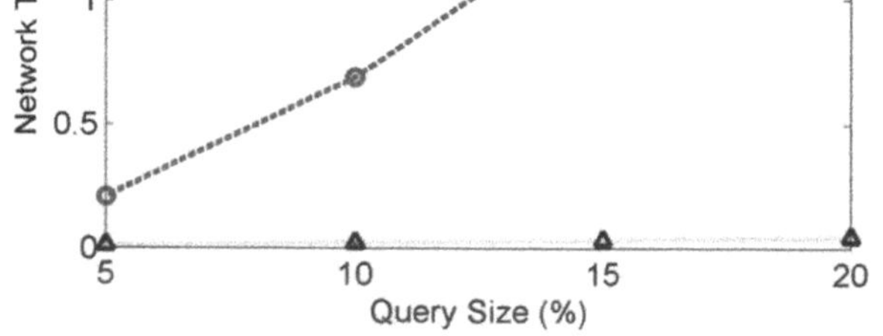

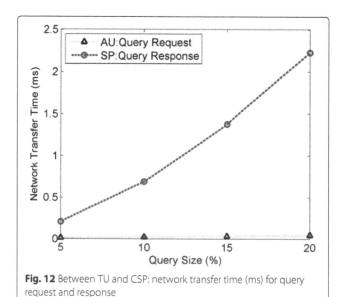

Fig. 12 Between TU and CSP: network transfer time (ms) for query request and response

In DISC, the leaf nodes are searched sequentially for query Hilbert values so that the exact points can be returned. Therefore, varying the node capacity of DISC would result in identical communication cost. Whereas, DISC* has a higher communication cost in comparison to DISC as the entire leaf nodes are returned as part of the query result. Hence, increasing the node size in DISC* would increase the communication cost as well. It is clear that the average communication cost increases linearly as the query size increases due to the increase in number of points returned. The result is decrypted at the user-end using the AES key. The OL and NE dataset results are displayed here, while the rest of the datasets follow a similar trend.

The proposed retrieval scheme is compared with the CRT technique (the R^*-tree index structure is built and encrypted using AES), and shown in Fig. 13. This is an appropriate comparison, since the R^*-tree achieves the same query time complexity as these schemes. It is demonstrated that our method is at least twice as fast as we require only one round-trip between the CSP and TU, which minimizes the communication overhead. It can be seen in experiments that the communication cost increases as the size of the spatial dataset increases. Moreover, for query sizes greater than 15%, there is a sharp increase in the communication cost of **CRT** due to the amount of messages exchanged between the user and server, which is dominated by the depth of the R^*-tree utilized. This is due to the fact that in CRT, the query is processed at both the user and server side, resulting in multiple rounds of communication. Moreover, CRT returns entire leaf nodes to the user, while using DISC, the

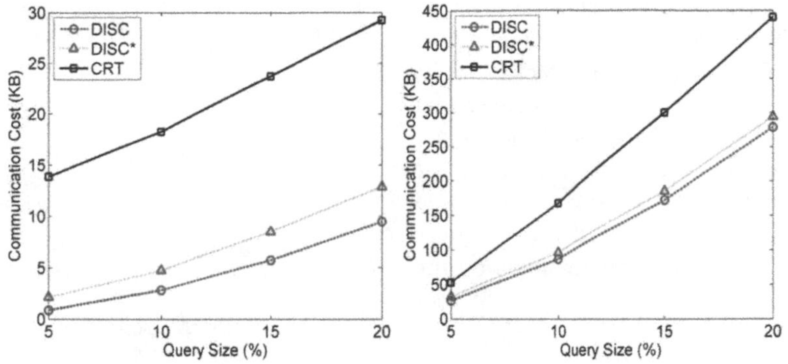

Fig. 13 DISC and DISC* vs. CRT: Effect on communication cost (KB) with different query sizes (Datasets: OL & NE)

server is able to retrieve the relevant data points in the leaf nodes based on the query Hilbert values. Even DISC* is able to achieve highly efficient queries, while hiding the ordering of data points within each leaf node.

Dynamic updates at the CSP

Dynamic updates are initiated by the DO and transmitted to the CSP. The CSP executes the updates on the encrypted index based on the Hilbert value of the given update. The DISC scheme allows dynamic updates on encrypted data by preserving the order of data (using OPE) in the encrypted leaf and non-leaf nodes, but preserving the parent-child relationships by not encrypting the pointers. To the best of our knowledge, none of the prior works provide the update characteristic in their retrieval schemes. The main advantages of the Hilbert R-tree is its ability to handle dynamic updates. The CRT [5] technique does not allow updates and only handles static data, as the tree split/merge procedure cannot be applied on AES encrypted data in the R^*-tree.

Experiments were performed on DISC for all dynamic update operations and the only communication cost entailed is the request sent from the DO to the CSP, where the update is handled. For instance, the insertion of a new object and overflow handling is peformed using the Hilbert value of the new data point. Whereas in DISC*, updates cannot be performed entirely at the CSP as the leaf nodes are encrypted using AES which does not allow comparison operations. In Fig. 14, we show the communication cost for three types of insert operations. First, the DO sends the update request which is just an encrypted Hilbert value. For the sake of simplicity, the simple insert update is explained in detail in "Secure dynamic updates" section. The CSP responds by returning the affected leaf node and the DO returns the updated encrypted nodes. In the case of overflow and sibling insert, multiple rounds of communication are required as neighboring leaf nodes are also sent to the DO. Further details on the more complex insert operations can be found in [29]. The other update operations, delete and modify, follow a similar exchange of data as insert and excluded for brevity. After analysis, the most costly operation was modify, followed by delete and lastly insert.

Conclusions

Data outsourcing has attracted much attention recently due to the emergence of cloud computing. Cloud computing virtualizes storage and computing resources at the server and provides data to trusted users. However, securing the outsourced data in the untrusted cloud server has security concerns. In this work, we are trying to strike a balance between data confidentiality and efficient query processing at the cloud service provider. We propose the DISC retrieval scheme, which has a dynamic encrypted index for spatial data at the CSP. The index is encrypted using the OPE technique, as it allows comparison operations on encrypted data at the server. Moreover, DISC allows dynamic updates at the CSP. An enhanced and

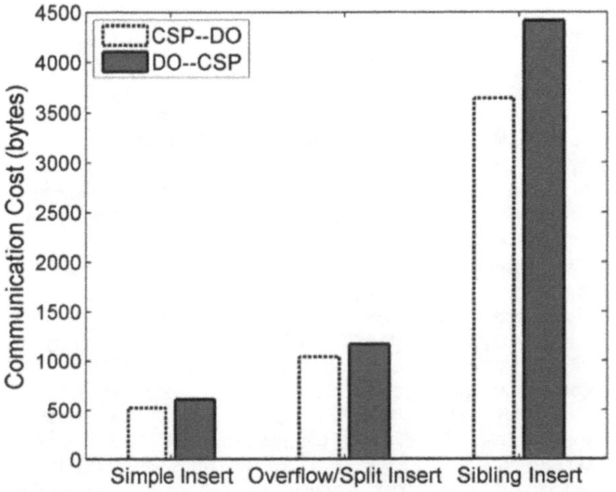

Fig. 14 Communication cost (bytes) between DO and CSP for an INSERT update

secure version, DISC*, is proposed as well. Several attack models are defined and it is shown that our scheme provides proven security against well-known attacks. Lastly, experiments were conducted and it is demonstrated that the DISC retrieval scheme improves the range query performance and is superior to existing cryptographic approaches. In conclusion, the retrieval scheme proposed in this paper enables users to retrieve spatial range query responses efficiently and allows dynamic updates on the encrypted index.

Authors' contributions
All the listed authors made intellectual contributions to the research. AT implemented the solution, conducted the experiments and, was responsible for preparing and editing the manuscript. All authors read and approved the final manuscript.

Competing interests
The authors declare that they have no competing interests.

Author details
[1]Research Institute of Sciences & Engineering, University of Sharjah, Sharjah, United Arab Emirates. [2]Department of Electrical & Computer Engineering, University of Sharjah, Sharjah, United Arab Emirates. [3]Department of Computer Science, University of Sharjah, Sharjah, United Arab Emirates.

References
1. Yu S, Wang C, Ren K, Lou W (2010) Achieving secure, scalable, and fine-grained data access control in cloud computing. In: IEEE Infocom, 2010 Proceedings. IEEE, San Diego, pp 1–9
2. Xu H, Guo S, Chen K (2014) Building confidential and efficient query services in the cloud with rasp data perturbation. IEEE Trans Knowl Data Eng 26(2):322–35
3. Hu H, Xu J, Ren C, Choi B (2011) Processing private queries over untrusted data cloud through privacy homomorphism. In: IEEE 27th International Conference on Data Engineering. IEEE, Hannover, pp 601–612
4. Zhao G, Rong C, Li J, Zhang F, Tang Y (2010) Trusted data sharing over untrusted cloud storage providers. In: IEEE Second International Conference on Cloud Computing Technology and Science (CloudCom). IEEE, Indianapolis, pp 97–103
5. Yiu ML, Ghinita G, Jensen CS, Kalnis P (2010) Enabling search services on outsourced private spatial data. VLDB J 19(3):363–84. Springer
6. Lawder JK, King PJH (2001) Querying multi-dimensional data indexed using the hilbert space-filling curve. ACM Sigmod Record 30(1):19–24
7. Khoshgozaran A, Shahabi C (2007) Blind evaluation of nearest neighbor queries using space transformation to preserve location privacy. In: Advances in Spatial and Temporal Databases. Springer, Boston, pp 239–257
8. Ku WS, Hu L, Shahabi C, Wang H (2013) A query integrity assurance scheme for accessing outsourced spatial databases. Geoinformatica 17(1):97124. Springer
9. Wang P, Ravishankar CV (2013) Secure and efficient range queries on outsourced databases using r-trees. In: 2013 IEEE 29th International Conference on Data Engineering (ICDE). IEEE, Brisbane, pp 314–325
10. Agrawal R, Kiernan J, Srikant R, Xu Y (2004) Order preserving encryption for numeric data. In: Proceedings of the 2004 ACM SIGMOD International Conference on Management of Data. ACM, Paris, pp 563–574
11. Wang B, Li M, Wang H (2016) Geometric range search on encrypted spatial data. IEEE Trans Inform Forensics Secur 11(4):704–719
12. Liu Z, Chen X, Yang J, Jia C, You I (2016) New order preserving encryption model for outsourced databases in cloud environments. J Netw Comput Appl 59:198–207
13. Pub NF (2001) 197: Advanced encryption standard. Federal Inform Process Stand Publ 197:441–0311
14. Damiani E, Vimercati S, Jajodia S, Paraboschi S, Samarati P (2003) Balancing confidentiality and efficiency in untrusted relational dbmss. In: Proceedings of the 10th ACM Conference on Computer and Communications Security. ACM, Washington, pp 93–102
15. Hore B, Mehrotra S, Tsudik G (2004) A privacy-preserving index for range queries. In: Proceedings of the Thirtieth International Conference on Very Large Data Bases. VLDB. pp 720–731
16. Hore B, Mehrotra S, Canim M, Kantarcioglu M (2012) Secure multidimensional range queries over outsourced data. VLDB J Int J Very Large Data Bases 21(3):333–358. Springer-Verlag New York, Inc.
17. Hacigümüs H, Iyer B, Mehrotra S (2002) Providing database as a service. In: 18th International Conference on Data Engineering, 2002. Proceedings. IEEE, San Jose, pp 29–38
18. Batten LM, Abawajy J, Doss R (2011) Prevention of information harvesting in a cloud services environment. In: CLOSER 2011: Proceedings of the 1st International Conference on Cloud Computing and Services Science. INSTICC, Noordwijkerhout. pp 66–72
19. Kim HI, Hong ST, Chang JW (2014) Hilbert-curve based cryptographic transformation scheme for protecting data privacy on outsourced private spatial data. In: 2014 International Conference on Big Data and Smart Computing (BIGCOMP). IEEE, Bangkok. pp 77–82
20. Kim HI, Hong S, Chang JW (2015) Hilbert curve-based cryptographic transformation scheme for spatial query processing on outsourced private data. Data Knowl Eng 104(2016):32–44. Elsevier
21. Talha AM, Kamel I, Aghbari ZA (2015) Enhancing confidentiality and privacy of outsourced spatial data. In: 2015 IEEE 2nd International Conference on Cyber Security and Cloud Computing (CSCloud). IEEE. pp 13–18
22. Ku WS, Hu L, Shahabi C, Wang H (2009) Query integrity assurance of location-based services accessing outsourced spatial databases. In: Advances in Spatial and Temporal Databases. Springer, Aalborg. pp 80–97
23. Wong WK, Cheung DW-L, Kao B, Mamoulis N (2009) Secure knn computation on encrypted databases. In: Proceedings of the ACM SIGMOD International Conference on Management of Data. ACM, Providence, pp 139–152
24. Lu Y (2012) Privacy-preserving logarithmic-time search on encrypted data in cloud. In: NDSS, San Diego
25. Gentry C, et al (2009) Fully homomorphic encryption using ideal lattices. In: STOC, Bethesda Vol. 9. pp 169–178
26. Yiu ML, Assent I, Jensen CS, Kalnis P (2012) Outsourced similarity search on metric data assets. IEEE Trans Knowl Data Eng 24(2):338–52
27. Moon B, Jagadish HV, Faloutsos C, Saltz JH (2001) Analysis of the clustering properties of the hilbert space-filling curve. IEEE Trans Knowl Data Eng 13(1):124–141
28. Boldyreva A, Chenette N, ONeill A (2011) Order-preserving encryption revisited: Improved security analysis and alternative solutions. In: Advances in Cryptology–CRYPTO 2011. Springer, Santa Barbara, pp 578–595
29. Kamel I, Faloutsos C (1993) Hilbert r-tree: An improved r-tree using fractals. Proceedings of the 20th International Conference on Very Large Data Bases, Santiago, Chile, September 1994, pp 500–509
30. Chung KL, Tsai YH, Hu FC (2000) Space-filling approach for fast window query on compressed images. IEEE Trans Image Process 9(12):2109–16
31. Goldreich O (2004) Foundations of Cryptography: Volume 2, Basic Applications, Cambridge university press
32. Real Spatial Datasets. http://www.cs.utah.edu/~lifeifei/SpatialDataset.htm
33. Georgiou S, Tsakalozos K, Delis A (2013) Exploiting network-topology awareness for vm placement in iaas clouds. In: Third International Conference on Cloud and Green Computing (CGC), 2013. IEEE, Karlsruhe. pp 151–158
34. Chen YC, Nahum EM, Gibbens RJ, Towsley D, sup Lim Y (2012) Characterizing 4g and 3g networks: Supporting mobility with multi-path tcp. University of Massachusetts Amherst, Tech. Rep
35. Popa RA, Redfield C, Zeldovich N, Balakrishnan H (2011) Cryptdb: protecting confidentiality with encrypted query processing. In: Proceedings of the Twenty-Third ACM Symposium on Operating Systems Principles. ACM, Cascais, pp 85–100

3

Dynamic multidimensional index for large-scale cloud data

Jing He[1,3], Yue Wu[1], Yunyun Dong[2], Yunchun Zhang[3] and Wei Zhou[3*]

Abstract

Although several cloud storage systems have been proposed, most of them can provide highly efficient point queries only because of the key-value pairs storing mechanism. For these systems, satisfying complex multi-dimensional queries means scanning the whole dataset, which is inefficient. In this paper, we propose a multidimensional index framework, based on the Skip-list and Octree, which we refer to as Skip-Octree. Using a randomized skip list makes the hierarchical Octree structure easier to implement in a cloud storage system. To support the Skip-Octree, we also propose a series of index operation algorithms including range query algorithm, index maintenance algorithms, and dynamic index scaling algorithms. Through experimental evaluation, we show that the Skip-Octree index is feasible and efficient.

Keywords: Cloud storage, Multidimensional index, Distributed index, Skip-Octree, Skip list, Octree

Introduction

Large-scale data management is a crucial aspect of most Internet applications. Emerging cloud computing [1–3] systems can provide users with cheap and powerful facilities for storage. As an attractive paradigm, cloud applications are required to deliver scalable and reliable management as well as process extensive data efficiently. However, most existing cloud storage systems generally adopt a distributed hash table (DHT) approach to index data, in which the data are then organized in the form of key-value pairs [4]. Thus, current cloud systems can only support keyword searches and access data through "point-query".

However, using only point queries is insufficient. Many multidimensional requirements exist for certain applications. For example, in location-based services, users often need to find an object based on its longitude, latitude, and time. In addition, they must query multiple attributes to return results immediately. Single key-value queries have clearly been unable to meet this demand. As a current solution, we can run a batch program such as a Hadoop task and scan all datasets to obtain results.

Multidimensional data structures are of considerable interest in many fields, including computational geometry, computer graphics, and scientific data visualization. Researchers have proposed multidimensional data structures such as R-tree [5], Quadtree [6, 7], and Octree [8], all of which enable efficient performance in data storage and searching systems. Quadtree is commonly used in the two-dimensional space, whereas Octree is more popular in the three-dimensional space common in many application systems. However, these traditional data indexes are normally used in a single machine or the peer-to-peer (P2P) system. Currently, with the emergence of the era of big data [9], the traditional data indices have several disadvantages such as lower storage capacity and slower efficiency.

Based on the aforementioned analysis, we have determined that the current cloud storage system performs poorly with respect to multidimensional and range queries. In addition, although traditional Octree conducts multidimensional searches effectively, it is unable to support the needs of today's big data. This is our motivation for integrating the multidimensional Octree into and developing an auxiliary dynamic index structure in a cloud environment.

This study proposes a dynamic index framework for multidimensional data in a cloud environment called Skip-Octree. Skip-Octree uses the concept behind a skip

* Correspondence: zwei@ynu.edu.cn
[3]National Pilot School of Software, Yunnan University, Kunming, Yunnan 650091, P.R. China
Full list of author information is available at the end of the article

list to improve the efficiency of the traditional Octree, and adopts double-layer Skip-Octree to construct an efficient and flexible cloud index. The main contributions of this study are listed as follows:

(1) A double-layer cloud index based on skip list and Octree is proposed in this study. To the best of our knowledge, ours is the first study to construct an auxiliary cloud index using an Octree structure. This combined index is decentralized and scalable.
(2) The skip lists are used to complete the hierarchical query of underlying Octrees. They also realize the linear indexing in a multidimensional indexing mechanism and speed up the searching process.
(3) Index maintenance algorithms and dynamic index scaling algorithms for load balancing are proposed in this study. The experiment results show the Skip-Octree index is feasible and efficient.

The remainder of this paper is organized as follows. Section 2 reviews related work. Section 3 describes the skip list, Octree, and presents a new framework of Skip-Octree on their basis. Section 4 illustrates the design of the relevant algorithms regarding Skip-Octree. Section 5 conducts tests for the algorithms related to the architecture and discusses the results of our experiments. Concluding remarks are given in Section 6.

Related works

Some existing cloud storage systems include: Google's Bigtable [10], GFS [11], and its open source implementation Hadoop [12], Amazon's Dynamo [13], and Facebook's Cassandra [14]. As a de facto standard for cloud storage systems, Hadoop has been widely used in many businesses including Yahoo, Linkedin, and Twitter. On a large scale, Hadoop allows multiple petabytes of data storage across hundreds or thousands of physical storage servers or nodes. However, lower performance of complex queries (such as range and multidimensional queries) in Hadoop presents an obstacle in its development.

Recent studies have shown that an index can dramatically improve the performance of cloud storage systems. Several studies [15–23] focusing on efficient indexes in cloud storage systems have been conducted. The study in [15] proposed a Trojan index to improve runtime performance. Its injects technology at the appropriate places by means of user defined functions (UDFs) only that affect Hadoop internally. In general, the embedded-index model is a kind of tight coupling solution. It integrates the index itself into a Hadoop framework closely to achieve high performance block selection. To decouple an index and storage system, a generalized search tree for MapReduce systems was designed in study [16]. In study [17], a global distributed B-tree index was built to organize large-scale cloud data. This method has high scalability and fault tolerance. However, it consumes considerable memory space to cache index information in the client, and it is unsuitable for processing multidimensional queries. The studies in [18, 19] proposed an improved B+ tree index. This solution adopt a double-layer index framework. The B+ tree index is built for each local data node that indexes only data on that node. By means of an adaptive algorithm, a proportion of the local B + tree nodes are published to the global index. They are efficient for single attribute queries. An R tree and content-addressable-network (CAN)-based multidimensional index schema called RT-CAN was proposed in study [20]. In RT-CAN, a CAN [21] overlay is constructed on top of the local R-tree indexes. In addition, a dynamic index node selection algorithm and cost model were proposed for RT-CAN. This solution provides high performance for multi-attribute queries. Similar to RT-CAN, a VA-file and CAN-based index framework was presented in study [22], which improves query performance by eliminating false positive queries in RT-CAN. The study in [23] adopted a compressed bitmap index to construct a cloud index, which can save considerable storage cost compared to other index structures.

Although some multidimensional indexes exist in cloud environments, an Octree-based multidimensional indexing remains nonexistent.

Octree is a kind of extended Quadtree data structure, which was proposed by Dr. Hunter in 1978 and is widely used for three-dimensional space. It is most often used to partition a three-dimensional space by recursively subdividing it into eight octants. Its tree structure has an advantage in terms of spatial decomposition, so it has been widely applied in the past years. The study of Octree has mainly focused on the analysis and improvement of traditional Octree algorithms. Meanwhile, Octree has also often been used in many 3D applications [24, 25]. The use of Octrees for 3D computer graphics was pioneered by Donald Meagher at Rensselaer Polytechnic Institute, as described in the study in [26]. In the study in [27], the author proposes a hybrid spatial index structure called ORSI, which is based on Octree and R tree. The experimental results show that the hybrid structure has more advantages than previous use of R tree on a 3D spatial index.

Current big data applications such as 3D spatical are a burden on traditional data indexes, not only in terms of space, but also high cost of storage. In addition, current cloud storage systems usually adopt a key-value model to organize data to retrieve data efficiently. This model only supports exact matching and thus does not work well with multidimensional data applications. Therefore, building a dynamic cloud storage index framework for multidimensional data is necessary.

In this study, we propose a novel skip list and Octree-based dynamic index. As far as we know, ours is the first work to set up an auxiliary cloud index using a skip list and Octree structure.

Framework of the Skip-Octree index

In cloud storage systems, a whole dataset is distributed and stored on multiple data servers. Therefore, query performance is mainly affected by two aspects. One is the manner in which to locate the corresponding data servers that stored user required data effectively. The other is the manner in which to improve the efficiency of data access on each local data server. In this study, a new double-layer cloud indexing framework based on Octree and skip list is proposed.

Background of Octree and skip list

Octree is a type of multidimensional data structure with which a multidimensional data space is recursively divided into eight equal subspaces (namely quadrants) until a quadrant contains only one data object. In addition, Octree is an adopted tree-based storage structure. For an Octree, an original data space is represented as a root node. Then, eight quadrants which act as eight children nodes of the root are generated by space partition. However, under the condition in which data is both sparsed and skewed, the query performance of Octree is worse than sequence retrieve. Hence, the compressed Octree was proposed in the study in [28]. In a compressed Octree, all empty paths are removed. Compared with R tree [29], the space division method of compressed Octree is simpler, and no space overlap occurs. Therefore, compressed Octree is used to index local data in this study. For simplicity, the compressed Octree is also called Octree in our cloud index framework.

The skip list [30] is a randomized data structure that organizes elements with hierarchical ordered link lists. Thus, it is an extension of the ordered list. Because query processing on each layer can skip many elements, a skip list can provide adequate query performance with a balanced binary tree. In addition, because a randomized algorithm is adopted to maintain balance rather than employing strictly enforced balancing, the insertion and deletion operations in a skip list are much simpler and considerably faster than the balanced binary tree. Furthermore, skip list is well suited to parallel computation applications. The insertion can be performed in parallel using different positions of the ordered list without rebalancing the global data structure. Skip list has been embedded in some popular key-value store databases such as Leveldb and Redis.

Strictly speaking, skip list is not a search tree, but its expected time complexity is $O(\log_2 n)$, which is similar to a binary search tree. In our Skip-Octree, the idea of skip list is utilized to accelerate the data retrieval efficiency of Octree.

Skip-Octree index specification

Octree is an efficient three-dimensional space partition method. However, in a cloud environment, extensive data can enlarge Octree to such an extent that it becomes inaccessible. In this section, our proposed index structure called Skip-Octree is described. Skip-Octree provides a hierarchical view of the compressed Octree to allow for logarithmic expected-time querying.

Design of Skip-Octree

Based on the randomizing idea of a skip list, the original dataset is randomly divided into subsets with a probability of 1/2. In addition, an individual Octree is constructed for each dataset.

In Fig. 1, Q_0, Q_1, and Q_2 are three datasets, where Q_0 is the original dataset, Q_1 contains approximately half the data of Q_0 and which is a subset of Q_0, and Q_2 is a subset of Q_1. The query request is processed from right to left, that is, from the smallest Octree to the largest. For each non-empty subspace, a pointer links it between different layers of the Octree. For example, if a user wants to search a keyword k, the hierarchical Octree index performs this query request at Q_2. Then, because k is not found on Q_2, this query request is redirected to Q_1. Finally, Q_0 receives this query request and obtains k. Because this query procedure has similar properties to those of a skip list, the hierarchical Octree is essentially a skip list reconstruction.

Definition of Skip-Octree The Skip-Octree is defined by a sequence of subsets Li of the input points S with $L_0 = S$ and builds a compressed Octree Qi for each Li. For $i > 0$, Li is sampled from L_{i-1} by maintaining each point with a probability of 1/2. For each Li, a compressed Octree Qi is built for the points in Li. Therefore, Qi can be seen as forming a sequence of levels in the skip list such that L_0 and $Ltop$ are the bottom and top levels, respectively.

As Fig. 2 illustrates, a skip list is a randomized data structure in which level 0 is denoted as L_0 that records all original data. In the same manner, L_1 records approximately half of the data of L_0 and L_2 records approximately half those of L_1. In Skip-Octree, L_0, L_1, and L_2 correspond to the three hierarchal Octree Q_0, Q_1, and Q_2. The multidimensional data space is partitioned by Octree to obtain multiple level subspaces. The skip list is used to organize these hierarchical data points and accelerate query performance. In a skip list, the same nodes between the upper and lower layers are associated with the pointer. Thus, with the pointer pointed to the root node in the topmost layer, we can find the specific keyword by having the pointer move down. In addition, with the locality sensitive hashing function [31], the

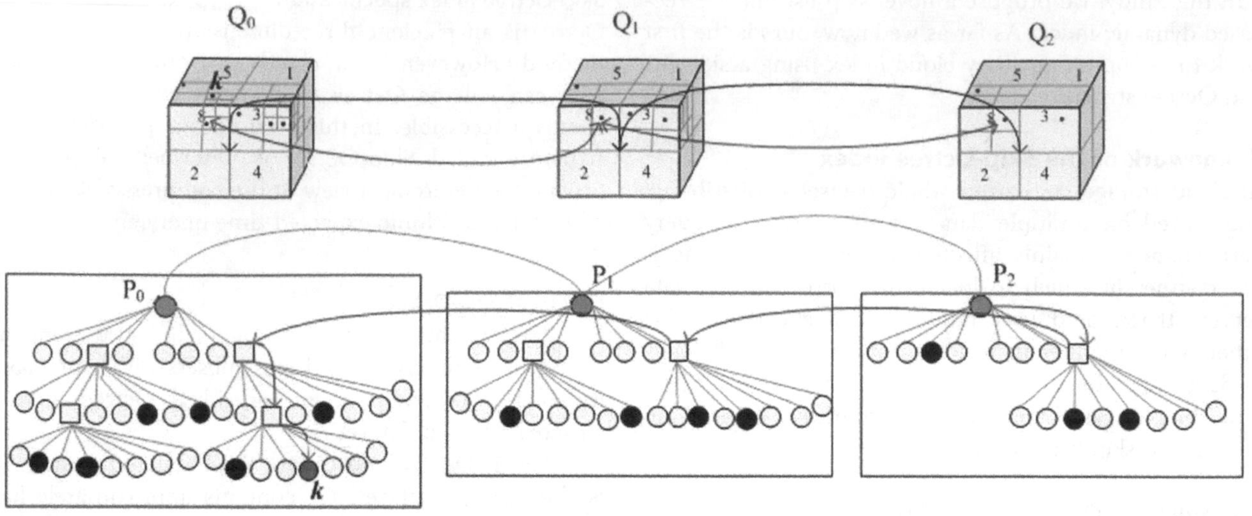

Fig. 1 Overview of a hierarchical Octree

points that belong to the same quadrant in the Octree map to the adjacent position of the skip list sequence.

Time complexity Given a point x, the searching time for x in a randomized multidimensional Skip-Octree of n points is $O(log_2n)$.

Proof Assume n points exist in a multidimensional data space with a probability of ½. The original dataset is divided into at most log_2n subsets. Thus, the layers of the Skip-Octree are log_2n. The query proceeds in a top-down fashion from the root consuming $O(log_2n)$ time. Simultaneously, the query proceeds forward on each layer only if the search key x is smaller than the current keyword. Otherwise, it skips down to the next layer according to the parent-child link. The forward move time is $O(1)$. Therefore, the search time for x in Skip-Octree is $O(log_2n)$ overall.

Extend Skip-Octree to index cloud data

In a distributed storage system, a large-scale dataset is usually divided into multiple small data units (known as data shards) by means of horizontal partitioning. These data shards are then stored in different computer nodes in the cloud computing environment based on the principle of load balancing. To improve query performance, a traditional global distributed index can be built for the whole dataset. However, with respect to big data, the global distributed index itself consumes much more memory space, and maintaining the index becomes difficult. Therefore, a double-layer hierarchical structure is adopted in our Skip-Octree-based cloud index. The overall framework of our Skip-Octree-based cloud index is shown in Fig. 3.

In the upper layer, the whole data space is partitioned into multiple subspaces according to the Octree structure. Each local data server is then assigned some of these subspaces. In the lower layer, a Skip-Octree is built

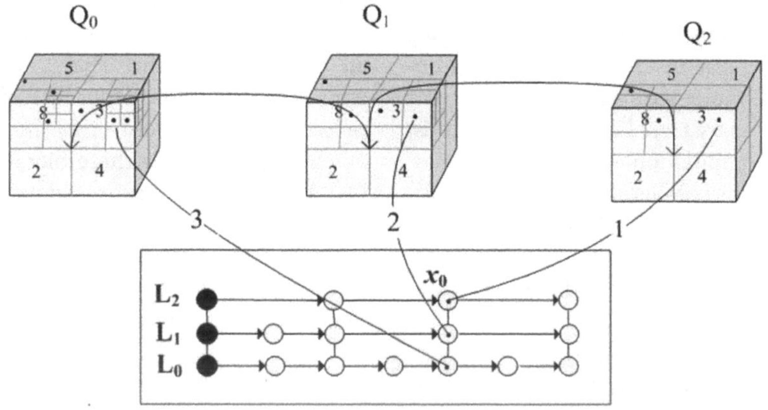

Fig. 2 Structure of Skip-Octree

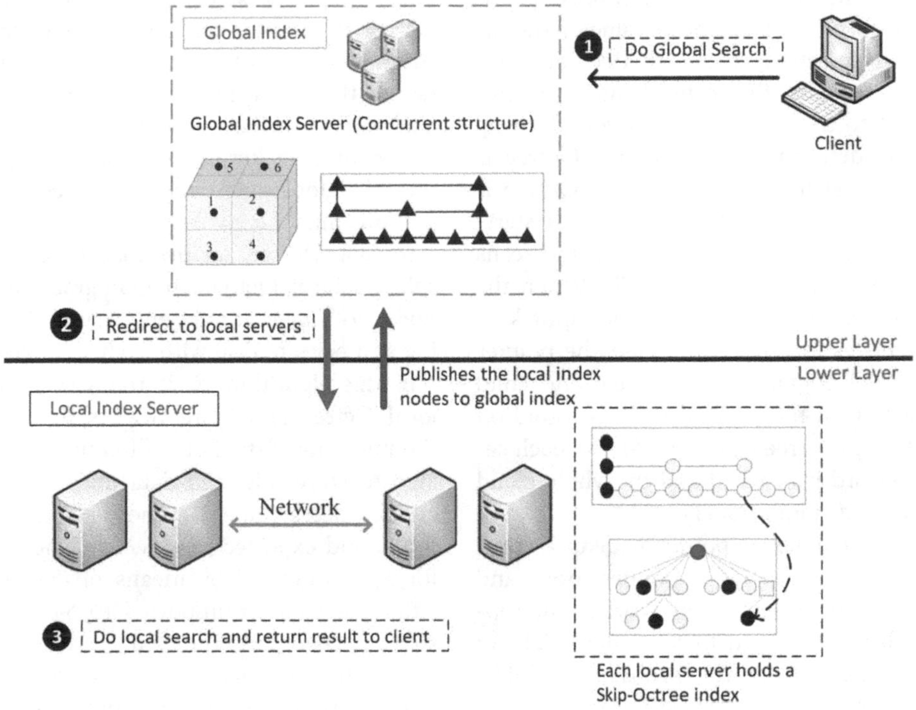

Fig. 3 Framework of Skip-Octree-based cloud index

to index data stored in each local data server. In addition, every local Skip-Octree publishes some of its own index nodes to construct a global Skip-Octree index. By combining the aforementioned two layer indexes, scanning data nodes that do not contain query results can be mostly avoided.

The query process is divided into three phases as shown in Fig. 3: (1) A query request is first send to the global index server, which performs index retrieval on global Skip-Octree to find the local data servers that may contain the query results; (2) the query request is then redirected to the corresponding local data servers; (3) finally, each selected local data server begins retrieving the data on its own local indexes, and returns the query results to the end user.

Index operating strategy

Range query processing

Range queries are widely used in cloud applications. For example, when we want to know product sales within a certain period, the search condition is a multidimensional range. In this case, the keyword index is unable to meet the user demand efficiently.

Skip-Octree can support multidimensional queries. Because we use Octree to store the data in the underlying structure. The general steps of this algorithm are as follows:

Algorithm 1 illustrates the global index process of a range query in the Skip-Octree framework. First, the function *lookup* is used to access the upper global servers to locate the first index node whose keyword is longer than *Rmin*. This index node is then mapped to the specific node of the local server (Lines 1–4). Second, the query message is forward to *Ni*'s neighbor, which invokes a similar algorithm to determine whether it is a node whose range satisfies the search range. This operation is conducted repeatedly until we find the range that is beyond the search range (Lines 5-11). Finally, local index retrieval is performed on the corresponding local data server (Line 12).

Index maintenance

In practice, the performance of inserting and deleting data also must be considered in the Skip-Octree architecture. In a cloud environment, the index maintenance process mainly consists of two steps. First, the global index server calculates the hash values of required keywords (inserting or deleting) according to the evaluation function, and then searches for the specific quadrants that contain those keywords. Second, a local index maintenance process is performed on each located local data server.

Because the skip list is a randomized data structure, the number of levels of an inserted keyword x set as random, which is generated by a random function *randomLevel()*.

Algorithm 2 provides a detailed description of the data inserting process on a cloud Skip-Octree. The locating phase (Lines 1-3) is similar to the query process previously discussed. By calculating the hash value of the input keyword, we can find the quadrant that contains this coordinate. Simultaneously, the central node of this quadrant is mapped to the root node of the underlying local server. It next determines whether the Octree is empty; it starts the local index process if the Octree is not empty (Lines 4–5). The local index retrieval starts from the root node of the highest level Octree, and scans the skip list from the top down (Lines 6-7). When the value of the current pointer is less than the input keyword, the pointer moves forward. Otherwise, the pointer skips to the next level containing the parent and child links until the position of the new keyword is found on the lowest level of Skip-Octree (Lines 8-14). For each selected level, the keyword is inserted and the whole cloud Skip-Octree is refreshed (Lines 15-21).

For a given set which has n points in Skip-Octree, each level requires O(1) time for a pointer move and keyword comparison. Furthermore, the search time top-down on the skip list is $O(\log_2 n)$ because the height of the skip list is $O(\log_2 n)$ under the probability of 1/2. Therefore, the efficiency of inserting data on Skip-Octree is $O(\log_2 n)$.

The process of deleting data is similar to that of inserting data in Skip-Octree. It must be noted that if only one keyword is deleted on a certain level in the Skip-Octree, the height of the skip list must be modified. The specific algorithm is detailed as follows:

As Algorithm 3 illustrates, the input keyword is converted to the form of a hash key by the global index in Skip-Octree. The local data server that contains this key word is then located (Lines 1-3). In the local index, because the same keyword may appear on different levels of the skip list, Lines 4-14 are used to find the position of the input keyword *X*. If this keyword is not found, the deletion operation cannot be performed (Line 15). Otherwise, this keyword is removed from the local index. In addition, in the event a link list in the Skip-list is empty, the height of this skip list is reduced (Lines 16-21). Finally, the whole cloud Skip-Octree is refreshed (Lines 22-24). Similar to the data insertion operation, the efficiency of data deletion on Skip-Octree is $O(\log_2 n)$.

Dynamic index scaling

In a distributed system, the greater the amount of data that a machine processes, the bigger is its index. Simultaneously, load balancing is a major problem. To solve this, our Skip-Octree framework is dynamically scaled. This means a local data server can migrate some of its data to other servers or merge together the data of a local data server. In this manner, the parallel load balancing processing of multiple servers is realized. Furthermore, a statistical approach is used in Skip-Octree to monitor the load status of the cloud systems. After a local data server periodically sends its load statistics to the global index server, statistical information is analyzed at the global server to determine the loading factor for each local server. Based on these loading factors, the global index server decides whether certain migrations must be invoked.

In Skip-Octree, an overloaded local data server can split its local Octree, then migrate some of its Octree nodes to a new or adjacent server. We offer the following strategies to deal with such splits in Octree:

In this algorithm, S_1 is the server that must split its local Octree and S_2 represents the server that accepts the migration data. First, a temporary list *newList* is created to store migrated data during the data transformation process (Line 1). Then, all data within l in S_1 is found and exported to *newList* (Lines 2-6). The skip list for S_1 is modified by means of data removal (Line 7). After the data are imported to S_2, the Octree on S_1 is split into two parts (Lines 8-9). At last, because location information is changed on the local index, the global index is refreshed for each published local index node (Lines 10-11). The function of refreshGlobal(*newlist[i]*) consists of two steps: locate the original published index node, and update its meta-index information with new local index data.

Figure 4a represents the original Octree on Server 3, and Fig. 4b is the structure of the split operation when completed. Given a three-dimensional data space, much data are in the third and eighth quadrants. Initially, all data are stored on the same server. However, big data may lead to index memory overflow. Therefore, some data on Server 3 must be transferred to another data server. In Fig. 4b, the whole data space is divided into two subspaces. The data within the eighth quadrant is migrated to Server 4. Server 3 saves the remaining data.

In addition to the split operation, the Skip-Octree framework offers a merging algorithm, which is used to accumulate data from different local data servers. As previously discussed, the splitting algorithm can transfer some Octree data to a new or adjacent server. After migrating, our merging algorithm can help combine migrating with current data. Moreover, if a local server crashes, we can use the merging algorithm to transfer the data derived from it to another available local server before removing it from the Skip-Octree framework.

Algorithm 5 describes the process of data merging in Skip-Octree. Here, S_1 is the server that needs to transfer its local Octree, whereas S_2 is the server that accepts the migrated local Octree. First, all data in S_1 is located and buffered in a temporary *migrateList* (Line 1). Second, the function *insertValue()*, which finds the proper position for inserted data, is called to insert each data set from

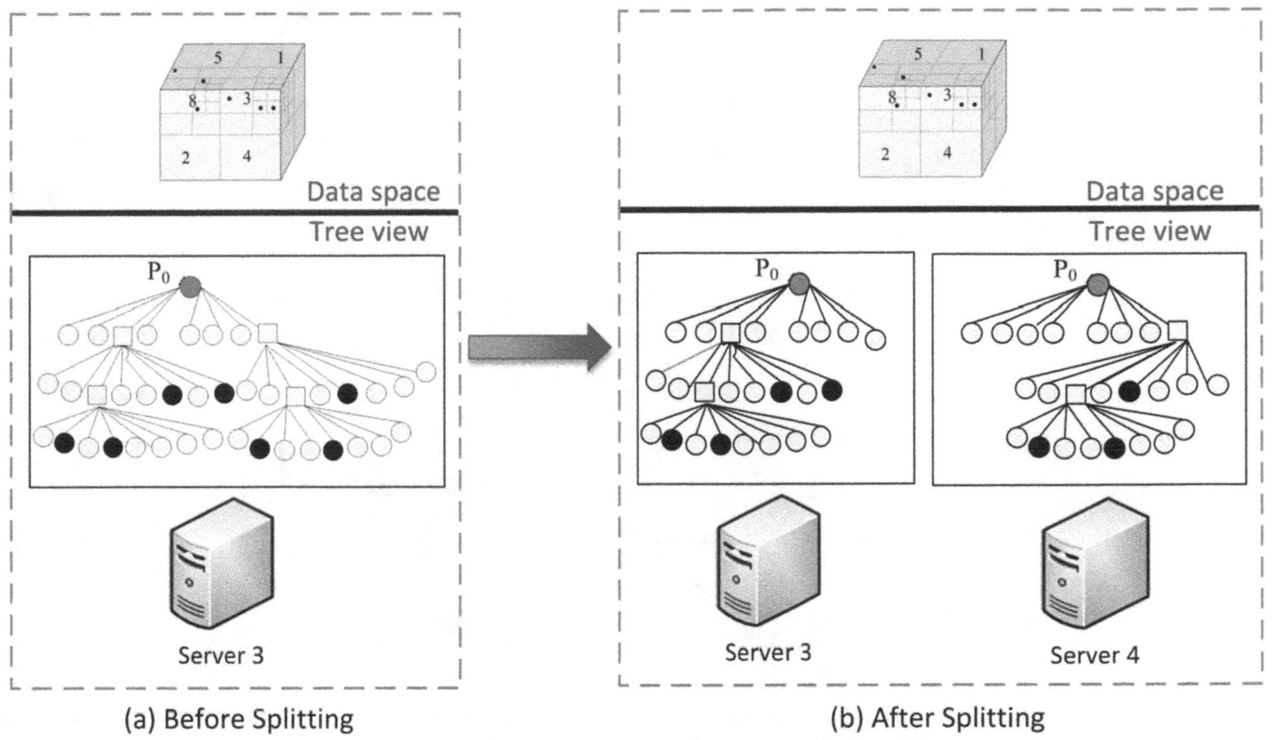

Fig. 4 Process of Octree splitting

migrateList to S_2 (Line 2-9). During the process of inserting data, determining whether the migrating data repeat with the data in S_2 is crucial. Each duplicated value is removed (Lines 5-8). If the indexNode is a published node, the relevant global index node must be refreshed (Lines 9-11). Finally, the Octree in S_2 is refreshed to ensure normal operation after merging, and the storage space of S_1 is released because empty (Line 12–13).

Experimental evaluation

To evaluate the performance of Skip-Octree architecture, we developed a simulator extended from Peersim [32]. The testing computer had an Intel Core i5 4200 M, 2.4 GHz CPU, 8 GB RAM, and a 320 G disk space running CentOS6.0 (64 bit). It was used to simulate different data nodes that extend from 10000 to 50000. In the simulator, the number of server nodes is set to 16, the type of keywords is a string, and the length of a keyword is 24. At each query, the the number of nodes is 500. For comparison, we also conducted an experiment using a traditional Octree. To guarantee the accuracy of the experimental data, we calculated the average of 10 runs of each experiment.

Figure 5 shows the performance comparison of three-dimensional range queries between Skip-Octree and traditional Octree. In this experiment, given 16 local data servers, the amount of data first increased from 1000, then grew in multiples of 1000. The search range was a radius of 0.1 cubes. We can see that Skip-Octree performs better than does the traditional Octree. The reason is that skip list realizes a hierarchical Octree structure with probability of 1/2. Through skip list, extensive data can be found rapidly without searching a huge Octree. This experiment also confirmed the feasibility of Skip-Octree's multidimensional indexing structure.

Index maintenance performance is a crucial indicator used to evaluate the effectiveness of an index structure. As shown in Fig. 6, eight data servers were created to build the cloud storage environment. As the amount of inserted data increased, the response time of the deletion operation increased. However, when the amount of data was the same, Skip-Octree always consumed less time than did the traditional Octree. Because Skip-Octree realized hierarchal Octree, considerable useless data was ignored during the deletion process.

The insertion operation in Skip-Octree is similar to that of the deletion. As shown in Fig. 7, when the amount of inserted data is small, Skip-Octree consumes nearly the same amount of time as does the traditional Octree. When the amount of inserted data increases, the Skip-Octree shows its performance advantage. The reason is that the skip list can more quickly determine inserted data positions by ignoring lots of data.

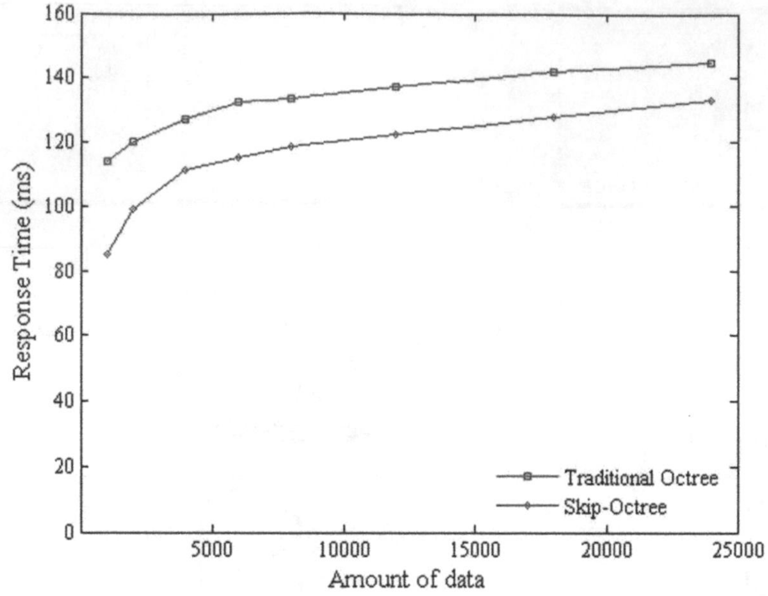

Fig. 5 Performance of range query

To achieve load balancing for the cloud storage environment, our Skip-Octree is dynamically adjusted by means of splitting and merging. In this experiment, the number of data servers was set to eight, and the amount of data increased from 10000 to 40000. Figure 8 shows a performance comparison of a given range query between a static Skip-Octree and dynamic adjusting Skip-Octree. Obviously, dynamic Skip-Octree was more efficient than static Skip-Octree, as load balancing is critical for a distributed storage system. Moreover, with each increase in the amount of data, the amount of time consumed for dynamic Skip-Octree actually decreased. The reason is that when executing a given query request in a determined cluster, if the amount of data is small, the number of local data servers selected by a dynamic skip list is greater. Otherwise, with an increasing scale of stored data, the required data are just a small portion of the entire dataset, with the resulting set stored in a few data servers. The retrieval time for a small number is less than for a large number of local indexes.

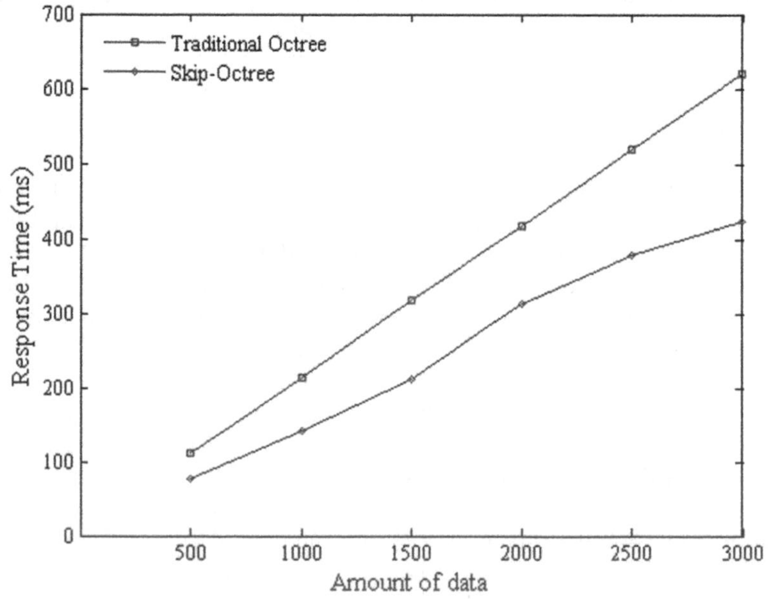

Fig. 6 Performance of the deletion process

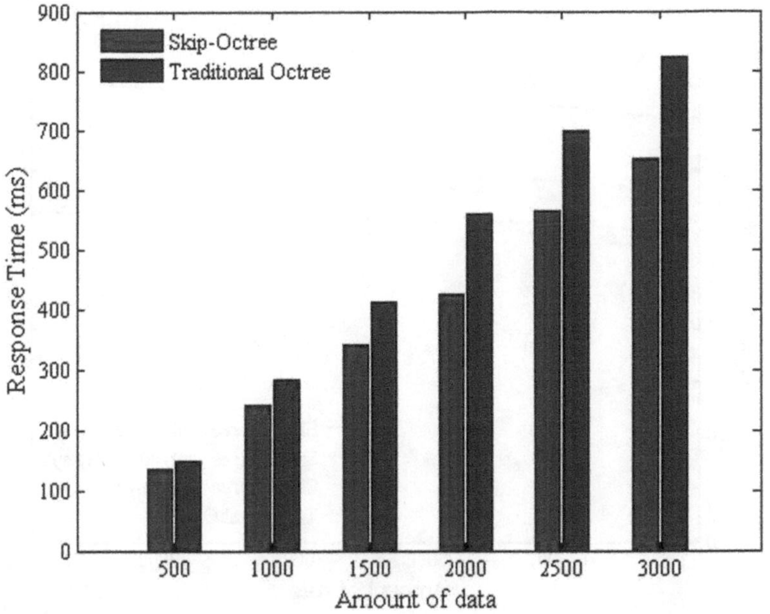

Fig. 7 Performance of the insertion process

The Skip-Octree is a double-layer cloud index that has more complex structure than a traditional single-layer index. In this experiment, the performance of a double-layer Skip-Octree was evaluated. As a comparison, a Skip-Octree having only an upper layer, a Skip-Octree having only a lower layer, and the traditional Octree were tested under the same conditions. Figure 9 shows 16 local data servers present in the cloud storage system, and the amount of data increases from 1000 to 50000. Our test queried 500 sets of data within the whole dataset. The double-layer Skip-Octree is the most efficient among them. The Skip-Octree having only an upper layer consumes more time than the traditional distributed Octree. This is because the upper layer index is built only of a global Skip-Octree, and the index is too deep when the amount of data is large. Although the traditional Octree is stored in multiple servers, its query speed is faster than that of Skip-Octree having only an upper layer.

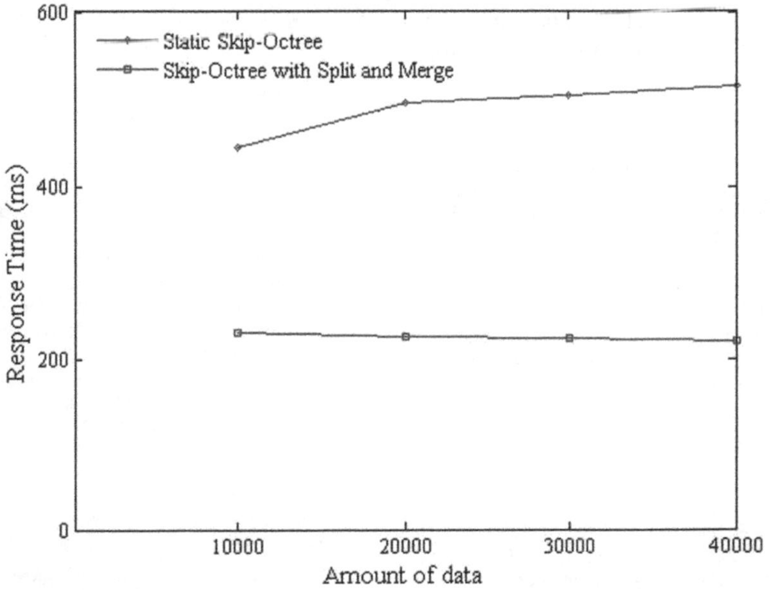

Fig. 8 Performance of the split and merge operations

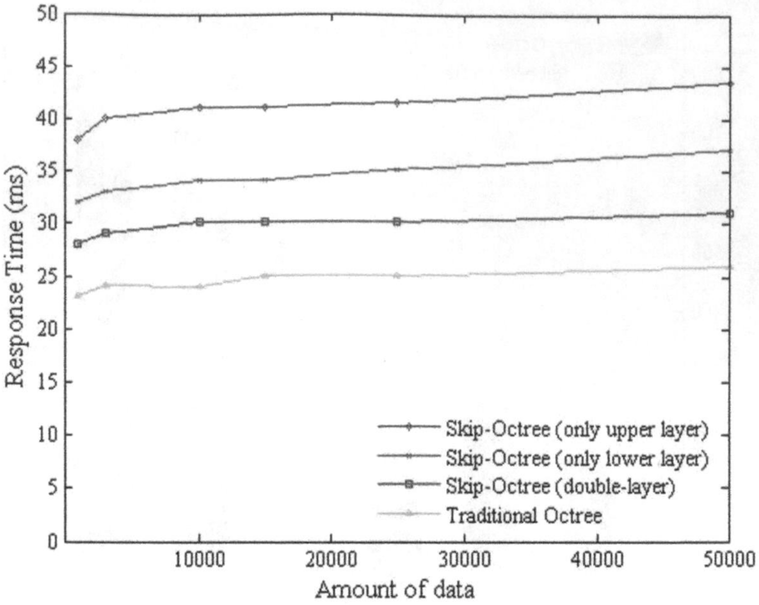

Fig. 9 Availability testing for a double-layer cloud index

Conclusion

This study provided a new multidimensional data index framework, called Skip-Octree, which combines the best features of two well-known data structures: Octree and skip lists. Some index operating algorithms that include multidimensional range querying, data insertion and deletion, and index splitting and merging were also proposed in this study. The experimental results show that our Skip-Octree is efficient. However, because a cloud storage system usually supports both transactional and data analysis operations simultaneously, frequent updates will conflict with data queries, thereby reducing data query efficiency. Means to enhancing data consistency in order to ensure query efficiency is a topic of future research.

Acknowledgments

This work is supported by the National Nature Science Foundation of China (61363021, 61540061), Science Research Foundation of Yunnan Province Education Department (2014Y013) and the Youth Program of Applied Basic Research Programs in Yunnan Province (2012FD0047).

Authors' contributions

Author JH provided the idea of this paper, carefully designed the framework, and drafts the manuscript. Author YD and YZ performed the experiments and presented performance analysis. Author YW and WZ reviewed and edited the manuscript. All authors read and approved the final manuscript.

Competing interests

The authors declare that they have no other competing interests.

Author details

[1]School of Computer Science and Engineering, University of Electronic Science and Technology of China, Chengdu, Sichuan 611731, P.R. China. [2]Research Center of Western Yunnan Development, Yunnan University, Kunming, Yunnan 650091, P.R. China. [3]National Pilot School of Software, Yunnan University, Kunming, Yunnan 650091, P.R. China.

References

1. Armbrust M, Fox A, Griffith R et al. (2010) A view of cloud computing. Commun ACM 53(4):50–58
2. Chauvel F, Song H, Ferry N et al. (2015) Evaluating robustness of cloud-based systems. J Cloud Comput 4(1):1–17
3. Hashem IAT, Yaqoob I, Anuar NB et al. (2015) The rise of big data on cloud computing: Review and open research issues. Inf Syst 47:98–115
4. Yang Y (2015) Attribute-based data retrieval with semantic keyword search for e-health cloud. J Cloud Comput 4(1):1–6
5. Kao B, Lee SD, Lee FKF et al. (2010) Clustering uncertain data using voronoi diagrams and r-tree index. IEEE Trans Knowl Data Eng 22(9):1219–1233
6. Nandi U, Mandal JK (2013) Efficiency and Capability of Fractal Image Compression With Adaptive Quardtree Partitioning. Int J Multimedia Its Appl 5(4):53–66
7. Eppstein D, Goodrich MT, Sun JZ (1997) The Skip Quadtree: A Simple Dynamic Data Structure for Multidimensional Data. J Comput 20(9):849–854
8. Zeng M, Zhao F, Zheng J et al. (2013) Octree-based fusion for realtime 3D reconstruction. Graph Model 75(3):126–136
9. Labrinidis A, Jagadish HV (2012) Challenges and opportunities with big data. Proc VLDB Endowment 5(12):2032–2033
10. Chang F, Dean J, Ghemawat S et al. (2008) Bigtable: A distributed storage system for structured data. ACM Trans Comput Syst 26(2):1–26
11. Ghemawat S, Gobioff H, Leung S-T (2003) The Google file system. ACM SIGOPS Operating Syst Rev 37(5):213–223
12. The Apache Software Foundation: Hadoop. http://hadoop.apache.org/. Accessed 22 June 2016.
13. Decandia G, Hastorun D, Jampani M et al. (2007) Dynamo: Amazon's highly available key-value store. In: The 21st ACM Symposium on Operating Systems Principles. ACM Press, New York, pp 205–220
14. Laskhmam A, Malik P (2010) Cassandra: a decentralized structured storage system. ACM SIGOPS Operating Syst Rev 44(2):35–40
15. Dittrich J, Quian'e-Ruiz J-A, Jindal A, Kargin Y et al. (2010) Hadoop++: Making a Yellow Elephant Run Like a Cheetah (Without It Even Noticing). Proc VLDB Endowment 3(1):518–529
16. Lu P, Chen G, Ooi BC et al. (2014) ScalaGiST: scalable generalized search trees for mapreduce systems [innovative systems paper]. Proc VLDB Endowment 7(14):1797–1808
17. Aguilera MK, Golab W, Shah MA (2008) A practical scalable distributed b-tree. Proc VLDB Endowment 1(1):598–609
18. Wu S, Jiang D, Ooi BC et al. (2010) Efficient B-tree Based Indexing for Cloud Data Processing. Proc VLDB Endowment 3(1):1207–1218
19. Zhou W, Lu J, Luan Z et al. (2014) SNB-index: a SkipNet and B+ tree based auxiliary Cloud index. Clust Comput 17(2):453–462

20. Wang J, Wu S, Gao H et al. (2010) Indexing multi-dimensional data in a cloud. In: Proceedings of the 2010 ACM SIGMOD International Conference on Management of data. Indianapolis, Indiana, USA., pp 591–602
21. Ratnasamy S, Francis P, Handley M et al. (2002) A scalable content-addressable network. ACM Sigcomm Comput Comm Rev 355(4):161–172
22. Cheng CL, Sun CJ, Xu XL et al. (2014) A Multi-dimensional Index Structure Based on Improved VA-file and CAN in the Cloud. Int J Autom Comput 11(1):109–117
23. Lu P, Wu S, Shou L et al. (2013) An efficient and compact indexing scheme for large-scale data store. In: 2013 IEEE 29th International Conference on Data Engineering (ICDE)., pp 326–337
24. Haber E, Schwarzbach C (2014) Parallel inversion of large-scale airborne time-domain electromagnetic data with multiple OcTree meshes. Inverse Problems 30(5):055011
25. Vo AV, Truong-Hong L, Laefer DF et al. (2015) Octree-based region growing for point cloud segmentation. ISPRS J Photogramm Remote Sens 104:88–100
26. Meagher D (2012) High-speed image generation of complex solid objects using Octree encoding., USPO, Retrieved 20 September 2012
27. Weijie GU, Jishui WANG, Hao SHI et al. (2011) Research on a Hybrid Spatial Index Structure. J Comput Info Syst 7(11):3972–3978
28. Aluru S, Sevilgen FE (1999) Dynamic compressed hyperoctrees with application to the N-body problem. In: *Proc.* In: 19th Conf. Found. Softw. Tech. Theoret. Comput. Sci., 1738., pp 21–33
29. Gaede V, Gunther O (1998) Multidimensional access methods. ACM Comput Surv 30(2):170–231
30. Xie Z, Cai Q, Jagadish H V, et al. (2016) PI: a Parallel in-memory skip list based Index. arXiv preprint arXiv:1601.00159.
31. Paulevé L, Jégou H, Amsaleg L (2010) Locality sensitive hashing: A comparison of hash function types and querying mechanisms. Pattern Recogn Lett 31(11):1348–1358
32. Montresor A, Jelasity M (2009) PeerSim: A scalable P2P simulator. In: IEEE 9th International Conference on Peer-to-Peer Computing. IEEE, New York, pp 99–100

4

An autonomic prediction suite for cloud resource provisioning

Ali Yadavar Nikravesh, Samuel A. Ajila* and Chung-Horng Lung

Abstract

One of the challenges of cloud computing is effective resource management due to its auto-scaling feature. Prediction techniques have been proposed for cloud computing to improve cloud resource management. This paper proposes an autonomic prediction suite to improve the prediction accuracy of the auto-scaling system in the cloud computing environment. Towards this end, this paper proposes that the *prediction accuracy of the predictive auto-scaling systems will increase if an appropriate time-series prediction algorithm based on the incoming workload pattern is selected.* To test the proposition, a comprehensive theoretical investigation is provided on different risk minimization principles and their effects on the accuracy of the time-series prediction techniques in the cloud environment. In addition, experiments are conducted to empirically validate the theoretical assessment of the hypothesis. Based on the theoretical and the experimental results, this paper designs a self-adaptive prediction suite. The proposed suite can automatically choose the most suitable prediction algorithm based on the incoming workload pattern.

Keywords: Cloud resource provisioning, Auto-scaling, Decision fusion technique, Structural risk minimization, Empirical risk minimization, Multi-layer perceptron, Multi-layer perceptron with weight decay, Workload pattern, Cloud computing

Introduction

The elasticity characteristic of cloud computing and the cloud's pay-as-you-go pricing model can reduce the cloud clients' cost. However, maintaining Service Level Agreements (SLAs) with the end users obliges the cloud clients to deal with a cost/performance trade-off [1]. This trade-off can be balanced by finding the minimum amount of resources the cloud clients need to fulfill their SLAs obligations. In addition, the cloud clients' workload varies with time; hence, the cost/performance trade-off needs to be justified in accordance with the incoming workload. Auto-scaling systems are developed to automatically balance the cost/performance trade-off.

There are two main classes of auto-scaling systems in the Infrastructure-as-a-Service (IaaS) layer of the cloud computing: *reactive* and *predictive*. Reactive auto-scaling systems are the most widely used auto-scaling systems in the commercial clouds. The reactive systems scale out or in a cloud service according to its current performance condition [2]. Although the reactive auto-scaling systems are easy to understand and use, they suffer from neglecting the virtual machine (VM) boot-up time which is reported to be between 5 and 15 min [3]. Neglecting the VM boot-up time results in the under-provisioning condition which causes SLAs violation. Predictive auto-scaling systems try to solve this problem by forecasting the cloud service's future workload and adjusting the compute and the storage capacity in advance to meet the future needs.

The predictive auto-scaling systems generate a scaling decision based on the future forecast of a performance indicator's value. Therefore, to improve the accuracy of the predictive auto-scaling systems, researchers have strived to improve the accuracy of the prediction techniques that are being used in the auto-scaling systems (see [4] for a comprehensive overview of the auto-scaling prediction techniques). According to [4], the most dominant prediction technique in the IaaS layer of the cloud auto-scaling domain is time-series prediction. Time-series prediction techniques use the historical values of a performance indicator to forecast its future value. Although in recent years many innovative time-series prediction techniques have

* Correspondence: ajila@sce.carleton.ca
Department of Systems and Computer Engineering, Carleton University, 1125 Colonel By Drive, Ottawa K1S 5B6, ON, Canada

been proposed for the auto-scaling systems, the existing approaches neglect the influence of the performance indicator pattern (i.e., how the performance indicator values change over time) on the accuracy of the time-series prediction techniques. This paper proposes an autonomic prediction suite using the decision fusion technique for the resource provisioning of the IaaS layer of the cloud computing environment. The proposed suite identifies the pattern of the performance indicator and accordingly selects the most accurate technique to predict the near future value of the performance indicator for better resource management. The central hypothesis in this paper that serves as the fusion rule of the prediction suite is:

The prediction accuracy of the predictive auto-scaling systems is impacted positively by using different prediction algorithms for the different cloud workload patterns

In order to lay out the theoretical groundwork of the prediction suite, this paper first examines the influence of the cloud service's incoming workload patterns on the mathematical core of the learning process. Previous studies on the predictive auto-scaling techniques in the IaaS layer of cloud computing [2, 5, 6] are limited to the experimental evaluation. To the best of our knowledge, none of the research efforts in the predictive auto-scaling domain has investigated the theoretical foundations of the predictive auto-scaling techniques. Establishing a formal foundation is essential to obtain a solid and more generic understanding of various auto-scaling prediction algorithms. Thus, to support the proposed prediction suite, this paper performs a formal study of the theories that have been used in the predictive auto-scaling systems. Further, this paper investigates the components that theoretically affect the accuracy of the models. The theoretical investigation provides a formal analysis and explanation for the behaviors of the time-series prediction algorithms in the cloud environment with different workload patterns. In addition, this paper proposes four sub-hypotheses in section Theoretical investigation of the hypothesis.

According to the theoretical discussion, the risk minimization principle that is used by the time-series prediction algorithms affects the algorithms' accuracy in the environments with the different workload patterns (see Section Theoretical investigation of the hypothesis). Furthermore, to experimentally validate the formal discussion, this paper examines the influence of the workload patterns on the accuracy of three time-series prediction models: the Support Vector Machine (SVM) algorithm and two variations of the Artificial Neural Network (ANN) algorithm (i.e., Multi-Layer Perceptron (MLP) and Multi-Layer Perceptron with Weight Decay (MPLWD)). The SVM and the MLPWD algorithms use Structural Risk Minimization (SRM) principle, but the MLP algorithm uses Empirical Risk Minimization (ERM) principle to create the prediction model. Comparing the MLP with the MLPWD algorithm isolates the influence of the risk minimization principle on the prediction accuracy of the ANN algorithms. Therefore, comparing the MLP with the MLPWD shows the impact of the risk minimization principle on the prediction accuracy of the ANN algorithms. In addition, since the SVM and the MLPWD algorithms use the same risk minimization approach, comparing the SVM algorithm with the MLPWD algorithm isolates the influence of the regression model on the prediction accuracy.

This paper enhances the preciseness of our previous experimental results in [2] by isolating and studying the impact of the risk minimization principle on the prediction accuracy of the regression models in regards to the changing workload patterns. The main contributions of this paper are:

- Proposing an autonomic prediction suite which chooses the most suitable prediction algorithm based on the incoming workload pattern,
- Providing the theoretical foundation for estimating the accuracy of the time-series prediction algorithms in regards to the different workload patterns,
- Investigating the impact of the risk minimization principle on the accuracy of the regression models for different workload patterns, and
- Evaluating the impact of the input *window size* on the performance of the risk minimization principle.

TPC-W web application and Amazon Elastic Compute Cloud (Amazon EC2) are respectively used as the benchmark and the cloud infrastructure in our experiments. It should be noted that this paper is scoped to the influence of the workload patterns on the prediction results at the IaaS layer of the cloud computing. Other IaaS management aspects (such as the VM migration and the physical allocation of the VMs) are out of the scope of this paper.

The remainder of this paper is organized as follows: Background and related work section discusses the background and the related work. In Self-adaptive workload prediction suite section a high level design for the self-adaptive prediction suite is proposed. Theoretical investigation of the hypothesis section, describes the principles of the learning theory and mathematically investigates the hypothesis. Section Experimental investigation of the hypotheses presents the experimental results to support the theoretical discussion. The conclusion and the possible directions for the future research are discussed in Conclusions and future work section.

Background and related work

In this section, the background concepts that are used in the paper and the related work are introduced. Sub-section Workload is an overview of the workload concept and its patterns. Sub-sections Decision making and Prediction techniques provide an overview of the most dominant auto-scaling approaches in two broad categories: decision making and prediction techniques.

Workload

The term workload refers to the number of the end user requests, together with their arrival timestamp [4]. Workload is the consequence of the end users accessing the cloud service [7]. According to [4, 7, 8], there are five workload patterns in the cloud computing environments:

- *Static workload* is characterized by a constant number of requests per minute. This means that there is normally no explicit necessity to add or remove the processing power, the memory or the bandwidth for the workload changes (Fig. 1).
- *Growing workload* represents a load that rapidly increases (Fig. 2).
- *Periodic workload* represents regular periods (i.e., seasonal changes) or regular bursts of the load in a punctual date (Fig. 3).
- *On-and-off workload* represents the work to be processed periodically or occasionally, such as the batch processing (Fig. 4).
- *Unpredictable workloads* are generalization of the periodic workloads as they require elasticity but are not predictable. This class of workload represents the constantly fluctuating loads without regular seasonal changes (Fig. 5).

Resource allocation for the batch applications (i.e., on-and-off workload pattern) is usually referred to as scheduling which involves meeting a certain job execution deadline [4]. Scheduling is extensively studied in the grid

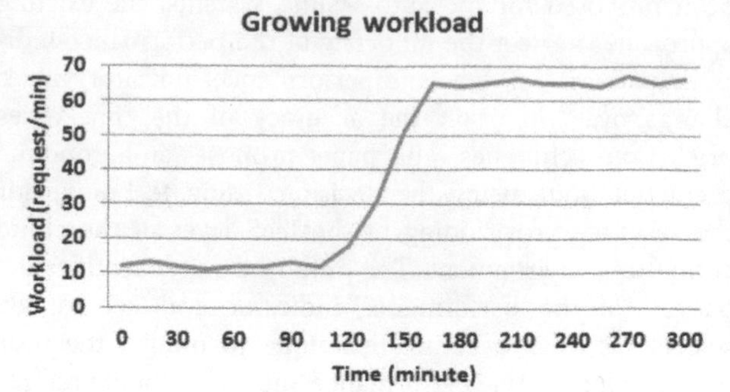

Fig. 2 Growing workload pattern

environments [4] and also explored in the cloud environments, but it is outside of the scope of this paper. Similarly, the cloud services with a stable (or static) workload pattern do not require an auto-scaling system for resource allocation per se. Therefore, this paper considers cloud services with the *periodic*, *growing*, and *unpredictable* workload patterns.

Decision making

The authors in [4] group the existing auto-scaling approaches into five categories: rule based technique, reinforcement learning, queuing theory, control theory, and time-series analysis. Among these categories, the time-series analysis focuses on the prediction side of the resource provisioning task and is not a "decision making" technique per se. In contrast, the rule-based technique is a pure decision making mechanism while the rest of the auto-scaling categories play the *predicator* and the *decision maker* roles at the same time.

The rule based technique is the only approach which is widely used in the commercial auto-scaling systems [9–11]. The popularity of this approach is due to its simplicity and intuitive nature. The rule based approaches typically have six parameters: an upper threshold (*thrU*), a lower threshold (*thrL*), *durU* and *durL* that define how long the condition must be met to trigger a scaling action, and *inL* and

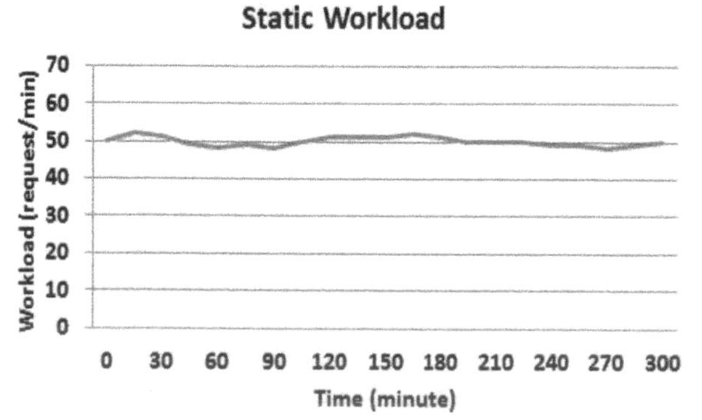

Fig. 1 Static workload pattern

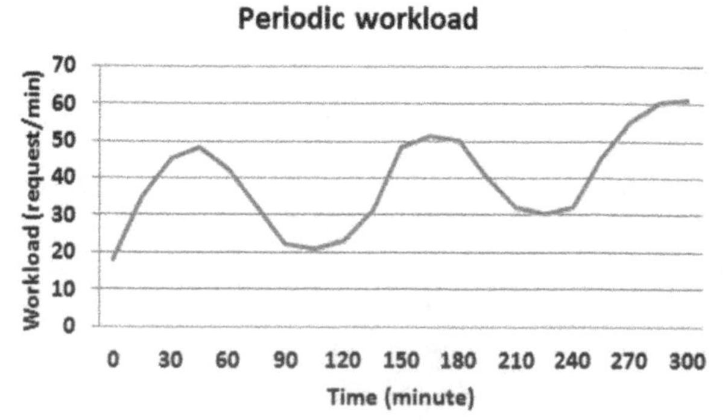

Fig. 3 Periodic workload pattern

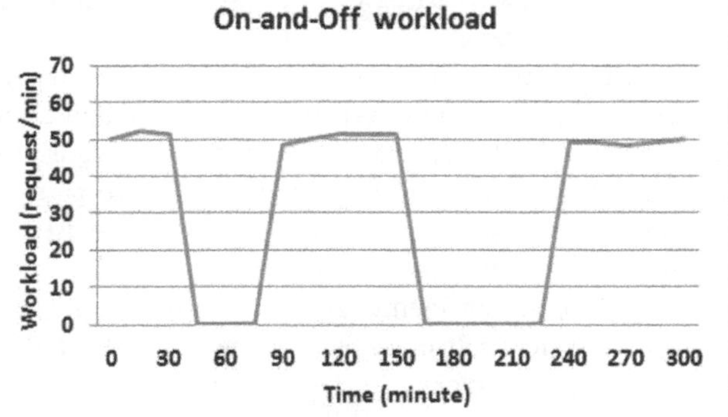

Fig. 4 On-and-off workload pattern

inU which indicate the cool down periods after the scale out and scale in actions [4]. The performance of the rule based technique highly dependents on these parameters. Therefore, finding the appropriate values for these parameters is a tricky task. A common problem in the rule based auto-scaling, which occurs due to an inappropriate threshold value, is the oscillations in the number of the leased VMs. In fact, the *durU* and the *durL* parameters are introduced to decrease the number of the scaling actions and reduce the VM oscillations. Some researchers have proposed alternative techniques to address the VM oscillation problem. For instance, the work in [12] uses a set of four thresholds and two durations. Moreover, some research works (such as [13]) have adopted a combination of the rules and a voting system to generate the scaling actions.

Prediction techniques

The most dominant prediction technique in the cloud auto-scaling domain is the time-series analysis [4]. In order to use the time-series analysis for the cloud auto-scaling purposes, a performance indicator is periodically sampled at fixed intervals. The result is a time-series containing a sequence of the last observations of the performance indicator. The time-series prediction algorithms extrapolate this sequence to predict the future value.

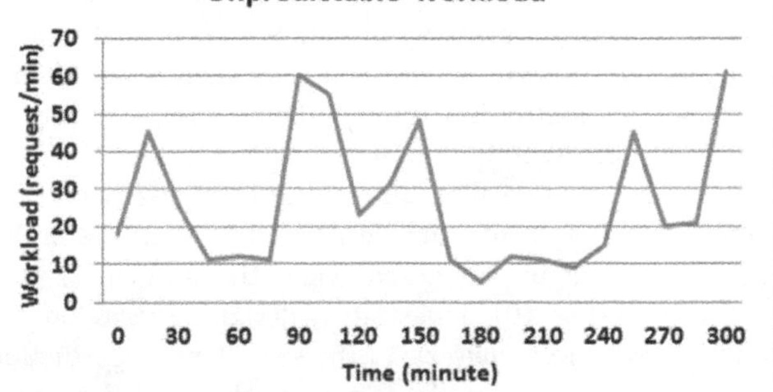

Fig. 5 Unpredictable workload pattern

Some of the time-series prediction algorithms that are used in the existing cloud resource provisioning systems are Moving Average, Auto-regression, ARMA, exponential smoothing, and machine learning approaches [4].

Moving average generally generates poor results for the time-series analysis [4]. Therefore, it is usually applied only to remove the noise from the time-series. In contrast, auto-regression is largely used in the cloud auto-scaling field. The results in [13] show that the performance of the auto-regression algorithm depends on the monitoring interval length, the size of the history window, and the size of the adaptation window. ARMA is a combination of the moving average and the auto-regression algorithms. The authors in [14] use ARMA to predict the future workload. Machine learning algorithms are used in [3] and [6] to carry out the prediction task in the cloud resource provisioning problem. The authors in [6] verify the Artificial Neural Networks (ANN) and the Linear Regression (LR) algorithms to predict the future value of the CPU load. The results in [6] conclude the ANN prediction model surpasses the LR algorithm in terms of prediction accuracy in the auto-scaling domain. In addition, the authors in [3] compare the SVM, the ANN and the LR algorithms and show the SVM algorithm outperforms the ANN and the LR algorithms to predict the future CPU utilization, response time, and throughput of a cloud service. Furthermore, the authors in [15] propose a self-adaptive method that uses a decision tree to assign the incoming workload to one of the forecasting methods based on the workload characteristics. According to the results of [15] the overall prediction accuracy increases by using different prediction algorithms for different workloads. However, to the best of our knowledge, none of the research works in the predictive auto-scaling domain investigates the theoretical foundations of the correlation between the different workload patterns and the accuracy of the prediction algorithms. Therefore, this paper performs a formal study of the theories that are closely related to the regression models used in the predictive auto-scaling systems and investigates the workload characteristics that affect the accuracy of the regression models.

Self-adaptive workload prediction suite

This section proposes a high level architectural design of the self-adaptive workload prediction suite. The self-adaptive suite uses the *decision fusion* technique to increase the prediction accuracy of the cloud auto-scaling systems. Decision fusion is defined as the process of fusing information from individual data sources after each data source has undergone a preliminary classification [16]. The self-adaptive prediction suite aggregates the prediction results of multiple time-series prediction algorithms to improve the final prediction accuracy. The different time-series prediction techniques use different *risk minimization* principles to create the prediction model. The theoretical analysis shows that the accuracy of a risk minimization principle depends on the complexity of the time-series. In addition, since the complexity of a time-series is defined by its corresponding workload pattern, the theoretical analysis concludes that the accuracy of a regression model is a function of the workload pattern (see Theoretical investigation of the hypothesis section).

Furthermore, Experimental investigation of the hypotheses section experimentally confirms the theoretical conclusion of Theoretical investigation of the hypothesis section. In the experiment two versions of an ANN algorithm (i.e., multi-layer perceptron (MLP) and multi-layer perceptron with weight decay (MLPWD)) and the Support Vector Machine (SVM) algorithm are used to predict three groups of time-series. Each time-series group represents a different workload pattern. The objective of the experiment is to investigate the correlation between the accuracy of the risk minimization principle and the workload pattern.

The ANN algorithms are identical except that MLPWD uses the *structural risk minimization* principle and MLP uses the *empirical risk minimization* principle to create the prediction model. Moreover, the SVM algorithm uses the *structural risk minimization* principle to create the prediction model. The experimental results show (see Experimental investigation of the hypotheses section):

- To predict the future workload in an environment with the unpredictable workload pattern it is better to use MLP algorithm with a large sliding window size.
- To predict the future workload in an environment with the periodic workload pattern it is better to use MLPWD algorithm with a small sliding window size.
- To predict the future workload in an environment with the growing workload pattern it is better to use SVM algorithm with a small sliding window size.

The self-adaptive prediction suite uses the experimental results as the fusion rule to aggregate the SVM, the MLP, and the MLPWD prediction algorithms in order to improve the prediction accuracy of the cloud auto-scaling systems. The prediction suite senses the pattern of the incoming workload and automatically chooses the most accurate regression model to carry out the workload prediction. Each workload is represented by a time-series. To identify the workload pattern, the proposed self-adaptive suite decomposes the incoming workload to its components by using Loess package of the R software suite [17]. The Loess component decomposes a workload to its *seasonal, trend,* and *remainder* components. If the workload has strong seasonal and trend components which repeat at fixed intervals, then the workload has periodic pattern. If the trend of the component is constantly increasing or decreasing, then the workload has growing pattern. Otherwise the workload has unpredictable pattern.

The self-adaptive suite constantly monitors the characteristics of the incoming workload (i.e., seasonal and trend components) and replaces the prediction algorithm according to a change in the incoming workload pattern. To this end, the autonomic system principles are used to design the self-adaptive workload prediction suite.

The goal of an autonomic system (Fig. 6 is to make a computing system self-managed. The field is motivated by the increasing complexity in the software systems due to objects change, environmental influence, and ownership cost of software [18, 19]. The idea is that a self-managed system (i.e., an autonomic system) must be attentive to its internal operation and adapt to the *behavior* change in order to produce *future* actions.

A typical autonomic system consists of a context, an autonomic element, and a computing environment [20–22]. In addition, the autonomic system receives the goals and gives the feedback to an external environment. An autonomic element regularly senses the sources of change by using the *sensors.* In the prediction suite, the sensor is the change in the workload pattern (Fig. 7).

In this paper, the autonomic system architecture is adopted for the cloud auto-scaling system architecture. The mapping between the two is presented in Fig. 8.

The presented cloud auto-scaling architecture consists of the cloud workload context, the cloud auto scaling autonomic system, and the cloud computing scaling decisions. The cloud workload context consists of two meta-autonomic elements: workload pattern and cloud auto scaling. In addition, a component for autonomic manager, knowledge, and goals is added to the architecture.

The cloud workload usage represents the "real world usage context" while the scaling decisions represents the "computing environment" context. It is important to note that an autonomic system always operates and executes within a context. The context is defined by the environment and the runtime behavior of the system. The purpose of the autonomic manager is to apply the domain specific knowledge to the cloud workload patterns and the appropriate predictor algorithm (Fig. 9) in order to facilitate the prediction. The autonomic manager is constructed around the analyze/decide/act control loop. Figure illustrates a detailed presentation of the cloud auto-scaling autonomic element.

The cloud auto-scaling autonomic elements (workload patterns and predictor) are designed such that the architecture can be implemented using the strategy design pattern [23] (Fig. 10). The strategy design pattern consists of a *strategy* and a *context.* In the self-adaptive prediction suite the prediction model is the strategy and the workload pattern is the context. A context passes all data (i.e.,

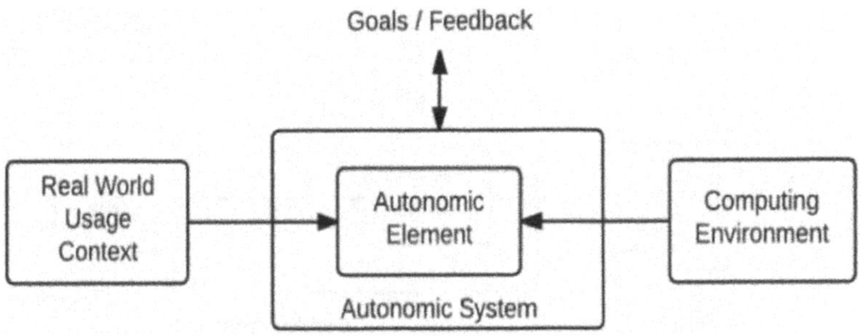

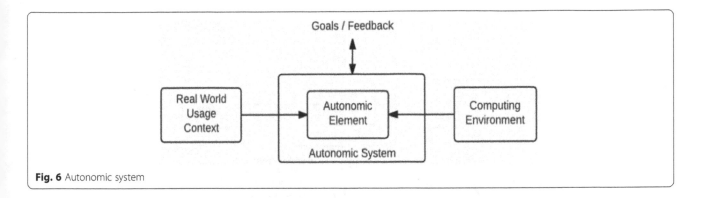

Fig. 6 Autonomic system

the workload pattern) to the strategy. In the prediction suite, the context passes itself as an argument to the strategy and lets the strategy call the context as required. The way this works is that the context determines the workload pattern and passes its pattern interface to the strategy's interface. The strategy then uses the interface to invoke the appropriate algorithm based on the workload pattern interface. All of these functions are realized at runtime automatically.

A careful examination of the strategy design pattern (Fig. 10) shows that the context is in turn designed by using the template design pattern. The intent of the template design pattern is to define the skeleton of an algorithm (or a function) in an operation that defers some steps to subclasses [23].

In a generic strategy design pattern, the context is simply an abstract class with no concrete subclasses. We have modified this by using the template pattern to introduce the concrete subclasses to represent the different workload patterns and to implement the workload pattern context as an autonomic element. This way, the cloud workload pattern is determined automatically and the pattern interface is passed on to the predictor autonomic element which then invokes the appropriate prediction algorithm for the workload pattern. After which the training is carried out and the testing (i.e., the prediction) using the appropriate algorithm is done.

Theoretical investigation of the hypothesis

Machine learning can be classified into the supervised learning, semi-supervised learning, and unsupervised learning. The supervised learning deduces a functional relationship from the training data that generalizes well to the whole dataset. In contrast, the unsupervised learning has no training dataset and the goal is to discover the relationships between the samples or reveal the latent variables behind the observations [5]. The semi-supervised learning falls between the supervised and the unsupervised learning by utilizing both of the labeled and the unlabeled data during the training phase [24]. Among the three categories of the machine learning, the supervised learning is the best fit to solve the prediction problem in the auto-scaling area [5]. Therefore this paper investigates the theoretical foundation of the supervised learning.

To accept or reject the hypothesis, we start with the formal definition of the machine learning and then explore the risk minimization principle as the core function of the learning theory. The definitions in the following sub-sections are taken from [25].

Formal definition of the machine learning process

Vapnik describes the machine learning process through three components [25]:

1. A *generator* of random vectors x. The generator uses a fixed but unknown distribution $P(x)$ to independently produce the random vectors.
2. A *supervisor* which is a function that returns an output vector y for every input vector x, according to a conditional distribution function $P(y|x)$. The conditional distribution function is fixed but unknown.

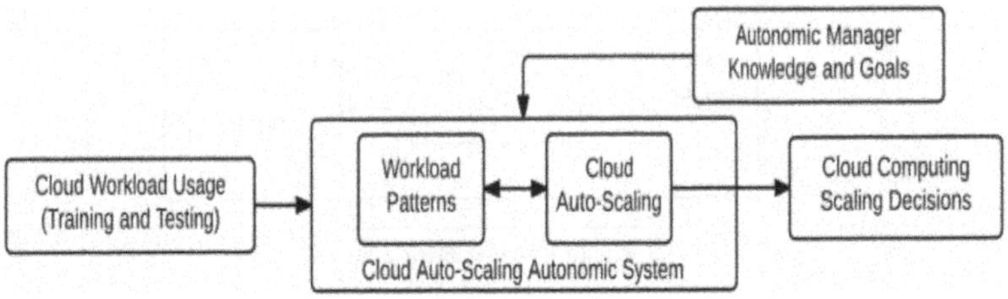

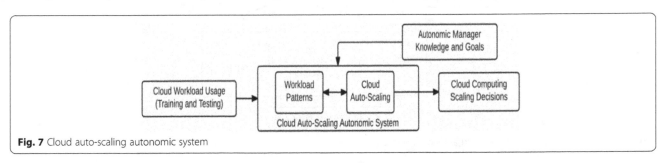

Fig. 7 Cloud auto-scaling autonomic system

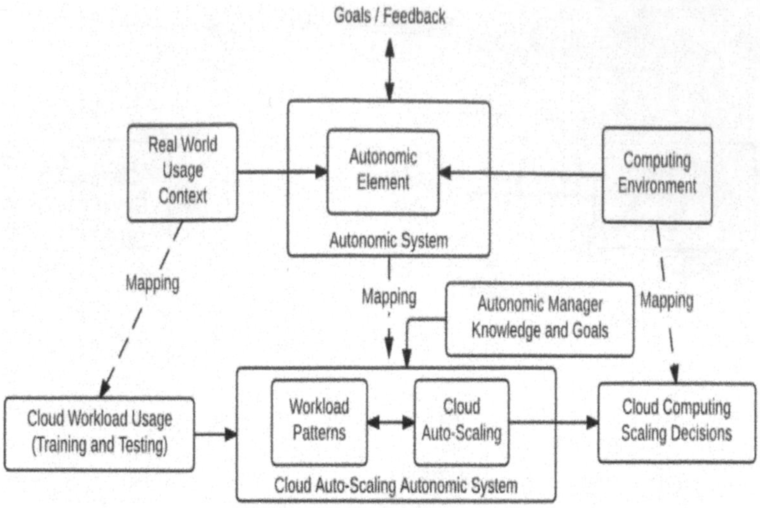

Fig. 8 Mapping classical autonomic system to cloud auto-scaling autonomic system

3. A learning machine that is capable of implementing a set of functions $f(x, w), w \in W$, where x is a random input vector, w is a parameter of the function, and W is a set of abstract parameters that are used to index the set of functions $f(x, w)$ [25].

The problem of learning is choosing from a given set of the functions, the one which best approximates the supervisor's response. The selection is based on a training set of l independent observations:

$$(x_1, y_1), \ldots, (x_l, y_l) \tag{1}$$

The machine learning technique objective is to find the best available approximation to the supervisor's response. To this end the loss $L(y, f(x, w))$ between the supervisor response y with respect to a given input x and the response $f(x, w)$ provided by the learning machine should be measured. The expected value of the loss, given by the *functional risk* is [25]:

$$R(w) = \int L(y, f(x, w))dP(x, y) \tag{2}$$

To improve the accuracy, the functional risk $R(w)$ should be minimized over a class of functions $f(x, w)$, $w \in W$. The problem in minimizing the functional risk is that the joint probability distribution $P(x, y) = P(y|x)P(x)$ is unknown and the only available information is contained in the training set.

In the predictive auto-scaling problem domain, the *Predictor* component corresponds to the learning machine of the learning process. The goal is to find the most accurate predictor, which is the learning machine with the minimum functional risk. Components of the formal learning process can be mapped

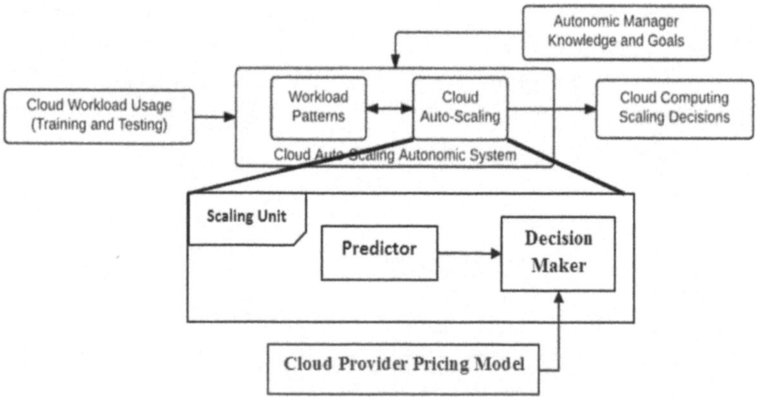

Fig. 9 Projection of the cloud auto-scaling autonomic element

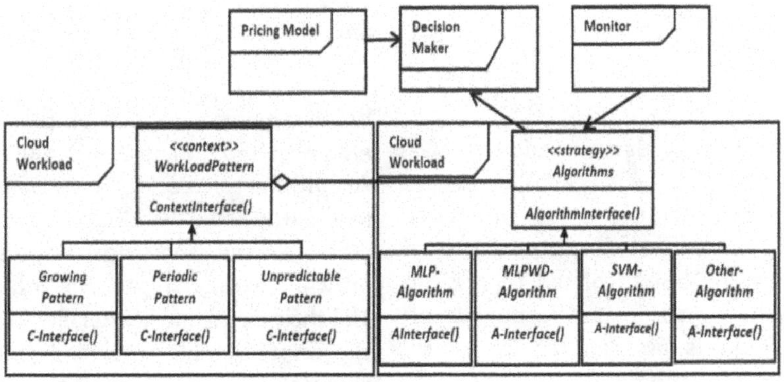

Fig. 10 Design of autonomic elements (Cloud workload pattern and predictor) using strategy design patter

to those of the predictive auto-scaling problem as follows:

- Supervisor's response is analogous to the time-series of workload values which is determined by $P(x, y)$.
- Independent observations are equivalent of the training dataset and indicate the historical values of the workload.
- Learning machine maps to the *Predictor* component.

In the auto-scaling problem domain, $P(x, y)$ refers to the workload distribution. Suppose that we have a set of candidate predictor functions $f(x, w)$, $w \in W$ and we want to find the most accurate function among them. Given that only the workload values for the training duration are known, the functional risk $R(w)$ cannot be calculated for the candidate predictor functions $f(x, w)$, $w \in W$; hence, the most accurate prediction function cannot be found.

Empirical risk minimization

To solve the functional risk problem, the functional risk $R(w)$ can be replaced by the empirical risk [25]:

$$E(w) = \frac{1}{l}\sum_{i=1}^{l} L(y_i, f(x_i, w)) \tag{3}$$

The empirical risk minimization (ERM) assumes that the function $f(x_i, w_l^*)$, which minimizes $E(w)$ over the set $w \in W$, results in a functional risk $R(w_l^*)$ which is close to minimum.

According to the theory of the uniform convergence of empirical risk to actual risk [26], the convergence rate bounds are based on the *capacity* of the set of functions that are implemented by the learning machine. The capacity of the learning machine is referred to as VC-dimension (for Vapnik-Chervonenkis dimension) [27] that represents the complexity of the learning machine.

Applying the theory of uniform convergence to the auto-scaling problem domain concludes that the convergence rate bounds in the auto-scaling domain are based on the complexity (i.e., VC-dimension) of the regression model that is used in the *Predictor* component.

According to the theory of the uniform convergence, for a set of indicator functions with VC-dimension h, the following inequality holds [25]:

$$R(w) < E(w) + C_0\left(\frac{l}{h}, \eta\right) \tag{4}$$

With confidence interval [25]:

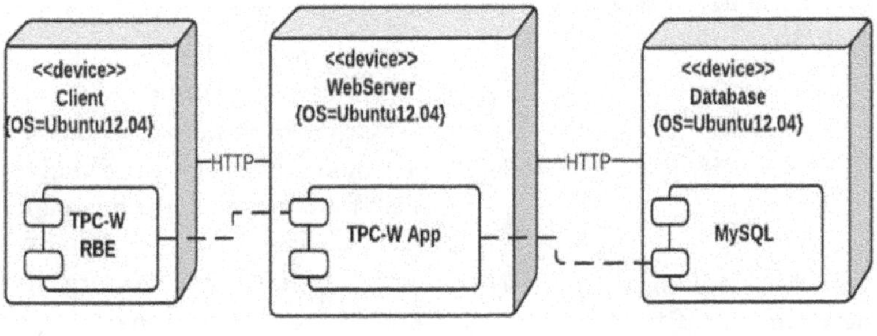

Fig. 11 Experimental setup

$$C_0\left(\frac{l}{h},\eta\right) = \sqrt{\frac{h(ln\frac{2l}{h}+1)-\ln\eta}{l}} \quad (5)$$

where l is the size of the training dataset, h is the VC-dimension of the regression model, e is the Euler's number, and $(1 - \eta)$ is the probability of the validity of Eq. (4) for all $w \in W$.

Equation (4) determines the bound of the regression model's error. Based on this equation, the probability of error of the regression model is less than the frequency of error in the training set plus the confidential interval. According to Eq. (4) the ERM principle is good to be used when the confidence interval is small (i.e., the functional risk is bounded by the empirical risk).

Structural risk minimization

Equations (4) and (5) show the bound of the regression model's error and the confidence interval. In Eqs. (4) and (5), l is the size of training dataset and h is the VC-dimension or the complexity of the regression model. According to Eq. (5) when $\frac{l}{h}$ is large, the confidence interval becomes small and can be neglected. In this case, the functional risk is bounded by the empirical risk, which means the probability of error on the testing dataset is bounded by the probability of error on the training dataset.

On the other hand, when $\frac{l}{h}$ is small, the confidence interval cannot be neglected and even $E(w) = 0$ does not guarantee a small probability of error. In this case to minimize the functional risk $R(w)$, both $E(w)$ and $C_0\left(\frac{l}{h},\eta\right)$ (i.e., the empirical risk and the confidence interval) should be minimized simultaneously. To this end, it is necessary to control the VC-dimension (i.e., complexity) of the regression model. In other words, when the training dataset is complex, the learning machine increases the VC-dimension to shatter[1] the training dataset. By increasing the VC-dimension, the regression model becomes strongly tailored to the particularities of the training dataset and does not perform well to new data (the overfitting situation).

To control the VC-dimension, structural risk minimization principle (SRM) is used. SRM uses a nested structure of subsets $S_p = \{f(x, w), w \in W_p\}$ such that:

$$S_1 \subset S_2 \subset \ldots \subset S_n \quad (6)$$

The corresponding VC-dimensions of the subsets satisfy:

$$h_1 < h_2 < \ldots < h_n \quad (7)$$

Therefor the structural risk minimization (SRM) principle describes a general model of the capacity (or complexity) control and provides a trade-off between the hypothesis space complexity (i.e., the VC-dimension) and the quality of fitting the training data.

Workload pattern effects on prediction accuracy of empirical and structural risk minimizations

According to Workload section, there are three workload patterns in the cloud computing environment: periodic, growing, and unpredictable. The periodic and the growing workload patterns follow a repeatable pattern and their trend and seasonality is predictable. Contrariwise, the unpredictable workload pattern does not follow a repeatable trend. Thus, the unpredictable workload pattern is more complex than the growing and the periodic patterns, which suggests using a regression model with a higher VC-dimension to forecast the unpredictable pattern. From the discussions in sections Formal definition of the machine learning process to Summary and Workload, we propose the following sub-hypotheses in addition to our main hypothesis in the introduction:

- Hypothesis 1a: The structural risk minimization principle performs better in the environments with the periodic and growing (i.e., predictable) workload patterns.
- Hypothesis 1b: The empirical risk minimization principle performs better in the environments with the unpredictable workload pattern.
- Hypothesis 1c: Increasing the window sizes does not have a positive effect on the performance of the structural risk minimization principle in the cloud computing environments.
- Hypothesis 1d: Increasing the window size improves the performance of the empirical risk minimization principle in the unpredictable environments and has no positive effect on the performance of the empirical risk minimization principle in the periodic and the growing environments.

Making these sub-hypotheses provides a basis for proving the main hypothesis of this research. To systematically prove the sub-hypotheses, this section provides a theoretical reasoning to explain the empirical and the structural risk minimization principles behaviors in regards to the different workload patterns in the cloud computing environment.

As shown in Empirical risk minimization section, $\frac{l}{h}$ determines whether to use the empirical or the structural risk minimizations. In this paper we assume the training dataset size (i.e., , l) is static, therefore for the small values of h, $\frac{l}{h}$ fraction is large. In this case, the confidence interval is small and the functional risk is bounded by the empirical risk.

In environments with the predictable workload patterns (i.e., periodic or growing) the training and the testing datasets are not complex. Thus, in such environments h is small and the empirical and the structural risk minimizations perform well. However, it is possible that the empirical risk minimization becomes over fitted against the training dataset. The reason is that, although the periodic and the growing workloads follow a repeatable pattern, it is highly probable that some of the data points in the training dataset do not follow the main pattern of the time-series (i.e., noise data). The noise in the data increases the complexity of the regression model. Increasing the complexity (i.e., VC-dimension) increases the confidence interval as well as the probability of error (see Eq. (5)), which reduces the ERM accuracy. On the other hand, the SRM principle controls the complexity by neglecting the noise in the data, which reduces the confidence interval. Therefore, in the environments with the periodic and the growing workload patterns the SRM approach is expected to outperform the ERM approach (hypothesis 1a).

The same reasoning applies to the environments with the unpredictable workload pattern. In the unpredictable environments there is no distinctive workload trend and none of the data points should be treated as the noise. In the unpredictable environments, the ERM approach increases the VC-dimension to shatter all of the training data points. However, since the training and the testing datasets follow the same unpredictable pattern, increasing the VC-dimension helps the prediction model to predict the fluctuations of the testing dataset, as well. On the contrary, the SRM approach controls the VC-dimension to decrease the confidence interval. Therefore, the SRM approach cannot capture the fluctuating nature of the unpredictable workload pattern and trains a less accurate regression model compared to the ERM approach (hypothesis 1b).

In the machine learning domain, window size refers to the input size of the prediction algorithm. Increasing the window size provides more information for the prediction algorithm and is expected to increase the accuracy of the prediction model. However, increasing the input size makes the prediction model more complex. To manage the complexity, the SRM approach compromises between the accuracy and the VC-dimension. Therefore, increasing the window size does not necessarily affect the accuracy of the SRM prediction model. (Hypothesis 1c).

Furthermore, because the ERM approach cannot control the complexity of the regression model, increasing the window size increases the VC-dimension of the prediction model. In the predictable environments (i.e., the periodic and the growing patterns) the training and the testing datasets are not complex and the ERM principle is able to capture the time-series behaviors by using smaller window sizes. However, increasing the window size in the predictable environments increases the noise in the training dataset which causes a bigger confidence interval, and reduces the accuracy of the prediction model. On the other hand, due to the fluctuations in the unpredictable datasets, none of the data points in the training dataset should be considered as a noise. Therefore, in the unpredictable environments increasing the window size helps the ERM principle to shatter more training data. However, since the training and the testing datasets follow the same unpredictable pattern, increasing the window size improves the ERM precision to predict the fluctuations of the testing dataset, as well (hypothesis 1d).

Experimental investigation of the hypotheses section experimentally investigates the theoretical discussion of this section and evaluates the four sub-hypotheses.

Summary

The research in the learning theory provides a rich set of knowledge in learning the complex relationships and patterns in the datasets. Vapnik et al. show that the proportion of the training dataset size to the complexity of the regression model determines whether to use the empirical or the structural risk minimizations [25]. In the auto-scaling domain, the *Predictor* component corresponds to the learning machine of the leaning process. Therefore, to improve the accuracy of the *Predictor* component, the risk minimization principle should be determined based on the complexity of the prediction techniques (i.e., the VC-dimension) and the training dataset size. The workload pattern complexity is the main driving factor of the *Predictor* component's VC-dimension. Four sub-hypotheses are introduced in order to experiment the risk minimization principles vis-à-vis the different workload patterns.

Experimental investigation of the hypotheses

The main goal of the experiment presented in this section is to verify the empirical and the structural risk minimization principles behaviors in the environments with the periodic, growing, and unpredictable workload patterns. There are various learning algorithms that have been used as the predictor for the auto-scaling purposes (see Prediction techniques section) which use either the empirical or the structural risk minimizations. In our previous work (see [2]) the SVM algorithm which is based on the structural minimization and the ANN algorithm which uses the empirical minimization principle were used. Our experimental results in [2] showed that in the environments with the periodic and the growing workload patterns the SVM algorithm outperforms the ANN algorithm, but ANN has a better accuracy in forecasting the unpredictable workloads. These results support the theoretical discussion in Evaluation metrics section. However, in this paper the goal is to zero-in on two different implementations of the ANN algorithm in order to compare the effect of the structural and the empirical risk minimizations on the ANN prediction accuracy. Therefore, in this experiment two implementations of the ANN algorithm (i.e., MLP and MLPWD) are used to isolate the influence of the risk minimization principle on the prediction accuracy. MLP uses the ERM principle and MLPWD uses the SRM principle. In addition, since both of the MLPWD and the SVM algorithms use the SRM principle, the accuracy of the MLPWD is compared with the SVM accuracy to isolate the impact of the regression model structure on the accuracy of the machine learning algorithms.

Sections Multi-layer perceptron with empirical risk minimization, Multi-layer perceptron with structural risk minimization, and Support vector machines briefly explain MLP, MLPWD, and SVM algorithms, respectively. Sections Training and testing of MLP and MLPWD, Evaluation metrics, and Experimental results describe the experiment and the results.

Multi-layer perceptron with empirical risk minimization

There are different variations of the Artificial Neural Network (ANN), such as back-propagation, feed-forward, time delay, and error correction [5]. MLP is a feed-forward ANN that maps the input data to the appropriate output.

A MLP is a network of simple neurons that are called perceptron. Perceptron computes a single output from the multiple real valued inputs by forming a linear combination to its input weights and putting the output through a nonlinear activation function. The mathematical representation of the MLP output is [25]:

$$y = \varphi\left(\sum_{i=1}^{n} w_i x_i + b\right) = \varphi\left(W^T X + b\right) \qquad (8)$$

where W denotes the vector of weights, X is the vector of inputs, b is the bias, and φ is the activation function.

The MLP networks are typically used in the supervised learning problems. Therefore, there is a training set that contains an input–output set similar to Eq. (1). The training of the MLP refers to adapting all the weights and biases to their optimal values to minimize the following equation [25]:

$$E = \frac{1}{l}\sum_{i=1}^{l} (T_i - Y_i)^2 \qquad (9)$$

where T_i denotes the predicted value, Y_i is the actual value, and l is the training set size. Equation (9) is a simplified version of Eq. (3) and represents the empirical risk minimization.

Multi-layer perceptron with structural risk minimization

The general principle of the structural risk minimization can be implemented in many different ways. According to [28] there are four steps to implement the structural risk minimization (see section Structural risk minimization), of which the first step is to choose a class of functions with hierarchy of nested subsets in ordered of the complexity. Authors of [25] suggest three examples of the structures that can be used to build the hierarchy of the neural networks.

- Structure given by the architecture of the neural network.
- Structure given by the learning procedure
- Structure given by the preprocessing.

The second proposed structure (i.e., given by the learning procedure) uses "weight decay" to create a hierarchy of the nested functions. This structure considers a set of the functions $S = \{f(x, w),\ w \in W\}$ that are implemented by a neural network with a fixed architecture. The parameters {w} are the weights of the neural network. Nested structure is introduced through $S_p = \{f(x, w),\ ||w|| \le C_p\}$ and $C_1 < C_2 < \ldots < C_n$, where C_i is a constant value that defines the ceiling of the norm of the neural network weights. For a convex loss function, the minimization of the empirical risk within the element S_p of the structure is achieved through the minimization of [29]:

$$E\left(w, \gamma_p\right) = \frac{1}{l}\sum_{1}^{l} L(y_i, f(x_i, w)) + \gamma_p ||w||^2 \qquad (10)$$

The nested structure can be created by appropriately choosing Lagrange multipliers $\gamma_1 > \gamma_2 > \ldots > \gamma_n$. According to Eq. (10), the well-known weight-decay procedure refers to the structural minimization [25].

Training the neural networks with the weight decay means that during the training phase, each updated weight is multiplied by a factor slightly less than 1 to prevent the weight from growing too large. The risk minimization equation for the Multi-Layer Perceptron with Weight Decay (MLPWD) algorithm is [29]:

$$E = \frac{1}{l}\sum_{i=1}^{l} (T_i - Y_i)^2 + \frac{\lambda}{2}\sum_{i=1}^{l} w_i^2 \qquad (11)$$

Authors of [29] have shown that the conventional weight decay technique can be considered as the simplified version of the structural risk minimization in the neural networks. Therefore, in this paper we use MLPWD algorithm to study the accuracy of the structural risk

Table 1 Hardware specification of servers for experiment

	Memory	Processor	Storage
Client	1 GB	4 core	8 GB
Web server	1 GB	4 core	8 GB
Database	2 GB	8 core	20 GB

minimization for predicting the different classes of workload.

Support vector machines

Support Vector Machine (SVM) is used for many machine learning tasks such as pattern recognition, object classification, and regression analysis in the case of the time series prediction. Support Vector Regression (SVR), is the methodology by which a function is estimated by using the observed data. In this paper the SVR and the SVM terms are used interchangeably.

SVM uses Eqs. (12) and (13) to define the prediction functions for the linear and the non-linear regression models, respectively [6]:

$$f(x) = (w.x) + b \tag{12}$$

$$f(x) = (w.\varphi(x)) + b \tag{13}$$

where, w is a set of weights, b is a threshold, and ϕ is a kernel function.

If the time-series is not linear, the regression model maps the time-series x to a higher dimension feature space by using kernel function $\varphi(x)$. Then the prediction model performs the linear regression in the higher dimensional feature space. The goal of the SVM training is to find the optimal weights w and the optimal threshold b. There are two criteria to find the optimal weights and the optimal threshold. The first criterion is the *flatness* of the weights, which can be measured by the Euclidean norm (i.e., minimize $||w||^2$). The second criterion is the error generated by the estimation process of the value, also known as the empirical risk, which is to be minimized. The overall goal is to find a regression function $f(x, w)$ which minimizes the structural risk R_s [6]:

$$R_s = E + \frac{\lambda}{2}||w||^2 \tag{14}$$

Table 2 MLP and MLPWD configurations

Parameter Name	MLP Value	MLPWD
Learning Rate (ρ)	0.3	0.3
Momentum	0.2	0.2
Validation Threshold	20	20
Hidden Layers	1	1
Hidden Neurons	(attributes + classes)/2	(attributes + classes)/2
Decay	False	True

Table 3 SVM configuration

Parameter Name	Value
C (complexity parameter)	1.0
kernel	RBF Kernel
regOptimizer	RegSMOImproved

where, E is the empirical risk, and $||w||^2$ represents the flatness of the weights of the regression function. The scale factor λ is the regularization constant and is often referred to as the capacity control factor. The scale factor λ is useful for reducing the complexity of the regression model to prevent the overfitting problem.

Experimental setup

In this experiment workload represents the web service requests arrival rate. Workload is a key performance indicator of a given web service that can be used to calculate other performance indicators (such as utilization, and throughput) of that web service. Furthermore, monitoring workload of a web service is straightforward and can be carried out by using instrumentation technique. Therefore, in this experiment workload of the web service is the target class of the prediction techniques.

The goal of this experiment is to compare the accuracy of the MLP, the MLPWD, and the SVM algorithms for predicting the periodic, the growing, and the unpredictable workload patterns. The required components to conduct this experiment are: a benchmark to generate the workload patterns, an infrastructure to deploy the benchmark, and an implementation of the prediction algorithms. Java implementation of TPC-W [30] and Amazon EC2 are used as the benchmark and the infrastructure, respectively. In addition, the implementation of Multi-Layer Perceptron and Support Vector Machine algorithms in WEKA tool is used to carry out the prediction task.

The MLP algorithm in WEKA tool [31] has various configuration parameters including a parameter to switch on/off the weight decay feature (i.e., *decay* parameter). Therefore, to use the empirical risk minimization the default value of the *decay* parameter (i.e., off) is used. Also, to use the structural risk minimization, the *decay* parameter is switched on.

The TPC-W benchmark emulates an online book shop and is implemented on 3-tier architecture. As shown in Fig. 11, the experimental setup consists of three virtual machines running on Ubuntu Linux. Table 1 shows the details of the virtual machines. Note that to decrease the experiment complexity, the experiment is limited to monitoring the performance of the web server tier in and it is assumed that the database is not a bottleneck. For this reason, a relatively powerful virtual machine is dedicated to the database tier.

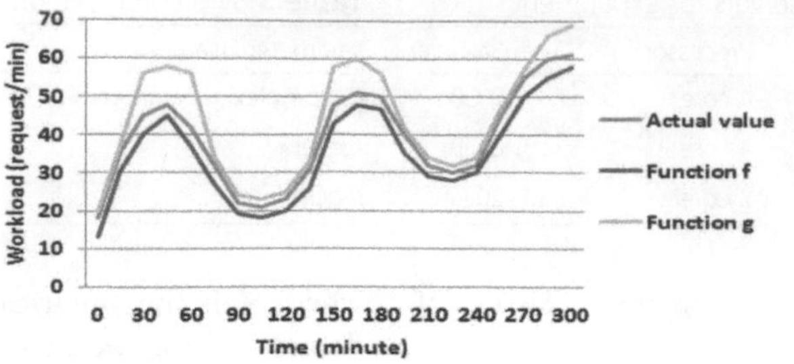

Fig. 12 RMSE vs. MAE

On the client side, a customized script is used along with the TPC-W workload generator to produce the growing, the periodic, and the unpredictable workload patterns. In this experiment workload represents the webpage requests arrival rate. Each of the workload patterns is generated for 500 min. To improve accuracy of the results, the experiment is repeated 10 times for each workload pattern. On the web-server machine, the total number of the user requests is stored in the log files every minute. This results in 10 workload trace files, for each of the workload patterns. Each of the workload trace files has 500 data points. We refer to the workload trace files as the *actual workloads* in the rest of this paper.

Training and testing of MLP and MLPWD

In our previous work [1] we proved that in the auto-scaling domain the optimum training duration for the ANN and the SVM algorithms is 60% of the experiment duration. Therefore, in this experiment the first 300 data points (i.e., 60%) of the actual workload trace files are considered as the training datasets and the rest 200 data points are dedicated to the test.

Another important factor in the training and the testing of the time-series prediction algorithms is the *dimensionality* of the datasets (i.e., the number of the features that exist in the dataset). In this experiment, the actual datasets have only one feature, which is the number of the requests that arrive at the cloud service per minute. Therefore, in order to use the machine learning prediction algorithms *sliding window* technique is used. The sliding window technique uses the last k samples of a given feature to predict the future value of that feature. For example, to predict value of b_{k+1} the sliding window technique uses $[b_1, b_2, \ldots, b_k]$ values. Similarly, to predict b_{k+2}, the sliding window technique updates the historical window by adding the actual value of b_{k+1} and removing the oldest value from the window (i.e., the sliding window becomes $[b_2, b_3, \ldots, b_{k+1}]$). Setting the sliding window size is not a trivial task. Usually the smaller window sizes do not reflect the correlation between the data samples thoroughly, while using the bigger window size increases the chance of the overfitting. Thus, in this experiment the effect of the sliding window size on the prediction accuracy of MLP and MLPWD is studied, as well.

To reduce the probability of the overfitting problem, the cross-validation technique is used in the training phase. Readers are encouraged to see [32] for more details about the cross-validation technique. Table 2 shows the configuration of the MLP and the MLPWD algorithms in this experiment. Configuration of the SVM algorithm is shown in Table 3.

Evaluation metrics

Accuracy of the experimental results can be evaluated based on the different metrics such as Mean Absolute Error (MAE), Root Mean Square Error (RMSE), PRED (25) and R2 Prediction Accuracy [33]. Among these metrics, PRED(25) only considers the percentage of the observations whose prediction accuracy falls within 25% of the actual value. In addition, R2 Prediction Accuracy

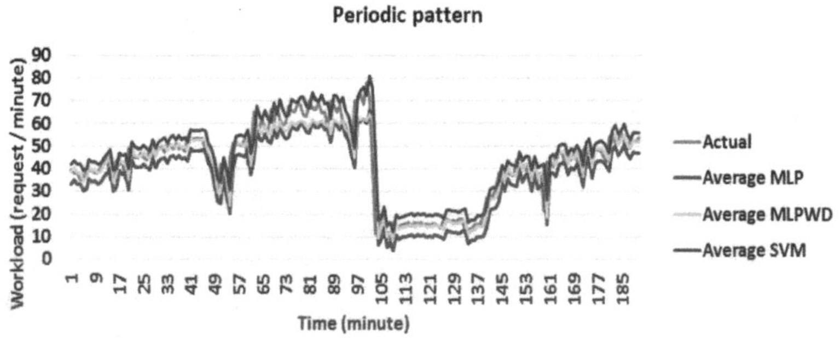

Fig. 13 Sample prediction results (periodic pattern)

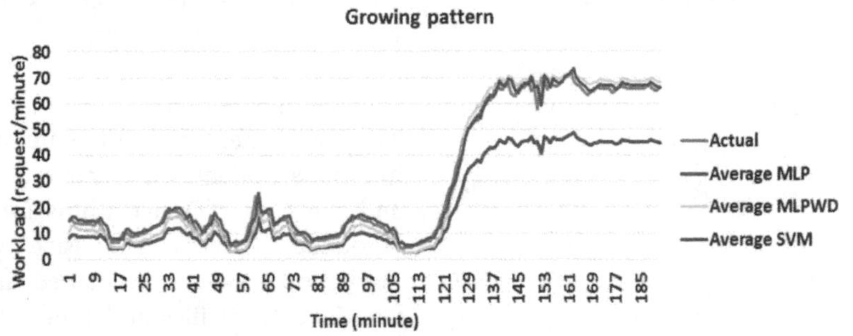

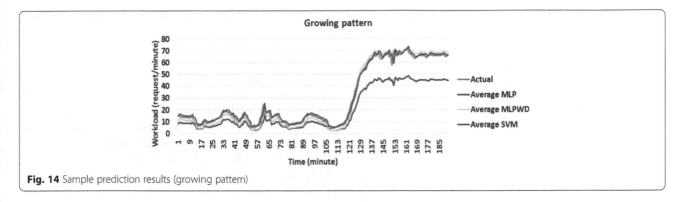

Fig. 14 Sample prediction results (growing pattern)

is a measure of the goodness-of-fit, which its value falls within the range [0, 1] and is commonly applied to the linear regression models [6]. Due to the limitations of PRED (25) and R2 Prediction Accuracy, the MAE and the RMSE metrics are used in this paper. The formal definitions of these metrics are [33]:

$$MAE = \frac{1}{n}\sum\nolimits_{i=1}^{n} |YP_i - Y_i| \tag{15}$$

$$RMSE = \sqrt{\frac{\sum\nolimits_{i=1}^{n} (YP_i - Y_i)2}{n}} \tag{16}$$

where YP_i is the predicted output and Y_i is the actual output for ith observation, and n is the number of the observations for which the prediction is made. The MAE metric is a popular metric in statistics, especially in the prediction accuracy evaluation. The RMSE represents the sample standard deviation of the differences between the predicted values and the observed values. A smaller MAE and RMSE value indicates a more effective prediction scheme.

The MAE metric is a linear score which assumes all of the individual errors are weighted equally. Moreover, the RMSE is most useful when the large errors are particularly undesirable [34].

In the auto-scaling domain, a regression model that generates a greater number of small errors (function *f* in Fig. 12) is more desirable than a regression model that generates a fewer number of the large errors (function *g*

Table 4 MAE and RMSE values (periodic pattern)

Phase	Window size	Average MAE			Average RMSE		
		MLP	MLPWD	SVM	MLP	MLPWD	SVM
Training	2	6.88	4.16	4.65	8.55	6.65	7.31
	3	6.7	4.12	4.62	8.32	6.32	7
	4	6.5	4.11	4.62	8.12	6.12	6.99
	5	5.95	4.05	4.52	8	6.44	6.8
	6	5.78	4.02	4.52	7.56	6.12	6.7
	7	5.68	3.88	4.32	7.5	6.2	6.7
	8	5.68	3.95	4.3	7.12	6.21	6.6
	9	5.51	4.02	4.3	6.9	6.18	6.8
	10	4.98	4	4.31	6.52	6.18	6.7
Testing	2	6.2	6	6	8.31	8	8.1
	3	6.3	5.9	6	8.31	7.9	7.98
	4	6.3	5.8	6.1	8.34	7.9	8.05
	5	6.99	5.9	6.2	8.62	7.8	8.15
	6	7.15	5.7	6.1	8.77	7.4	8
	7	7.25	5.72	6	9.12	7	7.71
	8	7.98	5.75	6	9.15	7	7.65
	9	8.56	5.66	5.8	10.36	7.1	7.5
	10	9.2	5.58	5.7	11.89	6.9	7.6

Table 5 MAE and RMSE values (growing pattern)

Phase	Window size	MAE			RMSE		
		MLP	MLPWD	SVM	MLP	MLPWD	SVM
Training	2	2.5	2.1	1.7	3.9	4.02	3.8
	3	2.8	2.3	1.75	3.9	3.82	3.7
	4	2.7	2.3	1.8	4.1	3.87	3.6
	5	2.7	2.5	1.8	3.98	3.89	3.7
	6	2.6	2.4	1.8	3.88	3.71	3.6
	7	2.7	2.4	1.81	3.84	3.81	3.6
	8	2.66	2.33	1.78	3.78	3.62	3.5
	9	2.8	2.22	1.78	3.95	3.7	3.3
	10	2.57	2.25	1.78	4	3.7	3.4
Testing	2	3.77	3	2.5	4.4	4	3.7
	3	3.85	3.6	2.5	4.91	4.21	3.7
	4	3.55	3.5	2.6	4.92	4.5	3.65
	5	3.64	3.41	2.4	4.71	4.22	3.6
	6	3.89	3.42	2.3	4.52	4.31	3.7
	7	3.84	3.31	2.2	5.11	4	3.7
	8	3.95	3.02	2.2	5.52	3.99	3.4
	9	4.12	3	2.2	5.98	3.95	3.5
	10	4.1	2.8	2.2	6.02	3.9	3.7

Table 6 MAE and RMSE values (unpredictable pattern)

Phase	Window size	MAE			RMSE		
		MLP	MLPWD	SVM	MLP	MLPWD	SVM
Training	2	1.4	1.74	1.81	2.6	2.9	3.15
	3	1.42	1.73	1.73	2.61	2.88	3.2
	4	1.43	1.72	1.78	2.59	2.87	3.31
	5	1.4	1.73	1.75	2.55	2.89	3.15
	6	1.35	1.69	1.73	2.4	2.91	3.19
	7	1.46	1.66	1.72	2.48	2.98	3.2
	8	1.44	1.65	1.74	2.31	2.74	3.2
	9	1.48	1.66	1.66	2.2	2.65	3.16
	10	1.44	1.65	1.68	2.15	2.74	3.17
Testing	2	2.6	2.82	3.12	3.01	3.41	3.31
	3	2.5	2.8	3.1	3	3.4	3.64
	4	2.34	2.77	2.9	3	3.38	3.7
	5	2.21	2.76	2.88	2.98	3.41	371
	6	1.98	2.44	2.89	2.9	3.42	3.78
	7	1.65	2.4	2.85	2.8	3.21	3.88
	8	1.42	2.1	2.91	2.7	3.2	3.9
	9	0.98	2.11	2.92	2.4	3.11	4.1
	10	0.98	2.1	2.9	2.2	2.8	4.18

in Fig. 12). The reason is because the rule-based decision makers issue the scale actions based on the prediction values and to generate a *correct* scale action, the prediction should be *close enough* to the actual value. In other words, the rule-based decision makers are not sensitive to the small errors in the prediction results. Therefore, the smaller errors in the prediction results are negligible. Our previous work [1] investigates the sensitivity of the rule-based decision makers to the prediction results. As a result, in the cloud auto-scaling domain, the RMSE factor is more important than the MAE factor. However, considering both metrics (i.e., MAE and RMSE) provides a comprehensive analysis of the accuracy of the prediction models. The greater is the difference between RMSE and MAE the greater is the variance in the individual errors in the sample.

Experimental results

The experiment has three iterations and each of the iterations evaluates the accuracy of the SVM, the MLP and the MLPWD algorithms for predicting one of the workload patterns. For each workload pattern, the prediction models are trained and tested based on 10 workload trace files and their accuracy is measured by MAE and RMSE metrics. The overall accuracy of each prediction model is represented by its average MAE and RMSE metric values. Figures 12 ,13 and 14 show the average MLPWD, MLP, and SVM prediction results in the test phase (window size = 3 min) for the periodic, growing, and unpredicted workload patterns, respectively.

Tables 4, 5 and 6 present the training and the testing accuracy of the MLWPD, MLP, and SVM for predicting the periodic, the growing and the unpredictable workloads, respectively. The results are also plotted in Figs. 16, 17, 18, 19, 20, 21. Note that the MAE and RMSE values in Tables 4, 5 and 6 are the average of the MAE and RMSE results over 10 repetitions of the experiment for each of the prediction algorithms. The following subsections analyze the experimental results in regard to the four sub-hypotheses that are introduced in Section Workload pattern effects on prediction accuracy of empirical and structural risk minimizations.

Hypothesis 1.a: the SRM principle performs better in the environments with the predictable workload patterns

In the environments with the predictable workloads, the training and the testing datasets are not complex. Therefore, both of the ERM and SRM principles are accurate. For instance, in the environments with the periodic workload pattern (Fig. 15), the MAE and the RMSE values of the MLP and the MLPWD algorithms for window size = 2 are very close (see Table 4). Because the SRM neglects the noise data its accuracy is slightly better than the ERM. However, by increasing the window size the noise in the training data

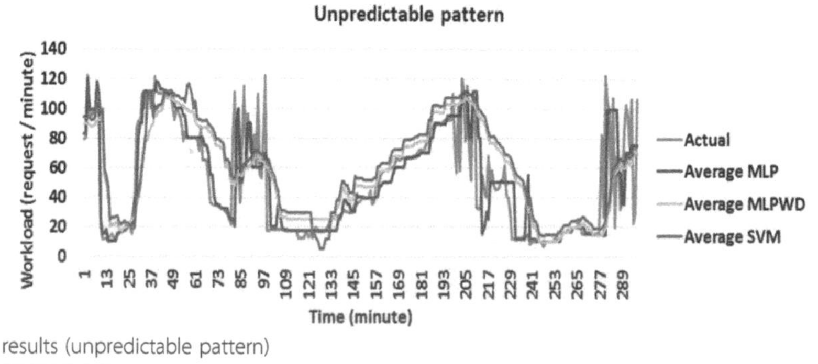

Fig. 15 Sample prediction results (unpredictable pattern)

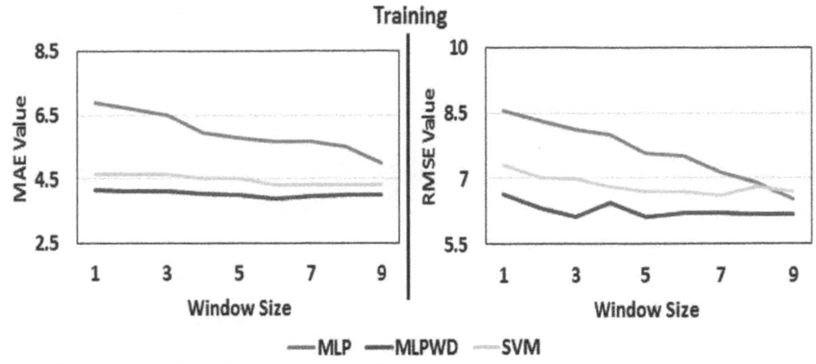

Fig. 16 MAE and RMSE values in the training phase (periodic pattern)

increases which reduces the accuracy of MLP, but because the MLPWD neglects the noise it's accuracy doesn't affect much.

Table 4, Figs. 16 and 17 show the prediction results for the periodic workload pattern. According to the results, the MLPWD algorithm outperforms the SVM and the MLP algorithms in the environments with the periodic workload pattern. The only difference between the MLPWD and the MLP algorithms is the risk minimization approach. Therefore, the results show that for the periodic workload pattern it is better to use the SRM principle.

Furthermore, the prediction results for the growing workload pattern are shown in Table 5, Figs. 18 and 19. The results show the SVM algorithm has better accuracy compared with MLPWD and MLP in the environments with the growing workload pattern. However, similar to the results of the periodic pattern, the MLPWD algorithm outperforms the MLP algorithm for predicting the growing workloads. This indicates that the SRM principle is more suitable compared to the ERM principle for predicting the growing workloads.

Based on the results, the SRM principle is more accurate than the ERM principle for forecasting the predictable workload patterns (i.e., the periodic and the growing workloads).

Hypothesis 1.b: the ERM principle performs better in the environments with the unpredictable workload patterns

According to Table 6, Figs. 20 and 21, the MLP algorithm has a better prediction accuracy compared with the SVM and the MLPWD algorithms in the environments with the unpredictable workload pattern. The MLP algorithm uses the ERM principle and tries to cover all of the training data. On the other hand, the MLPWD and the SVM algorithms use SRM principle and try to reduce the complexity by finding a smooth curve to cover the training data. Since the unpredictable data has a fluctuating nature, the SRM principle assumes some of the training data points are noise and removes them from the training dataset. As the result, in the environments with many fluctuations, the MLPWD and the SVM algorithms assume that the spikes are noise in the data. Therefore, the MLPWD and the SVM algorithms do not capture the spikes in the dataset. The result is that in the environments with the unpredictable workload pattern the MLP algorithm outperforms the MLPWD and the SVM algorithms. This confirms *hypothesis 1.b*.

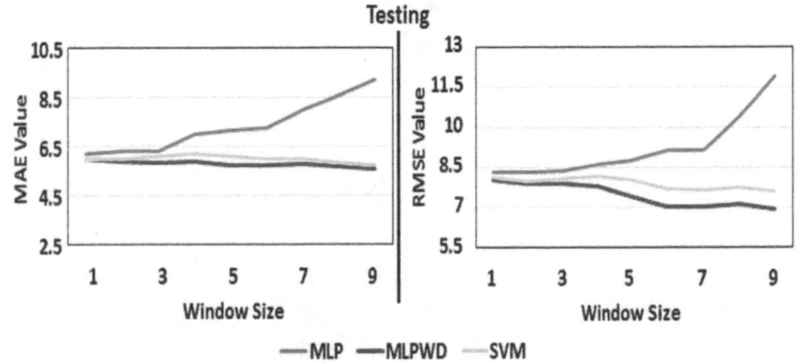

Fig. 17 MAE and RMSE values in the testing phase (periodic pattern)

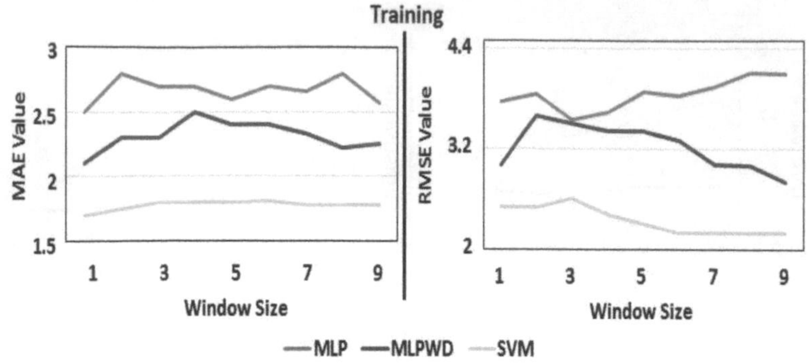

Fig. 18 MAE and RMSE values in the training phase (growing pattern)

Hypothesis 1.c: increasing the window sizes does not have a positive effect on the performance of the SRM principle

According to Tables 4 and 5 in the periodic and the growing environments increasing the window size does not affect the accuracies of the MLPWD and the SVM algorithms. The reason is because the SRM principle controls the prediction model's complexity by neglecting some of the training data points. As a result, increasing the window size neither increase nor decreases the accuracy of the prediction models.

By increasing the window size in the unpredictable environments the MLPWD accuracy slightly improves while the SVM accuracy slightly reduces (Table 6). However, the changes in the accuracies of the MLPWD and SVM in the unpredictable environments are negligible. Therefore, it can be concluded that for all of the workload patterns, increasing the window size has no substantial effect on the prediction accuracy of the SRM principle.

Hypothesis 1.d: Increasing the window size improves the performance of the ERM principle in the unpredictable environments and has no positive effect of the performance the ERM principle in the predictable environments.

Based on Fig. 16, for the smaller window sizes in the periodic environment the MLP accuracy is close to the MLPWD and the SVM accuracies. However, by increasing the window size, the MLP accuracy decreases. Similar to the results of the periodic pattern, in the environments with the growing workload pattern, the MLP prediction accuracy has a decreasing trend but does not change too much by increasing the window size. This is because increasing the window size of the MLP algorithm leads to the overfitting issue which decreases the MLP accuracy. As shown in Fig. 16, during the training phase the MLP accuracy increases by increasing the window size. This shows the MLP algorithm becomes over fitted to the training dataset by increasing the window size. The results confirm that in the environments with the periodic workload pattern, increasing the sliding window size has no positive effect on the prediction accuracies of the ERM principle.

Unlike the growing and the periodic patterns, increasing the window size has a positive effect on the prediction accuracy of the MLP algorithm in the environment with the unpredictable workload pattern. The reason is that in the unpredictable environments there are many fluctuations in the data; therefore, the ERM prediction models cannot extract the relationships between the features thoroughly. Thus, increasing the window size increases the input size of the algorithms, which improves the ERM's prediction accuracies.

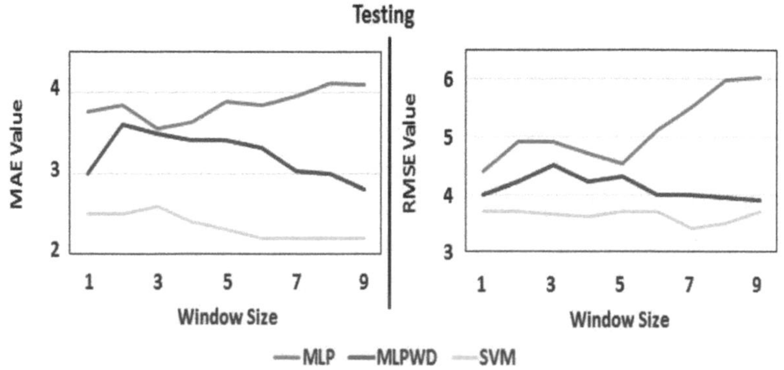

Fig. 19 MAE and RMSE values in the testing phase (growing pattern)

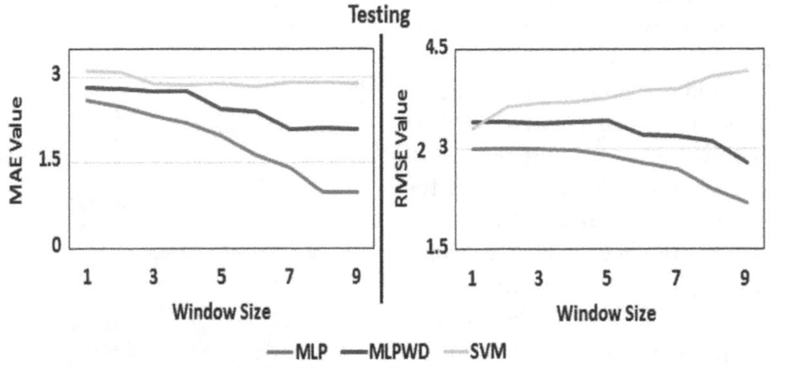

Fig. 20 MAE and RMSE values in the testing phase (unpredictable pattern)

Experimental results conclusion

The results of the experiments support the theoretical conclusion presented in Section Workload pattern effects on prediction accuracy of empirical and structural risk minimizations, which suggests the use of the SRM principle in the environments with the growing and the periodic workload patterns. In addition, the experimental results show that increasing the window size does not improve the SRM accuracy. On the other hand, for the environments with the unpredictable workload pattern, it is better to use the ERM principle with the bigger window sizes. According to the experimental results, Section Self-adaptive workload prediction suite proposes an autonomic prediction suite which chooses the most accurate prediction algorithm based on the incoming workload pattern.

Conclusions and future work

This paper proposed a self-adaptive prediction suite with an aim to improve the accuracy of predictive auto-scaling systems for the IaaS layer of cloud computing. The prediction suite uses the decision fusion technique and facilitates the selection of the most accurate prediction algorithm and the window size with respect to the incoming workload pattern. The proposed architecture used the strategy and the template design patterns which guarantees the automatic runtime selection of the appropriate prediction algorithm as well as detection of a suitable workload pattern and an appropriate window size. To lay out the theoretical foundation of the prediction suite, this paper proposed and evaluated a main hypothesis and four sub-hypotheses on the accuracy of several time-series prediction models in the IaaS layer of cloud computing. According to the main hypothesis, the prediction accuracy of the predictive auto-scaling systems can be increased by choosing an appropriate time-series prediction algorithm based on the incoming workload pattern.

To the best of our knowledge, the theoretical foundation of the predictive auto-scaling systems has not been investigated in the existing research works. Therefore, this paper performs a formal study of the theories that are closely related to the accuracy of predictive auto-scaling systems. To evaluate the main hypothesis, we have proposed four sub-hypotheses concerning the influence of the risk minimization principle on the prediction accuracy of the regression models in the environments with different workload patterns. To test these sub-hypotheses, the theoretical fundamentals of the prediction algorithms were investigated through analyzing the learning theory and the risk minimization principles.

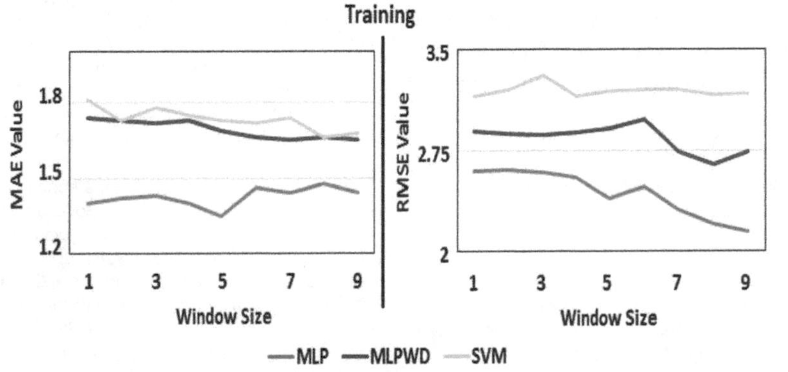

Fig. 21 MAE and RMSE values in the training phase (unpredictable pattern)

Based on the formal analysis, the structural risk minimization outperforms the empirical risk minimization for predicting the periodic and the growing workload patterns, but the empirical risk minimization is a better fit for forecasting the unpredictable workload pattern. Furthermore, experiments were conducted to validate the theoretical discussion. In the experiments, the influence of the risk minimization principle on the accuracy of the MLP and the MLPWD algorithms for predicting different workload patterns was examined. Moreover, the experiments compared the accuracy of the MLPWD and the SVM to isolate the impact of the regression model's structure on the prediction accuracy. The experimental results support the theoretical discussion. Also, the results show that increasing the sliding window size only has positive impact on the accuracy of the MLP algorithm in the environments with the unpredictable workload pattern. However, in other environments (i.e., growing or periodic workload patterns), increasing the window size does not improve the prediction accuracies of the MLP, MLPWD, and the SVM algorithms. The theoretical analysis and the experimental results demonstrated that using an appropriate prediction algorithm based on the workload pattern increases the prediction accuracy of the auto-scaling systems. Thus, based on the theoretical and experimental results in this paper, we can accept the main hypothesis that is, *the prediction accuracy of time-series techniques is positively impacted by using different prediction algorithms for the different cloud workload patterns.*

In the current work we assume that the database tier has no negative impact on the auto-scaling prediction accuracy. Investigating the impact of the database tier on the prediction accuracy warrants further research. In addition, we aim to investigate the relationship between the database tier auto-scaling and the workload patterns and the sliding window sizes. Finally, the autonomic elements in Fig. 10 will be re-designed to include more time series algorithms and possibly more work load patterns.

Endnotes

[1]*Shattering definition*: Model f with some parameter vector θ shatters a set of data points $(x_1, x_2, ..., x_n)$ if for all assignments of labels to the data points there exists a θ such that the model f makes no error evaluating that set of data points.

Acknowledgements
We will like to express our thanks to departmental technical and administrative staff who provided resources and supports to the AYN during his PhD research work.

Authors' contributions
This research work is primarily based on AYN's PhD research and thesis report which was co-supervised by SAA and CL. All authors contributed to the technical aspects and the writing of the paper. AYN designed and implemented the experiments based on guidance from SAA and CL. All authors read and approved the final manuscript.

Competing interests
The authors declare that they have no competing interests.

References

1. Nikravesh AY, Ajila SA, Lung C-H (2015) Evaluating sensitivity of auto-scaling decisions in environments with different workload patterns, Proceedings of the 39th IEEE International Computers, Software & Applications Conference Workshops., pp 690–695
2. Nikravesh AY, Ajila SA, Lung C-H (2015) Towards an autonomic auto-scaling system for cloud resource provisioning, Proceedings of the 10th International Symposium on Software Engineering for Adaptive and Self-Managing Systems., pp 33–45
3. Ajila SA, Bankole AA (2013) Cloud client prediction models using machine learning techniques, Proceedings of the IEEE 37th Computer Software and Application Conference., p 143
4. Lorido-Botran T, Miguel-Alonso J, Lozano JA (2014) A review of auto-scaling techniques for elastic applications in cloud environments. Journal of Grid Computing 12(4):559–592
5. Bankole AA (2013) Cloud client prediction models for cloud resource provisioning in a multitier web application environment, Master of Applied Science Thesis, Electrical and Computer Engineering Department, Carleton University
6. Islam S, Keung J, Lee K, Liu A (2012) Empirical prediction models for adaptive resource provisioning in the cloud. Journal of Future Generation Computer Systems 28(1):155–165
7. Fehling C, Leymann F, Retter R, Schupeck W, Arbitter P (2014) Cloud computing patterns: fundamentals to design, build, and manage cloud applications, 1st edn. Springer-Verlag Wien publisher, ISBN 978-3-7091-1568-8
8. Workload Patterns for Cloud Computing (2010) [Online], Available http://watdenkt.veenhof.nu. Accessed 3 July 2010
9. Amazon Elastic Compute Cloud (Amazon EC2) (2013) [Online], Available http://aws.amazon.com/ec2/. Accessed 10 Feb 2013
10. RackSpace, The Open Cloud Company (2012) [Online], Available: http://rackspace.com. Accessed 12 June 2012
11. RightScale Cloud management (2012) [Online], Available: http://www.rightscale.com/home-v1?utm_expid=41192858-85.eCMJVCEGRMuTt8X6n9PcEw.1. Accessed 20 June 2012
12. Hasan MZ, Magana E, Clemm A, Tucker L, Gudreddi SLD (2012) Integrated and autonomic cloud resource scaling, Proceesings of IEEE Network Operation Management Symposium., pp 1327–1334
13. Kupferman J, Silverman J, Jara P, Browne J (2009) Scaling into the cloud, Technical report, Computer Science Department, University of California, Santa Barbara
14. Roy N, Dubey A, Gokhale A (2011) Efficient autoscaling in the cloud using predictive models for workload forecasting, Proceesings of 4th IEEE International Conference on Cloud Computing., pp 500–507
15. Herbst NR, Huber N, Kounev S, Amrehn E (2013) Self-adaptive workload classification and forecasting for proactive resource provisioning, Proceedings of the 4th ACM/SPEC International Conference on Performance Engineering., pp 187–198
16. Benediktsson JA, Kanellopoulos I (1999) Classification of multisource and hyperspectral data based on decision fusion. Journal of IEEE Transactions on Geoscience and Remote Sensing 37(3):1367–1377
17. Local polynomial regression fitting. [Online], Available: http://stat.ethz.ch/R-manual/R-devel/library/stats/html/loess.html. Accessed 10 Feb 2010
18. Garlan D, Schmerl B (2002) Model-based adaptation for self-healing systems, Proceedings of the 1st Workshop on Selfhealing systems., pp 27–32
19. Sterritt R, Smyth B, Bradley M (2005) PACT: personal autonomic computing tools, Proceedings 12th IEEE International Conference and Workshops on Engineering of Computer-Based Systems., pp 519–527
20. Bigus JP, Schlosnagle DA, Pilgrim JR, Mills WN III, Diao Y (2002) ABLE: a toolkit for building multiagent autonomic systems. IBM Syst J 41(3):350–371
21. Littman ML, Ravi N, Fenson E, Howard R (2004) Reinforcement learning for autonomic network repair, Proceedings of International Conference on Autonomic Computing., pp 284–285
22. Dowling J, Curran E, Cunningham R, Cahill V (2006) Building autonomic systems using collaborative reinforcement learning. Journal of Knowledge Engineering Review 21(03):231–238
23. Gemma E, Helm R, Johnson R, Vlissides J (1994) Design patterns: elements of reusable object-oriented software, 1st edn. Addison-Wesley Professional publisher, ISBN 0201633612 (22nd printing, July 2001)

24. Wang S, Summers RM (2012) Machine learning and radiology. Journal of Medical Image Analalysis 16(5):933–951
25. Vapnik V (1922) Principles of risk minimization for learning theory, Proceedings of Advanced Neural Information Processing Systems Conference., pp 831–838
26. Vapnik V, Chervonenkis A (1978) Necessary and sufficient conditions for the uniform convergence of means to their expectations. Journal of Theory Probability 3(26):7–13
27. Sewell M (2008) VC-Dimension, Technical report, Department of Comuter Science University of Collage London
28. Sewell M (2008) Structural risk minimization, Technical report, Department of Computer Science, University College London
29. Yeh C, Tseng P, Huang K, Kuo Y (2012) Minimum risk neural networks and weight decay technique, Proceedings of 8th International Conference on Emerging Intelligent Computing Technology and Applications., pp 10–16
30. TPC-W benchmark. [Online]. Available: http://www.tpc.org/tpcw/. Accessed 10 Feb 2010
31. Hall M, Frank E, Holmes G, Pfahringer B, Reutemann P, Witten IH (2009) The WEKA data mining software. Newsletter of ACM SIGKDD Explorations 11(1):10–18
32. Trevor H, Tibshirani R, Friedman RJ (2009) The elements of statistical learning: data mining, inference, and prediction, 2nd edn. Springer Series in Statistics publisher, ISBN 978-0-387-84858-7
33. Witten I, Frank E (2011) Data mining practical machine learning tools and techniques with Java implementations, 3rd edn. Morgan Kaufmann publisher, ISBN 978-0-12-374856-0 (pbk)
34. Chai T, Draxler R (2014) Root mean square error (RMSE) or mean absolute error (MAE) – arguments against avoiding RMSE in the literature. Journal of Geoscience Model Development 7(1):1247–1250

5

Optimal and suboptimal resource allocation techniques in cloud computing data centers

Mohamed Abu Sharkh*, Abdallah Shami and Abdelkader Ouda

Abstract

Cloud service providers are under constant pressure to improve performance, offer more diverse resource deployment options, and enhance application portability. To achieve these performance and cost objectives, providers need a comprehensive resource allocation system that handles both computational and network resources. A novel methodology is introduced to tackle the problem of allocating sufficient data center resources to client Virtual Machine (VM) reservation requests and connection scheduling requests. This needs to be done while achieving the providers' objectives and minimizing the need for VM migration. In this work, the problem of resource allocation in cloud computing data centers is formulated as an optimization problem and solved. Moreover, a set of heuristic solutions are introduced and used as VM reservation and connection scheduling policies. A relaxed suboptimal solution based on decomposing the original problem is also presented. The experimentation results for a diverse set of network loads show that the relaxed solution has achieved promising levels for connection request average tardiness. The proposed solution is able to reach better performance levels than heuristic solutions without the burden of long hours of running time. This makes it a feasible candidate for solving problems with a much higher number of requests and wider data ranges compared to the optimal solution.

Keywords: Clouds, Resource allocation, Analytical models, Systems simulation, Communication system traffic, Communication system operations and management, Web and internet services, Virtual machines, Systems solution design

Introduction

The appeal of cloud computing for clients comes from the promise of transforming computing infrastructure into a commodity or a service that organizations pay for exactly as much as they use. This idea is an IT corporation executive's dream. As Gartner analyst Daryl Plummer puts it: *"Line-of-business leaders everywhere are bypassing IT departments to get applications from the cloud .. and paying for them like they would a magazine subscription. And when the service is no longer required, they can cancel that subscription with no equipment left unused in the corner"* [1]. The idea that centralized computing over the network is the future, was clear to industry leaders as early as 1997. None other than Steve Jobs said: *"I don't need a hard disk in my computer if I can get to the server faster .. carrying around these non-connected computers is byzantine by comparison"* [1]. This applies as well to organizations purchasing and planning large data centers.

However, performance remains the critical factor. If - at any point- doubts are cast over a provider's ability to deliver the service according to the Service Level Agreements (SLAs) signed, clients will consider moving to other providers. They might even consider going back to the buy-and-maintain model. Providers are under constant pressure to improve performance, offer more diverse resource deployment options, improve service usability, and enhance application portability. A main weapon here is an efficient resource allocation system. As in Fig. 1, in the cloud scenario, clients are able to rent Virtual Machines (VMs) from cloud providers. Providers offer several deployment models where VM configuration differs in computing power, memory, storage capacity and

*Correspondence: mabusha@uwo.ca
Department of Electrical and Computer Engineering, Western University, London, Canada

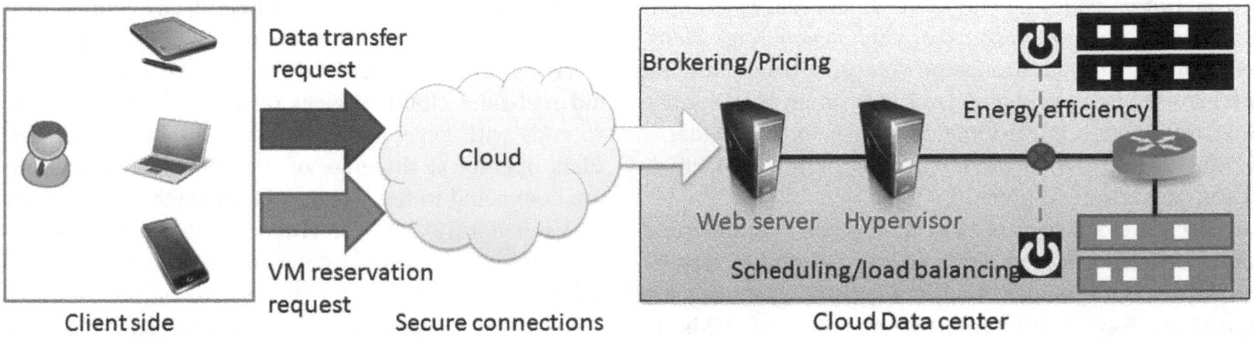

Fig. 1 Cloud simulated environment and components

platform just to name a few factors. During the rental period, clients require network capabilities. Clients will have data frequently exchanged between client headquarters (or private clouds) and VMs or between two client VMs. The aim here for a scheduler is to schedule VM reservation requests and connection requests in the fastest possible way while using the data center resources optimally. This task is getting even harder with the emergence of the big data concepts. IBM summarized big data challenges into 4 different dimensions referred to as the 4 Vs: Volume, Velocity, Variety, and Veracity [2]. With most companies owning at least 100 TB of data stored and with 18.6 billion network connections estimated to exist now [2], resource allocation efficiency has never been so important.

When faced by the task of designing a resource allocation methodology, many external and internal challenges should be considered. An attempt to summarize these challenges can be found in [3]. External challenges include regulative and geographical challenges as well as client demands related to data warehousing and handling. These limitations result in constraints on the location of the reserved VMs and restrictions to the data location and movements. External challenges also include optimizing the charging model in such a way that generates maximum revenue. Internal challenges discussed in [3] include also data locality issues. The nature of an application in terms of being data intensive should be considered while placing the VMs and scheduling connections related to this application.

To achieve these performance and cost objectives, cloud computing providers need a comprehensive resource allocation system that manages both computational and network resources. Such an efficient system would have a major financial impact as excess resources translate directly into revenues.

The following sections are organized as follows: a discussion of the related research efforts is introduced in the following section leading to this paper's contribution. Detailed model description is given in "Model description" section. "Mathematical formulation" section presents the mathematical formulation of the problem. The heuristic methods are presented in "Heuristic solution" section. The suboptimal solution is presented in "Suboptimal solution" section. Results are shown and analyzed in "Results" section. Finally, "Conclusion" section concludes the paper and conveys future work.

Related work

Previous attempts were made to optimize a diverse set of cloud resources. In [4], Dastjerdi and Buyya propose a framework to simplify cloud service composition. Their proposed technique optimizes the service composition on the basis of deployment time, cost and reliability preferred by users. The authors exploit a combination of evolutionary algorithms and fuzzy logic composition optimization with the objective of minimizing the effort of users while expressing their preferences. Despite including a wide range of user requirements in the problem modeling and providing an optimization formulation along with a fuzzy logic heuristic, [4] tackles the problem from the user's prospective rather than the provider's. The main goal is to provide the best possible service composition which gives the problem a brokering direction instead of the focus on cloud data center performance. SLA conditions are considered an input guaranteed by the cloud provider regardless of how they are achieved.

Wei et al. [5] address Quality of Service (QoS) constrained resource allocation problem for cloud computing services. They present a game-theoretic method to find an approximate solution of this problem. Their proposed solution executes in two steps: (i) Step 1: Solving the independent optimization for each participant of game theory; (ii) Step 2: Modifying the multiplexed strategies of the initial solution of different participants of Step 1 taking optimization and fairness into consideration. The model in [5] represents a problem of competition for resources in a cloud environment. Each system/node/machine represents a resource that has a corresponding cost and execution time for each task. More granularity is needed in terms of considering the multiple degrees of computational and network resources when scheduling. Memory, storage, computational powers and bandwidth (at least) should be considered separately in an ideal model. Moreover, network resource impact is not considered thoroughly in [5]. Also, no detailed discussion for Virtualization scenarios was given.

In [6], Beloglazov et al. define an architectural framework in addition to resource allocation principles for energy efficient cloud computing. They develop algorithms for energy efficient mapping of VMs to suitable physical nodes. They propose scheduling algorithms which take into account QoS expectations and power usage characteristics of data center resources. This includes, first, allocating VMs using modified best fit decreasing method and then optimizing the current VM allocation using VM migration. Considering challenges migration might cause in terms of performance hiccups caused by copying and moving delays and scheduling challenges along with provider vulnerability for SLA violations [7], a solution that minimizes the need for VM migration is a preferable one. In addition, no deadline for tasks is considered in that work.

Duan et al. [8] formulate the scheduling problem for large-scale parallel work flow applications in hybrid clouds as a sequential cooperative game. They propose a communication and storage-aware multi-objective algorithm that optimizes execution time and economic cost while fulfilling network bandwidth and storage requirements constraints. Here, the computation time is modeled as a direct function of the computation site location and the task instead of using a unified unit for task size. Memory was not used as a resource. Task deadlines are not considered. The goal is to complete a set of tasks that represent a specific application. This model is closer to job execution on the grid rather than the model more common in the cloud which is reserving a VM with specific resource requirements and then running tasks on them. Moreover, the assumption presented is that data exchange requests can run concurrently with the computation without any dependency.

One more variation can be seen in [9] in which two scheduling algorithms were tested, namely , green scheduling and round robin. The focus was energy efficiency again but the model offered contains detailed network modeling as it was based on NS-2 network simulator. The user requests are modeled as tasks. Tasks are modeled as unit requests that contain resource specification in the form of computational resource requirements (MIPs, memory and storage) in addition to data exchange requirements (these include values representing the process files to be sent to the host the task is scheduled on before execution, data sent to other servers during execution and output data sent after execution). There was no optimization model offered. In [10], an energy-efficient adaptive resource scheduler for Networked Fog Centers (NetFCs) is proposed. The role of the scheduler is to aid real-time cloud services of Vehicular Clients (VCs) to cope with delay and delay-jitter issues. These schedulers operate at the edge of the vehicular network and are connected to the served VCs through Infrastructure-to-Vehicular (I2V) TCP/IP-based single-hop mobile links. The goal is to exploit the locally measured states of the TCP/IP connections, in order to maximize the overall communication-plus-computing energy efficiency, while meeting the application-induced hard QoS requirements on the minimum transmission rates, maximum delays and delay-jitters. The resulting energy-efficient scheduler jointly performs: (i) admission control of the input traffic to be processed by the NetFCs; (ii) minimum-energy dispatching of the admitted traffic; (iii) adaptive reconfiguration and consolidation of the Virtual Machines (VMs) hosted by the NetFCs; and, (iv) adaptive control of the traffic injected into the TCP/IP mobile connections.

In [11], an optimal minimum-energy scheduler for the dynamic online joint allocation of the task sizes, computing rates, communication rates and communication powers in virtualized Networked Data Centers (NetDCs) that operates under hard per-job delay-constraints is offered. The referred NetDCs infrastructure is composed from multiple frequency-scalable Virtual Machines (VMs), that are interconnected by a bandwidth and power-limited switched Local Area Network (LAN). A two step methodology to analytically compute the exact solution of the CCOP is proposed. The resulting optimal scheduler is amenable of scalable and distributed online implementation and its analytical characterization is in closed-form. Actual performance is tested under both randomly time-varying synthetically generated and real-world measured workload traces.

Some of the more recent works include the FUGE solution [12]. The authors present job scheduling solution that aims at assigning jobs to the most suitable resources, considering user preferences and requirements. FUGE aims to perform optimal load balancing considering execution time and cost. The authors modified the standard genetic algorithm (SGA) and used fuzzy theory to devise a fuzzy-based steady-state GA in order to improve SGA performance in terms of makespan. The FUGE algorithm assigns jobs to resources by considering virtual machine (VM) processing speed, VM memory, VM bandwidth, and the job lengths. A mathematical proof is offered that the optimization problem is convex with well-known analytical conditions (specifically, KarushKuhnTucker conditions).

In [13], the problem of energy saving management of both data centers and mobile connections is tackled. An adaptive and distributed dynamic resource allocation scheduler with the objective of minimizing the communication-plus-computing energy consumption while guaranteeing user Quality of Service (QoS) constraints is proposed. The scheduler is evaluated for the following metrics: execution time, goodput and bandwidth usage.

When looking at the solutions available in the literature, it is evident that each experiment focuses on a few aspects of the resource allocation challenges faced in the area. We try to summarize the different aspects in Table 1.

An ideal solution would combine the features/parameters in Table 1 to build a complete solution. This would include an optimization formulation that covers computational and network resources at a practical granularity level. Dealing with bandwidth as a fixed commodity is not enough. Routing details of each request are required to reflect the hot spots in the network. That applies for computational resources as well. CPU, memory and storage requirements constitute a minimum of what should be considered. Moreover, A number of previous efforts concentrate on processing resources while some focus on networking resources. The question arising here is: How can we process client VM reservation requests keeping in mind their data exchange needs? The common approach is to perform the VM placement and the connection scheduling separately or in two different consecutive steps. This jeopardizes the QoS conditions and forces the provider to take mitigation steps when the VM's computational and network demands start colliding. These steps include either over provisioning as a precaution or VM migration and connection preemption after issues like network bottlenecks start escalating. Minimizing VM migration incidents is a major performance goal. Off-line VM migration, however fast or efficient it may be, means there is a downtime for clients. This does not really comply with a demanding client environment where five 9's availability (99.999% of the time availability) is becoming an expectation. As for online migration, it pauses a load with more copying/redundancy required. These challenges associated with VM migration cause cloud computing solution architects to welcome any solution that does not include migration at all.

This shortcoming calls for a resource allocation solution that considers both demands at the same time. This solution would consider the VM future communication demands along with computational demands before placing the VM. In this case, the network demands include not only the bandwidth requirements as a flat or a changing number, but also the location of the source/destination of the requested connection. This means the nodes/VMs that will (most probably) exchange data with the VM. As these closely tied VMs are scheduled relatively near each other, network stress is minimized and the need to optimize the VM location is decreased dramatically.

In this work, we aim to tackle the problem of allocating client VM reservation and connection scheduling requests to corresponding data center resources while achieving the cloud provider's objectives. Our main contributions include the following:

1- *Formulate the resource allocation problem for cloud data centers in order to obtain the optimal solution.* This formulation takes into consideration the computational resource requirements at a practical granularity while considering the virtualization scenario common in the cloud. It also considers conditions posed by the connection requests (request lifetime/deadline, bandwidth requirements and routing) at the same time. An important advantage of this approach over approaches used in previous efforts is considering both sets of resource requirements simultaneously before making the scheduling decision. This formulation is looked at from the providers' perspective and aims at maximizing performance.

2- *Make the formulation generic in a way that it does not restrict itself to the limited environment of one data center internal network.* The connection requests received can come from one of many geographically distributed private or public clouds. Moreover, the scheduler is given the flexibility to place the VMs in any of the cloud provider's data centers that are located in multiple cities. These data centers (clouds) represent the network communicating nodes. The complete problem is solved using IBM ILOG CPLEX optimization library [14].

3- *Introduce multiple heuristic methods to preform the two phases of the scheduling process.* Three methods are tested for the VM reservation step. Two methods are tested for scheduling connections. The performance of these methods is investigated and then compared to some of the currently available methods mentioned earlier.

4- *Introduce a suboptimal method to solve the same problem for large scale cases.* This method is based on a technique of decomposing the original problem into two separate sub-problems. The first one is referred to as master problem which performs the assignment of VMs to data center servers based on a VM-node relation function. The second one, termed as subproblem, performs the scheduling of connection requests assigned by master problem. This suboptimal method achieves better results than the heuristic methods while getting these results in more feasible time periods in contrast to the optimal formulation.

Model description

We introduce a model to tackle the resource allocation problem for a group of cloud user requests. This includes the provisioning of both computational and network resources of data centers. The model consists of a network of data centers nodes (public clouds) and client nodes (private clouds). These nodes are located in varying

Table 1 A comparison of cloud resource allocation efforts

Reference/ Feature	[4]	[5]	[6]	[7]	[8]	Proposed solution
Optimization model offered	Yes	Yes	No	Yes	No	Yes
Perspective	User/broker	Provider	Provider	Provider	Provider	Provider
Computation resources	VM types (generic)	Computational node (no memory)	CPU, Memory and Storage	Computational node (no memory)	CPU, Memory and Storage	CPU, Memory and Storage
Network resources	amounts of data	Does not affect execution time	No	BW & amounts of data	BW, source & destination	BW, source & destination
Scheduling considers both network & computational resources	No	No	No	Yes	No	Yes
Request deadline/ lifetime	No	Yes	No	No	Yes	Yes
VM modeling	VMs & VM appliances offered	No	VM placement & migration considered	No	VM placement & migration considered	VM placement considered

cities or geographic points as in Fig. 2. They are connected using a network of bidirectional links. Every link in this network is divided into a number of equal lines (flows). It is assumed that this granularity factor of the links can be controlled. We also assume that each data center contains a number of servers connected through Ethernet connections. Each server will have a fixed amount of memory, computing units and storage space. As an initial step, when clients require cloud hosting, they send requests to reserve a number of VMs. All of these VMs can be of the same type or of different types. Each cloud provider offers multiple types of VMs for their clients to choose from. These types vary in the specification of each computing resource like memory, CPU units and storage. We will use these three types of resources in our experiment. Consequently, each of the requested VMs is allocated on a server in one of the data centers. Also, the client sends a number of requests to reserve a connection. There are two types of connection [15, 16] requests: 1- A request to connect a VM to another VM where both VMs were previously allocated space on a server in one of the data centers (public clouds). 2- A request to connect a VM to a client node. Here, the VM located in a data center node connects to the client headquarters or private cloud. The cloud provider-client network is illustrated in Fig. 2. For every request, the client defines the source, destination, start time and duration of the connection. Thus, the objective becomes to minimize the average tardiness of all connection requests. A sample of client requests is shown in Table 2. Requests labeled "Res" are VM reservation requests. Requests labeled "Req con" are connection requests between a VM and a client node or between 2 VMs. An example of the VM configuration is shown in Table 3 [17, 18].

Mathematical formulation

To solve the problem of resource scheduling in cloud computing environment, we introduce an analytical model where we formulate the problem as a mixed integer linear problem. We model the optimization problem of minimizing the average tardiness of all reservation connection requests while satisfying the requirements for virtual connection requests of different clients. This model is solved using IBM ILOG CPLEX software for a small set of requests.

Notations

Environment and network parameters are described below. The set of VMs and the set of servers are represented by VM and Q respectively. M_{qm} represents the amount of resources (e.g. memory) available on a server where $q \in Q$ and $m \in \{memory(mem), CPU\ unit(cu), storage(sg)\}$ such that $M_{qm} = 30$ indicates that available memory on server q is 30 GB assuming that m denotes a specific type of required resource, i.e., memory on a server. K_{vm} is used to represent the amount of resources needed for every requested VM such that $K_{vm} = 7$ indicates that the VM $v \in VM$ requires 7 GB of memory assuming that m denotes memory resource on a server. The set of network paths and the set of links are represented by P and L respectively. a_{lp} is a binary parameter such that $a_{lp} = 1$ if link $l \in L$ is on path $p \in P$; 0 otherwise. In our formulation, fixed alternate routing method is used with a fixed size set of paths available between a node and any other node. These paths represent the alternate paths a request could be scheduled on when moving from a server residing in the first node to a server residing in the other node. b_{qcp} is a binary parameter such that $b_{qcp} = 1$

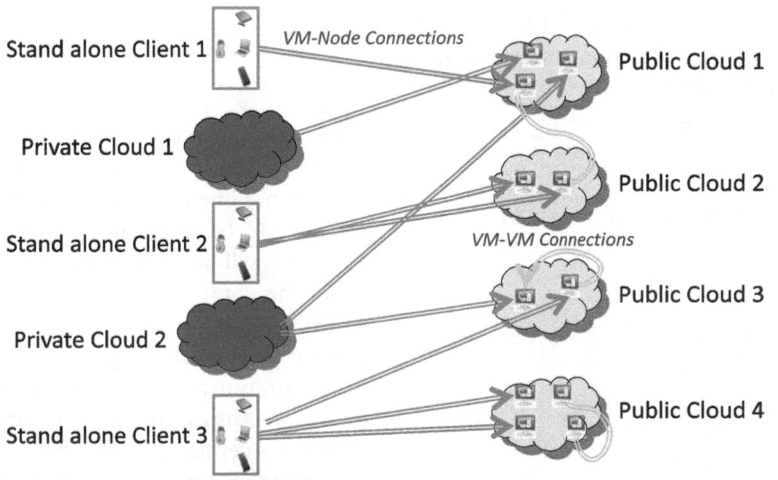

Fig. 2 An example of a cloud provider-client network: clients can connect from their private clouds, their headquarters or from a singular machine on the Internet. The provider data centers represent public clouds

Table 2 An example of a set of resource allocation requests

Client	Request	Type	Start	Duration	Source	Destination
C-1	Res VM1	High-CPU	T=10	125	-	-
C-2	Res VM2	High-Storage	T=15	400	-	-
C-1	Res VM3	Standard	T=20	150	-	-
C-2	Res VM4	High-Memory	T=10	70	-	-
C-1	Req con	VM-VM	T=15	10	VM1	VM3
C-1	Req con	VM-C	T=18	20	VM3	C1
C-2	Req con	VM-VM	T=25	8	VM4	VM2
C-2	Req con	VM-C	T=30	30	VM4	C2

if path $p \in P$ is one of the alternate paths from server, $q \in Q$ to server, $c \in Q$; 0 otherwise. I represents a set of connection requests. Every connection request, $i \in I$ is specified by a source (s_i), a destination (d_i), requested start time (r_i) and connection duration (t_i). $TARD$ represents the allowed tardiness (accepted delay) for each connection request. The formulation covers scenarios in which networks can divide a link into shares or streams to allow more flexibility with the formulation and cover a wide set of situations. The set of shares (wavelengths in the case of an optical network) could contain any number of wavelengths based on the problem itself. The set λ is the set of all available wavelengths in the network. The parameter h used in constraint 6 indicates a large number that helps to ensure the solution is derived according to the conditions in the constraint. In addition, the binary parameter W_{ij} indicates if request i is scheduled before request j. Using this parameter ensures constraint 6 is tested only once for each pair of requests.

Decision variables

F_i is an integer decision variable which represents the scheduled starting time for connection request, $i \in I$. X_{vq} is a binary decision variable such that $X_{vq} = 1$ if $v \in VM$ is scheduled on server $q \in Q$. Y_{ipw} is a binary decision variable such that $Y_{ipw} = 1$ if request, $i \in I$ is scheduled on path, $p \in P$ and wavelength, $w \in \lambda$.

Objective function

The problem is formulated as a mixed integer linear programming (MILP) problem. The objective of the MILP is minimizing the average tardiness of client connection requests to and from VMs. Tardiness here is calculated as the difference between the requested start time by the client (represented by r_i) and the scheduled start time by the provider (represented by F_i). The solver looks for the solution that satisfies clients in the best way while not harming other clients' connections. The solution works under the assumption that all clients requests have the same weight/importance to the provider. The objective function of the problem is as follows:

$$MIN \sum_i (F_i - r_i) \qquad i \in I, \tag{1}$$

Constraints

The objective function is subjected to the following constraints:

$$\sum_{q \in Q} X_{vq} = 1, \qquad v \in VM, \tag{2}$$

$$\sum_{p \in P} \sum_{w \in \lambda} Y_{ipw} = 1, \qquad i \in I, \tag{3}$$

$$\sum_{v \in VM} X_{vq} \times K_{vm} <= M_{qm}, \quad q \in Q, m \in \{m, c, s\}, \tag{4}$$

$$Y_{ipw} + (X_{s_i q} + X_{d_i c} - 3b_{qcp}) <= 2, \quad i \in I, q \in Q, c \in Q, p \in P, w \in \lambda, \tag{5}$$

$$\sum_{p \in P} [(t_i \times a_{lp} \times Y_{ipw}) + (h \times a_{lp} \times Y_{ipw}) + (h \times a_{lp} \times Y_{jpw})] + F_i - F_j + h \times W_{ij} <= 3h, \quad i,j \in I, l \in L, w \in \lambda, \tag{6}$$

$$W_{ij} + W_{ji} = 1, \qquad i,j \in I, \tag{7}$$

$$X_{vq}, Y_{ipw}, W_{ij} \in \{0, 1\}, \tag{8}$$

$$F_i - r_i >= 0, \qquad i \in I, \tag{9}$$

$$F_i - r_i <= TARD, \qquad i \in I, \tag{10}$$

$$F_i, r_i >= 0, \qquad i \in I. \tag{11}$$

In Eq. (2), we ensure that a VM will be assigned exactly to one server. In (3), we ensure that a connection request will be assigned exactly on one physical path and one wavelength (stream/share of a link). In (4), we guarantee that VM will be allocated on servers with enough capacity of the computational resources required by the VMs. In (5), we ensure that a connection is established only on one of the alternate legitimate paths between a VM and the communicating partner (another VM or client node). In (6), we ensure that at most one request can be scheduled on a certain link at a time on each wavelength and that no other requests will be scheduled on the same link and wavelength until the duration is finished. Constraint (7) ensures constraint 6 will only be tested once for each

Table 3 VM configuration for the 3 instance (VM) types used in the experiment as offered by Amazon EC2 [17]

Instance type	Standard extra large (SXL)	High memory extra large (MXL)	High CPU extra large (CXL)
Memory	15 GB	17 GB	7 GB
CPU (EC2 units)	8	6.5	20
Storage	1690 GB	490 GB	1690 GB

pair of requests. It indicates that request *i* will start before request *j*. In Eqs. (9) and (10), we ensure that the scheduled time for a request is within the tardiness window allowed in this experiment.

Heuristic solution

Heuristic model

The proposed model in this paper tackles the resource allocation challenges faced when provisioning computational resources (CPU, memory and storage) and network resources. A central controller manages these requests with the objective of minimizing average tardiness and request blocking. The solution aims at solving the provider's cost challenges and the cloud applications performance issues.

For every request, the client defines the source, destination, start time and duration of the connection. Thus, this problem falls under the advance reservation category of problems.

The central controller (could be a Software Defined Networking controller (SDN) [19, 20] for example) keeps the data tables of the available network paths, available server resources and connection expiration times in order to handle newly arriving requests. The controller then allocates the requested VMs on servers according to the method or policy used. It updates the resource availability tables accordingly. After that, the controller schedules and routes connection requests to satisfy the client requirements. Network path availability tables are also updated. As an initial objective, the controller aims at minimizing the average tardiness of all the advance reservation connection requests. Also, a second objective is minimizing the number of the blocked requests. This objective is to be reached regardless of what path is used. Heuristic policies/techniques proposed aim at getting good, although not mathematically optimal, performance metric values while providing this feasible solution within acceptable amounts of time.

Heuristic techniques for minimizing tardiness

The allocation process is divided into two consecutive steps:

1- Allocation of VMs on data center servers. Here, all the VM reservation requests are served based on server resource availability before any connection request is served.

2- Scheduling of connection requests on the available network paths. This happens after all VMs have been allocated resources and started operation on the servers.

For the first subproblem, three heuristic techniques were evaluated. For the second step (subproblem), two heuristic techniques were tested. For a complete experiment, one heuristic for each subproblem is used. These heuristics are divided as follows.

VM reservation heuristic techniques

a) Equal Time Distribution Technique (ED):
In this heuristic, TM_i is the total time reserved by connection requests from the virtual machine VM_i (sum of the connection durations). Next, the share of one server is calculated by dividing the total time units all the VMs have requested by the number of servers. This is based on the assumption that all servers have the same capacity (for computational and network resources). Then, for each server, VMs are allocated computation resources on the corresponding servers one by one. When the server is allocated a number of VMs that cover/consume the calculated server share, the next VM is allocated resources on the following server and the previous steps are repeated. The algorithm is described in pseudo code in Fig. 3.

b) Node Distance Technique (ND):
First, the average distance between each two nodes is calculated. The two nodes furthest from each other (with maximum distance) are chosen. Then, the maximum number of VMs is allocated on the servers of these two nodes. Next, the remaining nodes are evaluated, the node with maximum average distance to the previous two nodes is chosen. The same process is repeated until all the VMS are scheduled.

```
Input: Virtual machine set VM, Server
            set Q, connection request set R
Output: Allocation of VMs on servers,
            TM_i has the total connection time
            requested by VM_i
for TM_i ∈ TM do
    TM_i = 0
end for
for VM_i ∈ VM do
  for R_j ∈ R do
    if R_j.source = VM_i or R_j.dest = VM_i then
      TM_i = TM_i + R_j.duration
    end if
  end for
end for
TM_total = Σ_i TM_i
ServerShare = TM_total /|Q|
i = 0
for S_j ∈ Q do
  ThisServerShare = ServerShare
  while S_j isNotFull and ThisServerShare > TM_i
  do
    Schedule VM_i on S_j
    ThisServerShare = ThisServerShare − TM_i
    i = i + 1
  end while
end for
```

Fig. 3 Equal time distribution heuristic technique

The algorithm is described in pseudo code in Fig. 4. *fillNode* is a function that basically tries to schedule as many VMs as possible on the called node until the node's resources are exhausted. *fillNode* is illustrated in Fig. 5.

c) Resource Based Distribution Technique (RB):
In this heuristic, the choice of the server is based on the type of VM requested. As shown in Table 3, three types of VMs are used in the experiment: i) High Memory Extra Large (MXL) has high memory configuration; ii) High CPU Extra Large (CXL) has a high computing power; iii) Standard Extra large (SXL) is more suited to typical applications that need a lot of storage space. Depending on the type of VM requested by the client, the heuristic picks the server with the highest amount of available corresponding resources. The VM then is allocated resources on that server. This causes the distribution to be more balanced.

Connection reservation heuristic techniques

a) Duration Priority Technique (DP):

```
Input: Virtual machine set VM, Server
          set Q, Node set N, Path set P,
          where P_ijk is path k between nodes
          i and j, NP is afixed Number of paths
          between node i and node j
Output: Allocation of VMs on servers
for N_i ∈ N do
   for N_j ∈ N do
      A[i][j] = Σ_k^NP P_ijk.Length/NP
   end for
end for
Pick 2 nodes x, y with max A[x][y]
U = {x, y}
RemVMs = |VM|
RemVMs = fillNode(x, RemVMs)
RemVMs = fillNode(y, RemVMs)
while U ≠ N and RemVMs > 0 do
   maxDist = 0
   for N_i ∈ NandN_i ∉ U do
      avgDist = 0
      for B_j ∈ U do
         avgDist = avgDist + A[B_j][N_i]
      end for
      if avgDist > maxDist then
         maxDist = avgDist
         NextNode = N_i
      end if
   end for
   RemVMs = fillNode(NextNode, RemVMs)
   U = U ∪ {NextNode}
end while
```

Fig. 4 Node distance heuristic technique

```
Function :fillNode
Input: Virtual machine set VM, Node x,
          RequestedVMs, server set Q
Output: servers in node x filled with max
          VMs possible
i = |VM| − RemVMs
for S_j ∈ Q and S_j residing in Node x do
   while S_j isNotFull and i < |VM| do
      Schedule VM_i on S_j
      i = i + 1
   end while
end for
return i
```

Fig. 5 Function: fillNode

In this heuristic, connections with the shortest duration are given the priority. First, connection requests are sorted based on the requested duration. The following step is to pick the connection with the shortest duration and schedule it on the shortest path available. This step is repeated until all connection requests are served. The algorithm is described in pseudo code in Fig. 6.

b) Greedy Algorithm (GA):
In this heuristic, illustrated in Fig. 7, scheduling is based on the connection Requested Start Time (RST). Connection requests with earlier RST are scheduled on the first path available regardless of the path length.

Complexity analysis of the heuristic solutions

The resource allocation problem in a cloud data center is a variation of the well known knapsack problem. The knapsack problem has two forms. In the decision form –

```
Input: Path set P where P_xyk is path k
          between nodes x and y,
          and connection request set R
Output: Scheduling of network connection
          requests on network paths
Sort R in descending order based onR_i.duration
for R_i ∈ R do
   for t = R_i.RST to MaxTimeUnits do
      Pick shortest path P_xyk where R_i.source =
      x and R_i.destination = y
      if P_xyk isAvailable(t, R_i.duration) then
         Schedule R_i on P_xyk at time unit t
         Move to next request
      end if
   end for
end for
```

Fig. 6 Duration priority heuristic technique

```
Input: Path set P
        where P_xyk is path k between nodes
        x and y is Server set Q, connection
        request set R, NP is Number of paths
        between node x and node y
Output: Scheduling of network connection
        requests on network paths
Sort R in descending order based on R_i.RST
(requested start time)
for R_i ∈ R do
    for t = R_i.RST to MaxTimeUnits do
        x = R_i.source
        y = R_i.destination
        for k = 0 to NP do
            if P_xyk isAvailable(t, R_i.duration) then
                Schedule R_i on P_xyk at time unit t
                Move to next request
            end if
        end for
    end for
end for
```

Fig. 7 Greedy heuristic technique

which is considered less difficult - as it is NP-Complete- the question is: Can an objective value of at least K be achieved without exceeding a specific weight W? The optimization form of the problem – which is the form we try to solve in this work - tries to optimize the possible objective value. The optimization form is NP-Hard. This means it is at least as hard as all the NP problems. There is no current solution in polynomial time for this form.

This motivated the introduction of the heuristic algorithms. It might be of interest to the reader to visit the complexity of the introduced heuristic algorithms.

First, we revisit the variables covered in this analysis. VM represent the VM set, N represent the set of nodes, S is the set of servers, R is the set of connection requests, T is the allowed tardiness per request and D is the average duration of a connection. This analysis is offered with the sole purpose of being an approximation of the time complexity to show that these algorithms run within polynomial time and in turn- can be practically used by large scale cloud networks. Looking at the introduced algorithms one by one, we find that Equal time distribution has a complexity of $O(|VM||R| + |S|)$. Node distance algorithms runs in $O(|N^3| + |S| + |V|)$. Resource based distribution runs in $O(|V||S|)$ which constitutes the quickest among the 3 VM placement algorithms we introduced. As for connection scheduling heuristics algorithms, Duration priority runs in $O(|R|.lg|R| + |R|.T.D)$ or $O(|R|.(1 + lg|R| + T.D)$. Finally, the greedy connection scheduling algorithm runs in $O(R.T.D)$. Therefore, all the mentioned algorithms run in polynomial times and can yield a result for large scale problem in practical time periods.

Suboptimal solution

Although an optimal solution can be obtained using the formulation in "Mathematical formulation" section, this is only feasible for small scale problems. Even when using a 5-node network with 4 servers and 7 links connecting them, the number of optimization variables can be as big as 5000 variables when scheduling 50 requests that belong to 5 VMs. On the other hand, heuristic methods achieve feasible solution in relatively quick times but the solution quality cannot be proven. This motivates us to move to the next step which is finding a method that achieves a suboptimal solution. The method introduced here is based on a decomposition technique. We illustrate the method in Fig. 8. The steps go as follows.

1- In Step 1, a set of known connection requests are preprocessed to generate interdependency measurements. This is figured out by calculating the frequency of communications between each two points in the network. To be more specific, the frequency of the connection requests between each VM_i and VM_j is calculated as well as the frequency of connection requests between VM_i and $node_k$ which represent a private cloud. This gives us an indication of which direction most of the VM's connections go. This is closely correlated with the dependencies this VM has and should ideally affect where it is scheduled.

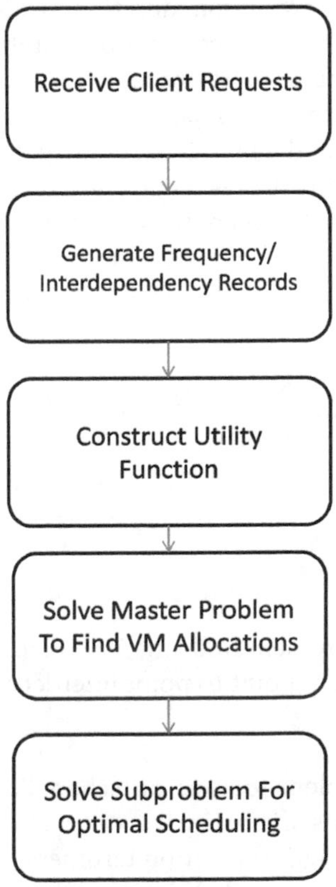

Fig. 8 The suboptimal method step by step

2- In the second step, a utility function is constructed based on the connection frequency values generated in step 1. The utility function serves as the objective function of the master problem that allocates VMs on hosts.

3- Next, a master problem in which we handle the assignment of VMs to servers and connections to specific paths without scheduling them is generated. In other words, we solve for the decision variable X_{vq} without considering any scheduling constraints. This produces a feasible assignment for VMs that aims at scheduling interdependent VMs close to each other.

4- After getting the VM assignment locations, A subproblem in which we try to find the optimal scheduling for the input connections under these specific VM assignment conditions. In other words, we solve for the decision variable Y_{ipw}, F_i in the subproblem. The minimum tardiness produced from the subproblem is the objective value we are looking for. As in any decomposition based optimization, the success of the decomposition technique depends on the way the solution of the master problem is chosen. We formulate the master problem and the subproblem as follows.

Master problem formulation

We first introduce Distance function. It represents the distance between two nodes measured by the number of links in the shortest path between them. A frequency function based on connection duration is also added. This is a function where the connection duration is preferred as dominant factor. The frequency function is a value that will represent interdependency between two VMs or between a VM and a private cloud (client node). Another alternative here is depending on the number of connections requested between these two points rather than the total amount of connection time. Once we calculate the frequency function values, the utility function is constructed as:

$$MIN \sum_{v\in VM} \sum_{u\in VM} \sum_{s\in Q} \sum_{q\in Q} (Freq_{vu} \times Distance_{sq} \times X_{vs} \times X_{uq}), \quad (12)$$

Subject to

$$(2), (4). \quad (13)$$

The master problem finds the VM allocation that maximizes the value of point to point interdependency.

Subproblem

As the subproblem focuses on scheduling, its objective function is the same as in the optimal form, i.e., minimizing the average connection tardiness. In this case, the final value of the relaxed objective will come directly from the solution of the subproblem. The difference is that the subproblem already knows where the VMs are allocated and is scheduling connections accordingly. The objective of the sub-problem is as follows.

$$MIN \sum_{i} (F_i - r_i) \qquad i \in I, \quad (14)$$

Subject to

$$(3), (5) - (11). \quad (15)$$

Results

Simulation environment

The problem is simulated using a discrete event based simulation program and solved on a more practical scale using the heuristic search techniques discussed in the previous sections. The network used for the experiment is the NSF network (in Fig. 9). It consists of 14 nodes of which 3 are data center nodes and the rest are considered client nodes [21]. Nodes are connected using a high speed network with a chosen link granularity that goes up to 3 lines (flows) per link. Fixed alternate routing method is used with 3 paths available between a node and any other node. Server configuration and request data parameters are detailed in Table 4. Preemption of connection requests is not allowed in this experiment.

Heuristics

As explained in the previous sections, every experiment includes two phases and hence two heuristics are needed: one to schedule VMs on servers and the other to schedule connection requests. The five techniques explained earlier yield 6 possible combinations. However, We chose to show the results from the best 4 combinations (best 4 full-solutions). This is due to space constraints. The 4 chosen combinations cover all the 5 heuristics. The simulation scenarios and combined heuristics used for the two subproblems are as follows.

1-ED-GA: Equal Time Distribution technique and Greedy algorithm.
2-RB-DP: Resource Based Distribution technique and Duration Priority technique.
3-ED-DP: Equal Time Distribution technique and Duration Priority technique.
4-ND-DP: Node Distance technique and Greedy algorithm.

In Figs. 10 and 11, the 4 methods' performances are compared in terms of the blocking percentage. This is measured as the request load increases. Figure 10 shows a comparison of the percentage of blocked requests (requests that could not be scheduled) where the allowed tardiness parameter value is very small (1 time unit). This means that this scenario resembles request requirements

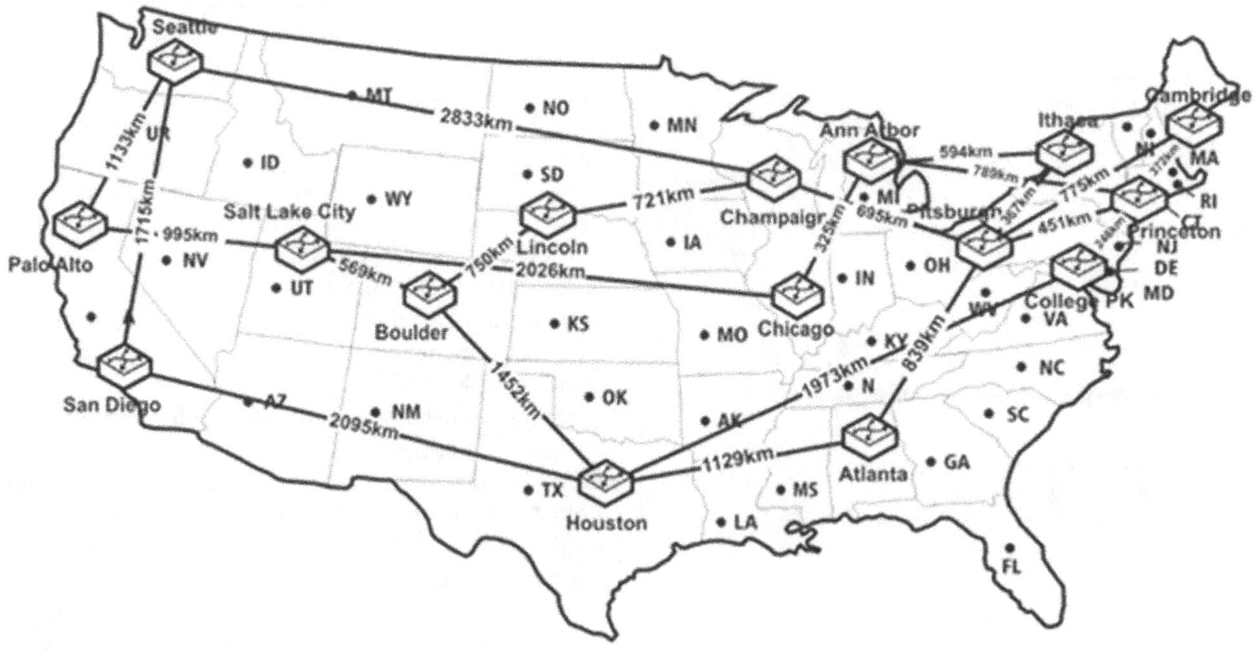

Fig. 9 The NSF network of 14 nodes [29]

imposing close to real time scheduling. The x axis represents request load which is measured by λ/μ. λ represents the arrival rate and μ represents the service rate. Figure 11 shows the same comparison when the allowed tardiness per request is large (30000 time units). In both scenarios, it is noticed that ED-DP and RB-DP methods have shown a clear advantage by scoring consistently lower blocked requests. The common factor for these 2 methods is using DP to schedule connections. Therefore, this indicates a clear advantage of using DP over GA when scheduling connection requests in tight or real time conditions. In addition, As seen in Fig. 11, RB-DP has shown a decent advantage over ED-DP in terms of blocking percentage.

Table 4 Experiment parameter configuration

Parameter	Value
Total number of servers	132
Servers/ data center	44
VM reservation requests	200
Connection requests	10000
RST distribution	Poisson with Lambda = 10
Connection duration distribution	Normal with mean = 200 time units
Source and destination distribution	Uniform
Allowed tardiness per request	ranging from 1 to 500 time units
Total experiment time	70,000 time units

Regarding the other performance metric, average tardiness per request, the measurements are shown in Fig. 12. The figure shows a comparison of the average tardiness per request produced when using the four methods. Allowed tardiness in that experiment is small (25 time unit). Once more, ED-DP and RB-DP methods have shown a clear advantage by scoring consistently lower tardiness per request. Also, it is noticed from the figure the ED-DP produces slightly better results (less average

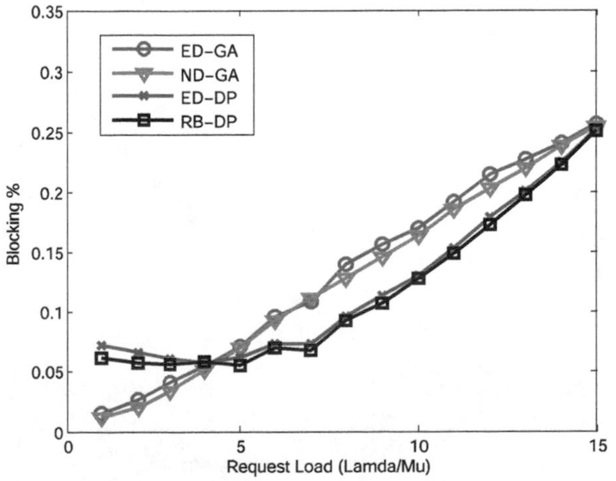

Fig. 10 Request Blocking results for scheduling methods (allowed tardiness/request =1 time units)

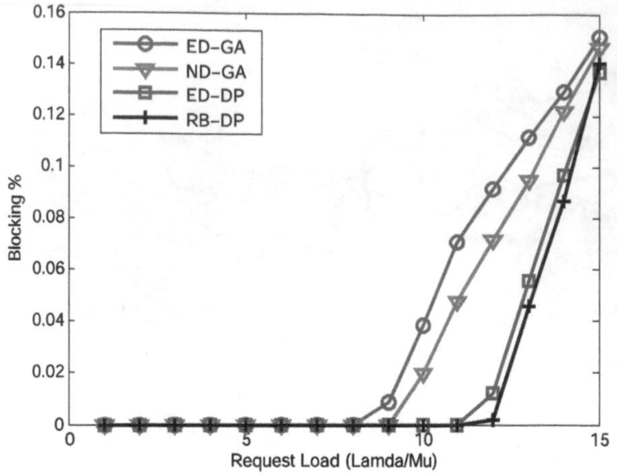

Fig. 11 Request Blocking results for scheduling methods (allowed tardiness/request =30,000 time units)

tardiness) than RB-DP. Therefore, using RB-DP method is more suitable to scenarios where there is an emphasis on serving the largest number of requests. On the other hand, using ED-DP is more suitable to scenarios where the individual request performance or service level is prioritized over serving more requests.

Relaxed solution results

With regards to the network we tested on, a 5-node network was used in these tests with 2 as data center nodes and the rest as client nodes (private clouds). Four servers were used in the tests with 2 servers in each data center. To connect the nodes in the physical network, 7 links were used and 20 different paths were defined. Two alternate routing paths were defined for each couple of nodes. The input contained data corresponding to 5 VM instances. The choice of this network is due to two factors. First, condensing requests in an architecture with limited resources puts the network under high load to eliminate the effect the network capacity would have on the result. This would allow more control by eliminating any factors related to network design or node distribution that might ease the pressure on the scheduling algorithm. This way, the problem size is controlled directly using only the parameters we are testing for which are the number of requests, their specification and their distribution. Second, it makes it easier to compare results and execution times of relaxed solution to those of the optimal solution.

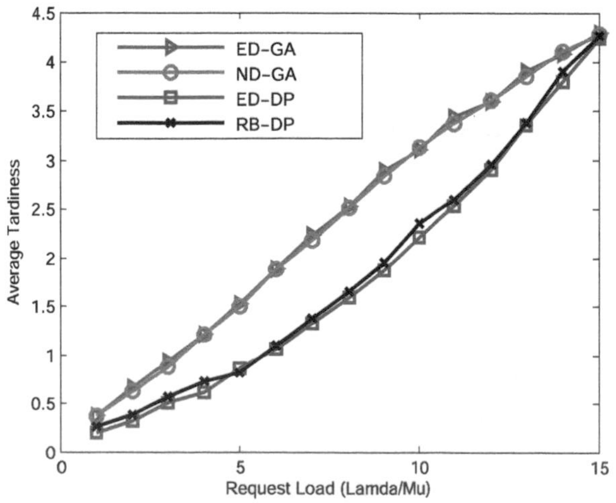

Fig. 12 Request average tardiness results for scheduling methods (allowed tardiness/request =25 time units)

For the connection requests coming from the clients, as in [22], their arrival rate values were set according to a Poisson process. The connection request lifetime (duration) was normally distributed with an average of 100 time units and the total number of connection requests was gradually increased from 20 up to 3000 requests. Every connection request is associated with a source, a destination, a requested start time and a duration. The source nodes/VMs were uniformly distributed.

To evaluate the optimal and relaxed solutions, we used the IBM ILOG CPLEX optimization studio v12.4. Both the optimal and relaxed solution were programmed using Optimization Programming Language (OPL) and multiple testing rounds were performed. Both solutions were tested for multiple values of normalized network load.

Table 5 shows a comparison between the objective values obtained using the optimal scheme vs. the values obtained from the relaxed (decomposed) scheme for small scale problems (up to 200 requests). While the optimal solution was able to schedule all requests without any delay (tardiness), the relaxed solution achieved an acceptable average tardiness in comparison. As noticed from the table, the execution times for the optimal scheme are slightly better for small data sets, but as the number of requests grows, the difference in execution times becomes evident. This goes on until the optimal solution becomes infeasible while the relaxed solution still executes in a relatively short period. The maximum number of requests the optimal solution is able to solve depends on the machines used and the network load parameters used to generate the input data.

Concerning large scale problems, the experimental results shown in Table 6 illustrate that the relaxed solution has achieved an acceptable average tardiness in comparison to the optimal solution. The effect of increasing the problem size on the value of average tardiness when using the relaxed solution is evident. The average tardiness achieved is less than 10% of the average request duration (lifetime). This is well within the bound set in [23] for acceptable connection tardiness which is half (50%) the lifetime or requested duration of the connection. This is

Table 5 Optimal vs. relaxed solution values and execution times

Number of requests	Network load	Optimal solution		Relaxed solution	
		Average tardiness value	Execution time	Average tardiness value	Execution time
30	0.86	0	3 s	5.73	8.14 s
50	0.86	0	7 s	10.12	9 s
200	0.86	0	2 min 24 s	10.785	1 min 2 s

also a considerable improvement over the performance of the heuristic solution which is shown in the same table (average tardiness values around 20% of request lifetime). The table also shows an increase in the average tardiness when increasing the number of requests (problem size). This is due to the fact that tardiness accumulates as priority is given to the request arriving earlier. In terms of execution time, as the number of requests grow, the difference in execution time between the optimal and relaxed solutions becomes evident. The optimal solution becomes infeasible while the relaxed solution still executes in a relatively short period scheduling 3000 requests in around in a period between 8–11 minutes depending on the network load.

To illustrate the impact of the allowed tardiness parameter on the request acceptance ratio, the results in Table 7 are presented. Using the heuristic solution with the combination RB-DP, the table shows the increase in the acceptance ratio as we increase the allowed tardiness per request for a specific network load.

To measure the acceptance ratio, we introduced a maximum waiting period parameter (or allowed tardiness as discussed in previous sections). This parameter represents the period of time a connection request will wait to be served before it is considered blocked. For that, an ideal value is the same value used in [23], namely, half the request lifetime. In other words, If the connection waited for more than 50% of its duration and it was not scheduled then it is blocked or not served. Table 6 shows the acceptance ratio and the average tardiness for requests with an average duration of 100 time units.

Considering this scenario where requests with high tardiness are blocked presents a trade off between average connection tardiness and the percentage (or number) of blocked connections. It is noticed that the average tardiness decreases as we remove the requests with high tardiness and consider them blocked. An average tardiness of less than 2% of a request lifetime can be guaranteed if we are willing to sacrifice 13% of the requests as blocked.

Deciding weather to use this scenario or not is up to the cloud solution architects. This depends on the client sensitivity to the precision/quality vs. the speed of achieving results.

Comparison with previous solutions

When planning the comparison between the proposed solution and solutions available in the literature, we are faced with a challenge. As discussed in detail in "Related work" section, the available solutions are diverse in terms of the parameters considered and the covered dimensions of the cloud resource allocation problem. This limits the number of solutions that can realistically be used to solve this particular flavor of the problem. However, we were able to use the algorithms implemented in [6] (Modified best fit decreasing method) and [24, 25] (GREEN scheduling) to solve the same problem and compare their performance to the method we developed. The focus was: network capacity (minimizing blocking percentage) and performance (when blocking is not an issue, minimizing the average tardiness per served request is a priority). This comparison was performed for a smaller network first, in order to explore the stress effect on a cloud network. Then, the same comparison is performed for a larger more realistic network scenario. As in the previous experiments, the tests were performed for different problem sizes and various levels of allowed tardiness per requests.

Small network results

Figure 13 compares the three algorithms' performance in terms of request blocking percentage for different

Table 6 Execution times & average tardiness for connection requests for large scale problems when increasing the average connection duration to 100 Time units

Network load	Heuristic solution (RB-DP) Average tardiness (percentage of duration/lifetime)	Relaxed solution average tardiness	Relaxed solution execution time
0.86	19.81%	2.88%	8 min 21 s
0.93	21.18%	6.36%	8 min 54 s
1	22.54%	9.08%	11 min 31 s

Table 7 Connection requests acceptance rate for different network loads using the relxed solution

Allowed tardiness (percentage of request lifetime or duration)	50%	200%	1000%
Acceptance rate	86%	87%	100%
Average tardiness for accepted requests	1.98%	16.72%	219.767%

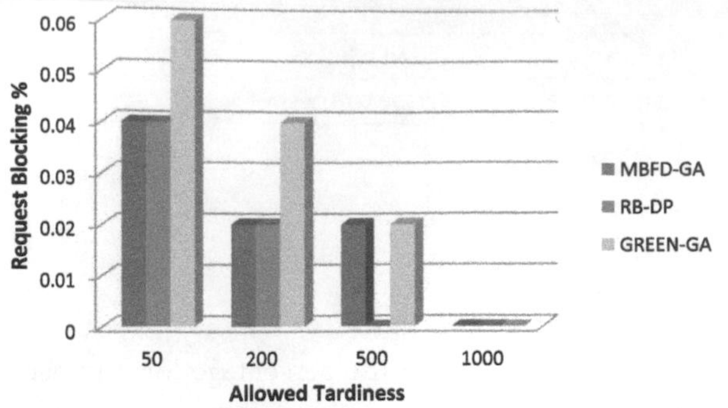

Fig. 13 Request blocking percentage results for 3 scheduling algorithms measured for 4 different allowed tardiness cases

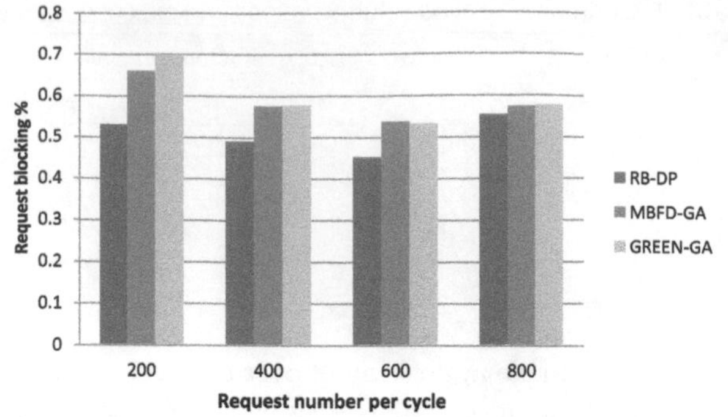

Fig. 15 Request blocking percentage results for scheduling methods with allowed tardiness=5 units (very low)

scenarios as the allowed tardiness level increases. The figure shows that our technique (RB-DP) performs consistently better (lower blocking percentage) than Green scheduling algorithm. It also shows that RB-DP performs at the same level as MBFD for low allowed tardiness levels before showing an advantage for high allowed tardiness. Figure 14 presents results for the other metric, average request tardiness. Figure 14 shows that RB-DP starts by performing on the same level of the other two algorithms and while we increase the allowed tardiness level for requests, RB-DP shows clear advantage (as seen in the last case of allowed tardiness =1000 time units). The effect of increasing the allowed tardiness is basically eliminating the need to schedule each request as soon as it arrives (to avoid blocking requests) Instead, it focuses the experiment on showing the algorithm that can serve/schedule requests in the most efficient way and this, in turn, decreases the average tardiness per requests.

Large network results

The same trends carry on while testing on large scale networks (the NSF network). In Fig. 15, blocking percentage is shown for the three algorithms for different problem sizes. Problem size here is represented by the number of requests submitted to the central controller per cycle (arrival rate). These results are shown for allowed tardiness level = 5 time units (very low level) which adds extra pressure to serve requests within a short period of their arrival and focuses the algorithms work on serving the highest number of requests not on tardiness levels. In Fig. 16, the same results are shown for a higher number of requests ranging from 3000 to 10,000 requests per cycle. This confirms that our experimental results are consistent when the network is exposed to higher load that is close to or exceeds its capacity. Looking at both figures, they show that our technique (RB-DP) performs consistently better than the other two algorithms under high loads.

Figure 17 explores the performance of the algorithms in the specific case of high allowed tardiness levels.

RB-DP offers clear advantage in terms of the blocking percentage metric for various allowed tardiness levels.

Moving to the second metric, Fig. 18 shows the performance of the three algorithms in terms of average request tardiness while changing the allowed tardiness levels (or request lifetime). RB-DP performs on a comparable level to the other two algorithms for small allowed tardiness levels and then exceeds the performance of MBFD starting medium levels of request lifetimes and then clearly

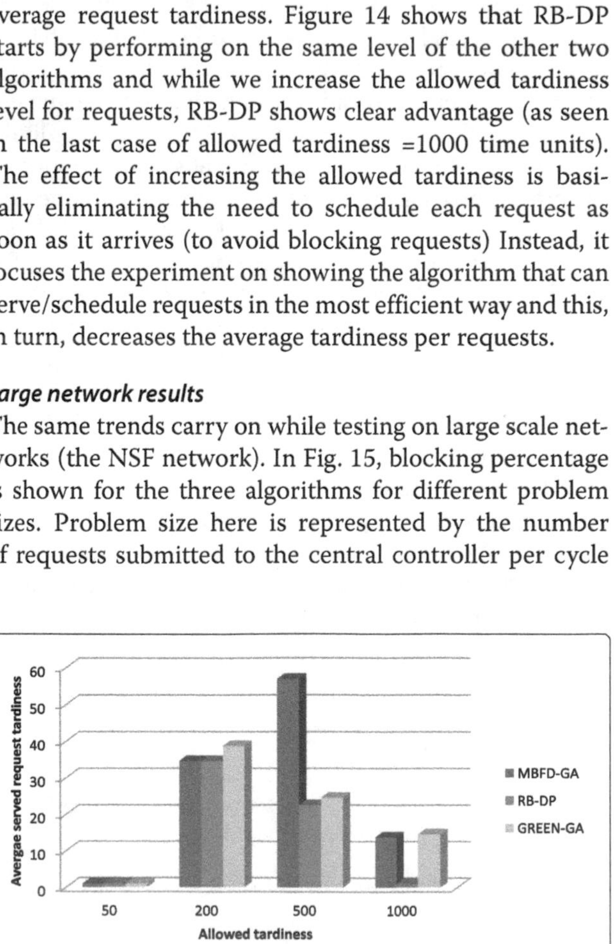

Fig. 14 Request average tardiness results for 3 scheduling algorithms measured for 4 different allowed tardiness cases

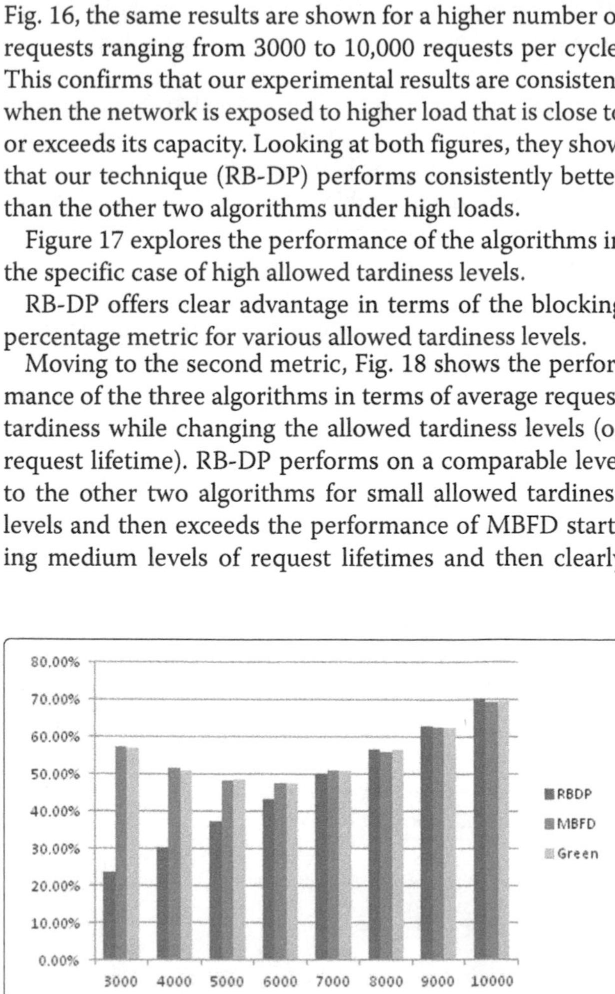

Fig. 16 Request blocking percentage results for 3 scheduling algorithms for a large number of requests per cycle (1–10k)

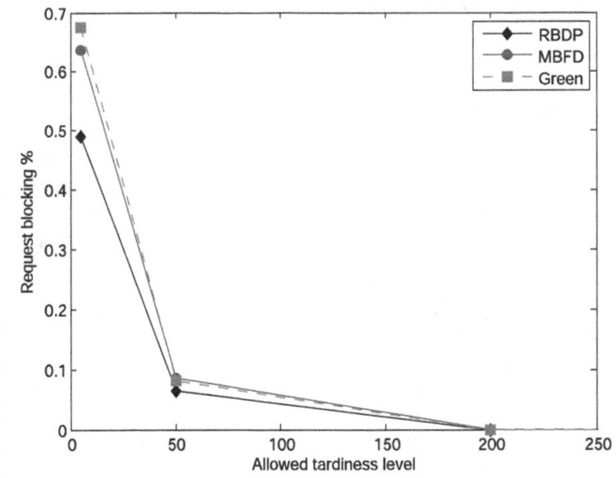

Fig. 17 Request blocking percentage results for scheduling methods while changing allowed tardiness levels

exceeds both algorithms with the higher levels starting 400 time units.

These results prove the potential our solution has in terms achieving better performance in both blocking percentage (more accepted connection requests and less network congestion) and average tardiness (better Quality of Service conditions for cloud users).

Conclusion

We introduced a comprehensive solution to tackle the problem of resource allocation in a cloud computing data center [26]. First, the problem was formulated as a mixed integer linear model. This formulation was solved using an optimization library for a small data set. However, finding the optimal solution for larger more practical scenarios is not feasible using the optimal mathematical formulation. Therefore, we introduced 5 heuristic methods to tackle the two sides of the problem, namely VM reservation and connection scheduling. The performance of these techniques was analyzed and compared. Although the solution scale issue is solved, a heuristic solution does not offer optimality guarantees. This constituted the motivation to introduce a suboptimal solution. The solution contained 4 steps that exploited the VM interdependency as a dominant factor in the VM allocation process. This allows us to solve the scheduling phase optimally in the following step which causes the solution to improve considerably. The relaxed solution achieved results matching with parameters preset in the literature for average connection tardiness. The results were also shown for the scenario where request blocking is allowed. Results were achieved without sacrificing the computational feasibility which shows our method to be a valid solution for reaching acceptable connection tardiness levels. Furthermore, the proposed solution was compared to two of the prominent algorithms in the literature. The proposed solution was shown to be advantageous in terms of minimizing both average request tardiness and blocking percentage for multiple cloud network scenarios. This makes it a strong candidate to be used in cloud scenarios where the focus is on metrics like more accepted connection requests and less network congestion or request average tardiness (better quality of service conditions for cloud users).

In the future, we plan to use our scheme to experiment with other important objectives of the cloud provider [27, 28]. Maintaining privacy while processing and communicating data through cloud resources is a critical challenge. Privacy is a major concern for users in the cloud or planning to move to the cloud. Improving data privacy metrics is not only important to clients, but also critical for conforming with governmental regulations that are materializing quickly. This means that a resource allocation system should extend its list of priorities to include privacy metrics in addition to typical performance and cost metrics. Constraints on the data handling, data movement and on scheduling locations should be seen. The privacy extends to data on resources required by the cloud clients. We have investigated some of the topic's challenges at length in [3]. Our next step is to extend our model to explore these possibilities. This would add a different dimension to give a competitive advantage to cloud providers which offer the expected level of privacy to prospective clients.

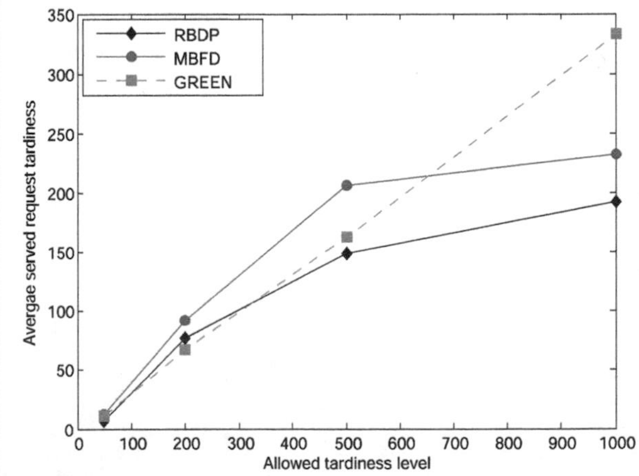

Fig. 18 Request average tardiness results for scheduling methods (allowed tardiness/request = 25 time units)

Acknowledgments
The authors would like to thank Dr. Rejaul Choudry for his contribution to the code implementation and related work section. The authors would also like to thank Dr. Daehyun Ban from Samsung for his insightful feedback.

Funding
This work is supported in part by the Natural Sciences and Engineering Research Council of Canada (NSERC-STPGP 447230) and Samsung Global Research Outreach (GRO) award.

Authors' contributions

Dr. Mohamed Abu Sharkh reviewed the state of the art of the field, did the analysis of the current resource allocation techniques and their limitations. He formulated the problem in optimal and suboptimal forms, implemented the simulator presented in this paper, and performed the experiments as well as analysis. Prof. Abdallah Shami initiated and supervised this research, lead and approved its scientific contribution, provided general input, reviewed the article and issued his approval for the final version. Dr. Abdelkader Ouda provided general input and reviewed the article. All authors read and approved the final manuscript.

Competing interests

The authors declare that they have no competing interests.

References

1. Mckendrick J 12 Most Memorable Cloud Computing Quotes from 2013, Forbes Magazine, [Online]. Available: https://www.forbes.com/sites/joemckendrick/2013/12/08/12-most-memorable-cloud-computing-quotes-from-2013/#7c88fe2330af. Accessed Feb 2017
2. IBM's The big data and analytics hub, The 4 Vs of the Big Data, IBM, [Online]. Available: http://www.ibmbigdatahub.com/infographic/four-vs-big-data. Accessed Feb 2017
3. Abu Sharkh M, Jammal M, Ouda A, Shami A (2013) Resource Allocation In A Network-Based Cloud Computing Environment: Design Challenges. IEEE Commun Mag 51(11):46–52
4. Dastjerdi AV, Buyya R (2014) Compatibility-aware Cloud Service Composition Under Fuzzy Preferences of Users. IEEE Trans Cloud Comput 2(1):1–13
5. Wei G, Vasilakos AV, Zheng Y, Xiong N (2010) A game-theoretic method of fair resource allocation for cloud computing services. J Supercomput 54(2):252–269
6. Beloglazov A, Abawajy J, Buyya R (2012) Energy-aware resource allocation heuristics for efficient management of data centers for cloud computing. Futur Gener Comput Syst, Elsevier 28(5):755–768
7. Abu Sharkh M, Kanso A, Shami A, hln P (2016) Building a cloud on earth: a study of cloud computing data center simulators. Elsevier Comput Netw 108:78–96
8. Duan R, Prodan R, Li X (2014) Multi-objective game theoretic scheduling of bag-of-tasks workflows on hybrid clouds. IEEE Trans Cloud Comput 2(1):29–42
9. Guzek M, Kliazovich D, Bouvry P (2013) A holistic model for resource representation in virtualized cloud computing data centers. In: proc CloudCom, vol. 1. IEEE. pp 590–598
10. Shojafar M, Cordeschi N, Baccarelli E (2016) Energy-efficient adaptive resource management for real-time vehicular cloud services. IEEE Trans Cloud Comput PP(99):1rgy
11. Cordeschi N, Shojafar M, Baccarelli E (2013) Energy-saving self-configuring networked data centers. Comput Netw 57(17):3479–3491
12. Shojafar M, Javanmardi S, Abolfazli S, Cordeschi N (2015) FUGE: A joint meta-heuristic approach to cloud job scheduling algorithm using fuzzy theory and a genetic method. Clust Comput:1–16. http://link.springer.com/article/10.1007/s10586-014-0420-x
13. Shojafar M, Cordeschi N, Abawajy JH (2015). In: Proc. of IEEE Global Communication Workshop (GLOBECOM) Workshop. IEEE. pp 1–6
14. IBM IBM CPLEX Optimizer [Online]. Available: http://www-01.ibm.com/software/commerce/optimization/cplex-optimizer/. Accessed Feb 2017
15. Kantarci B, Mouftah HT (2012) Scheduling advance reservation requests for wavelength division multiplexed networks with static traffic demands. In: proc. IEEE ISCC. IEEE. pp 806–811
16. Wallace TD, Shami A, Assi C (2008) Scheduling advance reservation requests for wavelength division multiplexed networks with static traffic demands. IET Commun 2(8):1023–1033
17. Amazon Amazon Elastic Compute Cloud (Amazon EC2), [Online]. Available: https://aws.amazon.com/ec2/. Accessed Feb 2017
18. Maguluri S, Srikant R, Ying L (2012) Stochastic Models of Load Balancing and Schedulingin Cloud Computing Clusters. In: proc. IEEE INFOCOM. IEEE. pp 702–710
19. Jammal M, Singh T, Shami A, Asal R, Li Y (2014) Software defined networking: State of the art and research challenges. Elsevier Comput Netw 72:74–98
20. Hawilo H, Shami A, Mirahmadi M, Asal R (2014) NFV: state of the art, challenges, and implementation in next generation mobile networks (vEPC). IEEE Network 28(6):18–26
21. Abu Sharkh M, Shami A, Ohlen P, Ouda A (2015) Simulating high availability scenarios in cloud data centers: a closer look. In: 2015 IEEE 7th Int Conf Cloud Comput Technol Sci (CloudCom). IEEE. pp 617–622
22. Abu Sharkh M, Ouda A, Shami A (2013) A Resource Scheduling Model for Cloud Computing Data Centers. In: Proc. IWCMC. pp 213–218
23. Chowdhury M, Rahman MR, Boutaba R (2012) Vineyard: virtual network embedding algorithms with coordinated node and link mapping. IEEE/ACM Trans Netw 20(1):206–219
24. Kliazovich D, Bouvry P, Khan SU (2013) Simulation and performance analysis of data intensive and workload intensive cloud computing data centers. In: Kachris C, Bergman K, Tomkos I (eds). Optical Interconnects for Future Data Center Networks. Springer-Verlag, New York. ISBN: 978-1-4614-4629-3, Chapter 4
25. Kliazovich D, Bouvry P, Khan SU (2011) GreenCloud: a packet level simulator of energy-aware cloud computing data centers. J Supercomput 16(1):65–75. Special issue on Green Networks
26. Armbrust M, Fox A, Griffith R, Joseph A, Katz R, Konwinski A, Lee G, Patterson D, Rabkin A, Stoica I, Zaharia M (2009) Above the Clouds: A Berkeley View of Cloud Computing. Tech. Rep. UCB/EECS-2009–28. EECS Department, UC Berkeley
27. Foster I, Zhao Y, Raicu I, Lu S (2008) Cloud Computing and Grid Computing 360-Degree Compared. In: proc. GCE Workshop. IEEE. pp 1–10
28. Kalil M, Meerja KA, Refaey A, Shami A (2015) Virtual Mobile Networks in Clouds. Adv Mob Cloud Comput Syst:165
29. Miranda A, et al. (2014) Wavelength assignment using a hybrid evolutionary computation to reduce cross-phase modulation. J Microw Optoelectron Electromagn Appl 13(1). So Caetano do Sul http://dx.doi.org/10.1590/S2179-10742014000100001

6

Critical analysis of vendor lock-in and its impact on cloud computing migration: a business perspective

Justice Opara-Martins*, Reza Sahandi and Feng Tian

Abstract

Vendor lock-in is a major barrier to the adoption of cloud computing, due to the lack of standardization. Current solutions and efforts tackling the vendor lock-in problem are predominantly technology-oriented. Limited studies exist to analyse and highlight the complexity of vendor lock-in problem in the cloud environment. Consequently, most customers are unaware of proprietary standards which inhibit interoperability and portability of applications when taking services from vendors. This paper provides a critical analysis of the vendor lock-in problem, from a business perspective. A survey based on qualitative and quantitative approaches conducted in this study has identified the main risk factors that give rise to lock-in situations. The analysis of our survey of 114 participants shows that, as computing resources migrate from on-premise to the cloud, the vendor lock-in problem is exacerbated. Furthermore, the findings exemplify the importance of interoperability, portability and standards in cloud computing. A number of strategies are proposed on how to avoid and mitigate lock-in risks when migrating to cloud computing. The strategies relate to contracts, selection of vendors that support standardised formats and protocols regarding standard data structures and APIs, developing awareness of commonalities and dependencies among cloud-based solutions. We strongly believe that the implementation of these strategies has a great potential to reduce the risks of vendor lock-in.

Keywords: Cloud computing, Vendor lock-in, Enterprise migration, Cloud adoption, Cloud API's, Interoperability, Portability, Standards, DevOps

Introduction

Cloud computing is to offer an opportunistic business strategy to enterprises (small or large), to remain competitive and meet business needs [1–3]. Whilst this seems like an attractive proposition for both public and private companies, a number of challenges remain inadequately addressed. A recent survey conducted by [4] reported security and vendor lock-in as major barriers to cloud adoption across the United Kingdom (UK) market. The European Network and Information Security Agency (ENISA) and European Commission (EC) have recognized the vendor lock-in problem as a one of the greatest obstacles to enterprise cloud adoption [5].

The reviews of existing literature [6–12] have shown that previous studies have focused more on interoperability and portability issues of cloud computing when lock-in is discussed. Amongst many problems being discussed are: the lack of standard interfaces and open APIs [13], the lack of open standards for VM format [14] and service deployment interfaces [15], as well as lack of open formats for data interchange. These issues result in difficulties in integration between services obtained from different cloud providers as well as between cloud resources and internal legacy systems [16]. Consequently, this renders the interoperability and portability of data and application services difficult. The emergent difficulty is a direct result of the current differences between individual cloud vendors offerings based on non-compatible underlying technologies and proprietary standards. In essence, cloud providers often propose their own solutions and proprietary interfaces for access to resources and services. This heterogeneity of cloud provider solutions (i.e. hardware and software) and

* Correspondence: joparamartins@bournemouth.ac.uk
Faculty of Science and Technology, Bournemouth University, Bournemouth, UK

service interfaces is a crucial problem since most of the current resources bind the customer to stick with one cloud technology due to high cost in porting the applications and data to a different provider's interface. The heterogeneity in cloud computing is simply the existence of differentiated hardware, architectures, infrastructure, and technology used by cloud providers. Many cloud vendors provide services based on custom-built policies, infrastructure, platforms, and APIs that make the overall cloud landscape heterogeneous. Such variations cause interoperability, portability, and integration very challenging.

Following the principle that compatible interfaces are important in a cloud environment, two implementations of the same cloud service may store and process data very differently. This may well also involve storing derived and implementation specific data differently [17]. Without proper definitions for import and export formats, a set of data from one service implementation will probably be meaningless when imported into another cloud service. For example, a cloud service may be accessed and used by a wide variety of clients, including mobile, desktops and even tablet PCs. However, the information created and consumed by those services can still be limited to a single vendor if a proprietary data format is used. Further, this can create a degree of instability and data incompatibility issue as interfaces to the functionality may be proprietary, and thus any solution that is built to leverage the functionality provided cannot be easily migrated to a competitive cloud service offering [15]. So, while customers might be able to access and use the services from a variety of clients, the ability to move seamlessly from one vendor to another may be difficult because of other dependencies such as different data formats. Clearly, this problem has an impact on interoperability and data portability between clouds.

At the core of all these problems, we can identify concerns about consumers' demand to migrate data to and from different clouds (data portability), and interoperability between clouds. Research has already addressed movability and migration on a functional level [18, 19]. However, migration is currently far from being trivial. The two main reasons are the lack of world-wide adopted standards or interfaces to leverage the dynamic landscape of cloud related offers [14], and absence of standards for defining parameters for cloud applications and their management. Without an appropriate standardized format, ensuring interoperability, portability, compliance, trust, and security is difficult [12]. Standards continue to rapidly evolve in step with technology. Hence, standards may be at different stages of maturity and levels of acceptance. But, unless the standards are well-accepted and widely used, such standards remain a questionable solution [20]. In other words a partially adopted standard would represent a poor solution. Essentially, this explicit lack of standards to support portability and interoperability among cloud providers stifles the market competition and locks customers to a single cloud provider [21]. To expatiate further, potential difficulties (by primarily technological means) in achieving interoperability and portability lead to lock-in – resulting in customer dependency on the services of a single cloud computing provider [22]. From a legal stance, the dependency can be aggravated by the abusive conduct of a cloud computing provider within the meaning of Article 102 TFEU (Treaty on the Functioning of the European Union) [18], where other providers are excluded from competing from the customers of the initial cloud provider. In such situations, limitations to interoperability and portability could be seen as an abuse by a dominant provider using this practice as a technical means to stifle (i.e. monopolize) competition. Such practices distort competition and harm consumers by depriving them of better prices, greater choices and innovation. Hence, the competition law has the role of ensuring competition is maintained and enforced in the market by regulating anti-competitive conduct by cloud providers. To this end, it can be concluded that cloud interoperability (and data portability) constraints are potential results of anti-competitive environment created by offering services with proprietary standards.

Vendor lock-in

The vendor lock-in problem in cloud computing is the situation where customers are dependent (i.e. locked-in) on a single cloud provider technology implementation and cannot easily move in the future to a different vendor without substantial costs, legal constraints, or technical incompatibilities [23]. To substantiate further from the lenses of a software developer, the lock-in situation is evident in that applications developed for specific cloud platforms (e.g. Amazon EC2, Microsoft Azure), cannot easily be migrated to other cloud platforms and users become vulnerable to any changes made by their providers [24]. Actually, the lock-in issue arises when a company, for instance, decides to change cloud providers (or perhaps integrate services from different providers), but is unable to move applications or data across different cloud services because the semantics of resources and services of cloud providers do not match with each other. This heterogeneity of cloud semantics [25] and cloud Application Program Interfaces (APIs) creates technical incompatibility which in turn leads to interoperability and portability challenges [26]. This makes interoperation, collaboration, portability and manageability of data and services a very complex and elusive task. For these reasons, it becomes important from the view point of the business to retain the flexibility to change providers according to business concerns or even keep in-house some of the components that are less mission-critical due to security related risks. Interoperability and portability among cloud providers can avoid the problem of vendor lock-in. It is the way toward a more competitive market for cloud providers and customers.

Lock-in affects cloud migration

Interoperability and portability are essential qualities that affect the cloud under different perspectives [7, 13], due to the risk of vendor lock-in. While many studies cite vendor lock-in as a major barrier to cloud computing adoption [3, 27–32], yet due to its complexity, a lack of clarity still pervades. Without a clear insight into how such complex decision is made to avoid lock-in, it is difficult to identify gaps where further research is beneficial for business adopters. Existing solutions and studies addressing the lock-in problem have predominantly been technological oriented, where the focus is on knowledge garnered through logical deduction and technical expertise. Such approach is compromised by ignoring organisations' awareness and perception of the lock-in problem. For example, how is cloud lock-in experienced or understood from the business stance? Limited in-depth studies exist to investigate the complexity of cloud lock-in problem within enterprise organisations. Likewise the customers, who are willing to choose the cloud services without being strictly bond to a specific solution, are mostly neglected. Advances in cloud computing research have in recent years resulted in a growing interest for migration towards the cloud. But due to concerns about the risks of vendor lock-in, as noted by [33], organisations would particularly welcome standards that address application migration (e.g. Open Virtualization Format (OVF)) and data migration (e.g. Amazon S3 API) because such standards mitigate lock-in concerns. Various standardisation solutions from different industry bodies have been developed for increasing interoperability and portability within diverse cloud computing services [32, 34]. However, initiatives by multiple standard bodies, researchers, and consortiums could indirectly lead to the possibility of multiple standards emerging with possible lack of consensus, thereby deteriorating the lock-in problem even further.

In spite of these legitimate concerns and technical complexity, our study aims to answer the following two questions of interest to business adopters: *1)* "How to avoid being locked-in to a single cloud provider? *2)* How easy and secure is it to deploy existing cloud artefacts (e.g. software applications, databases, data, virtual servers etc.) on another service provider's platform without modification to the artefacts – which would reduce the financial benefit of the migration?" The former applies more to companies who have migrated or are looking to adopt more cloud solutions, whereas the latter is closely related to companies considering moving core systems into the cloud environment. Giving answers to these questions is deceptively easy and straightforward, but the reality is different. Presently, for many companies, there is a large amount of sensitive data and IT assets in-house which can deter them to migrate to the cloud due to risks of vendor lock-in, security and privacy issues. For these reasons, it becomes not only critical to consider security and privacy concerns but also related issues such as integration, portability, and interoperability between the software on-premise and in the cloud [35], should be taking into account. Therefore, organisations must be aware of appropriate standards and protocols used by cloud providers to support data/application movability. Moreover, the ease of moving data across (i.e. portability) cloud providers' platform mandates data to be in a compatible format [34], and includes the need to securely delete the old storage [36]. In other words, the ability to move data/application about is of crucial importance, as much as the effort involved in actually moving – inability to achieve this portends large as a management issue for cloud computing. To further complicate matters, maintaining compliance with governmental regulations and industry requirements adds another layer of considerations to the management of data. Whether or not organisations can easily shift their data/application about seamlessly, still remains one of the biggest issues facing cloud adoption across diverse industries. Based on our findings, we propose strategic solutions that enterprises can follow to avoid entering into vendor lock-in situations.

Methodology

Research design

To explore factors that contribute to a lock-in situation in cloud computing, epistemologically, our study design in this paper consists of two distinct phases, as depicted in Fig. 1.

Phase 1: pilot interview study

In the pilot study, qualitative data were collected through the use of open-ended interviews with IT practitioners to explore the business-related issues of vendor lock-in affecting cloud adoption. Five participants from different industry sectors and organizations were purposely selected for in-depth interviews. They included a security expert, cloud advisor, IT technician, business end user, and an IT manager. The purpose was to explore the cloud lock-in problems, and explore the

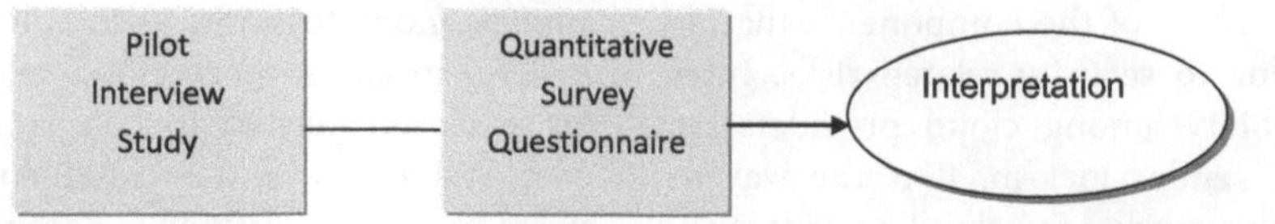

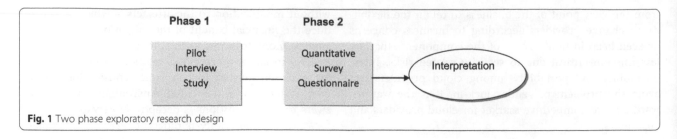

Fig. 1 Two phase exploratory research design

prevalence of its dimensions, by gaining a range of insights from different IT professionals.

Each interview data collected was transcribed verbatim, and the data was analysed using the Nvivo 8 QSR software package for data storage, coding, and theme development [37]. Due to the participatory and time consuming nature of this pilot phase, it was deemed important that each interview be given considerable time for analysis. Seven themes emerged in relation to participants' perception of vendor lock-in problem and how this affects their migration and adoption decisions. The themes were; (1) standards, (2) interoperability in the cloud environment, (3) the need for portability, (4) integration challenges, (5) contract exit strategy, (6) data ownership (7) security and privacy issues. The analysis of the responses across the seven themes showed the participants' priority of the themes. As a result, data portability and interoperability concerns were the most discussed theme in relation to vendor lock-in. However, participants were less interested to divulge about the security and contract exit strategies, including data ownership and privacy risks. Subsequent to the pilot interviews a questionnaire was designed for a survey. The main issues raised at the interviews were incorporated into the questionnaire.

Phase 2: quantitative survey questionnaire

The goal of phase 2 was to identify and evaluate the risks and opportunities of vendor lock-in which affect stakeholders' decision-making about adopting cloud solutions. This phase of the research design is based on an online survey tool [38]. Participants were selected and invited by e-mail to participate in the survey. The aim of the survey was an in-depth study of the effect of vendor lock-in in migration of enterprise IT resources to the cloud (Additional files 1 and 2).

Questionnaire data collection

The target population mainly consists of large corporations and small to medium-sized enterprises (SMEs) located in the United Kingdom (UK). Participants in the survey varied between IT professionals, managers and decision-makers within their respective business enterprise. A total of 200 companies were invited to participate in the survey. Overall, 114 participants responded and completed the online survey, which constituted a satisfactory response rate of 57 %. To supplement for a higher response rate as possible and to avoid skewing the data, a paper-based questionnaire was administered in person to participants at conferences and workshops. 12 completed responses were received, giving a good response rate of 63 %. Prior to presenting the findings of the survey, it should be pointed out that the questionnaire comprised of many questions, however only those which revealed important issues of lock-in are presented and discussed in context. For the purpose of analysis, Table 1 presents a socio-demographic profile of the companies and participants in the survey. As shown in Table 1, the samples were slightly dominated by organisations sized between 251 and 500 employees, and majority came from ICT organisations, followed by education, consumer business, public sector and healthcare.

Organisations in the survey

In Fig. 2, a vast majority of the respondents were IT managers and CIOs. These are the key people responsible for

Table 1 Socio-Demographic profile of participant organisation

Organisation Size	Percentage
1–24	7 %
25–50	12 %
51–250	28 %
251–500	39 %
Over 501 Employees	14 %
Total:	100 %
Industry Sector	Percentage
Construction sector	3.5 %
Consumer Business	10.5 %
Education sector	15.8 %
Financial services	4.4 %
ICT services	17.5 %
Production & Manufacturing	7.0 %
Public sector & Healthcare	11.4 %
Services industry	10.5 %
Other	19.3 %
Total:	100

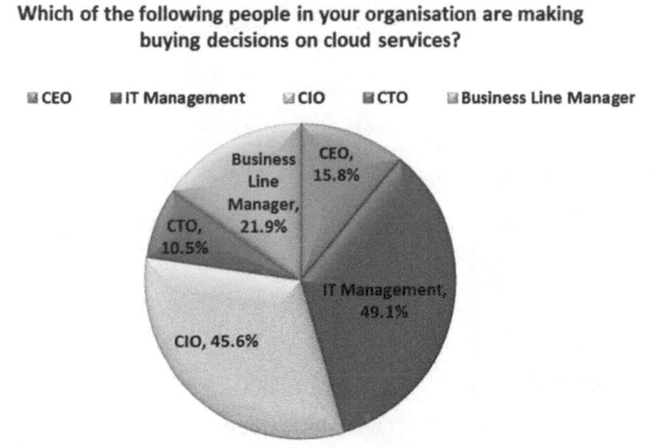

Fig. 2 Sample profile of participants

making buying decisions in the cloud adoption process. This indicates that the role of IT manager in most organisations is still considered paramount as opposed to premise that the advent of cloud computing will make IT management obsolete – that is, some of the existing IT management roles will be moved to cloud providers [39]. Arguably this is not the case today as pointed by [40]. Cloud computing is seen as a viable deployment model within the context of UK organisations IT strategy, but it is not seen as the only viable model. Most organisations foresee the continued use of on-premise IT alongside cloud-based services for the foreseeable future, evolving into a prevalence of hybrid IT estates.

Findings

The analysis of the results show over 49 % of top level IT managers influence the decisions for adopting cloud services. This confirms that cloud computing adoption in the UK is seen as a viable IT deployment model. Moreover, more than half (50.9 %) of the organisations polled in the study are already using cloud services for at least one application domain within their organisation. The higher majority (69 %) utilise a combination of cloud services and internally owned applications (i.e. hybrid IT) for organisation's needs (Fig. 3).

Adoption of cloud computing by UK businesses

The survey affirms that the concept of using cloud computing services to address the business IT needs has established a mainstream deployment across organisations of various sizes. To further substantiate this matter, interestingly about 36 % of participants confirmed using a hybrid (public and private) cloud deployment model as opposed to a private cloud. Only 46 % of UK firms participated in the survey use public cloud services, in spite of the associated security risks (Fig. 4). The rate of adoption has been motivated by numerous indicators for effective cloud deployment decision. The most cited reasons for adopting cloud computing includes better scalability of IT resources (45.9 %), collaboration (40.5 %), cost savings (39.6 %) and increased flexibility (36.9 %). This suggests that organisations are allured to utilising cloud services due to the perceived business benefits of cost savings, IT flexibility and business agility.

The business benefits of cloud migration

In addition to the reasons for why the cloud model has achieved a mainstream deployment status across UK organisations, identifying the actual benefits of cloud computing is critical to further our understanding of motivations to migrate to cloud-based services. As shown in Fig. 5, the majority of the respondents identified capacity and scalability (70.3 %), increased collaboration, availability, geography and mobility as benefits for migration. However, further analysis have shown, from a business stance, that for organisations with more than

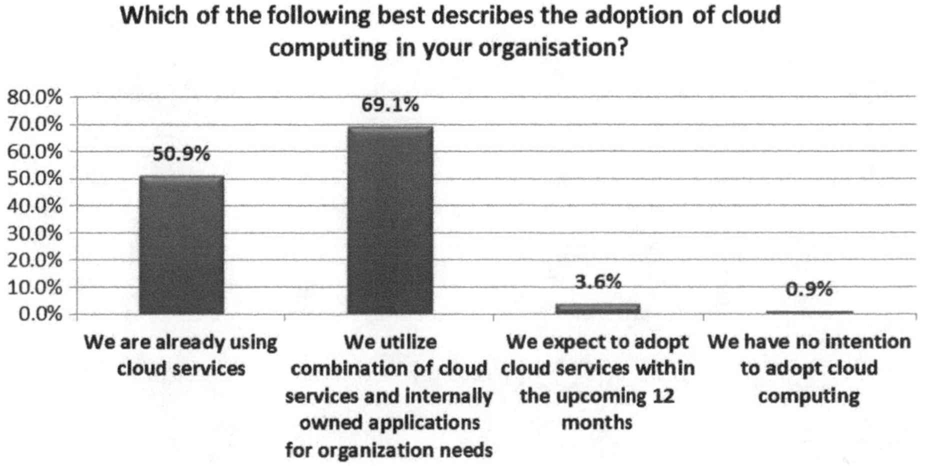

Fig. 3 Cloud adoption maturity in UK

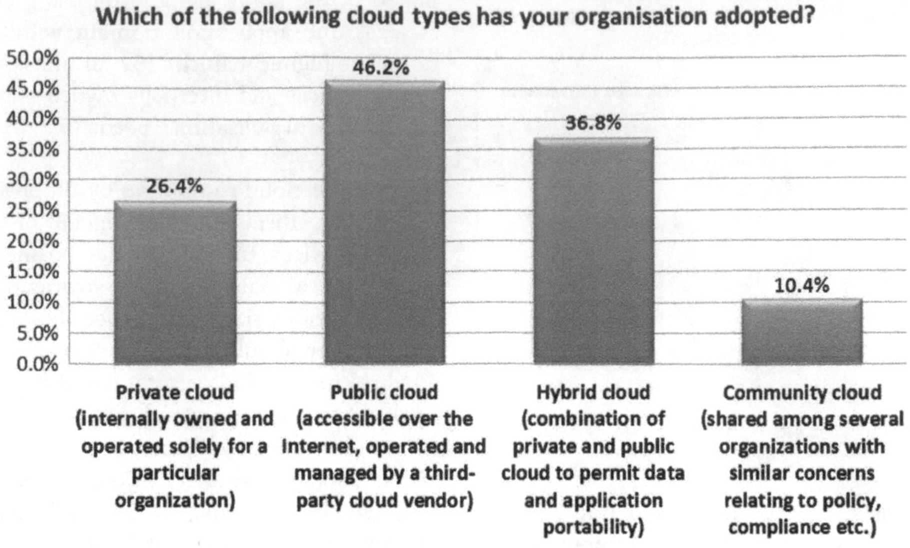

Fig. 4 Service deployed models

250 employees, the three most important realised benefits reported by participants are reduced infrastructure cost, ubiquity, and increased collaboration respectively. This indicates that the business benefits of migrating to the cloud vary across different organisation sizes. Moreover, the results also show slight difference between the motivations for adoption and the actual benefits realised from using cloud services.

Challenges to cloud implementation for UK businesses

In order to identify the factors that have an impact on cloud implementation and purchasing decisions, this study explored "what are the greatest barriers for implementing cloud computing for organisations?" Fig. 6 shows the barriers identified by the participants. Respondents identified systems and data security risks, loss of control and over dependence on a single cloud provider (35.1 %) as core existing barriers to future cloud implementation. To confer from this result, the security is still a major concern for UK businesses in implementing cloud solutions. In fact, this is due to lack of trust [11], often associated with worries about loss of control (i.e. in terms of system availability and business continuity risks), as indicated by (48.6 %) participants in the study. For instance, some organisations are worried about security within the cloud (i.e. data centres), while others feel that moving data into different geographies can have regulatory (compliance) implications. Besides, another barrier to

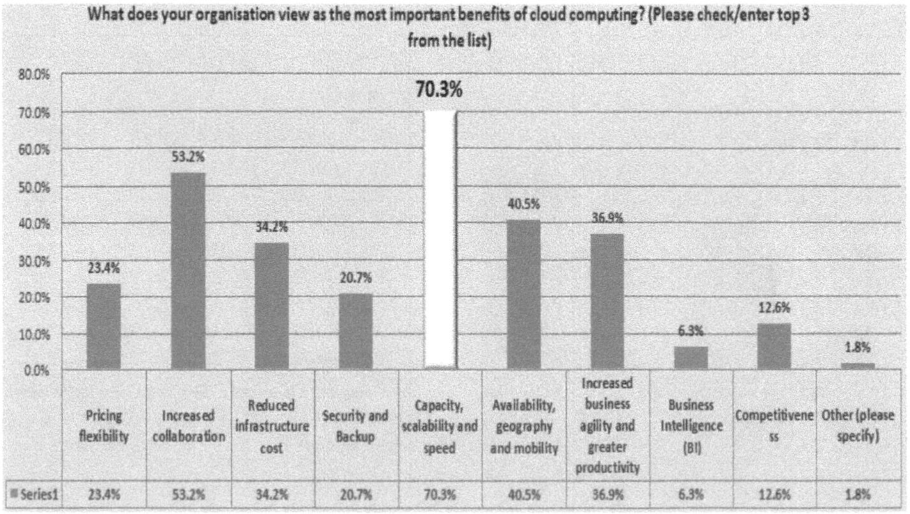

Fig. 5 Benefits of cloud computing to UK Enterprises

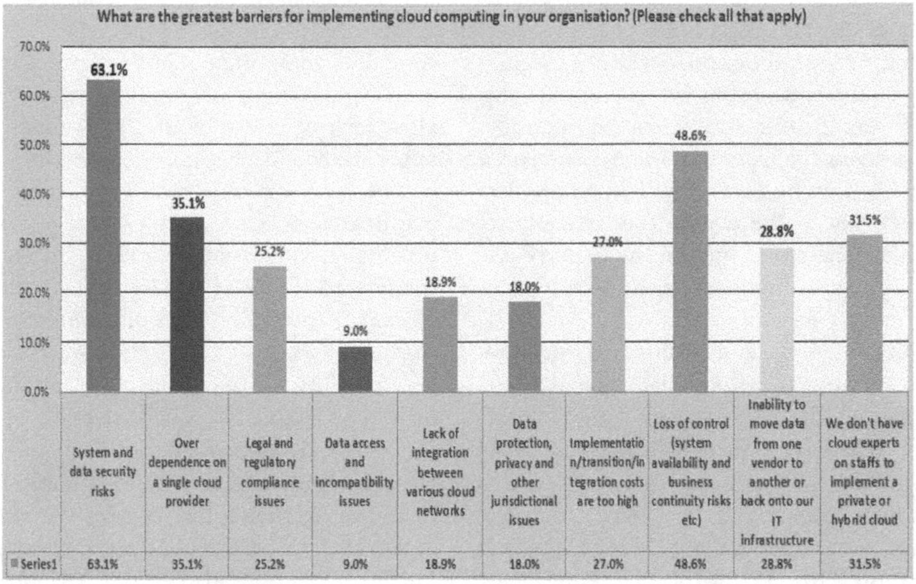

Fig. 6 Barriers to cloud implementation in the UK

cloud implementation evident in Fig. 6 is legal and regulatory compliance issues (25.2 %). Moreover, the findings tie in with a recent study published by [41], of which (57 %) participants identified "the biggest challenge in managing data security and privacy is compliance". However, regarding systems and data security risks (63.1 %), cloud service providers can demonstrate their compliance with, and adherence to, industry-accepted standards for data security and integrity. In essence, this will show transparency in practice and capability, and also assist the establishment of trust for organisations to implement/deploy their most critical, data-intensive functions and processes in the cloud.

Cloud application usage and service adoption among UK organisations

In order to identify the opportunities which may affect stakeholders' and decisions for or against cloud migration, this study explored which applications have adopted from cloud services, which local applications are considered for moving to the cloud. It also explored which applications for whatever reason, were not intended to adopt from the cloud model. The findings presented herein continue to validate cloud solutions as being pervasive options across UK organisations and industry sectors. The results in Fig. 7 suggest that general purpose applications such as email and messaging,

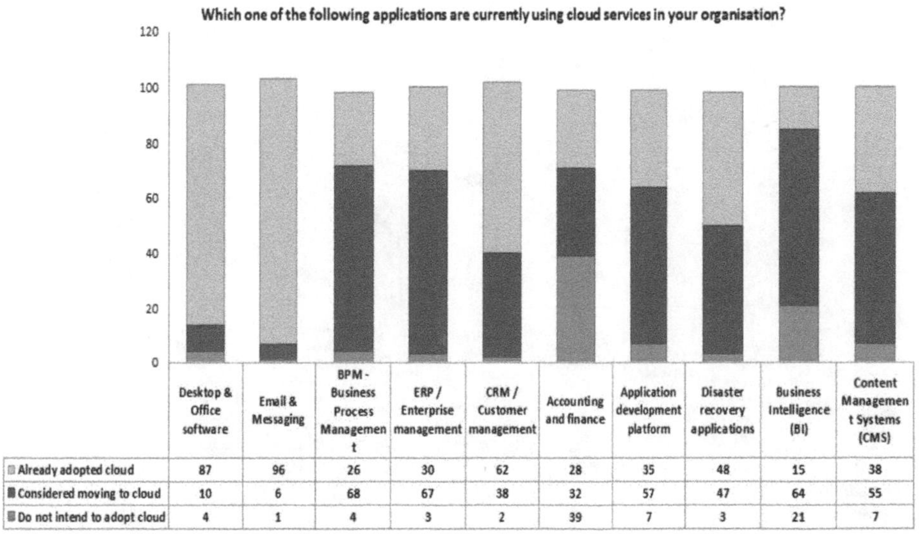

Fig. 7 Cloud-based CRM and ERP service adoption rates soar

desktop and office software, etc. have all adopted the cloud delivery model. It should be noted that the widespread and reckless sign of adoption could pose significant risks, as the cloud computing era is still evolving. This is further reinforced by respondents who consider moving business process management (68 %), enterprise management (67 %), and business intelligence applications (64 %) respectively to the cloud. This certainly reflects the impact that the cloud has on the delivery and use of enterprise software applications, as identified by respondents.

The one application which is identified by most respondents as not suitable for cloud deployment is accounting and finance (39 %), perhaps due to data security concerns. Moreover, further data analysis in cloud adoption rate across organisations, realised that larger enterprises find disaster recovery, (ERP) and business process management applications (BPM) as the best fit for cloud migration. However, for smaller enterprises, the adoption of (non-mission critical) cloud-based applications mirrors their use of email messaging, desktop hosting and Customer Relationship Management (CRM) applications for collaboration. Remarkably, the lower cost and flexibility that cloud-based applications offer is ideal for small businesses, as they are agile and often run with teams that are spread over wide geographical regions. In essence, these applications are better suited for online delivery [42].

Vendor lock-in concerns and challenges in cloud migration

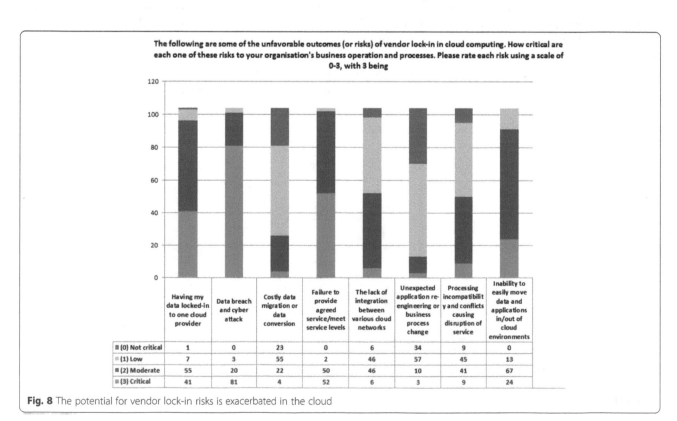

As cloud computing adoption rate soars across the UK market, the risks of vendor lock-in is also prevalent. How lock-in critically affects an organisations' business application and operation in the cloud cannot be overemphasized or underestimated. For example, Fig. 8 paints a clear admonitory picture of how UK businesses rate the risks of vendor lock-in against the decision to migrate/adopt cloud services. The risks (in Fig. 8) were identified from the initial pilot interviews and also from the literature [9–11, 13]. Moreover, the following risks (i.e. inability to move data and applications in/out of cloud environments, data ownership and cyber breaches) in Fig. 8 were critical themes that emerged from the unstructured interviews with IT practitioners. The results in Fig. 8, highlights that besides the risks of data breach and cyber-attack, or failure to meet agreed service levels, UK businesses are also concerned about having corporate data locked-in to a single cloud provider. These concerns affect the wider business functions where an enterprise is using cloud to perform essential business activities to keep operations running.

In the study it was deemed paramount to first assess participants current perception of the term "vendor lock-in" in the context of cloud computing. As shown in Fig. 9, only 44 % of respondents indicated to have a basic understanding of the term. This indicates that whilst UK

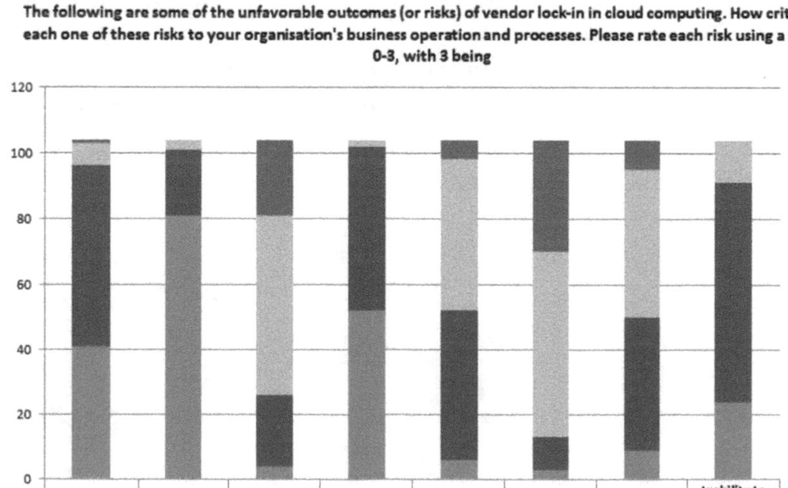
The following are some of the unfavorable outcomes (or risks) of vendor lock-in in cloud computing. How critical are each one of these risks to your organisation's business operation and processes. Please rate each risk using a scale of 0-3, with 3 being
120
100
80
60
40
20
0

	Having my data locked-in to one cloud provider	Data breach and cyber attack	Costly data migration or data conversion	Failure to provide agreed service/meet service levels	The lack of integration between various cloud networks	Unexpected application re-engineering or business process change	Processing incompatibility and conflicts causing disruption of service	Inability to easily move data and applications in/out of cloud environments
(0) Not critical	1	0	23	0	6	34	9	0
(1) Low	7	3	55	2	46	57	45	13
(2) Moderate	55	20	22	50	46	10	41	67
(3) Critical	41	81	4	52	6	3	9	24

Fig. 8 The potential for vendor lock-in risks is exacerbated in the cloud

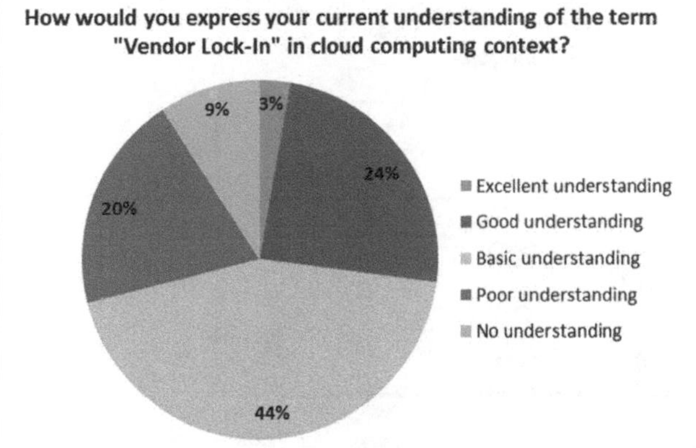

Fig. 9 UK Business perception of vendor lock-in

organisations are rapidly migrating and adopting cloud services, only a few (3 %) had exceptional knowledge. This means the lack of clarity on the problem of vendor lock-in still pervades. In part, this gap of knowledge means that organisations are not aware of the inherent lock-in problem within the cloud environment. However, the result implies that organisations with basic knowledge may not yet have experienced a cloud lock-in situation. A possible explanation for this may be attributed to the immaturity of the cloud computing ecosystem. If organisations' previous experiences in IT are compatible with the existing information and the infrastructure, then the degree of lock-in introduced by service providers will be consistent with the current knowledge and practice. Hence, in order to develop a comprehensive understanding to manage the risks associated with lock-in, organisations must first define what the lock-in means to them. This requires mapping and cross-examining the challenges of lock-in with different cloud service types (i.e. infrastructure, platform and software) and deployment models (i.e. public, private or hybrid). Comprehending the term "vendor lock-in" is critical to further our understanding. In agreement with the definition of vendor lock-in provided in [2] by Armbrust et al., in Table 2 as many as 71 % of the participants claimed vendor lock-in risks will deter their organisations from adopting more cloud services, although some respondents were unsure.

Core risk factors of lock-in

In an effort to highlight factors which may affect future cloud migration decisions, participants were requested to identify practical challenges of lock-in they encountered when using cloud services. These issues relate to lack of integration points between existing management tools (47.7 %), incompatibility issues with on-premise software, and inability to move to another service provider or take data in-house (Fig. 10). Overall, the results indicate that these challenges closely relate to interoperability and data portability issues prevalent in the cloud environment. Moreover further results show that a significant majority (76.6 %) of participants were unsure of relevant (existing or emerging) standards to support interoperability across clouds and portability of data from one cloud provider to another.

Table 2 Response indicator suggest Lock-in is a deterrent to Cloud migration

Definitely yes	Possibly yes	Not sure	No
9 %	71 %	11 %	9 %

To confer from Fig. 10, the main challenges associated with cloud lock-in are integration and incompatibility issues, followed by data portability. However, as shown in Fig. 11, when asked to identify best practices to minimize lock-in risks in cloud migration, most business respondents identified the following as top mitigation strategies: (a) making well-informed decisions before selecting vendors and/or signing cloud contracts (66.4 %); (b) the need for an open environment for continuous competition between providers in the cloud service market (52.3 %); (c) use of standard software components with industry-proven interfaces (39.3 %). Equally, in the case of managing the risks of vendor lock-in, it is encouraging to note that respondents expressed by a substantial majority are slightly (39.4 %), moderately (33.7 %), and quite likely (22.1 %) to use a cloud computing risk management framework to manage vendor lock-in risks and compliance requirements effectively. Furthermore, this indicates that UK businesses require effective and efficient strategies to manage lock-in risk(s) prevailing in the cloud ecosystem.

UK organisations view on cloud lock-in

Business strategies for avoiding vendor lock-in

This section summarises both the desires and experiences of the participants who contributed to this study. Moreover, this section presents strategic approaches for mitigating the risks and challenges of lock-in in cloud migration.

Awareness of the commonalities among cloud providers

To refer back to the first research question of interest to business adopters stated in section 1.1. UK business decision makers are rightly concerned about the risks of being locked into a single cloud service provider and the implications of such a risk including not having a clear exit strategy. There is a need for these organisations to understand what the exit strategy looks like, even if it is unlikely that they will exit in the near future – besides, no company would want to buy into a service where they feel they had no alternative provider. In this

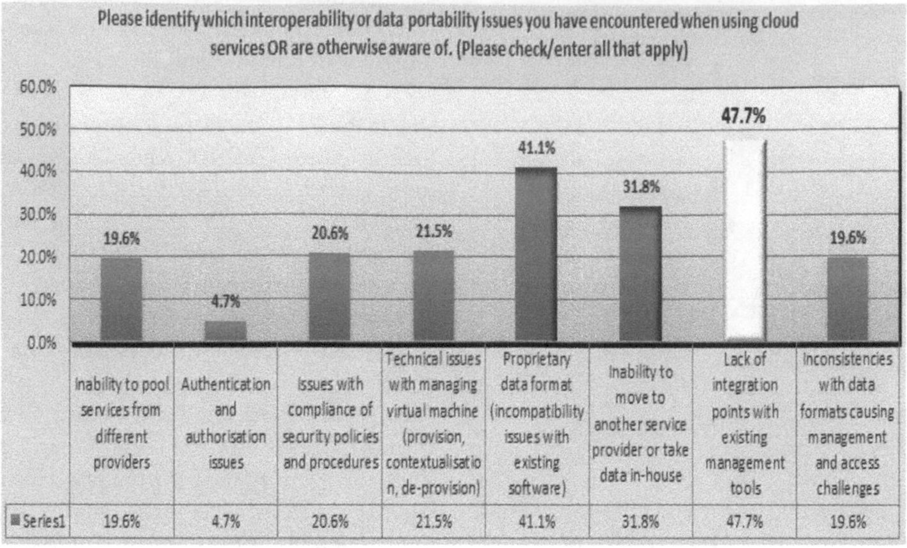

Fig. 10 Practical challenges of vendor lock-in in cloud migration

connection, one possible strategy will require decision-makers to possess a comprehensive understanding of the heterogeneity that exist between cloud semantics and the cloud interfaces. This often requires an awareness of the commonalities (i.e. complexities and dependencies) among services offered by cloud providers and standards used. By clearly understanding this, organisations will realise how the cloud's loose structure can affect data/application movability and security of data sent in it. This can be done by having an in-depth understanding of how data and application components are handled and transmitted in the cloud environment. When this is well understood and harnessed (at pre contractual phase), the benefits to the organisations become apparent (at post migration phase). Additionally, enterprises can be more interoperable and avoid vendor lock-in strategically by selecting vendors, platforms, or services that support more standards and protocols (as further discussed below in Section 4.1.3). This is essentially important in the vendor selection process as it enables organisations to maintain a favourable mix of cloud providers and internal support. These strategies can help

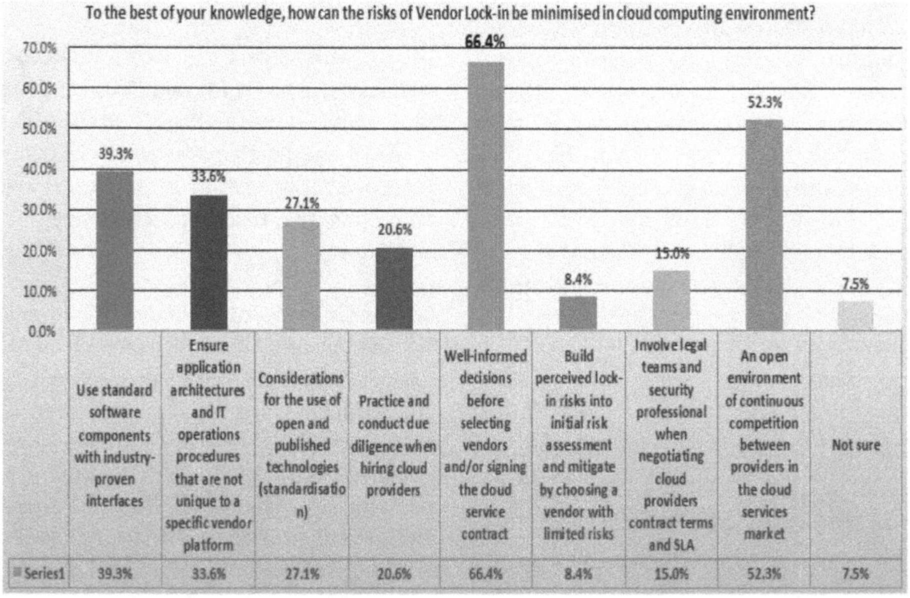

Fig. 11 Current best practice for mitigating cloud lock-in risks

organisations to form a plan for an efficient and effective migration and adoption process. Actually, having a clear understanding of the disparity between cloud semantics and service interfaces offered by different cloud vendors can help significantly to reduce the effects of vendor lock-in.

Substantial training and stakeholder engagement is necessary to develop an understanding and agree solutions on specific lock-in concerns [43–45]. Otherwise, cloud services offered to enterprises may not be properly assessed for potential lock-in risks before decisions are made to use the service [46]. Moreover, the results in Fig. 6 indicate a general lack of understanding and awareness of lock-in problem in the cloud. The low response gained from participants who identified over dependence on a single cloud provider (35.1 %) and difficulty to move data back in-house or across to a different cloud provider (28.8 %) platform illustrates the unawareness of practitioners on the potential effect of cloud lock-in problem. To infer from this result, it appears the risk of dependency is a more significant barrier than data lock-in. This seems counter intuitive considering the practical challenges associated with the data lock-in when extending the use of cloud in the enterprise. However, the probable explanation is that presently most organisations are too reliant on cloud providers for operational and technical support [47], thus they fail to fully prepare to deal with unexpected and undesirable data lock-in issues in the cloud (referring to Fig. 10). As pointed out by Bradshaw et al. [28], lock-in will become more of an issue as the cloud computing market matures. In agreement, Lipton in [48] admits that the complexity and cost of switching (or porting) a cloud service to a different provider is often under-appreciated until it is too late. Therefore it can be claimed that as long as corporate data is not locked-in moving to another cloud provider is just a matter of enduring a switching cost. Such cost can be reduced by employing best practices such as choosing cloud providers that support: (i) the use of standardised APIs wherever possible; (ii) wide range of programming languages, application runtimes and middleware; (iii) as well as ways to archive and deploy libraries of virtual machine images and preconfigured appliances. Overall, these findings suggest respondents do not currently have sufficient understanding on possible technical and non-technical issues of lock-in that can occur in the cloud environment. Thus, it is recommended that organisations remain meticulous when making decisions towards the selection of vendors, taking into consideration potential difficulties associated with switching vendors. However, it is probable for organisations to suffer financial loss if they did not make a strategically correct vendor selection decision from the very onset.

Well-informed decision making

The study has found that for UK organisations, when it comes to evaluating the business risks of vendor lock-in for or against cloud migration, surprisingly, a vast majority (66.4 %) of respondents said making well-informed decisions before selecting vendors and/or signing the cloud service contract is an extremely important part of the decision-making process (refer to Fig. 11). This signifies that as cloud computing becomes more widely used for various applications across different industry sector[s] and size[s], UK businesses are finding it extremely important to understand ways to maximize benefits and minimize the risks of lock-in. In essence, this is particularly important given the plethora of vendors in the market place today, with each offering businesses proprietary cloud-based services and contracts that have different specification (and legal agreements). In regard to the interpretation of this finding, our study suggests that the vetting process for selecting vendors is a critical aspect for effective cloud migration with minimized risk of lock-in. Moreover, such finding exemplify the need for organisations to look beyond the vendor selection phase, and focus on constantly monitoring any development or changes in the cloud that may impact data security or hinder interoperability and portability – thus facilitating a lock-in situation. However, the findings (in Fig. 11) also reveal a gap in understanding, regarding how organisations should manage the risks of vendor lock-in. A sign of lack of understanding is explained by a smaller percentage (8.4 %) of participants identifying the need to build perceived lock-in risks into initial risk assessment. This is quite enlightening, in spite of the relevance of this strategy in the vendor selection phase. Possible interpretation of these may be attributed to the general lack of understanding and experience (on the part of IT and business managers) in respect of technical aspects of complex distributed cloud-based solutions.

Standards and cloud-based solutions

The impact caused by vendor lock-in problem due to lack of standards is what enterprises should be wary about when considering migration to cloud computing [29]. Despite the number of studies in recent years underlining the high relevance of standards in cloud computing, unfortunately this study reveals that most UK organisations still lack a comprehensive understanding on the importance of standards in minimising lock-in risks. In fact, as pointed out by [49], there are two ways a business can achieve the full potential of cloud computing (i) either by changing providers according to their needs (ii) prioritising or simply combining different solutions to get the best of the breed services. However, this will require standards and interoperability to be supported by all providers, but it is often not the case. An informative example in this context is seen in research in [50], arguing that many cloud providers are concerned with the loss of customer that may come with standardisation initiatives which may flatten profits, and do not regard the solution favourable. Based on our research findings, from a business perspective, we suggest the following as key measures to improve customer retention and engender trust in enterprise cloud migration: 1) the quality of service (QoS) guarantee, 2) data protection and metadata ownership, 3) contract termination, as well as 4) data export functionality. Furthermore, as discussed in our previous study [4], in the absence of standardisation, UK businesses willing to outsource and combine a range of services from different cloud providers to achieve maximum efficiency, irrefutably, will experience difficulty when trying to get their in-house systems to interact with the cloud. Likewise, the lack of standardisation also brings disadvantages, when migration, integration or exchange of computer resources is required. This is consistent with the research findings presented in this paper (see Fig. 10). Unsurprisingly these issues were identified from a business perspective, considering the important role of standards in at least mitigating such concerns. Hence, business stakeholders' should be aware that decisions to adopt or move resources to the cloud require adequate risk analysis for potential lock-in. Based on this analysis and the evidence in Fig. 10, we believe there are opportunities that exist for the regulatory and standard bodies to take the necessary action. One potential solution would be to standardise the APIs in such a way that businesses (or SaaS developers for example) could deploy services and data across multiple cloud providers. Thus, the failure of a single cloud provider/vendor would not take all copies of corporate data with it.

Standard initiatives Cloud-specific standards are regularly proposed as a way to mitigate vendor lock-in and achieve portability and interoperability [50]. It is expressed in [51] that many providers are concerned with customer churn rate that may come with standardisation. But according to [52], unless there is a well-accepted and widely used standard, it remains a questionable solution. Therefore as a partially adopted standard would represent a poor solution [53], many cloud vendors now support the creation and adoption of new standards by proposing them to standardisation groups. Clear examples of such cloud-specific standards are OASIS CAMP [54] for PaaS and TOSCA [55] for IaaS. Both specifications aim at enhancing the portability and interoperability of applications across different clouds. We review the two OASIS cloud-specific standards (TOSCA and CAMP) and their potential for dealing with the lock-in problem.

TOSCA The Topology and Orchestration Specification for Cloud Applications (TOSCA) [55], is an emerging standard that enhances service and application portability in a vendor-neutral ecosystem. TOSCA specification describes a meta-model for defining IT services. This metamodels defines both the structure of a service (topology model of a service) and its operational aspects (such as how to deploy, terminate, and manage this service). Service templates are interpreted by a TOSCA-compliant environment (e.g. OpenTOSCA [56]), which operates the cloud services and manages their instances [54].

Managing cloud services requires extensive, mostly manual effort by the customers. Further, important cloud properties (such as self-service and rapid elasticity) can only be realised if service management is automated. In this aspect, TOSCA allows application developers and operators (DevOps) to model management best practices and reoccurring tasks explicitly into so-called plans (i.e. Workflows). TOSCA plans use existing workflow languages such as Business Process Model and Notation (BPMN) [57, 58] or the Business Process Execution Language (BPEL) [59]. To increase portability, TOSCA allows service creators to gather into plans those activities necessary to deploy, manage, and terminate the described cloud service. TOSCA also enables a cloud service creator to provide the same plan or implementation artefact in different languages (e.g. a plan can include the same functionality twice – in BPEL and BPMN). An application ported to the cloud using TOSCA can be composed of services provided by different cloud providers and a user can decide to a specific service with a similar one from a different vendor.

CAMP Cloud Application Management for Platforms (CAMP) is an Oasis cloud-specific standard designed to ease the management of applications across platforms offered as a service (PaaS) [54]. The CAMP standard defines a self-service management API that a PaaS offering presents to the consumer of the platform. The specified CAMP API provides a resource model to describe the main components of any platform offer. For instance, independent software vendors can exploit this interface to create tools and services that communicate with any CAMP-compliant cloud platform via the defined interfaces. Likewise, cloud vendors can also leverage these interfaces to develop new PaaS offerings, or adapt the existing ones, which would be compliant with independent tools. Thus, cloud users save time when deploying applications across multiple cloud platforms.

At present, the effort of deploying applications with vendor-specific tools across multiple PaaS cloud platforms is a non-trivial task. Developers and system operators often face the barrier of redeploying applications to other providers' platform because tools are incompatible. However, this can be simplified using the CAMP interface common to both source and target platforms. To simplify the deployment efforts and support migration across multiple cloud platforms, CAMP defines the Platform Deployment Package (PDP). A PDP is an archive containing a plan file together with application content files such as web archives, database schemas, scripts, source code, localization bundles, icons etc. This archive can be used to move an application and its components from platform to platform, or between a development environment and an operative target platform.

Portable hybrid IT environment

To infer from discussion in the preceding section, the vendor lock-in risk is a valid concern for organisations migrating to the cloud. Considering that lock-in is undesirable, and cannot be eradicated, then how can businesses mitigate its associated risks when migrating to the cloud? From a portability perspective, it becomes critical that organisations' data is sharable between providers, since without the ability to port data or application, it would become simply impossible to switch cloud service providers at all [60, 61]. Cloud portability is a salient consideration to enable organisations migrate a cloud-deployed asset to a different provider and it is a direct benefit of overcoming vendor lock-in [62]. Generally, reconfiguration of systems and applications to achieve interoperability is time/resource consuming and may require a considerable amount of expertise, which could be challenging for some organisations. Therefore, from a business perspective, portability should be seen as a key aspect to consider when selecting cloud providers as it can both help mitigate lock-in risks, and deliver business benefits. This means allowing applications, systems and data components to continue to work correctly when moved between cloud providers' (hardware and/or software) environments [35]. Indeed, the need for organisations to easily switch cloud providers with their data alongside have been a consistent theme throughout the discussion presented hitherto.

To expatiate on the question stated above, it is helpful to view the situation from a business perspective after deploying a SaaS cloud service such as CRM (which according to Fig. 7, 52 % of organisations have already adopted the cloud model). Suppose these organisations use the SaaS CRM and over time, perhaps, the terms of use or the price of the cloud-based CRM service become less attractive, compared to other SaaS providers or with the use of an in-house CRM solution. If the organisation decides to change providers for whatever reason, data portability aspects must be considered. For SaaS cloud services, data formats and contents are handled by the service provider thereby making data portability a major consideration. The issue of importance in a SaaS-level migration is the compatibility of the functional interface presented to end-users and any API made available to other customer applications. In order to alleviate this problem, the APIs made available by the SaaS service should be interoperable with the interface provided by the on-premise application or data that is being replaced. On the other hand, the data handled by one vendor's software should be importable by the second vendor's software, which implies both applications have to support the common format. Standard APIs for various application types will also be required. If the APIs are not interoperable, any customer application or data using the APIs will need to be changed as part of the migration process.

Data portability is usually of most concern in a SaaS, since in these services, the content, data schemas and storage format are under the control of the cloud service provider. The customer will need to understand how the data can be imported into the service and exported from the service. Further, SaaS applications also present interoperability barriers. The lack of adoption of standard APIs for SaaS applications makes switching from one SaaS application to another difficult as it involves a change in the interface. This also applies to any application or system belonging to the cloud service customers that use APIs offered by the SaaS application. Data synchronization is another concern, encountered in cloud interoperability and not in data portability [63]. To further substantiate this argument, we elucidate on the need for a portable hybrid environment by highlighting two main categories of portability scenarios encountered in current cloud service market: 1) porting legacy applications or data; and 2) porting cloud native applications or data. In scenario 1, due to dependence on particular technologies and data organisation, the legacy software assets currently require a significant amount of effort to be invested in porting them into the cloud environment. Whereas in scenario 2, even when applications and data are written from scratch for a cloud environment, they are usually locked and targeted for a specific cloud [63]. Thus, the effort of porting in a different cloud is usually a onetime exercise [63]. However, in both scenarios, the main problem is that there must be a capability to retrieve customer data from the source cloud service and also a capability to import customer data into the target cloud service. Thus, data portability is based on import and export functionality from cloud data services for data structures. This is commonly done through the existence of some API (or web interface) associated with the cloud service – it may be a generic API or a specific API, unique to the cloud service.

In light of such challenges, [64] claims that ensuring data portability is a major challenge for enterprises due to the large number of competing vendors for data storage and retrieval. The ability to move data also emerges as a management issue for cloud computing. Therefore, in response to the question of data movability, it is important to note that the API used for the source service may not be the same as the API used for the target service and that different tooling may be required in each case. The main aspects of data portability are the syntax and semantics of the transferred data. The syntax of the data should ideally be the same for the source service and the target service. However, if the syntax does not match (i.e., the source may use JSON syntax, but the target may use XML), it may be possible to map the data using commonly available tools. If the semantics of the transferred data does not match between the source and target services, then data portability is likely to be more difficult or even impossible. However, this might be achieved by the source service supplying the data in exactly the format that is accepted by the target service. Therefore, on a long term, achieving data portability will depend on the standardization of import and export functionality of data and its adoption by the providers. The aim is to minimize the human efforts in re-design and re-deployment of application and data when moving from one cloud to another. To this end, it becomes vital that any enterprise cloud migration project can be carried out without any disruption to data availability since data is an organisation's most critical, ubiquitous, and essential business asset [29].

Observations

This paper confirms that UK organisations are increasingly adopting cloud services, and it also reveals that they have been progressively migrating services perceived as non-mission critical (i.e. where lock-in and security risks seem lower) such as general purpose applications suites, email and massaging applications. This strategy used allows the organisations to get a feel for how the cloud environment works before fully committing themselves. However, this is generally not the case for organisations surveyed. A lesser minority (see Fig. 7) seem to have adopted core systems in the cloud (e.g. ERP and CRM), including accounting and finance applications. At present, as indicated by the Cloud Industry Forum [39], cloud providers or vendors are better placed, if they ensure such capabilities like the trial or "test and see" strategy (whether completely free or paid for time limited pilot) is made available within their go-to-market strategy. It is worth underlining that, free of charge or low cost does not necessary mean free of lock-in risks or low proprietary lock-in risk. Organisations must be cautious of potential areas of lock-in traps and take adequate measures to mitigate their exposure; e.g. choice of operating environment, programming models, API stack, data portability etc. Further, businesses should take heed of other legal, regulatory, or reputational risks that may exist. This is vitally important if the data involved is not just for testing, but constitutes real corporate data, perhaps even confidential or personal data. It is interesting to note that 28 % of organisations surveyed have already adopted the cloud model for hosting accounting and finance applications (refer to Fig. 7).

On a conclusive note, it is believed that the discussions presented herein, above all, indicate hypothetically that vendor lock-in risks will reduce cloud migration, which in turn affects the widespread adoption of cloud computing across organisations (small or large). Thus an emerging research agenda arises as to investigate: 1) ways to come up with multijurisdictional laws to support interoperability and portability of data across cloud providers platform, along with effective data privacy and security policies; and 2) novel ideas of avoiding vendor dependency on the infrastructure layer, platform, and through to the application layer as lock- cannot be completely eliminated, but can be mitigated. However, these require, not just tools and processes, but also strategic approaches – attitude, confidence, comfort, and enhanced knowledge of how complex distributed cloud-based services work. Sometimes the inhibitor to cloud adoption and migration in most organisations, in principle, are the attitude, knowledge, and confidence of the paramount decision makers. Thus, for most organisations today, the challenge is clear that they simply do not understand potential effect of lock-in to the business. While the business benefits of cloud computing are compelling, organisations must realise that achieving these benefits are consistent with ensuring the risks of vendor lock-in and security implication of such risk is clearly understood upfront. When identified, such risks should be mitigated with appropriate business continuity plans or vendor selection, prior to migration to the cloud.

Potential of DevOps tools for avoiding vendor lock-in

Issues with cloud lock-in surpass those of technical incompatibility and data integration. Mitigating cloud lock-in risks cannot be guaranteed with a selection of individual open (technology-centric) solutions or vendors. Instead, the management and operation of cloud services to avoid lock-in should be addressed at a standardised technology-independent manner. In this respect, we present a concise discussion on the potential of DevOps [65] and of tools (such as Chef, Juju and Puppet) that support interoperable management.

DevOps is an emerging paradigm [66] to eliminate the split and barrier between developers and operations personnel. Automation underlies all the practices that constitute DevOps. The philosophy behind DevOps is to bring agile methodologies into IT infrastructure and service management [65]. This is achieved by implementing the concept of "Infrastructure as Code" (IaC) using configuration management tooling. An automation platform is what provides the ability to describe an infrastructure as code. IaC automations are designed to be repeatable, making the system converge to a desired state starting from arbitrary states [67, 68]. In practice, this is often centred on the release management process (i.e., the managed delivery of code into production), as this can be a source of conflict between these two groups often due to different objectives [68]. DevOps approaches can be combined with cloud computing to enable on-demand provisioning of underlying resources (such as virtual servers, database, application middleware and storage) in a self-service manner. These resources can be configured and managed using DevOps tools and artifacts. As a result, end-to-end deployment automation is effectively enabled by using the DevOps approaches in cloud computing environments [69]. Tools are emerging that address building out a consistent application or service model to reduce the proprietary lock-in risks stemming from customized scripting while improving deployment success due to more-predictable configurations. Today, several applications provisioning solution exists that enable developers and administrators to declaratively specify deployment artefacts and dependencies to allow for repeatable and managed resource provisioning [56]. Below, we review some DevOps tools among the currently available ones that may help enterprises simplify their application release circle.

Chef Chef is a configuration management framework written in Ruby [70]. Chef uses an internal Domain Specific Language or DSL to express configurations. Configuration definitions (i.e. ruby-scripts) and supporting resources (e.g. installation files) in Chef are called recipes. These recipes are basically scripts written in DSL to express the target state of a system [71]. Chef manages so called nodes. A node is an element of enterprise infrastructure, such as a server which can be physical, virtual, in the cloud, or even a container instance running a Chef client [72]. Chef provides APIs to manage resources on a machine in a declarative fashion. Chef recipes are typically declarative (resources which define a desired state) but can include imperative statements as well. Combining a Chef system together with cloud infrastructure automation framework makes it easy to deploy servers and applications to any physical, virtual, or cloud location. Using Chef, an organization can configure IT from the operating system up; applying system updates, modifying configuration files, restarting any necessary system services, applying and configuring middleware and applications.

Puppet Puppet is an open source configuration and management tool implemented in Ruby [47] that allows expressing in a custom declarative language using a model-based approach [73]. Puppet enables deploying infrastructure changes to multiple nodes simultaneously. It functions the same way as a deployment manager, but instead of deploying applications, it deploys infrastructure changes. Puppet employs a declarative model with explicit dependency management. One of the key features of Puppet is reusability. Modules can then be reused on different machines with different operating systems. Moreover, modules can be combined into configuration stacks.

Juju Juju is a cloud configuration, deployment and monitoring environment that deploy services across multiple cloud or physical servers and orchestrate those services [74]. Activities within a service deployed by Juju are orchestrated by a Juju charm, which is a deployable service or application component [75].

In summary, as applications evolve to function in the cloud, organizations must reconsider how they develop, deploy, and manage them. While cloud computing is heavily used to provide the underlying resource, our review shows that DevOps tools and artefacts can be used to configure and manage these resources. As a result, end-to-end deployment automation is efficiently enabled by employing DevOps approaches in cloud environments. But, cloud providers such as Amazon and cloud frameworks such as OpenStack provide cost-effective and fast ways to deploy and run applications. However, there is a large variety of deployment tools and techniques available [76]. They differ in various dimensions, most importantly in the metamodels behind the different approaches. Some use application stacks (e.g., AWS OpsWorks2 or Ubuntu Juju) or infrastructure, others use lists of scripts (e.g., Chef run) or even PaaS-centric application package descriptions such as Cloud Foundry manifests. This makes it challenging to combine different approaches and especially to orchestrate artefacts published by communities affiliated with the different tools, techniques, and providers. Nevertheless, these solutions are highly desirable because some communities share a lot of reusable artefacts such as portable scripts or container images as open-source software [77]. Prominent examples are Chef Cookbooks, Puppet modules, Juju charms, or Docker images. Adopting a configuration management tool implies a significant investment in time and/or money [78]. Nevertheless, before making such an investment, an informed choice based on objective criteria is the best insurance that an enterprise has picked the right tool for its environment, as the focus is on deploying predefined application stacks across several (virtual or physical) machines.

Discussion and conclusion

In this paper a comprehensive analysis of vendor lock-in problems was discussed and the impact to companies as a result of migration to cloud computing was explored. A survey was conducted and revealed that the cloud paradigm has greatly impacted on many organisations subsequent to migrating IT and business applications to the cloud due to vendor lock-in. In fact, the study has shown that, while organisations are eager to adopt cloud computing due to its benefits, there is equally an urgent need for avoiding vendor lock-in risks. Moreover, the results of our study have highlighted customers' lack of awareness of proprietary standards which prohibit interoperability and portability when procuring services from vendors. The complexity and cost of switching providers is often under-appreciated until implementation. Business decision makers are often unaware of how to tackle this issue. Our findings offer cloud computing consumers, service providers, and industry practitioners a better understanding of the risk of lock-in embedded in the complex, technologically interdependent and heterogeneous cloud systems. In this respect, our research points to the need for more sophisticated policy approaches that take a system-wide perspective to alleviate the current vendor lock-in problem which affects interoperability and portability. Furthermore, our findings show that within many organisations in the study, a lack of clarity on the problem space of vendor lock-in still pervades. This lack of knowledge poses a significant barrier to obscure the potential effect the vendor lock-in problem could have on enterprise applications migrated to and operating in cloud platforms. Hence, to be protected against such risks when migrating to the cloud environment, companies require standards, portability, and interoperability to be supported by providers. However, this is currently difficult to achieve as explored in this paper. Fundamentally, the difficulty is attributed to the vendors' APIs which control how cloud services are harnessed, as cloud APIs are not yet standardized, making it complex for customers to change providers. Some cloud providers are concerned with the loss of customers that may come with standardisation initiatives which may then flatten their profits and do not regard the solution favourable. Therefore, we propose the following strategic approaches to address the issues: (i) create awareness of the complexities and dependencies that exist among cloud-based solutions; (ii) assess providers' technology implementation such as API and contract for potential areas of lock-in; (iii) select vendors, platforms, or services that support more standardised formats and protocols based on standard data structures; and (iv) ensure there is sufficient portability. In our future work, we will explore interoperability and portability constraints which affect enterprise application migration and adoption of SaaS clouds.

Competing interests

The authors declare that they have no competing interests.

Authors' contributions

All listed authors made substantive intellectual contributions to the research and manuscript. JOM was responsible for the overall vendor lock-in research including drafting the manuscript, analysis and interpretation of study results. RS, FT and JOM contributed to the design of methodology used. RS and FT participated in the critical and technical revisions of the paper including editing the final version, also helping with the details for preparing the paper to be published. RS and FT coordinated and supervised the project related to the paper and also gave final approval of the version to be published. All authors read and approved final manuscript.

Authors' information

Justice Opara-Martins is a PhD candidate at Bournemouth University where he graduated with an MSc in Wireless and Mobile Networks. He holds a BSc (Hons.) in Information and Communication Technology. He is a member of the British Computer Society (BCS), IBM Academic Initiative and Association for Project Managers (APM). His research interests include cloud computing, virtualization and distributed systems.
Reza Sahandi completed his PhD at Bradford University in the United Kingdom in 1978. He has been a senior academic at various Universities in the United Kingdom for many years. He is currently Associate Dean at Bournemouth University. His research areas include multimedia and network systems, wireless remote patient monitoring and cloud computing.
Feng Tian received the PhD degree from Xi'an Jiaotong University, China. Currently he is an Associate Professor Bournemouth University (BU), United Kingdom. He was an Assistant Professor in Nanyang Technological University in Singapore before joining BU in 2009. His current research interests include computer graphics, computer animation, augmented reality, image processing and cloud computing.

Acknowledgements

The research leading to these results is supported by Bournemouth University (DEC) Doctoral Scholarship funding. Additionally, the authors would like to thank the Faculty of Science and Technology for providing additional financial support to enhance the quality of this manuscript.

References

1. Andrikopoulos V, Binz T, Leymann F, Strauch S (2013) How to Adapt Applications for the Cloud Environment: Challenges and Solutions in Migrating Applications to the Cloud. Springer Comput J 95(6):493–535
2. Armbrust M, Fox A, Griffith R, Joseph AD, Katz R, Konwinski A, Lee G, Patterson D, Rabkin A, Stoica I, Zaharia M (2009) Above the Clouds: A Berkeley View of Cloud Computing. Commun ACM 53(4):50–58
3. Buyya R, Yeo CS, Venugopal S, Broberg J, Brandic I (2009) Cloud computing and emerging IT platforms: Vision, hype, and reality for delivering computing as the 5th utility. Futur Gener Comput Syst 25(6):599–616
4. Sahandi R, Alkhalil A, Opara-Martins J (2013) Cloud Computing from SMEs Perspective: A Survey Based Investigation. J Inf Technol Manag Publ Assoc Manag XXIV(1):1–12, ISSN #1042-1319
5. Loutas N, Kamateri E, Bosi F, Tarabanis KA (2011) Cloud Computing Interoperability: The State of Play. In: CloudCom., pp 752–757

6. Toosi AN, Calheiros RN, Buyya R (2013) Interconnected Cloud Computing Environments: Challenges, Taxonomy and Survey. ACM Computing Survey 5:Article A
7. Di Martino, B. Cretella, G. Esposito, A. (2015) Classification and Positioning of Cloud Definitions and Use Case Scenarios for Portability and Interoperability, in Future Internet of Things and Cloud (FiCloud), 3rd International Conference on, pp.538–544, doi: 10.1109/FiCloud.2015.119
8. Di Martino, B. Cretella, G. Esposito, A. Sperandeo, R.G., (2014) Semantic Representation of Cloud Services: A Case Study for Microsoft Windows Azure, in Intelligent Networking and Collaborative Systems (INCoS), 2014 International Conference on, pp.647–652, doi: 10.1109/INCoS.2014.76
9. Satzger B, Hummer W, Inzinger W (2013) Winds of Change: From Vendor Lock-in to the Meta Cloud. IEEE Internet Comput 1:69–73
10. Binz T, Breiter G, Leyman F, Spatzier T (2012) Portable cloud services using tosca. IEEE Internet Comput 3:80–85
11. Petcu D, Macariu G, Panic S, Craciun C (2013) Portable cloud applications-from theory to practice. Futur Gener Comput Syst 29(6):1417–1430, https://doi.org/10.1016/j.future.2012.01.009
12. Ardagna, D., Di Nitto, E., Casale, G., Petcu, D., Mohagheghi, P., Mosser, S., Matthews, P., Gericke, A., Ballagny, C., D'Andria, F. and Nechifor, C.S., (2012) Modaclouds: A model-driven approach for the design and execution of applications on multiple clouds. In Proceedings of the 4th International Workshop on Modelling in Software Engineering (pp. 50–56). IEEE Press.
13. The OpenGroup Consortium. Available from: http://www.opengroup.org
14. Ferry, N. Hui Song Rossini, A Chauvel, F. Solberg, A. (2014) CloudMF: Applying MDE to Tame the Complexity of Managing Multi-cloud Applications, in Utility and Cloud Computing (UCC), 2014 IEEE/ACM 7th International Conference on, pp.269–277, doi:10.1109/UCC.2014.36
15. Silva, G.C, Louis M. R, and Radu, C. (2013) A Systematic Review of Cloud Lock-in Solutions. Cloud Computing Technology and Science (CloudCom), IEEE 5th International Conference on. Vol. 2. IEEE.
16. Edmonds, A. Metsch, T. Papaspyrou, A. Richardson, A. (2012) Toward an Open Cloud Standard, in Internet Computing, IEEE, vol.16, no.4, pp.15–25 doi: 10.1109/MIC.2012.65
17. Toosi, A. Rodrigo N. C, and Buyya, R. (2014) Interconnected Cloud Computing Environments: Challenges, Taxonomy, and Survey. 47, 1, Article 7 47 pages. http://dx.doi.org/10.1145/2593512
18. Behrens, P, (2015) The Ordoliberal Concept of 'Abuse' of a Dominant Position and its Impact on Article 102 TFEU. Nihoul/Takahashi, Abuse Regulation in Competition Law, Proceedings of the 10th ASCOLA Conference Tokyo 2015, Forthcoming. Available at SSRN: http://ssrn.com/abstract=2658045
19. Leymann F et al (2011) Moving Applications to the Cloud: An Approach Based on Application Model Enrichment. Int'l J Cooperative Information Systems 20(3):307–356
20. Shan C, Heng C, Xianjun Z (2012) Inter-cloud operations via NGSON. IEEE Commun Mag 50(1):82–89, January
21. Toivonen, M., 2013. Cloud Provider Interoperability and Customer Clock-In. In *Proceedings of the seminar* (No. 58312107, pp. 14–19). Available from: https://helda.helsinki.fi/bitstream/handle/10138/42910/cbse13_proceedings.pdf?sequence=2#page=17
22. Moreno-Vozmediano R, Montero R, Llorente I (2012) Key Challenges in Cloud Computing to Enable the Future Internet of Services, IEEE Internet Computing., 18 May, Available from: http://doi.ieeecomputersociety.org/10.1109/MIC.2012.69
23. Michael A, Armando F, Rean G, Anthony DJ, Randy HK, Andrew K, Gunho L, David AP, Ariel R, Ion S, Matei Z (2010) A view of cloud computing. Commun ACM 53(4):50–58
24. Sitaram D, Manjunath G (2012) Moving To the Cloud: Developing Apps in the New World of Cloud Computing. Elsevier, USA
25. Loutas N, Peristeras V, Bouras T, Kamateri E, Zeginis D, Tarabanis K (2010) Towards a Reference Architecture for Semantically Interoperable Clouds. In: IEEE Second International Conference on Cloud Computing Technology and Science., pp 143–150
26. Rodero-Merino L, Vaquero LM, Gil V, Galán F, Fontán J, Montero RS, Llorente IM (2010) From infrastructure delivery to service management in clouds. Futur Gener Comput Syst 26(8):1226–1240
27. Petcu D, Vasilakos AV (2014) Portability in clouds: approaches and research opportunities. Scalable Comput Practice Experience 15(3):251–270
28. Bradshaw D, Folco G, Cattaneo G, Kolding M, (2012) Quantitative estimates of the demand for cloud computing in Europe and the likely barriers to up-take. IDC Interim Tech. Report. SMART 2011/0045. http://cordis.europa.eu/fp7/ict/ssai/docs/study45-d2-interim-report.pdf Accessed 29 Dec 2014
29. Opara-Martins J, Sahandi R, Tian F (2014) Critical review of vendor lock-in and its impact on adoption of cloud computing', International Conference on Information Society (i-Society), pp.92-97, doi: 10.1109/i-Society.2014.7009018
30. Badger L, Grance T, Patt-Corner R, Voas J (2011) Cloud Computing Synopsis and Recommendations [draft] (Special Publication 800-146). National Institute of Standards and Technology. http://csrc.nist.gov/publications/drafts/800-146/Draft-NIST-SP800-146.pdf Accessed 24 Jan 2015
31. Ahronovitz M et al. (2010) Cloud Computing Use Cases: Introducing Service Level Agreements. Use Cases Discussion Group, White Paper V4.0. http://www.cloud-council.org/Cloud_Computing_Use_Cases_Whitepaper-4_0.pdf Accessed 8 Feb 2015
32. Liu X, Ye H (2008) A Sustainable Service-Oriented B2C Framework for Small Businesses. In 4th IEEE International Symposium on Service Oriented Systems Engineering (SOSE'08), Taiwan, December.
33. Miranda J, Guillen J, Murillo J (2012) Identifying Adaptation Needs to Avoid the Vendor Lock-in Effect in the Deployment of Cloud ServiceBased Applications (SBAs). WAS4FI I-Mashups September 19 Bertinoro, Italy.
34. Petcu D (2011) Portability and Interoperability between Clouds: Challenges and Case Study. In: Towards a Service-Based Internet, vol 6994. Springer, Berlin Heidelberg, pp 62–74
35. Lewis GA (2013) Role of standards in cloud-computing interoperability. In: 46th Hawaii International Conference on System Sciences (HICSS)., pp 1652–1661
36. Hogan M, Liu F S A, Tong J (2011) NIST Cloud Computing Standards Roadmap. NIST Special Publication 500-291, July. http://www.nist.gov/itl/cloud/upload/NIST_SP-500-291_Jul5A.pdf Accessed 7 Jan2015
37. NVivo qualitative data analysis software; QSR International Pty Ltd. Version 8, 2008.
38. Survey Monkey, (2014) Online Survey Development Tool. https://www.surveymonkey.com Accessed 17 Sept 2014
39. Alkhalil A, Sahandi R, John D (2013) Migration to Cloud Computing-The Impact on IT Management and Security. In 1st International Workshop on Cloud Computing and Information Security, Atlantis Press.
40. Cloud Industry Forum (2014) The Normalisation of Cloud in a Hybrid IT market – UK Cloud Adoption Snapshot & Trends for 2015. Cloud UK, Paper 14. http://www.aspect.com/globalassets/images/uk-documents/aspect—cif-wp.pdf Accessed 17 Nov 2014
41. KPMG (2013) Breaking through the Cloud Adoption Barriers. Cloud Providers Survey https://www.kpmg.com/LU/en/IssuesAndInsights/Articlespublications/Documents/breaking-through-the-cloud-adoption-barriers.pdf Accessed 24 Nov 2014
42. Dubey A, Wagle D (2007) Delivering software as a service. The McKinsey Quarterly (May), pp. 1–12
43. Premkumar G, Michael P (1995) Adoption of computer aided software engineering (CASE) technology: an innovation adoption perspective. SIGMIS Database 26(2-3):105–124
44. Eder L, Igbaria M (2001) Determinants of intranet diffusion and infusion. Omega 29(3):233–242
45. Daylami N, Ryan T, Olfman L, Shayo C (2005) System sciences. HICSS '05, Proceedings of the 38th Annual Hawaii International Conference, Island of Hawaii, 3-6 January.
46. T. Binz, F. Leymann, and D. Schumm (2012) "CMotion: A Framework for Migration of Applications into and between Clouds," Proc. Int'l Conf. Service-Oriented Computing and Applications, IEEE Press, pp. 1–4.
47. Dutta A, Peng GCA, Choudhary A (2013) Risks in enterprise cloud computing: the perspective of IT experts. J Comput Inf Syst 53(4):39–48
48. Lipton P (2013) Escaping Vendor Lock-in with TOSCA, an Emerging Cloud Standard for Portability, CA Technology Exchange 4, 1
49. Leimbach T, Hallinan D, Bachlechner D, Weber A, Jaglo M, Hennen L, Nielsen R O, Nentwich M, StrauB S, Lynn T, Hunt G (2014) Potential and Impacts of Cloud Computing Services and Social Network Websites. Publication of Science and Technology Options Assessment. http://www.europarl.europa.eu/RegData/etudes/etudes/join/2014/513546/IPOL-JOIN_ET(2014)513546_EN.pdf Accessed 14 Nov 2014
50. Govindarajan A, Lakshmanan L (2010) Overview of Cloud Standards. Springer Computer Communications and Networks Journal, London, pp 77–89
51. Petcu D (2011) Portability and interoperability between clouds: Challenges and case study. In: Towards a Service-Based Internet, vol. 6994 LNCS. Springer Berlin Heidelberg, Poland, pp 62–74

52. Lewis, G (2013) Role of standards in Cloud Computing Interoperability. In: 4th Hawaii International Conference on System Sciences Jan, pp. 1652–1661.
53. Shan, C. Heng, and Z. Xianjun (2012) Inter-cloud operations via NGSON. In: IEEE Communications Magazine, vol. 50, no. 1, pp. 82–89.
54. OASIS Cloud Application Management for Platforms, version 1.0. (2012) Available from: https://www.oasis-open.org/committees/download.php/47278/CAMP-v1.0.pdf
55. OASIS Topology and Orchestration Specification for Cloud Applications (TOSCA) Version 1.0, Committee Specification Draft 04 (2012).
56. OpenTOSCA (2015) Available from: http://www.iaas.uni-stuttgart.de/OpenTOSCA
57. Breitenbucher, U., Binz, T., Kèpes, K., Kopp, O., Leymann, F., and Wettinger, J. (2014) Combining Declarative and Imperative Cloud Application Provisioning based on TOSCA. In IC2E. IEEE.
58. Business Process Model and Notation (BPMN) Version 2.0. OMG (2011)
59. OASIS (2007) Web Services Business Process Execution Language (BPEL) Version 2.0
60. Parameswaran AV, Chaddha A (2009) Cloud Interoperablility and Standardization. Infosys, SETLabs Briefings 7(7):19–26
61. Cisco Systems, (2010) Planning the Migration of Enterprise Applications to the Cloud. A Guide to your migration Options and Best Practices, Technical report. http://www.cisco.com/en/US/services/ps2961/ps10364/ps10370/ps11104/Migration_of_Enterprise_Apps_to_Cloud_White_Paper.pdf Accessed 1 Dec 2014
62. Mell P, Grance T (2009) The NIST Definition of Cloud Computing, Technical report
63. Petcu D, Vasilakos AV (2014) Portability in clouds: Approaches and research opportunities. Scalable Comput Pract Exp 15(3):251–270. doi:10.12694/scpe.v15i3.1019
64. Buyya R, Ranjan R, Calheiros RN (2010) InterCloud: Utility-oriented federation of cloud computing environments for scaling of application services, Proceedings of the 10th International Conference on Algorithms and Architectures for Parallel Processing (ICA3PP 2010), Busan, South Korea. Springer, Germany, pp 328–336
65. Humble J. and Farley D. (2010) Continuous Delivery: Reliable Software Releases through Build, Test, and Deployment Automation. Addison-Wesley Professional.
66. Wettinger J, Breitenbücher U, Leymann F (2014) DevOp Slang—bridging the gap between development and operations. In: Villari M, Zimmermann W, Lau KK (eds) Service-Oriented and Cloud Computing. Lecture Notes in Computer Science, vol. 8745. Springer, Berlin Heidelberg, pp 108–122
67. Hummer, W, Rosenberg, F., Oliveira, F and Eilam, T., (2013) Automated testing of chef automation script. In: Proceedings of ACM/IFIP/USENIX 14th International Middleware Conference
68. Nelson-Smith, S. (2011) Test-Driven Infrastructure with Chef. O'Reilly.
69. Wettinger J, Gorlach K, Leymann F (2014) Deployment aggregates—a generic deployment automation approach for applications operated in the cloud. In: IEEE 18th International Enterprise Distributed Object Computing Conference Workshops and Demonstrations (EDOCW)., pp 173–180
70. Nelson-Smith, S. (2011). Test-Driven Infrastructure with Chef. O'Reilly Media, Inc.
71. Sabharwal N, Wadhwa M (2014) Automation through Chef Opscode: A Hands-on Approach to Chef
72. Ruby (2016) Available from: https://www.ruby-lang.org/en/
73. Puppet Labs (2015) Open Source Puppet. Available from https://puppetlabs.com/puppet/puppet-open-source
74. Ubuntu Juju (2015) Available from: https://juju.ubuntu.com
75. Wettinger, J., Breitenbücher, U., Leymann, F (2014) Standards-based Devops automation and integration using tosca. In: Proceedings of the 7th International Conference on Utility and Cloud Computing (UCC 2014), pp. 59–68. IEEE Computer Society
76. Gunther, S., Haupt, M., and Splieth, M. (2010) Utilizing Internal Domain-Specific Languages for Deployment and Maintenance of IT Infrastructures. Technical report, Very Large Business Applications Lab Magdeburg, Fakultat fur Informatik, Otto-von-Guericke-Universitat Magdeburg
77. J. Wettinger, V. Andrikopoulos, S. Strauch, and F. Leymann (2013) "Enabling Dynamic Deployment of Cloud Applications Using a Modular and Extensible PaaS Environment," in Proceedings of IEEE CLOUD. IEEE Computer Society, pp. 478–485.
78. Delaet T, Joosen W, Vanbrabant B (2010) A Survey of System Configuration Tools. In: Proceedings of the 24th Large Installations Systems Administration (LISA) conference

7

Energy-efficient service-oriented architecture for mobile cloud handover

Qassim Bani Hani* and Julius P. Dichter

Abstract

Mobile cloud computing uses features to deliver outsourcing data to remotely available mobile devices. However, the flexible nature of the mobile device is a critical challenge for the mobile cloud computing environment. The mobile phone significantly degrades the data transfer performance when initiating the handover process. Thus, an energy-efficient handover process could improve the quality of service (QoS). Here, we introduce a secure energy-efficient and quality-of-service architecture (EEQoSA) for the handover process in the mobile cloud computing environment. The proposed architecture involves four layers: application, the Internet protocol multimedia subsystem (IPMS), communication, and media with connectivity layers.

These four layers collectively handle the energy-efficiency, security and QoS parameters. Existing service-oriented architectures designed for mobile cloud computing are based on the symmetric encryption cryptography to support different media services. However, this approach easily allows an adversary to expose the symmetric key and gain access to private data. Thus, our proposed architecture uses the secure and strong authentication (SSA) process at the IPMS layer by protecting the media services from unauthorized users, as the IPMS is the central layer that could be the entry point for an adversary. Furthermore, to extend the mobile lifetime during the handover process, an energy detection (ED) model is deployed at the communication layer to detect the energy level of the mobile device prior to the handover initialization process. The media with the connectivity layer supports the secure handover process using a priority enforcement module that allows only legitimate users to complete the re-registration process after initiating the handover. Finally, the architecture is tested using the CloudSim simulation environment and validated by a comparison with other known service-oriented architectures.

Keywords: Mobile cloud computing, Efficient handover process, Service-oriented architecture, Energy detection, Secure and Strong authentication priority enforcement module

Introduction

Mobile cloud computing is an evolving platform in which data storage and data handling are performed outside of the mobile device [1]. Mobile cloud applications transport the data through the mobile device into the cloud servers, attracting many mobile subscribers [2]. Mobile cloud computing is promoted as a promising platform to support different media services [3, 4]. Additionally, the use of smartphones has increased the importance of mobile cloud computing considerably, as the data stored on the mobile cloud servers is easily accessible anytime and anywhere except network and services are unattainable. Today, the usage of mobile subscribers continues to increase due to the provision of new exciting features, such as GPS navigation, MP3, MP4, multimedia messaging services, dispatching emergency responders, Bluetooth, built-in projector personal digital assistant functions, streaming video, camcorders, memory card readers, and instant messaging [5, 6]. These additional smartphone features have been utilized to facilitate the acquisition of outsourcing data (e.g., contractual-execution for the exchange of agreed services) from mobile cloud servers. However, mobility is one of the key challenges for mobile cellular phones [7, 8]. This issue is apparent when

* Correspondence: qbanihan@my.bridgeport.edu
Department of Computer Science & Engineering, University of Bridgeport, Bridgeport, CT 06604, USA

a mobile device initiates the handover process, which leads to a reconnection process and in turn to additional energy being consumed. In addition, the data-exchange performance may degrade or be hacked by an attacker because the attacker can install its malicious node into the entry point of the access point (AP) or base station (BS). Thus, the mobility management process should be properly addressed prior to accessing the mobile cloud computing environment [9, 10]. Several mobility management approaches have been proposed to handle the handover process in cloud computing [11–13]. However, these existing approaches still use the traditional methods to obtain the cloud services from the servers. As a result, excess energy consumption and quality of service (QoS) degradation occur.

Handover management and interference mitigation problems for the mobile cloud computing environment were examined in [14]. Thus, a low-complexity management approach is introduced to combine the cloud radio access network with small cells. Fast mobility Internet Protocol version-6 (FMIPv6) was introduced to handle the handover process in mobile cloud computing [15]. The protocol reduced the handover latency and packet loss using buffering and tunneling procedures. As a result, these mechanisms work well in the ad hoc wireless network but could suffer in the mobile cloud computing environment [16–18]. A service-aware location updated paradigm was introduced to identify the frequency and location of mobile devices without using the periodic registration update (PRU) [19]. A service-oriented architecture was introduced for the heterogeneous cloud network to handle the handover management process, which combines the features of cloud computing and the heterogeneous small cell network. However, the architecture particularly focuses on the cloud computing extenuation management process. A robust architecture that can improve the handover process in the mobile cloud computing environment is urgently needed [20]. Furthermore, adversaries attempt to attack sensitive data during the handover process and slow down the services [21, 22]. As a result, the privacy, integrity and authentication of the legitimate users are compromised [23]. Secure packet authentication was introduced to restrict the access of adversaries to mobile cloud computing during the handover process. However, such authentication provides minimal user-privacy support [24]. The architecture attempts to reduce the handover computational cost but not the energy consumption. Existing proposed mechanisms for the handover process in mobile cloud computing focus on reducing the computational cost, flow of the media contents and network connectivity. Hence, the architecture must properly support the energy-efficient handover process while maintaining secure communications and improving the QoS parameters in mobile cloud computing.

Thus, we introduce a state-of-art, service-oriented architecture comprised of four layers: application, the Internet protocol multimedia subsystem (IPMS), communication and media with connectivity. These four layers collectively help the mobile device access the cloud computing resources efficiently. Furthermore, this paper presents a priority enforcement module, which allows only legitimate users to complete the re-registration process after initiating the handoff and thus enables reliable data access and content delivery. A substantial amount of energy and bandwidth are saved through the fast and seamless handoff process. Furthermore, this paper outlines the secure and strong authentication (SSA) to secure the services available on the IPMS layer (e.g., web, videoconference, video-on-demand, Internet, fax, email, telephone, and voice over IP service). In addition, the SSA helps store the key on different mobile clouds, making it difficult for the attacker to break the key. Finally, this paper discusses the energy detection model that calculates the energy consumption of the mobile device when initiating the handoff (as this model provides the updated energy status of the mobile phone). The remainder of this paper is organized as follows: Energy-efficient, service-oriented architecture section presents the energy-efficient, service-oriented architecture designed for the handover process (including the strong secure authentication and priority-based module), Experimental setup and simulation results section presents the simulation results and analysis, and the paper is concluded in Conclusion section.

Energy-efficient, service-oriented architecture

Mobile cloud computing aims to provide mobile devices with appropriate and rapid access to the data on the mobile cloud server. The handover process is one of the major challenges in the mobile cloud computing environment. The mobile handover process introduces problems because of the limited energy, restricted processing capability, wireless connectivity, and security threats. As a result, these factors could lead to performance degradation [25]. Furthermore, low-bandwidth and less reliable transmission can affect the handover process and thus have a significant effect on the QoS [26, 27]. The security threats caused by the handoff process affect several functions of mobile applications. Therefore, maintaining the confidentiality and privacy in mobile

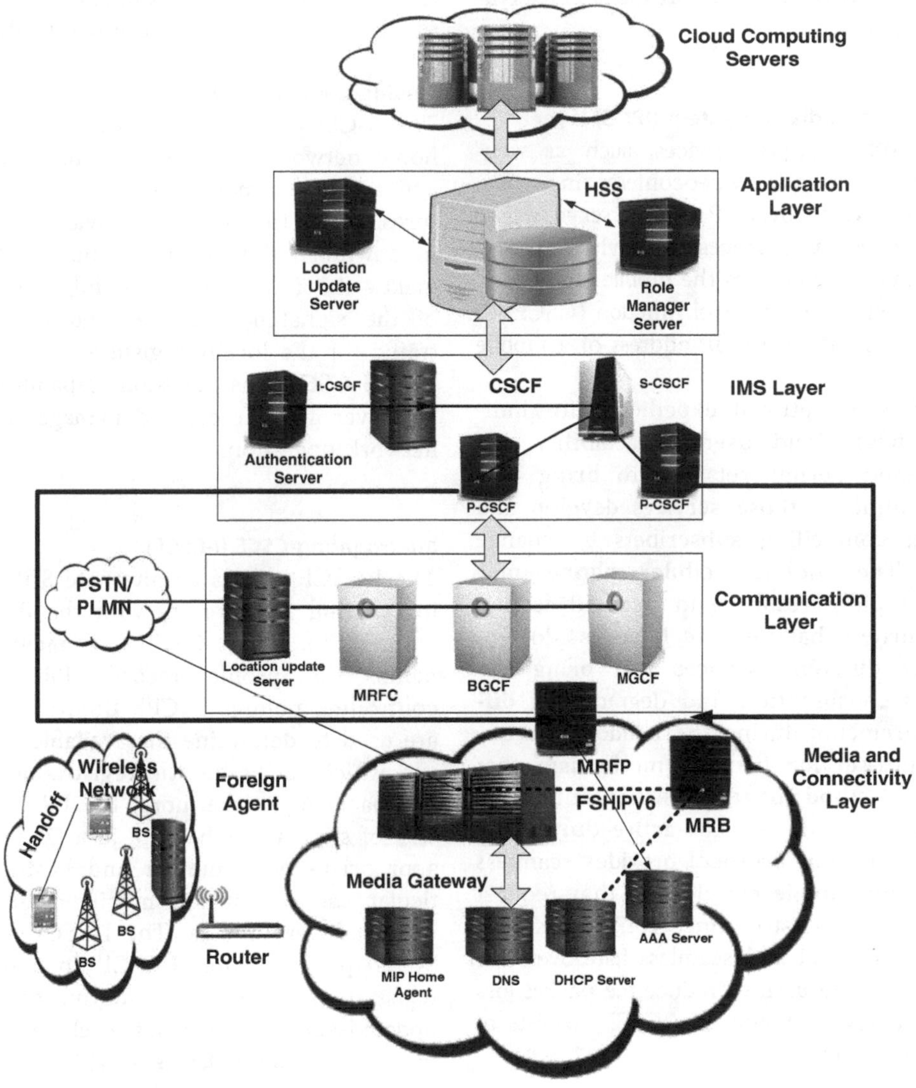

Fig. 1 Secure, energy-efficient and quality-of-service-supported service-oriented architecture

cloud computing is unpredictable. Thus, there is a high demand for secure and energy-efficient architectures to support the handover process in the mobile cloud computing environment. Understanding such an important need for a secure and energy-efficient handover and maintaining these apprehensions as the top priority, we introduce an energy-efficient and secure service-oriented architecture to support an effective handover that evades data loss and security concerns. The architecture is composed of four layers, as shown in Fig. 1.

- Application layer
- IPMS layer
- Communication layer
- Media with connectivity layer

Application layer

This layer constitutes the home subscriber server (HSS) that interconnects with the cloud computing servers as an enterprise server. The HSS also links to the IPMS layer to successfully maintain data communication. The HSS involves the subscription-related information (SRI) server, location update (LU) server and role manager server. The mobile cloud user profiles are stored in the SRI, and the LU stores the mobile cloud user's current location. Prior to transferring the cloud data to a legitimate mobile cloud user, encryption is performed for secure data communication. The attribute-based model is used to support the HSS encryption at the application layer.

Internet protocol multimedia subsystem (IPMS) layer

The IPMS layer offers utility services, such as web-browsing, video-on-demand, videoconferencing, fax, email, Internet, and voice over IP (VoIP) service. The IPMS involves the registration process, which helps obtain updated location information from the mobile cloud user. The IPMS uses a call session control function (CSCF) to bind a public user identity to the IP address of a mobile cloud user.

The IPMS offers exceptional expediency for individual and business cloud users. Tractability and expandability would permit retailers to bring new cloud services online as those services develop and advance without compelling subscribers to change carriers often. The mobile cellular phone may change location rapidly, resulting in frequent session handoff. The current handoff mechanisms do not properly support different services that bring unnecessary energy consumption and degrade the different QoS requirements during the handoff process. We apply a multi-service handoff mechanism that applies the list method of the Session Initiation Protocol (SIP) to keep all services active during the handoff. Furthermore, our protocol provides seamless mobility support for mobile cloud users that request real-time services (such as streaming, VoIP, and shared game playing). Thus, rapid and seamless handovers for the MIPv6 (FSMIPv6) are used to reduce the packet loss and extend the handover latency. The CSCF consists of the following components:

- Proxy-CSCF (P-CSCF)
- Serving-CSCF (S-CSCF)
- Interrogating-CSCF (I-CSCF)

Proxy-CSCF (P-CSCF)

The session initiation protocol proxy is the entry point to be used to connect with the IPMS layer. The P-CSCF can be used with either a foreign network or home network. The P-CSCF is comprised of the session frame controller (SFC), which is used to establish the user network interface. Hence, the features of the SFC help protect the IPMS. The P-CSCF is assigned to the IPMS prior to registration and is not altered during the entire process. The P-CSCF also accepts the encrypted signal and declines the unencrypted signal to help protect the communication. Furthermore, the P-CSCF consists includes a policy decision function, which helps maintain the QoS of the media resources. The policy decision function fully organizes the bandwidth utilization.

Serving-CSCF (S-CSCF)

The S-CSCF controls the session and is fixed in the home network. It maintains the registration process and sets the timer by involving two significant features. First, the S-CSCF provides the interface used to download the profile of mobile cloud device and makes the implication. Second, it supports the trail of the signaling messages and monitors all of the traffic for the locally registered mobile cloud devices. The S-CSCF has decision capability regarding the handover and directs and manages the policy of the network operation.

Interrogating-CSCF (I-CSCF)

The I-CSCF acts as an alternate SIP. It is responsible for sharing the identity with the domain name system (DNS). The I-CSCF also includes two components: the profile record (PR) and the name controlling pointer (NCP). Both of these components are used to determine the available remote cloud server, which facilitates the registration process for the SIP packets. Furthermore, the PR has the additional task of stipulating the data in a DNS, which traces an appropriate port number and hostname of the particular service when a mobile cloud device initiates the handover process. The I-CSCF also forwards the SIP request to the S-CSCF to refresh the exiting registration process and informs the network of the updated status of the mobile cloud device. Therefore, the mobile cloud device is able to complete the re-registration process efficiently.

The secure and strong authentication (SSA) process is used in this layer to protect the web, videoconferencing, video-on-demand, Internet, fax, email, telephone, and VoIP services. The authentication process is performed using the SSA algorithm. The cloud service server only has an idea about the encryption but requires full authentication support to protect different types of services. The authentication key is fragmented and stored on different cloud servers, making it difficult for an adversary to collect all the fragmented parts to access the services. Even if the adversary obtains all pieces of the key, it is incapable of recognizing the key patterns used. The SSA can easily secure our services and confidential data from the adversary in mobile cloud computing. When a mobile user intends to gain access to the service in this strong authentication process, the key from the cloud service server is required. The key acquisition process is detailed in Algorithm 1.

Algorithm 1: Key acquisition process using the SSA

1. Initialization: { U_i= user, C_{ss} = cloud service server
   A_s = authentication server, M_{cu}: mobile cloud user, L_{mcu}: legitimate mobile cloud user; S: services}
2. Input: { token, C_{ss}}
3. Output: {S}
4. M_{cu} requests =>C_{ss} // The mobile cloud user requests an authentication process to be performed by the cloud service server
5. C_{ss} forwards =>A_s// The cloud service server redirects the request of the mobile cloud user to the authentication server
6. A_s issues token =>M_{cu}// The authentication server issues the token to the mobile cloud user if it is a legitimate mobile cloud user
7. M_{cu}maps token to C_{ss} // The issued token is compared with the profile of the mobile cloud user
8. Set access to C_{ss} // Access is given to different cloud service servers to collect the keys to use for authentication purposes in steps 9–11
9. Key $_1$ =>C_{s1}
10. Key $_2$ =>C_{s2}
11. Key $_3$ =>C_{s3}
12. If $M_{cu} \in L_{mcu}$ then // If the keys collected by the mobile cloud user are authentic, then access is granted for the service in step 13; otherwise, it is denied in step 14
13. Grant access to S otherwise
14. Deny S
15. end if

The authentication process starts with the request of the mobile cloud user. The request is sent to the cloud service server (main server). Upon receipt of the request, the cloud service server redirects it to the authentication server, and the authenticity of the mobile cloud user is verified based on the stored profile on the authentication server. If the mobile cloud user is found to be a legitimate user, then the server issues the token; otherwise, the request is dropped, and the user is considered to be an adversary. If the mobile cloud user is legitimate, a token is given to the cloud service server. In response, the cloud service server checks the information and decides, based on that information, whether to grant the user access to other servers to collect the remaining segments of the key. If the mobile cloud user is illegitimate, then it blocks the user. If the mobile cloud user possesses the valid key, and the key from the user matches the cloud server, then the cloud service server provides the user with access to use the resources. The complete SSA process is shown in Fig. 2.

Communication layer

This layer routes the data and synchronizes the media and IPMS layers. It consists of the media gateway controller function (MGCF), media resource function controller (MRFC) and breakout gateway control function (BGCF). The BGCF acts as the SIP proxy, which is responsible for processing the request to route the data from the S-CSCF whenever it determines that a session cannot be established using a DNS. Furthermore, the BGCF contains the routing features based on the telephone records.

The MGCF is considered as the SIP endpoint and manages the call exchange between the bearer-independent call control (BICC) and SIP. The MRFC is the signaling component that infers information looming from the S-CSCF with an application server (AS) to manage the MRFP. During this process, determination of the energy consumption is of high significance to route and synchronize the data. Furthermore, the location update server initiates the re-registration process, which is comprised of two levels: periodic re-registration (PRR) and re-

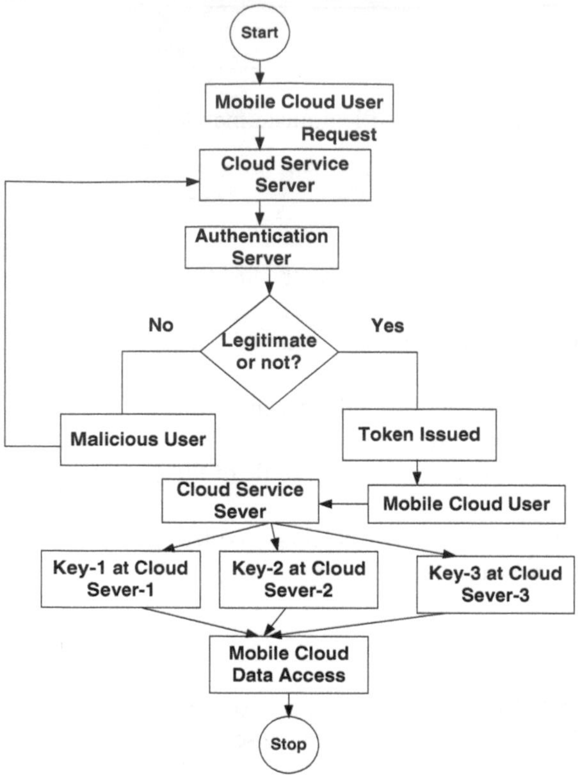

Fig. 2 Secure and strong authentication process for mobile cloud computing

registration for change capabilities (RRCC). The PRR and RRCC levels involve the messaging process to complete the re-registration. Hence, the energy for the re-registration process should be calculated after completion of the handover process to help determine the remaining power of the mobile device.

Energy Consumption for the Re-Registration Process

When the mobile device initiates the handover process, the re-registration and re-attachment processes with a new AP require a sufficient energy level to complete the handover process. When the distance between the mobile phone and its old attached AP 'A_p' is smaller than the threshold distance 'Th_d', the energy consumption of the mobile device should be counted before the handover completion process. Hence, we first determine the energy of the mobile device prior to the handover process.

$$E_{in1} = D_s \left\{ \pi' Th_d^2 \gamma P_s + \sum_{i=0}^{\pi' Th_d^2 \gamma} \epsilon\beta \left(A_x - A_i\right)^2 + \left(B_x - B_i\right)^2 \right\} \quad (1)$$

When the distance between the mobile phone and its old attached AP 'A_n' is larger than the threshold distance 'Th_d', the energy consumption for the package transmission by the mobile device can be calculated using Eq. (2). Eq. (2) is the exponential time of Eq. (1). Reducing the time needed to perform the handover process can lower the energy consumption.

$$E_{ah1} = D_s \left[\Psi - \pi' Th_d^2 \gamma P_s + \sum_{i=0}^{\Psi - \pi' Th_d^2 \gamma} \epsilon\rho \left\{ \left(A_x - A_i\right)^2 + \left(B_x - B_i\right)^2 \right\}^2 \right] \quad (2)$$

Equations (3) and (4) describe the energy consumed from the mobile nodes to receive the RESPONSE message from the APs/BS. The condition of receiving the range of APs/BS is similar to receiving the RESPONSE message. Thus, Eqs. (3) and (4) are related to the receiving energy. We can determine when the mobile device is far from the APs/BS when the number of long-distance handovers is twice the number of mobile devices. The conclusions drawn from Eq. (3) are well established.

$$E_{in2} = D_s \left\{ \pi' Th_d^2 \gamma P_r + \sum_{i=0}^{\pi' Th_d^2 \gamma} \epsilon\beta \left(A_x - A_i\right)^2 + \left(B_x - B_i\right)^2 \right\} \quad (3)$$

After the second handoff process, several mobile devices can join the nearest AP or BS.

$$E_{ah2} = D_s \left[\left(\Psi - \pi' Th_d^2\right) \gamma P_r + \sum_{i=0}^{\Psi - \pi' Th_d^2 \gamma} \epsilon\rho \left\{ \left(A_x - A_i\right)^2 + \left(B_x - B_i\right)^2 \right\}^2 \right] \quad (4)$$

The mobile device requires re-registration and sends the control messages 'M_c', which consumes energy. Eq. (5) is used to calculate the energy consumption of the mobile cloud server and mobile device 'E_{ms}'. We measure the energy consumption of the mobile cloud server because the mobile cloud server could potentially run out of power and thus would not be able to deliver the data to the mobile device. Here, the APs/BS are independent in our calculation. Furthermore, the energy of the APs/BS is unbounded, which provides an indication of the broadcasting and receiving energy such that a calculation is not required.

$$E_{ms} = M_c \left[\Psi(1 - w_t) \gamma P_s + \Psi * w_t * \gamma P_r + \sum_{i=0}^{\Psi(1-w_t)\gamma} \epsilon\beta \left(A_y - A_i\right)^2 + \left(B_y - B_i\right)^2 \right] \quad (5)$$

By combining Eqs. (1), (2), (3), (4) and (5), we obtain the total energy consumption 'E_t' from the mobile device and cloud mobile server while initiating the handover process.

$$E_t = (E_{ms} + E_{ah1} + E_{ah2} + E_{in2} + E_{in1}) \quad (6)$$

A description of the notations is given in Table 1.

Media with connectivity layer (MCL)

This layer offers media- and connectivity-related functionalities (e.g., voice stream and tome, including rapid handover). The MCL is comprised of the media resource function controller (MRFC) and the media resource agent (MRA). The MRFC mixes the media streams and handles the shared resources. The MRA controls the existing media resource function information and forwards the appropriate information to the authentication server. The MRA also contains queries and in-line modes. In the query mode, the MRA organizes the calls by obtaining the reply of the in-line mode and media resource function. Furthermore, the MRA enables the SIP request. Thus, the handover process is managed effectively. The MRFC and MRA modules are interrelated with IPv6 to ensure proper handover. Additionally, the MRA is coupled to the Dynamic Host Configuration Protocol (DHCP) server to support the handover process, as shown in Fig. 3. The media gateway is linked with the DNS. The MRFP is connected to the authentication, authorization, and accounting (AAA) servers. We deploy a rapid, seamless handoff process for the mobile cloud user for QoS provisioning. The priority enforcement module (PEM) provides the context-based administration to apply the application-layer security and arrangement. It also enforces the network access procedures and guidelines based on the mobile cloud service user roles, app flows, device types and location. Furthermore, the PEM offers user-level responsiveness for all traffic across the network.

Table 1 Notations used in this work and their descriptions

Notation	Description
E_{in1}	Energy of the mobile device before the first handover process
D_s	Data sent
Th_d	Threshold distance
γ	Number of mobile nodes accessing the same BS or AP for registration
P_s	Packet size sent by the sender
P_r	Packet size sent by the receiver
β	Number of mobile devices in the range of APs/BS that want to initiate handover
A_x, B_x	Location information of the AP/BS
A_i, B_i	Location information of the nodes
Ψ	Range of the APs/BS
E_{ah1}	Energy of the mobile device after the first handover process
ρ	Number of mobile devices in the range of APs/BS that want to initiate the re-registration process
M_c	Control messages
E_{ms}	Energy consumption of the mobile cloud server and a mobile device
w_t	Wait time for the re-registration process

Rapid, Seamless handover procedure

A mobile cloud device can change its attachment from its respective home domain. This could lead to re-attachment with another domain and the possibility of several handovers during the process. The handover process affects the QoS parameters including the end-to-end delay and packet loss. Handing this situation to the mobile cloud computing environment, we introduce the fast, seamless handover mobile IPv6 (FSHIPv6) to support the mobility management. The FSHIPv6 includes the mobility management utilities to reduce the unexpected signaling load within the intra domain when several mobile cloud users initiate the handover processes. As a result, the packet-drop and latency are greatly increased. In our approach, the handover process involves two states: periodic re-registration (PRR) and re-registration for change capabilities (RCC). In the PR, the mobile cloud device remains attached with same AP (AP)/BS to keep sending the data until it becomes attached with either another AP or BS. The timer is kept as active and ON during both steps. In the RCC, the mobile cloud user uses the utility features, and the attachment process is completed with another AP/BS.

The PR aims to identify whether the mobile cloud user is still registered with the home network. In this state, the home network begins the re-registration process because the registration timer has timed out. The RCC aims to intimate the change in the location of the mobile cloud user to the home network. During the re-registration process, the timer triggers the RCC, whereas the PR controls the changing parameters. The registration timer is required for both the RCC and PR to efficiently initiate the new session. In our proposed fast, seamless handover, the IPMS identifies the current registration status of the mobile cloud device. The process is also supported with the priority enforcement module (PEM) that reduces the traffic load when the handover is in progress, as this feature assigns the priority to each device based on the nature of the traffic. Furthermore, the IPMS also refreshes the registration timer during the session establishment process and cloud server-access. As a result, the time consumed for the PR can be reduced in our approach.

Experimental setup and simulation results

The performance of our proposed secure energy-efficient and quality-of-service architecture (SEEQoSA) is confirmed through the CloudSim simulation environment. The CloudSim simulator is installed on the Ubuntu Linux

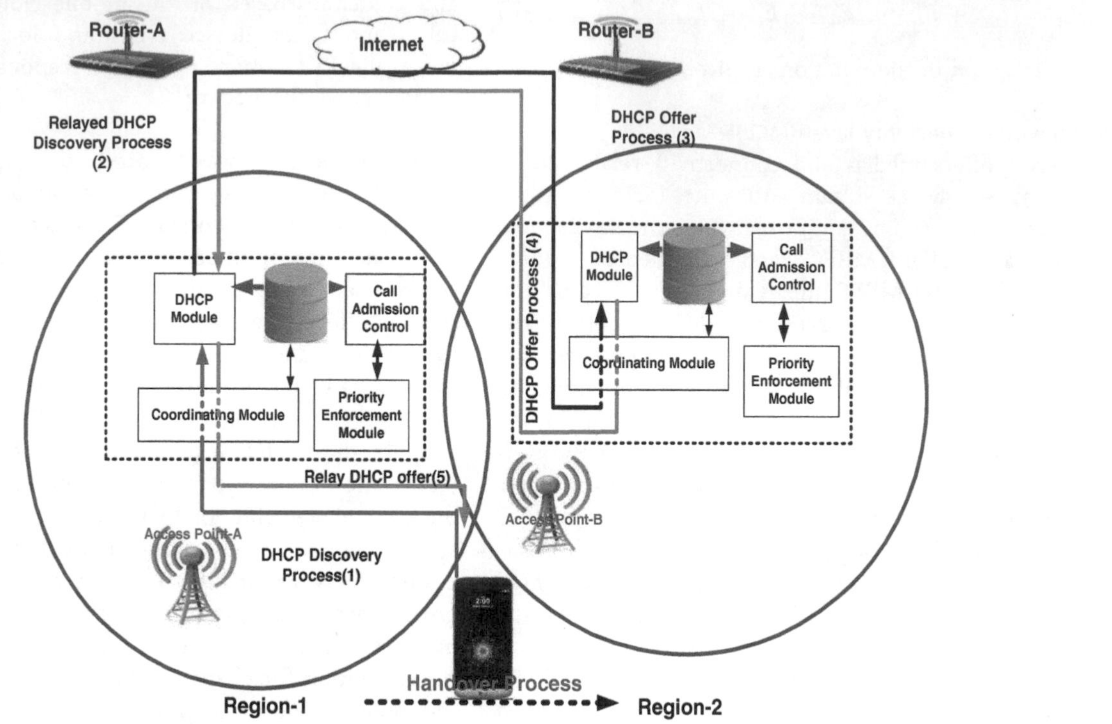

Fig. 3 DHCP server-supported handoff process

operating system. All the experiments are performed on a laptop with an Intel Pentium Dual-Core E6500 Wolfdale Dual-Core 2.93 GHz and 5 GB of RAM. The computing machine uses the 64-bit version of Windows 8.

The network size is approximately 1400 × 1800 m. At the application layer, 1900 chassis switches, 1452 line cards and 48 ports are deployed. At the IPMS layer, 230 chassis switches, 150 line cards, and 52 ports are used. A total of 64 servers with 20,000 mobile cloud devices are deployed and repeatedly perform the handover processes. Each mobile cloud device performs a maximum of 20 handover processes during the entire simulation time of 30 min. There are 256 and 16 racks deployed at the IPMS and application layers, respectively. Each rack consists of 128 hosts, and each host covers 16 processors with 164 GB of memory, 480 GB of storage, and a 300 GB of virtual disk space. We set a 280 GB bandwidth for the application layer, 100 GB for the IPMS layer, 20 GB for the communication layer and 7 GB for the media with the connectivity layer. The size of the packet with header is 1280 KB. Some of the parameters used are summarized in Table 2.

We analyzed the performance of the proposed (SEE-QoSA) that supports the handoff and then compared it with well-known service-oriented architectures designed for mobile cloud computing, including the market-oriented architecture for mobile cloud computing (MOMCC) [28], mobile cloud computing based on the

Table 2 Showing the simulation parameters and its description

Simulation parameter	Description
Machine	Intel Pentium Dual-Core E6500 Wolfdale Dual-Core 2.93 GHz
RAM	*5 GB*
Operating system	Windows 08 + *Ubuntu Linux*
Network size	1400 m × 1800 m
Chassis switches	1900
Line cards	1452
Ports	48
Servers	64
Mobile cloud devices	20000
Maximum number of handover	20
Simulation time	27 min
Racks at application layer	16
Racks at IPMS layer	256
Hosts	128 hosts in each rack
Processor	16 processors in each rack
Packet size	1280 KB
Processor memory	164 GB
Storage	480 GB
Virtual disk space	300 GB

service-oriented architecture (MCLSOA) [29], service-oriented heterogeneous resource sharing (SOHRS) [30], cloud-based semantic service-oriented content provisioning architecture (CSSCPA) [31] and the service-based arbitrated multi-tier infrastructure (SAMI) [32]. Based on the experimental results, the collected data were used in MATLAB to graph the following parameters:

- Energy Consumption
- Malicious Detection Probability
- Reliable Data Delivery
- Bandwidth Consumption
- Latency in the presence of a Malicious Node
- Average Throughput

Energy consumption

The lifetime of the networks depends entirely on the amount of energy available in the mobile phone [33, 34]. The lack of the energy significantly affects the performance and efficiency of the mobile cloud device including running applications on the cloud [35, 36]. Based on the experimental results, we observed that the energy consumption of the mobile devices increased when the mobile device initiated the handover process. The trend of energy consumption shows that our proposed SEEQoSA consumes overall less energy when compared with the SAMI, CSSCPA, SOHRS, MCLSOA and MOMCC approaches, as shown in Fig. 4. However, this impact of minor energy consumption in our case does not affect the mobile cloud data outsourcing and transfer because the mobile cloud device still has substantial energy to effectively perform its function. Our approach is particularly designed to support a wide-range of mobile devices. Most of the conventional approaches are not introduced to support the smaller number of mobile cloud users because many resources are required, making these approaches unsuccessful in real situations. Our SEEQoSA consumes 34.67 out of 50 Joules of energy after completing 4500 rounds for a maximum of 18 handover processes. On the other hand, other competing approaches consume 35.22–42.46 Joules with same number of handovers and rounds. The location update server is deployed with our approach to determine the location of the mobile device and to initiate the re-registration after the handover. As a result, the IPMS acquires the updated request from the top layer (application layer), which could save additional time and lead to a lower energy consumption.

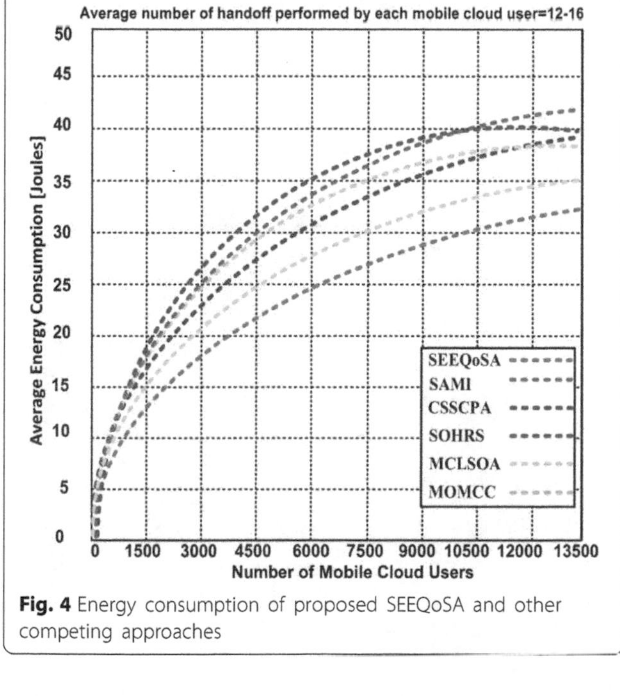

Fig. 4 Energy consumption of proposed SEEQoSA and other competing approaches

Malicious detection probability

Recently, the security of mobile cloud computing has been subjected to a high level of threat, leading to security cracks. Therefore, the probability of detecting malicious intent should be determined. We demonstrate the performance of our proposed SEEQoSA and its comparison with other competing approaches for malicious probability detection in Fig. 5. When the number of malicious mobile cloud users increased in this experiment, the malicious detection probability began to drop. However, our SEEQoSA approach had an edge over other contending approaches. The malicious detection probability decreased by only 5.36% with 108 malicious mobile cloud devices, whereas the malicious detection probability decreased by 10.86–18.24% for contending approaches. Therefore, these results indicate that our approach is superior to other approaches for detecting

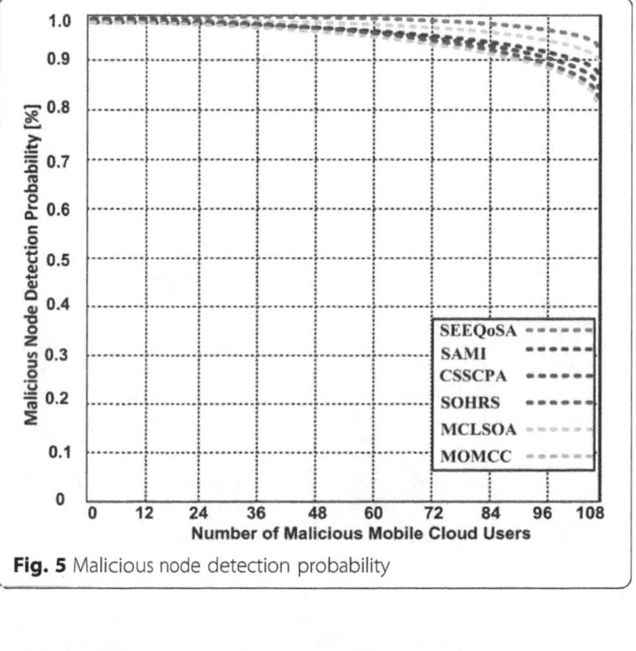

Fig. 5 Malicious node detection probability

malicious users. The secure and strong authentication algorithm in our approach provides privacy protection because the keys are fragmented and stored on different servers. Hence, it is more difficult for an adversary to gain access to all of the cloud servers. If any adversary tries to exploit the mobile cloud servers, then an adversary is recognized as an illegitimate user, and as a result, it is not permitted by the role manager. Therefore, the SSA helped to identify the probability of the malicious mobile device, whereas the contending approaches either deploy no proper secure authentication or apply fragile authentication mechanisms that can only secure the traditional networks but are not appropriate for mobile cloud computing [37, 38].

Reliable data delivery

There is a large probability of data loss when the mobile device initiates the handover process. The delivery of reliable data is of high significance because the performance of the architecture depends on how much data can be reliably delivered to the end user. The trends in the reliable data delivery for our proposed algorithm and other contending approaches are plotted in Fig. 6. The trend shows that the reliable data delivery of the SEEQoSA steadily evolves and ranges between 99.08 and 99.68% with 9000 mobile cloud devices and a maximum of 16 handovers. A lower reliable data delivery rate is observed for the competing approaches and ranges between 97.64 and 99.16%. In Fig. 7, we increased the number of mobile cloud devices up to 13,500; the data delivery rate is slightly reduced in our case to values of 98.74–99.45%, whereas the contending approaches have a rate of 95.23–99.17% in the same scenario with similar parameters. The results prove that our SEEQoSA outperforms other contending approaches in terms of the reliability of data transfer when the number of the mobile cloud devices increases.

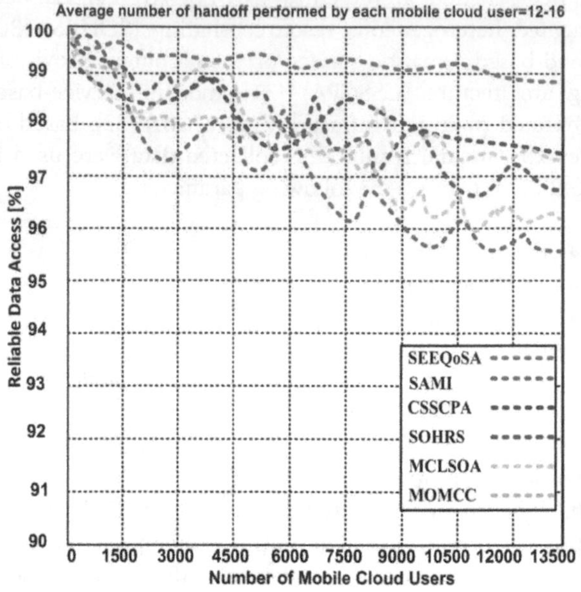

Fig. 7 Reliable data delivery of proposed SEEQoSA and other competing approaches with 13,500 mobile cloud users

Bandwidth consumption

We determined the bandwidth utilization of the SEEQoSA and compared it with those of the SAMI, CSSCPA, SOHRS, MCLSOA and MOMCC in Fig. 8. The SEEQoSA

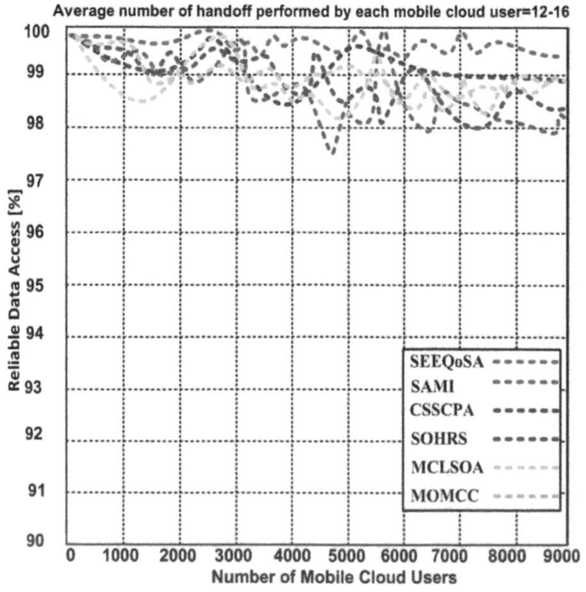

Fig. 6 Reliable data delivery of proposed SEEQoSA and other competing approaches with 9000 mobile cloud users

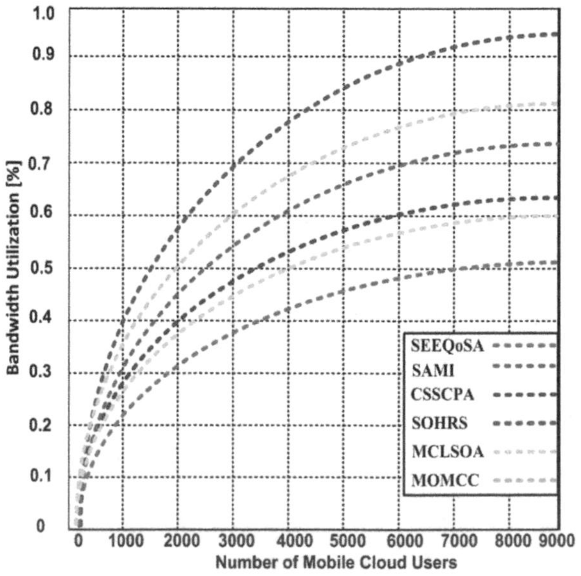

Fig. 8 Bandwidth utilization of proposed SEEQoSA and other contending approaches with 9000 mobile cloud users

consumes less bandwidth than the contending approaches during the mobile cloud handover initialization process. The results show that the bandwidth consumption increases with increases in the number of the mobile cloud devices. The bandwidth consumption of the other approaches depends on the number of available mobile cloud devices that attempt to initiate the handover and re-registration processes. The results confirm that the SEEQoSA approach consumes 53.07% of the total assigned bandwidth with 9,000 mobile cloud devices, whereas the competing approaches consume 59.8–94.37% of the entire assigned bandwidth. When we increase the number of mobile cloud devices to 13,500, the SEEQoSA consumes 56.3% of the bandwidth, whereas the contending approaches consume 73.98–99.24%, as shown in Fig. 9. The SOHRS had the greatest bandwidth consumption compared to the other approaches, and the SEEQoSA, which uses the simple registration process, had the lowest bandwidth consumption. The significance of the SEEQoSA is to incorporate the PEM, which assigns priority to the mobile cloud device when initiating handover based on the nature of the network traffic.

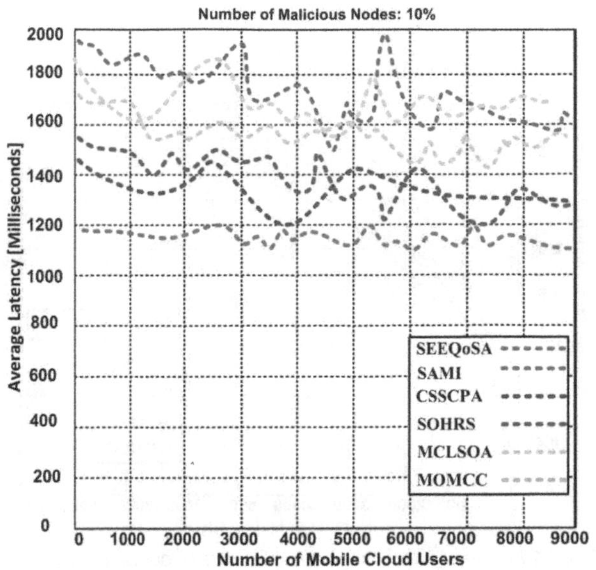

Fig. 10 Latency of our proposed SEEQoSA and other competing approaches: SAMI, CSSCPA, SOHRS, MCLSOA and MOMCC in presence of 10% malicious nodes

Latency in the presence of a malicious node

Cloud latency specifies the delay between a response of the cloud service provider and a client request and significantly affects the communication performance (which can be particularly susceptible to the latency for several reasons). The latency is less predictable but is difficult to determine in cloud computing. In Fig. 10, the latency of our proposed SEEQoSA is compared to those of other competing approaches (SAMI, CSSCPA, SOHRS, MCLSOA and MOMCC) with 10% of the nodes being malicious and attempting to affect the hops in the router. The simulation results indicated that our proposed SEEQoSA has a minimum latency of 1,150 ms (which is nearly stable for the cloud users), whereas the other competing approaches have a higher latency of 1,254–1,834 ms. Factors affecting the latency include the number of the hops in the router or ground-to-satellite communication hops that target the server. Thus, the latency can cause serious damage for multiple cloud services. Our approach is supported by the priority enforcement module and communication module, which help handle the flow of the packets and detect the malicious nodes available on each hop.

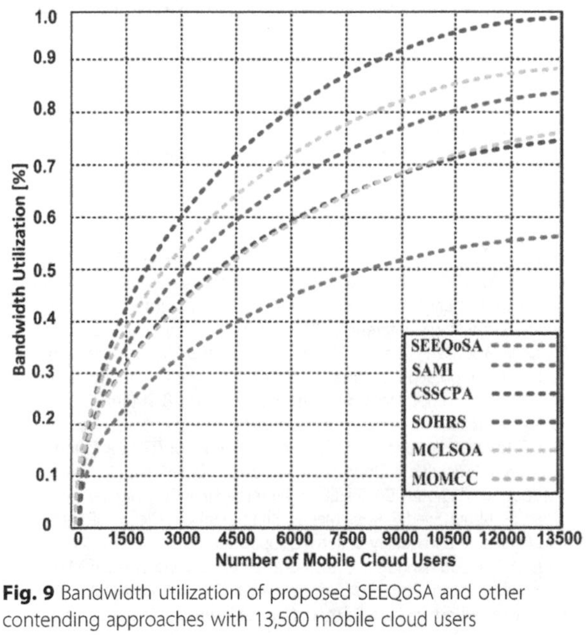

Fig. 9 Bandwidth utilization of proposed SEEQoSA and other contending approaches with 13,500 mobile cloud users

Average throughput

The key measurement of the network performance is the throughput. The throughput indicates the average amount of bandwidth data that can be transmitted through the network per unit time. Throughput is not always considered as a critical factor for cloud-based software applications [39]. The average throughput performance is shown in Fig. 11, illustrating that our proposed SEEQoSA has an advantage over other competing approaches. The SEEQoSA has a throughput of 3.9 MB/s, whereas the other approaches have throughputs of 3.01-3.46 MB/s. The SOHRS produced the minimum throughput among all the approaches. The improved throughput in our approach is due to the fast and seamless handoff based on the dynamic host configuration protocol (DHCP), which involves the new priority

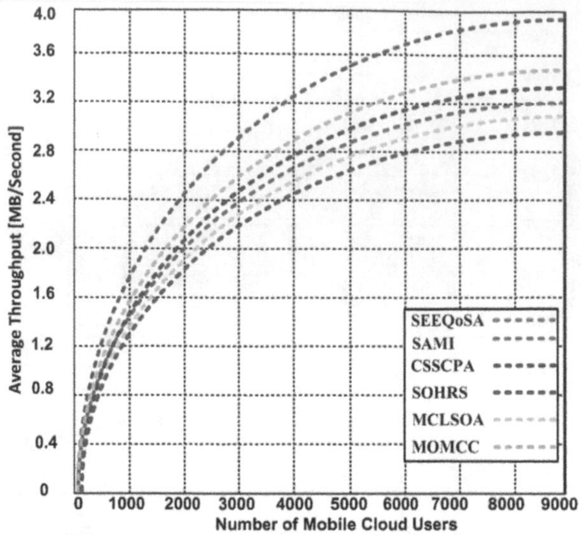

Fig. 11 An average throughput performance of our proposed SEEQoSA and other competing approaches: SAMI, CSSCPA, SOHRS, MCLSOA and MOMCC

enforcement module that allows only legitimate users to complete the re-registration process after initiating the handoff. This approach enables reliable data access and content delivery with a higher throughput.

Conclusion

This study introduced the SEEQoSA to achieve an efficient handover process in mobile cloud computing. The proposed paradigm consists of four layers: application, IPMS, communication and media with connectivity. The application layer serves as the enterprise server to control the operations of the other three layers. The IPMS provides different services, such as web, videoconferencing, and video-on-demand. The communication layer handles the faster re-registration process to avoid unexpected delays and data loss. Furthermore, the communication layer involves an energy-efficient detection model to determine the energy of each node when initiating the handoff process. The media with connectivity layer consists of the priority-based module, which allows only legitimate users to complete the re-registration process after initiating the handover and reduces the occurrence of extended delays during the handover. The architecture is implemented using C++, and the code is converted to the object tool command language (OTCL) run on the CloudSim platform. The results confirm the validity of our proposed architecture and comply with the QoS and energy-efficiency parameters. The architecture aims to facilitate energy-efficient and QoS-supported handoff processes. The simulation results validate that the SEEQoSA achieves a 5.5–12.8% higher malicious node detection probability with an 8.2–42.2% lower bandwidth consumption compared to other known approaches. The SEEQoSA consumes 0.67–7.87% less energy with 12–16 handover processes over 5,000 rounds. Furthermore, it has also a 0.7–1.4% higher data delivery rate compared to other service-oriented architectures.

The results confirm that the SEEQoSA is a more suitable choice for mobile phones when initiating the handover process in a cloud computing environment. In the future, we will determine possible malicious attacks on the SEEQoSA and will propose appropriate solutions.

Acknowledgements

We are also thankful to anonymous reviewers for their valuable feedback and comments for improving the quality of the manuscript.

Authors' contributions

This research work is part of QBH. dissertation work. The work has been primarily conducted by QBH under the supervision of JPD. Extensive discussions about the algorithms and techniques presented in this paper were carried between the two authors over the past year. Both authors read and approved the final manuscript.

About the Authors

Qassim Bani Hani is pursuing towards his Ph.D., Department of Computer Science and Engineering University of Bridgeport, Bridgeport, at the CT. Qassim's interests are in Cloud computing, Cloud computing mobility, and Cloud localization. He has authored and coauthored several technical refereed papers in various conferences, and journal articles. He is IEEE member.

Julius Dichter is an Associate Professor in the department of Computer Science and Engineering at the University of Bridgeport in Connecticut. He received his M.S. degree from the University of New Haven and the Ph.D. from the University of Connecticut in the area of parallel computing optimization. He has authored and coauthored several technical refereed and non-refereed papers in various conferences, journal articles, and book chapters in research and pedagogical techniques. His research interests include parallel and distributed system performance, security of the cloud computing, algorithms and object-oriented systems. Dr. Dichter is a member of IEEE, ACM, and ISCA.

Competing interests

The authors declare that they have no competing interests.

References

1. Yuan H, Kuo C-CJ, Ishfaq A (2010) Energy efficiency in data centers and cloud-based multimedia services: An overview and future directions. In: Green Computing Conference, 2010 International., pp 375–382
2. Shiraz M, Abdullah G, Rashid Hafeez K, Rajkumar B (2013) A review on distributed application processing frameworks in smart mobile devices for mobile cloud computing. Communications Surveys & Tutorials, IEEE 15 3:1294–1313
3. Rizvi S, Razaque A, Katie C (2015) Third-Party Auditor (TPA): A Potential Solution for Securing a Cloud Environment. In: Cyber Security and Cloud Computing (CSCloud), 2015 IEEE 2nd International Conference., pp 31–36
4. Razaque, Abdul, Syed S. Rizvi, Meer J. Khan, Hani QB, Dichter JP, Parizi RM (2017) "Secure and quality-of-service-supported service-oriented architecture for mobile cloud handoff process." Computers & Security 66:169-184
5. Othman M, Sajjad Ahmad M, Samee Ullah K (2014) A survey of mobile cloud computing application models. IEEE Communications Surveys & Tutorials 16 1:393–413

6. Wang S, Dey S (2013) Adaptive mobile cloud computing to enable rich mobile multimedia applications. IEEE Transactions on Multimedia 15(4):870–883
7. Shekhar S, Viswanath G, Michael RE, KwangSoo Y (2012) Spatial big-data challenges intersecting mobility and cloud computing. In: Proceedings of the Eleventh ACM International Workshop on Data Engineering for Wireless and Mobile Access., pp 1–6
8. Sanaei Z, Abolfazli S, Gani A, Buyya R (2014) Heterogeneity in mobile cloud computing: taxonomy and open challenges. IEEE Communications Surveys & Tutorials 16(1):369–392
9. Zhang H, Chunxiao J, Julian C, Victor CM L (2015) Cooperative interference mitigation and handover management for heterogeneous cloud small cell networks. IEEE Wireless Communications 22 3:92–99
10. Gani A, Nayeem GM, Shiraz M, Sookhak M, Whaiduzzaman M, Khan S (2014) A review on interworking and mobility techniques for seamless connectivity in mobile cloud computing. J Netw Comput Appl 43:84–102
11. Chiu K-L, Yuh-Shyan C, Ren-Hung H (2011) Seamless session mobility scheme in heterogeneous wireless networks. International Journal of Communication Systems 24 6:789–809
12. Ferretti S, Vittorio G, Fabio P, Elisa T (2010) Seamless support of multimedia distributed applications through a cloud. In: Cloud Computing (CLOUD), 2010 IEEE 3rd International Conference., pp 548–549
13. Chen Y-S, Kun-Lin W (2011) A cross-layer partner-assisted handoff scheme for hierarchical mobile IPv6 in IEEE 802.16 esystems. Wireless Communications and Mobile Computing 11 4:522–541
14. Razaque A, Rizvi SS (2017) Privacy preserving model: a new scheme for auditing cloud stakeholders. J Cloud Comput 6:1–7.
15. Ryu S, Lee K, Mun Y (2012) Optimized fast handover scheme in Mobile IPv6 networks to support mobile users for cloud computing. J Supercomput 59(2):658–675
16. Keke G, Qiu M, Zhao H, Tao L, Zong Z (2016) Dynamic energy-aware cloudlet-based mobile cloud computing model for green computing. J Netw Comput Appl 5:46–54
17. Rakpong K, Niyato D, Wang P, Hossain E (2013) "A framework for cooperative resource management in mobile cloud computing." IEEE J Sel Areas Commun 31;(12):2685 2700.
18. Lee D, Lee H, Park D, Jeong Y-S (2013) Proxy based seamless connection management method in mobile cloud computing. Clust Comput 16(4):733–744
19. Qi Q, Liao J, Cao Y (2014) Cloud service-aware location update in mobile cloud computing. Communications, IET 8(8):1417–1424
20. Qi H, Abdullah G (2012) Research on mobile cloud computing: Review, trend and perspectives. In: Digital Information and Communication Technology and it's Applications (DICTAP), 2012 Second International Conference., pp 195–202
21. Mayuri K, Ranjith KS (2014) A Novel secure handover mechansim in PMIPV6 networks. International Journal of Information Technology Convergence and Services 4(4):1
22. Razaque A, Saty Siva Varma N, Suharsha V, Dinesh Kumar A, Dammannagari Nayani R, Poojitha A, Divya V, Vamsee Sai M (2016) Secure data sharing in multi-clouds. In: Electrical, Electronics, and Optimization Techniques (ICEEOT), International Conference., pp 1909–1913
23. Rizvi S, Razaque A, Cover K (2015) Cloud Data Integrity Using a Designated Public Verifier. In: High Performance Computing and Communications (HPCC), 2015 IEEE 7th International Symposium on Cyberspace Safety and Security (CSS), 2015 IEEE 12th International Conferen on Embedded Software and Systems (ICESS), 2015 IEEE 17th International Conference., pp 1361–1366
24. Suo H, Zhuohua L, Jiafu W, Keliang Z (2013) Security and privacy in mobile cloud computing. In: Wireless Communications and Mobile Computing Conference (IWCMC), 2013 9th International., pp 655–659
25. Abolfazli S, Sanaei Z, Ahmed E, Gani A, Buyya R (2014) Cloud-based augmentation for mobile devices: motivation, taxonomies, and open challenges. IEEE Communications Surveys & Tutorials 16(1):337–368
26. Jiang Y, Hu X, Sen W (2014) Transformation Matrix for Time Discretization Based on Tustin's Method. Math Probl Eng 2014:9
27. Márquez-Barja J, Calafate CT, Cano J-C, Manzoni P (2011) An overview of vertical handover techniques:Algorithms, protocols and tools. Comput Commun 34(8):985–997
28. Abolfazli S, Zohreh S, Muhammad S, Abdullah G (2012) MOMCC: market-oriented architecture for mobile cloud computing based on service oriented architecture. In: Communications in China Workshops (ICCC), 2012 1st IEEE International Conference., pp 8–13
29. Gutierrez M, Andres F, Neco V (2011) Mobile Cloud Computing based on service oriented architecture: Embracing network as a service for 3 RD party application service providers. In: Kaleidoscope 2011: The Fully Networked Human?-Innovations for Future Networks and Services (K-2011), Proceedings of ITU., pp 1–7
30. Nishio T, Ryoichi S, Tatsuro T, NarayanB M (2013) Service-oriented heterogeneous resource sharing for optimizing service latency in mobile cloud. In: Proceedings of the first international workshop on Mobile cloud computing & networking., pp 19–26
31. Yee KY, Yilun C, Flora ST, Ang Wee T, Rajaraman K (2011) Cloud-based semantic service-oriented content provisioning architecture for mobile learning. Journal of Internet Services and Information Security 1 1:59–69
32. Sanaei Z, Saeid A, Abdullah G, Muhammad S (2012) SAMI: Service-based arbitrated multi-tier infrastructure for Mobile Cloud Computing. In: Communications in China Workshops (ICCC), 2012 1st IEEE International Conference., pp 14–19
33. Rizvi S, Karpinski K, Razaque A (2015) Novel architecture of self-organized mobile wireless sensor networks. J Comput Sci Eng 9(4):163–176
34. Razaque A, Elleithy KM (2014) Energy-efficient boarder node medium access control protocol for wireless sensor networks. Sensors 14(3):5074–5117
35. Guan L, Xu K, Meina S, Junde S (2011) A survey of research on mobile cloud computing. In: Computer and Information Science (ICIS), 2011 IEEE/ACIS 10th International Conference., pp 387–392
36. Kumar K, Yung-Hsiang L (2010) Cloud computing for mobile users: Can offloading computation save energy? Computer 43(4):51–56
37. Alizadeh M, Saeid A, Mazdak Z, Sabariah B, Kouichi S (2016) Authentication in mobile cloud computing: A survey. J Netw Comput Appl 61:59–80
38. Chow R, Markus J, Ryusuke M, Jesus M, Yuan N, Elaine S, Zhexuan S (2010) Authentication in the clouds: a framework and its application to mobile users. In: Proceedings of the 2010 ACM workshop on Cloud computing security workshop., pp 1–6
39. Razaque A, Rizvi SS (2016) Triangular data privacy-preserving model for authenticating all key stakeholders in a cloud environment. Computers & Security 62:328–347

8

Tackling uncertainty in long-term predictions for host overload and underload detection in cloud computing

Dorian Minarolli[1*], Artan Mazrekaj[2] and Bernd Freisleben[3,4]

Abstract

Dynamic workloads in cloud computing can be managed through live migration of virtual machines from overloaded or underloaded hosts to other hosts to save energy and/or mitigate performance-related Service Level Agreement (SLA) violations. The challenging issue is how to detect when a host is overloaded to initiate live migration actions in time. In this paper, a new approach to make long-term predictions of resource demands of virtual machines for host overload detection is presented. To take into account the uncertainty of long-term predictions, a probability distribution model of the prediction error is built. Based on the probability distribution of the prediction error, a decision-theoretic approach is proposed to make live migration decision that take into account live migration overheads. Experimental results using the CloudSim simulator and PlanetLab workloads show that the proposed approach achieves better performance and higher stability compared to other approaches that do not take into account the uncertainty of long-term predictions and the live migration overhead.

Keywords: Virtual machine live migration, Long-term resource prediction, Probabilistic model, Cloud computing

Introduction

Cloud computing is a promising approach in which resources are provided as services that can be leased and released by users through the Internet in an on-demand fashion [1]. One of the widely used cloud computing service models is Infrastructure as a Service (IaaS) [2] where raw computing resources are provided in the form of Virtual Machines (VMs) to cloud consumers charged for the resources consumed. Virtualization approaches such as Xen [3] and VMware [4] allow infrastructure resources to be shared in an effective manner. VMs also make it possible to allocate resources dynamically according to varying demands, providing opportunities for the efficient use of computing resources, as well as the optimization of application performance and energy consumption.

One of the main features virtualization technology offers for dynamic resource allocation is live migration of VMs [5]. It allows cloud providers to move away VMs from overloaded hosts to keep VM performance to SLA levels and to dynamically consolidate VMs to fewer hosts to save energy when the load is low. Using live migration and applying online algorithms that make live migration decisions, it is possible to manage cloud resources efficiently by adapting resource allocation to VM loads, keeping VM performance levels according to SLAs and lowering energy consumption of the infrastructure.

An important problem in the context of live migration is to detect when a host is overloaded or underloaded. Most of the state-of-the-art approaches are based on monitoring resource usage, and if the actual or the predicted next value exceeds a specified threshold, then a host is declared as overloaded. However, live migration is an expensive action, expressed as VM performance violations. The problem with existing approaches is that basing decisions for host overload detection on a single resource usage value or a few future values can lead to hasty decisions, unnecessary live migration overhead and stability issues.

A more promising approach is to base live migration decisions on resource usage predictions several steps ahead in the future. This not only increases stability by

*Correspondence: dminarolli@fti.edu.al
[1]Department of Computer Engineering, Polytechnic University of Tirana, Tirana, Albania
Full list of author information is available at the end of the article

performing migration actions only when the load persists for several time intervals, but also allows cloud providers to predict overload states before they happen. On the other hand, predicting further into the future increases the prediction error and the uncertainty, thus diminishing the benefits of long-term prediction. Another important issue is that live migration actions should only be performed if the penalty of SLA violations is larger than the penalty of the live migration overhead.

In this paper, a new approach for host overload and underload detection is presented based on long-term resource usage predictions that take into account the prediction uncertainty and the live migration overhead. More specifically, the paper makes the following contributions:

- A novel approach to dynamically allocate resources to VMs in an IaaS cloud environment is presented. It combines local and global VM resource allocations. Local resource allocation means allocating CPU resource shares to VMs according to the current load. Global resource allocation means performing live migration actions when a host is overloaded or underloaded in order to mitigate VM performance violations and reduce the number of hosts to save energy.
- A novel approach based on long-term resource usage predictions is presented to detect when a host is overloaded or underloaded. For long-term predictions, a supervised machine learning approach based on Gaussian Processes [6] is used.
- To take into account the uncertainty of long-term predictions for overload detection, a novel probabilistic model of the prediction error is built online using the non-parametric kernel density estimation [7] method.
- To take into account VM live migration overheads, a novel decision-theoretic approach based on a utility function is proposed. It performs live migration actions only when the predicted utility value (penalty) of SLA violations is greater than the utility value of live migration overhead.

The proposed approach is experimentally compared to other approaches: (a) an approach that relies on short-term predictions, (b) an approach that makes long-term predictions without taking into account prediction uncertainty, (c) an approach that makes long-term predictions taking into account prediction uncertainty, but not applying decision theory for considering live migration overhead, and (d) a the state-of-the-art approach based on Local Regression Detection [8] for host overload detection. Experimental evaluations based on the CloudSim [9] simulator and PlanetLab [10] workloads show that the proposed approach achieves better performance and stability compared to the other approaches.

The paper is organized as follows. "Resource manager architecture" section presents the overall architecture of the resource management approach. "VM agent" section discusses the functionality of the VM agent. "Host agent" section explains the duties of the host agent: probabilistic and decision-theoretic overload, underload and not-overload detection. "Global agent" section presents the global agent, and "VM SLA violation" section discusses VM SLA violation metrics. In "Experimental evaluation" section, the experimental evaluation is presented. Related work is discussed in "Related work" section. The last section concludes the paper and outlines areas for future research.

Resource manager architecture

This work focuses on managing an IaaS cloud in which several VMs run on physical hosts. The overall architecture of the resource manager and its main components are shown in Fig. 1. There is a VM agent for each VM that determines the resource shares to be allocated to its VM in each time interval. There is a host agent for each host that receives the resource allocation decisions of all VM agents and determines the final allocations by resolving any possible conflicts. It also detects when a host is overloaded or underloaded and transmits this information to the global agent. The global agent initiates VM live migration decisions by moving VMs from overloaded or underloaded hosts to not-overloaded hosts to mitigate SLA violations and reduce the number of hosts. In the following sections, a more detailed discussion is provided for each of the components of the resource manager.

VM agent

The VM agent is responsible for local resource allocation decisions by dynamically determining the resource shares to be allocated to its own VM. Allocation decisions are made in discrete time intervals where in each interval the resource share to be given in the next time interval is determined. In this work, the time interval is set to 10 seconds to adapt quickly to changing load. The interval is not set to less than 10 seconds, since in long-term prediction this would increase the number of time steps to predict into the future, lowering the prediction accuracy. This time interval value is also used in previous work [11] for long-term prediction, where the same reasoning is used to make it possible to predict further into the future. Setting a larger time interval can lead to inefficiencies and SLA violations due to the lack of quick adaptation to the load variation. This dynamic allocation of resource shares permits the cloud provider to adapt the resources given to each VM according to the current load, thus keeping the required performance level with the minimum resource costs. Our work focuses on CPU allocation, but in principle the approach can be extended to other resources as

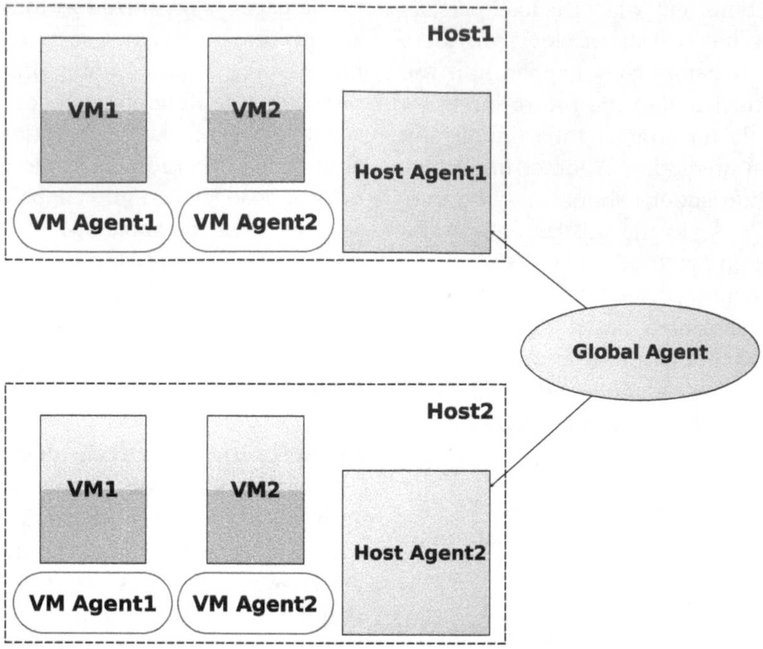

Fig. 1 Resource manager architecture

well. More specifically, for CPU share allocation, the CPU CAP setting that most modern virtualization technologies offer is used. The CAP is the maximum CPU capacity that a VM can use, given as a percentage of the total capacity, which provides good performance isolation between VMs.

To estimate the CPU share allocated to each VM, first the value of the CPU usage for the next time interval is predicted. Then, the CPU share is calculated as the predicted CPU usage plus 10% of the CPU capacity, similar to previous work [12]. By setting the CPU CAP to leave 10% room above the required CPU usage allows us to account for prediction errors and reduces the possibility of performance-related SLA violations. To predict the next CPU usage value, a time series forecasting technique, based on the history of previous CPU usage values, is used. More specifically, a machine learning approach based on Gaussian Processes [6] is employed. Although for local resource allocation only a one step ahead prediction is needed, our VM agent predicts several steps ahead into the future to support overload detection through long-term prediction.

Host agent

One of the duties of the host agent is to play the role of an arbitrator. It gets the CPU requirements from all VM agents, and by resolving any conflicts between them, it decides about the final CPU allocations for all VMs. Conflicts can arise when the CPU requirements of all VMs exceed the total CPU capacity. If there are no conflicts, the final CPU allocation is the same as the allocations requested by the VM agents. If there is a conflict, the host agent computes the final CPU allocations according to the following formula:

$$FinalA = \frac{A}{SumA} * TotalCapacity \tag{1}$$

where *FinalA* is the final allocation, *A* is the required allocation, *SumA* is the sum of all VMs' requested allocations and *TotalCapacity* is the total CPU capacity.

Another duty of the host agent, which is the main focus of this work, is to detect whether the host is overloaded or underloaded. This information is passed to the global agent that then initiates live migration actions for moving VMs away from overloaded or underloaded hosts according to the global allocation algorithm.

Overload detection

For overload detection, a long-term time series prediction approach is used. Long-term prediction in the context of this work means predicting 7 time intervals ahead into the future. A straightforward way for host overload detection is as follows. A host is declared as overloaded if the actual and the predicted total CPU usage of 7 time intervals ahead into the future exceed an overload threshold. The predicted total CPU usage of a time interval into the future is estimated by summing up the predicted CPU usage values of all VMs of the corresponding time interval. The value of predicting 7 time intervals into the future is chosen such that it is greater than the estimated average live migration time (around 4 time intervals). In this work, the average live migration time is assumed to be known and its value of 4 time intervals is estimated by averaging over all VM live migration times over several simulation experiments. In real world scenarios, this value is not known in advance, but it can be estimated based on the previous history of live migration times. Another more fine-grained approach would be to apply VM live migration modelling [13] for live migration time prediction based on relevant VM parameters. Based on this estimated live migration time, the number of time steps to predict into the future can be set to a value greater than the migration time. This is done in order to signal overload states that last longer than the live migration time. Performing live migration actions for overload states that last less than the live migration time is useless, since in this case the live migration action does not eliminate the overload state. Having a larger value than 7 time intervals is not really useful either, since this can lead to skipping some overload states that do not last long, but that can be eliminated by live migration actions. Some preliminary experiments have shown that increasing the number of prediction time intervals further into the future does not increase the stability and performance of the approach. The overload threshold value is determined dynamically based on the number of VMs and is related to the VM SLA violation metric, as explained in "VM SLA violation" section .

Underload detection

The host agent also detects whether a host is underloaded in order to apply dynamic consolidation by live migrating all its VMs to other hosts and turning off the host to save energy. Here, long-term time series predictions of CPU usage are also used. The host is declared as underloaded if the actual and the predicted total CPU usage of 7 time intervals ahead into the future are less than an underload threshold. Again, the value of 7 time intervals is long enough to skip short-term underload states, but not too long as to miss any opportunity for consolidation. The underload threshold value is a constant value, and in this work it is set to 10% of the CPU capacity, but it can be configured by the administrator according to his or her preferences for consolidation aggressiveness.

Not-overload detection

To make live migration decisions, the global agent needs to know the hosts that are not overloaded in order to use them as destination hosts for VM live migrations. A host is declared as not overloaded if the actual and the predicted total CPU usage of 7 time intervals ahead into the future is less than the overload threshold. The actual and the predicted total CPU usage of any time interval is estimated by summing up the actual and predicted CPU usage of all existing VMs plus the actual and the predicted CPU usage of the VM to be migrated. The purpose is to check whether the destination host remains not overloaded after the VM has been migrated.

Uncertainty in long-term predictions

Overload or underload detection based on long-term predictions carries with it the uncertainty of correct predictions, which can lead to erroneous decisions. To take into account the uncertainty of long-term predictions, the above detection mechanisms are augmented with the inclusion of a probabilistic distribution model of the prediction error.

First, the probability density function of the prediction error for every prediction time interval is estimated. Since the probability distribution of the prediction error is not known in advance and different workloads can have different distributions, a non-parametric method to build the density function online is required. In this work, a non-parametric method for probability density function estimation based on kernel density estimation [7] is used. It estimates the probability density function of the prediction error every time interval based on a history of previous prediction errors. In this work, the probability density function of the absolute value of the prediction error is used. Since there are 7 time interval predictions into the future, 7 different prediction error probability density functions are built online.

Probabilistic overload detection

Based on the probability density function of the prediction error, it can be estimated probabilistically, for each predicted time interval, if the future total CPU usage will be greater than the overload threshold. In the following, for convenience, the future total CPU usage is just called the future CPU usage. This is achieved by Algorithm 1 that returns true or false with some probability whether the future CPU usage will be greater than the overload threshold.

First, the algorithm finds the probability that the future CPU usage will be greater than the overload threshold. If the predicted CPU usage is greater than the overload threshold, the difference, called max_error, between the predicted CPU usage and overload threshold, is found. For the future CPU usage to be greater than the overload threshold, the absolute value of the error (i.e., the difference between predicted and future value) should be less than max_error. Based on a cumulative distribution function of the prediction error, the probability that the prediction error is less than max_error, i.e., the future CPU usage is greater than the overload threshold, is found. Since it can happen that the future CPU usage will be greater than the overload threshold, and also that the prediction error will be greater than max_error, the

Algorithm 1: IsUtilizationOver

```
if Pred_Total_Util >= OverThreshold then
    max_error=Pred_Total_Util - OverThreshold
    probability=CumulativeProbability(max_error)
    probability=(probability+1)/2
end
else
    max_error=OverThreshold - Pred_Total_Util
    probability=CumulativeProbability(max_error)
    probability=(probability+1)/2
    probability=1-probability
end
probability=(probability)*100
randnum=rand.nextInt(100)
if randnum < probability then
    return true
end
else
    return false
end
```

probability that this happens, given as (1-probability)/2, is added to the calculated probability to yield the final probability (probability+1)/2. If the predicted CPU usage is less than the overload threshold, by the same approach, first, the probability that the future CPU usage will be less than the overload threshold is found. Then, the probability that the future CPU usage will be greater than the overload threshold is given as (1-probability). Finally, the algorithm returns true with the estimated probability.

Algorithm 1 returns the overload condition probabilistically only for a single prediction time interval. Therefore, to declare the host as overloaded, the actual CPU usage should exceed the overload threshold, and the algorithm should return true for all 7 prediction time intervals in the future.

The interpretation of taking into account prediction uncertainty in overload detection is as follows. Although CPU prediction can lead to values above the overload threshold, there is some probability, due to the uncertainty of prediction, that the CPU utilization will be lower than the threshold. This means that for some fraction of the time the host will not be considered as overloaded. This increases the stability of the approach, as shown by the lower number of live migrations for the probabilistic overload detection approach, compared to other approaches. Furthermore, when CPU prediction is lower than the overload threshold, there is some probability that the CPU utilization will be greater than the threshold. This means that for some fraction of the time the host will be considered as overloaded. In summary, we can say that the host is considered as overloaded or not in proportion to the uncertainty of prediction, which is the right thing to do, as supported by our good experimental results compared to approaches that do not take prediction uncertainty into account.

Algorithm 2: IsUtilizationNotOver

```
if Pred_Total_Util >= OverThreshold then
    max_error=Pred_Total_Util - OverThreshold
    probability=CumulativeProbability(max_error)
    probability=(probability+1)/2
    probability=1-probability
end
else
    max_error=OverThreshold - Pred_Total_Util
    probability=CumulativeProbability(max_error)
    probability=(probability+1)/2
end
probability=(probability)*100
randnum=rand.nextInt(100)
if randnum < probability then
    return true
end
else
    return false
end
```

Probabilistic not-overload detection

To take into account the uncertainty of long-term predictions in detecting whether a host is not overloaded, Algorithm 2 is proposed. It returns true, with some probability, if the future CPU usage of some prediction time interval will be less than the overload threshold. The host is declared as not overloaded if the actual CPU usage is less than the overload threshold, and Algorithm 2 returns true for all 7 prediction time intervals in the future.

Probabilistic underload detection

To detect whether a host is underloaded, Algorithm 3 is proposed. It returns true, with some probability, if the future CPU usage of some prediction time interval will be less than the underload threshold. The host is declared as underloaded if the actual CPU usage is less than the underload threshold, and Algorithm 3 returns true for all 7 prediction time intervals into the future.

Decision-theoretic overload detection

The above improvements make it possible to take into account the uncertainty of long-term predictions in the detection process, but do not take into account the live migration overhead. In this section, a further approach, based on decision theory, is presented that performs live

Algorithm 3: IsUtilizationUnder

```
if Pred_Total_Util >= UnderThreshold then
    max_error=Pred_Total_Util - UnderThreshold
    probability=CumulativeProbability(max_error)
    probability=(probability+1)/2
    probability=1-probability
end
else
    max_error=UnderThreshold - Pred_Total_Util
    probability=CumulativeProbability(max_error)
    probability=(probability+1)/2
end
probability=(probability)*100
randnum=rand.nextInt(100)
if randnum < probability then
    return true
end
else
    return false
end
```

migration actions only if SLA violations due to future host overload states are greater than the penalty of VM live migration.

Applying decision theory requires us to define a utility function that should be optimized. In this work, the utility function value represents the penalty of the host SLA violation or the penalty of live migration overhead. A SLA is a contract between the cloud provider and the cloud consumer that defines, among others, the performance level the cloud provider should conform to and the penalty costs of violating it. In this work, a host SLA violation is defined as the situation when the total CPU usage of the host exceeds the overload threshold for 4 consecutive time intervals. The penalty of host SLA violation is the percentage of the CPU capacity that the total CPU usage exceeds the overload threshold for all 4 consecutive time intervals. The penalty value can be converted to a monetary value with some conversion function, but here it is treated as a CPU capacity percentage value.

Since each VM live migration is associated with some performance degradation, a penalty value for each VM live migration action can be defined in a SLA contract. More concretely, a SLA violation penalty value (expressed also as a percentage of the CPU capacity) for each time interval during VM live migration is defined. The VM live migration SLA violation penalty is defined as the sum of all SLA violation penalties for all time intervals that the VM live migration lasts.

The proposed decision-theoretic approach tries to minimize the host SLA violation penalty (utility value), taking into account the VM live migration SLA violation penalty. In the following, the term utility value will be used instead of host SLA violation penalty. First, the expected utility value of the future host overload state is estimated. The expected utility is given by the sum of the expected utility values of all 4 consecutive future time intervals from interval 4 to interval 7. It is started from time interval 4 instead of time interval 1 in order to capture an overload state before it happens and eliminates it through VM live migration that takes, on the average, 4 time intervals.

If the future CPU usage is known, then the utility of a time interval can be given just as the difference between future CPU usage and the overload threshold. Since only the predicted CPU usage is known, the expected utility value of one time interval can be calculated as follows. First, the CPU usage interval between the total CPU capacity and the overload threshold is divided into a fixed number of levels (5 in this work). Then, the CPU usage above the overload threshold (i.e., the utility value) of each level is calculated as shown in Algorithm 4.

Algorithm 4: LevelUsage

```
Interval=100-OverThreshold
Delta=Interval/UsageLevels
Start=OverThreshold+Level*Delta
return ((Start+(Delta/2))-OverThreshold)
```

In Algorithm 4, *Interval* is the CPU usage interval width above the overload threshold, *Delta* is the CPU usage interval width of the corresponding level, *Level* is the level number (from 0 to 4), whose utility value will be found, *UsageLevels* is the total number of levels and *Start* is the CPU usage of the start of level interval. The algorithm returns as the utility value the CPU usage value taken from the middle of the level interval. Algorithm 4 is run for each possible level to find its utility value.

Second, for any time interval, the probability that the CPU usage of some level will indeed be the future CPU usage is calculated by Algorithm 5.

Start and *Delta* are calculated as in Algorithm 4, *Pred_Util* is the total predicted CPU usage of the corresponding time interval, *CumProbability*() represent the cumulative distribution function used to find the probability that the prediction error is less than a certain value and *prob* represents the probability that the CPU usage of the corresponding level will be the future CPU usage. The algorithm considers three possible situations in which the level interval can be: one in which the interval does not include the predicted CPU usage and is below it, one in which the interval includes the predicted CPU usage, and one in which the interval does not include the predicted CPU usage and is above it. In each case, based on the cumulative distribution function of the prediction error,

Algorithm 5: LevelProbability

```
End=Start+Delta;
if Pred_Util > End then
    prob=(CumProbability(Pred_Util - Start) -
    CumProbability(Pred_Util - End))/2
end
else if (Pred_Util <=End)AND(Pred_Util>=Start)
then
    prob1=CumProbability(Pred_Util - Start)/2
    prob2=CumProbability(End - Pred_Util)/2
    prob=prob1+prob2
end
else
    prob=(CumProbability(End - Pred_Util) -
    CumProbability(Start - Pred_Util))/2
end
return prob
```

the probability that the future CPU usage value will fall inside the level interval is calculated. Since the probability density function of the absolute value of the prediction error is used, the probability that the prediction error is less than a certain value but on the other side of the predicted CPU usage should be excluded from the calculations. Therefore, the estimated probability should be divided by two.

The expected utility of each time interval into the future is given by the sum, over all levels, of the product of the level utility value (the level CPU usage) with the corresponding probability of getting that CPU usage value (level probability). The expected utility of a future host overload state is given as the sum of the expected utilities of 4 consecutive time intervals into the future starting from time interval 4. The host is declared as overloaded and therefore a VM live migration action should be taken if the expected utility (which is the expected host SLA violation penalty) of the future overload state is greater than the live migration SLA violation penalty.

One point that should be stressed is that the above decision is based on the short-term optimization of the utility value but does not consider the long-term utility value accumulation that can result from utility values of overload states that are less than live migration SLA violation penalties but over time can accumulate to bigger values. To address this issue, the utility values of overload states that are less than the live migration SLA violation penalty are accumulated, and at each time interval, a check is made. If the accumulated utility value is greater than the live migration SLA violation penalty, than a VM live migration action is performed regardless whether there is no overload state at that time interval. The same modification is also added to the probabilistic detection approaches explained in the "Probabilistic overload detection", "Probabilistic not-overload detection" and "Probabilistic underload detection" sections.

Decision-theoretic not-overload detection

To detect whether the destination host is not overloaded after a possible VM live migration, a check is made whether the expected utility of 4 consecutive future time intervals starting from interval 4 is greater than zero. If it is zero, then the host will be not overloaded after a VM live migration and can serve as a destination of the VM.

Decision-theoretic underload detection

To detect whether a host is underloaded, the same approach of probabilistic underload detection that is presented in "Probabilistic underload detection" section is used. The utility value is not used for underload detection, since it represents a host SLA violation that can happen only when the host is in the overload state.

Global agent

The global agent makes global resource allocation decisions by live migrating VMs from overloaded or underloaded hosts to other hosts to reduce SLA violations and energy consumption. It gets notifications from the host agent if a host will be overloaded or underloaded in the future and performs the appropriate VM live migration action if it is worth the cost.

The global agent applies the general resource allocation algorithm used in previous work [8] for global VM resource allocation and the Power Aware Best Fit Decreasing (PABFD) [8] algorithm for VM placement, with the following modifications. For overload or underload detection, our approaches presented above to apply long-term prediction with uncertainty consideration are used. For VM selection, the Minimum Migration Time (MMT) [8] policy is used, but with the modification that only one VM is selected for migration in each decision round even if the host can possibly remain overloaded after migration. This is done to reduce the number of simultaneous VM live migrations and the associated overhead. For the consolidation process, unlike the previous work [8] that considers all hosts excluding overloaded and turned off hosts, we consider only underloaded hosts that are detected by the proposed approaches based on long-term prediction. From the list of underloaded hosts, the ones that have lower average CPU usage of previous history values are considered first. As VM live migration destinations, the hosts detected as not overloaded by the presented approaches with long-term predictions are chosen.

VM SLA violation

Since it is difficult for the cloud provider to measure a performance violation metric outside VMs that depends on the performance metric of various applications, such as response time or throughput, we defined a general SLA violation metric that can be easily measured outside VMs. It is based only on VM resource usage. More specifically, it is called VM SLA violation and represents the penalty of the cloud provider for violating the performance of the VMs of the cloud consumer. The performance of an application running inside a VM is at an acceptable level if the required VM resource usage is less than the resource share allocated.

Following the previous argument, a VM SLA violation is defined to happen if the difference between the allocated CPU share and CPU usage of a VM is less than 5% of the CPU capacity for 4 consecutive time intervals. For example, if the CPU share allocated to a VM is 35% of the CPU capacity and the actual CPU usage is more than 30% for 4 consecutive time intervals, then there is a VM SLA violation. The idea of this definition is that application performance gets worse as the required CPU usage is near to the allocated CPU share. The penalty of a VM SLA violation is the CPU share by which the actual CPU usage exceeds the 5% threshold difference from the allocated CPU, for all 4 consecutive time intervals. Although the SLA violation penalty is defined in terms of CPU usage, it can be easily converted to a monetary value by some conversion function. Thus, one of the goals of the global agent is to mitigate VM SLA violations by providing sufficient free CPU capacity through VM live migration, in order to have the CPU share allocation above the required usage by more than 5% for each VM.

Having defined the VM SLA violation metric, the overload threshold can be defined as follows. It is calculated dynamically based on the number of VMs. Let us define N as the number of VMs on a host. To avoid a VM SLA violation, each VM should have more than 5% capacity above CPU usage, so the total free CPU capacity of the host should be more than $N * 5\%$. Based on this, the overload threshold is calculated as the total CPU capacity (100%) minus $N*5\%$. This means that the overload threshold represents the CPU usage level above which some VMs will have SLA violations.

Experimental evaluation

In this section, an experimental evaluation of the proposed approach is presented. First, the experimental setup is described. Then, the experimental results are discussed.

Experimental setup

To conduct controllable and repeatable experiments in a large cloud infrastructure, the CloudSim [9] simulator is used. It is a well known simulator that permits the simulation of dynamic VM resource allocation and energy consumption in virtualized environments. We have made several modifications and extensions to CloudSim in order to integrate the proposed approach and to provide support for setting the CPU CAP to VMs for local resource allocation.

A virtualized data center with 100 heterogeneous hosts is simulated in our experiments. Two types of hosts are simulated, each with 2 CPU cores. One host has CPU cores with 2,100 MIPS and the other one has CPU cores with 2,000 MIPS, while both have 8 GB of RAM. One host simulates the power model of the HpProLiantMl110G4 Xeon3040 computer, and the other one simulates the power model of the HpProLiantMl110G5 Xeon3075.

In the beginning of the simulation, on each host, on the average, 3 VMs (leading to a total of 300 VMs) are scheduled. Four types of VMs are used, and each VM requires one VCPU. Three VMs require a maximum VCPU capacity of 1000 MIPS, while the other one requires 500 MIPS. Two VMs require 1740 MB of RAM, one requires 870 MB, and the last one requires 613 MB. To test realistic workloads, the CPU usage data of real VMs running on the PlanetLab [10] infrastructure are chosen to simulate VM workloads. Each VM runs one application (cloudlet in CloudSim terminology) and the cloudlet length, given as the total number of instructions, is set to a large value in order to prohibit cloudlets to finish before the experiment ends. The experiment is run for 116 time intervals, and the duration of a time interval is set to 10 seconds. The overload detection approach that does not apply prediction error probability modelling yields the same results every time it is run with the same workload, while the probabilistic approaches lead to different results. This prevents running repeated experiments with the same workload in order to compare the two approaches in a fair manner. For this reason, a small random value from a normal distribution with 0 mean and 0.001 standard deviation is added to the CPU usage value of the PlanetLab workload for each time interval. This adds enough perturbation for the experiment to give different results for different runs, as required.

For long-term time series prediction, the WEKA [14] machine learning framework with Gaussian Processes for regression is used through its Java API. A history of previous CPU usage data with a length of 20 samples is used for prediction and forecasting model training. To keep the simulation time to acceptable levels, the forecasting model is trained every 5 time intervals with new CPU usage data. For kernel density estimation, the empirical probability distribution implementing the Variable Kernel Method with Gaussian Smoothing of the Apache Commons Math 3.6 API [15] is used. A history of previous prediction errors with a length of 30 samples is used for probability density function model training, which is done in each time interval.

Experimental results

In this section, experimental results of comparing six different approaches are presented. The first one called NO-Migrations (NOM) is the approach that just allocates CPU resources locally to VMs, but does not perform live migration actions. The second one called Short-Term Detection (SHT-D) detects an overload state if the actual and the predicted CPU usage values of the next two time intervals in the future are above the overload threshold. Also, to detect not-overload and underload states, the actual and predicted CPU values for the next two time intervals into the future are used. This approach represents detection based on short-term CPU usage predictions and is expected to be quite sensitive to short spikes of overload conditions. The third approach called Long-Term Detection (LT-D) bases overload, underload and not-overload detections on long term CPU usage predictions of the next 7 control intervals into the future. The fourth approach called Long-Term Probabilistic Detection (LT-PD) bases overload, underload and not-overload detections on long-term CPU usage predictions of the next 7 control intervals into the future, but takes into account prediction uncertainty through prediction error probability distribution modelling. The next approach called Long-Term Decision Theory Detection (LT-DTD) bases overload, underload and not-overload detections on long-term CPU usage predictions of the next 7 control intervals into the future, but takes into account prediction uncertainty and live migration overhead by applying decision theory. The last approach called Local Regression Detection (LR-D) is one of the approaches used in related work [8] that uses the local regression technique to predict the resource usage in the future. We selected it as a representative state-of-the-art technique, since it achieves the best performance as shown by the authors [8] compared to other techniques that use static or adaptive utilization thresholds.

In our evaluation, the following performance metrics are used:

- VM SLA violation (VSV) as explained in "VM SLA violation" section represents the penalty of the cloud provider for each VM. It is important to stress that a VM SLA violation can also happen because of wrong local CPU share allocations as a result of wrong CPU predictions. In the experiments, only a VM SLA violation, as a result of shortage of CPU capacity due to overload states of hosts, is shown.
- Energy consumption (E) of the data center for the whole experimental time measured in KWh.
- Number of VM live migrations (NM) for the whole experimental time.
- Since there is a trade-off between energy consumption and SLA violations, another metric that integrates both VM SLA violations and energy in a single value is defined. This is called the Utility metric and is given by the formula below:

$$Utility = \frac{CVSV}{NOM\_CVSV} + \frac{Energy}{NOM\_Energy} \quad (2)$$

where *CVSV* is the cumulative VSV value of all VMs for the whole experimental time, *Energy* is the energy consumption, *NOM_CVSV* is the cumulative VSV value of the NOM approach, *NOM_Energy* is the energy consumption of the NOM approach. Both *NOM_CVSV* and *NOM_Energy* are used as reference values for the normalization of the respective metrics. Normalization is performed to permit the integration of two metrics with different measuring units in a single utility function. The best approach is the one that achieves the minimal Utility value.
- Another metric that also has been used in previous work [8] and can capture both energy and VM SLA violations is ESV. This metric is given by:

$$ESV = E * CVSV \quad (3)$$

where E is energy consumption and *CVSV* is the cumulative VSV value of all VMs for the entire experimental time.

The simulation experiment is run for two different load levels called LOW and HIGH and three different VM live migration SLA violation penalties, mp=2%, mp=4% and mp=6% (MP2, MP4, MP6). For convenience, in the following, the term VM live migration SLA violation penalty is shortened to live migration penalty. By load level we mean the CPU usage consumed by each VM. The loads LOW and HIGH are taken by multiplying the PlanetLab CPU usage values for each time interval with a constant value of 8 and 14, respectively. Each of the previously given live migration penalties represents the migration penalty of one time interval. The experiment is repeated five times for each combination of approach, load level and migration penalty, and the results are exposed to a statistical ANOVA analysis.

In Fig. 2, the cumulative VM SLA violation penalty (cumulative VSV) for each approach averaged over all combinations of load levels and migration penalties is shown. The cumulative VSV value is the sum of VSV values of all VMs for the whole experimental time. It is evident from the graph that the LT-DTD and LT-PD approaches that consider prediction uncertainty achieve lower VM SLA violation levels than the other approaches, with statistical significance, as shown by the ANOVA analysis. On the other hand, we see that LR-D performs better than SHT-D, but similar to LT-D with no statistically significant difference. This is expected, since both techniques apply prediction of resource usage into the future, but without taking prediction uncertainty into

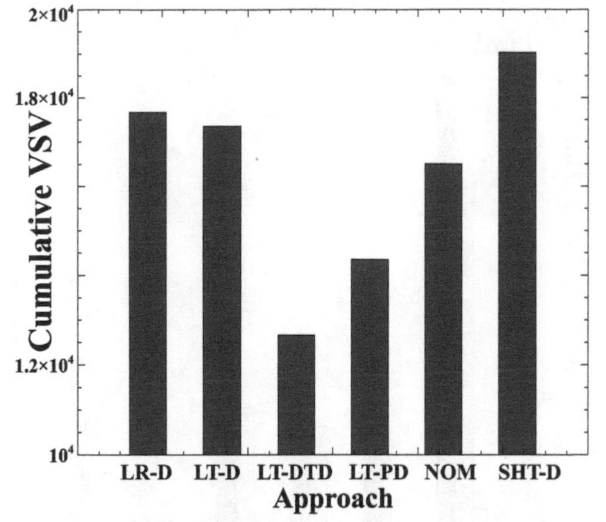

Fig. 2 Cumulative VSV over all loads and migration penalties

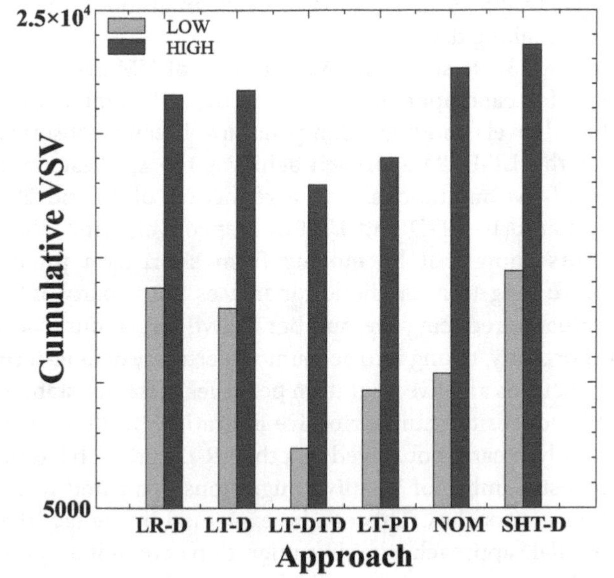

Fig. 3 Cumulative VSV over all migration penalties for two load levels

account. This shows that considering long-term prediction uncertainty in decision-making is useful for lowering VM SLA violations. More importantly, the LT-DTD approach achieves the lowest level of VM SLA violations compared to the other approaches, confirming the conclusion that applying decision theory to take into account live migration penalty can result in better performance. For example, the LT-DTD approach decreases the cumulative VSV value relative to the LT-D approach by 27% and relative to LT-PD by 12%. Furthermore, by comparing LT-D with SHT-D, applying long-term predictions even without considering prediction uncertainty can lower VM SLA violations.

To see the effect the load level has on VM SLA violations, in Fig. 3 the cumulative VSV value is shown, averaged over all migration penalties, for each approach and the two load levels. First, it can be observed that for each approach, increasing the load increases the VM SLA violations, which is expected since there is more contention for resources. Again, we can see that for both load levels, the LT-DTD approach achieves the lowest VSV value compared to the other approaches. More importantly, the reduction in VSV value by going from high load to low load is larger for the LT-DTD approach than for the other approaches. For example, the reduction in VSV value from high to low load for the LT-D approach is 40%, while for LT-DTD it is 59%. Furthermore, it can be observed that for low load both LR-D and LT-D are worse even compared to the non-migration case, and only for high loads they show better results, with statistical significance, as indicated by the ANOVA tests. This shows that when the load is low, it is not worth, at least with respect to VM SLA violations, to perform live migration actions without taking into account prediction uncertainty.

To understand how different approaches behave regarding the migration penalty, Fig. 4 shows the cumulative VSV value for each approach, averaged over two load levels and three migration penalties. In general, for all approaches, increasing the migration penalty results in increased VM SLA violation values, which is expected since the migration penalty is part of the VM SLA violation value calculation. It is evident that LT-DTD is more robust and does not really follow this trend, as shown by statistically not significant differences of the cumulative VSV values between MP2 and MP4. This is because the

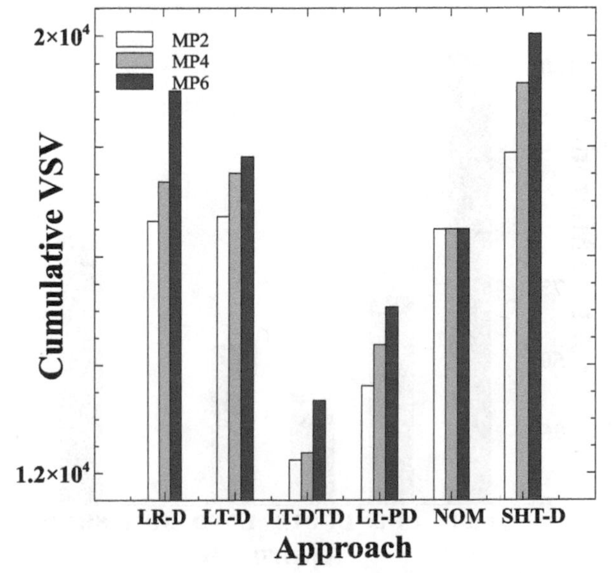

Fig. 4 Cumulative VSV over all loads for three migration penalties

LT-DTD approach takes into account migration penalties when making decisions.

In Fig. 5, we show the total number of VM live migrations for each approach, averaged over all combinations of load levels and migration penalties. It can be observed that the LT-DTD approach achieves the smallest number of live migrations with a reduction of 46 and 29% compared to LT-D and LT-PD, respectively. First, these results show that by moving from short-term prediction to long-term prediction increases the stability of the approach, reducing the number of live migrations. More importantly, taking into account uncertainty of long-term predictions and live migration penalties increases stability and reduces the number of live migrations further. Interestingly, it can be observed that the LR-D approach has the highest number of VM live migrations compared to the other approaches. This can be explained by the fact that the LR-D approach takes live migration actions if only one predicted usage point in the future is above the threshold, while the other approaches check several points into the future.

In Fig. 6, we show for each approach how the number of live migrations is affected by the load level. In general, apart from LT-DTD and LT-D, increasing the load level increases the number of live migrations, which can be explained by the fact that more live migrations are required to deal with increased load. The LT-DTD approach shows more stability by not increasing the number of live migrations with increased load, and since this still results in better VSV values compared to the other approaches (as shown in Fig. 3), this is a desirable behavior. The LT-D approach shows a slight increase in the number of live migrations, but this is not statistically significant, as shown by an ANOVA analysis.

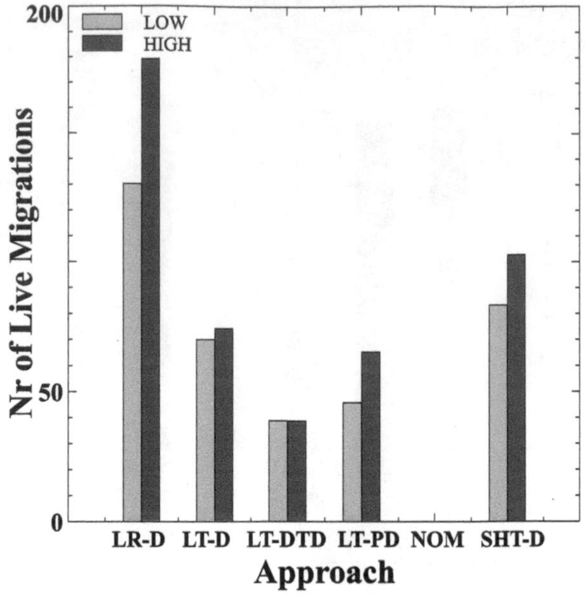

Fig. 6 Number of live migrations over all migration penalties for two load levels

Figure 7 shows for each approach how the number of live migrations changes by varying the migration penalty. Unlike other approaches, both LT-DTD and LT-PD show decreased numbers of live migrations by increasing the migration penalty. The LT-DTD approach shows a decreased number of live migrations when moving from MP2 to MP4, and this can be explained by the fact that

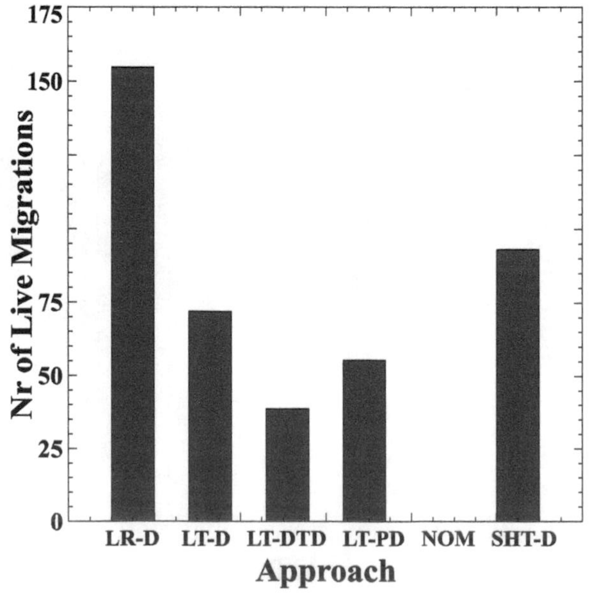

Fig. 5 Number of live migrations over all loads and migration penalties

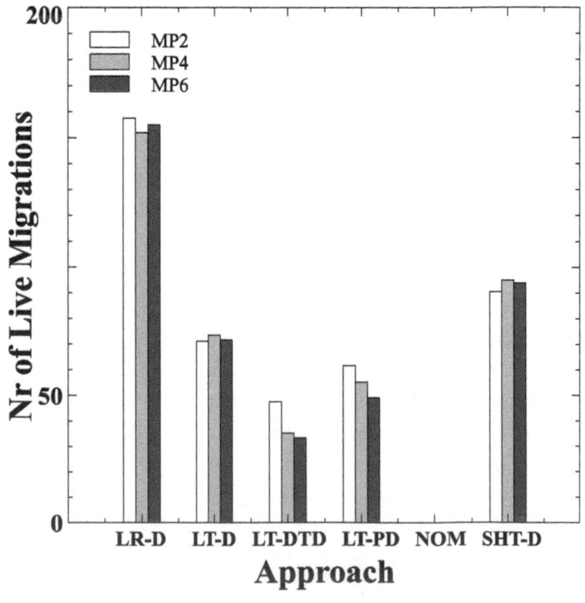

Fig. 7 Number of live migrations over all loads for three migration penalties

it takes the migration penalty into account when making live migration decisions. This behavior has the benefit of using the migration penalty as a parameter to control the aggressiveness of the consolidation process. On the other hand, the decreased number of live migrations for the LT-DP approach, at least for MP2 to MP6, which is statistically significant, does not have an apparent explanation since this approach does not take into account the migration penalty in decision making. The only explanation is that this behavior is caused because the LT-PD approach also takes into account utility value accumulation in decision making the same way as LT-DTD does, as explained in "Decision-theoretic overload detection" section . To test this claim and to check whether also the LT-DTD approach achieves the above behavior due to this this modification, an experiment has been conducted to measure the number of live migrations for three migration penalties with low load. The experiment is run for LT-PD and LT-DTD, but without taking into account utility value accumulation.

The results of the experiment are shown in Fig. 8. It is evident that for LT-PD, increasing the migration penalty does not change the number of live migrations, supporting the claim that the above behavior is caused only by taking into account utility value accumulation in decision making. However, for LT-DTD, increasing the migration penalty decreases the number of live migrations, showing that this behavior is due to the decision-theoretic approach adopted by it.

Figure 9 shows the energy consumption of the data center for the whole experimental time for each approach

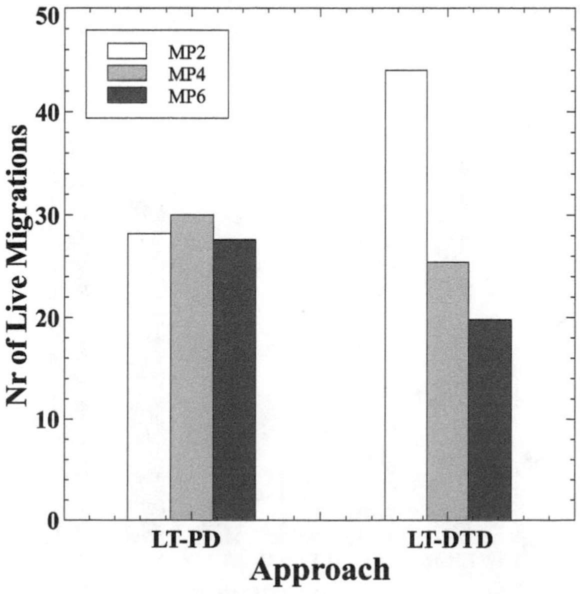

Fig. 8 Number of migrations for LT-PD, LT-DTD for three migration penalties

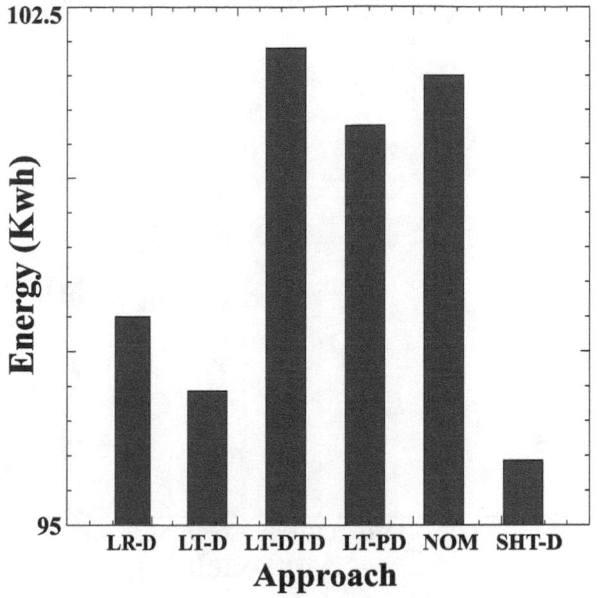

Fig. 9 Energy over all load levels and migration penalties

averaged over all combinations of load levels and migration penalties. It is evident that the LT-DTD approach shows a slight increase in energy consumption compared to the other approaches. For example, it increases energy consumption by 5 and 0.30% compared to LT-D and NOM, respectively. Although the LT-DTD approach saves less energy, the improvement in the VM SLA violation values outweighs the decrease in energy savings, as shown by the results of the Utility metric. The LR-D, LT-D and SHT-D aproaches achieve more energy savings than the LT-DTD approach at the expense of higher VM SLA violations, resulting in worse ESV and Utility values.

In Fig. 10, we show for each approach how the energy consumption is affected by the load level. It can be observed, as expected, that increasing the load increases the energy consumption for all approaches. Decreased energy consumption with a decrease in the load level can be explained by the fact that low load creates more opportunities for consolidation and turning off hosts.

From the above argument it can be expected that by decreasing the load level further, LT-DTD can save energy compared to NOM. To test this claim, another experiment is conducted with load lower than LOW load, which is called Very LOW (VLOW). VLOW is taken by multiplying the PlanetLab CPU usage values for each time interval by a constant value of 2. The migration penalty is set to MP4. The experiment is repeated for 5 times for each of the LT-DTD and NOM approaches.

The average energy consumption and Utility values are shown in Table 1. The Utility value is shown to understand if any possible energy savings are achieved at the expense of VM performance.

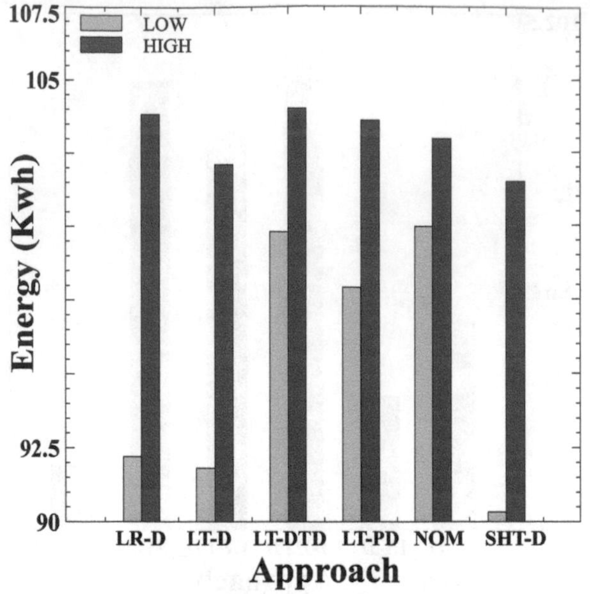

Fig. 10 Energy over all migration penalties for two load levels

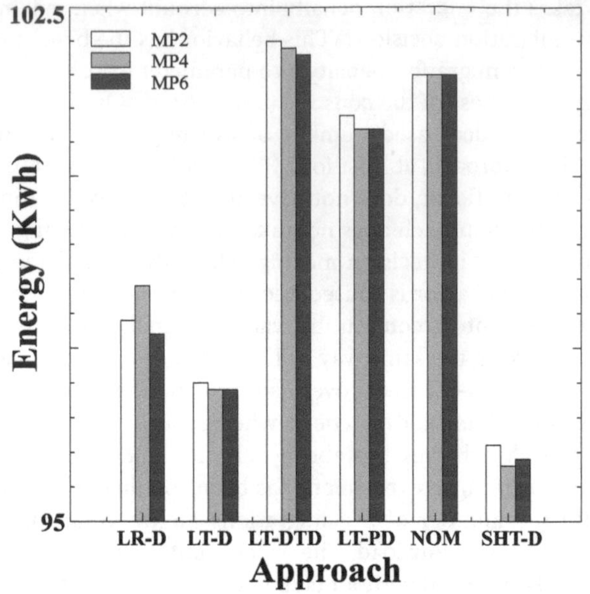

Fig. 11 Energy over all loads for three migration penalties

The LT-DTD approach achieves energy savings of 22.8% compared to NOM, with a better Utility value. This shows that when the load decreases, the LT-DTD approach gives more priority to the consolidation process, reducing the number of hosts and saving energy. On the other hand, when the load increases, it gives more priority to the load balancing process by saving less energy but lowering the VM SLA violations.

In Fig. 11, we show for each approach how the energy consumption is affected by migration penalty. An ANOVA statistical analysis indicates, for each approach, no statistically significant differences of energy value between different migration penalty cases. This shows that the migration penalty has no significant effect on energy consumption.

To understand better the trade-off between energy savings and performance of VMs, in Fig. 12 we present the Utility for each approach over all load levels and migration penalties. The Utility is the metric that indicates improvements in both energy savings and VM SLA violations and can serve as the metric of measuring the overall performance. It can be observed that the LT-DTD approach achieves the lowest Utility value compared to other approaches with statistical significance, as shown by an ANOVA analysis. It improves the Utility by approximately 9.4% and 4.3% compared to LT-D and LT-PD approaches, respectively. These results show that although the LT-DTD approach achieves slightly less energy savings, it improves the SLA violations, thus finding the best performance-energy trade-off. With respect to the Utility value, the LR-D approach performs better than the SHT-D approach, but slightly worse than the LT-D approach. This is because the LR-D approach achieves

Table 1 Energy and utility for two approaches with MP4 penalty and VLOW load

Approach	Energy (KWh)	Utility value
LT-DTD	70.2	0.79
NOM	91	0.88

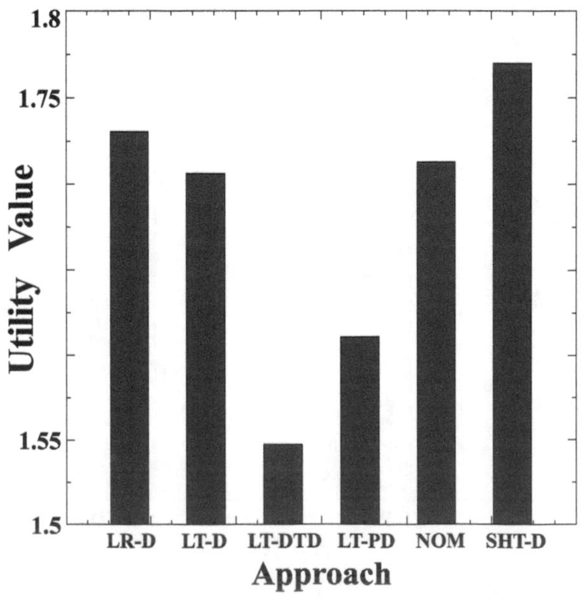

Fig. 12 Utility value over all loads and migration penalties

less energy savings than the LT-D approach with similar SLA violations, as shown in Figures 2 and 9.

Figure 13 shows for each approach how the Utility is affected by the load levels. It can be observed that increasing the load increases the Utility value, since both energy consumption and SLA VM violations are increased. For each load level, the LT-DTD approach achieves the lowest Utility value compared to the other approaches. Similar to the case of the cumulative VSV value, it is also evident that for high load, the LR-D and LT-D approaches achieve comparably equal Utility values and show improvements compared to the NOM case with statistical significance.

Figure 14 shows for each approach the effect that the migration penalty has on the Utility. In general, for all approaches it can be observed that increasing the migration penalty increases the Utility, since it increases the VM SLA violation penalty. However, similarly to the VSV value, the LT-DTD approach seems to be more resistant in increasing the Utility. This can be observed at least for the case of moving from MP2 to MP4 where there are no statistically significant differences resulting from the ANOVA analysis.

In Figs. 15, 16 and 17, the overall ESV value, the ESV value for two load levels and the ESV value for three migration penalties, are shown, respectively. For display convenience, the ESV value in the graphical illustration is divided by 10.000. It can be observed that the ESV value shows the same trend as the Utility value. The LT-DTD approach achieves the lowest ESV value compared to the other approaches with statistical significance, as shown by the ANOVA analysis. Similarly to the Utility value, the LR-D approach performs comparably equal with LT-D and better than NOM and SHT-D with statistical significance, especially for high loads. Furthermore, regarding the ESV, the LT-DTD approach seems to be more resistant with respect to increasing the ESV value with an increased live migration penalty.

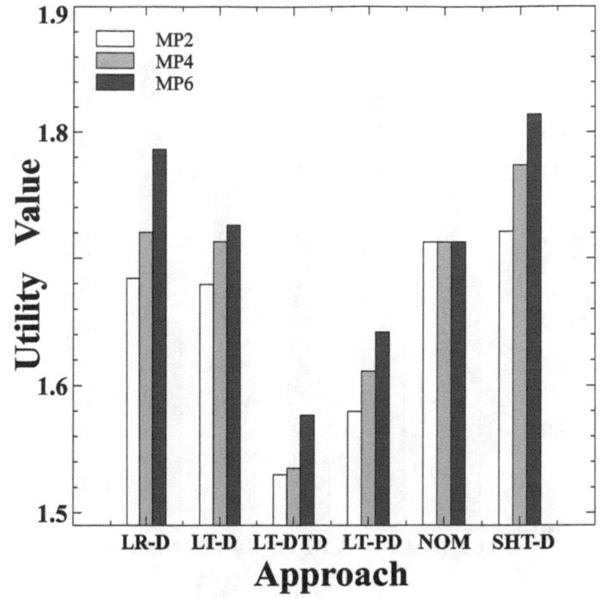

Fig. 14 Utility value over all loads for three migration penalties

Related work

There are many works in the literature on dynamic resource allocation in cloud computing, tackling the

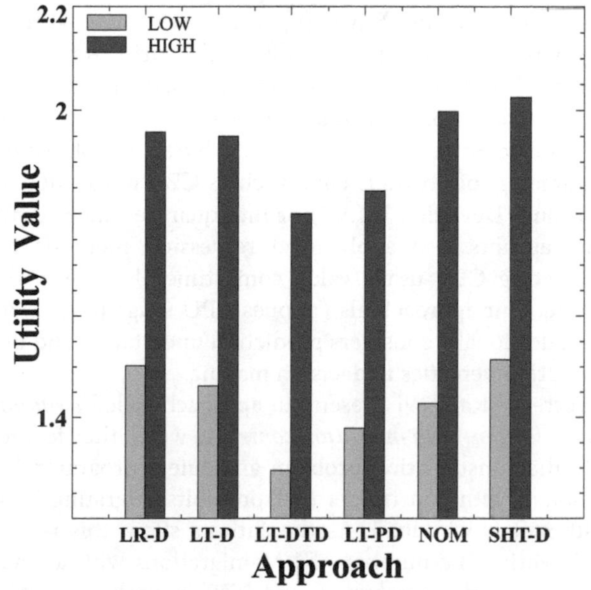

Fig. 13 Utility value over all migration penalties for two load levels

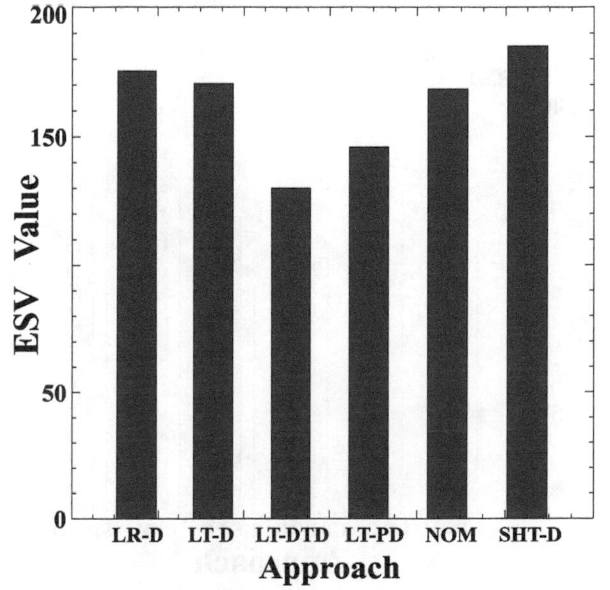

Fig. 15 ESV value over all loads and migration penalties

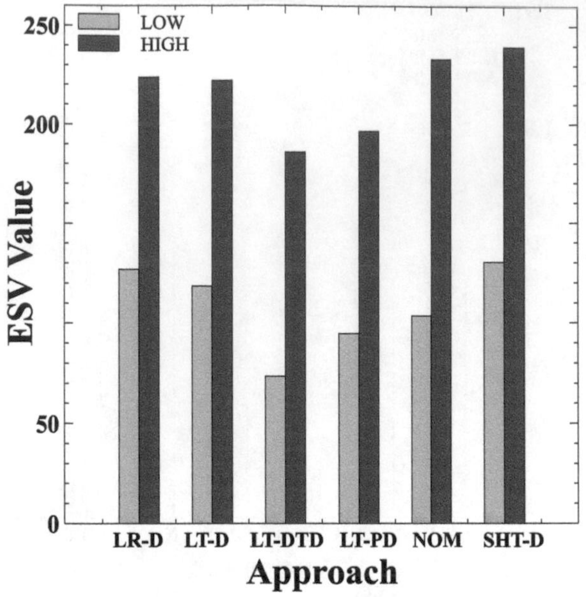

Fig. 16 ESV value over all migration penalties for two load levels

problem from different angles. Therefore, we cannot provide an exhaustive treatment of related work, but focus mainly on the aspects of VM resource demand prediction and host overload detection.

Several works apply VM live migration to allocate resources to VMs for overload mitigation or consolidation of VMs to fewer hosts. For example, Wood et al. [16] propose an approach called *Sandpiper* for overload detection and live migration of VMs from overloaded hosts to not overloaded ones. Their overload detection approach declares a host as overloaded if the past k resource usage values and the next predicted one exceed a given threshold. They use a greedy algorithm that live migrates heavy loaded VMs to least loaded hosts.

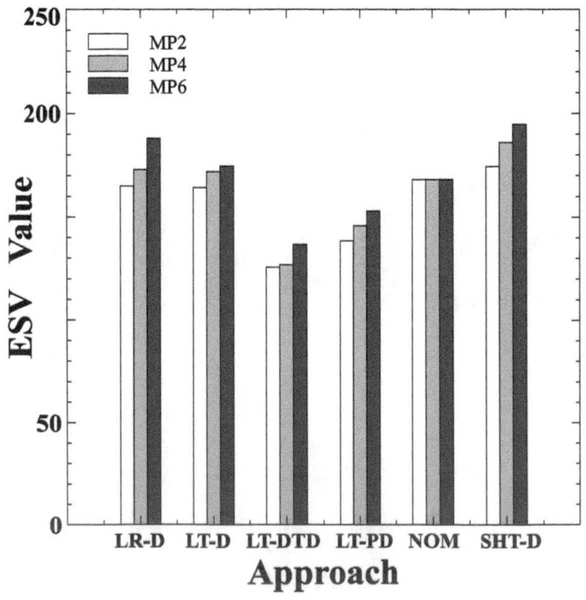

Fig. 17 ESV value over all loads for three migration penalties

Similarly, Khanna et al. [17] propose an approach for dynamic consolidation of VMs based on live migration. Their approach for host overload detection is also based on resource usage exceeding a threshold value. Their goal is to minimize the number of hosts by maximizing the variance of resource capacity residuals. This is achieved by ordering VMs in non-decreasing order of their resource usage and migrating the least loaded VM to the least residual resource capacity host.

Beloglazov et al. [18] propose energy-aware heuristic algorithms for dynamic allocation of VMs to hosts based on live migration. They decide on the overload or underload state of a host based on whether the CPU usage is higher or lower than the overload or underload thresholds, respectively. The authors apply a modified Best-Fit-Decreasing (BFD) heuristic to pack VMs to fewer hosts, which takes into account the power increase of hosts.

All the above approaches base host overload or underload detection on current or short-term predictions of resource usage and static usage thresholds, which can be sensitive to short spikes of load that can cause stability problems and unnecessary live migrations. In contrast, our approach bases overload or underload detection on long-term predictions of CPU usage by taking into account prediction uncertainty, which results in stability and efficient live migration actions, as shown by the experimental results.

Several other works apply more sophisticated approaches than just static usage thresholds. For example, Beloglazov and Buyya [8], as a continuation of their previous work [18], present different heuristics for host overload and underload detection based on statistical analysis of historical resource usage data. They propose to use adaptive usage thresholds based on statistical parameters of previous data, such as CPU usage Median Absolute Deviation (MAD) or interquartile range (IQR). The authors also apply local regression methods for predicting CPU usage value some time ahead into the future. Our approach also applies CPU usage prediction, but additionally considers prediction uncertainty and live migration penalties in decision making.

Ferreto et al. [19] present an approach called *dynamic consolidation with migration control* in which they formulate the consolidation problem as a linear programming problem with constraints that prohibits migrating VMs with steady workload. As the authors show, this results in lowering the number of VM migrations with a small increase in the number of hosts. Their work is complementary to our work, since it tries to avoid unnecessary migrations, but can not provide stability if the data center is running only variable load VMs.

Gong and Gu [20] propose a dynamic consolidation approach called Pattern-driven Application Consolidation (PAC) based on extracting patterns of resource usage called signatures using signal processing approaches such as Fast Fourier Transform (FFT) and dynamic time warping (DTW). Based on extracted signatures, they perform dynamic placements of VMs to the hosts that have the highest match between VM resource usage signature and host free capacity signature. Their work focuses on periodic global consolidation for VM resource usage patterns that show periodicity. The authors also consider on-demand VM migrations for instantaneous overloads, but in contrast to our approach, they base overload detection on a single resource usage value exceeding a static threshold.

Andreolini et al. [21] propose an approach for host overload detection in which a host is declared as overloaded when there is a substantial change in the load trend of the host, as a result of applying the CUSUM algorithm. Their goal is similar to the goal of our work for providing a robust and stable approach avoiding unnecessary live migrations, but their load change point detection requires past history usage data to be available, at which point the SLA violations have already happened. In contrast, our approach applies long-term prediction to avoid violations before they happen.

Beloglazov and Buyya [22] propose an approach for host overload detection based on Markov chains and optimization of inter-migration time with Quality of Service (QoS) constraints. The goal of their approach is finding the solution (migration probabilities of each state) of an optimization problem to maximize inter-migration time while keeping the Overload Time Fraction (OTF) metric inside certain values. To take into account dynamic and non-stationary workloads, the authors apply a multi-size sliding window approach. Similarly, we also propose an approach for host overload detection, but in contrast, we apply long-term prediction techniques taking into account the VM live migration penalty. Another difference is that we tackle a different performance metric, i.e., minimization of SLA violations of each VM, while Beloglazov and Buyya focus on keeping the percentage of time that a host is overload inside certain constraints.

There are several works that apply VM resource demand prediction techniques for resource allocation in cloud computing. For example, Gong et al. [23] and later Shen et al. [11] propose an approach for VM fine-grained resource allocation based on resource demand prediction. They base their resource demand prediction on two methods: a) Fast Fourier Transform to find periodicity or signature of resource demand and b) a state based approach using Markov chains. Similarly to our approach for overload detection, they apply these methods for long-term prediction of host resource conflicts. If they predict a conflict, they apply a live migration action to resolve it, taking into account the migration penalty. As the authors point out, using a multi-step Markov model to predict further into the future lowers the prediction accuracy. This is exactly the problem we tackle in this paper by taking into account uncertainty of long-term prediction to deal with low prediction accuracy.

Islam et al. [24] propose resource prediction approaches based on machine learning. More specifically, they propose and experiment with Linear Regression and an Error Correction Neural Network. They show experimentally the superiority of the neural network in making more accurate predictions, but they do not apply their techniques to host overload detection or in general for VM resource allocation.

Farahnakian et al. [25] propose a prediction technique based on linear regression to detect if a host is overloaded or underloaded. They train a model based on past CPU utilization history and predict the next CPU utilization. Based on this prediction, they detect if a host is overloaded or underloaded and apply VM live migration to move VMs to other hosts. The problem with their approach is that they base their overload or underload detection technique on short-term CPU utilization prediction which is susceptible to oscillatory load. In contrast, we apply long-term prediction augmented with uncertainty estimation to provide a more stable approach.

Khatua et al. [26] propose an approach for VM load prediction several time steps into the future by applying an Auto-regressive Integrated Moving Average (ARIMA) model. They apply their approach for horizontal scaling in cloud settings. If an overload situation is detected, based on some threshold value, then the number of VMs is increased. Also, their approach does not consider the uncertainty and prediction errors in their model of long-term prediction, which is important for increasing the quality of allocation decisions.

Ashraf et al. [27] propose a load prediction approach for VM resource allocation and admission control of multi-tier web applications in cloud computing. Their prediction method is based on a two step procedure. In the first step, a so called load tracker, based on Exponential Moving Average (EMA), constructs a representative view of the load by filtering the noise. In the second step, a load predictor based on linear regression takes as input the representative view of the load produced by load tracker and provides as output the predicted load value in some interval k in the future. They apply a hybrid reactive-proactive approach to calculate a weighted utilization. Through a linear interpolation, the authors mix the measured and the predicted value, by including a weight factor *w* that depends on the prediction error. In contrast to their work, our approach to prediction is different. We apply a long-term prediction method directly to the past resource utilizations and consider long-term prediction uncertainty through prediction error probability distribution. Furthermore, their approach is applied for horizontal VM scaling and admission control of multi-tier web applications, while we tackle the problem of host overload detection and mitigation through VM live migration.

Qiu et al. [28] propose an approach for VM load prediction based on a deep learning prediction model. More specifically, this model is composed of two layers, the Deep Belief Network (DBN) and a regression layer. The DBN is used to extract the high-level workload features from the past VM resource utilizations, while the regression layer is used to predict the future load values. The authors evaluate experimentally only the prediction accuracy of the approach, but do not apply it on any VM resource allocation problem. In contrast, we propose and evaluate a complete approach for VM resource allocation problem through long-term resource prediction and VM live migration.

Conclusion

In this paper, a novel approach for VM resource allocation in a cloud computing environment has been presented. It allocates resources locally by changing the CPU share given to VMs according to the current load. Global resource allocation is performed by migrating VMs from overloaded or underloaded hosts to other hosts to reduce VM SLA violations and energy consumption. For overload or underload host detection, long-term predictions of resource usage are made, based on Gaussian processes as a machine learning approach for time series forecasting. To take into account the prediction uncertainty, a probability distribution model of the prediction error is constructed using the kernel density estimation method. To consider the VM live migration overhead, a decision-theoretic approach is applied.

We can draw the following conclusions. First, making long-term predictions of resource demand can increase stability and overall performance of a cloud. Second, making overload detection decisions proportional to uncertainty of predictions is the right thing to do, as supported by our experimental results. Third, taking into account both prediction uncertainty and live migration overhead by applying decision-theoretic optimization methods yields the best decisions and improves the performance further.

There are several areas for future work. First, we want to point out that our approach is based on a long-term prediction model that relies on historical load patterns. This means that our prediction model cannot easily predict sudden and sharp increases of the load (i.e., load bursts). This issue is out of scope of this paper, but it can be addressed by focusing on load burst detection techniques ([29–31]). Thus, an interesting area of future work is combining load burst detection techniques with load prediction techniques to deal with a large variety of cloud load patterns. Second, in addition to the currently used scheme of predicting the next CPU usage value for local resource allocation, more sophisticated schemes based on control theory [32, 33], Kalman filters [34] or fuzzy logic [35, 36] can be explored. Third, a distributed resource allocation approach should be investigated, where each host agent makes live migration decisions in cooperation with nearby host agents. A distributed approach is suitable for large scale cloud infrastructures where centralized optimization complexity and single point of failure are important factors to consider. In distributed approaches, the problem is how local agents with a limited view should coordinate each other to achieve a global optimization objective. Finally, investigating long-term prediction of the usage of multiple resources (e.g., CPU, memory and I/O bandwidth) and their interdependencies in allocation decisions is an interesting area of future work.

Abbreviations

ARIMA: Auto-regressive integrated moving average; BFD: Best-fit-decreasing; DBN: Deep belief network; DTW: Dynamic time warping; EMA: Exponential moving average; FFT: Fast fourier transform; IaaS: Infrastructure as a service; IQR: Interquartile range; LT-D: Long-term detection; LT-DTD: Long-term decision theory detection; LT-PD: Long-term probabilistic detection; MAD: Median absolute deviation; MMT: Minimum migration time; NOM: No-migrations; OTF: Overload time fraction; PAC: Pattern-driven application consolidation; PABFD: Power aware best fit decreasing; SHT-D: Short-term detection; SLA: Service level agreement; VM: Virtual machine; VSV: VM SLA violation

Acknowledgements

This work is supported by the German Research Foundation (DFG, SFB 1053 - MAKI), by the LOEWE initiative (Hessen, Germany) within the NICER project and and the Albanian Government (Excellence Fund).

Authors' contributions

DM provided the main idea of the paper, designed and coded the main algorithms in the simulator, performed some of the experiments and their statistical analysis and wrote the first draft of the manuscript. AM revised the manuscript and added some of the related works, helped finding bugs and revised the code, adapted the local regression algorithm and performed some of the experiments and statistical analysis. BF revised the algorithms and the experimental statistical data analysis, critically reviewed and edited the manuscript. All authors read and approved the final manuscript.

Competing interests

The authors declare that they have no competing interests.

Author details

[1]Department of Computer Engineering, Polytechnic University of Tirana, Tirana, Albania. [2]Department of Contemporary Sciences and Technologies, South East European University, Tetovo, Macedonia. [3]Department of Mathematics & Computer Science, Philipps-Universität Marburg, Marburg, Germany. [4]Department of Electrical Engineering & Information Techology, TU Darmstadt, Darmstadt, Germany.

References

1. Zhang Q, Cheng L, Boutaba R (2010) Cloud computing: state-of-the-art and research challenges. J Intern Serv Appl 1(1):7–18
2. (2011) Amazon elastic compute cloud (amazon ec2). http://www.vmware.com/. Accessed 5 Jul 2016
3. Barham P, Dragovic B, Fraser K, Hand S, Harris T, Ho A, Neugebauer R, Pratt I, Warfield A (2003) Xen and the art of virtualization. In: Proc. 19th ACM Symposium on Operating Systems Principles. ACM, New York. pp 164–177
4. (2016) VMWare, Inc. http://www.vmware.com/. Accessed 7 Jul 2016
5. Clark C, Fraser K, Hand S, Hansen JG, Jul E, Limpach C, Pratt I, Warfield A (2005) Live migration of virtual machines. In: Proc. 2nd Conference on Symposium on Networked Systems Design and Implementation. USENIX Association, Berkeley. pp 273–286
6. Rasmussen CE, Williams CKI (2005) Gaussian Processes for Machine Learning (Adaptive Computation and Machine Learning). The MIT Press, Cambridge
7. Scott DW (1992) Multivariate density estimation : theory, practice, and visualization. In: Wiley series in probability and mathematical statistics : Applied probability and statistics section. Wiley-Interscience, New York, Chichester, Brisbane
8. Beloglazov A, Buyya R (2012) Optimal online deterministic algorithms and adaptive heuristics for energy and performance efficient dynamic consolidation of virtual machines in cloud data centers. Concurr Comput Pract Experience 24(13):1397–1420. doi:10.1002/cpe.1867
9. Calheiros RN, Ranjan R, Beloglazov A, De Rose CAF, Buyya R (2011) Cloudsim: A toolkit for modeling and simulation of cloud computing environments and evaluation of resource provisioning algorithms. Software: Practice & Experience 41(1):23–50
10. Park K, Pai VS (2006) Comon: A mostly-scalable monitoring system for planetlab. ACM SIGOPS Oper Syst Rev 40(1):65–74
11. Shen Z, Subbiah S, Gu X, Wilkes J (2011) Cloudscale: Elastic resource scaling for multi-tenant cloud systems. In: Proceedings of the 2nd ACM Symposium on Cloud Computing. ACM, New York, NY. pp 1–14
12. Minarolli D, Freisleben B (2014) Cross-correlation prediction of resource demand for virtual machine resource allocation in clouds. In: Proc. 6th International Conference on Computational Intelligence, Communication Systems and Networks (CICSYN '14). IEEE Computer Society, Washington. pp 119–124
13. Akoush S, Sohan R, Rice A, Moore AW, Hopper A (2010) Predicting the performance of virtual machine migration. In: Proceedings of the 10th IEEE International Symposium on Modeling, Analysis and Simulation of Computer and Telecommunication Systems. IEEE Computer Society, Washington. pp 37–46
14. Hall M, Frank E, Holmes G, Pfahringer B, Reutemann P, Witten IH (2009) The weka data mining software: An update. ACM SIGKDD Explor Newsl 11(1):10–18
15. Commons Math: The Apache Commons Mathematics Library (2016). http://commons.apache.org/. Accessed 10 Jul 2016
16. Wood T, Shenoy P, Venkataramani A, Yousif M (2009) Sandpiper: Black-box and gray-box resource management for virtual machines. Comput Netw 53(17):2923–2938
17. Khanna G, Beaty K, Kar G, Kochut A (2006) Application performance management in virtualized server environments. In: Proc. 10th IEEE/IFIP Network Operations and Management Symposium (NOMS 2006). IEEE Computer Society, Washington. pp 373–381
18. Beloglazov A, Abawajy JH, Buyya R (2012) Energy-aware resource allocation heuristics for efficient management of data centers for cloud computing. Future Generation Comp Syst 28(5):755–768
19. Ferreto TC, Netto MAS, Calheiros RN, Rose CAFD (2011) Server consolidation with migration control for virtualized data centers. Future Generation Comp Syst 27(8):1027–1034. Elsevier B.V., Amsterdam
20. Gong Z, Gu X (2010) Pac: Pattern-driven application consolidation for efficient cloud computing. In: Proc 2010 IEEE International Symposium on Modeling, Analysis and Simulation of Computer and Telecommunication Systems. IEEE Computer Society, Washington. pp 24–33
21. Andreolini M, Casolari S, Colajanni M, Messori M (2009) Dynamic load management of virtual machines in cloud architectures. In: CloudComp, Springer, Lecture Notes of the Institute for Computer Sciences, Social Informatics and Telecommunications Engineering, vol 34. Springer, Berlin. pp 201–214
22. Beloglazov A, Buyya R (2013) Managing overloaded hosts for dynamic consolidation of virtual machines in cloud data centers under quality of service constraints. IEEE Trans Parallel Distrib Syst 24:1366–1379
23. Gong Z, Gu X, Wilkes J (2010) Press: Predictive elastic resource scaling for cloud systems. In: Proc. International Conference on Network and Service Management (CNSM'10). IEEE Computer Society, Washington. pp 9–16
24. Islam S, Keung J, Lee K, Liu A (2012) Empirical prediction models for adaptive resource provisioning in the cloud. Future Gener Comput Syst 28(1):155–162
25. Farahnakian F, Liljeberg P, Plosila J (2013) Lircup: Linear regression based cpu usage prediction algorithm for live migration of virtual machines in data centers. In: Proceedings of the 2013 39th Euromicro Conference on Software Engineering and Advanced Applications. IEEE Computer Society, Washington. pp 357–364
26. Khatua S, Manna MM, Mukherjee N (2014) Prediction-based instant resource provisioning for cloud applications. In: Proceedings of the 2014 IEEE/ACM 7th International Conference on Utility and Cloud Computing. IEEE Computer Society, Washington. pp 597–602
27. Ashraf A, Byholm B, Porres I (2016) Prediction-based vm provisioning and admission control for multi-tier web applications. J Cloud Comput 5:1–21
28. Qiu F, Zhang B, Guo J (2016) A deep learning approach for vm workload prediction in the cloud. In: 2016 17th IEEE/ACIS International Conference on Software Engineering, Artificial Intelligence, Networking and Parallel/Distributed Computing. IEEE Computer Society, Washington. pp 319–324
29. Lassnig M, Fahringer T, Garonne V, Molfetas A, Branco M (2010) Identification, modelling and prediction of non-periodic bursts in workloads. In: Proceedings of the 10th IEEE/ACM International Conference on Cluster, Cloud and Grid Computing. IEEE Computer Society, Washington. pp 485–494
30. Mehta A, Dürango J, Tordsson J, Elmroth E (2015) Online spike detection in cloud workloads. In: Proceedings of the 3th IEEE International Conference on Cloud Engineering. IEEE Computer Society, Washington. pp 446–451
31. Zhu Y, Shasha D (2003) Efficient elastic burst detection in data streams. In: Proceedings of the 9th ACM SIGKDD International Conference on Knowledge Discovery and Data Mining. ACM, New York. pp 336–345
32. Minarolli D, Freisleben B (2011) Utility-driven allocation of multiple types of resources to virtual machines in clouds. In: Proc. 13th IEEE Conference on Commerce and Enterprise Computing (CEC'11). IEEE Computer Society, Washington. pp 137–144
33. Padala P, Shin KG, Zhu X, Uysal M, Wang Z, Singhal S, Merchant A, Salem K (2007) Adaptive control of virtualized resources in utility computing environments. In: Proc. 2nd ACM SIGOPS/EuroSys European Conference on Computer Systems (EuroSys '07). ACM, New York. pp 289–302
34. Kalyvianaki E, Charalambous T, Hand S (2009) Self-adaptive and self-configured cpu resource provisioning for virtualized servers using kalman filters. In: Proceedings of the 6th International Conference on Autonomic Computing. ACM, New York. pp 117–126
35. Minarolli D, Freisleben B (2013) Virtual machine resource allocation in cloud computing via multi-agent fuzzy control. In: Proc. 3rd International Conference on Cloud and Green Computing (CGC'13). IEEE Computer Society, Washington. pp 188–194
36. Rao J, Wei Y, Gong J, Xu CZ (2011) Dynaqos: model-free self-tuning fuzzy control of virtualized resources for qos provisioning. In: Proc. 19th International Workshop on Quality of Service. IEEE Computer Society, Washington. pp 1–9

9

Data security in decentralized cloud systems – system comparison, requirements analysis and organizational levels

André Müller[1*], André Ludwig[2] and Bogdan Franczyk[1]

Abstract

Cloud computing has been established as a technology for providing needs-orientated and use-dependent IT resources, which now are being used more frequently for business information systems. Particularly in terms of integration of decentralized information systems, cloud systems are providing a stable solution approach. Still, data security is one of the biggest challenges when using cloud systems and a main reason why many companies avoid using cloud services. The question we are facing is how cloud systems for integration of decentralized information systems have to be designed, in terms of technology and organization, so that privacy laws of the cloud user can be guaranteed. This contribution summarizes the results of a system comparison of decentralized cloud systems in social networks, a requirements analysis based on a literature analysis, and a model for organizational levels of cloud systems, derived from the requirements analysis.

Keywords: Data security, Cloud system, Decentralized information system, Requirements, Organization levels

Introduction

Cloud computing receives a lot of attention in terms of research and in practice. Over the years, the use of cloud computing in businesses has been increasing [1]. Individual infrastructure, platform and software services, which are provided by a private computer center via a private cloud system or by an external hosted private cloud system, are now being used in particular [2]. Based on cloud computing technology, new forms of IT resource relocation and their needs-orientated and use-dependent provision via commercial services have been established. Moreover, cloud computing has a far-reaching potential for the transformation of business models and operative processes, especially supported through system integration [3].

In terms of business information systems, cloud computing is becoming more and more important. Business information systems, as a socio-technological man-machine system, describe the connection between technological components and business staff, in order to fulfill the work tasks [4] and to become the backbone of many modern worlds of employment. The need for decentralization and a technological as well as an organizational new-orientation of information system is increasing because of the increasing distribution of value-added processes via various companies, a faster and more flexible new-orientation of business partnerships, and an intensive integration of customers into value-added processes [5, 6]. Current developments in information technology and communication technology, including keywords, for example, such as "Internet of Things" [7], "Cyber Physical Systems" [8], "Emergent Software Systems" [9], or "Fog Computing" [10], are supporting a higher decentralization of information systems. In this context, cloud systems are offering an infrastructural solution. Via Internet connection and the provision of software solutions and integration solutions according to the "As-a-Service-Paradigma", various decentralized components of an information system can be integrated. Though cloud systems are a stable technological basis for the

* Correspondence: amueller@wifa.uni-leipzig.de
[1]Department of Business Information Systems, Leipzig University, Grimmaische Straße 12, 04109 Leipzig, Germany
Full list of author information is available at the end of the article

provision and cooperation of information systems, missing solutions in terms of data security are inhibiting the broad utilization of this technology in businesses.

Especially smaller and medium-sized companies are on the one hand interested in the use of cloud systems [2]; on the other hand they are afraid of using them since they show insufficient informational right to say in terms of storage location and legal security [11], and they are afraid of the "lock-in effects" [2] of external-hosted utilization. Further, new and unsolved challenges concerning data security arise because of the possibility for the collection and analysis of big, distributed data files, i.e., in terms of the "Big Data Context" [12]. Key provisions for data security are defined in the German privacy laws and are therefore an informational self-rule but those laws are only applicable to private individuals and hence not suitable for a reliable protection of business data. Service providers from non-EU countries do not fulfil these requirements and are therefore not suitable for reliable data protection. Consequently, solution approaches, which guarantee the fulfillment of data protection regulations on an organizational and professional level during the operation of the information systems and during the transfer of data between the information systems, are needed.

Our central and design-orientated research issue results from this motivation:

How must a cloud-based ecosystem for the integration of decentralized information systems be built technologically and in terms of organization, in order to guarantee cloud user their privacy laws? To answer this question, we base our method on the "Heuristical Theorizing" research approach [13]. In order to structure our problem, we analyzed solution concepts for the organization of cloud ecosystems from the application area of social networks via a system comparison. Following on that, we developed requirements for the support of decentralized systems through literature research. Derived from the results, various organizational levels for a division of roles in cloud-based ecosystems were developed. The research artifacts are summarized in the following contribution. In the next step, a first conceptual architecture draft and a technical proof-of-concept prototype based on the results is developed. The evaluation proceeds according to the quick-and-simple strategy of the FEDS framework [14].

The article is structured as follows: In section 2 basic terms are explained. In section 3 the system comparison is described. In section 4 the results of our literature research, from which the catalog of requirements is derived, are summarized. Section 5 shows basic forms of organizational decentralization derived from the system comparison and the catalog of requirements. In section 6 the results are discussed and the following steps are shown. The article closes with the summary in section 7.

Basic terms

In the following, the terms "decentralized information systems" and "cloud systems" are classified with regard to the development of decentralized cloud ecosystems.

Data security peculiarities in these systems are described afterwards. The term "information system" describes a socio-technical man-machine system, which embeds itself into the organizational, personnel and technical structures of an institution [15]. The system can be categorized fully through five characteristic features: human, user properties, operational tasks, technology, and information behavior phases [16]. Decentralized information systems extend the term "information system" since they include aspects of a decentralization of stakeholder groups, technological components, and process cycles beyond company boundaries.

Decentralization can't be reduced down to the distribution of technological resources within an infrastructure. Organizational decentralization means externalization of responsibilities, rights, and duties within a superordinate process. Technological decentralization describes the use of distributed systems and the externalization of software system components. Both ways of decentralization are strongly connected, changing dynamically, and can influence each other. Because of the complexity of the decentralized structures and relations, the openness, and dynamic of the changing value-added structures, information systems can also be called ecosystems [17].

The term "cloud system" describes a network-based computer system, which can be used for organizational and technological integration into decentralized information systems, based on cloud computing technology. Applications and data are loosely connected, they communicate via network, and translate organizational distributed business processes. Because of open interfaces and dynamic composition, a reconfiguration of the system is possible. Technological decentralization based on distributed applications has to be considered as a requirement of organizational decentralization.

Organization of rights, duties and tasks for data security represents a central component of information systems, and the same is true for cloud (eco-) systems. The aim is to protect user data from unauthorized access, transfer and commercialization by third parties. With today's authentication technologies, authorization technologies and encryption technologies, communication and protection from unauthorized data access can be guaranteed, but looking at it from an organizational view, the problem concerning data security cannot be solved. Here, control over data of the cloud services provider, or rather cooperation partner, lies with the recipient. Therefore, a decentralized data keeping in cloud systems has to make it possible for all parties to decide on their own which data security regulations apply to their own data. Their adherence has to be transparent and controllable. The cloud system has to be designed so that changing data access regulations can be determined by the cloud user. Further, technological requirements and country-specific laws as well as "aspects of trust" have to be able to be integrated into the data access management and data access rights management. Data security principles such as "a specific purpose", "transparency", and "reliability of data generation and processing" apply to decentralized cloud systems, too [18]. It was shown that a decentralization makes an increasing adherence to data security requirements possible since control over data and applications is transferred to the user [10, 19]. Deriving from this motivation, forms and gradations of decentralization and its suitability for fulfilling requirements beyond data security have to be analyzed.

System comparison

We carried out a system comparison in order to structure the problem and to identify the established solution approaches for the organization of cloud ecosystems.

The field of research of decentralized organized social networks is very suitable for this comparison since decentralized cloud systems are already widely spread in this field and the topic data security is of high significance. Further, various references already exist and can be used as a comparable object.

The system comparison includes eight social network concepts in total. These eight concepts were analyzed in terms of architecture, performance, security/data security, and benefit. The results of the comparison are summarized in Fig. 1. The solutions of the investigated concepts of PeerSoN [20], Priv.io [21], Safebook [22], and SuperNova [23] are based on a peer-to-peer approach. The concepts PrPl [24], SlopPy [25], and Vis-à-Vis [26] are based on distributed applications and on server solutions as well as cloud solutions that are self-managed by the user. As a common ground of these concepts, all parties are expected to run and manage their own cloud system. The eight already mentioned systems will now be explained shortly and examined with regard to their currently unsolved problems.

PeerSoN by Buchegger et al. [20] is a peer-to-peer approach that focuses on privacy. In order to protect user data, encryption following the public-key-method is used. Thus, data can only be accessed with the right key. In general, all data is stored on the respective local computer of the users. A lookup service helps finding users and with the interaction. If a user is not online, data cannot be updated. The problem of limited data availability can be solved by storing data temporarily on a friend's computer. This, however, affects the data security negatively. Direct communication takes place via external applications. **Persona** by Baden et al. [27] is a solution approach that uses a central storage service. Further, it uses attribute-based encryption with fine granular rules. With the help of a browser extension, it can be integrated into an already existing SNS. However, first performance measurements showed that loading a big amount of data can take relatively long (up to 10 s). **Priv.io** by Zhang and Mislove [21] is a cloud-based approach. For this, two components, i.e., priv.io core and priv.io applications, were developed. Priv.io core is a Java application, which allows to access and manipulate user data. In addition, it is used for communication with other users. Priv.io applications allow the usage of further applications in this ecosystem. In general, Priv.io uses attribute-based encryption. The Priv.io application

Name	Author(s)	Year	Architecture					Performance			Security/ Data Security			Benefit		
			P2P	Decentral	Cloud based	Data management by users	Massaging	Availability of data	Data transfer	Load and Process Delay	Encryption	Data caching	Relationship management	Costs	Complexity	Prototype
PeerSoN	Buchegger et al.	[2009]	●	◕	○	◑	○	◑	◕	◌	●	◑	○	◌	●	◑
Persona	Baden et al.	[2009]	○	○	○	○	◕	●	◑	◕	◕	○	○	◌	●	◑
Priv.io	Zhang & Mislove	[2013]	●	●	●	○	○	◕	◕	●	●	○	○	◕	●	◑
PrPl	Seong et al.	[2010]	○	◕	◑	◕	◌	◕	●	◑	◑	◕	◕	◕	◕	●
Safebook	Cutillo et al.	[2009]	◕	◕	○	◑	○	◑	●	◌	◕	○	◑ ◌	◕	●	◑
SlopPy	Gambs & Lolive	[2013]	○	◕	○	●	○	●	◕	◑	●	◑	○	◑	●	◑
SuperNova	Sharma & Datta	[2012]	●	●	○	◕	○	◕	●	◑	◕	●	◑	◌	●	◑
Vis-à-Vis	Shakimov et al.	[2011]	○	●	◕	●	○	◑	◑	◑	○	◌	○	◕	◕	◑

◌ No statement ○ Not / None ◑ Partial / Medium ◕ Mostly / High ● Full / Very High

Fig. 1 Results of the degree of the fulfillment of the system comparison characteristics

has to be able to run on every cloud as a web service. All data is stored by the cloud provider. Therewith, data availability is guaranteed and costs rise. **PrPl** by Seong et al. [24] introduces a software component named Personal Cloud Butler. It is operated by the user himself or provided by another provider. Therewith, various data security levels arise, depending on who operates the software. Different instances of the Butler communicate with each other in order to build a network. Further, it is possible to add data from other systems (e.g., from Facebook). This concept is mainly organized in a decentralized way since each instance has to be set up by a user without having a central unit. **Safebook** by Cutillo et al. [22] is a decentralization approach with Real-life trust. Here, the aim was to solve the problem of trust between users, the system and its operators. Like many other solution concepts, P2P technology is used for communication and the development of the network. The connection is implemented via a Matryoshka architecture, which checks the trust between the users. Communication is set up through a social network server. **SlopPy** by Gambs and Lolive [25] is an approach for storing encrypted data on so-called semi-trusted instances. Here, data is transferred to friends but can only be accessed with the right key. The communication takes place via an anonymous communication network. Here, the problem of low availability is addressed. **SuperNova** by Sharma and Datta [23] is a P2P solution approach with Super-Peers. In this approach, friends store data for higher availability. So-called Storekeepers hold key tasks and keep the network running. **Vis-à-Vis** by Shakimov et al. [26] is an extensive concept of a decentral cloud-based social network. Virtual Individual Servers (VIS) are operated by the user himself or rented from a cloud provider. These VISs consist of a storage layer and a processing layer, which communicate. That way, user data can be exchanged. The system is local- and group-based and can be compared to Diaspora*.

All network concepts either fully or partly implement data accessibility and transaction encryption. Further, absolute decentralization without gradation is required. Often, the need of the user for simple operations is not the focus of the approach [28].

From comparison it can be seen that already-existing solution approaches prefer peer-to-peer as a technological realization since it isn't necessary to trust in a centralized authority and moreover, data security requirements can be applied. Challenges arise especially in terms of accessibility of data in these approaches. Further, it can be seen that a decentralization solution is more complex in terms of application compared to a centralized solution. Data transfer is comparatively high in all solutions and the time for the transfer is likely to increase when the number of users increases.

Requirements analysis

In addition to the comparison of the system and for further structuring, we conducted a systematic literature research from which we derived requirements for the design of a cloud ecosystem that followed data security laws. The literature research was conducted in international A+, A and B information system journals, i.e., Information Systems Research, Management Information Systems Quarterly and Journal of Management Information Systems, based on the VHB ranking [29]. After following the method according to Denyer [30], a keyword search within the context of decentralization, information systems, and data security was used. Following that, titles and abstracts were selected. Ultimately, insights and requirements for the design of information systems were gained through extraction and synthesis.

Altogether, 14 contributions with a high relation to the topic were identified. Afterwards, 21 recommendations for the conception of data security in decentralized cloud systems were taken from these contributions. We then assigned these recommendations through content structuring to the fields of data security, trust, relationship management, and system design. All requirements were evaluated and adapted according to quality criteria. According to Pohl [31], quality criteria are: completeness, transparency, correctness, clarity, understandability, consistency, controllability, evaluation, topicality, and atomicity. That way, it was possible to identify unspecified issues and to correct them in a targeted way. These requirements were completed by six further requirements, which were taken from the results of the system comparison and the information of the relevant authors. The first catalog of requirements consists of 27 requirements and is summarized in Table 1.

"Basic system requirements" describes basic requirements for future conceptions.

It becomes clear that a central authority, so-called "Trusted Party", represents an especially expedient solution approach [32]. However, this means that a first restriction concerning decentralization takes place since a jointly agreed on neutral and trustworthy authority is now needed. Further, it should still be the aim to make preferably low costs possible and to use already-existing offers at the current market.

That way, through a distribution of service provisions and the respective specialization of service providers, a high-quality overall offer is created. External user data storage can be mentioned as an example. Additionally, an all-inclusive new development can be avoided. An alternative level of data security can be adapted, aimed at various target groups for future participants [33, 34]. When using external resources, it is necessary to ensure availability as far as possible [35].

"Data security" sets a special focus on data security aspects and their application within information systems.

Table 1 Catalogue of requirements

ID	Description
CO	Basic system requirements
CO1	System as central authority of trust ("Trusted Party")
CO2	Use of services offered at the market, which need little user configuration
CO3	Basic use of system without user costs
CO4	Alternative selection of data security level
CO5	Provide possibility for data encryption on storage medium
CO6	Integration of user management
CO7	Complete availability of necessary resources in the form of data
DS	Data Security
DS1	Data security has to be highlighted visually for the user
DS2	Control over data usage with an option for (automatic) deletion
DS3	Simple rights management to avoid conflicts
DS4	User anonymity within the system
DS5	Personal data protection through user or authority for data management
DS6	Attached protection policies for data
DS7	Co-data security for jointly created user data (Co-Privacy)
DS8	Recommendation for data security settings
TR	Trust
TR1	Centralization of trust
TR2	Creation of trust of the user (i.e., via support from other user)
RM	Relationship Management
RM1	Support for contact management
RM2	Automatic derivation of relations
SY	System Design
SY1	High number of data sources through a high abstraction of the access layer
SY2	Concept for the availability and non-availability of user data
SY3	System robustness against attacks and incorrect data
SY4	Fine granular
SY5	Inoperability
SY6	Rights and interaction management based on relationships
SY7	High-performance search within the network
SY8	Self-presentation management (monitoring/feedback)

Basically, what is needed is all-inclusive data security control, involving high transparency and understandability for the user [36]. A simple rights management helps the user when defining rules. Through low complexity, better implementation and a reduction of wrong decisions are made possible [37]. To delete unused data, the system has to work automatically and in a transparent way for the user [38]. Attached protection policies, i.e., in form of meta data, assist when allocating data and make a theoretical transfer into another system possible [39]. Nowadays, data cannot only be assigned to one user because they consist of many different parts. Hence, it must be made possible that the so-called Co-Privacy is displayed and implemented conceptually in an information system [39].

The sector "Trust" explicitly requires decentralizing the Co-Privacy. Further, it is pointed out that trust has to be created, i.e., via other user [40]. For this, the relationship management has to be created. The management has to be able to automatically derive relations [39, 41].

The sector "system design" sets basic requirements for the system. Here, fine granularity, robustness, and interoperability are basic elements. Monitoring and feedback are helping the user when using the system. The high number of sources for external data represents the openness of the system [35, 39].

Organizational levels analysis

Various organizational levels for a division of roles in terms of data security in cloud (eco-) system can be derived from the system comparison and requirements analysis. Here, parties involved can act in different roles: infrastructure provider, user of infrastructure, or both. Moreover, trust toward other participants is extremely important—especially when talking about a high decentralization. This means new concepts of trust are needed and the situation can't be handled without the inclusion of the environment. Consequently, the government, as the most trustworthy authority, is to be involved in the consideration, acting within the legal framework. Based on these insights, an organizational model was created, which represents a network-of-relationships model of the various parties. All parties involved have different requirements and aims for the network, hence different forms of relationship constellations arise. Figure 2 summarizes the various forms of organizational decentralization.

Following, levels of organizational decentralization are explained. The model of organizational decentralization is divided into five stages, whereas the first stage (Level 0: None (Central)) doesn't contain any decentralization aspects. These levels correspond to the currently most common solution approach where all customer data is stored centrally. The shift to the next level represents another organizational structure.

Already existing system implementations and system approaches can be assigned to exactly one level. The higher the level, the higher the decentralization.

Level 0: Centralized

Level 0 is characterized by completely centrally organized applications and a range of services. Most recent

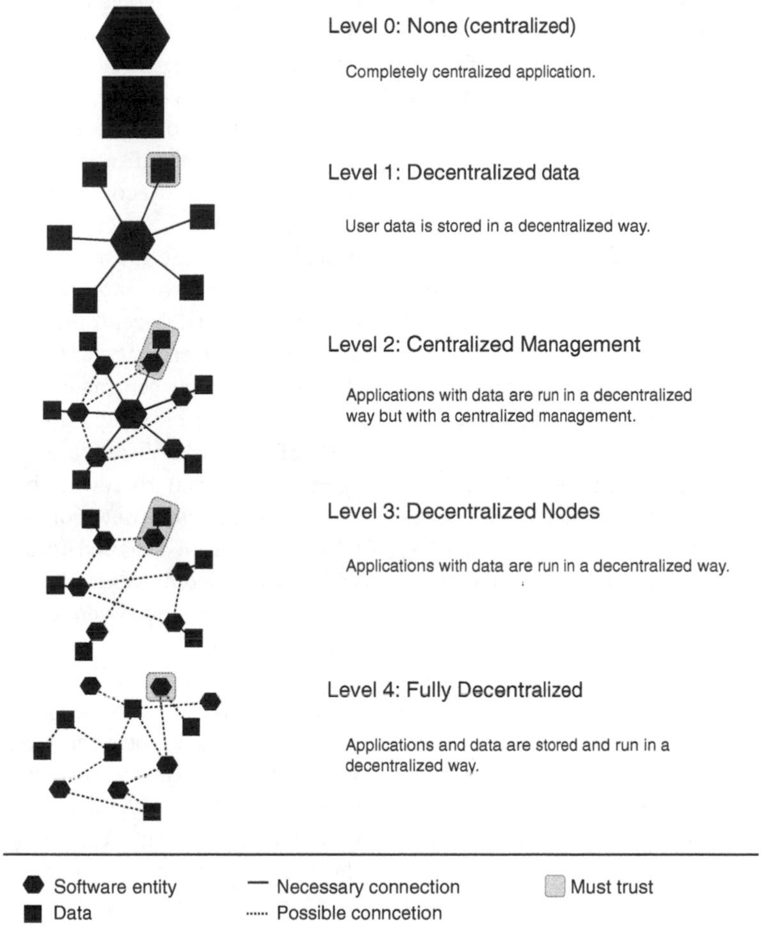
Level 0: None (centralized)
Completely centralized application.
Level 1: Decentralized data
User data is stored in a decentralized way.
Level 2: Centralized Management
Applications with data are run in a decentralized way but with a centralized management.
Level 3: Decentralized Nodes
Applications with data are run in a decentralized way.
Level 4: Fully Decentralized
Applications and data are stored and run in a decentralized way.
Software entity
Data
Necessary connection
Possible conncetion
Must trust

Fig. 2 Overview of organizational decentralization

Internet platforms can be assigned to this level. This is due to the fact that the creation of service offers can take place independent from the participants. Hence, it is possible to implement a system in a simple way without restrictions.

Another advantage for companies is that data can be kept as an economic asset within the application. Following this concept, responsibilities, rights, and duties do not have to be transferred to a third party. Participants need to trust the provider completely. This is being criticized by many customers at the moment [42].

Level 1: Decentralized data

On Level 1, a decentralization in terms of externalization of user data takes place. The cloud computing technology called "Storage Cloud" is suitable for the technological implementation since it enables an easy integration of data storage of user into the system. The centrally acting provider takes the roles of trustworthy authority and data management without storing any user data on their own. Complete trust dissolves partially and user takes on more rights and duties. For a high-quality range of services, a guarantee of data availability is essential.

Level 2: Centralized management

Level 2 is characterized by the relocation of applications and data to the participants and a centralized management. In many systems, a centralized Registry is used for the connection of the nodes in order to connect the participants with each other. The service-orientated paradigm is a typical example of this kind of organizational form. Further, the concept is implemented in the World Wide Web. The so-called "Domain Name" server redirects centralized-managed web addresses to the server. Here, it has to be considered that the centralized management needs to be trusted in terms of identity checks of the participants.

Level 3: Decentralized nodes

On Level 3, a centralized management of the network is missing so the participants need to organize the cooperation and interaction on their own. In the field of social networks, Diaspora* [43] is a representative that supports this concept. It has to be mentioned that self-managed nodes can raise difficulties for persons without technological knowledge. Basically, the principle follows the peer-to-peer approach. Some approaches use the principle of distributing data to various participants in order to achieve high-availability.

Level 4: Fully decentralized

The last stage, Level 4, describes a full decentralization of all components, meaning that data and applications are being stored and run separately. This concept can be found in the field of "Internet of Things" [7] and in the "Fog Computing-Paradigma" [10]. Currently, the implementation of this stage is subject to recent research. What's striking is that only the whole ecosystem needs to be trusted but not the centralized provider. Future research has to investigate if such a concept can work without a centralized management.

All described stages can be operated and implemented with various forms of technological decentralization. Hence, this is a clearly organizational model. For the evaluation of the introduced model, systems and concepts are being assigned to the respective levels. A falsification is displayed if a system can't be assigned to a level.

Results discussion and next steps

The results discussion is divided according to the presented artifacts of the analysis phase into the section "requirements catalog" and "organizational decentralization model."

The requirements catalog introduced in this contribution brings together insights from research and presents guidelines for a conceptualization of ecosystems with decentralized organized information systems. The primary criterion is the creation of trust between all members of the network (see: CO1). Therefore, extensive analysis of solution strategies regarding legal and technological aspects are needed. Since it was shown that the centralization of trust is the most successful variant, a peer-to-peer solution, as introduced in other concepts, is to be excluded completely. That way, a wide range of variants of possible system concepts is restricted implicitly. New insights coming from research and experience make it necessary to extend or rather adapt the collected requirements accordingly. Further, it has to be analyzed if all requirements can be realized within a system entirely. Here, a prototypical implementation of all requirements serves as the basis for an evaluation. The application of already existing solutions on the market (see: CO2) applies mainly to external data storage. The integration of many sources is very complex. Especially a full availability of resources (see: CO7) requires strategies in case of non-availability (see: SY2). Basically, the aim is to gain more control over personal data. In order to involve user more, a storage cloud solution is offered. For the user, this means additional expenses and giving away responsibility. Based on this, a first concept idea is seen in Fig. 3.

The organizational decentralization model is the first step toward a classification of roles and the increase of trust toward cloud ecosystems. For the evaluation of the developed model, already existing concepts and approaches from the current research were classified. The classification of the introduced systems into the model of organizational decentralization is split into a complete application sovereignty and data sovereignty, and into the usage of a central management. Safebook, and SuperNova can be assigned to Level 2. PeerSoN, Priv.io, PrPl, SlopPy und Vis-à-Vis do not need a central management and can therewith be assigned to Level 3. In case of falsification, new concepts have to be developed, which cannot be assigned to any level. Then, the model will be extended or adapted.

While categorizing systems, it could be seen that Level 1 (Decentralized Data) was not represented. The distribution of data, i.e., distributed in data bases, is a strategy used in practice in order to deposit data. It was seen that this kind of strategy does not occur in a relational context. Further, it was seen that there is a connection between the increase of decentralization and the decrease of necessary trust toward other participants. Hence, Level 0 provides absolute trust in the provider. In practice, trust in large providers is lost so other solution approaches try to reduce the necessary trust. Altogether, it was seen that in practice and with the current service range of Internet services, Level 0 is being used the most. To some extent, this is due to the fact that complexity of software application development increases to the same extent as decentralization. Concerning loosely-linked components, further increase of data transmission is expected.

In order to answer the presented questions, future research needs to choose a level of organizational decentralization and to implement this level into an exemplary information system. Challenges for all decentralized architectures are the fields of data security and availability. Further, a trustworthy authority (Trusted Party) needs to be installed while considering and analyzing all local circumstances concerning data security

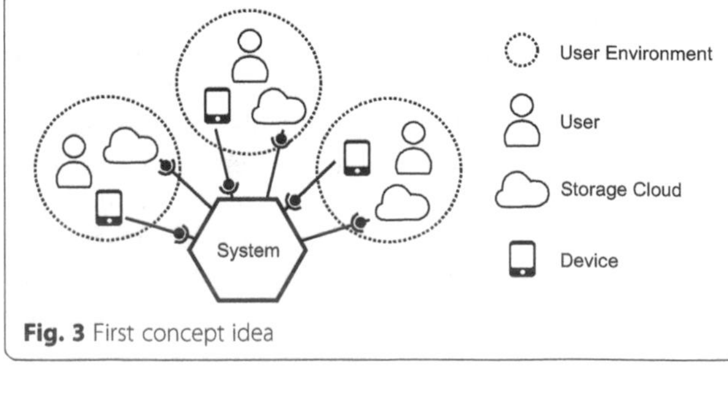

Fig. 3 First concept idea

guidelines and legislation. Therefore, the next research step consists of implementing a Proof-of-Principle and, following on that, a Proof-of-Concept prototype. The aim is to develop a system with low complexity and at the same time high data security. Here, the user needs to answer questions concerning the decrease of complexity and the increase of data security and acceptance.

Conclusion

This contribution introduced *research artifacts* in order to answer our research issue: *How must a cloud-based ecosystem for the integration of decentralized information systems be built technologically and in terms of organization, in order to guarantee cloud users their privacy laws?* In order to structure the problem, a system comparison from the field of social networks was carried out, and basic forms of the organization of cloud systems were analyzed. It became clear that peer-to-peer approaches as technological realization are favored since they do not require trust toward the centralized authority. Additionally, the users need to run their own systems. From the then conducted literature analysis, 27 requirements for the implementation of decentralized systems with the focus on data security were raised. It was shown that trust is a key element when it comes to data security aims and that users are becoming more involved in the process of creating services. Finally, various organizational levels for a division of roles in cloud-based ecosystems were introduced. The presented model can be used for the application of already existing concepts and as a support for the conceptualization of new approaches.

Acknowledgements

We acknowledge support from the German Research Foundation (DFG) and Universität Leipzig within the program of Open Access Publishing.

Authors' contributions

AM and AL carried out the literature review and the system comparison. AM did the requirements analysis and organizational levels analysis. AL introduced the FEDS framework for evaluation and was mainly part of the results discussion. BF provided useful insights and guidance and critically reviewed the manuscript. All authors read and approved the final manuscript.

Competing interests

The authors declare that they have no competing interests.

Author details

[1]Department of Business Information Systems, Leipzig University, Grimmaische Straße 12, 04109 Leipzig, Germany. [2]Kühne Logistics University, Großer Grasbrook 17, 20457 Hamburg, Germany.

References

1. Statista (2015) Einsatz von Cloud Computing in deutschen Unternehmen bis 2015 Umfrage Statista, http://de.statista.com/statistik/daten/studie/177484/umfrage/einsatz-von-cloud-computing-in-deutschen-unternehmen-2011/. Accessed 18 Aug 2016
2. IDC (2015) IDC Studie: Hybrid Clouds nehmen angesichts der Digitalen Transformation Fahrt auf in deutschen Unternehmen, http://idc.de/de/ueber-idc/press-center/63144-idc-studie-hybrid-clouds-nehmen-angesichts-der-digitalen-transformation-fahrt-auf-in-deutschen-unternehmen. Accessed 5 Aug 2016
3. BITKOM (2014) Wie Cloud Computing neue Geschäftsmodelle ermöglicht, https://www.bitkom.org/Publikationen/2014/Leitfaden/Wie-Cloud-Computing-neue-Geschaeftsmodelle-ermoeglicht/140203-Wie-Cloud-Computing-neue-Geschaeftsmodelle-ermoeglicht.pdf. Accessed 18 Aug 2016
4. Ropohl G (2009) Allgemeine Technologie. Eine Systemtheorie der Technik. Universität Karlsruhe Universitätsbibliothek, Karlsruhe
5. BMBF: Die neue Hightech-Strategie: Innovationen für Deutschland (2014)
6. BMWi, BMI, BMVI: Digitale Agenda 2014–2017. München (2014)
7. Atzori L, Iera A, Morabito G (2010) The Internet of Things: A survey. Comput Netw 54:2787–2805
8. Beetz K (2010) Die Wirtschaftliche Bedeutung von Cyberphysical Systems aus der Sicht Eines Global Players. In: Broy M (ed) Cyber-Physical Systems. Springer, Berlin Heidelberg, pp 59–66
9. Software-Cluster (2015) Emergente Software, http://www.software-cluster.com/de/forschung/themen/emergente-software. Accessed 24 Nov 2015
10. Vaquero LM, Rodero-Merino L (2014) Finding Your Way in the Fog: Towards a Comprehensive Definition of Fog Computing. SIGCOMM Comput Commun Rev 44:27–32
11. TecChannel (2014) Cloud Computing - der deutsche Mittelstand hinkt hinterher - TecChannel-Studie TecChannel.de, http://www.tecchannel.de/wege_in_die_cloud/2053924/cloud_studie_tc_2014_tx/index.html. Accessed 29 Jan 2016
12. Smith M, Szongott C, Henne B, Voigt Gv (2012) Big data privacy issues in public social media. In: 2012 6th IEEE International Conference on Digital Ecosystems and Technologies (DEST), pp 1–6
13. Gregory RW, Muntermann J (2014) Research Note—Heuristic Theorizing: Proactively Generating Design Theories. Inf Syst Res 25:639–653
14. Venable J, Pries-Heje J, Baskerville R (2014) FEDS: a Framework for Evaluation in Design Science Research. Eur J Inf Syst 25:77–89
15. Laudon K.C, Laudon J.P, Schoder D (2009) Wirtschaftsinformatik: Eine Einführung. Pearson Studium, München
16. Heinrich LJ, Heinzl A, Riedl R (2010) Wirtschaftsinformatik: Einführung und Grundlegung. Springer, Berlin
17. Moore JF (1997) The Death of Competition: Leadership and Strategy in the Age of Business Ecosystems. Harper Paperbacks, New York
18. Erklärung von Montreux: Ein universelles Recht auf den Schutz personenbezogener Daten und der Privatsphäre unter Beachtung der Vielfalt in einer globalisierten Welt. 27. Internationale Datenschutzkonferenz in Montreux, Montreux (2005)
19. Yeung C-MA, Liccardi I, Lu K, Seneviratne O, Berners-lee T (2009) Decentralization: The future of online social networking. In: In W3C Workshop on the Future of Social Networking Position Papers
20. Buchegger S, Schiöberg D, Vu L-H, Datta A (2009) PeerSoN: P2P Social Networking: Early Experiences and Insights. In: Proceedings of the Second ACM EuroSys WS on Social Network Systems. ACM, New York, pp 46–52
21. Zhang L, Mislove A (2013) Building Confederated Web-based Services with Priv.io. In: Proceedings of the First ACM Conference on Online Social Networks. ACM, New York, pp 189–200
22. Cutillo LA, Molva R, Strufe T (2009) Safebook: A privacy-preserving online social network leveraging on real-life trust. IEEE Commun Mag 47:94–101
23. Sharma R, Datta A (2012) SuperNova: Super-peers based architecture for decentralized online social networks. In: 2012 Fourth International Conference on Communication Systems and Networks (COMSNETS), pp 1–10
24. Seong S-W, Seo J, Nasielski M, Sengupta D, Hangal S, Teh SK, Chu R, Dodson B, Lam MS (2010) PrPl: A Decentralized Social Networking Infrastructure. In: Proceedings of the 1st ACM 2010, pp 8:1–8:8
25. Gambs S, Lolive J (2013) SlopPy: Slope One with Privacy. In: Di Pietro R, Herranz J, Damiani E, State R (eds) Data Privacy Management and Autonomous Spontaneous Security. Springer, Berlin Heidelberg, pp 104–117
26. Shakimov A, Lim H, Caceres R, Cox LP, Li K, Liu D, Varshavsky A (2011) Vis-à-Vis: Privacy-preserving online social networking via Virtual Individual Servers.

In: 2011 Third International Conference on Communication Systems and Networks (COMSNETS), pp 1–10

27. Baden R, Bender A, Spring N et al (2009) Persona: An Online Social Network with User-defined Privacy. Proceedings of the ACM SIGCOMM 2009 Conference on Data Communication. ACM (SIGCOMM '09), New York, pp 135–146. doi:10.1145/1592568.1592585. ISBN: 978–1–60558-594-9
28. Narayanan, A., Toubiana, V., Barocas, S., Nissenbaum, H., Boneh, D.: A Critical Look at Decentralized Personal Data Architectures. arXiv:1202.4503 [cs] (2012)
29. VHB (2015) Teilrating WI: Verband der Hochschullehrer für Betriebswirtschaft e.V, http://vhbonline.org/service/jourqual/vhb-jourqual-3/teilrating-wi/. Accessed 19 Nov 2015
30. Denyer D (2013) Doing a literature review in business and management, http://www.ifm.eng.cam.ac.uk/uploads/Research/RCDP/Resources/Working_with_literature_for_Cambridge.pdf. Accessed 19 Nov 2015
31. Pohl K (2008) Requirements Engineering: Grundlagen, Prinzipien,Techniken. dpunkt.Verlag GmbH, Heidelberg
32. Sarker S, Ahuja M, Sarker S, Kirkeby S (2011) The Role of Communication and Trust in Global Virtual Teams: A Social Network Perspective. J Manag Inf Syst 28:273–310
33. Williams P, Sion R (2013) Access Privacy and Correctness on Untrusted Storage. ACM Trans Inf Syst Secur 16, 12:1–12:29
34. Erway CC, Küpçü A, Papamanthou C, Tamassia R (2015) Dynamic Provable Data Possession. ACM Trans Inf Syst Secur 17, 15:1–15:29
35. Tigelaar AS, Hiemstra D, Trieschnigg D (2012) Peer-to-Peer Information Retrieval: An Overview. ACM Trans Inf Syst 30, 9:1–9:34
36. Tsai JY, Egelman S, Cranor L, Acquisti A (2011) The Effect of Online Privacy Information on Purchasing Behavior: An Experimental Study. Inf Syst Res 22: 254–268
37. Ni Q, Bertino E, Lobo J, Brodie C, Karat C-M, Karat J, Trombeta A (2010) Privacy-aware Role-based Access Control. ACM Trans Inf Syst Secur 13, 24:1–24:31
38. Karla J (2010) Can Web 2.0 Ever Forget? Bus Inf Syst Eng 2:105–107
39. Fogues R, Such JM, Espinosa A, Garcia-Fornes A (2015) Open Challenges in Relationship-Based Privacy Mechanisms for Social Network Services. Int J Hum Comput Interact 31:350–370
40. Liu D, Brass D, Lu Y, Chen D (2015) Friendships in Online Peer-to-Peer Lending: Pipes, Prisms, and Relational Herding. Manag Inf Syst Q 39:729–742
41. Davison RM, Ou CXJ, Martinsons MG (2013) Information technology to support informal knowledge sharing. Inf Syst J 23:89–109
42. IfD, glh, Institut für Demoskopie Allensbach, Centrum für Strategie und Höhere Führung: Cyber Security Report 2015: Ergebnisse einer repräsentativen Befragung (2015)
43. diaspora* (2016) Über - Das Projekt diaspora*, https://diasporafoundation.org/about. Accessed 25 Aug 2016

10

Nearby live virtual machine migration using cloudlets and multipath TCP

Fikirte Teka, Chung-Horng Lung* and Samuel A. Ajila

Abstract

A nearby virtual machine (VM) based cloudlet is proposed for mobile cloud computing (MCC) to enhance the performance of real-time resource-intensive mobile applications. Generally, when a mobile device (MD) discovers a cloudlet in the vicinity, it takes time to set up a VM inside the cloudlet before data offloading from the MD to the VM starts. The time between the discovery of the cloudlet and actual offloading of data is considered as the service initiation time. When multiple cloudlets are present in a nearby geographical location, initiating a service with each cloudlet may be frustrating for cloudlet users that moving from one location to another. In order to eliminate the delay caused by the service initiation time after moving away from the source cloudlet, this paper proposes a seamless live VM migration between neighbouring cloudlets. A seamless live VM migration is achieved with the prior knowledge of the migrating VM IP address in the destination cloudlet and more importantly with multipath TCP (MPTCP). We have performed a number of experiments to validate the proposed approach using Linux KVM hypervisor. The experimental results demonstrate the feasibility of the proposed approach and also show performance improvement. Specifically, there is almost zero downtime at the destination cloudlet after the migration is completed.

Keyword: Cloudlets, Mobile cloud computing, Multipath TCP, Virtual machine migration, Fog computing

Abbreviations: AP, Access Point; DHCP, Dynamic Host Configuration Protocol; HoA, Home Address; LAN, Local Area Network; MCC, Mobile Cloud Computing; MD, Mobile Device; MoA, Mobile Address; MPTCP, Multipath TCP; QoE, Quality of Experience; RTO, Retransmission Time Out; TCP, Transport Control Protocol; VM, Virtual Machine; VPN, Virtual Private Network; WAN, Wide Area Network

Introduction

The high demand for mobile applications has encouraged software and mobile developers to bring the desktop level applications to mobile devices (MDs). Although the computation and storage capacities and battery life time of MDs have improved considerably in recent years, mobile devices still remain resource-poor devices because of battery power, bandwidth, and capacity to handle resource-hungry applications. Most of the applications executing on MDs are real-time and interactive applications. In addition to offloading, a real-time application to a distant remote cloud through the Internet increases response time due to Wide Area Network (WAN) latency [1]. Latency affects MD users in two ways. Firstly is the quality of experience (QoE). As latency increases, the QoE degrades. Secondly is the faster drain of energy on MDs [2, 3]. Energy efficiency is also an important performance parameter for MDs. Therefore, maximizing the benefit of offloading applications for MDs can be achieved by minimizing the latency between the MDs and the servers. In order to do this, researchers have proposed resource-rich nearby servers which are connected to or integrated with wireless access points (AP) as a solution for MDs offloading. Examples include CLONECLOUD [4], MOCHA [5], MAUI [2], Odessa [6], COMET [7], and virtual machine (VM) based cloudlet [1]. In this way, the need for improving QoE and energy efficiency can be accomplished by low latency, one-hop, high bandwidth (BW) wireless access to the servers.

There are two types of offloading mechanisms in the literature. One is by partitioning applications and sending only resource-intensive instructions to servers and executing the rest of instructions on the MD itself. The

* Correspondence: chlung@sce.carleton.ca
Department of Systems and Computer Engineering, Carleton University, Ottawa, Ontario K1S 5B6, Canada

second mechanism is to send all the instructions to the server. The second mechanism needs to create a VM instance on the server for each MD to serve as shared infrastructure and to provide strong isolation between computations from different MDs. VM-based cloudlets [1] adopted the second approach.

The authors in [1] define a cloudlet as "a trusted, resource-rich computer or cluster of computers that's well-connected to the Internet and available for use by nearby MDs." Cloudlets are a disruptive technique in mobile computing. Cloudlets can provide low delay, high bandwidth access to high-end computing devices that are within one wireless hop, which can bring substantial value to new emerging applications [8, 9]. The concept of cloudlets is consistent with the recent concept of Fog computing [10–12] which focuses on the edge for mobile users so that mobile users can access computation-intensive services via short-distance and low-delay local connections. Further, cloudlets can also be considered as "second-class data centers" which are much more flexible and easier to maintain or replace compared to the traditional data centers [9].

This paper focuses on the VM-based cloudlets. The motivation of this research stems from the fact that MD users are not stationary, although they are getting benefit from the nearby static cloudlet servers. A frequent movement is common to a MD user but changing network location causes the following two problems:

- The first one is the change of MD IP address, which will terminate the existing transport control protocol (TCP) connection between the source cloudlet and the MD.
- The second problem is that MD needs to wait for another service initiation time before the offloading starts, if there is available nearby cloudlet in the new location. Service initiation time is the time from discovering the cloudlet to the time the offloading starts. Service initiation time has negative impact on QoE.

To address these two problems, we initially proposed [13] to replace TCP with MPTCP [14] for the first problem. Further, our proposed solution to the second problem is to perform a VM migration from the source cloudlet to the destination cloudlet to eliminate or reduce the extra service initiation time.

This paper is an extension of [13]. The main contributions of the paper include: First, the paper demonstrates in detail the capability of MPTCP to support live server VM migration over a wide area network (WAN). Without any code modification to MPTCP, a server VM can be migrated live seamlessly without interrupting the application running on the VM. Second, this paper proposes two interfaces to be used by the VM and to configure the destination IP address information before the VM is migrated. This approach has two advantages: seamless connection migration and zero network VM downtime after the migration is completed. This paper also discusses location identifier, possible neighbor database to facilitate migration decision making, and various scenarios. We also have added an algorithm to a Virtual Private Network (VPN) and an algorithm for migration decision making.

The rest of the paper is organized as follows; Section II describes the related works. Section III discusses our proposed VM migration for cloudlets using MPTCP. Section IV describes our experiments and demonstrates the results. Section V discusses decision making for VM migration. Finally, Section VI is the conclusions and future directions.

Background and related work

Various technical areas are related to this paper. This section introduces the basic concepts of those related areas, specifically cloudlets, live VM migration, MPTCP and Fog computing.

Computational offloading and cloudlets

Mobile Cloud Computing (MCC) brings together cloud computing, mobile computing, wireless networks, and cloud services to provide MD users rich computational resources. MCC overcomes the resource limitation of wireless MDs by leveraging fixed infrastructure. Resources, such as CPU, RAM, data storage and battery energy, are limited resources in MDs. Resource intensive applications, such as speech recognition, natural language processing, computer vision and graphics, machine learning, augmented reality, planning, and decision-making become common in MDs. In order to enhance the performance of these resource-intensive applications, offloading from the MDs to resource-rich servers in the vicinity or to a distant server is a common solution for mobile computing.

Research efforts [1, 2, 4] have shown that offloading applications to a *remote server* is not always the optimal solution for MDs. The latency between the MD and the server is a parameter that governs the performance of the system in terms of energy consumption and QoE. As latency increases the energy consumption of the MD increases and the QoE degrades. Using a *nearby server* instead of a remote server for offloading applications minimizes the network latency between the cloudlet and the MD.

There are basically two types of offloading mechanism. Executing resource-intensive application remotely by partitioning the application is the first method. This approach relies on the programmers to specify how to partition the program and to identify the instructions to be sent to the remote sever. The partitioning scheme has to adapt to the network condition and the availability of resources in real-time basis. For example, if a smartphone can access a remote server with a good wireless network connection, resource-intensive tasks can be executed remotely. If the energy cost to send the tasks remotely is higher due to poor wireless connection, the tasks will be executed locally on the smartphone. The following tools: CLONECLOUD [4], MOCHA [1], MAUI [2], Odessa [7], and COMET [7] adopt this approach.

The second offloading mechanism is to send the whole application to a VM instance identified in a remote server. No smart decision is required for this method. This approach reduces the burden on the application programmers because the applications do not need to be modified to take advantage of remote execution. If a remote server is available, the whole application is offloaded to the server; otherwise, the device executes the whole program locally. The authors in [1] proposed a VM-based cloudlet offloading approach.

There are two different methods to send the VM state to a cloudlet infrastructure. One is VM migration, in which an already executing VM is suspended, its processor, disk and memory states are transferred; and finally VM execution is resumed at the destination from the same point of suspension. The other approach is called dynamic VM synthesis which customizes a VM on demand. VM customization is time consuming, as the process includes the time to create VM disc space, install operating system and install a particular application. Delivering a service after all of the steps taken causes a great deal of delay. Minimizing VM customization time is the main objective of dynamic VM synthesis.

Fog computing

Fog computing, first proposed by Cisco [12], shares similar concept as cloudlets, as the emphasis is on the nearby cloudlets or edges. Fog computing extends the conventional cloud computing paradigm to the edge of the network that is close to the end users. Fog is also known as micro datacenter. Fog computing has received tremendous attention lately as the technology has the potential to bring the benefits of cloud computing closer to the users to leverage energy-rich, high-end computing, and low-latency.

Authors in [10–12] presented various scenarios for Fog computing. For instance, connected vehicles, smart grid, wireless sensor and actuator networks can benefit considerably from low-delay response using Fog computing [10]. Other potential scenarios include Internet of Things (IoT) and cyber-physical systems [11]. Fog computing can also facilitate augmented reality and real-time video analytics and mobile big data analytics that require intensive computations [12].

Fog computing is still in the early stage in terms of research and practical deployment. On the other hand, Fog computing addresses not only the technical aspects, but also the business concerns that exist for cloudlets. To effectively support Fog computing, a basic infrastructure for edge computing devices is essential and needs to be planned and managed by a network operator. The managed infrastructure can mitigate some of the issues that may occur for VM migration. For instance, the overlapping of cloudlets, and issues of handovers and IP address assignment can be effectively managed with pre-configured policies. Section III describes a simple pre-established network configuration policy that can help manage IP addresses for VM migration.

Live VM migration and network migration

VM migration, especially live VM migration, as mentioned in Section II.A, is useful for delay sensitive applications for MCC. Live VM migration, a key technology in virtualization, is the process of moving a running VM from one physical host to another with minimal downtime. For live VM migration, the service initiation time is a critical factor that causes delay. Service initiation time is the time from when the MD discovers a cloudlet to the time the MD starts offloading data. Four main steps are involved for the service initiation time: bind the MD with the cloudlet, transfer the VM overlay, decompress the VM overlay, and apply the VM overlay to the base VM to launch the VM. To minimize the service initiation time, Ha, et al. [15] applied four optimization techniques (Deduplication, Bridging the Semantic Gap, Pipelining, and Early Start) to minimize the delay significantly.

Live VM migration can be performed within a data center from one server to another or it can be performed across geographically distributed data centers. There are three key aspects to be considered in a live VM migration [16]: RAM state, storage and network migration. This paper focuses on the network migration aspect.

Network migration involves LAN migration and/or WAN migration. In LAN migration, the VM can retain its IP and MAC addresses after migration. The local switch needs to adjust the mapping for the VM's MAC address to its new switch port [17]. Over a WAN, retaining the same IP address before and after VM migration is a challenge. Extending the layer 2 connectivity over WAN is one solution, e.g., CloudNet [18]. This allows open network connections to be seamlessly redirected to the VM's new location.

Mobile IP is another approach that has been used for connection redirection [18] without the constraint of retaining the original IP address. The VM used two IP addresses; one is called the Home Address (HoA) and the other one is called Mobile Address (MoA). Every time the VM changes its location, the VM updates an agent of the new location. Traffic for the VM always goes through the HoA, and then HoA will redirect traffic to MoA. This causes additional delay for the traffic.

Multipath TCP (MPTCP)

To mitigate the VM migration delay and improve the robustness, another mechanism is to adopt MPTCP. MPTCP is a transport layer as opposed to a network layer and is a viable solution for live VM migration. The main idea is that even if the original IP address of a VM has changed, the connections remain established [19]. MPTCP is implemented for migration of a VM running a client application. Unlike the regular TCP/IP protocol, MPTCP is an IETF (Internet Engineering Task Force) protocol that allows *multiple interfaces* to be used *for a single application* and socket interface [14]. MPTCP is responsible for connection setup, transferring data between TCP connections, adding and removing subflows, and tearing down the session for one or more TCP connections. In MPTCP, a path is a sequence of links between a sender and a receiver and it is defined by 4-tuple source and destination address pair; a subflow is the same as TCP segments operating over an individual path; and an MPTCP connection is a one-to-one mapping between a connection and an application socket.

Other related work

Other approaches to cloudlet migration have been discussed in the literature. Li, et al. [20] discussed the lack of consistent network performance for mobile user while offloading; the optimal offloading decision becomes suboptimal due to MD user movement. The authors proposed a three-tier (Smartphone-cloudlet-cloud) architecture that tracks user locations using GPS and saves it in a centralized database found in a remote cloud. The location information helps to predict user's movement and to identify the energy efficient Wi-Fi AP. The real-time network performance between a smartphone and an AP and the server-side load are considered to make optimized offloading decisions. The approach considered multiple cloudlets and proposed a centralized cloudlet system which is different from the decentralized VM based cloudlet [1]. The research has focused only on energy saving. On the other hand, the paper does not mention how the state of the user's application could be transferred from one cloudlet to the other.

Kommineni, et al. [21] also considered more than one cloudlet in a nearby location. The authors claimed that in order to make the best cloudlet selection, the smartphone has to consider the processing speed and the available memory size of a cloudlet. In addition, the wireless network latency between a smartphone and an AP and the BW of a fixed network from the cloudlet to the remote server were considered crucial metrics for cloudlet selection. The real-time network performance is not considered in this paper.

Jararweh, et al. [22, 23] studied how using cloudlet through Wi-Fi could save energy of smartphones than accessing a remote cloud through 3G/4G. Even though this paper describes transferring the state of the offloaded application from one cloudlet to another while the user is moving, the offloading mechanism and the networking collaboration between cloudlets is not mentioned.

Seamless live VM migration for cloudlets with multipath TCP

This section presents our seamless live VM migration approach between cloudlets which is triggered by the relocation of an MD. Our goal is to develop a nearby VM-based approach for cloudlets to improve MCC communications. Two major benefits of our approach are proximity of servers to MDs minimizes latency and offloading to a remote server through minimum latency not only supports QoE, but also saves the energy of the MDs. Dynamic VM synthesis [21, 24] customizes VM on demand for cloudlet users. After service initiation time, the user starts offloading data to enhance the applications performance. Since the cloudlet is one hop away from the user, only a minimum delay is experienced as long as the user remains in the communication range of the cloudlet.

The first problem with the existing dynamic VM migration is that the MD's IP address is changed after it moves from one cloudlet to another. A new IP address for the MD will terminate the established TCP connection with the VM instance, which compels the MD to start a new TCP connection. QoE will be significantly affected or may not be acceptable in such a solution. The second problem occurs when accessing the source cloudlet from the destination cloudlet during the migration process. This approach involves the network latency (could be WAN latency) which defeats the purpose of using a cloudlet to have a short delay.

To address the aforementioned two issues, the following two key points are considered for this research:

- To avoid re-establishment of the TCP connection, the proposed solution uses MPTCP. Hence, it is possible keep the connection established after the MD changes its IP address, which can significantly reduce the delay.
- To ensure that traffic is forwarded between two cloudlets, creating a trusted network collaboration using a VPN for geographically nearby cloudlets is a solution.

MPTCP for seemless live VM migration

The transport protocol plays a crucial role in migration of a VM instance. The most commonly used transport layer protocol is TCP. TCP uses five tuples, *the source IP address, the destination IP address, the source port, the destination port and the protocol type* to identify a connection between a server and a client. If any of the five tuples changes during the lifetime of the TCP connection, the established connection will be closed abruptly. In order to continue the connection with the server, the client needs to initiate a new connection with TCP.

Over the WAN, VM migration is performed from one network to another, which forces the IP address of the VM to be changed. This forces the VM to restart all the established connections, which causes delay and unacceptable QoE.

As stated before, this paper proposes the use of MPTCP in both the client and the server to reduce the delay caused by TCP re-establishment. MPTCP works only if the migrating VM runs as a client application, since only the client can send a TCP SYN packet with the new IP address acquired after migration. Even if a server supports MPTCP, the server does not synchronize with the client automatically after the IP address is changed. In addition, the existing MPTCP does not meet all the requirements for VM migration unless the kernel code is modified specifically for VM migration. To resolve this limitation without modification of the MPTCP kernel code, this paper proposes another solution to support a live VM migration without having to re-establish a new TCP connection. The following explains the additions to MPTCP.

Migrating a server VM with MPTCP

If a VM server has only one virtual interface and if it is restarted, all the connections to the server will be lost regardless of the transport layer protocol used. This is how both MPTCP and TCP are designed. With TCP, the server will not actively initiate a connection with a client. Modifying the kernel implementation to meet this requirement (e.g., server could initiate the connection) is a solution, but this solution will cause a complication if a server initiates a connection with a client. The reason is that the client IP address may not be always the original IP address. For instance, in a network path that involves network address translation (NAT) box, the original IP address of the client is hidden.

Therefore, this paper proposes two additional features on top of MPTCP. The first feature is for the VM instance to have two virtual interfaces and the second feature is to construct it in a way that the VM instance knows its future IP address via a pre-configured policy for IP addresses.

Prior knowledge of the next IP address

In VM migration, this feature can be supported with a pre-established network configuration policy. IP address assignment can be achieved without much difficulty if the cloudlets are managed by the same network operator or cooperative network operators. Emerging techniques, such as Fog computing [10], can be used to seamlessly support the feature.

One of the possible policies is explained with the following example:

LAN IP address: 10.4.0.0/24
Broadcast IP: 10.4.0.255/24
MD IP address: The Evens (10.4.0.2/24, 10.4.0.4/24, ...).
VM IP address: The Odds (10.4.0.3/24, 10.4.0.5/24, ...).
Cloudlet IP address: 10.4.0.1/24
Reserved IP address: 10.4.0.224/24

The new VM IP address is the next odd IP address of the *paired* MD IP address. For instance, assume that the LAN IP address of the source (C1) and destination (C2) cloudlets are 10.4.0.0/24 and 10.5.0.0/24, respectively. The service was originally initiated at C1 with *paired* IP addresses, i.e., 10.4.0.2/24 for the MD and 10.4.0.3/24 for the VM. After the user changes location, the MD is assigned a new IP address, say 10.5.0.8/24. As soon as the VM is accessed with this new IP address, the VM knows that the new location IP address would be the next odd IP address which is 10.5.0.9/24.

The ADD_ADDR22 option from MPTCP [14] is used by the VM to inform the client that there is a new or additional IP address. To send the ADD_ADDR22 option, at least one active subflow is needed for the connection. Hence, this research proposes the VMs to have two virtual interfaces inside a cloudlet. One interface is to operate in the regular VM operation mode; the other works only after the VM is migrated.

Each VM inside of a cloudlet is configured with two virtual interfaces, e.g., Eth0 and Eth1. Usually, only Eth0 or Eth1 is used to communicate with the MD at a time. If Eth0 is up, then Eth1 is down. After a VM migration, the state of the two interfaces will exchange. Always, the interface with the DOWN state is intended to serve as the interface during migration. When a VM is accessed from a different IP address than the existing LAN IP address of the VM, the VM knows that the paired MD has changed the location. The VM then prepares the migration by turning on the interface that was in the DOWN state. The IP address for this new interface is determined by the paired MD IP address.

Although ADD_ADDR22 advertises the existence of the additional IP address, no subflow can be started with the additional interface before the VM is migrated. Since the IP address assigned to the additional interface is from a different LAN after migration, the VM is unreachable through this interface. But the connection

Table 1 Operation phases and status of the server VM

Operation Phases of VM	Interface Status		Number of Subflow
	Eth1	Eth0	
Normal operation time	Down	Up	1
After VM is accessed with different LAN IP address	Up (inactive)	Up	1
Right after migration is completed	Up	Up (inactive)	1
Normal operation time	Up	Down	1

from the MD will keep trying to create a new subflow with the new IP address of the VM.

The VM will be available through the additional interface right after the migration is completed. At this time the previously working interface becomes inactive. Since the MD knows the additional IP address of the VM which was advertised before migration, the MD initiates a connection through that interface. As soon as the new subflow is started, the previous interface will be taken down to make it ready for the next potential migration. Table 1 summarizes the operation mode of the VM and the interfaces status.

MD handover with MPTCP

A MD installed with MPTCP can be configured with three different operational modes based on requirements. Each operational mode identifies the handover mode as well. A device with one or more interfaces can select one of the handover modes based on the need.

Full-MPTCP mode

The full-MPTCP mode allows creating a TCP subflow with all active IP addresses. For instance, a MD integrated with both Wi-Fi and 3G/4G interfaces can benefit from the full-MPTCP mode using both interfaces at the same time to achieve the maximum throughput. If one of the interfaces goes down, the other active interface keeps working without any disruption.

Backup mode

In backup mode, MPTCP opens TCP subflows with all available interfaces just like the full-MPTCP mode. However, only a subset of interfaces is active for normal data transfer based on the priority of the interfaces. The MP_PRIO option (cf. Table 2) sent by the peer is used to identify the backup interface. As the other peer received the MP_PRIO option, MPTCP keeps the subflow open but never sends data unless the current active interface goes down.

Table 2 Summary of MPTCP signals

Signalling	Name	Function
MP_CAPABLE	Multipath TCP Capable	Checks the capability of the end host on establishing a MPTCP connection
MP_JOIN	Join Connection	Adds additional subflow to existing MPTCP connection
REMOVE_ADDR	Remove Address	Removes failed subflow
MP_PRIO	Multipath Priority	Inform subflow priority
MP_FASTCLOSE	Fast Close	Closes MPTCP connection abruptly.
ADD_ADDR22	Add Address	Informs the availability of additional IP address to the paired host

Single-path mode

Only a single subflow is active with this mode. MPTCP is able to keep the established connection open for retransmission time out (RTO) time after the active subflow is lost. This feature enables peer devices to continue data transfer with the open subflow after a new IP address is acquired for the same interface or from different interface. A handover for a smartphone can be from Wi-Fi to 3G/4G network after it is disconnected from the Wi-Fi network. Compared to the backup mode, this mode waits for two more round-trip times before the new MPTCP subflow is established and data can be sent.

Handover scenarios for MDs

This paper considers two MD handover scenarios for VM migration: (i) from Wi-Fi to Wi-Fi, and (ii) from Wi-Fi to 3G/4G to Wi-Fi. The following presents an analysis for these scenarios. The objective is to show that a handover is performed before the MPTCP connection is closed between the VM and the MD. Both the source and the destination cloudlets are assumed to be in the same VPN. This allows the MD and the VM to communicate using their LAN IP address through the WAN even if they exist in different cloudlet networks.

From Wi-Fi to Wi-Fi

Two geographically close Wi-Fi networks may overlap or may have a gap. The distance between the two Wi-Fi network regions may enable the MD to handover without any interruption if the MPTCP protocol is installed both in the MD and the server the MD is connected to. The role of the RTO in the MPTCP is to give enough time for the MD to acquire a new IP address and to resume the data transfer from where it has stopped without reestablishment of a new TCP connection if the application timeout is longer (applications are configured with their own response waiting time).

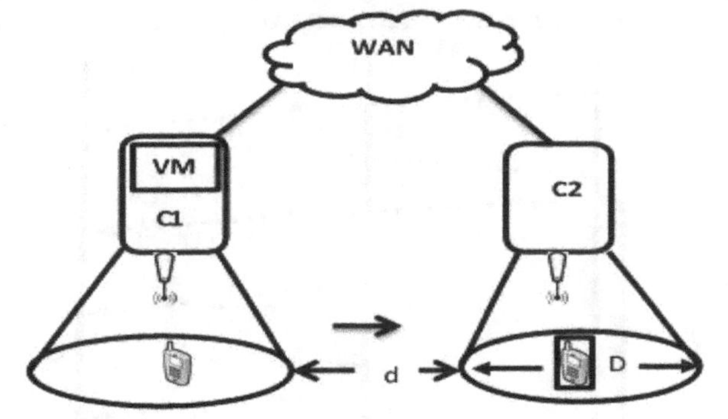

Fig. 1 Two Wi-Fi network regions separated with distance d

If two network regions overlap, for a MD moving from the source to the destination region, the time needed to create a new subflow with the MPTCP connection is the time for the MD to be assigned an IP address from the destination region.

In the case where there is no overlap between two cloudlet network regions, as shown in Fig. 1, the maximum distance *d* that a MD is allowed to catch up on the established MPTCP connection is calculated as

$$d = (RTO\text{–}RTT/2\text{–}T_{IP}) \times V_{hum} \qquad (1)$$

where d is the distance between the two cloudlet network regions, RTO is the retransmission timeout for the MPTCP connection, RTT is the round trip time between the access points (APs) through WAN, V_{hum} is the average human walking speed and T_{IP} is the time that the MD obtain a new IP address from the local Dynamic Host Configuration Protocol (DHCP). The RTO for the MPTCP protocol varies from 13 to 30 min [25]. The actual RTO value depends on the latency between the client and the server.

To guarantee that the new subflow is created before MPTCP connection timeouts, the minimum RTO value for MPTCP, i.e., 13 min (or 780 s) [25], is used to estimate the maximum distance between two cloudlet network regions before MPTCP retransmission timeout happens. This paper also assumes that the user walks with the average human walking speed of 1.2 m per second, i.e., $V_{hum} = 1.2$ m/s, based on research results in Civil Engineering [26]. Practically, when a user is using a MD, the walking speed generally is slower than the normal speed. In addition, to accommodate a wider range of variations or errors in estimating the maximum distance *d*, this paper discards the value of independent variables RTT and T_{IP} as listed in Eq. (1). Hence, $d <= RTO \times V_{hum} = 780 \times 1.2\ m/s = 936\ m$. The estimated distance can be used as a reference for network operators that provide cloudlet services or Fog computing to avoid delay due to the MPTCP timeout mechanism. For instance, the distance could be configured shorter than the calculated distance to ensure that MPTCP timeout will not happen.

If D/2 (see Fig. 1) is the Wi-Fi AP communication range in meters, D + d will be the maximum distance between two cloudlets that allows a handover of MDs before the established MPTCP connection timeouts. This calculation for maximum distance gives the ideal distance based on the transport layer protocol. However, applications may have their own session timeout values. Before the MPTCP connection gives up on waiting for a response, application session may timeout.

The MPTCP handover mode used for this scenario could be either full-MPTCP or single-path MPTCP. Both of these handover modes have the same performance, since only one subflow can be active at a time. Figure 2 shows the sequence diagram for the handover operation between the MD and the VM. Assume that the MD user was in the C1 network region, the left cloudlet as shown in Fig. 1. The VM instance is launched in the nearest cloudlet server (C1). As the user walks out of the region of C1 and is connected to cloudlet C2 on the right, MPTCP protocol handovers the established connection seamlessly. The sequence chart is explained as follows.

Steps 1–3 are the 3-way handshake of MPTCP between the VM and the MD with the MP_CAPABLE option. Duration A in Fig. 2 represents the period between MD and VM while MD remains in C1's coverage. T_t is the time that the MD spent without any network coverage which is less than the actual RTO of the connection.

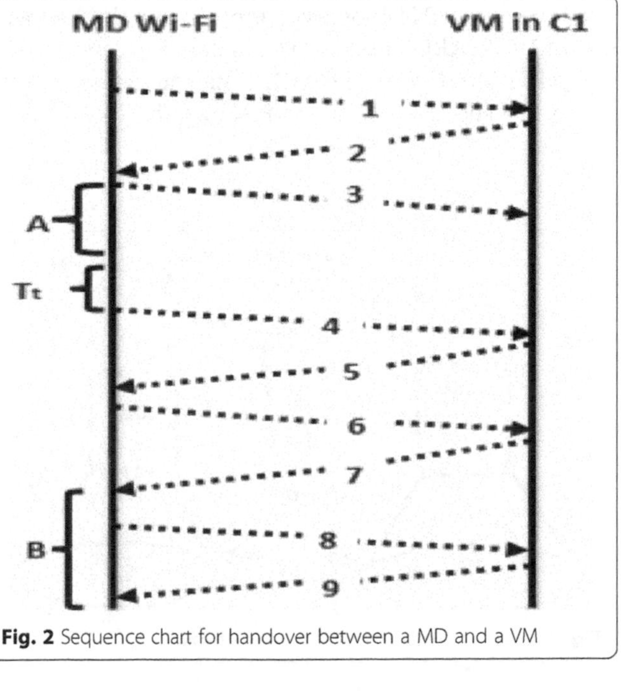

Fig. 2 Sequence chart for handover between a MD and a VM

After the MD is disconnected from C1 and connected with C2, C2 then assigns a new IP address to the MD. The new 3-way handshake starts at step 4 which is the TCP SYN packet with the JOIN option in MPTCP. Step 7 indicates an ACK for the JOIN subflow. Duration B represents data transfer using the new subflow. The REMOVE_ADDR option is sent from the MD to the VM in C1 to inform that its previous IP address is no longer available (step 8). Step 9 is an ACK message.

From Wi-Fi to 3G/4G to Wi-Fi

The ubiquitous nature of 3G/4G cellular network is one advantage over Wi-Fi networks. Devices with the 3G/4G capability can take the advantage of this feature to transfer data between Wi-Fi networks seamlessly with the help of MPTCP. The existence of a cellular network between two Wi-Fi networks, as shown in Fig. 3, does not change the maximum distance between two cloudlets for a potential live VM migration, see Eq. (1). The reason is that, for this scenario, some devices, e.g., tablets may only have Wi-Fi capability.

The handover mechanism is the same as that of the Wi-Fi to Wi-Fi network. But for a MD connected with the cellular network, all the three handover modes, full-MPTCP, backup, and single-path, can be used depending on the required performance by the user. For instance, if energy efficiency is more important than the throughput, the backup or the single-path mode can be used. However, the full-MPTCP handover mode provides a better throughput, since both the Wi-Fi and 3G/4G interfaces can be used simultaneously.

The sequence diagram for the backup handover mode is shown in Fig. 4 as an illustration. Steps 1–3 are the 3-way handshake of MPTCP between the VM and the MD with the MP_CAPABLE option. This subflow is started with the Wi-Fi interface of the MD. Data transfer starts with the Wi-Fi subflow (duration *A* shows the data transfer period) while the JOIN option of MPTCP protocol is sent through 3G/4G interface (steps 4–7). The JOIN option includes information which indicates that this particular subflow is a backup subflow. No data will be sent through this subflow unless the Wi-Fi subflow fails.

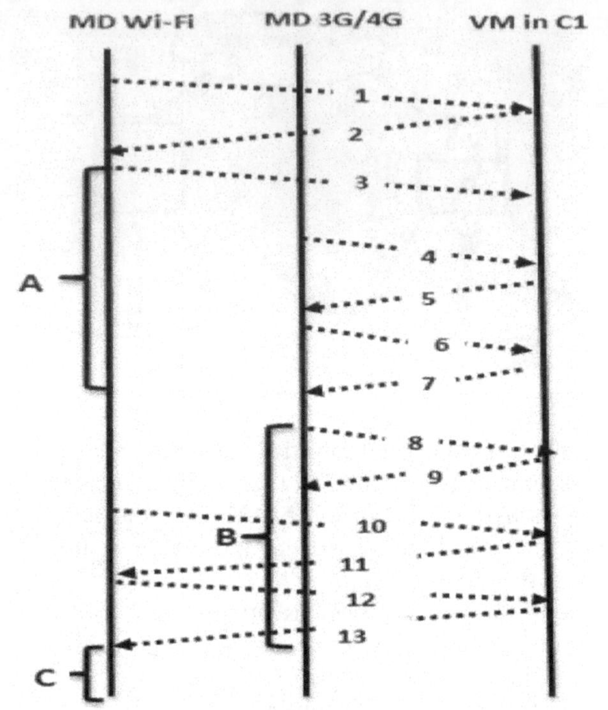

Fig. 4 Sequence chart for MPTCP backup handover mode for Wi-Fi to 3G/4G to Wi-Fi

As soon as the MD is disconnected from the Wi-Fi network, the data transfer shifts to the backup subflow (*B* denotes the data transfer duration). The REMOVE_ADDR (step 8) option is sent through the 3G/4G subflow to inform the VM that the previous IP address is no longer available. At step 9, an ACK message is sent from the VM to the MD.

After the second Wi-Fi AP assigns an IP address to the MD, the JOIN option is sent through the Wi-Fi interface of the MD with the new IP address (steps 10–13). Immediately after the Wi-Fi subflow is formed, the data transfer shifts from the 3G/4G subflow to the Wi-Fi subflow (*C* denotes the data transfer period). Then, the 3G/4G subflow remains as a backup.

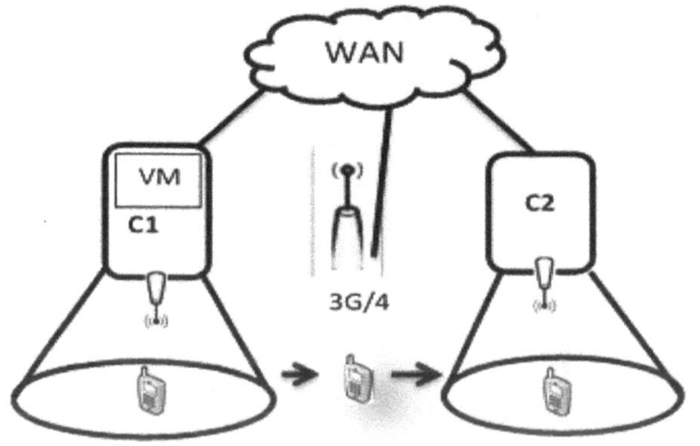

Fig. 3 A scenario with Wi-Fi and 3G/4G networks

Networking collaboration between cloudlets

If a service is available in different locations and if there is no collaboration between the two service providers, it is impossible to transfer the user state from one service location to the other seamlessly. For MCCs, Satyannarayanan, et al. [1] proposed cloudlet servers to be decentralized and

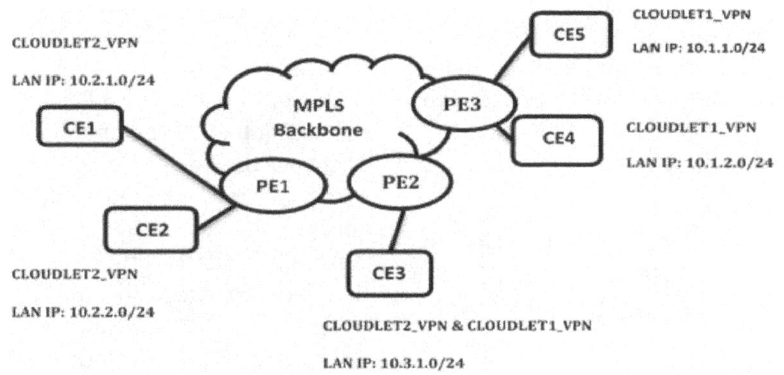

Fig. 5 VPN connections for cloudlets

managed only by the local businesses. In a scenario where multiple cloudlets are geographically close, it is impossible to make a seamless live VM migration from one cloudlet server to another if there is no collaboration between two cloudlets.

Hence, in this research, a VPN connection between cloudlets is proposed to allow a seamless live VM migration between two cloudlets. More detailed description is as follows.

VPN for cloudlets

Accessing a host remotely over the public network needs administrative permission and dedicated software that allows the remote user to access the host. In this research, the main objective is to migrate a VM between two cloudlets over the WAN. To meet this objective, each cloudlet must trust each other and there must be an administrative permission in each host to allow a VM migration from one cloudlet to the other. In order to create a secure networking collaboration between different sites of cloudlets, VPN is the most appropriate approach. Adoption of the popular peer model used in the field for VPN is proposed to meet the requirements.

As shown in Fig. 5, in a peer model VPN, there are two main types of routers, e.g., customer edge (CE) and provider edge (PE). Further, each CE is connected to a peer PE. To minimize the latency, we assume that cloudlets are capable of performing some functionalities of a CE. In other words, a cloudlet is connected directly to a PE. Hence, cloudlet and CE are used interchangeably in the context of VPNs in this paper.

A VPN is formed based on the geographical location of the CEs. If CEs are close enough for a walking distance, the CEs would form a VPN. From Fig. 5, CLOUDLET1_VPN and CLOUDLET2_VPN are established when a proximity cloudlet servers are found. CE1 and CE2 belong to CLOUDLET2_VPN and CE4, and CE5 belong to CLOUDLET1_VPN, respectively. CE3 is a member of both CLOUDLET1_VPN and CLOUDLET2_VPN.

Adding a cloudlet to a VPN

A cloudlet is added to a VPN if and only if it is near at least one cloudlet of the VPN. The maximum distance a cloudlet can have with at least another cloudlet from a VPN can be estimated using Eq. (1). The network coverage of the wireless network in meters plus 936 m (calculated using Eq. (1)) is the maximum distance one cloudlet should have with at least another cloudlet from a VPN. The algorithm to add a cloudlet in a VPN is defined below. *Dmax* is the maximum distance between two cloudlets to make a seamless handover. The existing cloudlet VPNs are represented by *VPNc*. *C* stands for a new cloudlet to be added to a VPN. *Dck* is the distance between cloudlet *C* and cloudlet *K*.

A new cloudlet candidate can be added to the existing VPNs at any time. Once the IP address space is assigned to VPN sites, merging a VPN will cause IP address overlaps or IP address change to each sites. If a cloudlet candidate is in between two VPNs, it would be a member of both VPNs but merging would not be performed. CE3 from Fig. 5 is an example.

```
Algorithm 1
Input: Dmax, VPNc, C
Output: VPNs where C is added as a new member
  for each VPN V ∈ VPNc
    for each cloudlet K ∈ V
      Add C to V, if Dck <= Dmax
      Update V
    end for
  end for
End Algorithm 1
```

Removing a cloudlet from a VPN will cause complication, if the cloudlet being removed is a neighbour for cloudlets far apart with a distance longer than *Dmax*. One VPN may be divided in two VPNs as a result of the removal of one cloudlet.

Location identifier

Packets coming to a cloudlet are filtered based on the source IP address. When a cloudlet is accessed from a different site, it is initiated to perform the VM migration. VM migration is triggered when a mobile IP address is changed based on the following two reasons:

- A cloudlet can be accessed with a different LAN IP address if it is in new location or if it is from a cellular network. After the original IP address of the MD is changed, the first cloudlet could not give the optimal performance anymore since WAN latency is involved between the MD and the first cloudlet.
- Since cloudlets are assumed to be owned by local businesses or organizations, the MD would benefit only if the user remains in the particular business area. For example, a coffee shop would allow users to access the cloudlet if users remain in the shop. Although users will not be disconnected as soon as they move out from the business area, there would be a time limit to allow the VM instance to be migrated. After all, the VM instance consumed a resource in a cloudlet and it has to be freed for the use of another customer.

Possible neighbour database

Each cloudlet maintains a possible neighbour database which helps make decision on VM migration. While joining a VPN the new cloudlet multicasts its presence to all VPN members. The other cloudlets receive and check the RTT with the new cloudlet. If RTT is in the acceptable range, the cloudlet is added to the possible neighbour database with the current RTT value. Since RTT is dependent on the real-time network condition, each cloudlet computes the RTT with their neighbour cloudlets. The RTT value is computed and the database is updated periodically, e.g., every minute or minutes. The following are the two main reasons for making the RTT an important parameter in forming the neighbour database.

The first reason is QoE. After the MD changes a location, it will access the previous cloudlet through the WAN. If the RTT between the previous and the current cloudlets is unacceptable, there is no need to provide the service. If the RTT is unacceptable, a new VM will be synthesised in the new location. This research work considers VM migration between cloudlets only if the RTT between the cloudlets is less than 150 msec.

The second reason is that RTT determines the TCP throughput. Ideally the maximum TCP throughput achievable is: *TCP Throughput = Receiver window size / RTT.* Iperf [14] application is used to measure the TCP throughput between two cloudlets as RTT increases. By default Iperf application sets the maximum server window size to 83.5Kbyte. The result is shown below in Fig. 6.

The throughput of TCP is inversely proportional to the VM migration time. As RTT increases between the cloudlets, the duration of VM migration would be unacceptable.

The VM migration decision is based on the neighbour database. When a cloudlet receives a packet from a remote LAN, it checks whether the network address matches any of the cloudlets in the possible neighbour database. The VM migration starts if and only if the cloudlet is found in the neighbour database.

Other VPN functionalities

To fully support cloudlet services, more VPN-related functionalities are needed. VPN-related techniques for cloudlets are beyond the scope of this paper. A detailed description on those functionalities can be found in [18].

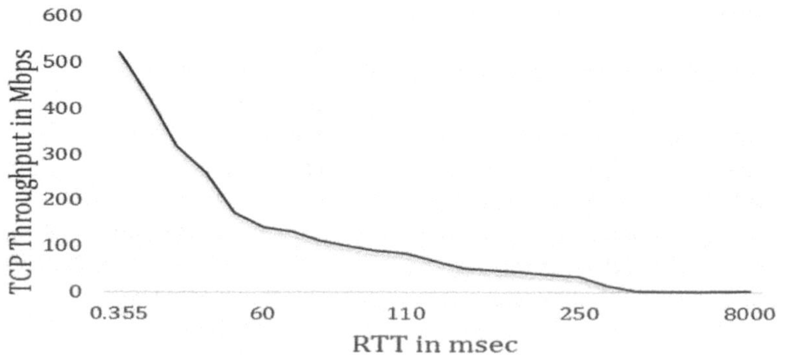

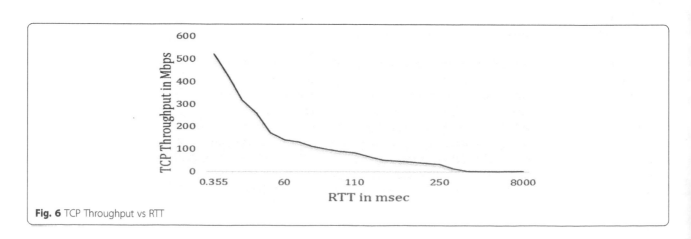

Fig. 6 TCP Throughput vs RTT

Table 3 VM specifications inside the Linux host

VM	Virtual CPU	RAM Size	Virtual Disk	Virtual Interface	Operating System
Cloudlets (VM1 & VM2)	4	8GB	40GB	2	Linux 3.11.10+ (64 bit)/ Ubuntu 12.04 LTS
MD (VM4)	2	4GB	40GB	2	Linux 3.11.10 + (64 bit)/ Ubuntu 12.04 LTS
Nested VM (VM3)	2	2GB	10GB	2	Linux 3.11.10.squeezemptcp (32 bit) / Debian 7.3.0

Experimental setup and results

This section presents experiments and results of live VM migration with a change of IP address using MPTCP.

Experiment environment

Experiments have been conducted using a 16GB RAM, core i7 Linux 3.11.10+ (Ubuntu 12.04 LTS) host. The cloudlet servers are emulated using VMs inside the Linux host. The VM monitor (or hypervisor) used is KVM with QEMU emulator [27] which uses a pre-copy RAM state migration mechanism [14].

Table 3 shows the specifications for the emulated components. Four VMs inside the Linux host are used for the experiment (see Table 3 and Fig. 7). VM1 and VM2 represent cloudlet 1 (C1) and cloudlet 2 (C2), respectively. The nested VM (VM3) inside C1 denotes the server VM instance used by the MD, and VM4 represents the MD.

Both wireless and wired transmission medium technologies are characterized by a VM bridged networking. The VMs networking in Fig. 7 emulates the cloudlets and the MD as shown in Fig. 1. In Fig. 7, VM4's Eth0 and Eth1 are used to emulate a single Wi-Fi interface of a MD. VM4 accesses VM3 through one interface at a time (Eth0 or Eth1). The movement of the MD is emulated by configuring VM4's interfaces to UP or DOWN state, as shown in Table 1.

For instance, if the MD is assumed to be in the communication range of C1 initially, only VM4's Eth0 will be at the ON state. The movement of the MD from C1 to C2 is imitated by configuring VM4's Eth0 to the DOWN state, then Eth1 to the UP state. Since most of the current Wi-Fi interface can connect to one AP at a time, the above mentioned method is suitable to represent a Wi-Fi interface for our objective.

MPTCP protocol is installed in all the VMs inside the Linux host in Fig. 7. A static routing protocol is used to forward traffic between the VMs. The LAN IP address connected to Br1 and Br2 of the Linux host is 10.1.1.0/24 and 10.1.2.0/24, respectively. Br0 of the Linux host associates the two cloudlets with 134.117.64.0/24 public IP address. The static routing on the VM4 changes automatically as the MD changes the coverage. The following example explains the scenario. Assume that the MPTCP connection is initially established with the VM4's Eth0 interface and the

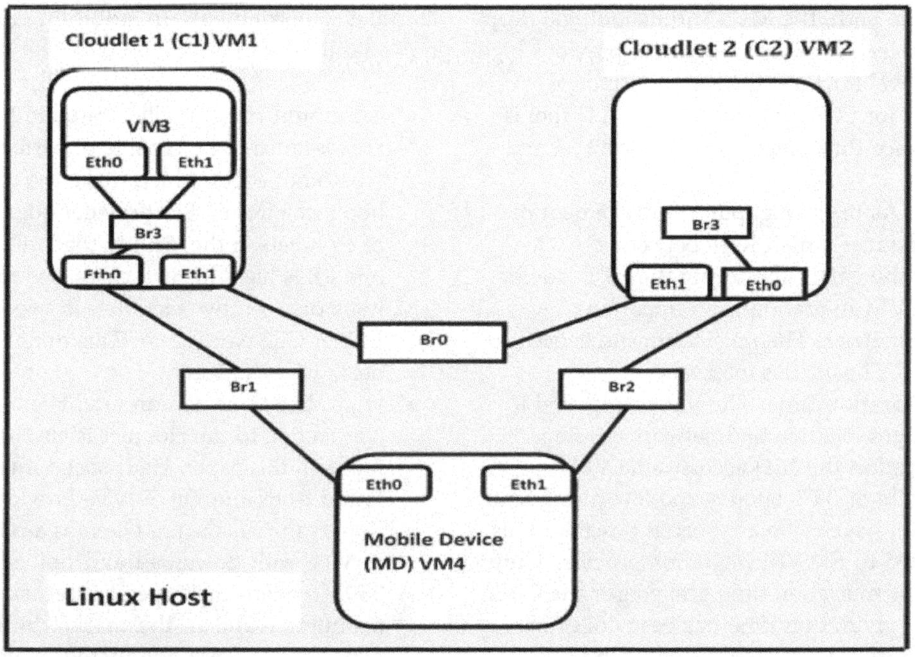

Fig. 7 Experiment using VMs and bridged networking inside a Linux host

VM3's Eth0 interface. The static routing forwards initial traffic as follows:

Eth0 of the VM4 → Br1 of the Linux Host → Br3 of VM1 → Eth0 of VM3.

After some time the VM4's Eth0 interface is taken down and then the Eth1 interface is turned on to emulate the movement of the MD from C1 to C2. This situation changes the static routing as follows:

Eth1 of the VM4 → Br2 of the Linux host → Br3 of VM2 → Br0 of the Linux host through Eth1 of VM2 → Br3 of VM1 through Eth1 of VM1 → Eth0 of VM3.

High bandwidth (BW) availability and low RTT latency between the MD and the cloudlet through Br1 and Br2 emulates a LAN. By varying the available BW and by introducing RTT latency between the two cloudlets, Br0 network emulates the WAN. Emulating WAN is achieved using the Linux traffic control (*tc*) command. Token Bucket Filter (*tbf*) queuing discipline provided by Linux is used to set the upload BW of an interface.

Performance metrics and measurements

QoE can be affected by various factors. This paper adopts four common metrics for performance evaluation.

- Throughput: Changing coverage from C1 to C2 exposed the MD to low throughput due to the WAN delay. If VM migration and the MD traffic share the same path, the MD's throughput will drop during the migration. Returning to the previous high throughput level for the MD is a performance measurement for the system. The *Iperf* [14] tool is used to measure throughput between the VM and the MD.
- RTT latency: As in throughput, the movement of the MD introduces a high RTT between the VM instance and the MD. Monitoring the RTT latency after the live VM migration is an important performance metrics. The *ping* command is used to measure the RTT with 1 s interval.
- Total VM migration time: The VM is migrated if the MD changes location and network coverage. The time duration the MD accesses the VM instance with high RTT latency and low throughput through WAN have to be as short as possible. This duration is tied to the VM migration process. The longer the VM migration time, the poorer the QoE. The total VM migration time has been collected. The VM migration is initiated using a Linux command, the time before and after the migration command completes is considered as the total VM migration time.
- VM down time: The VM downtime is part of the total VM migration time. A downtime is the time the VM is not accessible. The RAM state migration mechanisms, (both post-copy and pre-copy, [16]), have a VM downtime. Unacceptable VM downtime may be experienced based on the network condition between source and destination.

Network layer unavailability during VM migration is also investigated using the *ping* command. During migration, the VM is pinged with the original IP address and also with the expected next IP address (see Section III.A) at the same time. The VM downtime is the time the VM from the source is paused (no *ping* response) to the time the VM from the destination host starts running (*ping* response received). The downtime of the VM is measured with an interval of 10 msec. It is possible to minimize the interval to 1 msec but flooding of packets to a VM may influence the performance. For this reason, in this paper the VM downtime is known if only it is greater than 10 msec. Otherwise the down time is expressed as less than 10 msec.

Networking assumptions

This paper assumes that cloudlets are connected to high-speed Internet. The availability of high BW and low RTT latency between cloudlets in the vicinity are assumed throughout the experiment. The assumption of low RTT latency between cloudlets is supported by the geographical proximity between hosts for the cloudlet environment. In addition, low RTT is supported due to:

- Minimum Hops: As illustrated in Fig. 5, cloudlets are assumed to be capable of performing as CEs (customer edge), which make the cloudlets only one hop away from a PE (provider edge). The possibility of cloudlets in the vicinity that will be aggregated to one PE is high. In such cases, the total number of hops between two cloudlets is two, i.e., CE1 → PE1 → CE2 (see Fig. 5). This minimizes the total delay in each router.
- High data transmission rate: High-speed Internet connection to the cloudlet is also an assumption made in this paper. High-speed Internet services found from Internet Service Providers, such as Rogers in Canada, are taken as a reference. The service with download and upload speed of 350Mbps are high speed Internet connection products found in the market by the time the experiments were conducted, which represents low transmission delay.

Table 4 Baseline results for rtt and throughput

	RTT	Maximum Throughput
Between VM1 and VM2	0.382 msec	627 Mbps
Between VM3 and VM4	0.392 msec	160 Mbps

To assess the feasibility of low RTT latency and high throughput assumption, public servers which provide the *Iperf* application are used to measure the network layer RTT and the maximum throughput. By running *Iperf* client, RTT results were collected for *Iperf* servers around the world, including 71 ms for California, 119 ms for (Brabant Wallon) Belgium, and 143 ms (Saint Petersburg) Russia. All those servers are > 15 hops away from the host. Hence, it is fair to assume that that the RTT between the cloudlets can be less than 150 ms. We also varied RTT from 20 ms to 150 ms in the evaluation.

The following sub-sections show some results. The first set of results represents baseline performance. No application was running on the migrating VM, i.e., the migrating VM has all the resources or there is no resource sharing for this scenario.

Baseline performance for VM migration

The baseline performance of MPTCP was evaluated with a single path between VM1 and VM2 (as shown in Fig. 7). MPTCP acts like a regular TCP and there was no application running on the migrating VM (VM3). The purpose is to minimize the effect of latency and BW usage between VM3 and other applications and to maximize the performance.

The average measured network RTT latency between the VMs and the maximum throughput achieved for the experiment setup is shown in Table 4. *Iperf* is used to measure the throughput and the *ping* command is used to measure the average RTT. The receiver window size (RWS) is set to the default TCP window size which is 64KByte.

Without any application running on VM1, VM2, and VM3, migrating VM3 from VM1 to VM2, (see Fig. 7), takes 10.67 s and VM downtime is 243.46 msec on average. The total VM migration and the VM downtime are similar to the result reported in other research [28]. Figure 8 depicts the effect of VM3 migration on the throughput between VM1 and VM2. The period T in Fig. 8 represents the total VM migration time. During T, the result illustrates that the maximum throughput decreases and fluctuates once the VM migration is started.

Performance of live VM migration with MPTCP

This section presents the results for a seamless live VM migration using MPTCP. The TCP connection remains open after both VM3 and VM4 change their original IP addresses.

As it is presented in Section III.A, the prior knowledge of the IP address to be assigned for the migrating VM in the destination host enables a live server VM migration seamlessly with the MPTCP protocol. The migration is achieved with the change of the VM IP address. In addition, the results from the experiment also prove the seamless handover of the MD from C1 to C2 network using MPTCP.

Figure 9 illustrates the maximum throughput obtained between VM3 and VM4. The results are gathered from VM4, with *Iperf* server and *Iperf* client running on VM3 and VM4, respectively. The maximum available BW between VM1 and VM2 through Br0 was configured as 350 Mbps and the network RTT was 20 ms in this experiment. In Fig. 9, the time is divided into slots A, B, C, D, and E. The following paragraphs describe the situations for each time slot.

Time slot A is the time where VM4 initially accesses VM3 through VM1. During period A, VM3 resides inside VM1 and VM4 is directly connected to VM1. The MPTCP connection is established with the UP state interfaces and the IP addresses as shown in Table 5 before VM4 migration. The traffic flow between VM4 and VM3 is as follows:

Eth0 of the VM4 → Br1 of the Linux Host → Br3 of VM1 → Eth0 of VM3.

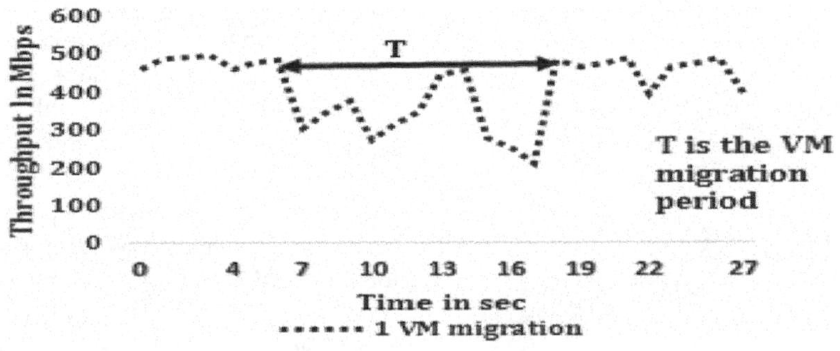

Fig. 8 Throughput between VM1 and VM2 when VM3 is migrating from VM1 to VM2

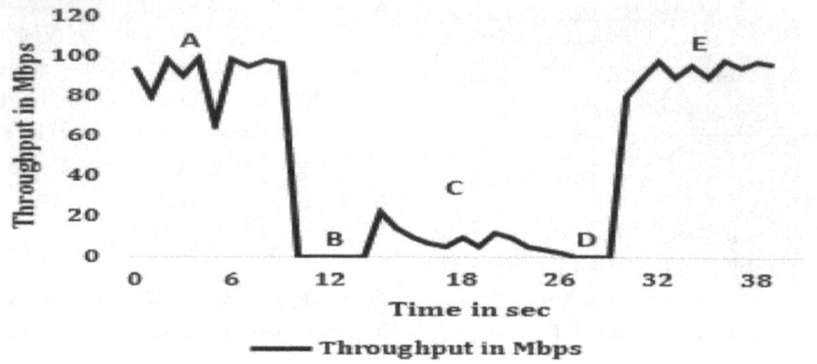

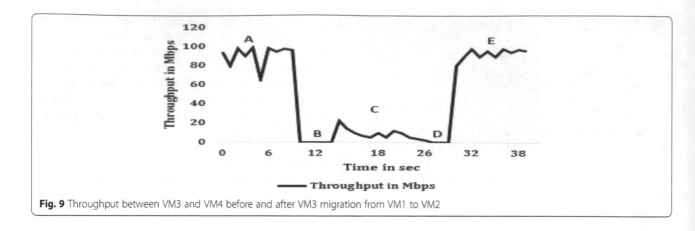

Fig. 9 Throughput between VM3 and VM4 before and after VM3 migration from VM1 to VM2

After some time, Eth0 of VM4 is taken down. Time slot B denotes the time where both the Eth0 and the Eth1 interfaces of VM4 are down (zero throughput for 5 s). This is to imitate the time a MD user walks from one Wi-Fi AP (access point) to another and the time the new Wi-Fi AP takes to connect and assign a new IP address for the real MD. If a real MD and Wi-Fi AP were used, the performance difference would be different in time slot B. The delay depends on the distance between the two WiFi network coverages and the walking speed of the user (See Fig. 1). For this experiment, the delay is configured to be 5 s. After 5 s downtime, the Eth1 interface of VM4 is changed to the UP state. During this time, VM4 is connected back to VM3 through VM2. The existing MPTCP connection adds a new subflow with the UP state and an IP address for Eth1, as presented in Table 3 after VM4 migration.

As we can see from Fig. 9, during time slot C, the application keeps running even after VM4 IP address has changed. The traffic between VM4 and VM3 flows as:

Eth1 of the VM4 → Br2 of the Linux host → Br3 of VM2 → Br0 of the Linux host through Eth1 of VM2 → Br3 of VM1 through Eth1 of VM1 → Eth0 of VM3.

During time slot C, the throughput decreases because of the involvement of the WAN between VM3 and VM4 (emulated via Br0) to keep the application running.

Table 5 Initial Interfaces and IP Addresses for VM3 and VM4

	Interface	Before VM4 migration		After VM4 migration	
		Interface state	IP address	Interface state	IP address
VM3	Eth0	UP	10.1.1.15/24	UP	10.1.1.15/24
	Eth1	DOWN	NONE	DOWN	NONE
VM4	Eth0	UP	10.1.1.14/24	DOWN	NONE
	Eth1	DOWN	NONE	UP	10.1.2.18/24

As soon as VM3 is accessed with the new IP address of 10.1.2.18/24 for MD (VM4), VM3 recognizes that VM4 has changed its original location (interface). The moving of MD to a new location or VM4 changing the initial IP address triggers the migration of VM3 from VM1 to VM2. This is done to minimize the latency and maximize the throughput between VM3 and VM4 by avoiding the traffic flow through the WAN. As the approach mentioned in Section III.A, the Eth1 interface of VM3 will be changed to the UP state and assigned with the next odd IP address (i.e., 10.1.2.19/24) to pair with the current VM4 IP address (10.1.2.18/24).

VM3 migration process is completed after time slot D. Time slot D indicates that during the time period, VM3 is inaccessible at the application level. The total VM migration time is 14.00 s. VM3 application level downtime is 3 s whereas the network layer downtime is only 204.3 msec.

Time slot E shows the time after VM3 migration is completed. The MPTCP connection adds a new subflow with the UP state and new IP addresses. At this time, the traffic between VM4 and VM3 follows the path:

Eth1 of the VM4 → Br2 of the Linux Host → Br3 of VM2 → Eth1 of VM3.

Time slots B, C, and D affect the performance of the entire system. Time slot B is determined by the geographical location of the cloudlets. If the network coverage of the cloudlets overlaps, minimum time slot B can be achieved. Time slots C and D depend on the VM migration process. The shorter these time slots are, the better the QoE.

The following sub-sections demonstrate the effect of maximum available BW and RTT latency on the performance of VM migration between VM1 and VM2 for time slots C and D. The results were based on the KVM hypervisor which is known for its shorter VM downtime than that of Xen Server, Hyper V and VMware [28].

Table 6 Total VM Migration Time (*in Seconds*)

		RTT			
		20 ms	50 ms	100 ms	150 ms
BW	350Mbps	14.00	16.62	29.44	42.02
	175Mbps	19.93	20.55	35.27	48.77
	60Mbps	43.74	46.79	48.35	50.13

Table 7 Network Layer VM Downtime (*in Milliseconds*)

		RTT			
		20 ms	50 ms	100 ms	150 ms
BW	350Mbps	204.53	860.81	1878.25	2811.18
	175Mbps	709.30	1273.41	2367.87	3564.01
	60Mbps	2483.76	3011.99	3547.25	3687.74

Total VM migration time and VM downtime

This experiment measures the total VM migration time (C + D) and VM network layer downtime by varying RTT and BW. The network RTT values used were 20 ms, 50 ms, 100 ms, and 150 m, and the BW values used for the experiments were 350Mbps, 175Mbps, and 60Mbps.

Results for total VM migration time and network layer VM downtime are shown in Tables 6 and 7, respectively. The results show that the total VM migration time and the VM downtime increase as the RTT latency increases with a fixed available BW between VM1 and VM2. It can also be observed that, as the available BW decreases, the migration time and VM downtime increases. The RTT effect is more noticeable for high BW, e.g., 175Mbps and 350Mbps than that for the low BW, e.g., 60Mbps.

Figures 10 and 11 show that the total VM migration time and the VM downtime increase as the RTT latency increases with a fixed available BW between VM1 and VM2. It can also be observed that as the available BW decreases, the migration time and VM downtime increases. The RTT effect is more noticeable for high BW, 175Mbps and 350Mbps than the low BW, 60Mbps. The following points explain the reasons for the results shown in Figs. 10 and 11.

- The total amount of memory configured for VM3 is 2GByte while the used amount of the memory is only 263MByte. The hypervisor used for this experiment is KVM. KVM only transfers the used

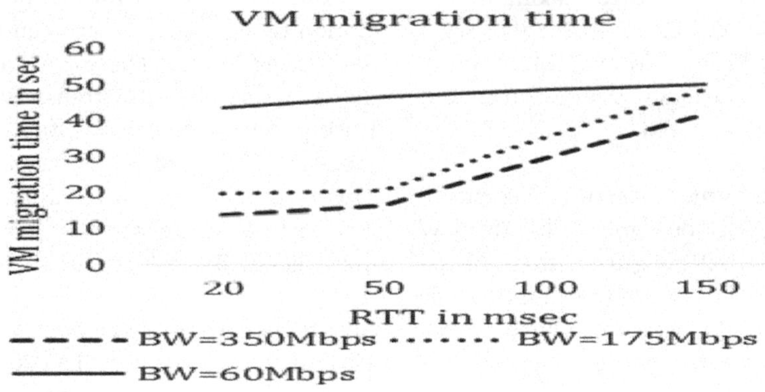

Fig. 10 Latency vs VM Migration Time

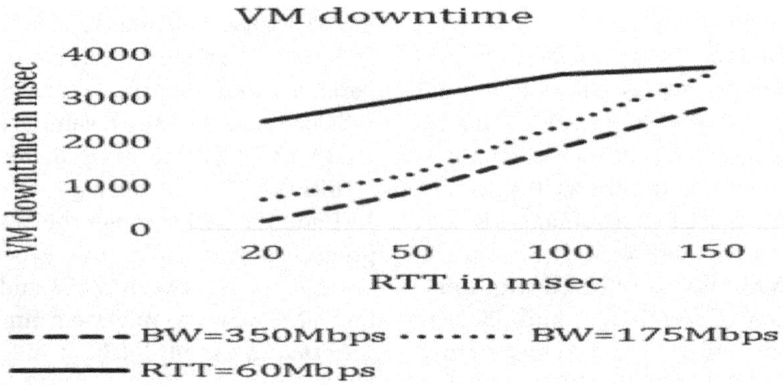

Fig. 11 Latency vs VM Downtime

memory and it has a way to abstract the free memory for migrating VM at the destination host. Recall from the baseline performance result, migrating more than 263MByte takes only 10.67 s. The estimated data transfer speed of KVM will be the used memory size divided by the migration time which is equal to 197.19Mbps. Note also that 197.19Mbps is the estimated speed, not the exact speed. To calculate the exact data transfer speed we need to know how many iterations KVM goes through and the data transferred in each iteration. During the baseline experiment, no application was running on the migrating VM; hence the estimated data transfer speed is close to the exact speed of KVM.

- If the available BW is less than 197.19Mbps, queuing delay will be introduced in addition to the RTT values between VM1 and VM2. As the total delay increases between VM1 and VM2, the data transmission speed decreases which increases the total VM migration time.
- The throughput for VM3 migration does not stay the same throughout the migration process. The TCP auto tuning is turned on, both on VM1 and VM2 and also the TCP stack on VM1 and VM2 is configured with minimum of 4Kbyte, maximum of 5394Kbyte, and 85Kbyte default receiver buffer size. When VM3 is migrated from VM1 to VM2, VM2 increases or decreases its window size to control the data flow between VM1 and VM2.

The VM migration is performed over the TCP protocol. The efficiency of TCP is determined by the BW delay product (BDP). If the BDP is greater than the receiver window buffer size, TCP data transmission will not be efficient. To identify the scenarios which do not use the available BW efficiently, the average receiver window buffer size has to be known. TCP performance analysis is given in the next sub-section.

Performance analysis and TCP

Performance analysis related to TCP is crucial for migration decision making and design, as MPTCP is built upon TCP. The throughput for VM3 migration fluctuates during the migration process, as the migration is performed over the TCP protocol and the TCP auto tuning was turned on. Further, TCP performance is also closely related to the receiver window size (RWS). The TCP stack on VM1 and VM2 was configured with minimum of 4KByte, maximum of 5394KByte, and 85KByte default RWS. The efficiency of TCP is KAI determined by the BW delay product (BDP). If the BDP is greater than the RWS, TCP data transmission is not efficient.

Table 8 The BDP results in KByte

		RTT			
		20 ms	50 ms	100 ms	150 ms
BW	350Mbps	854	2734	4272	6409
	175Mbps	427	1068	2136	3204
	60Mbps	146	366	732	1098

To identify the scenarios which do not use the available BW efficiently, the average RWS has to be known.

Table 8 shows the BDP values in KByte for the corresponding RTT and BW values. From the BDP results, when BW is 350Mbps and RTT is 150 msec, the data transmission is inefficient even when the RWS is at its maximum value, i.e. 6409Kbyte ((350Mbps × 150 msec) / (8 bits/Byte × 1024)) which is greater than 5394Kbyte (maximum system configured window size). For this particular case the data transmission speed is governed by the RWS and the RTT instead of the available BW. If BDP is greater than the RWS, the ideal maximum TCP throughput can be calculated as:

$$Max.\ TCP\ Thoughput = RWS/RTT \tag{2}$$

Based on the total VM size and the VM migration time (as shown in Table 4), we can estimate the data transmission speed or throughput (e.g., VM size/VM migration time), which in turn can be used to calculate the RWS using Eq. (2). The shaded area in Table 6 indicates the scenarios where the transmission speed is inefficient. During those periods, data transmission speed is determined by RTT and RWS instead of the available BW. This is also the reason for a similar high total VM migration time values when RTT = 150 msec regardless of the available BW values (see Table 4).

Latency and performance analysis

This subsection describes the latency performance analysis during the VM migration process and the experiments show that the RTT between VM3 and VM4 increases from its original value. The goal here is to show the bahaviour of the RTT during migration. The RTT values used in this experiment are 20 msec, 50mesc, 100 msec, and 150 msec and the maximum available BW used in this experiment are 350Mbps and 60Mbps.

Before analyzing the results as shown in Figs 12, 13, 14, 15, 16, and 17, some terms are defined below for clarity.

Initial RTT: The average RTT between the migrating VM and the MD through the WAN before the migration process is started. For this experiment, it would be the average RTT between VM3 and VM4 through Br0 before VM3 starts to migrate from VM1 to VM2.

Actual average RTT: is the average RTT between VM3 and VM4 during VM3 migration process from VM1 to VM2.

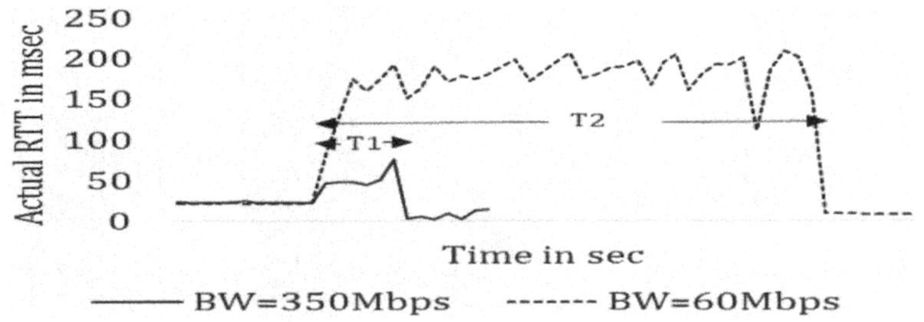

Fig. 12 Actual RTT during VM migration for initial RTT = 20 msec

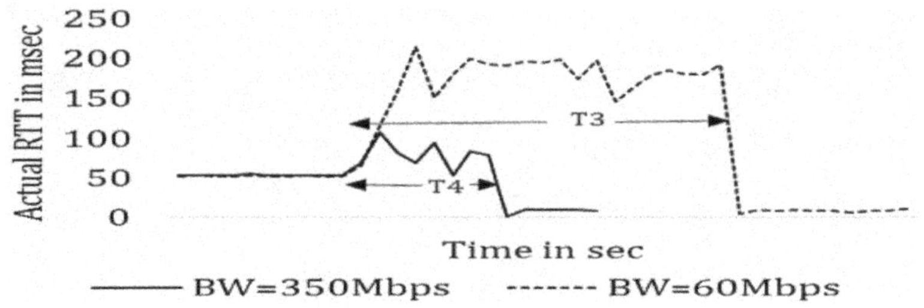

Fig. 13 Actual RTT during VM migration for initial RTT = 50 msec

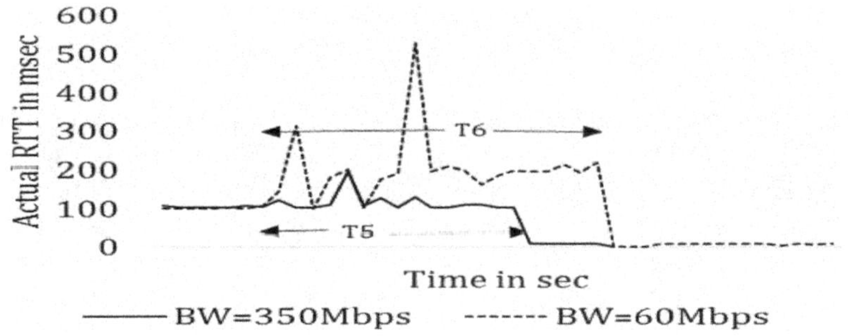

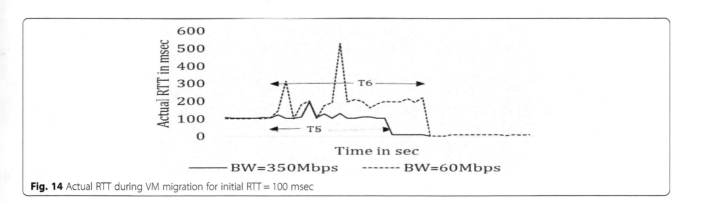

Fig. 14 Actual RTT during VM migration for initial RTT = 100 msec

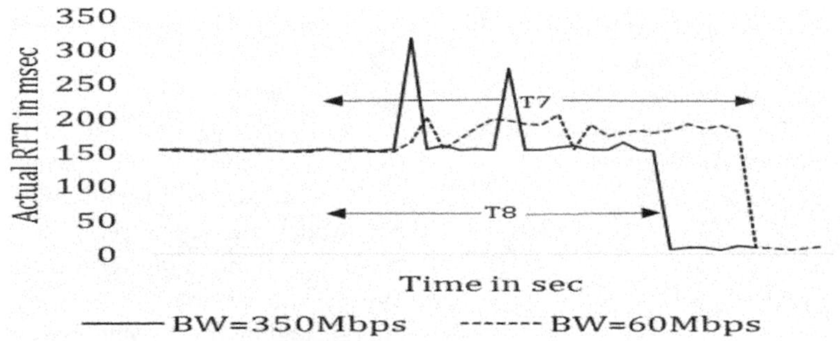

Fig. 15 Actual RTT during VM migration for initial RTT = 150 msec

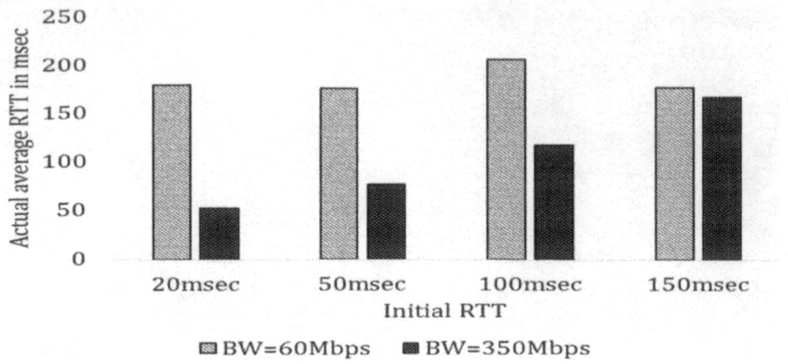

Fig. 16 Average RTT during migration process vs initial RTT

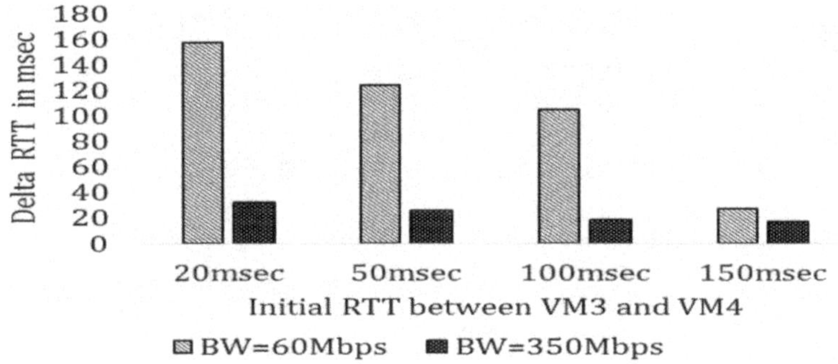

Fig. 17 Delta RTT vs the Initial RTT

Delta RTT: is the difference between the actual average RTT and the initial RTT.

Figures 12, 13, 14 and 15 show the actual RTT during VM migration for initial RTT of 20 msec, 50 msec, 100mesec and 150 msec respectively. The RTT was measured by using *ping* command with a 1 s interval. The objective is to show how much the latency increases when the VM starts to migrate. All the graphs show the results from the time when VM4 starts to access VM3 through the WAN. At the start, the low latency shows the RTT between VM4 and VM3 before VM3 migration process is started. The time durations are noted as T1, T2, T3, T4, T5, T6, T7 and T8 show the total VM migration time for different available BW and RTT values and the values for different Ti are given in Table 9. Figures 12, 13, 14 and 15 (i.e., T1, T4, T5, and T8) show that as the initial RTT increases, the duration of migration increases (cf. Table 9).

Table 9 Total VM migration time for the time duration shown in Figures 12, 13, 14 and 15

T1	T2	T3	T4	T5	T6	T7	T8
8.12 s	24.30s	24.0 s	9.91 s	15.62 s	25 s	26 s	23 s

Figure 16 summarizes the results in terms of the actual average RTT with respect to initial RTT of 20 msec, 50 msec, 100 msec, and 150 msec respectively. In the case of initial RTT of 150 msec cf. Figure 16), there is little or no difference in actual average RTT between the lower BW (i.e. 60Mbps) and the higher BW (i.e., 350 msec). For fixed latency, minimizing the available BW increases the VM migration time and the actual average RTT significantly. The significance is more noticeable for low latency. For low BW, 60Mbps, the actual average RTT is independent of the initial RTT. Regardless of the initial RTT, the actual average RTT reflects the same amount. For the high BW, 350 Mbps, the actual average RTT increases as the initial RTT increases. However, the amount of the RTT added to the initial RTT is not the same.

Figure 17 illustrates delta RTT as the initial RTT increases for the BW of 60Mbps and 350 Mbps. Delta RTT decreases as the initial RTT increases regardless of the available BW. Hence, having a low initial RTT before VM migration is not a guarantee for low RTT for migration. From the results, it is concluded that as long as there is a high available BW, the actual average RTT does not show much difference from the initial RTT.

Throughput performance analysis

One main advantage of using a nearby cloudlet is to achieve a high throughput. The result shown in Fig. 18 is the throughput achieved between VM3 and MD (VM4). The figure shows the throughput only after VM4 is directly connected to VM2. In Fig. 18, the time before t = 10 is the time when VM4 is connected to VM3 through the WAN. At t = 10, the migration process is manually started. The completion of the VM migration for various RTT values is depicted in Fig. 18.

Lower RTT values result in higher throughput, as observed in Fig. 18. The throughput of VM4 drops at t = 10 when migration starts. Specially, for RTT = 20 msec, the throughput decreases significantly at t = 13. On the other hand, the throughput starts to increase earlier when RTT is lower. Figure 19 demonstrates a five times increase in RTT (from 20 msec to 100 msce), the average throughput only decreases by 26.4 % (from 7.2Mbps to 5.3 Mbps). With RTT = 20 msec, however, the performance is better than all the other RTT values.

If the proposed MPTCP and prior knowledge of the migrating IP address are not used, the throughput of the MD user would be zero before the VM is launched in the new cloudlet. If a real application is used, a notice7able delay is inevitable during the VM migration process.

VM migration decision algorithm

The results show that it is impossible to guarantee fast VM migration over the WAN using only the bare hypervisor. Optimization techniques for WAN VM migration mentioned in other research efforts, such as [18], has to be adopted to make the system more efficient. In addition, a smart VM migration decision maker is desirable for better QoE. As the main objective is eliminating the service re-initiation time for the MD, an efficient service has to be provided during migration. All the performance metrics need to be considered before the VM migration starts. If the VM migration is predicted to result in worse performance than service re-initiation time, it is better for the MD to launch a new VM at the new location.

The type of applications running on the VM also determine the VM migration time. In this work, only *Iperf* application runs on the migrating VM. *Iperf* is a type of send and receive application which does not consume much of the CPU (maximum of 15 % of VM3 CPU). Thus, VM migration decision algorithm needs to consider the type of the application running on the VM in terms of resource (RAM, CPU, hard disc, and network) consumption and usage. For instance, RAM write intensive applications dirty memory pages frequently. A precopy migration works best only when memory pages can

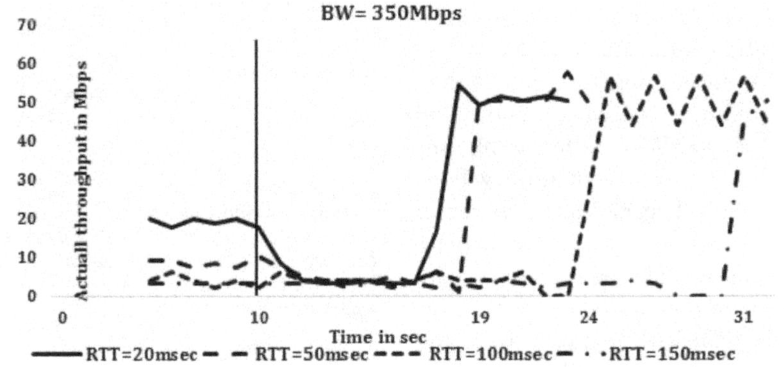

Fig. 18 Actual VM4 throughput during VM3 migration for 350Mbps

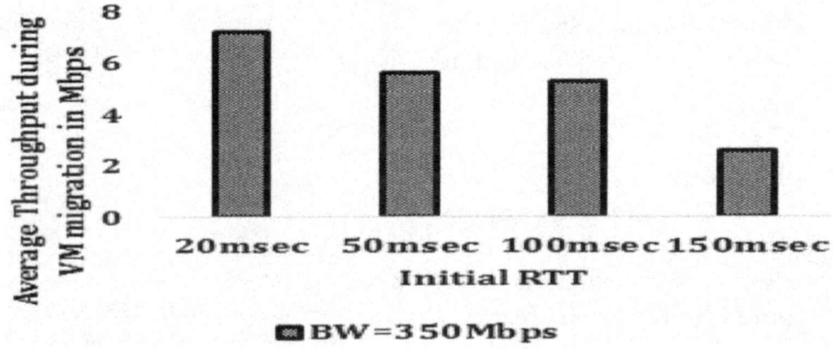

Fig. 19 Average throughput during VM3 migration

be copied to the destination host faster than they are dirtied. In addition, KVM will never finish live migration if the RAM page is dirtied with a speed of 32Mbps [28]. Therefore, for live migration to be beneficial, a decision algorithm plays an important role in determining if the live VM migration should proceed. The decision algorithm needs to consider factors such as RTT latency and available BW. The proposed VM migration decision algorithm is as follows:

```
Algorithm 2
Input: average RTT, initial RTT
Estimate Delta RTT  /* Delta RTT is the difference between the actual
                        average RTT and the initial RTT */
if (initial RTT + Delta RTT <= 150msec}
   then migrate the VM
   else if ((150msec < Initial RTT + delta RTT <= 1sec} and
          (estimated VM migration time < service initiation time))
      then migrate the VM
      else
          ignore VM migration
          notify user to start a new service
          destroy the VM instance
      end if
end if
End Algorithm 2
```

The algorithm considers three main parameters in making decision on the VM migration; the service initiation time, the VM migration time and the RTT during VM migration. If the RTT during migration is less than 150 msec, it means that the user is having a good QoE even through the WAN. Regardless of the total estimated VM migration time, the VM migration will be performed. There is no need to trigger VM migration, if the actual RTT during VM migration is greater than 1 s since the service becomes useless for the user.

The algorithm should be implemented in each cloudlet. The estimation of the total VM migration time and delta RTT can be achieved through profiling. Applications and network resources profiler need to be deployed in to the system which keeps track of all VM migration results. Over time, the profiler provides precise information. Each cloudlet also can share their profiles to learn a wide variety of situations within short time.

Conclusions and future directions

Live VM migration over the WAN includes migration of the RAM state, network, and storage. This paper presented an approach for live server VM migration using MPTCP. To realize the approach, two main features have been proposed: (i) a scheme for IP address assignment to reduce TCP downtime and (ii) two virtual interfaces were proposed for the VM migration; one interface operates during normal operation and the other one operates when a VM migration is triggered.

A number of experiments using emulation have demonstrated that the proposed approach can be realized to support actual live VM migration. Further, the paper investigated the performance of VM migration, including total live migration time, VM downtime, throughput, RTT and TCP protocol. In addition, the effect of various parameters has been investigated for further advancement in this fast growing field.

The experiment does not consider storage migration. Storage migration is influenced by the network resources (BW and RTT) and the disc I/O speed. If the available BW is less than the reading speed, it may take a long time for VM migration. In general, migrating storage would not be effective.

The concept of cloudlets is similar to the emerging Fog computing technology. Our proposed live VM migration between cloudlets can also be applied in a Fog computing environment, where a service running in a Fog can be migrated from one edge device to another as the MD is moving from one area to another. In Fog computing, cloudlets are most likely managed by the same network operator, which can effectively facilitate IP address assignment and other migration issues, including the business concerns. VM migration for Fog computing is worth investigating.

Acknowledgements

We would like to express our gratitude to Jerry Buburuz who provided resources and resolved all the technical errors we faced during the lab environment setup.

Authors' contributions

The work is primarily based on FT's Master's research and thesis, which was co-supervised by CL and SA. All authors contributed to the technical areas and the writings. FT designed and implemented the experiments. All authors read and approved the final manuscript.

Competing interests

The authors declare that they have no competing interests.

References

1. Satyannarayanan M, Bahl P, Caceres R, Davies N (2009) The case for VM-based cloudlets in mobile computing. IEEE Pervasive Comput 8(4):14–23
2. Cuervo E et al (2010) MAUI: Making Smartphones Last Longer with Code Offload". Proc. of the 8th Int'l Conf. on Mobile Systems, Applications, and Services, ACM, New York, pp 49–62
3. Flinn J (2012) Cyber Foraging: Bridging Mobile and Cloud Computing via Opportunistic Offload, Morgan & Claypool Publishers
4. Chun B-G, Ihm S, Maniatis P, Naik M, Patti A (2011) CloneCloud: Elastic Execution between Mobile Devices and Cloud". Proc. of the 6th Conf. on Computer Systems, ACM, New York, pp 301–314
5. Soyata T et al (2012) Cloud-Vision: Real-time Face Recognition using a Mobile-Cloudlet-Cloud Acceleration Architecture. Proc. of Symp. on Computers and Communications, Cappadocia, pp 59–66
6. Ra M, Sheth A, Mummert L, Pillai P, Wetherall D, Govindan R (2011) Odessa: Enabling Interactive Perception Applications on Mobile Devices. Proc. of the

Int'l Conf. on Mobile Systems, Applications, and Services (MobiSys), ACM, New York, pp 43–56
7. Gordon MS, Jamshidi DA, Mahlke S, Mao ZM, Chen X (2012) COMET: Code Offload by Migrating Execution Transparently. Proc. of the 10th USENIX Symp. on Operating Systems Design and Implementation (OSDI), Hollywood, pp 93–106
8. Ha K et al (2013) The Impact of Mobile Multimedia Applications on Data Center Consolidation. Proc. of the IEEE Int'l Conf. on Cloud Engineering, Redwood City, pp 166–176
9. Satyanarayanan M (2014) A brief history of cloud offload. GetMobile 18(4):19–23
10. Bonomi F, Milito R, Zhu J, Addepalli S (2012) Fog Computing and its Role in the Internet of Things. Proc. of the 1st Edition of the MCC Workshop on Mobile Cloud Computing, ACM, New York, pp 13–16
11. Yi S, Li C, Li Q (2015) A Survey of Fog Computing: Concepts, Applications, and Issues. Proc. of the Workshop on Mobile Big Data, ACM, New York, pp 37–42
12. Stojmenovic I, Wen S (2014) The Fog Computing Paradigm: Scenarios and Security Issues. Proc. of the Federated Conf. on Computer Science and Information Systems, Warsaw, pp 1–8
13. Teka FA, Lung C-H, Ajila S (2015) Seamless Live Virtual Machine Migration with Cloudlets and Multipath TCP. Proc. of the 39th IEEE Computer Software and Applications Conf. (COMPSAC), Taichung, pp 607–616
14. MPTCP, www.multipath-tcp.org, Last accessed in Nov, 2015
15. Ha K, Pillai P, Richter W, Abe Y, Satyanarayanna M (2013) Just-in-time Provisioning for Cyber Foraging". Proc. of the 11th Int'l Conf. on Mobile Systems, Applications, and Services, ACM, New York, pp 153–166
16. Hines M, Deshpande U, Gopalan K (2009) Post-copy live migration of virtual machines. SIGOPS Oper Syst Rev 43(3):14–26
17. Clark C, Fraser K, Hand S, Hansen JG (2005) Live Migration of Virtual Machines". Proc. of the 2nd Symp. on Networked Systems Design & Implementation, USENIX, Berkeley, pp 273–286
18. Wood T, Ramakrishnan KK, Shenoy P, van der Merwe J (2011) CloudNet: Dynamic Pooling of Cloud Resources by Live WAN Migration of Virtual Machines. Proc. of the 7th ACM SIGPLAN/SIGOPS Int'l Conf. on Virtual Execution Environments, ACM, New York, pp 121–132.
19. Nicutar C, Paasch C, Bagnulo M, Raiciu C (2013) Evolving the Internet with Connection Acrobatics". Proc. of the Workshop on Hot Topics in Middleboxes and Network Function Virtualization, ACM, New York, pp 7–12
20. Li J, Bu K, Liu X, Xiao B (2013) ENDA: Embracing Network Inconsistency for Dynamic Application Offloading in MCC". Proc. of the 2nd ACM SIGCOMM Workshop on Mobile Cloud Computing, ACM, New York, pp 39–44
21. Kommineni S, De A, Alladi S, Chilukuri S (2014) The Cloudlet with a Silver Lining". Proc. of 6th Int'l Conf. on Communication Systems & Networks, Bangalore, pp 1–4
22. Jararweh Y et al (2013) Resource Efficient Mobile Computing Using Cloudlet Infrastructure". Proc. of 9th Int'l Conf. on Mobile Ad-hoc and Sensor Networks, Dalian, pp 373–377
23. Jaraweh Y, Tawalbeh L, Ababneh F, Khreishah A, Dosari F (2014) Scalable Cloudlet-based Mobile Computing Model. Proc. of the 11th Int'l Conf. on Mobile Systems & Pervasive Computing, Niagara Falls, pp 434–441
24. Kondo T, Aibara R, Suga K, Maeda K (2014) A Mobility Management System for the Global Live Migration of Virtual Machine across Multiple Sites". Proc. of the 38th Int'l Computer Software and Applications Conf. Workshops (COMPSACW), Vasteras, pp 73–77
25. Paasch C et al (2012) Exploring Mobile/WiFi Handover with Multipath TCP. Proc. of the ACM SIGCOMM Workshop on Cellular Networks: Operations, Challenges, and Future Design, ACM, New York, pp 31–36
26. LaPlante JN, Kaeser TP (2004) The continuing evolution of pedestrian walking speed assumptions. ITE J 74:32–40
27. KVMQEMU, www.linux-kvm.org. Last accessed in Nov, 2015
28. Hu W et al (2013) A Quantitative Study of Virtual Machine Live Migration". Proc. of the 2013 ACM Cloud and Autonomic Computing Conf., Article No. 11, ACM, New York

11

Performance characterization and analysis for Hadoop K-means iteration

Joseph Issa

Abstract

The rapid growth in the demand for cloud computing data presents a performance challenge for both software and hardware architects. It is important to analyze and characterize the data processing performance for a given cloud cluster and to evaluate the performance bottlenecks in a cloud cluster that contribute to higher or lower computing processing time. In this paper, we implement a detailed performance analysis and characterization for Hadoop K-means iterations by scaling different processor micro-architecture parameters and comparing performance using Intel and AMD processors. This leads to the analysis of the underlying hardware in a cloud cluster servers to enable optimization of software and hardware to achieve maximum performance possible. We also propose a performance estimation model that estimates performance for Hadoop K-means iterations by modeling different processor micro-architecture parameters. The model is verified to predict performance with less than 5 % error margin relative to a measured baseline.

Keywords: Performance prediction, Performance analysis, Hadoop K-means Iterations

Introduction

Given the rapid growth in the demand of cloud computing [1, 2] and cloud data, there is an increasing demand in storing, processing and a retrieving large amount of data in a cloud cluster. The data can be either stored to a cloud network such as scientific data (i.e. Climate modeling, Fusion, Bioinformatics...etc) or use the cloud network for data-intensive tasks such as collecting experimental data, dumping data on parallel storage systems, run large scale simulations...etc. Cloud computing is an emerging technology used to deliver different types of resources known as services over the internet. Cluster computing [3–7] is a set of stand-alone computers connected together to form a single computing resource [8, 9]. This improves the performance and availability of a cloud cluster as compared to a single computer.

Hadoop was introduced as a solution to handle processing, storing and retrieving Big Data in a cloud environment which usually runs on a cluster of commodity machines. This cluster is composed of a master and slave nodes that process and compute data in parallel. It is important for processor architects to understand what processor micro-architecture parameters contribute to higher or lower performance. It is also important for benchmark developers to optimize the benchmark software for a given hardware to achieve maximum performance possible. Hadoop is an open-source framework with two main components: MapReduce [10], and Hadoop Distributed File System (HDFS). HDFS is the primary storage for Hadoop; it is highly reliable and uses sockets for communications and is used for distributed storage [11, 12]. One important feature of HDFS is the partitioning of data and computation using thousands of hosts, and the execution of application computations in parallel in a way it is close to their data [13–16]. Hadoop cluster scales with computation and storage capacity by adding more servers. For example, Yahoo Hadoop cluster uses 40,000 servers and stores 40 PetaBytes of application data. Hadoop HDFS is used for data protection and reliability by replicating the file content across multiple DataNodes. This replication increases the probability for locating computation near the needed data.

The MapReduce [17, 10] framework is used for parallel processing. MapReduce and HDFS are co-designed, co-developed and co-deployed. What this means is that we have a single set of servers where MapReduce and HDFS are deployed so there is no separate set of servers

Correspondence: joseph_issa@yahoo.com
Department of Electrical and Computer Engineering, Notre Dame University, Zouk Mosbeh, Lebanon

for HDFS to store data and a separate set of servers for processing data. One important aspect of MapReduce is that it's capability of moving compute to data (DataNode on which the data is located) and not the other way around. MapReduce knows where the data is placed in a cluster by working closely with HDFS. MapReduce consists of two main components, the JobTracker, and the TaskTracker. The JobTracker is the master and it is responsible for resource management such as tracking which nodes are up or down and how to deal with node failures. The TaskTracker is the slave, it gets direction from the JobTracker to run the tasks and report any failures and scheduling tasks.

Hadoop framework consists of several micro-benchmarks developed using MapReduce algorithm, in other words, it is a framework used to process large data sets in a distributed computing environment. The resource utilization for the benchmarks is categorized as IO-bound, CPU-bound, or in between. Table 1 summarizes the system resource utilization for each workload.

In this paper, we present a detailed performance characterization for Hadoop K-means iterations using different processor configurations. We also propose a performance projection model that projects and model performance by changing different processor architecture parameters such as the number of cores/threads, memory bandwidth, memory size, cycles-per-instruction (CPI) and memory latency [18, 19]. The remainder of this paper is organized as follows: In "Hadoop K-means Overview" section, we start with an overview of Hadoop K-means and Mahout K-means implementations. In "Related Work" section, compare our work to other published work of the same topic. In "Performance Characterization using Intel Xeon Based Platform" section we present a detailed performance characterization of Hadoop K-means for different key processor architecture parameters using Intel Xeon processor. In "Performance Characterization using AMD Interlagos Platform" section, we present a detailed performance analysis and characterization for Hadoop K-means using AMD Interlagos processor by analyzing the performance sensitivity to key processor architecture parameters. In "Performance Projection Model"' section we propose a performance projection model that projects processor performance and total runtime and finally we conclude and discuss future work.

Table 1 Workloads based on Hadoop framework: System Resource Utilization

Workloads	System Resource Utilization
WordSort	Sort Phase: IO-bound in the Reduce Phase: Communication-bound.
Word Count	CPU-bound
TeraSort	Map Stage: CPU-Bound
	Reduce stage: IO-bound
NutchIndexing	IO-bound with high CPU utilizations in the map stage. This workload is mainly used for web searching.
K-means	CPU-bound in the iteration, IO-bound in the clustering. It is used for machine learning and data mining.

Hadoop K-means overview

Hadoop is designed as a framework for processing (storing and appending) multi Petabytes of data sets in a distributed computing cluster systems. There are several components of Hadoop architecture, the first component is known as the NameNode which is responsible for storing the file system namespace. The second component of Hadoop architecture is the DataNodes which is responsible for storing blocks and hosting MapReduce computation. The JobTracker component is responsible for tracking jobs; also it is responsible for detecting any failures. All applications in Hadoop are based on MapReduce which was introduced by Google. MapReduce means that a given application can be broken down into smaller blocks that can run on any node. The application can run on systems with thousands on nodes to achieve better performance. Hadoop is a framework which consists of several micro-benchmarks. Some of these benchmarks are Sort, Word Count, TeraSort, K-means, and NutchIndexing. The file system in Hadoop is organized in a way that maps all the local disks in a cluster into a single file system hierarchy known as HDFS. Hadoop K-means is basically used for machine learning as well as data mining. It is divided into two main phases, the first phase is the iteration phase and the second phase is the clustering phase. In the iteration phase, the performance is a CPU-bound, which means the performance will increase if there is an increase in processing power such as an increase in the number of cores. In the clustering phase, the performance is IO-bound which means that the performance is limited and bounded by IO communication within a cluster. Clustering is a technique used to identify groups (clusters) within the input observation in such a way that the objects within each group will have high similarities and fewer similarities between other groups or clusters. The similarities metric in clustering algorithm uses distance measured only, similarities by correlation is not used in the clustering algorithm. K-means clustering generates a specific number of disjoint (non-hierarchal) clusters. The K-means method is numerical, unsupervised and iterative. K stands for K number of clusters and must be manually supplied by the user based on the input data.

Hadoop K-means version 2.7.0 is a clustering algorithm in which the input is a set of data points such as K with a set of points X1, X2....Xn. The variable K refers to how many clusters it needs to find. The algorithm starts by placing K centroids in a random location such as C1, C2...Ck. The algorithm will then repeat by executing the following steps below until convergence:

For each point X, find the nearest centroid C. This is done by computing the distance between Xi and Cj for every cluster centroid, then it pick the cluster J with minimum distance. It will then assign the point X to the cluster of the nearest centroid. For each cluster J = 1.....K, the algorithm will take the distance for every point in the selected cluster and average out the distance by using the following relation: $\mathbf{C(a)} = \frac{1}{n}\sum_{xi}^{cj}\mathbf{X(a)} \quad \mathbf{for\ a} = 1...\mathbf{d}$, where C(a) is the new centroid for cluster J. The algorithm keeps running them one after the other until none of the cluster assignment changes, so no points change cluster membership. At this point, the algorithm has converged so it stops there. The complexity of the Hadoop K-means iteration algorithm is given as a factor of:

$$O(\#\textbf{\textit{iterations}} \times \#\textbf{\textit{clusters}} \times \#\textbf{\textit{instances}} \times \#\textbf{\textit{dimensions}})$$

The number of iterations is determined by how many times it will run until the algorithm convergence. Another implementation of K-means is Apache Mahout [20] which is used as a machine learning software that allows applications to analyze a large set of data. Mahout uses Apache Hadoop power to solve a complex problem by breaking them up into multi-parallel tasks. Mahout offers three machine learning techniques which are Recommendation, Classification, and Clustering. Recommendations use user's information with community information to determine the likelihood of user's preference. For example, Netflix uses the Mahout Recommendation engine to suggest movies. Classification engine is used for example in classifying spam emails. It uses known data to determine how new data should be classified into a set of existing categories. So every time a user mark an email as 'spam' it directly influences the email Classification engine for providing future email spams. The last Mahout engine is clustering which is used for example to group different news of similar article together. This is mainly used by Google and other search engines. Clustering forms a group of similar data based on common characteristics. Unlike classifications, clustering does not group data into an existing set of known categories. This is particularly useful when the user is not sure how to organize the data in the first place.

Related work

Analyzing cloud computing performance is an important research topic that leads to several published papers. Map-Reduce clusters are becoming popular for a set of applications [21–23] in which large data processed is stored and shared as files in a distributed file systems.

Emanuel V in [24] presents an analytical model that estimates performance for a Hadoop online prototype using job pipeline parallelism method. In comparison, the projection model proposed in this paper projects performance and runtime using different processor micro-architecture parameters that are important parameters for processor architects to model performance. Furthermore, our model is verified to predict both performance and runtime with <5 % error margin for all tested cases. The performance projection model we present in this paper is flexible and can be implemented without the need for a simulator and sampling traces.

Dejun et al in [25], propose an approach to evaluate the response time and I/O performance. Ibrahim et al in [26], analyze Hadoop execution time on virtual machines. Stewart in [27] compares the performance of several data query languages. All their work is focused on different aspects for analyzing Hadoop performance. Our work complements performance analysis for Hadoop. We also present a prediction analytical model for performance which is the main focus of the research presented in this paper. There are several performance monitoring tools for Hadoop K-means. Salsa [28] for example is a DataNode/TaskTracker log analyzer which provides data and control flow execution on each node. Mochi [29] extracts job execution view from a DataNode/TaskTracker logs.

Therdphapiyanak et al in [30] proposed an implementation using Mahout/Hadoop for a large data set by pre-determining the appropriate numbers of K-means clusters. This is done by describing the appropriate number of cluster and the proper amount of entries in log files.

Jiang in [31] conducted an in-depth performance analysis for MapdReduce. The research presented optimization methods to improve performance. However, his research does not present an estimation model to translate the optimized methods presented into a performance prediction model.

Esteves et al, in [32] presented detailed performance analysis of Mahout K-means using large data sets running on Amazon EC2 instances. The performance gain in runtime was compared when running on a multi-node cluster.

Performance characterization using Intel Xeon based platform

Several measurements are conducted to analyze the performance sensitivity for Hadoop K-means iteration using Intel Xeon based platform.

1) Platform Configuration

The slave node configuration consists of software and hardware configuration. For slave node hardware

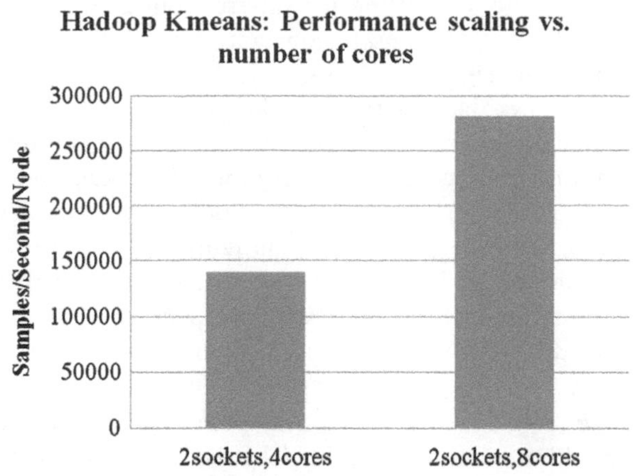

Fig. 1 Performance scaling vs. number of cores Hadoop K-means

configuration, we used 4 Intel platforms with the following setup:

2xIntel Core i7 CPU at 2.7GHz
32GB Memory (8x 4GB DIMMs) at 1066 MHz
Network controller using onboard 1GbE
Seagate disk at 1 TB 7200RPM
HDFS setup using 5x Intel 200GB SSDs on each system

The software configuration for the setup is as follows:

Disabled power management (including C-states)
Disabled Hyper-Threading
Enabled Prefetchers
Operating System used is Red Hat Enterprise Linux with Apache Hadoop version 1.2.1
1:1 Map slots
1:1 Reduce Slots: 1:1
Heap Size is 2GB

2) Problem Size requirements

The workload input size must run and scale on different processor architecture. We have to model it in a way to scale across different processors architectures using the baseline configuration with Intel Core i7 processor. In order to do that, we need the workload input size to be based on the number of active logical threads with fixed memory size per thread. The problem size relation in GB can be stated as

$$\text{Problem size} = (7/8) \times 2\text{GB} \times \text{ of threads} \quad (1)$$

The populated memory should scale as close as possible with JVM heap requirements. The metric used for measurement is the number of samples per unit time (seconds) per node. If the problem size varies, the runtime will not be consistent. So the problem size must have a fixed number of sample, for example, a problem size of 28GB is equal to 409.6 M sample.

3) Core and Socket Scaling

For socket scaling, we conduct measurements using one and two processor sockets for the same number of cores. For core scaling, we used two sockets but change the number of cores (4 cores and 8 cores) as shown in Fig. 1.

For core scaling, using four and eight cores, the performance scaling is linear; close to 2x going from four cores to eight cores. This means that Hadoop K-means performance scales linearly with a number of cores.

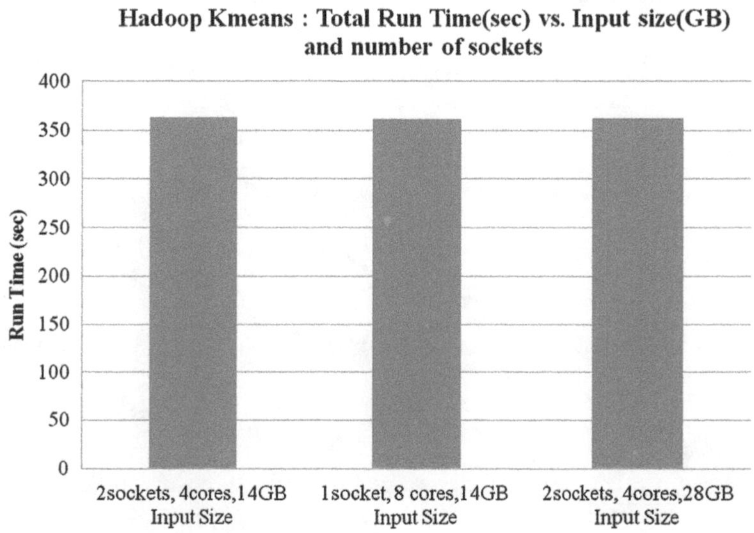

Fig. 2 Hadoop K-means: Total run-time (sec) vs. Input Size (GB) and number of sockets

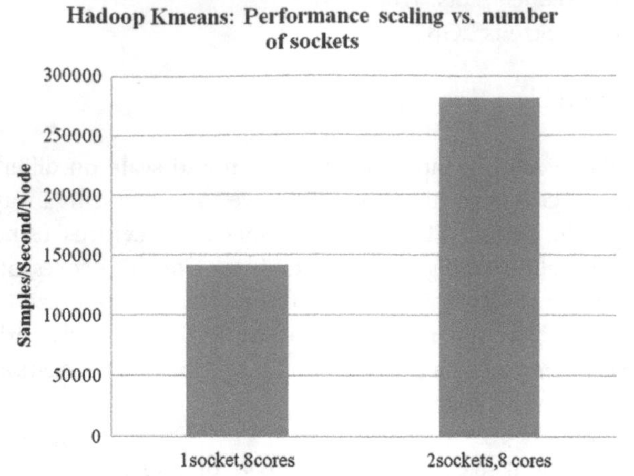

Fig. 3 Performance scaling vs. number of sockets

For socket scaling, using one and two sockets with eight cores on both, the performance scaling (Samples/Second/Node) shows a linear scaling is about 1.99x. We conclude that both socket and core scaling is 2x. The core scaling was adjusted accordingly using "Active Core Count" in BIOS while the socket scaling is achieved using the physical removal of a processor with associated memory. The Cycles-Per-Instruction (CPI) overall for the benchmark using different input sizes (14 GB and 28 GB) calculated is about 0.52 for 1 socket/8 cores, 2 sockets/8 cores, and 2 sockets/4 cores. The Execution Length (EL) for different configurations is constant ~ 262,000. The EL is defined by the total number of instructions executed per different cores. In this case, it is constant and doesn't change with respect to the change in the number of cores. The total runtime for different input sizes and different configurations is constant about 362 seconds as shown in Fig. 2.

This shows that the total runtime (seconds) is almost constant relative to a different number of sockets, the number of cores and the input data size. What change is the performance metric defined as Samples/Second/Node for different configurations as previously shown in Fig. 1 and Fig. 3. Next, we analyze core and socket scaling with respect to memory bandwidth (GB/sec) and performance as shown in Fig. 4.

From Fig. 4 we conclude that performance is correlated with memory bandwidth. That is the scaling in performance between 1 socket/8 cores/14GB input size to 2 sockets/4 cores/28GB is about 2x. Same is true for memory bandwidth; the scaling for the same configurations is also about 2x.

4) Core Frequency Scaling

Core frequency scaling is required so we can analyze how performance behaves with respect to higher core frequencies as shown in Fig. 5. The scaling between two or three core frequencies will indicate the performance change between these measured data points; so that we can use to model the performance with respect to the frequency change.

From Fig. 5, the performance is measured as a number of samples per second per node (samples/second/mode). The performance scaling from 2.1GHz to 2.4GHz (2.4/2.1 = 1.14) is about 1.13x (249100/220000) in performance, and from 2.4GHz to 2.7GHz (2.7/2.4 = 1.125) the performance scaling is about 1.12x (281300/249100).

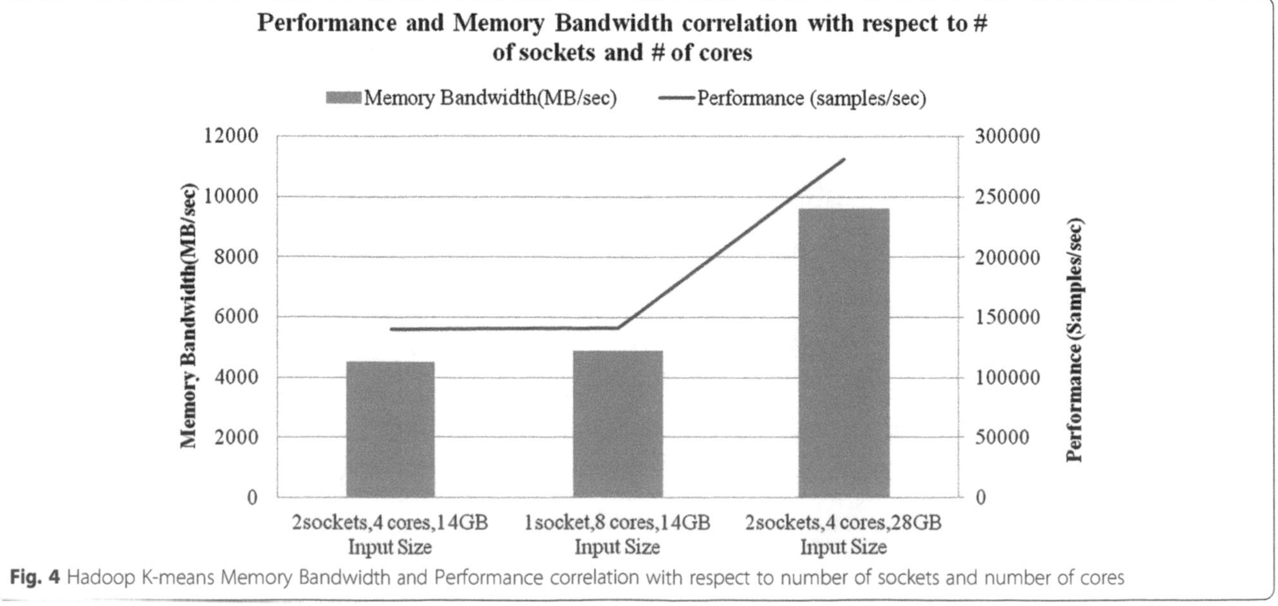

Fig. 4 Hadoop K-means Memory Bandwidth and Performance correlation with respect to number of sockets and number of cores

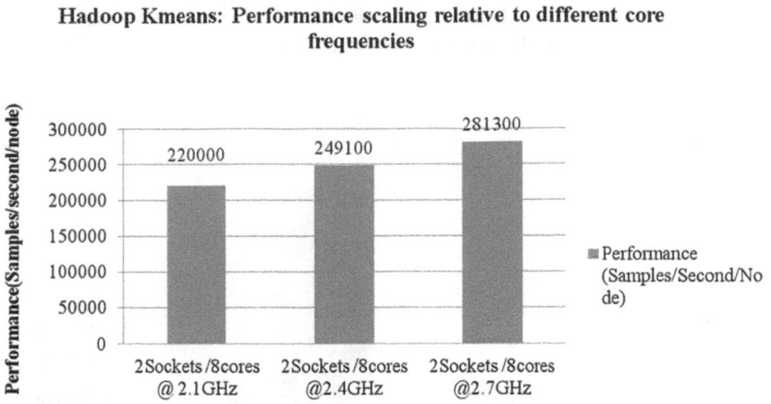

Fig. 5 Hadoop K-means: Performance vs. Core Frequency Scaling

However, the performance scaling from 2.1GHz to 2.7GHz (1.28) is about 1.27x (281300/220000). This shows that there is an excellent scaling between core frequency and performance so we can use this scaling factor for core frequency in the performance model. Memory bandwidth scales almost linearly with core frequency as shown in Fig. 6.

The scaling rate from 2.1GHz to 2.4GHz is 1.14x while the scaling rate for memory bandwidth is 8670/7600 = 1.14x. Similarly, the scaling for 2.1GHz to 2.7GHz is 1.28x and the memory bandwidth scaling is 9600/7600 = 1.26x. This shows that the scaling factor for memory bandwidth with respect to the scaling factor for core frequency is linear.

5) Hyper-Threading/Simultaneous Multi-Threading Scaling

Enabling the processor Hyper-Threading (HT) feature will enable an active core to execute two threads per core instead of one thread or Single Thread (ST). In our performance characterization, we found that enabling Simultaneous Multi-Threading (SMT) and scaling the workload with respect to thread count shows an average of 20 % increase in performance with all cores active.

In Fig. 7, SMT scaling for 2 sockets/4 cores shows 1.2x improvements in performance from Single Thread (ST) to HT with 1GB heap size. It also shows a 1.24x performance improvement from ST to HT with 2GB Heap size. For 2 sockets/8 cores, the improvement from ST to HT with 1GB heap size is 1.17x and for HT with 2GB heap sizes its 1.22x in performance improvement. Given that HT is enabled, the CPI for the kernel increases with an average of 40 % as compared to HT off, but the overall CPI is 0.97 on average.

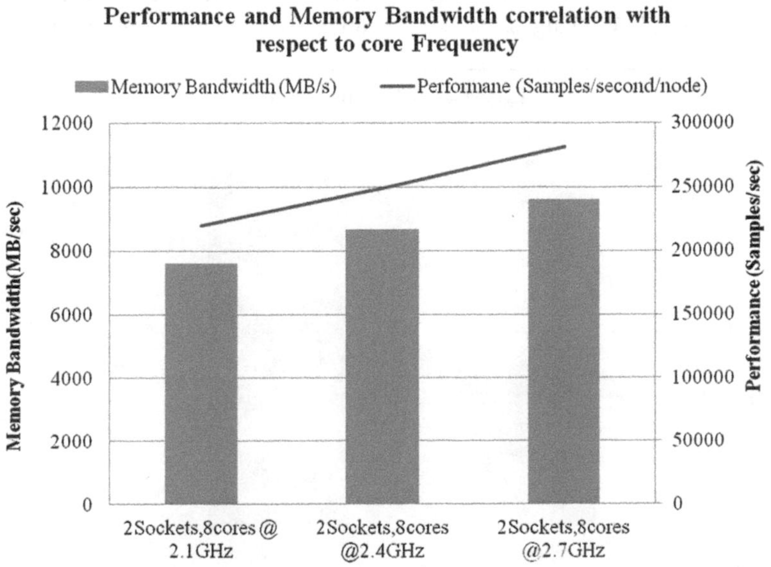

Fig. 6 Hadoop K-means Memory Bandwidth and Performance scaling with respect to different core frequencies

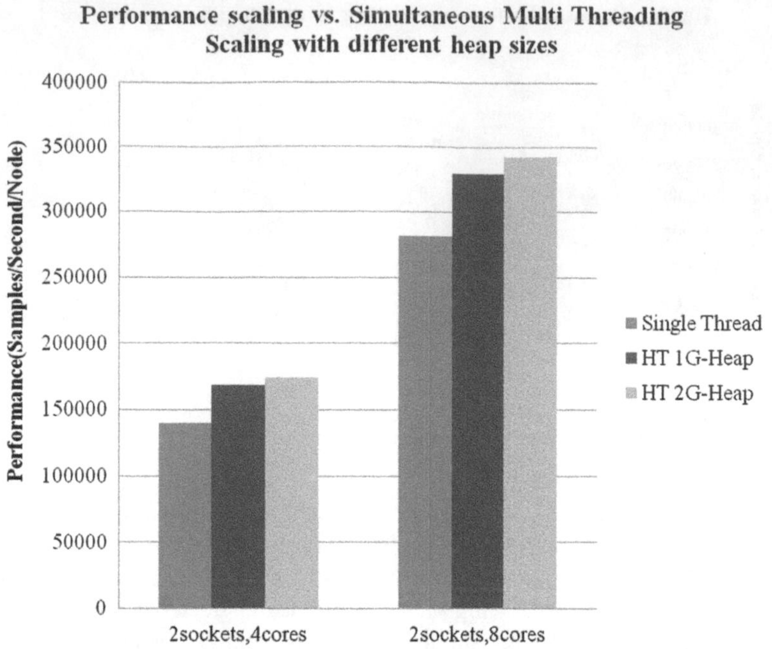

Fig. 7 Hadoop K-means: Performance vs. Simultaneous Multi-Threading scaling with different heap sizes

6) Last Level Cache Scaling

The capacity of Last Level Cache (LLC) does not have any impact on performance improvement. If the cache size is increased from 10 MB to 20 MB, the performance improvement is only 1.01x as shown in Fig. 8 using 2 sockets/4 and 8 cores processor configuration. So for Hadoop K-means workload it is not bounded by LLC. We conclude there is no performance improvement even if LLC size is increased above 20 MB.

The Message Passing Interface (MPI) is directly related to the LLC size. For 10 MB LLC size, the overall LLC MPI measured is 0.00111 using 2 sockets with 4 cores. For 20 MB LLC size, the MPI measured is 0.00097, this shows that MPI is affected by LLC size with about 14 % decrease with LLC 20 MB versus LLC 10 MB which is expected. For memory bandwidth, there is about 7 % lower in memory bandwidth utilization for the same performance with larger LLC.

7) Data Input Size Scaling

Data input size is a key factor that impacts performance for Hadoop K-means. We scaled input size and analyzed the change in execution run-time. The result is

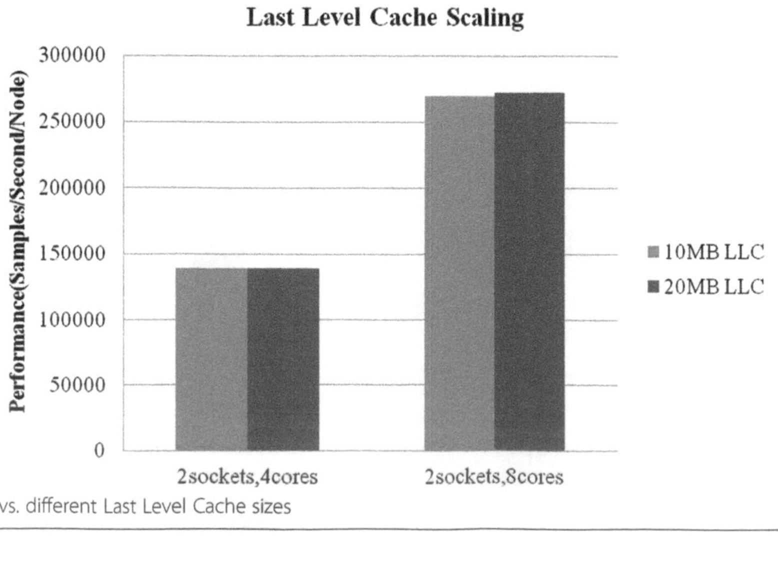

Fig. 8 Performance scaling vs. different Last Level Cache sizes

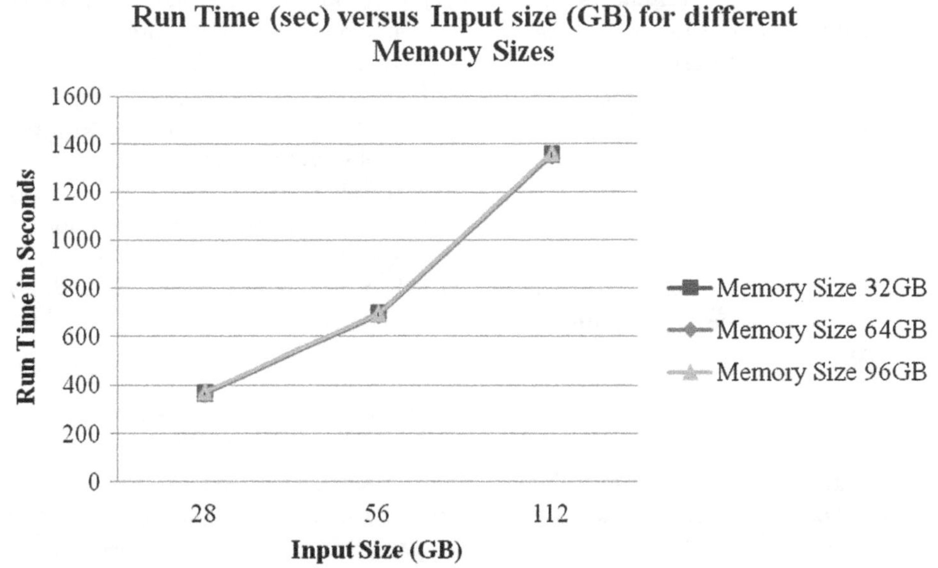

Fig. 9 Total run-time (sec) vs. different input sizes (GB) for different memory sizes (GB)

an increase of twice the input size results in about 1.9x increase in run-time. For example, the scaling factor for 56GB/28GB is 2x, and the scaling factor for run-time (695 sec/367 sec) is 1.9x. Figure 9 shows the input size scaling with respect to total run-time for different memory sizes. In this case, the memory size does not have any impact on total run-time, with less than 1 % variation for memory size 32GB, 64GB, and 96GB.

In summary, a 2x increase in input size will result in about 1.9x increase in execution time regardless of memory size. Figure 9 shows even more linear scaling going from 56GB to 112GB input size.

8) Memory and Heap Size Scaling

For memory scaling, there is almost a 1 % run-time variation between different memory sizes. This indicates there is no performance and run-time variation for Hadoop K-means for these three memory sizes (32GB, 64GB, and 96GB) as shown in Fig. 10.

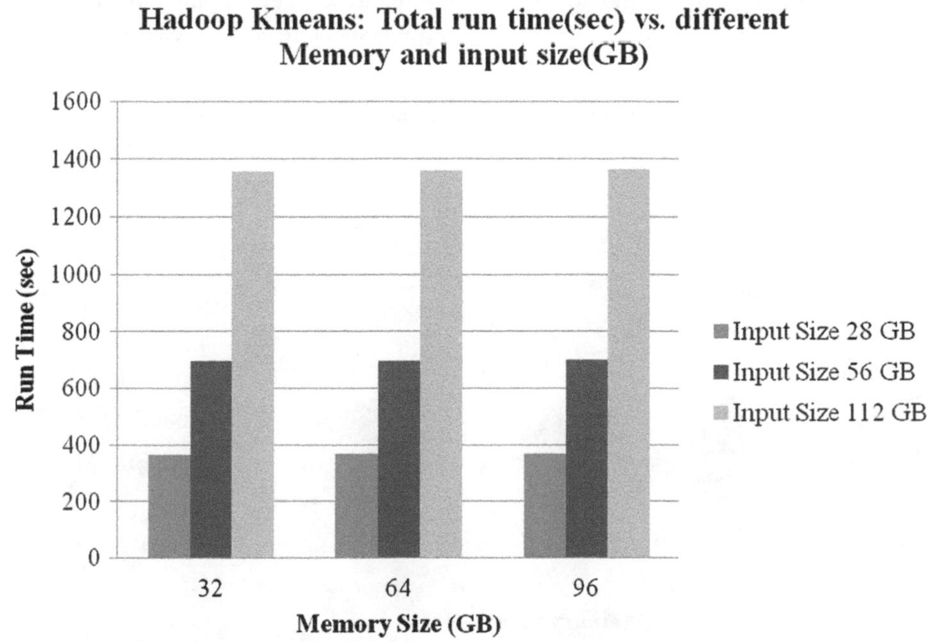

Fig. 10 Total run-time (sec) vs. different Memory and input sizes (GB)

The run-to-run variation for the run-time data collected for memory scaling is in the range of 1 %-3 % which is an expected run-to-run variation range. For heap size scaling, we used heap size of 1GB, 2GB, and 4GB. The run-time is almost the same for different input size as shown in Fig. 11.

Performance characterization using AMD interlagos platform

In this section, we implement performance analysis characterization for Hadoop K-means iteration using AMD Interlagos platform.

1) AMD Platform Setup

The slave node configuration consists of software and hardware configuration. For slave node hardware configuration, the following setup is used:

4x AMD Interlagos platforms (Bulldozer core)
Two different chassis: 2x HP Proliant and 2x Supermicro
CPU: 2x 2.60GHz ITL
Memory: Fixed at 1066 MHz for all configurations
32GB = 4x 8GB DIMMs (1-socket) and 64GB = 8x 8GB DIMMs (2-socket)
NIC: Onboard 1GbE (only 1 port in use)
For disk configuration, the System disk used is Seagate 1 TB 7200RPM (holds no HDFS data). The HDFS: 4x Intel 200GB SSDs on each system. All disks attached via an SAS controller.

For slave node software configuration, the following setup is used:

Power Now: Enabled, but frequency fixed via On Demand governor and Core Performance Boost disabled
Prefetchers: Enabled
Operating System: Red Hat Enterprise Linux 6.1 with Kernel version 2.6.32
Java: Sun 1.6.0_25
Hadoop distribution: 1.0.2 snapshot (based on Apache distribution)
Map Slots: 1:1 with active logical threads
Reduce Slots: 1:1 with active logical threads
Heap Size: 2GB

2) Problem Size Requirements

The workload needs to scale across all testing domains using different processor architectures. So the approach is to use a workload input size based on a number of active logical threads with fixed memory size per thread as indicated in Eq (1). The populated memory also scales as close as possible with JVM heap requirements. The metric used for measurement is samples/sec/node. The run-time is not a consistent metric if we are varying the problem size. A given problem size has a fixed number of samples (unit of work). Ex. 28GB problem size per node (without replication) = 409.6 M total samples. The metric calculated is Total Samples/Run-time/# of Nodes.

3) Hadoop K-means Performance Scaling with respect to thread Count

This experiment is implemented to scale performance with respect to thread count. The measurements were

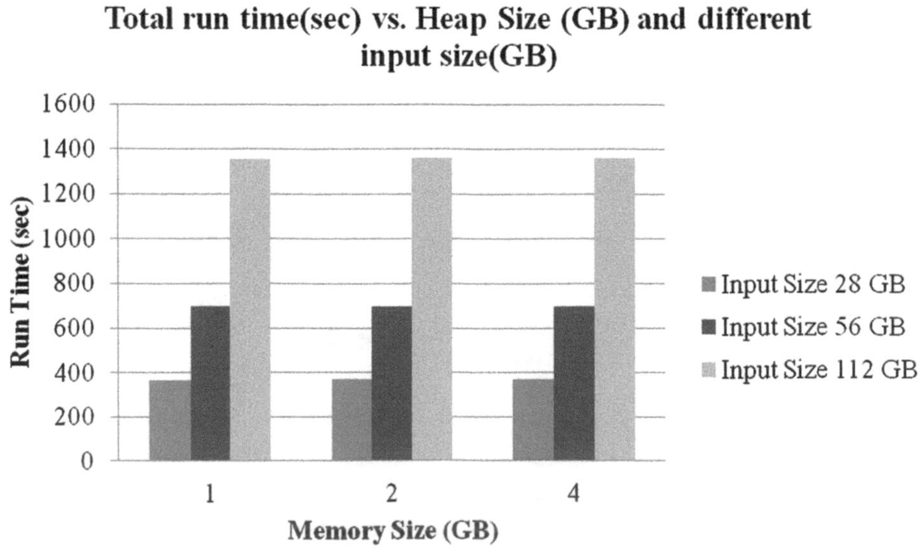

Fig. 11 Total run-time (sec) vs. heap and input size scaling

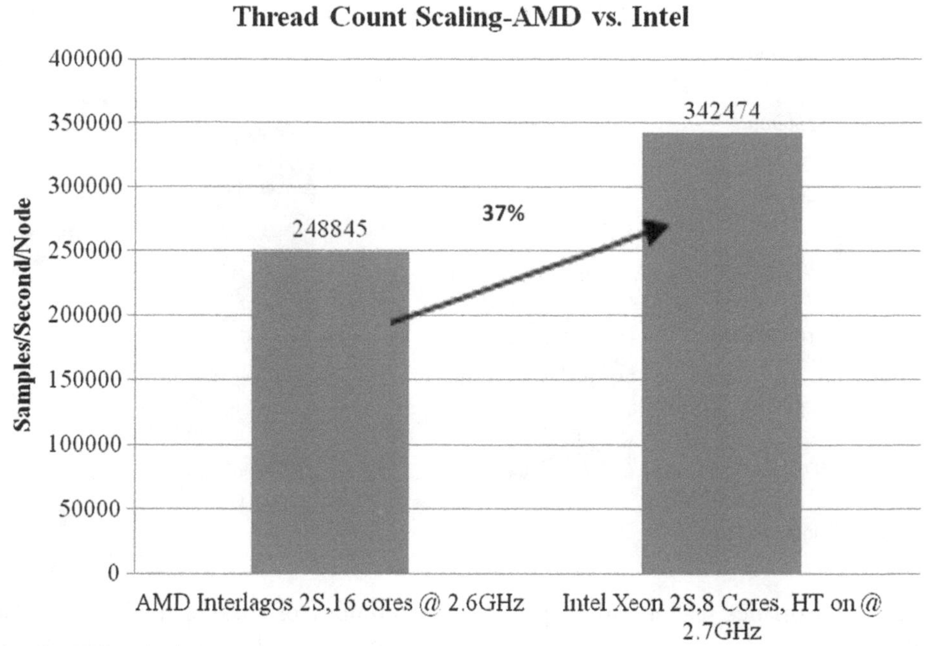

Fig. 12 Thread scaling for AMD vs. Intel

taken using Intel Xeon processor (2 sockets, 8 cores, Hyper-Threading On, at 2.7GHz core frequency) which gives a total of 32 threads versus AMD Interlagos (2 sockets, 16 cores, at 2.6GHz core frequency) which also gives a total of 32 threads. Comparing the performance for these two configurations, we conclude that there is a ~37 % lead for Intel Xeon compared to AMD Interlagos using the same thread count as shown in Fig. 12. Given the slight difference in core frequency (2.6GHz vs. 2.7GHz), our Hadoop K-means frequency scaling assessment indicates that the performance will be close to 34 % instead of 37 %.

The total run-time for Intel vs. AMD shoes that Intel Xeon total run-time is 35 % less (smaller the better) compared to AMD run-time as shown in Fig. 13. This is implemented for the same number of threads (32).

The CPI for Intel Xeon is measured at 0.96 versus 1.26 for AMD which means Intel CPI is ~24 % lower as compared to AMD.

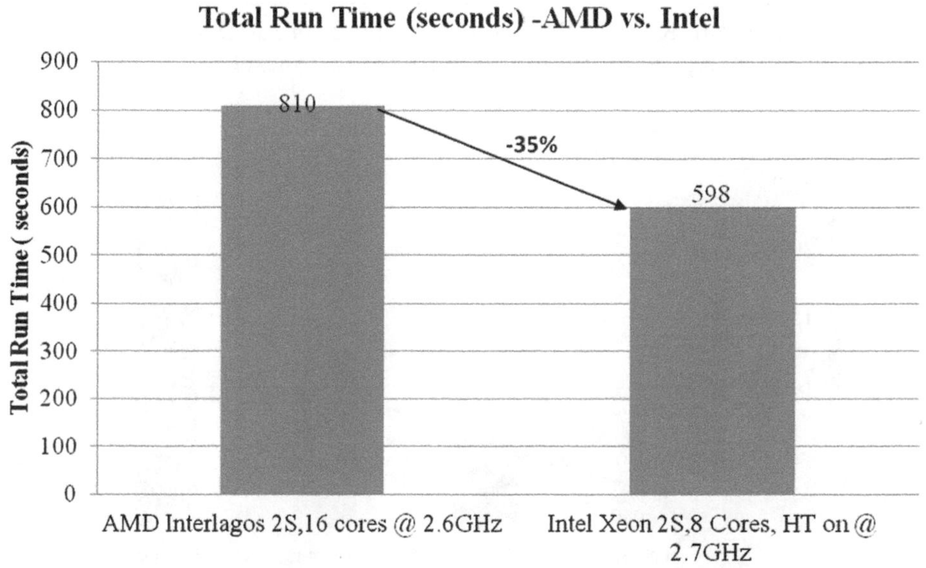

Fig. 13 Total run-time scaling for AMD vs. Intel for the same thread count

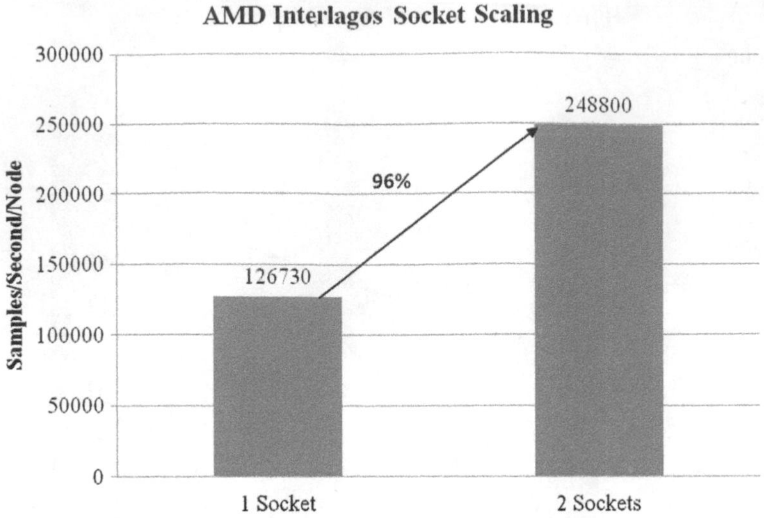

Fig. 14 Socket scaling for AMD Interlagos

4) Hadoop K-means Performance scaling with respect to thread count

Performance change with respect to a change in the number of sockets was implemented on AMD Interlagos system for one and two sockets.

From Fig. 14, we conclude that there is a linear scaling between one and two sockets on AMD Interlagos system. The performance rate change is 96 % going from one to two sockets. For Intel Xeon system, the performance is also about 98 % between one and two sockets configuration. This confirms the Hadoop K-means scales linearly with respect to the number of processor sockets. For the CPI scaling as the number of sockets doubles, the CPI change from one to two sockets is relatively flat around 1.22 for one socket versus 1.26 for two sockets. We conclude that CPI does not change significantly as the number of sockets doubles.

5) Hadoop K-means Performance Scaling for AMD with respect to core count using 2 sockets

Hadoop K-means performance scaling for AMD Interlagos using 2 sockets processor shows a linear scaling with respect to a change in a number of cores as shown in Fig. 15. The performance almost doubles when the number of cores doubles (Fig. 16).

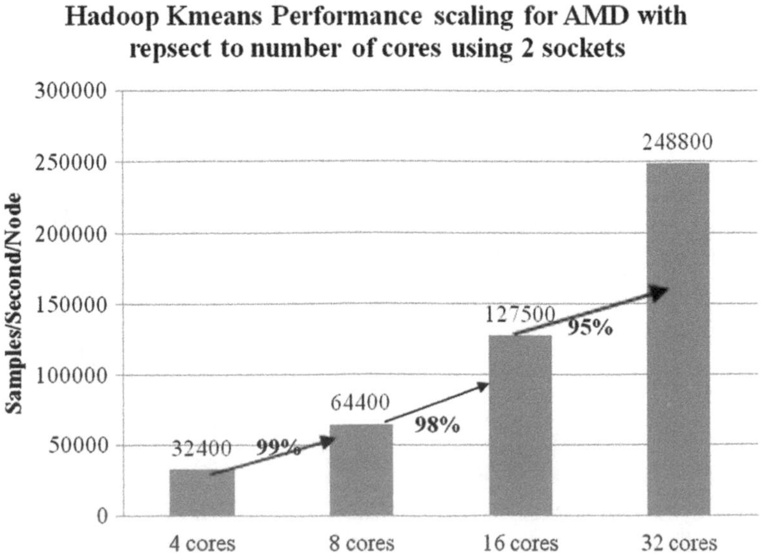

Fig. 15 Performance scaling with respect to change in number of cores for AMD Interlagos using 2 sockets

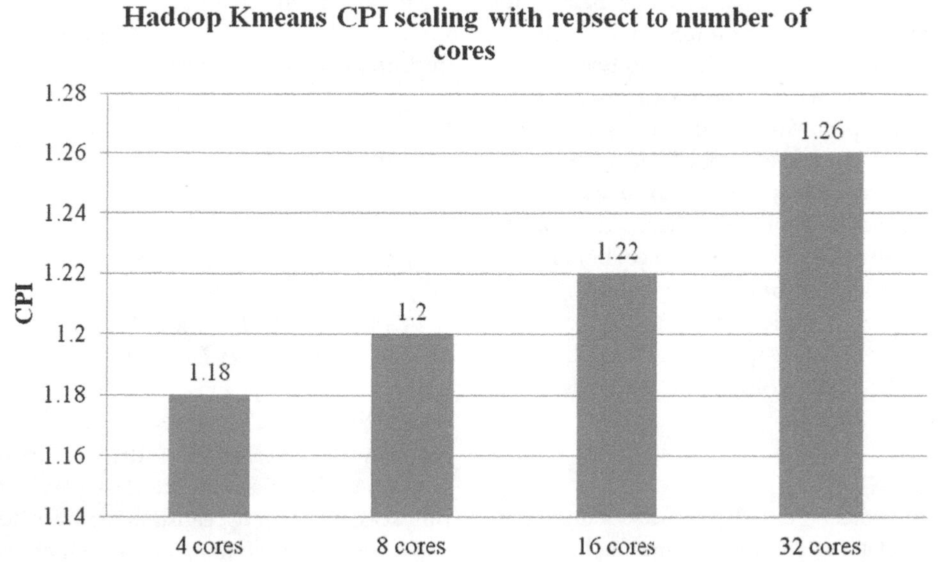

Fig. 16 CPI scaling with respect to change in number of cores for AMD Interlagos

The same measurement was implemented on Intel Xeon processor, and a similar conclusion can be concluded for Intel Xeon as performance doubles when the number of cores doubles. There is a slight increase in CPI when the number of cores doubles.

We conclude there is a slight increase in CPI when the number of cores increases at a non-linear rate.

6) Hadoop K-means Performance Scaling for AMD with respect to core frequency

The performance for Hadoop K-means scales almost linearly with respect to change in core frequency as shown in Fig. 17. For example changing core frequency from 2.0GHz to 2.3GHz (2.3/2.0 = 1.15 or 15 %) results in a 12 % increase in performance (225000/200100 = 1.12). Similarly changing the core frequency from 2.3GHz to 2.6GHz (2.6/2.3 = 1.13 or 13 %) will result in 1.105 change rate in performance (248800/225000 = 1.105 or 10.5 %). Note that the frequency scaling was achieved through Linux governor.

7) AMD Interlagos core and cluster scaling using one socket

The objective for analyzing performance with respect to a number of clusters and a number of cores is to understand the core-per-cluster impact on performance. From

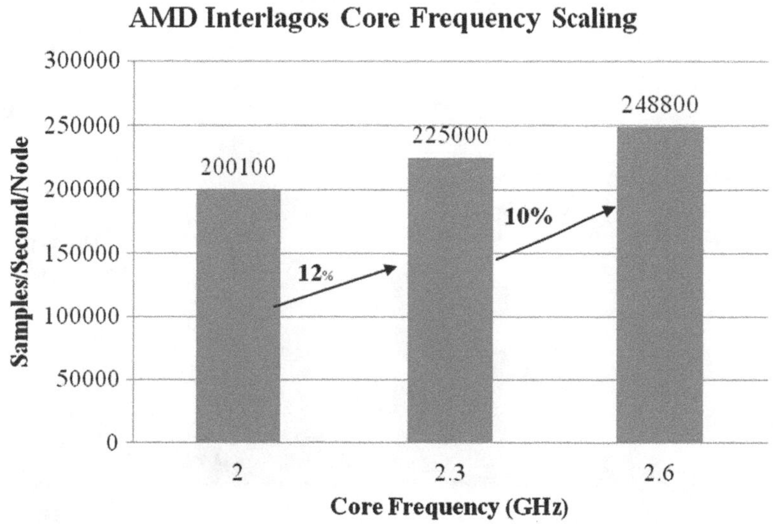

Fig. 17 AMD Interlagos Core frequency scaling

Fig. 18, we conclude there is a performance benefit for additional core per cluster. For example, in four cluster configuration, the change from one thread to two threads results in about 60 % increase in performance. Similarly for eight clusters, the performance benefits going from one thread to two threads is also about 60 %. However in one cluster configuration, the performance benefit going from one to two threads is almost doubled (>100 %). We can conclude that there is a performance benefit for additional core-per-cluster for most configurations.

There is an increase in performance going from one cluster to four clusters in a range of 4.4x, and the performance increases by ~2.2x going from four clusters to 8 clusters as shown in Fig. 18.

Performance model

In this section, we discuss a detailed processor performance projection model for Hadoop K-means based on the performance characterization we did in Section IV is used to derive the performance model. We start with defining the general equation for performance, the performance (samples/second) relation is derived as

$$Performance = \frac{core\ frequency \times Total\ \#\ of\ cores}{Execution\ Length \times CPI}, \quad (2)$$

and the total run-time in seconds is given by

$$Run\quad Time = \frac{Input\ Size}{\#\ of\ nodes \times Performance}. \quad (3)$$

The Execution Length (EL) is defined by the total number of instructions executed divided by measured performance baseline given as

$$Execution\quad Length = \frac{of\ instructions\ executed}{measured\ performance}. \quad (4)$$

The Cycles-per-Instruction is given as

$$CPI = CoreCPI + 0.5 \times MPI \times Memory\ Latency, \quad (5)$$

where the core CPI is defined as the CPI without the memory stall cycles added. In other words, it is the CPI with no cache misses in the Last Level Cache. Given that this scenario is not realistic, we have to add the cycles generated from memory misses which is the MPI multiplied by memory latency. The '0.5' factor used in Eq (5) to multiply the memory latency and MPI, is caused by memory cache miss which is referred to as a memory blocking factor. We expect the memory blocking factor to range from 0 to 1 for most processors. In case it is equal to 0, this means there are no memory misses at all which means that the CPI is equal to the CCPI. This is not a realistic scenario for this workload. On the other hand, if the memory blocking factor is '1', it means that there is 100 % miss rate, which is not a realistic scenario. Based on statistical analysis for memory a 0.5 value for blocking factor is used for Hadoop K-means. The model is verified to project performance (samples/second) and

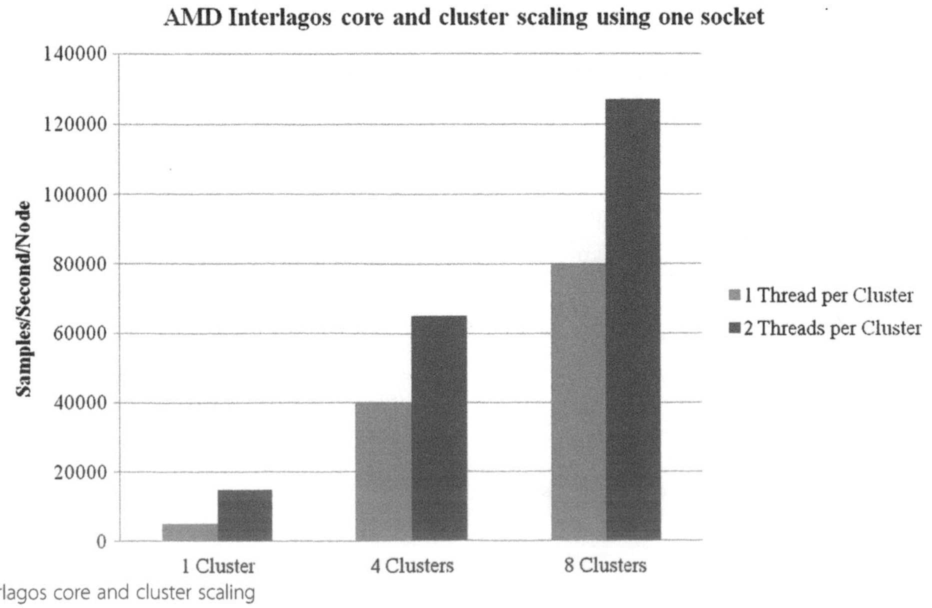

Fig. 18 AMD Interlagos core and cluster scaling

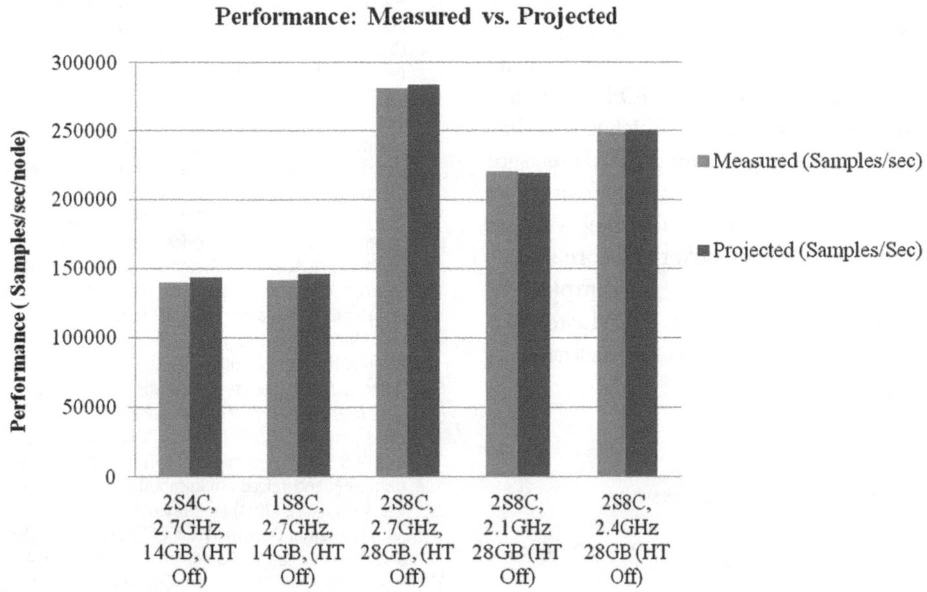

Fig. 19 Performance: Projected vs. Measured

run-time(seconds) with <5 % error margin for all tested cases as shown in Fig. 19 and Fig. 20.

From Fig. 19, the performance measured is compared to performance projected by the model. We verified different processor configurations such as different number of sockets, different number of cores, different core frequency, and different input sizes, with Hyper-threading set to off. All these variables are included in the performance model. The error variation is within expected range of < 5 %. Among all tested configurations in Fig. 19, the peak performance achieved is for 2 sockets, 8 cores, 2.7GHz core frequency with 28 GB input size.

For modeling run-time, the highest run-time is expected for the configuration with lowest core frequency which in this case is 2.1GHz as shown in Fig. 20. All tested cases for run-time (measured vs. projected) shows an error margin of <5 %.

Conclusion

In this paper, we presented a detailed performance characterization analysis for Hadoop K-means using Intel and AMD based processors. We also proposed a projection model for Hadoop K-means workload. The projection model is verified to project performance and runtime with 5 % error margin for all tested cases. The model is flexible to accept any changes in processor micro-architecture parameters and estimate performance or runtime. The model does not require any simulation which in turn requires trace based sampling for the workload. In future work, we can implement the same approach for different Hadoop framework workloads such as word count and

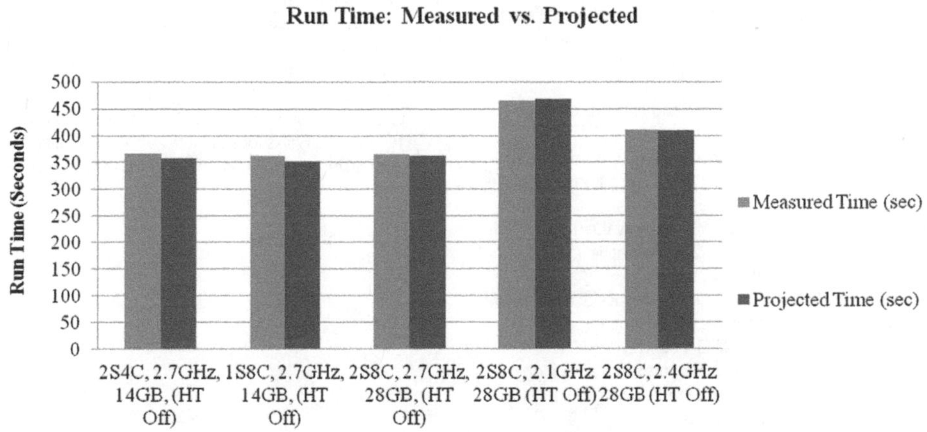

Fig. 20 Run-time: Projected vs. Measured

implement a full details performance characterization. The model can be expanded to include IO latency such as disk and network latency. The focus of this paper is on the processor performance excluding any IO latency, this is why the input size selected was 28GB which is less than the system memory size of 32GB. For AMD Interlagos versus Intel Xeon performance analysis, we conclude that there is about 38 % better performance for Intel Xeon as compared to AMD Interlagos. The socket and core scaling is almost linear in most measured cases, the sample conclusion applied to Intel Xeon Processor. For cluster-per-core scaling, there is about 60 % increase in performance for AMD Interlagos processor.

Competing interests

The authors declare that they have no competing interests.

Authors' contributions

The research presented in this paper is the result of individual work. The author read and approved the final manuscript.

Authors' information

Joseph A. Issa Dr. Issa joined the faculty of engineering at Notre Dame University in October 2013 as an assistant professor in the department of Electrical, Computer and Communication Engineering (ECCE). Dr. Issa research areas of interest include processor architecture, performance and power modeling for different processor architectures using different cloud computing and high-performance computation workloads. He teaches a number of subjects at Notre Dame University including computer processor architecture (MIPS, x86, and ARM), microprocessors, PIC microcontrollers and digital logic design. He received his B.E in computer engineering from Georgia Institute of Technology in 1996. He obtained his master's degree in computer engineering at San Jose State University in California in 2000 and received his Ph.D. in Computer Engineering from Santa Clara University in California in 2012.

References

1. Mak VW and Lundstrom SF (1990) Predicting performance of parallel computations. IEEE Trans. Parallel Distributed Systems, Online Journal
2. Mell P, Grance T (2011) The NIST definition of cloud computing. NIST Special Publication, online (800-145)
3. Dean J and Ghemawat S (2004) MapReduce: Simplified data processing on large clusters. 6th conference on Symposium on Opearting Systems Design & Implementation, Seattle, WA, USA
4. Fitzpatrick B (2004) Distributed caching with Memcached. Linux Journal 2004(124):5
5. Vianna E (2011) Modeling performance of the hadoop online prototype. International Symposium on Computer Architecture, Vitoria
6. Xie J (2010) Improving Map Reduce performance through data placement in heterogeneous Hadoop clusters. IEEE International Symposium on Parallel & Distributed Processing, Atlanta
7. Ishii M, Han J, Makino H (2013) Design and performance evaluation for hadoop clusters on virtualized environment. In: 2013 International Conference on Information Networking (ICOIN), pp. 244–249
8. Chao T, Zhou H, He Y, and Zha L (2009) A Dynamic MapReduce Scheduler for Heterogeneous Workloads. Techical paper online, IEEE Computer Society.
9. Ranger C, Raghuraman R, Penmetsa A, Bradski G, and Kozyrakis C (2007) Evaluating MapReduce for multi-core and multiprocessor systems. High-Performance Computer Architecture, Proc. IEEE 13th Int'l Symp. High Performance Computer Architecture, Scottsdale, AZ, USA
10. Dean J and Ghemawat S (2004) MapReduce: simplified data processing on large clusters. In Op. Systems Design & Implementation
11. Hendricks J, Sambasivan RR, and Sinnamohideenand S, Ganger GR (2006) Improving small file performance in object-based storage. Technical report, Carnegie Mellon University Parallel Data Lab, Online technical report
12. Berezecki M, Frachtenberg E, Paleczny M, Steele K (2011) Many-Core Key-Value Store. International Green Computing Conference and Workshops, Orlando, FL, USA
13. Mandal A et al (2011) Provisioning and Evaluating Multi-domain Networked Clouds for Hadoop-based Applications. Third International Conference on Cloud Computing Technology and Science, Athens, Greece
14. Shafer J, Rixner S, Cox AL (2010) The Hadoop distributed filesystem: Balancing portability and performance. IEEE International Symposium on Performance Analysis of Systems & Software, White Plains, NY, USA
15. Leverich J, Kozyrakis C (2010) On the energy (in)efficient of Hadoop clusters. ACM SIGOPS Operating systems Review, Indianapolis, IN, USA
16. Chun B (2010) An Energy Case for Hybrid Datacenters. ACM SIGOPS Operating System Review, Indianapolis, IN, USA
17. Wang G, Butt A, Pandey P, and Gupta K (2009) Using realistic simulation for performance analysis of MapReduce setups. LSAP. ACM, Munich, Germany
18. Issa J, Figueira S (2010) Graphics Performance Analysis Using Amdahl's Law. IEEE/SCS SPECTS, International Symposium on Performance Evaluation of Computer and Telecommunication System, Ottawa, ON, Canada
19. Issa J, Figueira S (2011) Performance and power-Consumption Analysis of Mobile Internet Devices. IEEE IPCC–International Performance Computing and Communications Conference, Austin, TX, USA
20. Apache Software Foundation: Official apache hadoop website: http://hadoop.apache.org. (2015)
21. Wiktor T et al (2011) Performance Analysis of Hadoop for Query Processing. International Conference on Advanced Information Networking and Applications, Fukuoka, Japan
22. Ekanayake J, Pallickara S, and Fox G (2008) MapReduce for data intensive scientific analysis. In: Fourth IEEE Intl. Conf. on eScience, pp. 277–284.
23. Chu C-T, Kim SK, Lin Y-A, Yu Y, Bradski G, Ng AY, and Olukotun K (2007) Map-Reduce for machine learning on multicore. NIPS, Vancouver, B.C., Canada, pp. 281–288.
24. Emanuel V (2011) Modeling Performance of the Hadoop online Prototype. ISCA, San Jose, CA, USA
25. Dejun J and Chi GPC (2009) EC2 Performance Analysis for Resource Provisioning of Service-Oriented Applications. International Conference on Service-Oriented Computing, Stockholm, Sweden
26. Ibrahim S, Jin H, Lu L, Qi L, Wu S, and Shi X (2009) Evaluating MapReduce on Virtual Machines: The Hadoop Case. International Conference on Cloud Computing, Bangalore, India
27. Stewart R (2010) Performance and Programmability of High Level Data Parallel Processing Languages. http://www.macs.hw.ac.uk/~rs46/papers/appt2011/RobertStewart_APPT2011.pdf
28. Tan J, Pan X, Kavulya S, Gandhi R, and Narasimhan P (2008) Salsa: Analyzing Logs as State Machines. In: Workshop on Analysis of System Logs.
29. Tan J, Pan X, Kavulya S, Gandhi R, and Narasimhan P (2009) Mochi: Visual Log-analysis Based Tools for Debugging Hadoop. In: HotCloud.
30. Therdphapiyanak J, Piromsopa K (2013) An analysis of suitable parameters for efficiently applying K-means clustering to large TCPdump data set using Hadoop framework. In: 10th International Conference on Electrical Engineering/Electronics, Computer, Telecommunications and Information Technology
31. Jiang DR, B. Ooi B, Shi L, and Wu S (2010) The performance of MapReduce: an in-depth study. Proceedings of the VLDB Endowment, Online Journal
32. Esteves RM, Pais R, Rong C (2011) K-means Clustering in the Cloud – A Mahout Test. In: IEEE Workshops of International Conference on Advanced Information Networking and Applications (WAINA), vol., no., pp.514-519, 22-25

12

Privacy preserving model: a new scheme for auditing cloud stakeholders

Abdul Razaque[1] and Syed S. Rizvi[2*]

Abstract

The Cloud computing paradigm provides numerous attractive services to customers such as the provision of the on-demand self-service, usage-based pricing, ubiquitous network access, transference of risk, and location independent resource sharing. However, the security of cloud computing, especially its data privacy, is a highly challengeable task. To address the data privacy issues, several mechanisms have been proposed that use the third party auditor (TPA) to ensure the integrity of outsourced data for the satisfaction of cloud users (CUs). However, the role of the TPA could be the potential security threat itself and can create new security vulnerabilities for the customer's data. Moreover, the cloud service providers (CSPs) and the CUs could also be the adversaries while deteriorating the stored private data. As a result, the objective of this research is twofold. Our first research goal is to analyze the data privacy-preserving issues by identifying unique privacy requirements and presenting a supportable solution that eliminates the possible threats towards data privacy. Our second research goal is to develop the privacy-preserving model (PPM) to audit all the stakeholders in order to provide a relatively secure cloud computing environment. Specifically, the proposed model ensures the quality of service (QoS) of cloud services and detects potential malicious insiders in CSPs and TPAs. Furthermore, our proposed model provides a methodology to audit a TPA for minimizing any potential insider threats. In addition, CUs can use the proposed model to periodically audit the CSPs using the TPA to ensure the integrity of the outsourced data. For demonstrating and validating the performance, the proposed PPM is programmed in C++ and tested on GreenCloud with NS2 by applying merging processes. The experimental results help to identify the effectiveness, operational efficiency, and reliability of the CSPs. In addition, the results demonstrate the successful rate of handling the negative role of the TPA and determining the TPA's malicious insider detection capabilities.

Keywords: Cloud computing, Privacy preserving model, Third party auditor, Cloud service provider, Cloud user, Authentication

Introduction

Cloud computing is an emerging IT environment that has significantly transformed everyone's vision of computing infrastructure, development models, and software distribution. Cloud computing is anticipated as the next generation high-tech paradigm for tomorrow's promise [1]. It provides several utilities as revolutionary gigantic paradigms where clients can remotely store valuable and confidential information as to avail from on-demand high quality computing resources [2]. While data outsourcing reduces the burden on the cloud users (CUs) from local storage and management, it brings several open problems related to the security and privacy of customer's outsourced data. On the other hand, cloud computing eradicates their physical control of data reliability and security, which can be addressed through the cooperation of three parties: the cloud service provider (CSP), the third party auditor (TPA) and the CU. Cloud computing has always been referred as virtualization of an existing server or data center. Subsequently, cloud computing is acknowledged as virtualization of existing data or data centers, providing multipurpose application support and enormous utility to remotely available users or clients [3]. This phenomenon leads to the cloud acting as a service, where services are provided upon request based on subscription or pay-per-use [4]. The cloud computing environment stores the

* Correspondence: srizvi@psu.edu
[2]Department of Information Sciences and Technology, Pennsylvania State University, Altoona, PA 16601, USA
Full list of author information is available at the end of the article

valuable information and offers attractive user applications with reliable service support [5]. With the emergence of new technology, new categories of clouds and services are introduced such as supercomputing as service (SCaaS) and high-performance computing as a service (HPCaaS).

From a security perspective, dealing with large amounts of data is a challenge. The security of CSPs has been investigated thoroughly from a storage standpoint [6–10]. Two highly sought CSP features that guarantee privacy protection are data availability and integrity. Since the CUs do not have physical access to the outsourced data, it raises the question of data privacy protection in cloud computing, particularly for users with very limited computing resources. Moreover, there are several other factors regarding the CSPs corruption that can deceitfully smash the CUs outsourced data [11]. For instance, a CSP can attempt to sustain its reputation by hiding the security incidents about the customer's lost data [12]. Cloud services can be financially advantageous; however, there is no guarantee that the stored data will be secure and available at all times. If this continues to be an issue and is not thoroughly examined, the cloud computing environment may never reach its full potential.

The massive amount of outsourced data, along with the CU's limited resources, can present a daunting challenge for auditors when examining a cloud service [13]. One solution to this problem is to maintain a very low level of cloud storage overhead using minimal data retrieval operations. Although we face these challenges, it is still of utmost importance to develop trust between the CUs and CSPs.

This is where TPAs could assist in guaranteeing the CU's data privacy. Through a fair and impartial auditing process as well as the preservation of the CU's computational resources, a higher standard could be set for trust in cloud services. This auditing process could also help in improving the QoS provided by cloud-based platforms and resources. In the field of data security and privacy, the possibility of an insider threat can not be avoided. This raises the concern that a TPA could be malicious. The TPA will have free and open access to the CU's data and the cloud services, which leaves the CU vulnerable to attacks. Therefore, to circumvent potential financial losses or insider threats, a strict check and balance process over the TPA performance should exist. To address all of these issues, there is a need for a privacy-preserving model (PPM) that can provide a mechanism to authenticate all cloud stakeholders (i.e., CSP, TPA and CU) in order to safeguard the cloud computing environment.

To address privacy concerns, researchers have introduced models to ensure data correctness and privacy protection using protocols across multiple peers and servers [14–17]. Many of these proposed protocols support public certifiable remote integrity checking process [18–20]. However, without proper implementation, public certifiable auditing would perpetrate CUs a false perception that their data were undamaged in the CSP's data-centers.

The first privacy-preserving public auditing using blind technique was proposed in [21]. In [21], the verifier disables the TPA from detecting the file blocks by disguising the proof with some randomness. Subsequently, authors in [22] show the exploitation of the vulnerabilities originating from [18] when specific file blocks possess low entropy as well as allowing CUs to audit the TPA themselves to ensure an honest auditing process. Secure auditable models have been proposed in [23–26] to ensure integrity of outsourced data.

Although these computing paradigms introduce the audibility process, but fail to address the security concerns of the three parties (i.e., CSP, CU, TPA). To address these issues from a security perspective, this paper presents a novel data PPM. Our work is one of the unique data privacy-preserving contributions with a focus on auditing the three entities to reduce the trust deficit between the cloud stakeholders and improve the reliability of the outsourced data. Our proposed scheme provides the capability and a complete methodology to keep checks and balances between each entity in order to minimize data corruption, preserve data privacy, and restrict the misuse of resources.

Our proposed model ensures that the TPA does not have an access to the stored data by assigning session keys for each auditing task. Once the auditing process is completed, the assigned session keys will be expired and returned to the pool. In addition, the CU uses the strong authentication mechanism (e.g., triple Data Encryption Algorithm and SHA-256) to protect its outsourced data from potential attacks. The aggregation and derivative properties of our model help the three stakeholders to maintain strong authentication processes. A CU sets its priorities, QoS requirements, and anticipate timeframe for the completion of each task within the provided services. If the CU is not satisfied with the agreed requirements, the model immediately would enable the CU to refer the issue of incorrectness and inaccuracy of the paid services to the CSP. This feature of our proposed scheme not only improves the CUs experience but also warns the CSP to keep updating the cloud services and maintaining the agreed QoS according to the service level agreement (SLA).

Research contributions

Our research contributions are as follows:

- We provide the bounded-time interval by using session keys for each individual auditing service, preventing malicious insiders from accessing the client's confidential data stored in cloud servers.
- We embed the mod derivation process to fully secure the encrypted-message mechanism for authentication purpose. This feature does not provide any opportunity for the TPA to become an adversary, while handling the entire auditing process of each individual CU.
- Our proposed model not only ensures that the allocated resources are correctively delivered to the CU but also looks for the malicious behavior of clients to protect the data of other CUs stored in cloud servers. Thus, our proposed scheme addresses the security issues related to cloud multitenancy.
- We demonstrate and validate the data privacy-preserving through various experiments. Our simulation results demonstrate the effectiveness, reliability, and operational efficiency of CSPs. In addition, the results show the success rate for controlling the malicious activities of TPA and validating the TPA's malicious insider detection capabilities.

Adversary model

Our primary contribution in this research work is the proposed PPM that provides separate mechanism for auditing each cloud entity. An illustration of the proposed model is shown in Fig. 1. The model begins with a CU obtaining desired services from a CSP for storing the data, as shown in step 1a of Fig. 1. In response, the CSP delivers the desired cloud services to the requesting CU after setting up the necessary SLA (step 1b of Fig. 1). On the other hand, the CU wants to ensure the privacy preservation of its outsourced data. Therefore, it provides the details of the obtained services to the TPA, as shown in step 2 of Fig. 1. To audit the services provided to the CU, the CSP issues the key to the TPA for each auditing session (step 3 of Fig. 1). Once the session key is assigned to the TPA, the TPA starts the auditing process, as shown in step 4 of Fig. 1. The CSP checks the integrity of the TPA to determine whether the assigned keys are in use for further processes or not (step 5 of Fig. 1). If a TPA attempts to use any session key for obtaining the customer's confidential information, this cannot be done since all issued sessions keys are only effective for a specific period of time for a given auditing session. Finally, the TPA provides the audit report to the CSP and the CU respectively, as shown in steps 6a and 6b of Fig. 1.

A malicious third party auditor (TPA)

A cloud environment involves two main entities: one is the service provider (i.e., the CSP) and the others are the service utilizers (i.e., the CUs). Both of these entities interact with each other using various tools and technologies (e.g., databases, networks, virtualization, operating systems, transaction management, resource scheduling, concurrency control, load balancing, and memory management). Not only the CUs utilize the services offered by the CSPs but also often outsource their sensitive data to the cloud servers. The use of various technologies and the fact that the customer's data is not in-house bring numerous security challenges. Among those security challenges, encryption and data integrity is ranked as one of the top concerns of most of the CUs by the research community [5]. To address the issue of

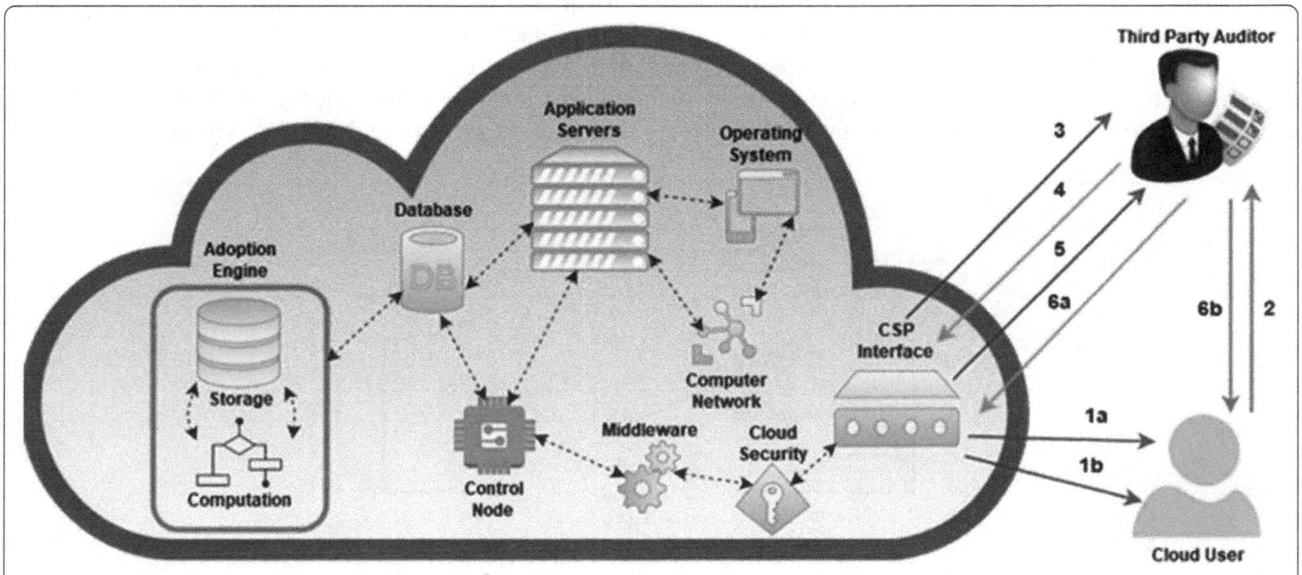

Fig. 1 Privacy-preserving service oriented architecture for cloud computing

data integrity and confidentiality, the use of a trusted TPA has been proposed by several researchers [11, 18]. It has been shown that the TPA can be very effective in performing several resource consuming tasks (such as checking the integrity of outsourced data and managing the encryption keys etc.) on behalf of CUs. Although the use of the TPA reduces significant computational burden on CUs, the possibility of malicious insiders at the TPA cannot be ignored. Therefore, there is clearly a need of a method that can be used to detect any malicious activities perform by the TPA. Since TPA servers as a proxy between the CUs and the CSPs, its integrity should be checked based on cloud services and customer's data. An illustration of the three entities (CUs, TPA, and CSP) is shown in Fig. 1.

A malicious cloud service provider (CSP)

To ensure the data confidentiality of customer's data, most of the existing work relies on the encryption-based schemes where the encrypted information can only be accessed by the entity (e.g., CU, CSP, and the TPA) that possess the encryption keys. Since CSPs may need to perform frequent computations on the customer's date for the offered services (e.g., data searches, modifications, additions, deletions and insertions), it is considered as a suitable candidate for holding and managing the encryption keys. In this way, the CU does not have to manage and assign the encryption key for each computation services provided by the CSPs. This also avoids the unnecessary delay that may cause due to the sharing/transmission of encryption keys between the CU and the CSP. However, it is unrealistic to assume that all CSPs are trustworthy. They can hide a data loss/leakage incident from CUs to maintain their high reputation. For instance, Byzantine failures, server conspiring attack, malicious data alteration, are some examples that may result a loss/leakage security incident. In a worst case scenario, a malicious CSP or malicious insiders at the CSP can exploit their own privileges by misusing the encryption keys to compromise the confidentiality of the customer's outsourced data, modify or even delete sensitive information without the knowledge of CUs. These malicious insiders can be categorized in two types. The first type is involved in debasing the stored CUs data files from individual servers. Once a server is compromised, a malicious insider can read and modify the contents of the customer's outsourced data. The second type of malicious insiders can compromise multiple data servers by taking advantage of multitenancy and collocation features of cloud environment. In either case, the confidentiality and the integrity of outsourced customer data is at high risk.

SLA violation by cloud user (CU)

In addition to the CSP, a CU can turn into a malicious entity by purposefully violating the terms and conditions of the SLA. Once a CU receives services from a CSP, it can sublet the services to other third-party organizations or individuals, which can raise serious security concerns and bring numerous management issues. Moreover, the subletting of cloud services to third-parties can slow down the service delivery process from the CSP site. All such malicious activities can severely affect the reputation of a CSP and can result into significant business loss. This clearly demands a periodic audit of CUs to detect any potential violations of SLA. For an unbiased and fair audit of CUs, a trusted TPA should be considered as the best candidate for this task.

Proposed privacy preserving model

We develop a new triangular data PPM to authenticate all the stakeholders (i.e., CU, CSP, and a TPA), as shown in Fig. 2. This model aims to ensure the integrity of the CU's data stored in the cloud data center, which can be retrieved on-demand at any time. Recent work has focused more on evaluating the reliability of the CSP in terms of its security and data privacy measures as well

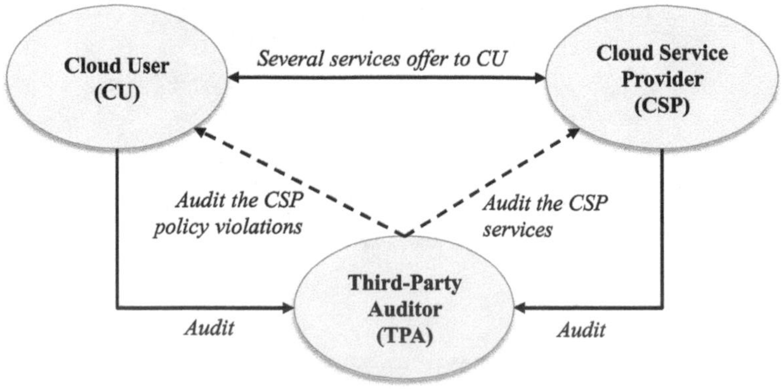

Fig. 2 A basic Cloud Computing Privacy-Preserving Authenticating Model

as its compliance with its SLA. However, little work has been done to evaluate the reliability of the CU and the TPA. Therefore, our proposed model evaluates the CU's integrity in terms of their ability to not violate any of the agreed upon rules defined and set by the CSP in the SLA. Furthermore, the TPA audits the services provided to the CU and ensures the TPA's integrity (i.e., the TPA is not disclosing the CU's contents from the information obtained through the auditing process).

The CU and the CSP provide a mechanism to audit the TPA. Thus, the CU verifies whether the TPA performs the assigned auditing within the given specification and the time frame. Furthermore, the CSP also verifies whether the TPA performs its auditing tasks using the assigned time-released session keys.

The proposed model performs the following functionalities. For each functionality of the cloud stakeholder, we provide a mathematical model to derive closed-form expressions. These functionalities are as follows:

- Service Types
- Malicious Insider and TPA
- CU Authentication for TPA through CSP
- CSP Authentication Process

Service types

This section discusses the types of services provided to the CU and derives a closed-form expression to reflect the correct delivery of cloud services. Let us assume that 'N' is the number of CUs in a given computing environment where each individual cloud customer (n_i) can obtain a maximum of K number of services from a CSP. The total number of CUs can be expressed as follows: $N = n_1, n_2, n_3, \ldots, n_n$.

A CU can access the cloud services that are within the SLA, since services beyond the SLA are restricted. Thus, the CSP can define security limitations 'L' for assigned services (K) such that each offered service (k_i) can have one or more limitations (i.e., L_i where $i = 1$ to K). Therefore, the security limitations (L) can be expanded up to the total number of services (K) offered by a CSP. This relationship can be expressed as follows:

$$L = [L_1, L_2, L_3, \ldots, L_K] \quad (1)$$

In our proposed model, CUs are allowed to define their own priorities, quality of service (QoS) requirements, and anticipate timeframes for the completion of several tasks within the organization. On the other hand, CUs are required to meet these specified requirements within the obtained services and the allotted timeframe defined in the SLA (i.e., allowed time that a CU can use services until the service-contract expires). We illustrate the allocated service time for the CU to use the cloud resources as follows:

$$\{A^x(k), k \in (1, 2, 3, \ldots, K)\} \quad (2)$$

where 'A^x' is the amount paid for each service for specific period of time, 'x' is the user that can access the service and 'k' is the type of service.

Let us consider that each service involves an arbitrary data set $Z = \{Z_1, Z_2, \ldots, Z_n\}$ that can be selected independently. Each query for every member of the data set is denoted by $Q_i = (q_i, f_i)$; for $i = 0,1,\ldots, n$ where $q_i \subseteq [n]$ is the sub set of the data-set member. Where f_i: specifies the function (e.g., max or sum). Thus, each query has an answer in the form defined as: $\Delta q_i = f_i(q_i)$. This can be applied to the subset of the data set entry as follows: $\{Z_j \mid j \in q_i\}$.

Theorem 1 *In the proposed PPM, CUs authorize the TPA to audit the obtained services by providing the few samples of services.*

Proof Let us prove that the paid amount for provided services to CUs are correctly stored on the CSP's server. Taking this into account, the confirmation process can be done as follows:

$$A_{dit} = \sum_{i=0}^{n} (A^x) \equiv \sum_{j=1}^{n} j(k_1) + j(k_2), \ldots, j(k_n) \gnapprox T_s \quad (3)$$

Equation (3) shows the total amount paid against all the services that are signed in the contract. The TPA compares the contracted services with the samples provided by CUs. The TPA based comparison can be shown in (4) as follows:

$$C_{sp} = \sum_{n=0}^{\infty} n(N) \cong C_{id} \left\{ \sum_{j=1}^{n} j(k_1) + j(k_2), \ldots, j(k_n) \right\} \gnapprox T_s \quad (4)$$

In Eq. (4), the CSP confirms the CU's identity with its record. If the CUs are legitimate, the TPA is allowed to compare the samples with the original services. This matching process can be shown in (5) as follows:

$$A_{dit} = \sum_{n=0}^{\infty} n(\omega) \cong T_s \quad (5)$$

In Eq. (5), the TPA initiates the matching process of signed contracts with the samples on record. If the samples match with the signed contracted services, the provided service types are considered as legitimate. Furthermore, the matching process helps increase the trust level of CSPs. The functional service type behavior is depicted in Fig. 3 and its used notations are described in Table 1.

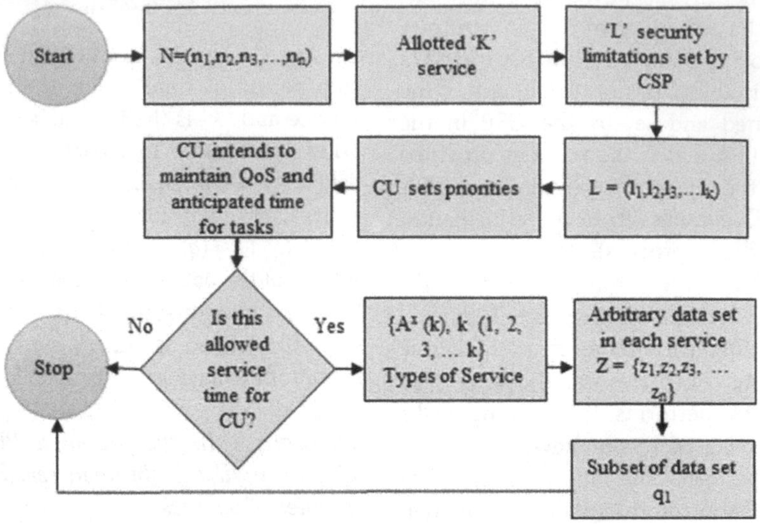

Fig. 3 Functional behavior of service-type to ensure the privacy-preserving authentication

Malicious insider and TPA

Let us assume that queries and their answers are protected by 'γ^{Φ}' for each entry 'Z_j' of malicious insiders which is bounded by the time interval of 'T_I'. An attacker can attempt to generate malicious entry 'Z_j' to capture the query and its protected answers during the bounded time interval. However, our objective is to prevent an attacker from exploiting the privacy of the protected 'γ^{Φ}' queries and answers. The method for protecting the information is to use the bounded-time with the session keys for each individual auditing-service. The CSP releases the session keys with the bounded-time for each auditing service. Once the auditing service is completed, the session keys will be returned and will not be regenerated until the CSP releases another poll of session keys.

In addition, the malicious insider could be a team member of the TPA or a CSP. As a result, their illicit attempt is not successful $Z_j \notin T_I$ to exploit the protected data $Z_j \in T_I$. Therefore, the sequence of queries and their answers are protected 'γ^{Φ}' from entry 'Z_j' due to bounded-time interval 'T_I'. These protected queries and answers can be written as follows:

$$\gamma^{\Phi}, j, T_I \; \{(q_1, q_2, ..., q_n), \; (a_1, \; a_2, ..., \; a_n)\} = \begin{cases} 1 \; if \; 1(1+\gamma^{\Phi}) \leq \dfrac{\beta \; (Z_j \in T_I \,|\sum_{i=0}^{n} f_i(q_i) \; = a_i}{\beta(Z_j \in T_I)} \leq (1+\gamma^{\Phi}) \\ 0 \quad Otherwise \end{cases} \tag{6}$$

where β: prediction of malicious insider.

Let $Z = \{Z_1, \; Z_2, ..., \; Z_n\}$ be the data set where Z_i is selected separately. This complies with the following statement as: (γ^{Φ}, β).

- The malicious insider poses the query as $Q_m = (q_m, f_m)$.
- The TPA decides whether to permit the query of a malicious attacker 'Q_m' or not. The TPA responds with the following expression $\Delta q_a = f_a(q_a)$.If Q_m is permitted, Δq_a is rejected, otherwise.
- Malicious insider is successful if $\beta = f_a(q_a)$

The malicious insider and TPA process is depicted in Fig. 4. Table 2 lists all the parameters used for malicious insiders and TPA modules.

Table 1 System parameters and definitions for service type

Notations	Description
A^x	Amount paid for each service for a particular period
f_i	Specifies the function (e.g., max or sum).
k	Service type
C_{sp}	Cloud service provider
L	Security limitations
N	The number of cloud users
$\Delta q_i = f_i(q_i)$	Correct answer of each query stored in a cluster
$Q_i = (q_i, f_i)$	Each query for every member of data set
x	The user that access the service
$n(\omega)$	Contracted services
$Z = \{Z_1, Z_2, \ldots, Z_n\}$	Arbitrary data set
$\{Z_j \mid j \in q_i\}$.	Subset of data-set entry
A_{dit}	Third party auditor
C_{id}	Identity of cloud users

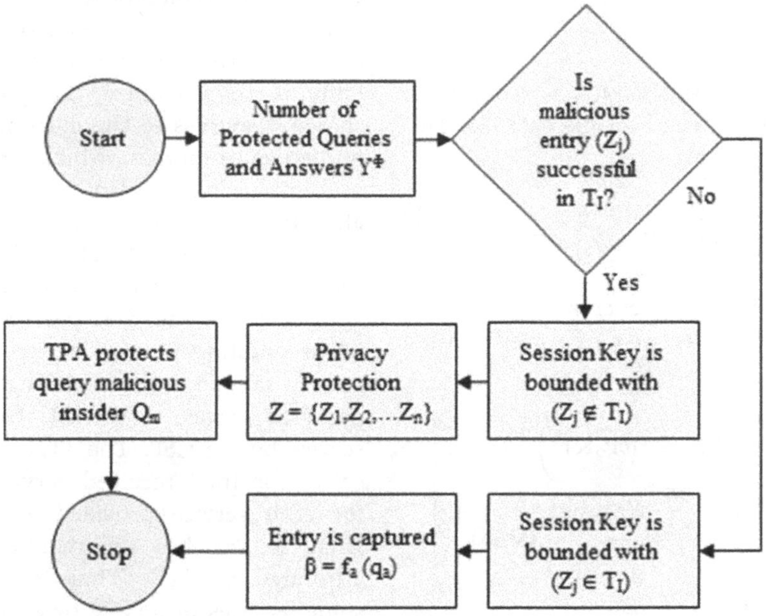

Fig. 4 Working process of malicious insider and TPA for guaranteeing the privacy-preserving authentication

CU authentication for TPA through CSP

Let us assume that 'φ' is the outsourced data file of the CU that consists of 'n' number of blocks: $n = \{b_1, b_2, b_3, ..., b_n\}$. The CU chooses the authentication message $M_a = \left(\iiint_{\varpi=0}^{n} \Delta s_\varpi + log_2 \acute{K}^n\right)$ using a secure and strong encryption scheme (e.g., AES Algorithm with SHA-256) that is modeled as '$\iiint_{\varpi=0}^{n} \Delta s_\varpi$' with '$log_2 \acute{K}^n$' size of the message. The chosen authenticated message by the CU is illustrated as follows:

$$M_a = \left[\left(\iiint_{\varpi=0}^{n} \Delta s_\varpi + \left(log_2 \acute{K}\right)^n\right)\{\dot{x}.\dot{y}(\nabla\beta\delta)\}\right] \quad (7)$$

where ϖ: random number assigning the initial value to product, $(\nabla\beta\delta)$: combination of two randomly chosen values consists of variable lengths and $\dot{x}.\dot{y}$: Quotient function that is used as a mod function. The detail of authenticated message with the encryption process is given as follows: Replacing the mod function $\dot{x}.\dot{y}$:

$$M_a = \left[\left(\iiint_{\varpi=0}^{n} \Delta s_\varpi + \left(log_2 \acute{K}\right)^n\right)\{f(z)(\nabla\beta\delta)\}\right]$$

Differentiation of $f(z)$ is required to model the mod derivation

$$M_a = \left[\left(\iiint_{\varpi=0}^{n} \Delta s_\varpi + \left(log_2 \acute{K}\right)^n\right)\left\{\frac{s(z)}{t(z)}(\nabla\beta\delta)\right\}\right]$$

Determining the equivalency of mod derivation to support encryption process yields:

$$M_a = \left[\left(\iiint_{\varpi=0}^{n} \Delta s_\varpi + \left(log_2 \acute{K}\right)^n\right)\left\{\frac{\Delta d}{\Delta dz}\frac{s(z)}{t(z)}(\nabla\beta\delta)\right\}\right]$$

Applying the product rule for mod derivation to secure the encryption process yields the following expression:

$$M_a = \left[\left(\iiint_{\varpi=0}^{n} \Delta s_\varpi + \left(log_2 \acute{K}\right)^n\right)\left\{t(z).\frac{\Delta d}{\Delta dz}[f(z)] + \frac{\Delta d}{\Delta dz}[t(z)].f(z).(\nabla\beta\delta)\right\}\right]$$

Simplifying the process to support the mod derivation and to show the division with two randomly generated numbers $(\nabla\beta\delta)$ for encryption is given as:

Table 2 System Parameters and Definitions for malicious insider and TPA

Notations	Description
$Q_m = (q_m, f_m)$	Query posed by a malicious insider
Q_m	Malicious attacker
T_I	Bounded time interval
(y^{Φ}, β).	Prediction of the malicious attacker against protected data (queries and answers)
y^{Φ}	Protected data comprising of query and answers
Z_j	The malicious insider entry
$Z_j \notin T_I$	Unsuccessful attempt
$Z_j \in T_I$	Successful attempt
$\Delta q_a = f_a(q_a)$	Response from TPA for malicious insider to authenticate itself
$\beta = f_a(q_a)$	Successful prediction of malicious insider

$$M_a = \left[\left(\iiint_{\varpi=0}^{n} \Delta s_{\varpi} + (log_2 \acute{K})^n\right)\left\{\frac{\frac{\Delta d}{\Delta dz}[s(z)] - \frac{\Delta d}{\Delta dz}[t(z)].f(z)}{t(z)}.(\nabla\beta\delta)\right\}\right]$$

Once again, the differentiation of $f(z)$ is required to hide the encryption and the length of the data file. This yields the following expression:

$$M_a = \left[\left(\iiint_{\varpi=0}^{n} \Delta s_{\varpi} + (log_2 \acute{K})^n\right)\left\{\frac{\frac{\Delta d}{\Delta dz}[s(z)] - \frac{\Delta d}{\Delta dz}[t(z)].\frac{s(z)}{t(z)}}{t(z)}.(\nabla\beta\delta)\right\}\right]$$

To show the complete message encryption to protect the CU from a malicious insider, we derive the following equation:

$$M_a = \left[\begin{array}{c}\left(\iiint_{\varpi=0}^{n} \Delta s_{\varpi} + (log_2 \acute{K})^n\right) \\ \left\{\frac{\frac{\Delta d}{\Delta dz}[s(z)].t(z) - \frac{\Delta d}{\Delta dz}[t(z)].s(z)}{[t(z)]^2}.(\nabla\beta\delta)\right\}\end{array}\right] \tag{8}$$

If a user is the legitimate CU, then a copy of $(\nabla\beta\delta)$ is generated at the server of a CSP. The CSP is required to identify the generated authentication message of a CU such that $M_a = \left(\iiint_{\varpi=0}^{n} \Delta s_{\varpi} + log_2 \acute{K}^n\right)$. The authentication message is generated by using a calculated aggregated authenticator to validate whether the message was generated by a legitimate CU. The resultant message is given as follows:

$$\acute{M}_a = \prod_{k=1}^{n} (\nabla\beta\delta) A_k \leq = \sum_{n=0}^{\infty} (\nabla\beta\delta)^N \tag{9}$$

where $(\nabla\beta\delta)^N$ represents the aggregated authenticator value.

Once the CU's authentication message matches with the aggregated authenticator of the CSP, the CU is considered as a legitimate client within the CSP's domain. The TPA can then obtain the secret key from the CSP for each authentication message of the CU to initiate the auditing process. Specifically, the TPA requires session keys for comparison of each audit. Thus, it will be harder for the TPA to expose the outsourced data file 'ϕ' of a CU once the auditing process is completed. If the TPA attempts to exploit the outsourced data file of a CU after the auditing process, it needs a new session key that is not assigned to the TPA by the CU. However, the TPA may experience the problem because the auditing process will be limited if auditing is required more than one time.

All possible secret keys should be able to overcome this drawback in advance. Once all fixed secret keys are exhausted, the CU can then retrieve and publish the data, which complies with the privacy-preserving requirements depicted in Fig. 5. Table 3 lists all the parameters used in the TPA module.

CSP authentication process

The CSP's integrity is of paramount importance for correct delivery of the services. The CSP's responsibility is to maximize the guarantee for providing shared resources to the customers. The CSP provides numerous resources, which are not only shared by multiple CUs, but also dynamically reallocated. This allocation of resources needs to be authenticated for the CU's satisfaction. Thus, the TPA not only audits the CU but also makes sure that the assigned service is correctly provided as per specification of the CU.

The auditing process begins when the TPA generates a sample "check message" $'C_m'$ against each provided service to the CU to confirm the provided service by the CSP. The TPA chooses a random value $'\forall\partial'$ for total received services $T_s = \{s_1, s_2, s_3, \ldots, s_n\}$ for each service provided as quantified in Eq. (1). Each service has different characteristics that are attributed by $'s_f'$. Thus, $s_f \in T_s$. The TPA checks some features of service by sending a "check message" $C_m = \{s_f, \ldots \forall\partial\}$ $s_f \in T_s$ to the CSPs server. Upon receiving the "check message", the server generates a response against "check message" to guarantee the storage of data correctly. Therefore, the server also selects the random number $\varpi \leftarrow \mathbb{R}_g$ and computes its value such as: $\forall\partial = (\rho, \ell)^{\varpi} \in \mathbb{R}_g$. The following parameters should be noted: s_f: features of each service, ρ: the service returned by cloud server, ℓ: order-set for the features of service, and $\mathbb{R}_g$: Random generator.

Let us assume that ρ^* represents the combination of sampled blocks that are specified in $'C_m'$, Thus, sampled check blocks can be described as:

$$\rho^* = \sum_{s_f \in T_s}^{s_n} \forall\partial L_k \tag{10}$$

In response to the sampled blocks, the server computes the requested service $'\rho'$ for the TPA to prove its integrity and ensure that the CU is correctly provided the requested services. To satisfy the TPAs requested query, the requested service should be delivered to the TPA using full encryption along with the sampled blocks. This compares the sampled blocks of requested service with the original service provided to the CU and can be expressed as follows:

$$\rho = \varpi + \sum_{s_f \in T_s}^{s_n} \forall\partial L_k + \left[\left(\iiint_{\varpi=0}^{n} \Delta s_{\varpi} + (log_2 \acute{K})^n\right)\right] \times \left\{\frac{\frac{\Delta d}{\Delta dz}[s(z)].t(z) - \frac{\Delta d}{\Delta dz}[t(z)].s(z)}{t(z)}.(\nabla\beta\delta)\right\} \tag{11}$$

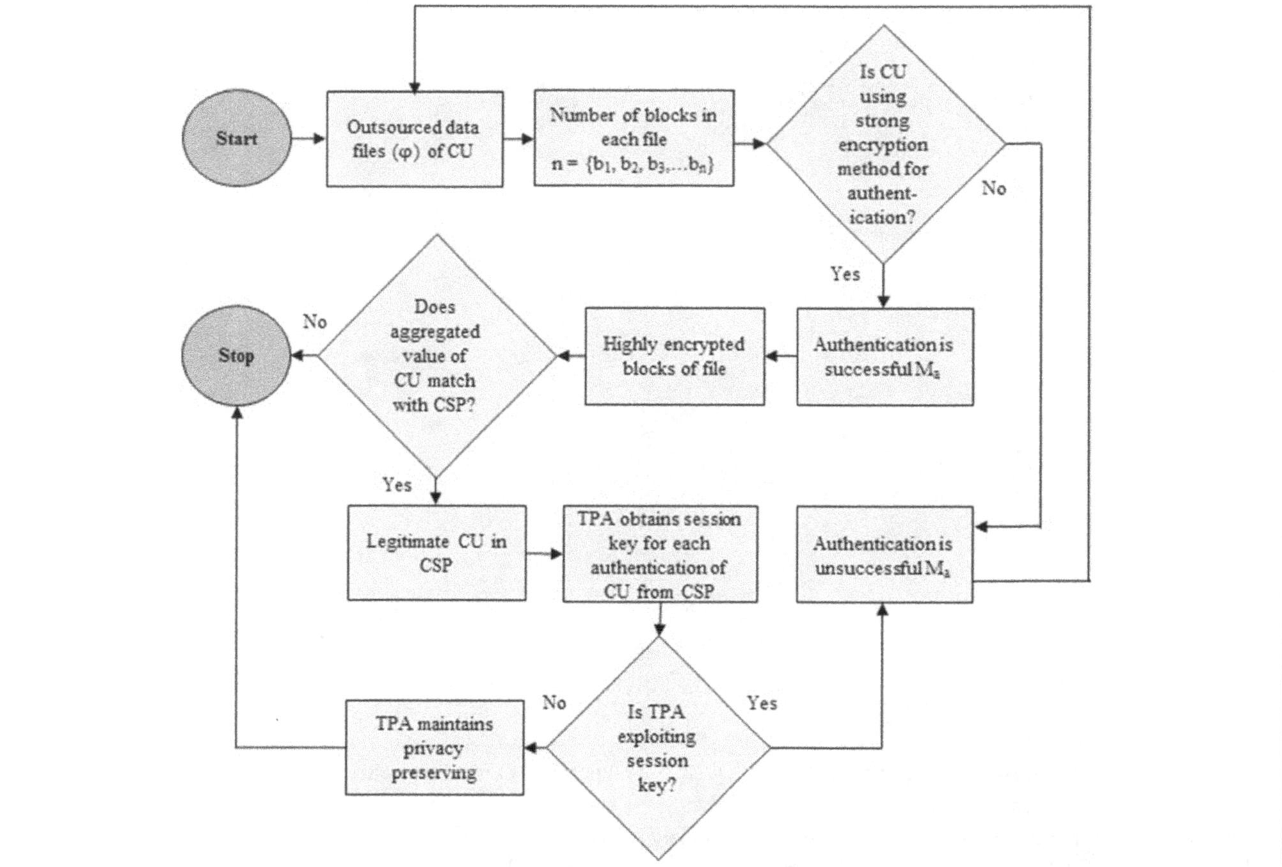

Fig. 5 Authentication of CU to maintain the privacy preserving process

If the CSP fails to provide the proper services according to the SLA, it may attempt to launch different kinds of attacks such as a forge attack, replay attack, distributed denial-of-service attack, etc.

To expose the attacks that are launched by a CSP, we examine if the "check message" 'C_m' or its data tag '$\aleph_t$' is bastardized. If they are corrupt, the TPA's verification request that determines the correctness of the service assigned to the CU cannot be processed. As a result, the server impersonates the original TPA's "check message" including its data tag '$\aleph_t$', and replaces them with the fake "check message" 'F_m' and fake tag 'F_t''. The impersonated message '$\nexists \mathbb{R}_m$' forwarded to the TPA with encryption can be defined as:

$$\nexists \mathbb{R}_m = \prod_{i=0}^{n} {}'\mathrm{O}\left(F_m, F_t\right)^{\mathrm{D}b_i} + \left[\left(\iiint_{\varpi=0}^{n} \Delta s_{\varpi} + \left(log_2 \acute{\mathrm{K}}\right)^n\right)\right] \times \left\{\frac{\frac{\Delta d}{\Delta dz}[s(z)].t(z) - \frac{\Delta d}{\Delta dz}[t(z)].s(z)}{t(z)}.(\nabla\beta\delta)\right\} \quad (12)$$

where, 'O: Output check-message, and $\mathrm{D}b_i$: Blocks of data sent in check-message.

Once the CSP forwards an encrypted impersonated message '$\nexists \mathbb{R}_m$' to the TPA, the TPA compares the CSP's message with (C_m, $\aleph_t$) to help determine a CSP's illegitimate action 'Ɽ' that is compared and shown in Fig. 6.

If Ɽ $= \left[\left\{\prod_{i=0}^{n} {}'\mathrm{O}(F_m, F_t)^{Db_i}\right\} \equiv \left(\varpi + \sum_{s_f \in T_s}^{S_n} \forall \partial L_k\right)\right]$, the CSP provides legitimate service(s) to the CU and fulfils the data-privacy requirements. On the other hand, if the above expression is not equivalent, it implies that the user data confidentiality is compromised and the CSP provides unstandardized services to the CU. Table 4 shows the parameters used for authenticating CSPs.

Table 3 System Parameters and Definitions of CU module for TPA

Notations	Description
$(\nabla\beta\delta)^N$	Aggregated authenticator value
$n = \{b_1, b_2, b_3, \ldots, b_n\}$	Number of data blocks
$\log_2 \acute{K}^n$	Size of the encrypted message
$\iiint_{\varpi=0}^{n} \Delta s_{\varpi}$	Secure and robust encryption method
$\dot{x}.\dot{y}\cdot$	Quotient function that is used as mod
φ	Outsourced data file of CU
ϖ	Random number

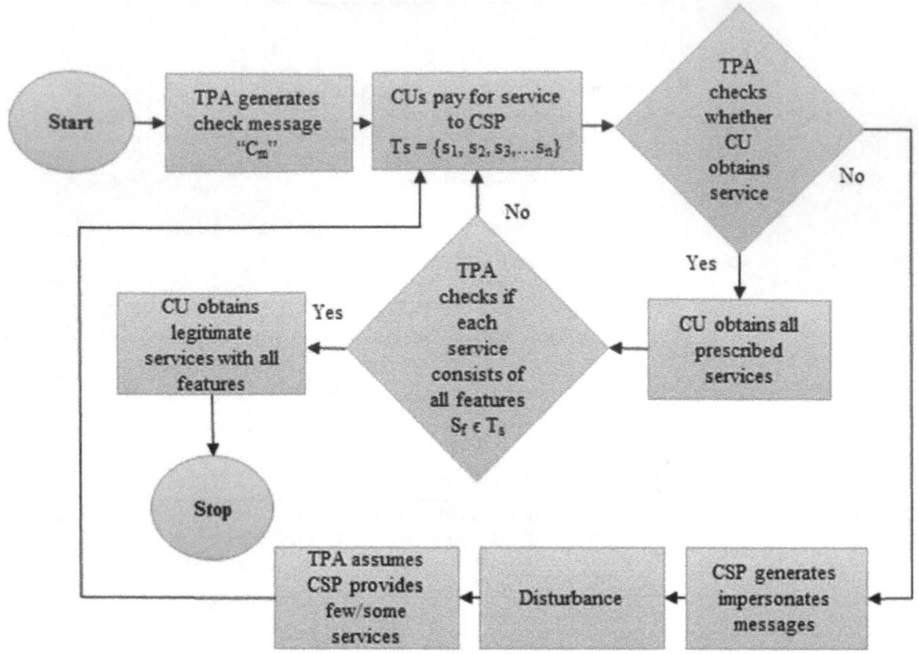

Fig. 6 Identifying the authentication process of CSP for fulfillment of data-privacy requirement

Experiments and performance evaluation

We test the performance of the proposed privacy-preserving model (PPM) involving the three entities (i.e., CSP, CU, and TPA). The proposed model is programmed in C++ and tested on the GreenCloud simulator, the extension of the Network Simulator 2 (NS2). The GreenCloud and NS2 are installed using the merging process. A 2.8 GHz Pentium Dual Core CPU with 5 GB RAM powered computer using a default Ubuntu 12.04 OS is used to run the experiments. The test machine uses a 64-bit version of Windows 8. The GreenCloud presents the repeatable and controllable environment to show the realistic behavior. We test the proposed model for different scenarios to demonstrate the validity of the three entities. Specifically, the following parameters are observed:

- Effectiveness of CSP
- Operational efficiency of CSP
- TPA malicious attempts and successful rate
- Reliability of CSP versus number of auditing

Effectiveness of cloud service provider (CSP)

In the first scenario, we investigate the effectiveness of the CSP based on the provided services to CUs. The effectiveness of the proposed PPM was evidenced in the obtained results which are relatively similar to the realistic environment. The PPM measured the performance of the CSP for ideal (PPM-I), expected (PPM-E), and worst-case (PPM-W) scenarios, as depicted in Figs. 7 and 8. We analyze the effectiveness of the CSP by increasing the number of provided services to the CU. As the number of services to CU is increased over the time, a slight decrease is observed in the effectiveness of the CSP. In all three cases, the proposed PPM demonstrates the realistic behavior of the CSP. The effectiveness of the CSP in the expected case was the reconfirmation that the PPM-E was not entirely approaching the theoretical maximum of the PPM-I. Similarly, in the case of PPM-W, the PPM-E performance was more realistic for the effectiveness of the CSP.

It was validated that the proposed model is well-ordered and remained bounded by a different number of services for most of the simulation time. Hence, it can be implied that the proposed PPM system remains stable in determining the effectiveness of the CSP. The reason for the performance degradation of the CSP was mainly the involvement of some impairing factors such as malicious insiders and outsiders that added into the system as more services are delivered by the CSP. If the role of the malicious adversary is entirely neglected, the effectiveness of the CSP could be much better. However, the possibility of all potential attacks on the CSP cannot be disregarded; otherwise, the effectiveness of a CSP in a realistic environment could not be analyzed in an organized way.

Operational efficiency of cloud service provider (CSP)

Both Figs. 9 and 10 demonstrate the operational efficiency of the CSP versus the number of users. The simulation results exhibit this by increasing the number of

Table 4 System Parameters and Definitions for the authentication process of CSP

Notations	Description
C_m	Check the message used by TPA to examine the correctness of contents stored on a cluster
Db_i	Blocks of data sent in check-message
(F_m, F_t)	Fake check message and fake tag generated by CSP if not provided the required service to CU
(γ^{Φ}, β).	Prediction of the malicious attacker against protected data (queries and answers)
γ^{Φ}	Protected data comprising of query and answers
Z_j	The malicious insider entry
$Z_j \notin T_l$	Unsuccessful attempt
$Z_j \in T_l$	Successful attempt
$\Delta q_a = f_a(q_a)$	Response from TPA for malicious insider to authenticate itself
$\beta = f_a(q_a)$	Successful prediction of malicious insider
s_f	The features of each service assigned to CU
$\varpi \leftarrow \mathrm{N}$	Generation of random number by TSP
ρ^*	Representing the combination of sampled blocks
$\mathbb{R}_g$	Random generator of TSP
$\nexists \mathbb{R}_m$	Impersonated message created by the server
'O	Output for check-message
$\aleph_t$	Data tag generated by TPA to validate the CSPs provided services to CU
$\mathbb{R}$	Determining the CSPs illegitimate action
$\frac{s(z)}{t(z)}$	Derivative of two quotients
$\forall \partial$	TPA chooses a random value for checking the CSPs provided service
ℓ.	Set of the features

CUs which decreases the operational efficiency for all three cases (i.e., PPM-I, PPM-E, and PPM-W), as shown in Fig. 10. The generated scenarios for determining the operational efficiency of the CSP is more realistic than expected for the proposed PPM. Therefore, we focus more on some of the limitations affecting the CSP such as rapid business changes, highly competitive markets, unpredictable economic environments, and dealing with more regulations. In accordance with our expectations, as the number of CUs increases (e.g., see Fig. 10), the overall operational efficiency for the three cases should fluctuate as compare to Fig. 9. However, the worst case scenario (PPM-W) profoundly affected the operational efficiency, as depicted in both Figs. 9 and 10.

In addition to an increase in the CUs and their respective services, the network and server delays also play a role in degrading the overall operational efficiency of the CSPs. The operational efficiency of the CSP could be improved, if we guarantee that all connections are protected prior to binding the cloud applications. For more accurate results, we need to know whether CUs are required to sign into a protected connection first, and then into the cloud application or if it is manageable and reachable ubiquitously.

TPA malicious attempts and successful rate

The primary challenge in protecting data privacy is to handle the malevolent role of the TPA. In the cloud storage system, the CUs host their data on the CSP's servers that can be accessed from anywhere. Due to data outsourcing, the TPA's fraudulence could damage the CSP's image. In addition, the confidential information of CUs could be exploited or leaked to adversaries. In Fig. 11, we demonstrate the malicious attempts of the TPA versus the successful malicious-detection of the proposed PPM.

While handling the malicious attempts of the TPA, different scenarios were generated for three different cases: ideal, expected, and worst. The PPM captured all the malicious attempts in an ideal case (PPM-I) and provided a success-rate reaching 100%. On the other hand, the PPM received the successful capturing rate of 96.6% and 88.3% for expected (PPM-E) and worst case (PPM-W) scenarios, respectively. The expected successful rate could be improved if a malicious insider did not help the TPA to gain access to sensitive information by recuperating the data blocks from a data proof. However, the malicious role of a CSP cannot be ignored, leaving the TPA's newly generated content keys useless against each CU's stored information. The simulation results are comparatively similar to a realistic environment and also confirm the correctness of the proposed PPM.

Reliability of cloud service provider versus number of auditing

The reliability of the CSP is a significant concern. When referring to the reliability of the CSP, it is mainly measured in terms of how secure the customer's data is at the data center and how securely the cloud services are delivered to the CUs. Figure 12 demonstrates the reliability of the CSP for different scenarios: an ideal, expected, and worst case. The primary goal of our experiment is to validate the PPM for various scenarios to evaluate the reliability ratio of the CSP versus the number of audits performed on the customer's data and the cloud services.

The simulation results show that the PPM-I produced 90.2% reliability of the CSP. However, in the expected and worst cases, the results show further decline in the reliability of the CSP as more auditing is done. Hence, the PPM-W confirmed the higher drop rate in the reliability of the CSP. Based on the number of auditing, the CSP will be able to maintain approximately 90.2% reliability for PPM-I, as shown in Fig. 12. In an expected

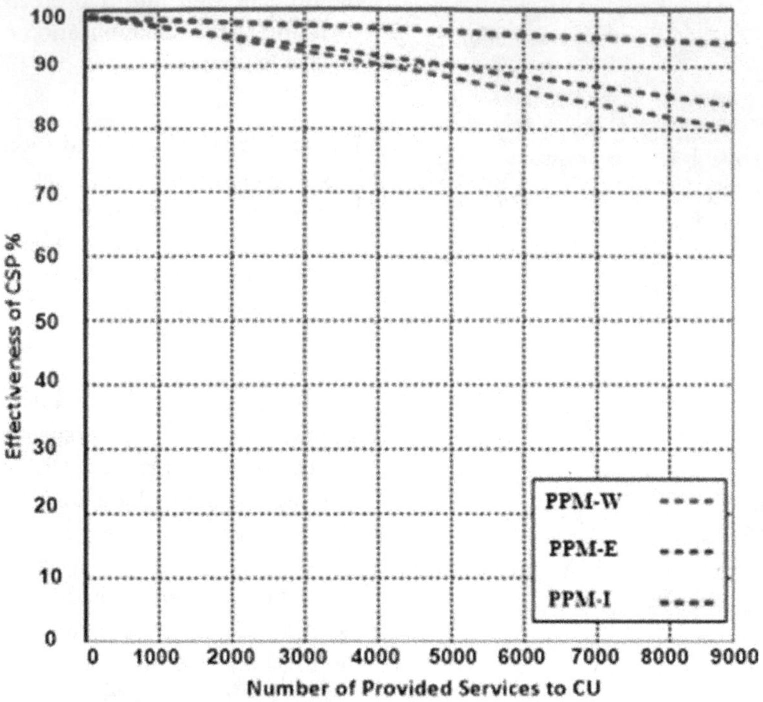

Fig. 7 Effectiveness of CSP VS relatively smaller number of services to Cloud Users

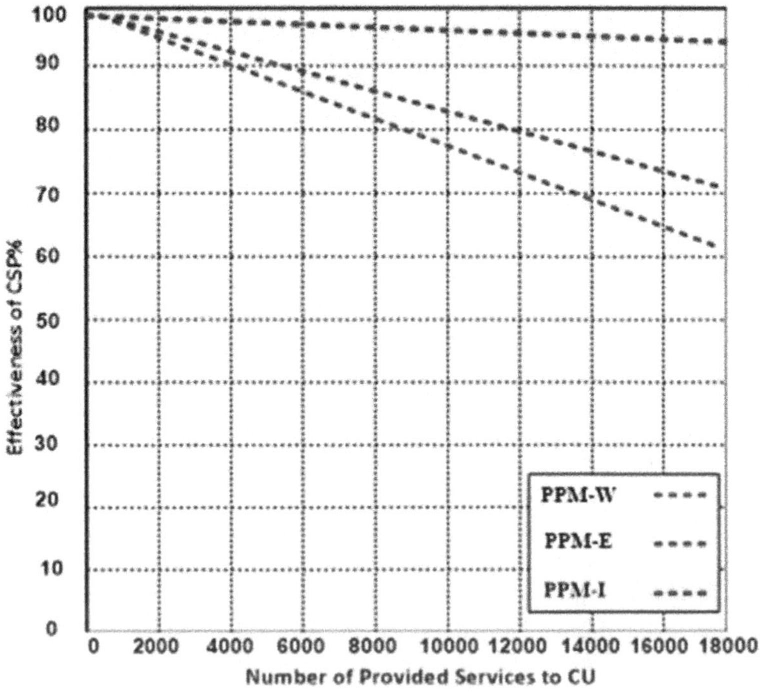

Fig. 8 Effectiveness of CSP VS relatively larger number of services to Cloud Users

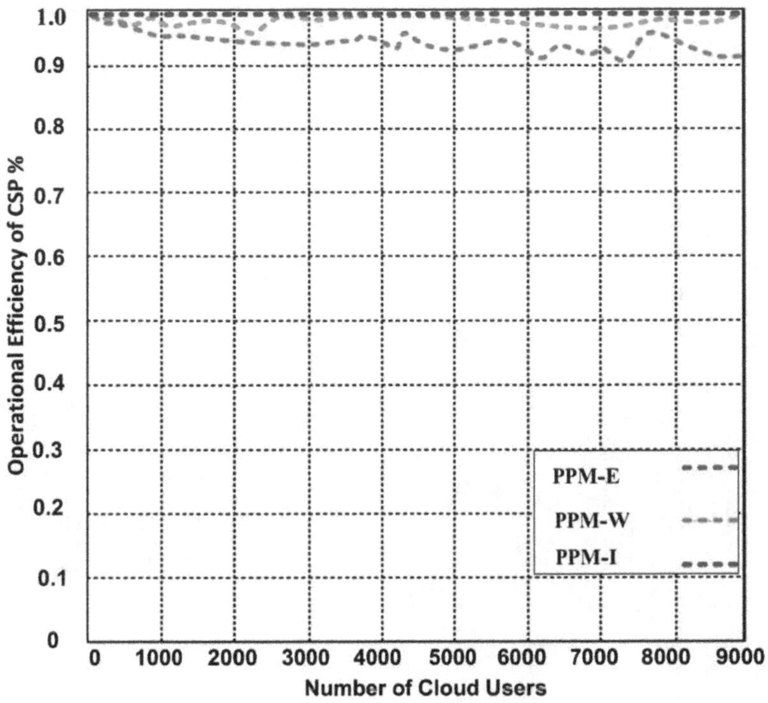

Fig. 9 Operational Efficiency VS number of cloud users (for a relatively smaller cloud network)

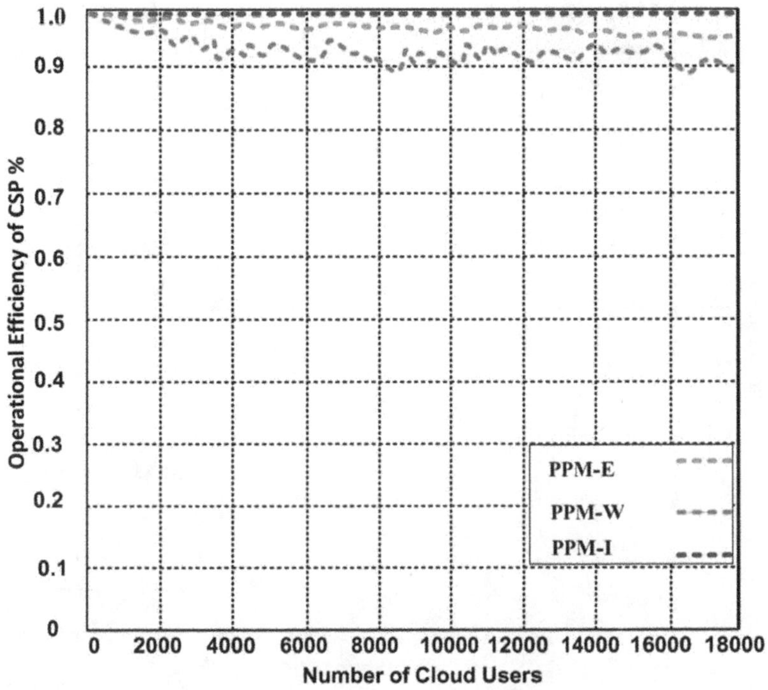

Fig. 10 Operational Efficiency VS number of cloud users (for a relatively larger cloud network)

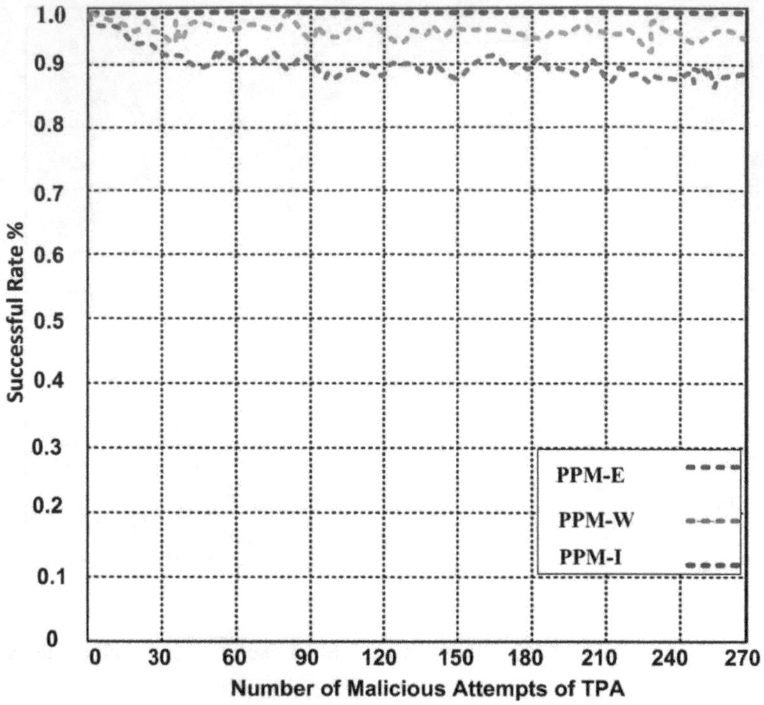

Fig. 11 Number of malicious attempts of TPA versus successful rate of detecting the malicious behavior

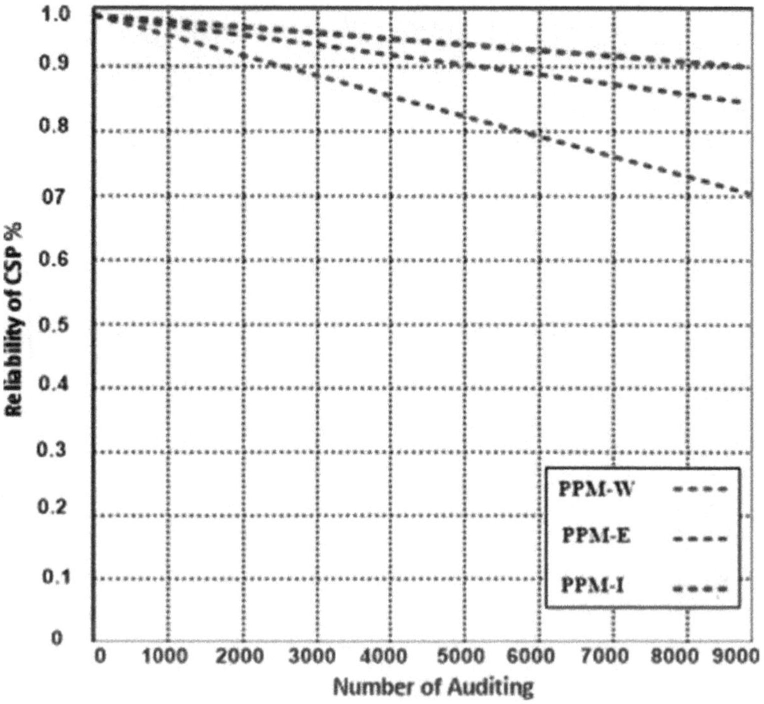

Fig. 12 Reliability of CSP on Number of Auditing

scenario (PPM-E), an approximately 85.2% reliability ratio was observed. In the third scenario, worse case (PPM-W), approximately 70% reliability of the CSP was noted. This simulated behavior implies that the PPM is capable of determining the reliability ratio of the CSP for all three cases. If a CSP is able to maintain an expected reliability ratio, the advantage of storing the confidential data with the CSP will greatly help in evolving the trust between CUs and service providers.

Related work

Most of the existing work [27–29] on the data privacy preservation is based on web services, which address the issues of data control and security in a cloud environment. This includes data access, data integrity, data recovery, data separation, data disposition, and data regulations [27]. Sengupta et al. [28] addressed the cloud security and privacy concerns such as data access, data compliance, and cloud hosted code. Rabai et al. [29] introduced a quantitative cloud security model which helps the subscribers and providers to measure the security risks related to the resources. The model assists the subscribers and providers to investigate and identify the security related issues. In addition, the model takes certain attributes into account when making the security decisions, such as economics, stakeholders, and heterogeneities. Yuhong et al. [30] proposed a new EnTrust framework which integrates the encryption and trust-based techniques to preserve the cloud's storage privacy. Specifically, the proposed framework contains three components: an encryption module, a trust evaluation module and a decision module.

Trusted third party protocols for securing the cloud computing environment were introduced in [31] and [32]. Zissis et al. [31] discussed the TPAs working principles and its security concerns. Thamizhselvan et al. [32] proposed a model that uses a third party security vendor that takes care of encryption and decryption of the data based on the CU's preferences. The public verifiability protocol without the use of a TPA was proposed in [33]. The protocol involves features that do not disclose any confidential information to the TPAs. The protocol demonstrated the accuracy and security parameters through formal analysis. Based on the experimental results, the authors claimed that the proposed protocol performed better in remote data cloud storage.

The trusted computing environment was proposed in [34], which involves the trusted computing module in the cloud computing environment. The trusted computing module focuses on the confidentiality, integrity, and the authentication. However, the module does not provide validation proof. A third party auditing protocol was introduced to keep online storage secure by encrypting the data before applying the hash functions using the symmetric-keys [25]. The auditor verifies the integrity of the received data and decrypts key at the server side. This proposed protocol experiences problems due to limited features that potentially exert an excessive overhead on the servers.

Rosa et al. [35] proposed a privacy-enhancement and trust-aware IdM mechanism which is based on the SAMLv2/ID-FF standards. The primary objective of this mechanism is to obtain an effective access control and identity management. A similar scheme was proposed by Siani et al. [36] to mitigate the data protection risks using a privacy management architecture. In their proposed architecture, the privacy manager is responsible to preserve the privacy for cloud computing technologies. Another privacy-preserving scheme was introduced in [37] for protecting the privacy of individuals in cloud computing environment. The authors attempt to induce the significance of privacy at all levels when designing, collecting, sharing, and processing the cloud's services. However, their research only focuseses on the notion of privacy, but no proof was provided to handle the data privacy issues.

Cong et al. [38] proposed a privacy-preserving public auditing system for data storage security in cloud computing. Specifically, the proposed system introduced the homomorphic linear authenticator with the random masking to prevent a TPA in accessing the contents of the customer's outsourced data during the auditing process. The proposed system enables a TPA to perform multiple auditing tasks in a batch processing mode for improved efficiency.

Hassan et al. [39] highlighted the fast adoption deferring-reasons for cloud security. Addressing this issue, a comprehensive cloud security framework was introduced to resolve the deferring reasons for cloud security. This framework involves the following modules: the policy integration module, access control, trust management, service management, authentication, heterogeneity management and identity management. Pelin et al. [40] proposed an authentication framework to detect the cloud computing entities such as cloud as user and services. The authors use the identity management module to address the privacy and identity issues. Recently, Abdul et al. [41] proposed a triangular data privacy-preserving scheme that supports public auditing with the capability of auditing all the key stakeholders for achieving optimal security in a cloud environment.

Conclusion

To guarantee data privacy in a cloud computing environment, it is essential to introduce a new scheme to authenticate the three cloud stakeholders (i.e., CSP, CU and TPA). Thus, the proposed triangle authentication process enables the three stakeholders to detect the negative role of each other. Another concern is how to design a privacy-preserving model to restrict the potential TPA vulnerabilities, control the malicious insider threats in CSPs, and determine the CUs deceitful role of distributing the obtained service to other clients. In this paper, we explored the integrity and privacy-related challenges among the three entities. To build a secure and efficient cloud computing environment, we extend and improve the existing CSP and TPA security models by leveraging the properties into a single triangular data privacy-preserving model to provide the auditing capability to all the key stakeholders. To support efficient and effective triangular auditing tasks, the scope of our privacy-preserving model is limited to: (a) guaranteeing the TPA's integrity, (b) administering the firm compliance of SLA by both the CSP and CUs, (c) authoring the exact use of allotted session keys for auditing the confidential data stored on the cloud's server, and (d) confirming the message authentication at the cloud service provider's side. The TPA audits the CSP to confirm the privacy of the CUs' outsourced data. The TPA also monitors the response provided by the CUs for the utilized services according to the SLA. Finally, an audit of the TPA is performed by both CSPs and CUs to reduce the probability of any possible malicious insider threats. To validate the correctness and soundness of the proposed work, an experimental analysis is conducted, which proves that the proposed PPM is highly efficient for preserving the data stored in the cloud computing environment.

Funding

This research project was not funded.

Authors' contributions

Both authors have equal contribution. Specifically, Dr. Razaque worked on Sections Proposed privacy preserving model and Experiment and performance evaluation. Dr. Rizvi worked on Sections Adversary model and Related work. Both authors read and approved the final manuscript.

Competing interests

The authors declare that they have no competing interests.

Author details

[1]Computer Science Department, New York Institute of Technology, New York, NY, USA. [2]Department of Information Sciences and Technology, Pennsylvania State University, Altoona, PA 16601, USA.

References

1. Rajkumar B, Yeo CH, Venugopal S, Broberg J, Brandic I (2009) Cloud computing and emerging IT platforms: vision, hype, and reality for delivering computing as the 5th utility. Futur Gener Comput Syst 25(6):599–616
2. Peter M, Grance T (2011) The NIST definition of cloud computing
3. Sumant R, Eloff M, Smith E (2010) The management of security in cloud computing. In: IEEE Information Security for South Africa (ISSA)., pp 1–7
4. Yong C, Buyya R, Jiangchuan L (2014) Cloud computing. China Communications, 11(4) China Institute of Communications (CIC) and the IEEE Communications Society (IEEE ComSoc), USA.
5. Toosi AN, Calheiros RN, Buyya R (2014) Interconnected cloud computing environments: challenges, taxonomy, and survey. ACM Comput Surv 47(1):7:1–7:47
6. Qian W, Wang C, Li J, Ren K, Lou W (2009) Enabling public verifiability and data dynamics for storage security in cloud computing. In: Computer Security–ESORICS. Springer, Berlin Heidelberg, pp 355–370
7. Rampal S, Kumar S, Kumar SA (2012) Ensuring data storage security in cloud computing. International Journal of Engineering And Computer Science, 2319–7242
8. Cong W, Wang Q, Ren K, Cao N, Lou W (2012) Toward secure and dependable storage services in cloud computing. IEEE Trans Serv Comput 5(2):220–232
9. Francesc S, Domingo-Ferrer J, Martinez-Balleste A, Deswarte Y, Quisquater J-J (2008) Efficient remote data possession checking in critical information infrastructures. IEEE Trans Knowl Data Eng 20(8):1034–1038
10. Zhuo H, Yu N (2010) A multiple-replica remote data possession checking protocol with public verifiability. In: 2010 Second International Symposium on Data, Privacy and E-Commerce (ISDPE)., pp 84–89
11. Kun H, Xian M, Fu S, Liu J (2014) Securing the cloud storage audit service: defending against frame and collude attacks of third party auditor. IET Commun 8(12):2106–2113
12. Mehul SA, Swaminathan R, Baker M (2008) Privacy-preserving audit and extraction of digital contents. IACR Cryptology ePrint Archive, Report 2008/186, 2008, http://www.hpl.hp.com/techreports/2008/HPL-2008-32R1.pdf. Accessed 10 Aug 2016
13. Glenn B, Mogull R (2009) Security guidance for critical areas of focus in cloud computing. Cloud Security Alliance 2(1):1–76
14. Qingji Z, Xu S (2011) Fair and dynamic proofs of retrievability. In: Proceedings of the first ACM conference on Data and application security and privacy., pp 237–248
15. Ari J, Kaliski BS (2007) PORs: proofs of retrievability for large files. In: Proceedings of the 14th ACM Conference on Computer and Communications Security., pp 584–597
16. Yevgeniy D, Vadhan S, Wichs D (2009) Proofs of retrievability via hardness amplification. In: Theory of cryptography. Springer, Berlin Heidelberg, pp 109–127
17. Kevin BD, Juels A, Oprea A (2009) Proofs of retrievability: theory and implementation. In: Proceedings of the 2009 ACM Workshop on Cloud Computing Security., pp 43–54
18. Cong W, Ren K, Lou W, Li J (2010) Toward publicly auditable secure cloud data storage services. IEEE Netw 24(4):19–24
19. Mohammed SH, Al-Haidari F, Salah K (2011) Edos-shield-a two-steps mitigation technique against edos attacks in cloud computing. In: 2011 Fourth IEEE International Conference on Utility and Cloud Computing (UCC)., pp 49–56
20. Hovav S, Waters B (2008) Compact proofs of retrievability. In: Advances in Cryptology-ASIACRYPT. Springer, Berlin Heidelberg, pp 90–107
21. Cong W, Wang Q, Ren K, Lou W (2010) Privacy-preserving public auditing for data storage security in cloud computing. In: IEEE INFOCOM., pp 1–9
22. Jia X (2011) Auditing the auditor: secure delegation of auditing operation over cloud storage. IACR Cryptology ePrint Archive, https://eprint.iacr.org/2011/304.pdf. Accessed 10 Aug 2016
23. Giuseppe A, Burns R, Curtmola R, Herring J, Kissner L, Peterson Z, Song D (2007) Provable data possession at untrusted stores. In: Proceedings of the 14th ACM Conference on Computer and Communications Security., pp 598–609
24. Bhagyashri S, Gurav YB (2014) Privacy-preserving public auditing for secure cloud storage. IOSR Journal of Computer Engineering (IOSR-JCE) 16(4):33–38
25. Mehul SA, Baker M, Mogul J, Swaminathan R (2007) Auditing to keep online storage services honest. In: Galen H (ed) Proceedings of the 11th USENIX Workshop on Hot Topics in Operating Systems (HOTOS'07). USENIX Association, Berkeley, p 6, Article 11
26. El-Booz SA, Attiya G, El-Fishawy N (2016) A secure cloud storage system combining time-based one-time password and automatic blocker protocol. EURASIP J Inf Secur 2016:13. doi:10.1186/s13635-016-0037-0
27. David C, Fatema K (2012) A privacy preserving authorisation system for the cloud. J Comput Syst Sci 78(5):1359–1373
28. Sengupta S, Kaulgud V, Sharma V (2013) Cloud computing security – trends and research directions. In: 2011 IEEE World Congress on Services, Washington DC, 2011., pp 524–531
29. Rabai LBA, Jouini M, Aissa AB, Mili A (2013) A cybersecurity model in cloud computing environment. Journal of Kind Saud University – Computer and Information Sciences 25(1):63–75
30. Yuhong L, Ryoo J, Rizvi S (2014) Ensuring data confidentiality in cloud computing: an encryption and trust-based solution. In: Proceedings of 23rd

IEEE Wireless and Optical Communication Conference (WOCC), Newark, NJ, May 2014., pp 1–6
31. Zissis D, Lekkas D (2012) Addressing cloud computing security issue. Futur Gener Comput Syst 28(2012):583–592
32. Thamizhselvan M, Raghuraman R, Gershon S, Victer Paul P (2015) A novel security model for cloud using trusted third party encryption. In: 2015 International Conference on Innovations in Information, Embedded and Communication Systems (ICIIECS), Coimbatore., pp 1–5
33. Zhuo H, Zhong S, Yu N (2011) A privacy-preserving remote data integrity checking protocol with data dynamics and public verifiability. IEEE Trans Knowl Data Eng 23(9):1432–1437
34. Shen Z, Tong Q (2012) The security of cloud computing system enabled by trusted computing technology. In: 2nd International Conference on Signal Processing Systems (ICSPS), Dalian, 2010., pp V2-11–V2-15
35. Rosa S, Almenares F, Arias P, Díaz-Sánchez D, Marín A (2012) Enhancing privacy and dynamic federation in IdM for consumer cloud computing. IEEE Trans Consum Electron 58(1):95–103
36. Siani P, Shen Y, Mowbray M (2009) A privacy manager for cloud computing. In: Cloud computing. Springer, Berlin Heidelberg, pp 90–106
37. Jian W, Zhao Y, Jiang S, Le J (2009) Providing privacy preserving in cloud computing. IEEE International Conference on Test and Measurement (ICTM'09) 2:213–216
38. Cong W, Chow SM, Wang Q, Ren K, Lou W (2013) Privacy-preserving public auditing for secure cloud storage. IEEE Trans Comput 62(2):362–375
39. Hassan T, Joshi BD, Ahn GJ (2010) Securecloud: towards a comprehensive security framework for cloud computing environments. In: 2010 IEEE 34th Annual Computer Software and Applications Conference Workshops (COMPSACW)., pp 393–398
40. Pelin A, Bhargava B, Ranchal R, Singh N, Linderman M, Othmane LB, Lilien L (2010) An entity-centric approach for privacy and identity management in cloud computing. In: 2010 29th IEEE Symposium on Reliable Distributed Systems., pp 177–183
41. Razaque A, Rizvi S (2016) Triangular data privacy-preserving model for authenticating all key stakeholders in a cloud environment. Comput Secur 62:328–347

An exploration of the determinants for decision to migrate existing resources to cloud computing using an integrated TOE-DOI model

Adel Alkhalil[1*], Reza Sahandi[2] and David John[2]

Abstract

Migrating existing resources to cloud computing is a strategic organisational decision that can be difficult. It requires the consideration and evaluation of a wide range of technical and organisational aspects. Although a significant amount of attention has been paid by many industrialists and academics to aid migration decisions, the procedure remains difficult. This is mainly due to underestimation of the range of factors and characteristics affecting the decision for cloud migration. Further research is needed to investigate the level of effect these factors have on migration decisions and the overall complexity. This paper aims to explore the level of complexity of the decision to migrate the cloud. A research model based on the diffusion of innovation (DOI) theory and the technology-organization-environment (TOE) framework was developed. The model was tested using exploratory and confirmatory factor analysis. The quantitative analysis shows the level of impact of the identified variables on the decision to migrate. Seven determinants that contribute to the complexity of the decisions are identified. They need to be taken into account to ensure successful migration. This result has expanded the collective knowledge about the complexity of the issues that have to be considered when making decisions to migrate to the cloud. It contributes to the literature that addresses the complex and multidimensional nature of migrating to the cloud.

Keywords: Cloud computing, Cloud migration, Decision-making process, Cloud migration factors, Cloud migration complexity, TOE, DOI

Introduction

Over the last decade, advances in computing have enabled cost-effective realisation of large-scale data centres [1]. It has led to computing being transformed to a model comprising services that are commoditised and delivered in a manner similar to traditional public utilities which stimulates a new paradigm – Cloud Computing. The emergence of this phenomenon fundamentally changed the way information systems are developed, deployed, scaled, supported, and paid for [2]. It has attracted many companies to migrate existing systems due to their promised advantages, particularly the reduction of capital expenses and the virtually infinite resource capacity that enhances businesses' agility [3]. Although cloud computing promises great benefits, it has not yet reached the maturity level that allows computing resources to be treated like commodities such as electricity as predicted by Buyya et al. [4]. Organisations are still reluctant to migrate their IT systems and services to the cloud due to concerns of losing control and other undesired outcomes [5]. Further, organisations are typically interested in moving only some of their systems to the cloud due to the difficulty of migrating the related applications, for example, safety-critical software [6]. Unlike start-up companies that develop systems from scratch, organisations planning to migrate existing legacy services to cloud computing often need the new services to be inter-

* Correspondence: a.alkalel@uoh.edu.sa
[1]Faculty of Computer Science and Engineering, University of Hail, Hail, Saudi Arabia
Full list of author information is available at the end of the article

operated with the existing systems [7]. This requires careful planning to avoid integration problem issues.

Being an important area for IT and business innovation, the adoption of cloud computing has received increasing attention in both practice and research [8]. Cloud computing is a fairly new provisioning model and a trend that involves continuing development of next-generation architecture. Therefore, most of the existing cloud studies are exploratory, descriptive, or case-based research [9]. For example, studies from [10–12] focus on the general conceptualization and definition of cloud computing, as well as strengths, weaknesses, opportunities and threats to the cloud computing industry. Further, many previous studies explored the business benefits and barriers for adoption. They focused mostly on the cost benefits, scalability, agility and the security issues, for examples see [13–17]. While these studies identified some factors that influence the decisions to migrate to the cloud, they were developed at an early stage of the evolvement of cloud computing. Further, the majority of them explored the factors affecting the adoption of cloud services while little attention was paid to the migration of legacy systems.

Many models and frameworks have been proposed to aid organisations with their decision to migrate to the cloud environment (e.g. [18–23]). Although significant contributions have been made by these works, there are still many aspects which require further support [24]. The main limitation in the proposed approaches is the separation of elements in the migration processes, that are connected and dependent on each other. Further, the existing support is usually limited to the selection of service providers such as [22] or to the adaption required for migrating applications such as [6]. Although evaluation of providers and their appropriate selection are critical, making an informed decision to migrate requires the analysis of a wide range of factors at early stages of the decision process. While the existing literature provides a fundamental understanding of cloud computing architecture, benefits and some issues, models and frameworks to support the migration and managing cloud services, research on drivers and barriers of the broad organizational adoption is still in early stages [5] and [9]. Therefore, this paper explores the issues that have increased the difficulties in organisations' decisions to migrate to the cloud. A two-stage survey was implemented for the exploration. This resulted in the identification of seven factors that contributed to the complexity of the decisions for migration. The analysis of the literature with regards to supporting the decision making process of companies when considering whether to migrate to the cloud shows that only some of those factors had been taken into account. The objective of this paper is to advance this further by empirically exploring the factors influencing the decision to migrate to the cloud. It proposes an integrated research model based on the Technology–Organization–Environment (TOE) framework and the Diffusion of Innovation theory (DOI).

Theoretical background

Migration to cloud computing

Migration to the cloud, for the purpose of this paper, can be defined as the transition process of all or part of an organisation's legacy IT resources, including: hardware, software, stored data, and business processes, from locally on-premises deployments behind its firewalls to the cloud environment where they can be managed remotely by a third party. The process also encompasses the shifting of IT resources between different cloud providers, which is known as cloud-to-cloud migration. The cloud migration process may involve retaining some IT infrastructure on-site [25].

Decision making process

Simon [26] developed a generic decision making process model. The model is divided into three major phases: Intelligence, Design, and Choice. The process starts with the intelligence phase in which the 'reality' of an organisation is examined. It involves problem identification and information gathering activities about the societal, the competitiveness, and the organisational environments. The design phase simplifies an organisation's "reality" and identifies relationships between variables, as well as setting the criteria for evaluating alternative courses of action. The choice phase is to select the most appropriate alternative course of action based on the criteria identified in the design phase. The model has been widely accepted and adopted for problem-solving [27]. Turban et al. [28] described the model as the most concise, yet complete characterisation of rational decision making. Decision Support Systems (DSSs) are an integral part of Simon's model. The following section presents an analysis of the exiting DSSs, designed to support the decision making process for migrating to cloud computing. We applied Simons' [26] model on the existing DSSs to examine the level of support they offer in each of the three levels.

Current level of support for decisions to migrate to the cloud

The evolution and also the increase in popularity of cloud computing has led to a significant raise and awareness of industrialists and academics for the support required for migration decisions. Cloud vendors and IT consultancy agencies have made many attempts to provide guidance and assessment tools to help decisions for migration, as evidenced by a number of published whitepapers (See for example, [29–31]). However, these attempts have either been developed for marketing purposes or are not publicly available, due to them being based on closed proprietary technologies that usually require consultancy contracts [32]. Nevertheless, a number of DSSs have been proposed to support migration, as illustrated in Table 1.

A review of the DSSs shows that the vast majority of them do not support the assessment of the current cloud environments and business processes. In other words, they focus on supporting migration at the choice level for selecting providers. Although evaluation of providers and their appropriate selection are critical, making an informed decision to migrate requires the analysis of a wide range of factors at early stages of a decision process. Companies should develop a good awareness of the cloud environment and its capabilities, regulations, potentials and threats, before coming to a decision. Almost none of the reviewed work studied so far had considered "the intelligence level" and only a few paid attention to "the design level" for decision-making by considering the need for services adaptations in order to make them cloud enabled. For example, Andrikopoulos et al. [6] considered the adaptation required to the applications for migrating to the cloud.

The review also shows a high level of interest for migration for the IaaS model followed by the SaaS while there is very limited attention to the PaaS. Additionally, the existing approaches focus on migration from on-premises to the cloud while there is a lack of interest for migration from one provider to another. This is an important aspect to be addressed to avoid the issue of vendor lock-in which is a concern for many [33].

Further, the majority of the existing DSSs are prototype-based, experimental or conceptual. Therefore, the provision of established DSSs to include relevant information can substantially aid the decision making process. Another problem is the dispersed information, which is required for decision making. Although the information is available, it is often time consuming to bring all the details together. Additionally, due to the development of the technology and the expansion of the services offered, the range of information that is required to be considered for migration is increasing. Further, the availability of a wide range of DSSs and tools may create uncertainty for decision makers, if they are used outside of a systematic process.

Table 1 A review of the existing cloud DSSs

Proposed approach	Cloud service	Factors taken into account	Method	Level of support
Suitability analysis for cloud computing [45]	Not specified	Size of the IT resources, the utilisation pattern of the resources, sensitivity of the data, and criticality of the service	ROI model	Design
CloudMIG [65]	PaaS and IaaS	Applications reengineering	Mathematical modelling	Design and Choice
Cloud adoption toolkit [18]	IaaS	Cost, characteristic social factors, political factors, performance, and practicalities	UML	Choice
DSS for migrating applications [21]	SaaS	Applications distribution, cloud providers selection, elasticity strategy, multi-tenancy requirements.	Three-tiered architecture	Design and Choice
DSS for migrating applications [66]	SaaS	Cost and providers' characteristic	Conceptual modelling	Choice
Applications adaptations for the cloud environment [6]	SaaS	The need for adaptation	Holistic approach	Design
partially migration of applications to the cloud [67]	SaaS	Hybrid deployment	Component placement a and AHP	Design and Choice
SMICloud [22]	Not specified	Accountability, agility, assurance, cost, performance, and security and privacy.	Component placement a and AHP	Choice
InCLOUDer [50]	SaaS	Applications adaptations and Accountability, agility, assurance, cost, performance, and security and privacy.	AHP	Design and Choice
DSS for migrating applications [68]	SaaS and PaaS	The database layer of an application	Step-by-step methodology	Design
CloudGenius [19]	IaaS	Cost, Performance, providers' characteristic	AHP and mathematical modelling	Choice
Configuration support [23]	IaaS	Cost and providers' characteristic	Feature model	Choice
Workflow Infrastructure migration [56]	IaaS	Cost and providers' characteristic	OPAL Simulation	Choice

Organisational adoption of innovation

The theoretical foundation for the exploration in this study is based on the TOE framework and DOI theory developed by Tornatzky and Fleischer [34] and Rogers [35] respectively, which are discussed below.

The Technology-organisation-environment framework

Although several frameworks have been developed for the adoption of ICT, the TOE is argued to be an integrative framework that provides a holistic approach and guidance [36]. The TOE framework consists of three dimensions of technology, organisation and environment that influence the process by which innovations are adopted (see Fig. 1). It serves as taxonomy for factors that facilitate or inhibit the adoption of technology innovations [37]. The framework has been used in the context of cloud commuting adoption as described by [17, 38, 39].

The technological dimension relates to what is available to an organization and focuses on how a certain technology influences the adoption process [34]. The organisational context looks at the structure and the processes in an organization that constrain or facilitate the adoption and implementation of innovations [34]. The external environmental context is also supported by Tornatzky and Fleischer [34] such as the industry, competitors, regulations, and relationships with governments.

The diffusion of innovation model

The research on adoption of innovation continued in order to provide richer and possibly more explanatory models [40]. A major contribution in this regard was the development of the Diffusion of Innovation model [35]. It has been widely used to explain IT adoptions. The model is concerned with the way that a new technological innovation progresses from creation to utilisation (see Fig. 2). It describes the patterns of adoption and the mechanisms for diffusion, as well as assisting to predict whether and how a new invention will be successful [35]. It has three main categories of factors that influence decisions to adopt innovations: Innovation Characteristics, Organizational Characteristics, and Individuals Characteristics. The innovation characteristics comprise the perceived attributes of the innovation that either encourage or hinder. Rogers [35] indicated that the five attributes of an innovation are: relative advantage, compatibility, complexity, trialability, and observability. Relative advantage refers to the level to which an advantage is perceived as better than the current system. Compatibility is the degree to which an innovation is perceived as being consistent with the existing values, past experiences and needs of potential adopters. Complexity relates to the perceived difficulty of understanding and using the innovation while trialability refers to the degree to which the innovation can be easily tried and tested over time. Finally, observability refers to the level to which the results of an innovation are visible to the technology adopter [35].

Research design

In order to answer the research questions, which focused on the exploration and support required for decision making for organisational migration to the cloud, a

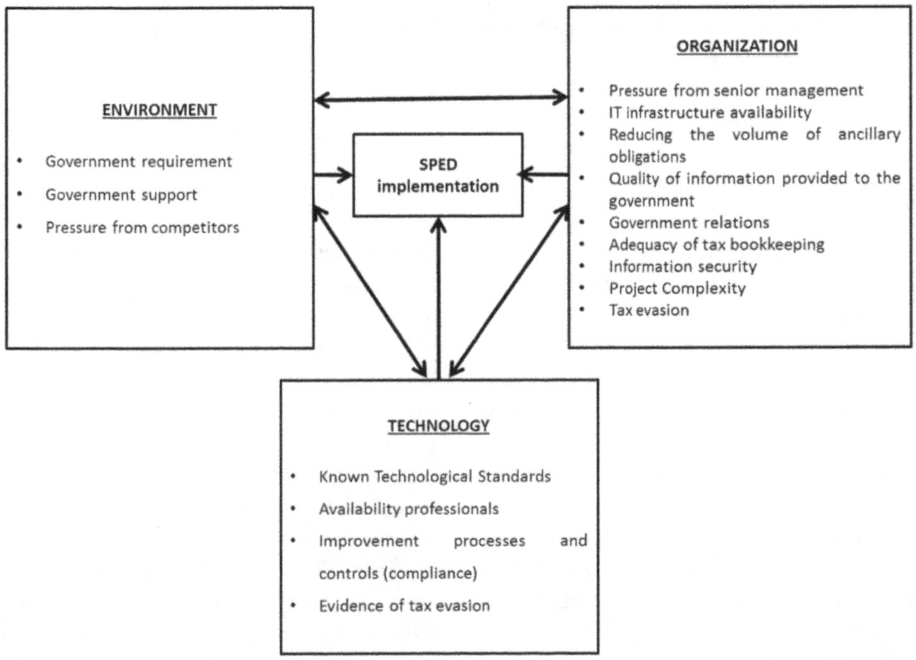

Fig. 1 The Technology-organisation-environment framework, Adapted from Tornatzky and Fleischer [34]

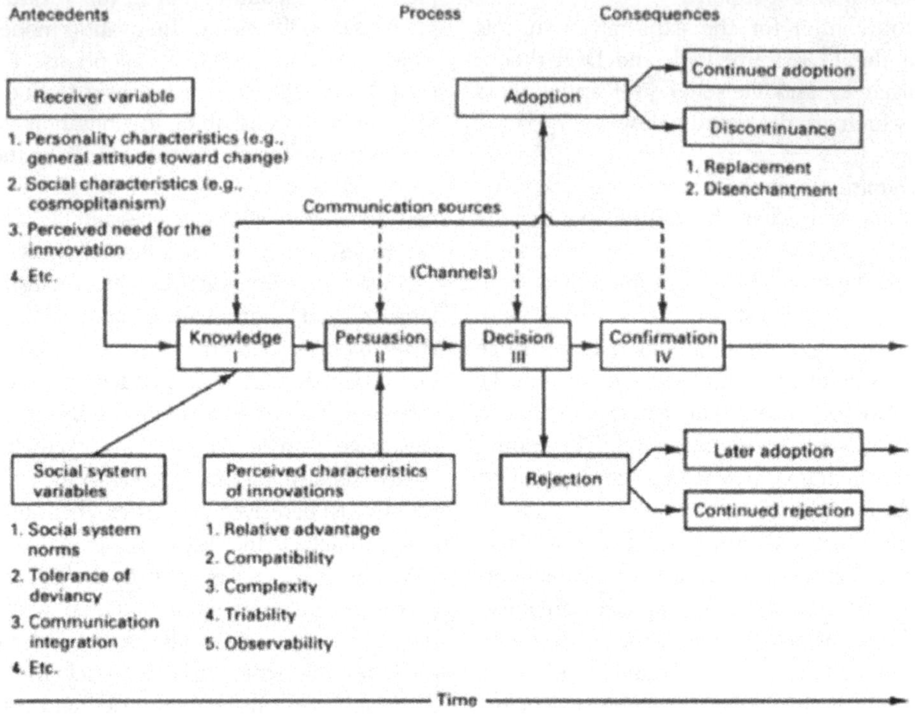

Fig. 2 The Diffusion of Innovation model, adapted from Rogers [35]

literature review was carried out. A number of factors and characteristics that increase the complexity of decisions to migrate were explored. The findings of the literature were supplemented with the implementation of a two-stage survey. The nature of the phenomenon studied in this research is comparatively new and is still evolving. Therefore, a sequential exploratory strategy was found to be the most appropriate way for gathering the needed data to answer the research questions. This strategy was tested using a two-stage survey that firstly gathered qualitative and then quantitative data (see Fig. 3).

Stage 1 was based on semi-structured interviews. Open ended questions were employed to ensure consistency, while it still allowed a degree of freedom and adaptability in obtaining the information from the interviewees. The interviews were conducted face-to-face and on average each lasted about an hour. There were 12 interviewees in total who included IT managers (4), security professionals (3), and technical leaders within cloud provider companies (5) who were selected based on their subject expertise. The choice of the interview technique was based on the belief that real life practitioners, in particular service providers can offer a richer understanding of the benefits and challenges for adopting cloud computing due to their related experience. The interviews were carried out to further gain insight into the factors, issues, and concerns about the migration decisions, as well as developing a foundation for further analysis. The interviewees included decision makers of organisations in respect of cloud services, as well as some security experts. Twelve interviewees is a relatively small number; however, the sample mainly targeted technical professionals who were working for cloud provider companies. The information they provided was based on their experience of dealing with large number of customers, and during the interviews, they used examples of migration of some projects which raised the quality and reliability of the information they were able to share. Based on the analysis of stage 1, as well as related literature, the research approach and hypotheses were formulated. In order to test the hypotheses, the stage 2 survey was implemented using an online survey questionnaire. Figure 3 shows the methodology adopted for this research.

Data analysis (the exploration phase)

Thematic analysis was used to analyse the qualitative data which was applied in six phases as suggested by [41]. The qualitative analysis enabled insights into challenges, issues, and factors that influence on the decision making process of whether to migrate to the cloud. To further specify these factors, the DOI and TOE frameworks were applied to the data. This resulted in findings within the following contexts: innovation characteristics, technology, organisation, and environment as shown in Table 2. The innovation characteristics was divided into four categories: relative advantages, compatibility, trialabilty, and probable risks. Participants indicated a number of advantages that can positively influence the decision to migrate to the cloud. They mostly agreed on cost

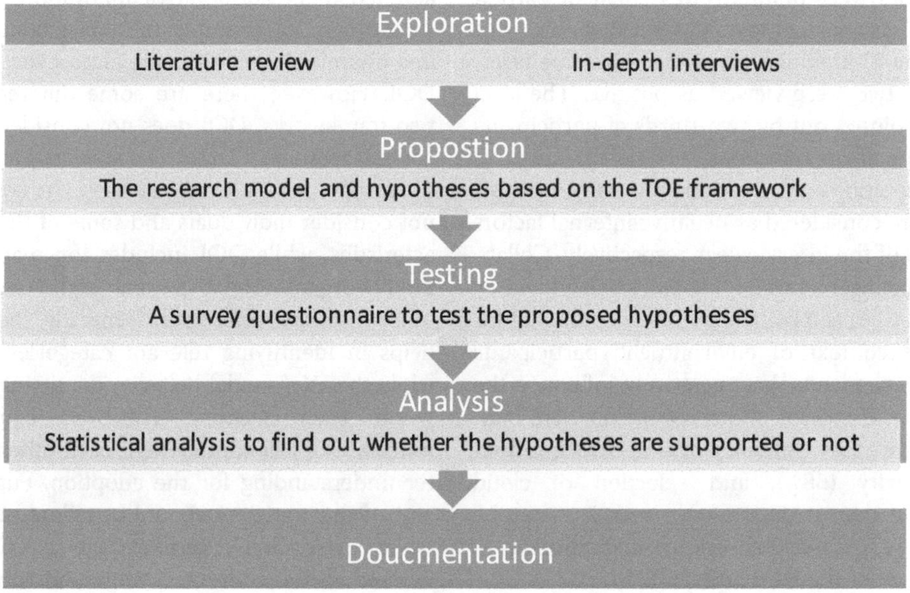

Fig. 3 Research design

reduction (91.6%) and agility (75%) followed by back-up (41.6%) and higher performance (41.6%) as positive drivers for migration. Further, two-thirds of the participants highlighted, testing advantages provided by the cloud as a positive driver for migration. On the other hand, participants reported a number of factors that increase risks and complexity (See Table 2). Lack of knowledge about the cloud environment was pointed out by all the cloud service providers interviewed in this study as a major issue that negatively influence the decision to migrate. Further, almost all the interviewees indicated there is a high level of concern for privacy and confidentiality regarding the adoption of cloud-based services. Within the technology context, participants indicated issues with compatibility and the difficulties of migrating large volume of legacy data as a negative influence on migration decisions. The impact on organisational culture, staff and interpretability issues were pointed out by 58% and the difficulties in

Table 2 The findings of stage 1 in the context of DOI and TOE

Context	Variable	Findings	Impact
Innovation Characteristics	Relative advantages (DOI)	Cost reduction, agility, back-up, and higher performance	Positive
	Complexity (DOI)	The lack of knowledge about the cloud environment, lack of skills for managing cloud-service, cost management problems, risks management, the immaturity of the cloud	Negative
	Triability (DOI)	Ease of testing	Positive
	Risks (DOI)	Concerns of privacy and confidentiality, vendor lock in, and loss of control	Negative
Technology	Compatibility (DOI)	Impact on organisational culture and staff, interpretability issues	Negative
	Size (TOE)	Difficulties in migrating large data	Negative
Organisation	Organisation readiness (TOE)	Level of expertise	Negative
	Internal social (TOE)	Need for adaptation, disruption to current business processes	Negative
	External social (DOI)	Collaboration	Positive
	Top management support (DOI)	Competitiveness, outsourcing culture, trust	Positive
Environment	Information sources (TOE)	Difficult access to information and complexity	Negative
	Regulation (TOE)	Concerns of legal implication, data ownership, and SLA	Negative
	Selection of cloud provider (TOE)	Selection of cloud services and providers is difficult, and Increasing number of cloud provider and their configuration	Negative

migrating large data were pointed out by half of participants. The organisational context was divided into four variables (see Table 2) in which two were viewed as negative and the other two were viewed as positive. The level of expertise was pointed out by two-thirds of participants as a negative factor of organisations readiness to migrate. The need for adaptation and disruption to current business processes were considered as negative internal factors by 66.6% and 50% of the interviewees respectively. Collaboration and top management support were considered by half of the interviewees as positive factors encouraging for migration. In the context of environment, participants pointed out three elements that negatively influence the decision to migrate. Concerns about regulation were indicated by 75% followed by difficulty of access to information and complexity (58%), and selection of cloud providers (50%). Further analysis of the interviews can be found in [42] and [43]. Table 2 shows the main findings of stage1 in the context of the DOI and TOE.

Proposed model and hypotheses

In this paper a model for identifying the determinants influencing the decision for cloud migration was developed (See Fig. 4). It is based on the integration of the characteristics contexts (organisation, innovation, individual, technology and environment) identified in the DOI and TOE frameworks. Combining more than one theoretical perspective was argued to enhance the understanding of adoption of innovative new technologies [44]. TOE and DOI have been widely accepted and adopted in IT adoption of innovation. They share some similarities, for example the consideration of technology and organisation context are almost the same in TOE and DOI. However, there are some differences between the two frameworks. DOI does not consider the environment context while in TOE, it is considered as part of organisational and technological context. In contrast, TOE does not consider individuals and some of the innovation characteristics, while DOI includes top management support in the organisational context and a wider range of the innovation characteristics. Generally, the TOE framework helps in identifying relevant categories for determinants while the DOI model helps in identifying specific variables within each category. Therefore, combining the two frameworks will complement each other and provide better understanding for the adoption. Further, in [41] it is argued that variables should be tailored to the characteristics of innovation. Therefore, the selection of variables is tailored to the context of migration to cloud computing. The variables were identified based on the analysis of the interviews in Stage 1, as well as the related literature. A hypothesis is created for each of the variables identified in the model, which are discussed in the following sections (Table 3 provides the list of the hypotheses).

Innovation characteristics

Relative advantages Migration to cloud computing can be a strategic decision for organisations to enhance the development of existing systems through improving

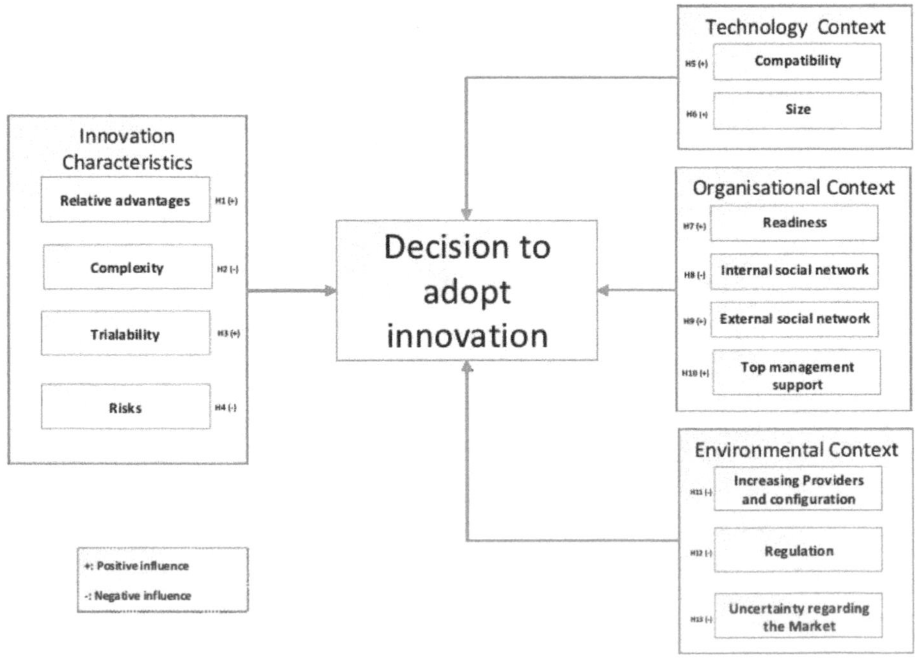

Fig. 4 The proposed model

Table 3 List of hypotheses

No	Hypotheses
H1	Organisations that perceive high relative advantages of cloud computing are more likely to migrate
H2	Perceiving cloud computing as a complex technology will negatively affect the decision to migrate
H3	Ease of testing in the cloud will positively influence the decision to migrate
H4	High perception of risks will negatively influence the decision to migrate
H5	The perception that cloud computing is less compatible with existing systems will negatively affect the decision to migrate
H6	High volumes of data are less likely to be migrated
H7	Organisations readiness will positively influence the decision to migrate to the cloud
H8	The impact of migration on the internal social network will negatively influence the decision to migrate
H9	The impact of migration on external social network will positively influence the decision to migrate
H10	Upper management support is positively related to the decision to migrate
H11	The process of selecting a cloud provider is difficult which negatively influences the decision to migrate
H12	Concerns about legal implication are negatively related to the decision to migrate
H13	Difficulties of information gathering will negatively influence the decision to migrate

scalability, flexibility, and time to market. The analysis of Stage 1 shows that cost reduction appears to be the strongest motivating factor from the participants' perspective for migration to cloud computing followed by agility. IT managers who participated in the survey believe that the need to implement a new service and finding cloud-based services to be the most economical choice are the main factors that drive cloud migration. It was also highlighted by participants in Stage 1 that for an organisation which wishes to set-up services more quickly, the cloud can offer what they cannot do internally. A cloud provider stated:

> *"One of the other things about the cloud that is attractive, but seems to come secondary to cost, but actually, is probably more important, is around agility and the ability to get new services much quicker than they can do internally."*

Enterprises can add or remove services as their businesses develop. In a technical sense, agile capabilities offered by the cloud enable enterprises to be much leaner. For example, a company in the UK decided to move to the cloud because they had a problem with agility, their internal processes and systems were too slow for what they wanted to do.

Cloud back-up was also highlighted by the participants as a perceived adavatage that can encourage organisations to migrate existing systems to the cloud. Cloud computing capabilities can enhance the availability of organisations systems by storing their data in a secure off-site backup. In the survey, a Technical Leader within a cloud provider company indicated that:

> *"It doesn't really make any sense to have an on-site facility that need maintenance with hardware that may fail, while it can be deployed in the cloud at a very low cost, higher performance and easy disaster recovery."*

Cloud back-up can significantly reduce the risk of impact as the two versions would be running at the same time in different locations with the ability of moving data across the two environments.

The analysis of the information in this section led to the formulation of the following hypothesis:

> H1: Organisations that perceive high relative advantages of cloud computing are more likely to migrate

Complexity The multi-user nature of cloud computing, as well as remote access, raises questions in respect of privacy and data confidentiality. Participants indicated that privacy and data confidentiality were their primary concerns in respect of the cloud environment. Further, interoperability was indicated by participants as the main perceived problem. Although cost reduction has been perceived as the main advatage that drives organisations to move to cloud computing, the analysis of stage 1 showed that the cost of cloud services emerged as an issue that some organisations faced when migrating to the cloud. Further, It was mentioned by the participants (cloud provider) that cost is the main reason for enterprises to back from the cloud. For example a cloud provider pointed out that "Costs are interesting because it's an instant attraction, but actually, very often clouds tends to be more expensive than people think it's going to be".

Cloud customers might need to pay for: data transfers in and out, storage of data in the cloud on a gigabyte per month basis, support, and additional availability. Therefore the combination of the charges a month actually become a considerable cost. A cloud provider pointed out that:

> "I think one of the first things to remember with a cloud is that many clients look at cloud as being a cheap option because they see a few cents per hour price. But that few cents per hour is usually the base

cost and then various additional services are added on, on top of it."

Further, cloud-based services are not always more economical than in-house provisions [45]. This depends upon the size of organisations and also on how long data is held. Usually, cloud computing is more cost effective for start-up companies or newly started organisations. On the other hand, companies that have large legacy-data will find migration more difficult and costly. For these organisations, cloud services would be more beneficial for the provision of new services, but not to replace or migrate already deployed services. The Reasons that emerged for moving back to locally managed IT resources are: migration to the cloud without having full knowledge of the cost of cloud-services; the cost of support; consultancy and other services which were expected to be provided without additional cost; cloud services running beyond working time, Failure on ROI; vendors' standards.

Participants also pointed out that the provision of cloud-based services is different from the traditional offering. The differences include the pricing and payment methods, performance monitoring, regulation and compliance, architecture, security, and service support. These differences require a certain expertise that enterprises do not usually have.

One interviewee from a cloud engineering company pointed out:

"The reason that we exist, and there are a growing number of these businesses, is because customers do not have the expertise to migrate to the cloud."

It also emerged from the interviews that cloud customers have high expections of the level of support. Many of the cloud services are self-administered whereas many customers are expecting 24/7 support.

A security analyst interviewed indicated that "a lack of knowledge about the cloud environment is the riskest part of migrating to the cloud". It was suggested by a number of interviewees that there is a need to develop an understanding about general security of the cloud environment. This will aid organisations to define their requirements and ensure a clear division of responsibilities with regard to Service Level Agreement (SLAs). It was noted that enterprises need to continually review the cloud market, due its dynamic costing nature and the services offered, for example, the cost of bandwidth will change, as will the cost of services. Therefore, it can be concluded that cloud computing has created more challenges for IT managers, because in the cloud IT management roles need to be shifted into technology implementation. The translation requires practical skills and an understanding of how to securely implement cloud services.

H2: Perceiving cloud computing as a complex technology will negatively affect the decision to migrate

Trialability Testing in the cloud environment emerged from the survey as an important advantage. Enterprises can use the virtual hardware for a period of time and then turn it off, whereas many organisations simply cannot afford to have, for example, ten spare physical servers available to be used for testing for a short time, and then turn them off.

H3: Ease of testing in the cloud will positively influence the decision to migrate

Risks The process of migration to the cloud may involve: a number of risks, loss of privacy, disruption to business processes, legal implications, problems with interoperability, data integrity, application portability, and security issues [20, 46–48]. The Cloud Security Alliance [49] identified 7 top threats in respect of cloud computing. These threats had led to wide concerns about the availability and accessibility of cloud based services. The IT managers and security professionals interviewed in this study expressed their concerns over security with regards to the migration of sensitive data. Further, the analysis showed concerns about potential risks to organisations that may include: loss of control, dependability, managing relationships with different cloud providers, liability, and business continuity and disaster recovery. For example, if an organisation is unable to access cloud services at a critical time, when it is largely depending on the cloud provider's customer service to provide information, this can lead to poor customer satisfaction. Therefore, it can be concluded that the possibility or even the perception of high risks can negatively affect the decision to migrate.

H4: High perception of risks will negatively influence the decision to migrate

Technology context

Compatibility Lack of standards in cloud computing usually raise interoperability, mobility, and manageability issues between cloud providers. This may increase the likelihood of vendor lock-in with possible economic impacts [33].

In cases where organisations need to implement a service tailored to their needs, cloud computing may only provide part of the solution. In such a case, the enterprise may require additional technical expertise to integrate the cloud solution with the in-house system – so-called 'hybrid cloud computing'.

Enterprises also need to evaluate the impact of migration to the cloud on the organisational culture and staff, due to possible unfamiliarity with the system and the environment. If a company wishes to migrate an existing system that has been developed and tailored over time with members of staff becoming accustomed to it, training would be required.

H5: The perception that cloud computing is less compatible with existing systems will negatively affect the decision to migrate

Size Organisations may need to predict their data volume as it has a direct impact on cost calculations. Usually, cloud computing is more cost effective for start-ups or newly started organisations [45]. On the other hand, companies that have large legacy-data will find migration more difficult and more expensive. For these organisations, cloud services, may be more beneficial for the provision of new services but not to replace, or migrate and deploy existing services.

H6: High volumes of data are less likely to be migrated

Organisation context

Readiness The heterogeneity of systems within organisations and their requirements have also affected the complexity of the decision making process when considering migration to cloud based solutions. Andrikopoulos et al. [6] pointed out that the decision whether to migrate, which cloud services to use and at which level to outsource is not trivial and that it largely depends on multiple factors that are specific to the context of each enterprise. Further, organisations have different business processes and interdependent criteria and constraints to consider when moving their systems to cloud environments [50]. The analysis of the Stage 1 also revealed that organisations have different expectations and understanding about the cloud environment.

The management related functions will become more important; for example, supplier relationships, service planning, contracts, negotiations, pricing, and procurement. These functions are required because enterprises need to maintain relationships with one or more cloud service providers that they have not used before. Further, organisations still need IT departments to monitor the cloud-based services and liaise with cloud providers for an effective system integration. Migration to the cloud will free IT managers from the burden of worrying about hardware, and they can focus on delivering better services. For example, one of the interviewees stated:

"So actually, it does change their perspective, but they actually focus on, 'what do my users need? What would be a better quality of service? What's a better performance time? And completely remove themselves from the hardware level."

The transformation of IT services has raised the need for new skills to deal with cloud-based services. It shifted roles and responsibilities from the local building and the support of internal resources to managing companies' systems in the cloud such as configuration, monitoring and integration of cloud services with the remaining on premise systems. These differences require a type of expertise that enterprises do not usually have.

H7: Organisations readiness will positively influence the decision to migrate to the cloud

Internal social network

The need for adapting existing services to be cloud enabled discussed in the interviews is a barrier against migrating existing systems to the cloud. According to [51] the systematic and efficient modernisation of legacy applications to exploit current cloud-based technologies remains a major challenge. Applications consist of several components that are connected with each other to comply with the application's functional and non-functional requirements [50]. These components need to be correctly adapted according to the target cloud environment. Failure or incorrect adaptation might result in difficulties in meeting some quality or economic requirements [50]. Typical adaptation problems range from compatibility and interoperability issues to licensing that may forbid organisations from moving registered software components.

Service performance may also be affected due to the increase in latency. These kinds of issues usually occur when a service component is shifted to the cloud while another dependent component is kept on-premises to meet security requirements [50]. Zhao and Zhou [52] identified the need for a holistic methodology from redesign and adaptation to application for special migration, architecture refactoring, integrated development environment and support migration of legacy applications to the cloud environment.

The security analysts interviewed in this study highlighted the importance of conducting risk analyses, because the business was originally based around a different type of architecture, and moving to the cloud could is seen as a dangerous way of doing business. The transfer may be risky and enterprises may need to adopt a different form of risk management going forward. However, if a business is newly-created, and it is based on the cloud and expands because of the cloud, then there should not be an issue.

Migrating an existing system may result in errors and significant costs to the changes involved. Organisations do not want to see disruptions to their business and many enterprises are anxious that system failure may affect their reputations. From the security analyst's perspective, the security experts interviewed in this study indicated that it is a risky move when a company that revolves around its central service, needs to give up what the entire business is anchored upon and move to a cloud solution. However, companies may use the migration as an opportunity to improve their systems and processes.

H8: The impact of migration on the internal social network will negatively influence the decision for migration

External social network

The cloud providers interviewed in this study indicated that cloud capabilities allow organisations to accomplish their business operations more effectively by sharing information and work cooperatively. The cloud environment offers platforms and tools in which information can be easily accessed internally and externally, thus enhancing collaboration with internal co-workers and external stakeholders.

Ferrer et al. [53] stated that economic factors are not sufficient for a highly dynamic environment in which relationships are created on an on-off basis with a possible high degree of anonymity between stakeholders. A broader perspective is required that should incorporate quality factors such as trust, reputation management and green assessment.

H9: The impact of migration on the external social network will positively influence the decision for migration

Top management support

Top management support plays an important role for the decision to migrate to cloud computing. It guides the allocation of resources, the integration of services, and the re-engineering of processes. Top management that recognizes the benefits of cloud computing are likely to allocate the necessary resources for its adoption and influence the organization's members to implement the change. When top management fails to recognize the benefits of cloud computing to the business, the management will be opposed to its adoption [54].

An outsourcing culture is a main factor for migration to cloud computing. Trust is a major factor that supports the decision-making for cloud migration, and an outsourcing culture can develop trust of migration systems to a third party.

H10: Upper management support is positively related to the decision to migrate

Environmental factors

Expansion in the number of services, providers and configurations Another factor that influences the complexity of migration decisions is the availability of vast numbers of cloud-based services that have different models, functionality, quality of service, costs, and configurations. The range of cloud-based services offered is growing simultaneously with the emergence of varying cloud service providers. Enterprises can find cloud based models of possibly everything from general-purpose applications such as email, and collaboration technologies to sales management and accounting software [55]. This rapid increase opens up new opportunities for designing new applications and enterprise architectures, new quality levels and capabilities. It increases the difficulty of choosing a provider and a service and renders the run-time adaptation and replacement of services almost impossible [20]. According to García-Galán et al. [56] there are over 100 public cloud providers associated with a considerable number of configurations, for example Amazon web services has 16,991 different configurations.

H11: The process of selecting a cloud provider is difficult which negatively influences the decision to migrate

Regulation The increase in the number of rules to regulate the adoption of cloud services, regulations and legal compliance violation has become a concern for many organisations.

Extensive concerns over regulation and legal compliance violations were indicated by the participants in Stage 1. Participants also registered concerns about the loss or misuse of data by others, SLA problems, data ownership and intellectual property rights. It was argued that enterprises need to ensure compliance with regulations. For example, one of the interviewees stated that:

"We have to be slightly careful with this when we're accepting payments online, we just have to be careful not to fall foul of things like tax, VAT and so on."

A cloud provider indicated that they used to run systems for various organisations that held credit card information. They removed all the payment card information from their servers because they were affected by regulations on payments and currently they link their system to a payment card service provider. Further, the interviewees showed concerns about the location of datacentres. If a company migrates to a multinational service provider, it may find some of its resources stored in other parts of the world, a situation that can create legal issues.

The simplicity of signing up new cloud based service contracts might result in SLA problems. SLA is a vital aspect in cloud computing. It includes agreements regarding the quality of service attributes, pricing, compliance to regulation, level of support, security and privacy guarantees, and others. Organisations need to review the general terms and conditions that providers usually include in SLAs.

H12: Concerns about legal implication are negatively related to the decision to migrate

Difficulties in information gathering about the cloud market Generally, information plays an important role in any decision making process, particularly during the intelligence and design phases of a decision making process. Participants perceived that there is a high level of availability of cloud related information. Although many organisations believe that cloud-related information can be easily obtained and is to some extent it is reliable, they do not find it easy to develop an understanding about the cloud environment. It can be due to the diversity of information sources and their complexity. This has resulted in uncertainty about the cloud market. It could be the reason for the issue of limited knowledge of customers in respect of the cloud environment.

H13: Difficulties of information gathering will negatively influence the decision for migration

Stage 2: testing the proposed model

To evaluate the proposed model, a survey questionnaire was conducted using a wide range of industries and organisations' sizes. The questions were based on the findings of Stage 1 (see Table 2) as well as the analysis of related literature. To ensure that the survey measured what was intended, a pilot survey was first conducted. Four participants were used for the pilot study. The feedback showed that the questions were understandable and the participants were able to provide the required answers, though a few amendments were suggested.

Zikmund [57] suggested that the target population is the entire group of subjects of interest who are defined by the research objectives. However, there is usually a considerable difference between the population that a researcher is attempting to study and their availably for sampling [58]. The sample population in this study are targeted professionals with experience in related disciplines and users. The sample in this study is convenient sampling in which the researcher attempted, as far as possible, to find participants from the target audience by distributing the questionnaire using various methods. The target audience were mainly invited by e-mails through personal contacts. The questionnaire was distributed to more than 1,000 professionals and potential users and 118 responses were received. Sixteen responses were incomplete, therefore they were eliminated from the analysis leaving 102 usable responses which is approximately ten per cent of the total population and consistent with what could be expected for a survey of this kind.

The population consisted of professionals who had been involved in cloud migration projects or they were researchers in the area. Participants were from organisations of different sizes and from a divers industry sectors. They included IT managers, software engineers, system analysts, and executive managers; in addition to cloud systems researchers. The survey reflected the issues which had been raised in Stage 1 affecting migration to cloud computing. Figure 5 shows demographic data of participants and their organisations.

The data was imported from the survey tool (survey Monkey) into an IBM SPSS sheet. The reliability of the questionnaire was calculated which was followed by exploratory factor analysis and confirmatory factor analysis. The constructs (relative advantages, complexity, testing, risks, compatibility, size, readiness, impact on internal social network, external social network, top management support, increasing service providers and configuration, regulatory, and uncertainty about the market) were measured using a five-point Likert scale on an interval level ranging from 1 (very low importance) to 5 (very high importance). To investigate how the determinants vary across different industries, organisation sizes, and relation to the cloud, the data was analysed, based on these indicators. For example, lower scores indicate low influence of a variable on the decision to migrate. However, the results show no major differences between different industries, therefore this paper discusses the overall results only.

Structural equation modelling

To test the research hypotheses, Structural Equation Modelling (SEM) [59] was used. SEM is a statistical approach for exploring the relationships between observed variables and latent variables. It includes two main components: the measurement model and the structural model. The measurement model shows relationships between latent variables and observed variables. It aims to provide reliability and validity, based on these variables. The structural model measures path strength and the direction of the relationships among the variables. It is first necessary to test the measurement

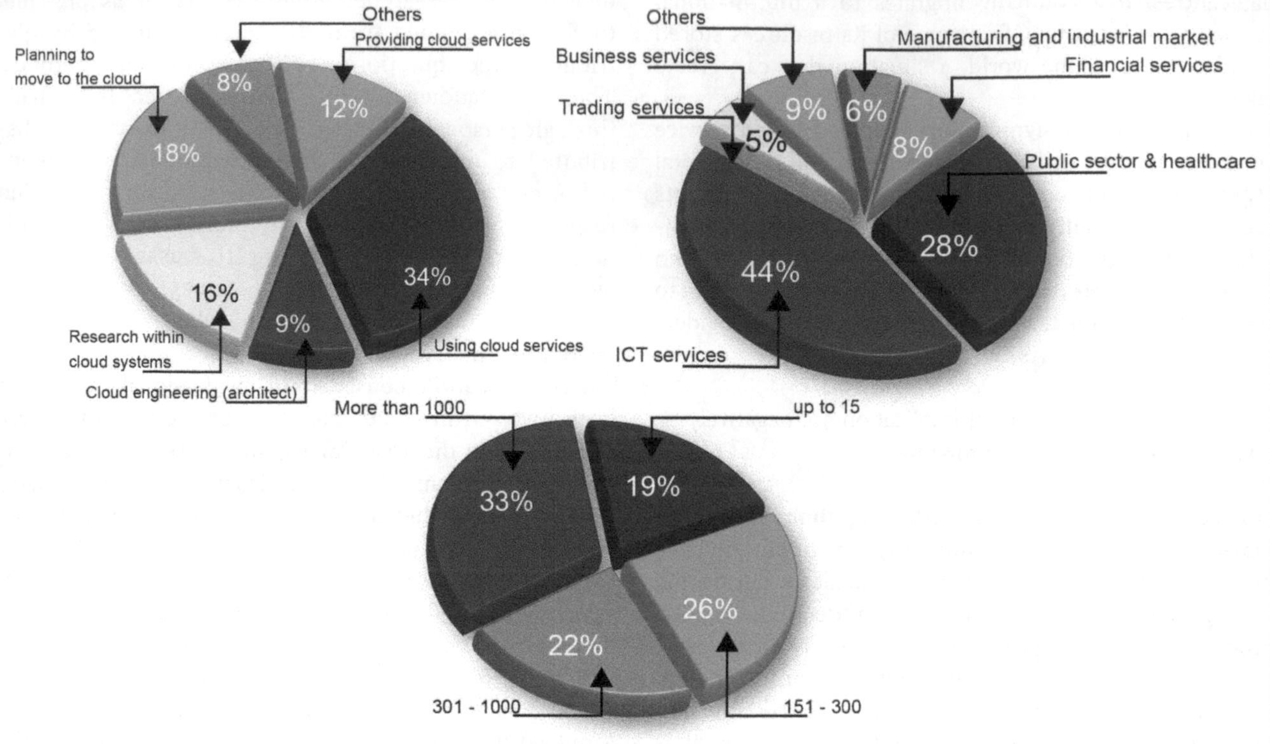

Fig. 5 Demographic of participants and their organisations

model and ensure that it has a satisfactory level of reliability and validity before exploring the significance of the relationships in the structural model.

Exploratory factor analysis

The result of applying the measurement model (reliability, convergent validity, discriminant validity, and descriptive statistics) are shown in Tables 4, 5, and 6. In order to test construct reliability for a set of two or more constructs (i.e. to examine internal consistency), the reliability of the scales was tested using composite reliability (CR) (more details may be found in [59]). The Cronbach's alpha [58] is a widely adopted method for testing CR. It generates coefficient values ranging between 0 and 1 with higher values indicating higher reliability of the indicators. Fornell and Larcker [60] indicated that CR should have a value greater than 0.70 for a respectable research quality. The calculation formula for CR is: (Σ standardised loading)2 / (Σ standardised loading)2 + Σ ε) where ε = error variance and Σ is summation.

Composite reliability analysis shows a Cronbach's "α" value of 0.773 for the 13 variables in the research model, which indicates high reliability and internal consistency (see Table 4). Further, the scale was factor analysed using principal component analysis.

In order to analyse the strength of association among the variables, the constructs validity was tested using the Bartlett's Test of Sphericity and the Kaiser-Mayer-Olkin (KMO) for the measure of sampling adequacy [61]. The result for Bartlett's test of Sphericity and the KMO value was 0.000 and 0.688 respectively (see Table 4). The latter value is more than 0.5, which shows a high level of sampling adequacy.

Examining the correlation (Table 5) shows the highest level of correlation between constructs regulation and top management (0.82). This is followed by correlation between compatibility and size of data (0.72) as well as regulation and increasing providers (0.77).

Discriminant validity refers to the extent to which a construct is truly distinct from other constructs [58]. A widely used statistical measure for discriminant validity

Table 4 Reliability of reflective constructs and KMO and Bartlett's Test

Reliability Statistics		
Cronbach's Alpha		N of Items
0.773		13
Results of the KMO and Bartlett's Test		
Kaiser-Meyer-Olkin Measure of Sampling Adequacy		0.688
Bartlett's Test of Sphericity	Approx. Chi-Square	414.500
	Degrees of freedom	78
	Sig.	0.00

Table 5 Correlation matrix

	RT	Cox	Testing	Risks	Compat	Size	Readyiness	Internal	External	Top management	Increasing providers	Regulate	Uncertinty
RT	1												
Cox	0.307185	1											
Testing	0.333801	0.20755	1										
Risks	0.432754	0.268197	0.206796	1									
Compat	0.220682	0.214349	0.227881	0.189518	1								
Size	0.276315	0.182915	0.208967	0.228618	0.793956	1							
Readyiness	0.267539	0.229533	0.219943	0.351581	0.234763	0.37207	1						
Internal	0.488697	0.144878	0.24622	0.354	0.157467	0.18358	0.1697743	1					
External	-0.03528	-0.08172	0.026308	0.060377	0.260662	0.22234	0.1640954	0.033231	1				
Top management	0.261611	0.336494	0.40907	0.345047	0.198847	0.27952	0.2820392	0.142431	0.063349	1			
Increasing providers	0.467624	0.432405	0.205529	0.352672	0.17559	0.26306	0.358264	0.311289	0.079038	0.287017103	1		
Regulate	0.446163	0.475076	0.39047	0.434137	0.234031	0.33847	0.3957604	0.276039	0.088055	0.828655065	0.774046124	1	
Uncertinty	0.302544	0.107049	0.045388	0.176953	0.047559	0.01458	0.2239462	0.229714	0.019811	0.203366383	0.183714333	0.241765	1

Table 6 Descriptive statistical

Variable	Minimum	Maximum	Median	Mean	Standard Deviation
I1 Cost Reduction	3.0	5.0	4.0	4.45	0.71
I1Agility	2.0	5.0	4.0	4.24	0.91
I1 Back-up	2.0	5.0	4.0	4.09	0.80
I1 Higher performance	2.0	5.0	4.0	4.20	0.68
I1 Average	2.25	5.0	4.0	4.24	0.77
I2 Lack of knowledge	2.0	5.0	4.0	4.18	0.83
I2 Cost management	2.0	5.0	4.0	3.54	1.04
I2 Risk management	3.0	5.0	5.0	4.66	0.58
I2 Average	2.0	5.0	4.0	4.12	0.86
I3 Testing	3.0	5.0	4.0	3.98	0.80
I4 Privacy and confidentiality	3.0	5.0	5.0	4.39	0.75
I4 Vendor lock in	1.0	5.0	4.0	3.72	1.03
I4 Loss of control	2.0	5.0	4.0	4.26	0.79
I4 Average	2.0	5.0	4.3	4.12	0.89
T1 Impact on culture and staff	1.0	5.0	5.0	3.49	0.94
T1 Interpretability issues	2.0	5.0	4.0	4.22	0.83
T1 Average	1.5	5.0	4.5	3.85	0.88
T2 Size	1.0	5.0	4.0	3.56	0.99
O1 Current IT infrastructure	1.0	5.0	4.0	4.15	0.77
O1 Level of expertise	1.0	5.0	3.0	3.71	0.90
O1 Average	1.0	5.0	3.5	3.92	0.99
O2 The need for adaptation	1.0	5.0	4.0	3.88	1.03
O2 Disruption to BP	1.0	5.0	4.0	3.84	0.91
O2 Average	1.0	5.0	4.0	3.86	0.97
O3 Collaboration	1.0	5.0	4.0	2.84	1.17
O4 Top management support	1.0	5.0	4.0	4.15	0.77
E1 Provider selection	1.0	5.0	4.0	4.24	0.84
E1 Increasing providers and configurations	1.0	5.0	4.0	4.16	0.78
E1 Average	1.0	5.0	4.0	4.20	0.81
E2 Legal implication	1.0	5.0	4.0	4.22	0.76
E2 IP	2.0	5.0	4.0	4.32	0.71
E2 SLA	2.0	5.0	4.0	4.20	0.81
E2 Average	1.6	5.0	4.0	4.25	0.76
E3 Accessibility	2.0	5.0	4.0	3.81	0.88
E3 Complexity	2.0	5.0	3.0	3.0	0.89
E3 Average	2.0	5.0	3.5	3.49	0.89

is a comparison of the Average Variance Extracted (AVE) with correlation squared [62]. In order to ensure discriminant validity, the AVE of two constructs must be more than the square of the correlation between the same two constructs. Our results show that AVE mean square root of each value variable is significantly greater than its correlation coefficient with other variables (see Table 5), thus discriminant validity is supported. Overall, the results show acceptable reliability, convergent validity and discriminant validity, which were appropriate for testing the research model.

Table 5 provides the correlation matrix for discriminant validity, which indicates the degree to which the constructs diverge from each other.

Confirmatory factor analysis

To test the stability of the scale, confirmatory factor analysis was employed using SEM to examine the hypothesized research model by performing a simultaneous test. A measurement model was developed using the AMOS tool and Maximum Likelihood Estimation (MLE) method was chosen for confirmatory factor analysis. MLE is a common estimation procedure used in SEM software. It does not require large sample size and the results of the method are reliable. Therefore, it is widely used in theoretical hypothesis testing. The structural model shows path coefficients results. It illustrates the extent of the mutual influence among variables. Path coefficient was calculated automatically by the tool. Figure 6 shows the standardized results for the structural model.

Results and discussion

The results of the analysis of Stage 2 reveal that 10 out of the 13 variables identified in the research model (see Fig. 4) significantly influenced the decision making for migrating to the cloud. Size of data volume, testing, and the impact on external network are not significant factors.

The Relative advantages factor is supported as a positive influence on the decision to migrate existing resources to the cloud. It has a significant ($p < 0.05$) and positive coefficient of 0.18, when considering migrating to the cloud. Within this variable the cost benefits factor was rated the highest (4.45) followed by agility (4.24), higher performance (4.20), and the back-up advantages (4.09) as shown in Table 6. This finding confirms the results found in similar previous studies that identified perceived advantages as the most influential factor for adopting cloud services (see for example: [9, 37, 38, 62, 63]). The realisation of the relative advantages shows that organisations perceive the cloud environment as a platform for rationalising expenditure and improving efficiency. Organisations need to review the cloud offers and appreciate how the advantages of the cloud provisions can be exploited in improve their business performances. This can lead to improvements in customer service, cost management, relationship with customers and stakeholders, management structure and policies, and business objectives.

The complexity of the cloud environment factor is confirmed in Stage 2 as a negative influence for the decision to migrate to the cloud, with path coefficient of (– 0.14). Within this variable organisations, perceived conducting a risk management for the migration as very difficult with an average rating of 4.47. This is followed by lack of

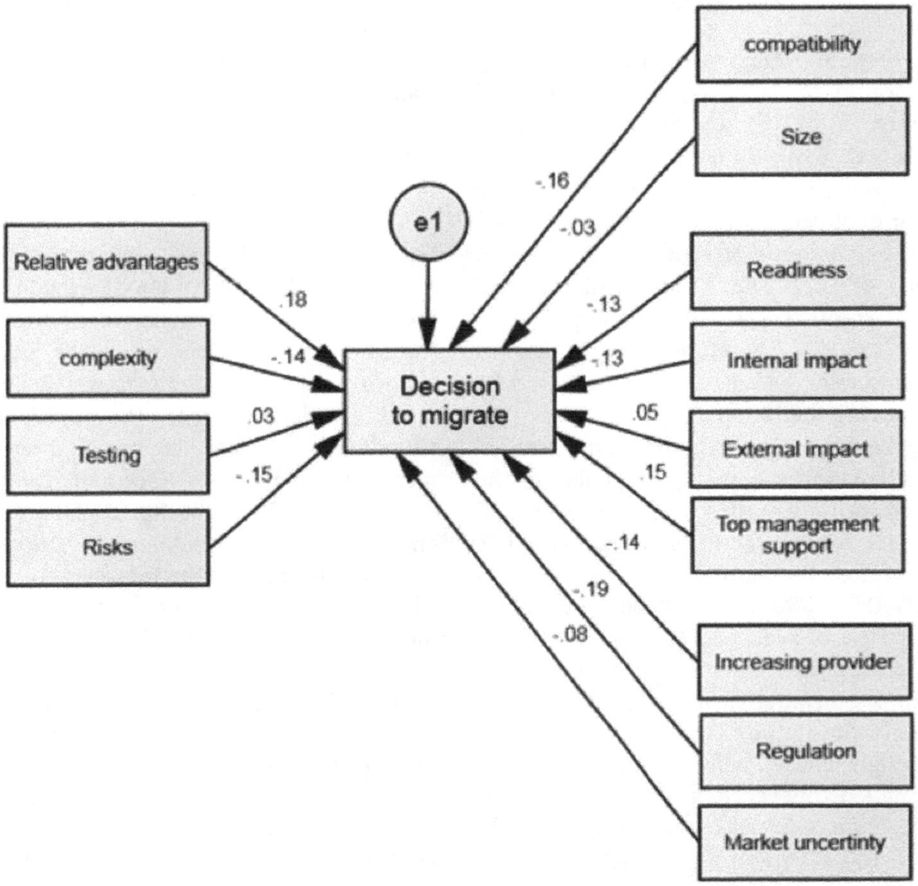

Fig. 6 Structural equation modelling using AMOS tool. e1: error variance

knowledge about the cloud environment with an average rating of 4.03 and the complexity of managing costs (3.62). Pervious works showed different results regarding the perceived complexity of cloud environment. Oliveira et al. [63] presented results in line with these findings; however, other studies suggested the opposite that the cloud environment is not perceived as a complex technology [13] and [64]. Cloud computing is a disruptive model of provisioning IT services, therefore perceiving it as complex environment is expected. The complexity can be mitigated by taking advantage of the testing facilities in the cloud that can allow organisations to be more familiar with the new environment. Further, the cloud is still in a growing phase and its complexity and risks are expected to be reduced.

Although ease of testing in the cloud environment is perceived by many as an advantage encouraging organisations to migrate to the cloud, it is not supported by our findings as a critical influencing factor for the decision to migrate. This may be due to the fact that the majority of the organisations who participated in this study are small and medium size (SME) and testing is not a critical factor for them. Further, testing would be more relevant to larger organisations such as universities and research centres which are not highly represented in this study.

The perception that migrating to the cloud is *a risky decision* factor is found to negatively affect companies' decisions to migrate to the cloud. This factor scored a path coefficient of - 0.15. Within this category privacy and confidentiality scored the highest with an average rate of 4.21 followed by the concerns of losing control rated at 4.09, and the concerns of vendor lock-in scored an average rating of 3.73. This result substantiates similar studies that conducted at the beginning of cloud adoption such as [13–15]. Therefore, security, fear of losing control, and vendor lock-in are still perceived by many as issues deterring migration.

Within the technology context, the *compatibility* factor is confirmed to as a negatively influence on the decision to migrate with a path coefficient of - 0.16 while the *size* of data volume factor is not supported as an important factor for the decision to migrate with a path coefficient of –0.03. Within this variable, impact on culture and staff scored an average rating of 3.49 and interpretability issues obtained 4.22. To manage the impact on staffing, organisations need to analyse the anticipated change to the staffing level, roles and expertise during the design phase, before commencing the process of migrating existing services to the cloud.

In respect of the organisational context, readiness, *the impact on internal networks*, and top management realisation of the business benefits factors have significant effects, with path coefficients of - 0.13, – 0.13, 0.15 respectively, while *the impact of external network* factor does not (0.05). This result shows that organisations that have higher levels of readiness require less adaptation, support from top management for cloud environment are more likely to migrate.

In the environment context, all variables have a significant effect, in particular the *regulation* factor, with a path coefficient of - 0.19 which is the highest influencing factor. The increasing service providers factor scored path coefficient of - 0.14 and the uncertainty about the market factor obtained - 0.08. Many organisations comply with regulators in their internal systems management, but by adopting cloud services, part of their service management can be shifted to the cloud service provider. In this scenario organisations need to know how to continue their compliance with the regulators which could be a challenge. Organisations need to review the general terms and conditions that providers usually include in SLAs. Companies need to review vendors' standard contracts, to see if their basic terms are sufficient for their organisational compliance requirements, and to ensure service providers' compliance with their regulators. Table 7 shows the results of testing the research hypotheses.

In order to improve trust in the cloud services, providers need to ensure privacy and data confidentiality of their customers. Further, complying with relevant standards would help in reducing the risks of vendor lock-in. This issue is partly caused by the lack of standardisation in cloud computing which was also indicated by participants as an issue that contributed to the complexity of cloud computing. In order to help organisations to decide whether to migrate to the cloud, there is a need to inform them about general security; whether the security of the infrastructure is resilient. The project manager should then move to the performance aspects by providing information about the opportunities and options which will meet the customer's requirements. The decision makers may not be interested in the technical details but it is important for them to see the business benefit. These items of information will allow enterprises to build confidence in the cloud service management. Based on this information, it should be possible to advise enterprises which cloud solution will be most suitable for them. Therefore, providers need to ensure the privacy and confidentiality of their customers' data, employ comprehensive costing models, in addition to complying with relevant standards to reduce the risks of vendor lock-in. These could remedy the high level of perceiving the migration to the cloud as a risky decision.

Contribution

This paper focused on the decision to migrate existing resources to the cloud. It empirically explored factors

Table 7 Results of hypotheses testing

No	Hypotheses	Coefficient	Result
H1 (+)	Organisations that perceive high relative advantages of cloud computing are more likely to migrate	0.18	Supported ($p < 0.05$)
H2 (−)	Perceiving cloud computing as a complex technology will negatively affect the decision to migrate	−0.14	Supported ($p < 0.05$)
H3 (+)	Ease of testing in the cloud will positively influence the decision to migrate	0.03	Not supported
H4 (−)	High perception of risks will negatively influence the decision to migrate	−0.14	Supported ($p < 0.05$)
H5 (−)	The perception that cloud computing is less compatible with existing systems will negatively affect the decision to migrate	−0.16	Supported ($p < 0.05$)
H6 (−)	High volumes of data are less likely to be migrated	−0.03	Not Supported
H7 (+)	Organisations readiness will positively influence the decision to migrate to the cloud	−0.13	Supported ($p < 0.05$)
H8 (−)	The impact of migration on the internal social network will negatively influence the decision to migrate	−0.13	Supported ($p < 0.05$)
H9 (+)	The impact of migration on external social network will positively influence the decision to migrate	0.05	Not Supported
H10 (+)	Upper management support is positively related to the decision to migrate	0.15	Supported ($p < 0.05$)
H11 (−)	The process of selecting a cloud provider is difficult which negatively influences the decision to migrate	−0.14	Supported ($p < 0.05$)
H12 (−)	Concerns about legal implication are negatively related to the decision to migrate	−0.19	Supported ($p < 0.05$)
H13 (−)	Difficulties of information gathering will negatively influence the decision to migrate	−0.8	Supported ($p < 0.05$)

influencing the decision to migrate by designing a model, based on TOE and DOI frameworks. The findings of this research has expanded the collective knowledge about the complexity of the issues that have to be considered when making decisions to migrate to the cloud. Seven determinants were identified that influence the complexity of decisions to migrate (see H2, H4, H5, H8, H11, H12, and H13 in Table 7). Some of the factors are similar to those which have been identified in previous studies that were conducted at an early stage of the evolution of cloud computing. This paper confirms that those factors are still being perceived as deterrent for migration. They are: H4, H5, and H12 while the other four are novel contributions unique to this paper. Further, the findings in this research are quite different compared to similar studies in that the majority of them explored the factors affecting the adoption of cloud services while this research focused on the migration of legacy systems.

The analysis in this paper shows that cloud computing is perceived by many as a valuable opportunity for business benefits such as cost reduction, agility, back-ups, and higher business performance. However, it identified a number of factors that increased the complexity of decisions to migrate. It highlighted how enterprises perceived the level of complexity of the cloud environment and the expertise required to design and manage cloud services. In particular, this research highlighted the lack of knowledge about the cloud environment. It also identified lack of expertise within organisations for design and management of cloud services. Further, our results confirm that cloud computing is in its early stages, and is still evolving. It also showed that financial benefits of cloud services vary and cost is found to be the main reason for enterprises that moved back from the cloud. Further, this study supported the view that since the emergence of cloud computing, security has been the main problem perceived by many organisations.

This study provides a better understanding of a wide range of factors that affect the decision making process for migration to the cloud. They can asset cloud DSS developers in the designing of systems that address their issue and concerns. Specifically, the application of the Simon's model for a systematic decision process for the cloud DSS shows that there is limited support at the intelligence and design phases. The analysis of this research shows a number of factors that require cloud DSS to provide support at intelligence (e.g. H2 in Table 7) and design (e.g. H5 in Table 7) levels. Therefore, this study contributes to the literature that addresses the complexity and multidimensional nature of migrating IT resources to the cloud.

Conclusion

Cloud computing is a new paradigm for emerging technologies. Migration to cloud computing is a strategic organisational decision that is complicated, dynamic, and highly unstructured. The cloud environment is still evolving; therefore, decision makers need to carefully evaluate the capabilities of cloud computing services to determine whether this style of computing will help them achieve their business goals. It requires the consideration and evaluation of a wide range of technical and organisational aspects. This research is aimed to support the decision making process for migrating existing resources to the cloud. It explored factors contributing to the complexity of the decision to migrate.

The review of current approaches for migration to the cloud revealed that, although many methods have been proposed to aid migration to it, the level of support offered by the existing DSS is not sufficient to enable decision makers to make informed decisions. Accordingly, many organisations are still finding it difficult to make decisions migrating existing resources to the cloud. This is mainly due to many complex factors that affect decision making to migrate to the cloud.

Understanding the level of complexity for making decisions to migrate aids the development of suitable resources and processes to simplify it. Accordingly, this paper extensively explored the factors affecting decision making. By integrating the innovation characteristics of the DOI and the TOE frameworks a model was developed. The model was empirically evaluated using the exploratory and confirmatory analysis, which identified the factors that have a significant positive or negative effect on the decision to migrate. A future work to enhance the findings of this study can be further examination of correlation between the identified variables. In addition, significant factors affecting migrations can be included in cloud DSSs.

Acknowledgements
The research leading to these results is supported by the faculty of science and Technology at Bournemouth University.

Authors' contributions
All listed authors worked closely throughout the development of this research and made major contributions. AA was responsible for literature review and data collection and analysis. Dr RS and Dr DJ contributed in the designing of the methodology including the design of the research instruments. All authors participated in drafting the manuscript, analysis and interpretation of study results. RS and DJ participated in the critical and technical revisions of the paper including editing the final version. They supervised the project related to the paper and also gave final approval of the version to be published. All authors read and approved final manuscript.

Authors' information
Adel Alkhalil is a recently PhD graduate from Bournemouth University, UK under supervision of Dr Reza Sahandi and Dr David John. In September 2016, Dr Alkhalil joined the faculty of computer science and engineering at the University of Hail, Saudi Arabia. His research interests include cloud computing, decision support systems, knowledge-based systems.
Reza Sahandi completed his PhD at Bradford University in the United Kingdom in 1978. He has been a senior academic at various Universities in the United Kingdom for many years. He is currently Associate Professor at Bournemouth University. He has supervised many PhD students. His research areas include multimedia and network systems, wireless remote patient monitoring and cloud computing.
David John completed his PhD at in the United Kingdom in 2002. Since then he has been an academic member in the faculty of computer science and engineering at Bournemouth University. His research interests include cloud computing, expressive Internet communication, assessing the effect cognitive style has on the perception of different modes of communication, and the evaluation of creative practice-based assessment methods.

Competing interests
The authors declare that they have no competing interests.

Author details
[1]Faculty of Computer Science and Engineering, University of Hail, Hail, Saudi Arabia. [2]Faculty of Science and Technology, Bournemouth University, Poole, UK.

References
1. Jennings B, Stadler R (2015) Resource management in clouds: Survey and research challenges. J Netw Syst Manag 23(3):567–619
2. Dhinesh Babu LD, Gunasekaran A, Krishna PV (2014) A decision-based pre-emptive fair scheduling strategy to process cloud computing work-flows for sustainable enterprise management. Int J Bus Inf Syst 16(4):409–430
3. Armbrust M, Fox A, Griffith R, Joseph AD, Katz R, Konwinski A, Zaharia M (2010) A view of cloud computing. Communications of the ACM 53(4):50–58
4. Buyya R, Yeo CS, Venugopal S, Broberg J, Brandic I (2009) Cloud computing and emerging IT platforms: Vision, hype, and reality for delivering computing as the 5th utility. Futur Gener Comput Syst 25(6):599–616
5. Phaphoom N, Wang X, Samuel S, Helmer S, Abrahamsson P (2015) A survey study on major technical barriers affecting the decision to adopt cloud services. J Syst Softw 103:167–181
6. Andrikopoulos V, Binz T, Leymann F, Strauch S (2013) How to adapt applications for the Cloud environment. Computing 95(6):493–535
7. Rai R, Sahoo G, Mehfuz S (2013) Securing software as a service model of cloud computing: Issues and solutions. International Journal on Cloud Computing: Services and Architecture (IJCCSA) 3(4):1–11
8. Oredo JO, Njihia JM (2015) Mindfulness and quality of innovation in cloud computing adoption, Int J Bus Manage, 10(1):144
9. Hsu PF, Ray S, Li-Hsieh YY (2014) Examining cloud computing adoption intention, pricing mechanism, and deployment model. Int J Inf Manag 34(4): 474–488
10. Buyya R (2009) Market-oriented cloud computing: Vision, hype, and reality of delivering computing as the 5th utility. In: 9Th IEEE/ACM International Symposium on Cluster Computing and the Grid, CCGRID
11. Mell P, Grance T (2009) The NIST Definition of Cloud Computing. Natl Inst Stand Technol 53(6):50
12. Leimeister S, Christoph R, Markus B, Helmut K (2010) The Business Perspective of Cloud Computing: Actors, Roles and Value Networks, European Conference on Information Systems
13. Low C, Chen Y, Wu M (2011) Understanding the determinants of cloud computing adoption. Ind Manag Data Syst 111(7):1006–1023
14. Wu WW (2011) Mining significant factors affecting the adoption of SaaS using the rough set approach. J Syst Softw 84(3):435–441
15. Sahandi R, Alkhalil A, Opara-Martins J (2012) SMEs' Perception of Cloud Computing: Potential and Security. In: Collaborative Networks in the Internet of Services. PRO-VE 2012. IFIP Advances in Information and Communication Technology, 380, Springer, Berlin, pp 186-195
16. Lin A, Chen N (2012) Cloud computing as an innovation: Perception, attitude, and adoption. Int J Inf Manag 32(6):533–540, Available from: http://www.sciencedirect.com/science/article/pii/S0268401212000539. Accessed 16 May 2016
17. Morgan L, Conboy K (2013) Factors affecting the adoption of cloud computing: an exploratory study., pp 1–12
18. Khajeh-Hosseini A, Greenwood D, Smith J, Sommerville I (2012) The Cloud Adoption Toolkit: Supporting cloud adoption decisions in the enterprise. Software - Practice And Experience 42(4):447–465
19. Menzel M, Ranjan R, Wang L, Khan S, Chen J (2014) Cloudgenius: A hybrid decision support method for automating the migration of web application clusters to public clouds. IEEE transactions on 64(5):1336–1348

20. Omerovic A, Muntes-Mulero V, Matthews P, Gunka A (2013) Towards a Method for Decision Support in Multi-cloud Environments. In: the fourth International Conference on Cloud Computing, GRIDs, and Virtualisation., pp 244–250
21. Andrikopoulos V, Song Z, Leymann F (2013) Supporting the Migration of Applications to the Cloud through a Decision Support System. In: IEEE Sixth International Conference on Cloud Computing., pp 565–572
22. Garg SK, Versteeg S, Buyya R (2013) A framework for ranking of cloud computing services. Futur Gener Comput Syst 626(4):1012–1023
23. Saez S G, Andrikopoulos V,Hahn M, Karastoyanova D, Leymann F, Skouradaki M, Vukojevic-Haupt K (2015) Performance and Cost Evaluation for the Migration of a Scientific Workflow Infrastructure to the Cloud, 5th International Conference of Cloud Computing and Service Science, CLOSER 2015, Lisbon, Portugal, pp 1-10
24. Gonidis F, Paraskakis I, Simons AJ (2014) Leveraging Platform Basic Services in Cloud Application Platforms for the Development of Cloud Applications. In: IEEE 6th International Conference on Cloud Computing Technology and Science., pp 751–754
25. Pahl C, Xiong H, Walshe R (2013) A comparison of on-premise to cloud migration approaches. In: European Conference on Service-Oriented and Cloud Computing ESOCC., pp 11–13
26. Simon HA (1977) The new science of management decision, 2nd edn. Prentice Hall, Englewood Cliffs (NJ)
27. Liu S, Duffy A, Whitfield R, Boyle IND (2010) Integration of decision support systems to improve decision support performance. Knowl And Inf Syst 22(3):261–286
28. Turban E, Aronson J, Liang TP (2005) Decision Support Systems and Intelligent Systems, 7th edn., Pearson Prentice Hall
29. Oracle (2012) Cloud Integration – A Comprehensive Solution. Oracle
30. Amazon EC2 (2015). Available from: https://d0.awsstatic.com/whitepapers/RDS/AWS_Database_Migration_Service_Best_Practices.pdf. Accessed 16 May 2016.
31. Accenture (2013) Putting the cloud to work with Accenture. Available from: https://www.accenture.com/t20150623T023251__w__/us-en/_acnmedia/Accenture/Conversion-Assets/DotCom/Documents/Global/PDF/Technology_2/Accenture-Putting-Cloud-Work-Acn.pdf. Accessed 16 May 2016.
32. Khajeh-Hosseini A, Sommerville I, Bogaerts J, Teregowda P (2011) Decision support tools for cloud migration in the enterprise. In: Proceedings - 2011 IEEE 4th International Conference on Cloud Computing, CLOUD., pp 541–548
33. Opara-Martin J, Sahandi R, Tian F (2016) Critical Analysis of Vendor Lock-in and its Impact on Cloud Computing Migration: A Business Perspective. Journal of Cloud Computing Advances, Systems and Applications 5:4, Available from: http://link.springer.com/article/10.1186/s13677-016-0054-z. Accessed 16 May 2016
34. Tornatzky LG, Fleischer M (1990) The processes of technological innovation. Lexington Books, Lexington, MA
35. Rogers EM (2003) Diffusion of innovations, 5th edn. Free Press, New York
36. Ramdani B, Chevers DA, Williams D (2013) SMEs' adoption of enterprise applications: A technology-organisation-environment model. Journal of Small Business and Enterprise Development 20(4):735–753
37. Gangwar H, Date H, Ramaswamy R (2015) Understanding determinants of cloud computing adoption using an integrated TAM-TOE model. J Enterp Inf Manag 28(1):107–130
38. Lian JW, Yen DC, Wang YT (2014) An exploratory study to understand the critical factors affecting the decision to adopt cloud computing in Taiwan hospital. Int J Inf Manag 34(1):28–36
39. Tashkandi AA, Al-Jabri, Ibrahim M (2015) Cloud Computing Adoption by Higher Education Institutions in Saudi Arabia International Conference on Cloud Computing. Riyadh, Saudi Arabia, Available from: http://ssrn.com/abstract=2624564. Accessed 16 May 2016
40. Prescott MB (1995) Diffusion of innovation theory: Borrowings, extensions and modifications from IT researchers. Data Base 26(2&3):16–19
41. Chau PYK, Tam KY (1997) Factors affecting the adoption of open systems: an exploratory study. MIS Q 21:1–24
42. Alkhalil A, Sahandi R, John D (2013) Migration to Cloud Computing-The Impact on IT Management and Security. In: 1st International Workshop on Cloud Computing and Information Security. Atlantis Press, Shanghai, China, pp 196–200
43. Alkhalil A, Sahandi R, John D (2014) Migration to Cloud Computing: A Decision Process Model. In th 25th Central European Conference on Information and Intelligent Systems, CECIIS-2014. Faculty of Organization and Informatics Varazdin, Varazdin. pp 17–19
44. Fichman RG (2004) Going beyond the dominant paradigm for information technology innovation research: emerging concepts and methods. J Assoc Inf Syst 5:314–355
45. Misra S, Mondal A (2011) Identification of a company's suitability for the adoption of cloud computing and modelling its corresponding Return on Investment. Mathematical And Computer Modelling 53(3):504–521
46. Motahari-Nezhad H R, Stephenson, B, Singhal S (2009) Outsourcing business to cloud computing services: Opportunities and challenges. IEEE Internet Computing, 10(4):1-17
47. Sahandi R, Alkhalil A, Opara-Martins J (2013) Cloud Computing from SMEs perspective: a Survey based Investigation. J Inf Technol Manag 24(1):1–12
48. Willcocks L, Venters W, Whitley E A (2011) Clear view of the cloud: The business impact of cloud computing. Available from: https://www.scribd.com/document/65119786/Accenture-Outlook-Clear-View-of-the-Cloud-Computing-The-Business-Impact-of-Cloud-Computing. Accessed 30 Dec 2016
49. CSA (2013) Practices for Secure Development of Cloud. Cloud security Alliance, Available from: http://www.safecode.org/publications/SAFECode_CSA_Cloud_Final1213.pdf. Accessed 10 July 2013
50. Juan-Verdejo A, Baars H, Kemper H, Surajbali B, Zschaler S (2014) InCLOUDer: A formalised decision support modelling approach to migrate applications to cloud environments. In: Proceedings - 40Th Euromicro Conference Series On Software Engineering And Advanced Applications, SEAA., pp 67–474
51. Bergmayr A, Bruneliere H, Canovas Izquierdo JL, Gorronogoitia J, Kousiouris G, Kyriazis D, Wimmer M (2013) Migrating legacy software to the cloud with ARTIST. In: IEEE Software Maintenance and Reengineering (CSMR), European Conference., pp 465–468
52. Zhao JF, Zhou JT (2014) Strategies and methods for cloud migration. Int J Autom Comput 11(2):143–152
53. Ferrer A, Hernández F, Tordsson J, Elmroth E, Ali-Eldin A, Zsigri C, Sirvent R, Guitart J, Badia R, Djemame K, Ziegler W, Dimitrakos T, Nair S, Kousiouris G, Konstanteli K, Varvarigou T, Hudzia B, Kipp A, Wesner S, Corrales M, Forgó N, Sharif T, Sheridan C (2012) OPTIMIS: A holistic approach to cloud service provisioning. Futur Gener Comput Syst 28:66–77
54. Amini M, Bakri A, Sadat Safavi N, Javadinia SA, Tolooei A (2014) The Role of Top Manager Behaviours on Adoption of Cloud Computing for Small and Medium Enterprises. Aust J Basic Appl Sci 8(1):490–498
55. Gogrid (2012) Cloud computing adoption slower than expected, Available from. http://www.gogrid.com/news/2012 February 22/cloud-computing-adoption-slower-thanexpected. Accessed 10 July 2013.
56. García-Galán J, Trinidad P, Rana O F, Ruiz-Cortés A (2016) Automated configuration support for infrastructure migration to the cloud, Futur Gener Comput Syst, 55, pp.200-212 Available from:http://www.sciencedirect.com/science/article/pii/S0167739X15000618. Accessed 1 June 2015.
57. Zikmund WG (2000) Business Research Methods, 6th edn. the Dryden Press, Chicago, IL
58. Hair JF, Anderson RE, Tatham RL, Black WC (1992) Multivariate Data Analysis, 3rd edn. Macmillan, New York
59. Hoyle RH (1995) The structural equation modeling approach: Basic concepts and fundamental issues. In: Hoyle RH (ed) Structural equation modeling: Concepts, issues, and applications. Sage Publications, Inc., Thousand Oaks, CA, pp 1–15
60. Fornell C, Larcker DF (1981) Evaluating structural equation models with unob-servable variables and measurement error. J Market Res 18(1):39–50
61. Beavers AS, Lounsbury JW, Richards JK, Huck SW, Skolits GJ, Esquivel SL (2013) Practical considerations for using exploratory factor analysis in educational research. Practical assessment, research & evaluation 18(6):1–13
62. Alshamaila Y, Papagiannidis S, Li F (2013) Cloud computing adoption by SMEs in the north east of England: A multi-perspective framework. J Enterp Inf Manag 26(3):250–275
63. Oliveira T, Thomas M, Espadanal M (2014) Assessing the determinants of cloud computing adoption: An analysis of the manufacturing and services sectors. Inf Manag 51(5):497–501, Available from: http://www.sciencedirect.com/science/article/pii/S0378720614000391. Accessed 16 May 2016
64. Borgman HP, Bahli B, Heier H, Schewski F (2013) Cloudrise: exploring cloud computing adoption and governance with the TOE framework. In: System Sciences (HICSS), 46th Hawaii International Conference on IEEE., pp 4425–4435
65. Frey S, Hasselbring W (2011) he cloudmig approach: Model-based migration of software systems to cloud-optimized applications. Int J Adv Softw 4, 3(4):342–353
66. Andrikopoulos V, Strauch S, Leymann F (2013) Decision Support for Application Migration to the Cloud. In: Proceedings of CLOSER'13., pp 149–155
67. Juan-Verdejo A, Baars H (2013) Decision support for partially moving applications to the cloud: the example of business intelligence. In: Proceedings of the 2013 international workshop on Hot topics in cloud services, ACM., pp 35–42
68. Strauch S, Andrikopoulos V, Karastoynova D (2014) Migrating Enterprise Applications to the Cloud: Methodology and Evaluation. International Journal Big Data Intelligence 1:127–140

14

Power management in virtualized data centers: state of the art

Auday Al-Dulaimy[1*], Wassim Itani[2], Ahmed Zekri[1,3] and Rached Zantout[4]

Abstract

Cloud computing is an emerging technology in the field of computing that provides access to a wide range of shared resources. The rapid growth of cloud computing has led to establishing numerous data centers around the world. As data centers consume huge amounts of power, enhancing their power efficiency has become a major challenge in cloud computing. This paper surveys previous studies and researches that aimed to improve power efficiency of virtualized data centers. This survey is a valuable guide for researchers in the field of power efficiency in virtualized data centers following the cloud computing model.

Keywords: Cloud computing, Data center, Virtualization, Power management, Power efficiency

Introduction

Cloud computing is an emerging model that delivers services over the Internet by providing access to a wide range of shared computational resources hosted in data centers. The growth of cloud computing model has led to establishing numerous data centers around the world that consume huge amounts of power. Therefore, eliminating any waste of power in cloud data centers is very necessary. This can be achieved by observing how power is delivered to the data centers' resources, and how these resources are utilized to serve users' jobs. Hence, the need for improving the existing resource allocation and management algorithms in cloud data centers, as well as proposing new ones, is highly required. This paper presents previous research works that aimed to improve power efficiency of virtualized data centers. It is a valuable guide for understanding the state of the art of how to manage the power consumed in such environments. Additionally, it leads to suggesting and adding new proposals for further enhancement.

This paper is structured as follows. The motivations and objectives of the paper are stated in the next section. Power and Energy section defines the terminology used throughout the paper. Power Consumption section explains the sources of power consumption. The section titled Power Efficiency Metrics lists and describes some power efficiency metrics. State of the Art in Power Management section describes the power management techniques in details. Finally, conclusions are drawn in the last section.

Motivations and objectives

Recently, numerous data centers were established around the world. These data centers consume large amount of energy.

In general, the consumed energy amount is resulting in:

1) Operating costs,
2) Carbon dioxide (CO_2) emissions.

This amount was estimated to be between 1.1 and 1.5 % of the total electricity use in 2010. It has increased by 56 % from 2005, and it will continue to increase in a rapid manner unless advanced energy efficient resource management algorithms are proposed [1, 2]. Beside, CO_2 emissions of the Information and Communication Technology (ICT) industry were accounted to be 2 % of the total global emissions. However, the CO_2 emissions affect the global warming [1].

Addressing the problem of high energy use is a significant issue due to its financial and environmental effects. So, it is important to improve the resource allocation algorithms and proposing new management approaches

* Correspondence: auday.aldulaimy@gmail.com; a.aldulaimy@student.bau.edu.lb
[1]Department of Mathematics & Computer Science, Beirut Arab University, Beirut, Lebanon
Full list of author information is available at the end of the article

which aim to enhance the power efficiency in the data centers.

This survey is a guideline for researchers in designing the energy aware algorithms that execute the users' jobs in cloud data centers.

Power and energy

In order to fully understand the relation between power and energy, and to comprehend their management techniques, some related terminology must be identified. So, fundamental terms are defined in this survey [3]:

Charge: *charge* is the quantity of electricity responsible for electric phenomena, expressed in Coulomb (C).

Current: *current* is the flow of electric charge transferred by a circuit per time unit, measured in Amperes (A):

$$a = \frac{\Delta c}{\Delta t} \tag{1}$$

Voltage: *voltage* is the work or energy required to move an electric charge, measured in Volt (V):

$$v = \frac{\Delta w}{\Delta c} \tag{2}$$

Power: *power* is the rate at which the work is performed by the system, measured in Watt (W):

$$P = \frac{\Delta w}{\Delta t} \tag{3}$$

Accordingly, power is calculated by multiplying the element current by element voltage:

$$P = \frac{\Delta w}{\Delta t} = \frac{\Delta w}{\Delta c} * \frac{\Delta c}{\Delta t} = v * a \tag{4}$$

Energy: *energy* is the total amount of work performed over a period of time, measured in Watt-hour (Wh):

$$E = P * \Delta t \tag{5}$$

From (4) and (5), it is obvious that both power and energy are defined in terms of the work that a system performs. It is very important to note the difference between power and energy. The reduction of power consumption does not necessarily lead to a reduction of the amount of energy consumed. For example, lowering the CPU performance by decreasing its voltage and/or frequency can result in a decrease in power consumption. In this case, completing the program execution may take a longer time. However, the consumed energy may not be decreased even by decreasing power consumption [1].

As discussed in detail in the following sections, power consumption can be reduced by applying Static Power Management (SPM), Dynamic Power Management (DPM), or even by applying both solutions to the system.

Power consumption

Generally, the power that any system consumes consists of two main parts [1, 4]: Static Power Consumption (SPC) and Dynamic Power Consumption, as shown in Fig. 1. A description of these two terms is presented in the following two sections.

Static Power Consumption (SPC)

Static power consumption is the power consumed by the system components. SPC is caused by leakage currents of the active circuits in the powered system. It is independent of clock rates and does not rely on usage scenarios. Instead, it is fundamentally specified by the type of transistors and the technology applied to the processor of the system.

The reduction of SPC requires reducing the leakage current, and this can be done in three ways [5]:

1) Reducing the supplied voltage. The renowned technique that has been applied to system components (e.g. CPUs, cache memories) is called Supply Voltage Reduction (SVR),
2) Reducing the size of the circuit in the system, either by designing circuits with fewer transistors, or by cutting the power supplies to idle components to reduce the effective transistor count,
3) Cooling the system by applying cooling technologies. Cooling technologies can reduce the leakage power by allowing circuits to work faster as electricity encounters less resistance at lower temperatures. Also, they eliminate some negative effects of high temperatures, specifically the

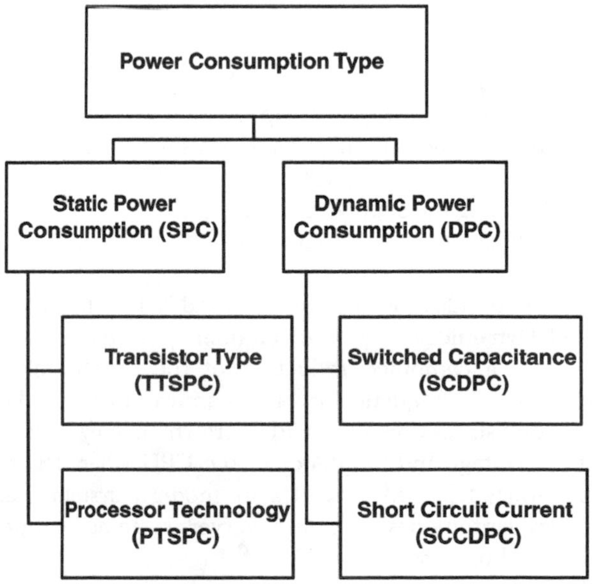

Fig. 1 Power consumption types

degradation of a chip's reliability and life expectancy.

The above three mentioned methods require improving the low-level system design, which lead to power reduction in SPC.

Dynamic Power Consumption (DPC)

Power consumption in this type results from the usage of system components. DPC is resulted by circuit activity. Mainly, DPC depends on clock rates, I/O activity, and the usage scenario. There are two sources of DPC; Switched Capacitance (SCDPC) and Short Circuit Current (SCCDPC) [5].

1) *SCDPC*: *SCDPC* is the major source of DPC. In this case, the consumed power is a byproduct of charging and discharging capacitors in circuits.
2) *SCCDPC*: *SCCDPC* is the minor source of DPC. The consumed power here results from the current switching between transistors. It approximately causes about 10–15 % of the total power consumption. However, this amount cannot be reduced without violating the system.

So, DPC can be defined as [1, 5–7]:

$$P_{Dynamic} = aCV^2f \tag{6}$$

where α represents the switching activity in the system, C is the physical capacitance, V is the voltage, and f is the CPU clock frequency of the system. The values of α and C are determined in the system design stage.

The DPC can be reduced by four methods [5]:

1) Reducing the switching activity.
2) Reducing the physical capacitance which depends on low level design parameters such as transistors sizes.
3) Reducing the supply voltage.
4) Reducing the clock frequency.

The core idea of the widely used DPM technique, called Dynamic Voltage and Frequency Scaling (DVFS), relies on a combined reduction of the supply voltage and/or clock frequency in a dynamical manner. This technique scales down the CPU performance by decreasing the voltage and frequency of the CPU when it is not fully utilized [8]. Most CPUs in modern systems (e.g. mobile, laptop, desktop, and server systems) support DVFS techniques.

Table 1 is a summary of the power consumption types [1, 4–5].

Table 1 A summary of power consumption types

Consumption Type	SPC	DPC
Results from:	The system components	The usage of the system components
Source:	The type of transistors and processor technology.	The short circuit current and switched capacitance.
Reason:	The leakage currents that are present in any active circuit of the powered system.	The circuit activity, Usage scenario, Clock rates, and I/O activity
Reduction:	Reducing the supplied voltage, Reducing the size of the circuits, Cooling the computer system.	Reducing the physical capacitance, Reducing the switching activity, Reducing the clock frequency, Reducing the supply voltage.

Power efficiency metrics

Different metrics are used to measure the power efficiency in data centers. Cloud providers have to use one or more metrics to estimate consumed power and overall performance. The researchers assessed the impact of applying their proposed strategies and algorithms in power management of data centers. These metrics can be classified as [9]:

1) Resource usage metrics: refer to the utilization of a certain resource (e.g. CPU, memory, bandwidth, storage capacity, etc.), concerning a component (node) or a set of components (node-group, rack).
2) Heat-aware metrics: use temperature as the main indicator for the behavior of a specific data center.
3) Energy-based metrics: refer to the amount of energy consumption during a certain period of time.
4) Impact metrics: that are used to assess the performance of data center in environmental and economic terms.

The following are examples of some metrics with their definitions:

i. *Total Energy Consumption*: *Total energy consumption* refers to the total power consumed by the data center over a certain period of time. It was measured in (W/h) and defined as:

$$TE_{DC} = \int_{t1}^{t2} TP_{DC}(t)dt \tag{7}$$

while TE_{DC} is the total energy consumed over a certain period of time, TP_{DC} is the total power consumed at a specific time.

ii. *Power Usage Effectiveness* (PUE): *Power Usage Effectiveness* refers to the ratio of the total power consumption in the data center and the power used by the IT equipment. PUE becomes the industry-preferred metric for measuring infrastructure energy efficiency for data centers, it is measured as [10]:

$$PUE_{DC} = \frac{TE_{DC}}{TE_{IT}} \tag{8}$$

iii. *Carbon Emission* (CE): *carbon emission* gives an indication about the amount of CO_2 emission in the data center. It uses Carbon Emissions Factor (CEF) and converts the total energy consumed to CO_2 emissions metric. CEF is a function of the participation of the different energy sources (e.g. carbon, gas, wind, solar, biomass, nuclear, etc.) which affect total electricity generation and the efficiency of conversion. Thus, this factor is different from one data center to another. CE is measured in kg CO_2 and can be defined as:

$$CE = TE_{DC} * CEF \tag{9}$$

iv. *Electricity Cost (EC)*: *electricity cost* converts the total energy consumed in the data center to a cost value by multiplying it by the price of electricity that differs from one data center to another. EC is measured in currencies (e.g. \$, €, and £) and can defined as:

$$EC = TE_{DC} * Price \tag{10}$$

State of the art in power management

Many research works have been done in the area of power management. Power management techniques can be divided into two main parts as shown in Fig. 2.

These techniques are discussed in more details in the next two sections.

Table 2 is a summary of the power management types [5, 11-14].

Static Power Management (SPM)

SPM determines the efficiency of the usage of the hardware components (e.g. CPU, memory, disk storage, network devices, and power supplies). The reduction in SPM is permanent. It includes all the optimization methods that are applied at the design of the logic, circuits, and architecture levels of the system [5].

Logic level optimization attempts to optimize the power of the switching activity of combinational and sequential circuits.

Circuit level optimization reduces the power of the switching activity of individual logic gates and transistors. This is usually done by utilizing a sophisticated gate design and transistor sizing.

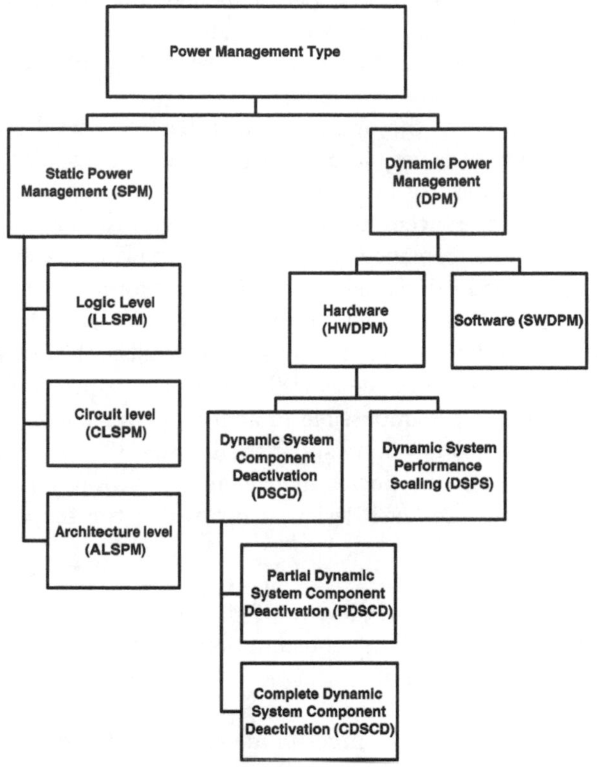

Fig. 2 Power management types

Architecture level optimization is achieved by mapping a high-level problem specification to a low-level design.

Low-power components are designed to save power and keep the system at an acceptable level of performance.

Many studies and SPM techniques have been proposed. The authors in [11] defined a novel system architecture, called fast array of wimpy nodes (FAWN). FAWN designed for low-power data intensive computing. In the proposed architecture, low-power CPUs combined with small amounts of local flash storage. The authors stated that such combination provides an efficient parallel data access in the system. In [12], the authors evaluated FAWN experimentally on various workloads. The results showed that the nodes with low-power CPUs are more efficient than conventional high-performance CPUs from the energy perspective. In [13], the authors defined a novel architecture, called Gordon, of

Table 2 A summary of power management types

Management Type	SPM	DPM
Level:	At the design of logic, circuits, and architecture levels	At the knowledge of the resource usage and application workloads
Reduction:	It is permanent	It is temporary
Implementation:	At the hardware level	At the hardware and software levels

low-power data-centric applications. Gordon can reduce the power consumption by utilizing low-power processors and flash memory. More details about the SPM techniques are available in [14].

In addition to the optimization in hardware-level system design, it is very important to carefully consider the implementation of programs that are to be executed on the system. Inaccurate software design can adversely affect the performance and may lead to power loss, even with perfectly designed hardware. Therefore, the code generation, the instructions used in the code, and the order of these instructions must be carefully selected, as they affect performance as well as power consumption.

Generally, it is impossible to analyze power consumption caused by any software at the hardware level [1, 15, 16]. However, the power management solution applied at the hardware level design is not within the scope of this survey.

Dynamic Power Management (DPM)

DPM optimizes energy consumption by utilizing a convenient knowledge of:

1) The available resources in the system and their usage.
2) The application workloads to optimize energy consumption.

Techniques in DPM allow a dynamic adjustment of the system's power states based on the system's current behavior. Additionally, they assume that the prediction of the workloads requirements is possible passable, which enables the adaptation of the future system behavior leading to perform the appropriate actions according to these requirements.

Thus, the reduction in DPM is temporary in the system, and it would last for an indefinite period of time according to the available resources and current workloads.

These techniques are distinguished by the level they are applied: hardware level or software level, as further explained in the next two sections.

Hardware Level Solutions

DPM techniques that are applied at the hardware level aim at reconfiguring the systems dynamically by designing methodologies to provide the requested services with a minimum number of active components or a minimum load on such components. The DPM techniques at a hardware level can selectively turn off the idle system components or reduce the performance of the partially unexploited ones. Also, it is possible to switch some components, such as the CPU, between active and idle modes to save energy [17, 18].

DPM at a hardware level can be divided into:

1) Dynamic System Component Deactivation (DSCD): which is subdivided into:
2) Dynamic System Performance Scaling (DSPS): DSPS techniques adjust the performance of the components dynamically according to the system state and the resources demands. These can be applied to system components to support the dynamic adjustment of their performance in a proportional manner with the power consumption. In addition to a complete deactivation approach, some components in the system (e.g. CPU) support increase or decrease in clock frequency along with adjustments of the supply voltage when the resource is not fully utilized. An example of DSPS is the DVFS technique [19] that is widely adopted in modern systems.
   i. Partial Dynamic System Component Deactivation (PDSCD): techniques are based on the idea of clock gating of parts of an electronic component.
   ii. Complete Dynamic System Component Deactivation (CDSCD): techniques are based on the idea of complete disabling for the components during periods of inactivity.

Software Level Solutions

A hardware level solution is very sophisticated. It is difficult to implement any modification or reconfiguration at this level. Therefore, shifting to the software level solutions is highly demanded.

There have been some proposed solutions for managing power consumption, such as Advanced Power Management (APM) performed by Basic Input/Output System (BIOS), firmware based, and platform-specific power management systems. But these solutions are hardware and platform-dependent.

The first attempt to address a software solution was made in 1996, when the first version of the Advanced Configuration and Power Interface (ACPI) was proposed. ACPI was a platform-independent interface. It improved the existing power and configuration standards for hardware devices and allowed operating systems to control power management and efficiently configured the hardware platform they ran on. ACPI has been widely accepted as a standard that brings DPM into the operating system (OS) control of all aspects of power management and device configuration [20, 21].

ACPI defines a number of power states. These states can be enabled in the system at runtime. Also, it gives software developers the ability to leverage the flexibility in adjusting the system's power states [1].

The states which are relevant in the context of DPM are:

i. *C-states*: *C-states* are the CPU power states C0, C1, C2, and C3. They denote the Operating State, Halt, Stop-Clock, and Sleep Mode respectively. Recently, deep power down states (e.g. C4, C5, C6, and C7) were introduced to define different levels of lower activity.
ii. *P-states*: *P-states* are the power-performance states when the processor is operating. P-states can be one of several states, and each state represents a specific combination setting of DVFS values. They are implementation-dependent, but P0 is always the highest performance one. If there is implementation-specific limit of n, then P_1 to P_n are successively lower performance states.

As mentioned earlier, data centers consume huge amounts of electrical power. Although DVFS technique can provide an efficient direction in managing power consumption of the CPU, more power reduction is required. The server consumes over 50 % of its actual peak power and up to 70 % in some cases, even when it is completely idle [22]. Switching PMs off is the only possible way to eliminate their SPC. These circumstances led to propose some solutions which are suit the data centers environment. Those solutions aimed to consolidate the workload to fewer PMs and deactivating the idle ones. The consolidation is a complicated problem. The performance of the applications can be affected from unnecessary consolidation. Therefore Quality of Service (QoS) requirements restricts consolidation. In general, QoS are defined in terms of Service Level Agreement (SLA) between cloud users (or their brokers) and cloud providers.

Many studies and approaches have been dedicated to enhance the power-efficiency in virtualized data centers.

Management techniques that take into account the concept of virtualized systems were first explored by Nathuji and Schwan in 2007 [23]. The authors examined ways of integrating power management mechanisms into the virtualized data center environments and presented a power management model for such environments, called VirtualPower, which controlled the power consumption of underlying platforms. A new technique, called "soft resource scaling", was applied in the model of that study. This technique emulated hardware scaling by providing less time for the VM to utilize a resource. It is a very efficient technique when hardware scaling is not supported. VirtualPower provided a set of virtualized power states, called VirtualPower Management (VPM) states, which were taken into account in all management actions. VirtualPower was able to modify model-specific registers (MSRs) in the PM and change the power states. Thus, an abstraction of (VPM) channels could be created. The channels then delivered guest VM power management actions as a set of 'soft' states that provided a virtual layer for application-aware management.

In the same year, Nathuji, Isci, and Gorbatov [24] pioneered in exploiting platform heterogeneity to improve the power management, while taking into account the emergence of the virtualization concept. They defined an intelligent workload allocation system that efficiently mapped workloads to the best fitted resources in heterogeneous platforms. The model consisted of three components: platform/workload descriptors, power/performance predictor, and allocator. The workload descriptor consisted of modules labeled by attributes, and a list of values for these attributes was provided. The platform descriptor consisted of individual modules representing system components that were used to convey information according to the PM's power management and hardware capabilities. The power/performance predictor used these descriptors to estimate the performance and power savings in the data center. Finally, the allocator used these predictions to map workloads to a specific type of platform. The allocator of the study evaluated the power efficiency tradeoffs of assigning a workload to many kinds of platforms, while each kind of platforms was associated with a cost metric. Jobs of the workloads were queued according to the values of the cost metric. Then, a mapping process was performed based on this queue with priority given to the job with the highest cost.

In [25], the authors investigated several previous solutions to the problem of high power consumption in data centers. Until then, there had not been any corresponding work on coordinating all these solutions. Hence, the authors characterized the existing solutions and classified them into hardware/software and local/global levels.

Then, the authors proposed their solution which was a model of multiple feedback controllers at various levels. The solution implemented in a distributed manner. Being the core level of that model, the Efficiency Controller (EC) was implemented in the system that served as a "container". This container was used as a reference to the controller depending on the desired part of its capacity. There was also a sensor to compare the value with the actual utilization of the container. By managing the actual resource utilization in the system and the reference value of the container, EC dynamically "resized the container". EC also monitored previous/former resource utilization and adjusted a processor P-state accordingly in order to match estimated demand. In this case, the consumed power was adapted to the total resource demand of the workloads in real time fashion. The second controller in that model, called Server Manager (SM), implemented the server level power capping. It measured the consumed power in the server and compared it with the power budget. The third controller, called Enclosure Manager (EM), implemented enclosure-level power capping. It monitored the total power consumption of the code enclosure and compared it with an enclosure-level power budget periodically. The forth controller, which implemented the group-level power capping, was called Group Manager (GM). It worked at either the rack level or the data center level. GM function is to compare the actual power consumption of the group with the group power budget. The final controller in the model was the Virtual Machine Controller (VMC). The function of VMC is to collect the resource utilizations of the individual VMs in the system and performed a new VM-to-Servers mapping to minimize the total power based on the utilization information. That model provided a feedback control loop to federate multiple power management solutions at different levels. However, the proposed architecture needs an extension to include coordination with other solutions in the performance domains.

The authors investigated the design and implementation of a power-aware application placement model under heterogeneous virtualized server environment in [26]. When matching the application containers to the PMs, the placement model considered the power and migration costs.

The authors divided this work into two parts: The first part presented methods to implement the placement of cost-aware application on real servers, while the second one presented an application placement framework, called (pMapper), to solve the problem of high power consumption and reduce this amount as much as possible. The architecture of that framework consisted of three managers (Performance Manager, Power Manager, and Migration Manager) and an Arbitrator. Performance Manager monitored the behavior of the workload and rearranged the VMs while taking into account both the current resource requirements and SLAs. It consulted a knowledge base for an application performance in addition to the cost of its VM migration from one machine to another. Power Manager monitored the current power consumption and adjusted hardware power states. It used the power model in the knowledge base to determine the placement, and thus could estimate the power for every placement scenario and suggest the server throttling. Migration Manager estimated the cost of moving from a given placement to a new one and issues instructions for VM live migration to consolidate the overall VMs of the application. Arbitrator, which was the central intelligence part in pMapper, received the estimations from the three managers, configured a space for the VM placements, computed the best VMs sizes, and implemented an algorithm to choose the best VM placement. Once the Arbitrator decided on the new configuration, the three managers executed the following operations respectively: VM sizing, server throttling and live migration.

The authors in [27] implemented a dynamic resource provisioning of VMs for web applications in virtualized server environments. In this study, the provisioning problem was defined as sequential optimization under uncertainty. The authors proposed a framework called Limited Look-ahead Control (LLC) to solve this problem. The framework monitored the process of VMs provisioning and calculated the switching costs resulting from this provisioning, then it encoded the corresponding cost value in the optimization problem. In order to reduce power consumption and maintain the SLA that was defined in term of the processing rate for each application, the work proposed an online controller to decide the number of PMs and VMs to be allocated to each job in the workload. In this case, it is possible to turn the PMs on and off upon the controller's decision which may vary according to workload types.

In [28], the authors designed a trace-based workload placement controller to optimize the VMs allocation based on historical information, while maintaining specific QoS requirements. Then, they proactively mapped the workload periodically to the PMs. The work traded off between the consumed power of the required resources and the number of migrations that may occur after VMs placement. This approach was based on the fact that the historic traces of any application offer a model for describing the future application behavior. Traces were used to decide how to consolidate the VMs workloads to the PMs. The workload trace-based approach was considered a proactive controller that caused the VMs of the workloads migration among PMs in order to consolidate the system periodically. In this work, the optimization algorithm was enhanced by reducing the total number of migrations that occurred during successive control intervals. In addition to the proactive controller, the study also introduced a reactive migration controller. It detected the overload/under-load conditions in the PM and initiated the VMs migration. It dynamically added and removed PMs to maintain a balance of supply and demand resources by turning PMs on and off. The controller's act was based on the real-time data collected from the resource usage. However, during the workload placement approach, this work did not consider the effect of cache sharing on power efficiency.

The authors in [29] proposed novel techniques for placement and power consolidation of VMs in the virtualized data centers. Most hypervisors (e.g. Xen and VMware) provide administrators that are able to adjust the minimum number of the required resources (min) and the maximum number of allowable resources for a VM (max). Values such as (min) and (max) are very useful in ensuring the intelligent distribution of resources between different workloads. Hence, this study leverages min, max and the shares parameters supported in virtualization technologies. The proposed techniques provided a tradeoff mechanism for power and performance when running heterogeneous workloads in data centers. They involved sorting physical machines (PMs) in an increasing order of the power cost per unit of capacity, wherein the objective function included power consumption and the utilization resulted from the execution of a specific VM, which was a priori assumption. The placement strategy then is to place all the VMs at their maximum resource requirements in a first-fit manner. An amount of 10 % of the capacity is leaved as a spare to handle any future growth of the resource usage.

The authors in [30] proposed a solution that facilitated coordination between the virtualization concept and the loosely couple platforms in data centers. This solution, known as vManage, provided an execution policy for better virtualization management. The design of vManager, which consisted of registry and proxy mechanisms, had several features such as a unified monitoring over platform and virtualization domains, the coordinators are able to interface with existing management controllers, easy portable across different hardware platforms with an independent implementation, and flexibility and extensibility in allowing new management solutions to participate in a "plug-and-play" manner. vManager is based on the concept of estimating "stability." In other words, it is based on the probability that a proposed VM reallocation will stay efficient for an appropriate future period of time. The predictions of future resource demands are computed using a probability function. This study provided an example of stability management and coordinated VM placement in the data center called the stabilizer, which is a plug-in' component. The VM placement policy considers the platform requirements as well as the requirements of the VM including CPU, memory, and network constraints. However, the proposed solution needs to be extended for larger scale data centers.

In [31], the authors tackled the problem of optimizing resource allocation for multitier applications in consolidated server environments. This was achieved by exploring a runtime cost-sensitive adaptation engine that weighed the potential benefits of automatic reconfiguration and their corresponding costs. The study suggested an offline cost model for each application to decide when and how to reconfigure the VMs. The model estimated the cost according to the changes in the utility for the application, which was a function of the response time for that application. This model improved the application response time and ameliorated the period over which the system remained functional in the new VM configuration.

In order to optimize resource allocation in data centers, the authors in [32] presented a multi-tiered resource scheduling scheme in that environment. This scheme, named RAINBOW, automatically provided on-demand capacities via resources flowing that indicated which resources were released by some VMs to be allocated to other VMs. The resource flowing was modeled using optimization theory and was resolved by the Simplex Method. Based on this model, the authors proposed a scheduling algorithm to optimize resource allocation and to ensure performance of some critical services, leading to reduction in consumed power. The proposed scheduling algorithm had three levels. The first was Application-Level scheduler: which dispatched requests across the VMs by applying VM migration; the second was Local-Level scheduler: which allocated resources of a PM to VMs according to their priorities; and the third was Global-level scheduler: which controlled the flow of resources among the applications.

In order to meet the QoS in this study, the resources were allocated to the applications according to the application priorities. In case of limited resources, the resources of low priority applications would be allocated to critical ones. The authors stated that performance of critical applications was guaranteed using this scenario. However, there is a need to analyze the effect and overhead caused by each tier of the proposed multi-tiered resource scheduling.

In [33], Stillwell, Schanzenbach, Vivien, and Casanova demonstrated the utilization of resource allocation management systems in virtualization technology for sharing parallel computing resources among competing jobs. The model focused on HPC applications. The authors defined the resource allocation problem considering a number of underlying assumptions and determined the complexity of each one. They also proposed a more general approach by eliminating some assumptions. The problem of resource allocation was formally defined as Mixed Integer Programming (MIP) model. The design of this model was based on two assumptions: first, the application required only one VM instance, and second, the computational power and memory requirements needed by the application were static. However, estimating accurate job resource requirements for jobs is a weak point in this work.

In [34], the authors investigated the problem of high power consumption in cloud data centers. They proposed an energy-aware resource provisioning that mapped the resources to the applications while meeting the SLA between the provider and the users. The study proposed visions, challenges, principles, and an architectural framework for energy-efficient model in virtualized data center environments. It focused on providing resources dynamically and how allocation algorithms could be improved via managing consumed energy among various data center infrastructures. The proposed framework consisted of three levels; *User level*: at this level, users or their brokers submit their service requests to the cloud. *Allocator level*: which acts as an interface between users and the cloud infrastructure. *Data center level*: represents the VMs and PMs.

The VM allocation process was divided into two parts. The first part was receiving new requests for VM provisioning. All VMs were sorted in decreasing order according to their current utilization, and then allocated each VM to a PM that expanded the minimum amount of increment in the consumed energy. The second part was optimizing the current allocation of VMs, which was further divided into two steps: selecting the VMs to be migrated and placing the selected VMs on new PMs.

In that study, the selection of the migrating VMs was heuristically achieved. Four heuristics were used; the first one was based upon setting an upper utilization threshold for PMs. The VMs were allocated to a PM when the placement process kept the total CPU utilization below that threshold. The other three heuristics were based on the idea of setting two thresholds for utilization, upper and lower. The total CPU utilization by all VMs had to remain between the setting two thresholds.

The four heuristics relied on three policies: the first was migrating the least number of VMs to minimize migration overhead. The second was migrating VMs that had the lowest usage of CPU to maintain utilization. The third policy was selecting the necessary number of VMs based on a uniformly distributed random variable.

In [35], the authors analyzed the cost of energy in virtualized data center environments. The virtualization concept inspired the authors to propose an energy-efficient framework dedicated to cloud architecture, and they called it Green Open Cloud (GOC). GOC was proposed for the next generation of Cloud data centers that support extra facilities, such as advanced reservation. GOC has the ability to aggregate the workload by negotiating with users. In this case, the idle PMs can be switched off for a longer period of time without the need for further negotiations with the users.

In [36], the paper presented the design and implementation of two VM management solutions: Distributed Resource Scheduler (DRS) and Distributed Power Management (DPM).

DRS managed the allocation of physical resources to a set of VMs by mapping these VMs to PMs. Additionally; it performed intelligent load balancing in order to enhance the performance. DRS provided a "what-if" mode to handle any changes in workloads or PM configuration. DRS solution performed four key resource-management operations: Computes the amount of resources requested by a VM based on the reservation, periodically balanced load across PMs by performing VM migrations, saved power by benefiting from DPM, and performed initial placement of VMs onto PMs.

DPM surpassed DRS in its ability to reduce the consumed power by consolidating VMs onto fewer number of PMs. DPM is able to power a PM off when the CPU and memory resources have low utilization. At the same time, it is able to power a PM on appropriately when demand on resources increases, or in order to maintain the constraints.

The researchers in [37] investigated the resource fragments which resulted from the imbalanced use of the PM resources. They mentioned that the problem of VMs to PMs placement should be solved according to a resource-balanced strategy. To characterize the resource usage of each PM, the authors proposed a multi-dimensional space model, while each dimension of the space corresponds to one dimensional resource. The whole space is partitioned into three domains, each with particular features, to elucidate the appropriateness of resource utilization for each VM placement process. The proposed model can be used as a guide in designing the resource-balanced VM placement algorithms. Based on this model, the researchers proposed their own energy efficient VM placement algorithm and called it (EAGLE). EAGLE was based on a tradeoff at each time-slot between balancing multi-dimensional resource utilization and reducing the total number of PMs during VMs placement. EAGLE checks the next resource usage state for each available PM and chooses the most suitable one. A new PM could be turned on to avoid any excessive resource fragments. This would decrease excessive resource fragments and further reduce the number of PMs on the long run. This algorithm resulted in a better utilization of resources, introduced less resource fragments and saved energy.

The trade-off between energy efficiency and SLA constraints were analyzed in [38]. The authors studied the users' utilization patterns and introduced a dynamic resource provisioning mechanism to over-allocate capacity in cloud data centers. The core concept of the proposed mechanism was to employ the resource utilization patterns of each user to eliminate any potential waste in utilization that might result from overestimation of resources requests. The over-allocate algorithm in this mechanism considered two different parameters: the predicted resource utilization based on historical data, and dynamic occupation to determine the maximum number of resources that could be allocated over the actual PM capacity. The PM capacity was calculated based on the cost-benefit analysis of deploying a specific instance into a particular server. It also allowed consolidating additional VMs in the same PM. A compensation mechanism to adjust resource allocation in cases of underestimation was also discussed in this study.

In his thesis [1], Anton Beloglazov proposed novel algorithms for distributed dynamic consolidation of VMs in virtualized cloud data centers. The thesis reduced amount of the total energy consumption under different workload requirements. Energy consumption was reduced by dynamically switching PMs on and off to meet the current resource demand. The author suggested a data center model and applied a VM placement algorithm that worked in this model. The data center model consisted of numerous PMs and had two types of managers to coordinate the VM management. The local manager residing on each PM as a module of the virtual machine management (VMM) and the global manager that resided as a master for a specific number of PMs. The decision to place the VM on a specific PM was made individually according to the communication between the local manager on the PM and the global managers.

The thesis also presented a novel approach that optimally solved the problem of host overload detection by maximizing mean inter-migration time. This approach was based on a Markov chain model and worked for any fixed workload and a given state configuration.

The authors in [39] investigated the VM provisioning as an essential technique in cloud computing. VM provisioning refers to providing VMs upon users' requests. The work proposed a power-aware VM provisioning model for both hard and soft real-time services. A real-time service (such as financial analysis, distributed databases, and image processing) was presented as real-time VM requests. It included many tasks, and each task was defined by some parameters. Therefore, when users made their requests to the cloud computing environment, appropriate VMs were allocated for executing those requests. Brokers were responsible for finding VMs for the users' requests. The requirements of the requested VMs were called Real-Time Virtual Machine (RT-VM) in this paper. Each RT-VM V_i included three parameters: utilization u_i, Million Instruction Per Second (MIPS) m_i , and deadline d_i. Such requirements imply that the real-time service is guaranteed if the allocated VM keeps providing a processing capacity of $u_i \times m_i$ amount by the specified deadline d_i. After defining their power model, the authors proposed a power aware framework including the following five steps: Requesting a VM, generating the RT-VM from real-time applications, requesting a real-time VM, mapping the physical processors, and finally, executing the real-time applications.

This study suggested the variable w_i as the remaining service time. The initial value of w_i is defined by $u_i \times m_i \times (d_i - t_s)$, at the submission time t_s. If V_i is provided with q_i MIPS rate for the period t_p, then, the value w_i is decreased by $q_i \times t_p$. In such case, V_i finishes its service when w_i becomes zero.

When a datacenter receives a RT-VM request from users or their brokers, it returns the price of providing the RT-VM service if it can provide real-time VMs for that request. Then, the users or brokers can select the VM with the minimum price among available VMs provided by the datacenters. Thus, the provisioning policy in this work was selecting the processing element with the minimum price to maximize user/broker profits. If the process element is able to schedule V_i, it estimates provisioning energy and cost. As the provisioning policy aimed to provide a lower price for the user, the proposed algorithm in this paper discovered the minimum-price processor. For the same price, less energy is preferable because it produces higher profit. Finally, a VM is mapped if V_i is schedulable on the datacenter. However, in this study, the soft real-time VM provisioning did not considered.

The authors in [40] stated the previous real time job scheduling algorithms were running in uncertain cloud environments. Those algorithms assumed that cloud computing environments were deterministic, and there were statistical pre-computed schedule decisions to be followed during the schedule execution. So this study introduced the interval number theory to describe the uncertainty of the cloud computing environment and the impact of uncertainty on the scheduling quality in a cloud data center. Accordingly, a novel scheduling algorithm, called Proactive and Reactive Scheduling (PRS), was presented. It dynamically exploited proactive and reactive scheduling methods for scheduling real-time jobs.

The proactive scheduling was used to build baseline schedules depending on redundancy, where a protective time cushion between jobs' finish time lower bounds and their deadlines was added to guarantee job deadlines. The reactive scheduling was triggered to generate proactive baseline schedules in order to account for various disruptions during the course of executions.

Some strategies were presented to scale the system's computing resources up and down according to workload to improve resource utilization and to reduce energy consumption for the cloud data center. These strategies were proposed to treat the following five events as disruptions:

1) a new job arrives;
2) the system becomes overloaded;
3) a new urgent job arrives or the waiting jobs become urgent;
4) a VM finishes a job;
5) some VMs' idle time exceeds the pre-established threshold.

However, estimating job execution time is main factor in the scheduling model proposed in this work. So, improving the precision of estimated job execution time may lead to better scheduling decisions.

The authors in [41] presented two scheduling algorithms for precedence-constrained parallel VMs in a virtualized data center. The proposed algorithms used a new insertion policy to insert VMs among previously scheduled ones. The new policy inserted VMs into already switched on low utilized PMs to increase their utilization, thus reducing the total number of switched on PMs that served the VMs, and therefore enhancing energy efficiency.

The first algorithm, called Virtualized Homogeneous Earliest Start Time (VHEST), was an extension of the well-known HEFT algorithm. HEFT scheduled VMs according to the non-overlapping insertion policy. VHEST was modified to use overlapping insertion policy to minimize the makespan.

It had two major stages: VM selection and PM Selection. At the first stage, VMs were sorted according to their priority, and then the VM with the highest priority was selected to be placed on PM. At the second stage, the selected VM was placed in the best PM that minimized the VM's start time by applying an overlapping-insertion policy.

The second algorithm, called Energy-Aware Scheduling Algorithm (EASA), solved a multi-objective problem. It improved the utilization of PMs and minimized the makespan. EASA also had two major stages: Local optimization and Global Optimization. The local optimization stage improved the utilization of the PMs. The global optimization stage reduced the number of switched on PMs by switching off the underutilized ones. However, the work did not support heterogeneous data centers.

An energy-aware resource provisioning framework for cloud data centers was proposed in [42]. The main functions of the proposed framework can be summarized into three points:

1) Predicting the upcoming number of the (VM) requests that would arrive to the cloud data center in a certain future period, associated with the requirements for each VM. The prediction approach relied upon monitoring past workload variations during a period of time. It combines machine learning clustering and stochastic theory to predict the number of the upcoming VM requests along with required resources associated with each request.
2) Estimating the number of PMs needed in the data center that will serve the upcoming users' requests. This estimation is based on the predictions of such requests.
3) Turning the unneeded PMs in the data center to the sleep mode by applying intelligent power management decisions in order to reduce the consumed energy.

In addition to the previous studies, various optimization methods such as, Ant Colony Optimization (ACO), Particle Swarm Optimization (PSO), and Genetic Algorithms (GA)) were used to improve resource utilization and reduce energy consumption in the virtualized data centers.

In [43], the researchers presented a framework to manage the VM placement in an IaaS environment. They defined an initial VM placement strategy and proposed multi-objective optimization algorithm based on (ACO) to determine the initial VMs placement. The proposed algorithm was an optimization method. It was able to achieve an optimal solution through efficient convergence by the constantly updated pheromone. The optimal solution was selected from a set of solutions using the exclusion method.

In [44], the authors designed a distributed ACO-based algorithm for solving the VM consolidation problem (VMCP). The algorithm iterated over a finite number of cycle. At each cycle, an item was selected for each ant to be packed in a bin. If the bin did not have enough space according to defined constraints, another bin was selected. At the end of each cycle, the best solution found was saved and pheromone evaporation was triggered to achieve the VM consolidation.

In [45], the authors proposed a multi-objective ACO to solve the problem of VM placement. The formulated multi-objective VM placement problem represented a permutation of VM assignment. The goal was to efficiently obtain a set of non-dominated solutions that reduced total power consumption resulting from resource wastage. This proposed model has two phases; Initialization phase: where the parameters and the pheromone trails were initialized. Iterative phase: in this phase, all VM requests were sent to the ants to start assigning VMs to the selected PMs. This was done by using a pseudo-random-proportional rule, which described the way each ant selected a particular next one VM pack into its current PM. Ants moved towards the most promising VMs based on information about the current pheromone concentration during the movement. Local and global pheromones were frequently updated. A local pheromone update was performed once an artificial ant built a movement. Then, a global update was performed with each solution of the current Pareto set after all ants had constructed their solutions.

The thesis in [46] focused on the IaaS cloud service model. This model offered compute infrastructure to cloud consumers by provisioning VMs on-demand. The thesis investigated the challenge of designing, implementing, and evaluating an energy-efficient IaaS cloud management system for private clouds. The author proposed four contributions:

1) IaaS Cloud Management system (Snooze): It was based on a self-configuring hierarchical architecture and performed VM management for distributed large-scale virtualized data centers by splitting the data center into independently managed groups of PMs and VMs. Snooze provided a holistic energy-efficient VM management solution. Particularly, it integrated a power management mechanism which automatically detected idle PMs, transitioned them into a power-saving state, and woke them up on demand.
2) VM Placement via ACO: an ACO-based VM placement algorithm was used to solve the problem of considering only a single resource to evaluate the PM load and VM resource demands while ignoring the other resources. In addition, ACO appealed to the VM placement problem due to its polynomial time worst-case complexity and convenience of parallelization.
3) VM Consolidation via Ant Colony Optimization: VM consolidation algorithms are required in order to enable continuous consolidation of already placed VMs on fewer PMs. This consolidation helped avoid resource fragmentation and further increases the data center resource utilization. Therefore, the researcher proposed a consolidation algorithm based on ACO to achieve both scalability and high data center utilization by applying VM consolidation.
4) Fully decentralized consolidation system based on an unstructured peer-to-peer network.

In [47], the authors proposed a VM consolidation scheme that focused on balanced resource utilization of servers across different computing resources with the goal of minimizing power consumption and resource wastage. This study presented an adaptation and integration of the ACO met heuristic with a balanced usage of computing resources. The degree of imbalance in the current resource utilization of a PM was captured and represented as a multi-dimensional server resource utilization, and then resources utilization are balanced using vector algebra.

The study in [48] proposed a PSO-based algorithm, which could successfully reduce the energy cost and the time for searching feasible solutions. The authors presented an environment of heterogeneous multiprocessors, which is similar to the environment of cloud data center, and they proposed a job to the processor assignment model that would work in that environment. During assigning jobs to the processors, the velocity of the particles (that represented the jobs) determined their positions. This velocity will affect the overall convergence of the PSO algorithm and the efficiency of the algorithm's global searching. The particle's position updates present the next position of the job. As the particle position updates, it indicated that it needed to adjust the number of processors that fit its requirements. Then, the proposed algorithm optimized the most feasible solution to in order to reduce energy consumption by assigning jobs to new processors or by exchanging their corresponding processors. However, there are many constraint conditions in the work, reducing them will make the work more convenient for solving the problem of real-time job scheduling.

In [49], the authors proposed a genetic algorithm for power-aware (GAPA) scheduling to find the optimal solution for the problem of VM allocation. In the proposed algorithm, a tree structure was used to encode chromosome of an individual job. The fitness function of GA calculated the evaluation value of each chromosome. The tree had three levels; Level 1: Consisted of a root node that did not have a significant meaning, Level 2: Consisted of a collection of nodes that represented a set of PMs, Level 3: Consisted of a collection of nodes that represented a set of virtual machines. Using this model, each instance of tree structure showed the VM to PM Allocation. However, the computational time of the GAPA is high, also deadline of jobs did not considered in the work.

In [50], the authors proposed a distributed parallel genetic algorithm (DPGA) of placement strategy for VMs deployment on cloud platform. The proposed algorithm had two stages: It executed the genetic algorithm in parallel and in a distributed manner on several selected PMs in the first stage to get several solutions. Then, it continued to execute the genetic algorithm of the second stage with solutions obtained from the first stage as the initial population. A relatively optimal job to VM mapping was obtained as a result of the second stage. The fitness value of GA chosen here was performance per watt.

In [51], the authors introduced a power efficient resource allocation algorithm for jobs in cloud computing data centers. The developed approach was also based on GA. Resource allocation was performed to optimize job completion time and data center power consumption. It considered a static scheduling of independent jobs on homogeneous single-core resources. The proposed algorithm, called Non-dominated Sorting Genetic Algorithm II (NSGA-II), was applied to cloud environments to explore space solutions and efficiently search for the optimal solution. The data center was modeled as three-tier fat-tree layers architecture: access, aggregation, and core layers. The access layer provided

Table 3 Studies of power efficiency improvement in virtualized data centers

Ref.	Virtualized Data Center		Environment		All Workload Types	Power Aware Scheduling		Resources					Approach		Scheduling		Technology/Method
	Single	Multiple	Homo	Hetero		Consider Cost	Consider Time	CPU	Memory	Storage	Network.	Cooling System	SW	HW	Offline	Online	
[23]	√		√		√			√					√	√		√	DVFS, SW-based Model, VM Consolidation, On/Off Switching.
[24]	√			√	√			√					√	√		√	DVFS, SW-based Model, VM Consolidation, On/Off Switching.
[25]	√		√		√	√		√					√	√		√	DVFS, SW-based Model, VM Consolidation, On/Off Switching.
[26]	√			√	√	√		√					√	√		√	DVFS, SW-based Model, VM Consolidation, On/Off Switching.
[27]	√		√		√			√	√				√			√	WS-based Model, On/Off Switching.
[28]	√		√		√			√	√				√			√	VM Consolidation, On/Off Switching.
[29]	√		√					√					√	√		√	DVFS, SW-based Model.
[30]	√		√		√		√	√	√		√		√		√		SW-based Model, VM Consolidation
[31]	√		√		√	√	√	√	√				√		√		SW-based Model
[32]	√		√		√			√	√				√			√	SW-based Model
[33]	√			√				√					√			√	SW-based Model, VM Consolidation
[34]	√			√	√	√		√					√	√		√	DVFS, SW-based Model.
[35]	√		√		√			√					√			√	SW-based Model, On/Off Switching.
[36]	√		√		√			√	√				√			√	SW-based Model, VM Consolidation, On/Off Switching.
[37]	√		√		√			√					√			√	SW-based Model, VM Consolidation.
[38]	√		√		√			√					√			√	SW-based Model, VM Consolidation, On/Off Switching.
[1]		√		√	√			√					√	√		√	DVFS, SW-based Model, VM Consolidation, On/Off Switching.
[39]	√			√	√	√		√					√	√		√	DVFS, SW-based Model.
[40]		√	√		√		√	√	√				√			√	SW-based Model.
[41]	√			√	√		√	√					√			√	SW-based Model, VM Consolidation.
[42]	√			√	√			√	√				√			√	SW-based Model.
[43]	√		√		√		√	√	√		√		√				ACO
[44]	√			√	√		√	√	√	√			√			√	ACO, VM Consolidation
[45]	√		√		√			√	√				√			√	ACO, VM Consolidation
[46]	√			√	√			√					√		√		ACO, VM Consolidation, On/Off Switching.
[47]	√		√		√			√	√		√		√			√	ACO, VM Consolidation, On/Off Switching.
[48]	√			√	√		√	√					√			√	PSO
[49]	√		√		√			√					√			√	GA
[50]	√		√		√	√		√					√			√	GA
[51]	√		√		√		√	√			√		√			√	GA

connection to servers which were arranged into racks with each rack being served by a single Top of the rack switch. Two fitness functions were used here: task completion time and data center power consumption. When the execution of the algorithm was completed and optimal Pareto solutions were obtained, it became possible to fine tune the trade-off between power consumption and execution time. Then, by using a procedure called ranking, the population of solutions were sorted heuristically into different non-domination levels. This procedure was repeated for every solution creating different groups or non-domination; an integer value called rank was assigned to each non-domination level. When applying selection and sorting, NSGA-II was able to deal with constraints. The solution with less constraint violation had a better rank.

Table 3 [1, 23-51] summarizes all the studies and techniques illustrated in this survey. The table compares the studies from many perspectives. It shows if the studies are applied in single or multiple data centers, Homogenous or heterogeneous environment, Specific or all types of jobs are used, if any other parameters are considered with enhancing the energy efficiency, the involved resources in enhancing the energy efficiency, HW or SW approach is applied with the study, the scheduling is online or offline, and finally, what is the used technology in each study?

Conclusion

By studying the research works mentioned in this survey paper, it can be concluded that:

1) In order to improve energy efficiency in DPM software solutions, the only two issues that have to be investigated in cloud data centers are: jobs or tasks to VMs allocation, and VMs to PMs placement.
2) The utilization of the PMs is a very important factor to be considered in proposing the resource management solutions. The PMs utilizations affect the energy efficiency in the cloud data centers. In general, the best energy efficiency occurs at optimal utilization and it drops as utilization decreases.
3) VM migrations usually occur when there is over/under utilization of the resources. Extra VM migration may affect the whole system performance, leading to further power consumption. So, VM management (e.g VM allocation and VM placement) is a very critical process that should be optimally done to avoid unnecessary VM migration.
4) Before proposing the energy aware scheduling algorithms, it is important to understand the capacity of the resources and the types of services provided by the cloud data centers to avoid any waste of the available resources capacities.
5) When proposing the energy aware algorithms, identifying the behaviors of cloud users' requests and common workloads patterns would improve the system performance, and therefore, enhance energy efficiency in the cloud data centers.
6) Although modern advances in hardware technologies have reduced energy consumption to some extent, many software approaches have been proposed for further improvements. The two directions must be considered as complementary approaches, and applying both of them (hardware and software) in any proposed model leads to more reduction in energy consumption in the cloud data centers.

We do believe that this survey is a good guideline for researchers in designing the energy aware algorithms that execute the users' jobs in cloud data centers.

Competing interests
The authors declare that they have no competing interests.

Authors' contributions
Auday explained the taxonomy and methodology, carried out the study on power efficiency in cloud data centers, and drafted the manuscript. Wassim discussed, revised and added sections to the manuscript. Ahmed and Rached provided notes and revised the manuscript and gave a useful feedback. All authors read and approved the final manuscript.

Acknowledgements
The authors wish to thank Dr Lama Hamandi for offering insightful suggestions and providing many references.

Author details
[1]Department of Mathematics & Computer Science, Beirut Arab University, Beirut, Lebanon. [2]Department of Electrical & Computer Engineering, Beirut Arab University, Beirut, Lebanon. [3]Department of Mathematics & Computer Science, Faculty of Science, Alexandria University, Alexandria, Egypt. [4]Department of Electrical & Computer Engineering, Rafic Hariri University, Beirut, Lebanon.

References
1. Beloglazov A (2013) Energy-efficient management of virtual machines in data centers for cloud computing, PHD thesis. Department of Computing and Information Systems, The University of Melbourne
2. Koomey J (2007) Estimating total power consumption by servers in the us and the world, Lawrence Berkeley National Laboratory, Technical Report
3. Dorf R, Svoboda J (2010) Introduction To Electric Circuits, 8 edn. John Wiley & Sons Inc, USA; ISBN: 978-0-470-52157-1
4. Orgerie A, Assuncao M, Lefevre L (2014) A survey on techniques for improving the energy efficiency of large scale distributed systems. ACM Comput Surv 46(4):1–35
5. Venkatachalam V, Franz M (2005) Power reduction techniques for microprocessor systems. ACM Comput Surv 37(3):195–237
6. Burd T, Brodersen R (1996) Processor design for portable systems. J VLSI Signal Processing 13(2–3):203–221
7. George J (2005) Energy-optimal schedules of real-time jobs with hard deadlines, Msc Thesis. Texas A&M University, Texas
8. Barroso LA, Hölzle U (2007) The case for energy-proportional computing. Computer 40(12):33–37
9. Cupertino L, Costa GD, Oleksiak A, Piatek W, Pierson J, Salom J, Sisó L, Stolf P, Sun H, Zilio T, part B (2015) Energy-efficient, thermal-aware modeling and

simulation of data centers: the coolemall approach and evaluation results. Ad Hoc Netw 25:535–553
10. Avelar V, Azevedo D, French A (2012) PUE: a comprehensive examination of the metric
11. Andersen D, Franklin J, Kaminsky M, Phanishayee A, Tan L, Vasudevan V (2009) FAWN: A Fast Array of Wimpy Nodes. In: 22nd ACM Symposium on Operating Systems Principles
12. Vasudevan V, Andersen D, Kaminsky M, Tan L, Franklin J, Moraru I (2010) Energy-efficient cluster computing with FAWN: workloads and implications. In: 1st International Conference on Energy-Efficient Computing and Networking
13. Caulfield A, Grupp L, Swanson S (2009) Gordon: using flash memory to build fast, power-efficient clusters for data-intensive applications. In: 14th international conference on Architectural support for programming languages and operating systems
14. Valentini G, Lassonde W, Khan S, MinAllah N, Madani S, Li J, Zhang L, Wang L, Ghani N, Kolodziej J, Li H, Zomaya A, Xu C, Balaji P, Vishnu A, Pinel F, Pecero J, Kliazovich D, Bouvry P (2013) An overview of energy efficiency techniques in cluster computing. Clust Comput 16(1):3–15
15. Tiwari V, Ashar P, Malik S (1993) Technology mapping for low power. In: 30rd design automation conference
16. Su CL, Tsui CY, Despain AM (1994) Saving power in the control path of embedded processors. IEEE Design & Test of Computers 11(4):24–31
17. Benini L, Bogliolo A, Micheli G (2000) A survey of design techniques for system-level dynamic power management. IEEE Transact Very Large Scale Integration Systems 8(3):299–316
18. Kuo C, Lu Y (2015) Task assignment with energy efficiency considerations for non-DVS heterogeneous multiprocessor systems. ACM SIGAPP Appl Comput Rev 14(4):8–18
19. Snowdon D, Ruocco S, Heiser G (2005) Power management and dynamic voltage scaling: myths and facts. In: The workshop on power aware real-time computing
20. Duflot L, Levillain O, Morin B (2009) ACPI: Design Principles and Concerns. In: the 2nd International Conference on Trusted Computing. Berlin
21. Toshiba, Compaq, Intel, Microsoft and PhoenixLTD (2013) Advanced configuration and power interface specification : Revision 5.0a
22. Fan X, Weber W, Barroso L (2007) Power provisioning for a warehouse-sized computer. In: the 34th annual International symposium on computer architecture
23. Nathuji R, Schwan K (2007) VirtualPower: coordinated power management in virtualized enterprise systems. ACM SIGOPS Oper Syst Rev 41(6):265–278
24. Nathuji R, Isci C, Gorbatov E (2007) Exploiting platform heterogeneity for power efficient data centers. In: The 4th International conference on autonomic computing
25. Raghavendra R, Ranganathan P, Talwar V, Wang Z, Zhu X (2008) No power struggles: coordinated multi-level power management for the data center. SIGARCH Compr Architecture News 36(1):48–59
26. Verma A, Ahuja P, Neogi A (2008) pMapper: power and migration cost aware application placement in virtualized systems. In: the 9th ACM/IFIP/USENIX International Conference on Middleware
27. Kusic D, Kephart J, Hanson J, Kandasamy N, Jiang G (2009) Power and performance management of virtualized computing environments via lookahead control. Clust Comput 12(1):1–24
28. Gmach D, Rolia J, Cherkasova L, Kemper A (2009) Resource pool management: reactive versus proactive or let's be friends. Comput Netw 53(17):2905–2922
29. Cardosa M, Korupolu M, Singh A (2009) Shares and utilities based power consolidation in virtualized server environments. In: the 11th IFIP/IEEE International Symposium on Integrated Network Management
30. Kumar S, Talwar V, Kumar V, Ranganathan P, Schwan K (2009) vManage: loosely coupled platform and virtualization management in data centers. In: the 6th International conference on autonomic computing
31. Jung G, Joshi K, Hiltunen M, Schlichting R, Pu C (2009) A cost-sensitive adaptation engine for server consolidation of multitier applications. In: the ACM/IFIP/USENIX International conference on middleware
32. Song Y, Wang H, Li Y, Feng B, Sun Y (2009) Multi-tiered on-demand resource scheduling for Vm-based data center. In: the 9th IEEE/ACM International symposium on cluster computing and the grid
33. Stillwell M, Schanzenbach D, Vivien F, Casanova H (2009) Resource allocation using virtual clusters. In: the 9th IEEE/ACM International symposium on cluster computing and the grid
34. Buyya R, Beloglazov A, Abawajy J (2010) Energy-efficient management of data center resources for Cloud computing: a vision, architectural elements, and open challenges. In: the International conference on parallel and distributed processing techniques and applications
35. Lefevre L, Orgerie A (2010) Designing and evaluating an energy efficient cloud. J Super Comput 51(3):352–373
36. Gulati A, Holler A, Ji M, Shanmuganathan G, Waldspurger C, Zhu X (2012) VMware distributed resource management: design, implementation, and lessons learned. VMware Tech J 1(1):45–64
37. Li X, Qian Z, Lu S, Wu J (2013) Energy efficient virtual machine placement algorithm with balanced and improved resource utilization in data center. Mathematical Computer Modeling 58(5–6):1222–1235
38. VIKRAM R, NEELIMA A (2013) Resource over allocation to improve energy efficiency in real-time cloud computing data centers. Int J Advanced Trends in Compr Sci Eng 2(1):447–453
39. Kim K, Beloglazov A, Buyya R (2011) Power-aware provisioning of virtual machines for real-time cloud services. Pract Experience Concurrency Computation 23(13):1491–1505
40. Chen H, Zhu X, Guo H, Zhu J, Qin X, Wu J (2015) Towards energy-efficient scheduling for real-time tasks under uncertain cloud computing environment. J Syst Softw 99:20–35
41. Ebrahimirad V, Goudarzi M, Rajabi A (2015) Energy-aware scheduling for precedence-constrained parallel virtual machines in virtualized data centers. J Grid Computing 13(2):233–253
42. Dabbagh M, Hamdaoui B, Guizaniy M, Rayes A (2015) Energy-efficient resource allocation and provisioning framework for cloud data centers. IEEE Trans Netw Serv Manag 12(3):377–391
43. Ma F, Liu F, Liu Z (2012) Multi-objective optimization for initial virtual machine placement in cloud data center. Journal of Information & Computational Science 9(16):5029–5038
44. Esnault A (2012) Energy-Aware Distributed Ant Colony Based Virtual Machine Consolidation in IaaS Clouds. Distributed, Parallel, and Cluster Computing [cs.DC]. HAL ID:dumas-00725215 version 1
45. Gao Y, Guan H, Qi Z, Hou Y, Liu L (2013) A multi-objective ant colony system algorithm for virtual machine placement in cloud computing. J Comput Syst Sci 79(8):1230–1242
46. E. Feller (2013) Autonomic and Energy-Efficient Management of Large-Scale Virtualized Data Centers, PhD Thesis. University of Rennes, ISTIC
47. Ferdaus M, Murshed M, Calheiros R, Buyya R (2014) Virtual Machine Consolidation in Cloud Data Centers Using ACO Metaheuristic. In: Euro-Par, the 20th International Conference of Parallel Processing. Porto, Portugal; Springer International Publishing, 306-317
48. Zhang W, Xie H, Cao B, Cheng A (2014) Energy-aware real-time task scheduling for heterogeneous multiprocessors with particle swarm optimization algorithm. Math Probl Eng 2014:Article ID 287475
49. Quang-Hung N, Nienz P, Namz N, Tuong N, Thoa N (2013) A genetic algorithm for power-aware virtual machine allocation in private cloud. Lecture Notes in Compr Sci 7804:170–179
50. Dong Y, Xu G, Fu X (2014) A distributed parallel genetic algorithm of placement strategy for virtual machines deployment on cloud platform. Sci World J 2014:Article ID 259139
51. Portaluri G, Giordano S, Kliazovich D, Dorronsoro B (2014) A power efficient genetic algorithm for resource allocation in cloud computing data centers. In: IEEE 3rd International conference on cloud networking

Permissions

All chapters in this book were first published in JoCCASA, by Springer International Publishing AG.; hereby published with permission under the Creative Commons Attribution License or equivalent. Every chapter published in this book has been scrutinized by our experts. Their significance has been extensively debated. The topics covered herein carry significant findings which will fuel the growth of the discipline. They may even be implemented as practical applications or may be referred to as a beginning point for another development.

The contributors of this book come from diverse backgrounds, making this book a truly international effort. This book will bring forth new frontiers with its revolutionizing research information and detailed analysis of the nascent developments around the world.

We would like to thank all the contributing authors for lending their expertise to make the book truly unique. They have played a crucial role in the development of this book. Without their invaluable contributions this book wouldn't have been possible. They have made vital efforts to compile up to date information on the varied aspects of this subject to make this book a valuable addition to the collection of many professionals and students.

This book was conceptualized with the vision of imparting up-to-date information and advanced data in this field. To ensure the same, a matchless editorial board was set up. Every individual on the board went through rigorous rounds of assessment to prove their worth. After which they invested a large part of their time researching and compiling the most relevant data for our readers.

The editorial board has been involved in producing this book since its inception. They have spent rigorous hours researching and exploring the diverse topics which have resulted in the successful publishing of this book. They have passed on their knowledge of decades through this book. To expedite this challenging task, the publisher supported the team at every step. A small team of assistant editors was also appointed to further simplify the editing procedure and attain best results for the readers.

Apart from the editorial board, the designing team has also invested a significant amount of their time in understanding the subject and creating the most relevant covers. They scrutinized every image to scout for the most suitable representation of the subject and create an appropriate cover for the book.

The publishing team has been an ardent support to the editorial, designing and production team. Their endless efforts to recruit the best for this project, has resulted in the accomplishment of this book. They are a veteran in the field of academics and their pool of knowledge is as vast as their experience in printing. Their expertise and guidance has proved useful at every step. Their uncompromising quality standards have made this book an exceptional effort. Their encouragement from time to time has been an inspiration for everyone.

The publisher and the editorial board hope that this book will prove to be a valuable piece of knowledge for researchers, students, practitioners and scholars across the globe.

List of Contributors

Hanshu Hong and Zhixin Sun
Key Lab of Broadband Wireless Communication and Sensor Network Technology, Ministry Education, Nanjing University of Posts and Telecommunications, Nanjing, China

Ayesha M. Talha
Research Institute of Sciences & Engineering, University of Sharjah, Sharjah, United Arab Emirates

Ibrahim Kamel
Department of Electrical & Computer Engineering, University of Sharjah, Sharjah, United Arab Emirates

Zaher Al Aghbari
Department of Computer Science, University of Sharjah, Sharjah, United Arab Emirates

Yue Wu
School of Computer Science and Engineering, University of Electronic Science and Technology of China, Chengdu, Sichuan 611731, P.R. China

Yunyun Dong
Research Center of Western Yunnan Development, Yunnan University, Kunming, Yunnan 650091, P.R. China

Jing He
School of Computer Science and Engineering, University of Electronic Science and Technology of China, Chengdu, Sichuan 611731, P.R. China
National Pilot School of Software,Yunnan University, Kunming, Yunnan 650091, P.R. China

Yunchun Zhang and Wei Zhou
National Pilot School of Software,Yunnan University, Kunming, Yunnan 650091, P.R. China

Ali Yadavar Nikravesh, Samuel A. Ajila and Chung-Horng Lung
Department of Systems and Computer Engineering, Carleton University, 1125 Colonel By Drive, Ottawa K1S 5B6, ON, Canada

Mohamed Abu Sharkh, Abdallah Shami and Abdelkader Ouda
Department of Electrical and Computer Engineering, Western University, London, Canada

Justice Opara-Martins, Reza Sahandi and Feng Tian
Faculty of Science and Technology, Bournemouth University, Bournemouth, UK

Qassim Bani Hani and Julius P. Dichter
Department of Computer Science & Engineering, University of Bridgeport, Bridgeport, CT 06604, USA

Dorian Minarolli
Department of Computer Engineering, Polytechnic University of Tirana, Tirana, Albania

Artan Mazrekaj
Department of Contemporary Sciences and Technologies, South East European University, Tetovo, Macedonia

Bernd Freisleben
Department of Mathematics & Computer Science, Philipps-Universität Marburg, Marburg, Germany
Department of Electrical Engineering & Information Techology, TU
Darmstadt, Darmstadt, Germany

André Müller and Bogdan Franczyk
Department of Business Information Systems, Leipzig University, Grimmaische Straße 12, 04109 Leipzig, Germany

André Ludwig
Kühne Logistics University, Großer Grasbrook 17, 20457 Hamburg, Germany

Fikirte Teka, Chung-Horng Lung and Samuel A. Ajila
Department of Systems and Computer Engineering, Carleton University, Ottawa, Ontario K1S 5B6, Canada

Joseph Issa
Department of Electrical and Computer Engineering, Notre Dame University, Zouk Mosbeh, Lebanon

Abdul Razaque
Computer Science Department, New York Institute of Technology, New York, NY, USA

Syed S. Rizvi
Department of Information Sciences and Technology, Pennsylvania State University, Altoona, PA 16601, USA

Adel Alkhalil
Faculty of Computer Science and Engineering, University of Hail, Hail, Saudi Arabia

Reza Sahandi and David John
Faculty of Science and Technology, Bournemouth University, Poole, UK

Auday Al-Dulaimy
Department of Mathematics & Computer Science, Beirut Arab University, Beirut, Lebanon

Wassim Itani
Department of Electrical & Computer Engineering, Beirut Arab University, Beirut, Lebanon

Ahmed Zekri
Department of Mathematics & Computer Science, Beirut Arab University, Beirut, Lebanon
Department of Mathematics & Computer Science, Faculty of Science, Alexandria University, Alexandria, Egypt

Rached Zantout
Department of Electrical & Computer Engineering, Rafic Hariri University, Beirut, Lebanon

Index

Printed in the USA
CPSIA information can be obtained
at www.ICGtesting.com
JSHW051415221024
72173JS00006B/1361

9 781632 407948